Beginning Site Server 3.0

Tim Huckaby
Mike Kendzierski
Jarrod Marshall
Brad Sherrell
Gopalakrishnan Sreeraman

Wrox Press Ltd. ®

Beginning Site Server 3.0

Published by Wrox Press Ltd, Arden House, 1102 Warwick Road, Acocks Green,
Birmingham, B27 6BH, UK
Printed in the United States
ISBN 1-861002-9-04

Trademark Acknowledgements

Credits

Authors
Jeff Hasan
Tim Huckaby
Mike Kendzierski
Jarrod Marshall
Brad Sherrell
Gopalakrishnan Sreeraman
Andreas Wallberg

Managing Editors
Victoria Hudgson
Joanna Mason

Technical Editors
Craig A Berry
Claire Fletcher
Lisa Stephenson
Lums Thevathasan

Development Editor
Sarah Bowers

Project Manager
Sophie Edwards

Technical Reviewers
Nick Apostolopoulos
Michael Corvese
Richard Harrison
Ron Landers
Sophie McQueen
Andrew Stopford
Peter Watt
John Wooton

Design/Layout
Tom Bartlett
Mark Burdett
Jonathan Jones
John McNulty

Figures
Jonathan Jones
Tom Bartlett

Cover
Chris Morris

Index
Allessandro Ansa
Martin Brooks
Andrew Criddle

About the Authors

Tim Huckaby

Tim Huckaby is the Founder and President of InterKnowlogy (www.InterKnowlogy.com). Interknowlogy's core competency is with Internet commerce interchange, business Internet systems and multi-tiered application software design and installation on Internet, Intranet and Extranet platforms.

Previously Tim was the architecture team Developer Lead at Microsoft for the Customizable Starter Sites during Microsoft's Site Server 3.0 product development. Since shipping the Site Server 3.0 product, Tim has been lead developer and/or lead architect on a number of large and successful e-commerce web sites. Tim was a presenter and speaker at Microsoft TechEd '99 North America, Europe, and Latin America conferences. Tim's presentation, "Gotchas, Tips and Tricks to developing a successful Site Server 3.0 Commerce site", received worldwide ratings in the top 10% in all 3 events at TechEd '99. Currently, Microsoft employees all over the world are delivering the presentation that Tim developed. Tim also has the highest rated keynote presentation at Microsoft Developer Days two years running. Tim regularly writes and performs technical editing duties for many magazines in addition to his various commitments to Wrox. Tim welcomes e-mail and can be reached at TimHuck@InterKnowlogy.com.

Mike Kendzierski

Mike Kendzierski, Director of Internet Services, works as a technical manager for B2Bgalaxy.com and is responsible for such systems that include Site Server, Oracle, Sun and BEA Systems. Mike brings extensive experience deploying and developing complex client-server and Internet e-commerce systems and is a regular speaker at technical conferences such as Microsoft Explorer and ASPDevCon on topics ranging from e-commerce systems to systems design and network architecture for high performance web sites. Mike is also a published technical author of over nine titles including Windows NT and BackOffice technologies such as Site Server and Internet Information Server. When he's not sipping coffee and reading magazines for free at Barnes & Noble he can be found roaming around aimlessly in Central Park or the Upper East Site in NYC. Mike welcomes e-mail, and can be reached at mkendzierski@att.net.

Dedication:

I'd like to dedicate this book to all of the people who have helped shape my career including Dave Rowe, Joe Stagner, Bruce Backa, Arnold Cohn, Norma Kroll and my parents. Somehow everything ended up working out fine and I just want to thank you for all of your help along the way! Each of you has had a significant role and I just wanted to say thanks.

This book wouldn't have been possible without the support from everyone from Wrox Publishing. I'd like to send out a special thank you to Sarah Bowers, Victoria Hudgson, Sophie Edwards, John Franklin, Claire Fletcher and Lums Thevathasan. You have all been a wonderful pleasure to work with and a great resource to have along the way.

I'd like to send a shout out to A.C, G-Funk and B-dawg for offering plenty of fun trips to pass the time and make life a lot more interesting during the course of the book. Jodi, I couldn't forget you either!

There are a lot more people I'd like to thank including Ed Pick, Shimon Yifrakh, Eric Farish, Ed Schroeder, Marty Horn and the entire team at B2Bgalaxy.com and USWeb/CKS Cornerstone. You guys are great and thanks for all of your support!

Jarrod Marshall

Jarrod Marshall resides in Nashville, Tennessee, where he is a consultant for G.A. Sullivan, a software development component based out of St. Louis, Missouri. Jarrod began programming at the age of 10 and over the last three years he has worked mostly with Internet-related applications and e-commerce. Jarrod plays bass guitar, and piano, and also enjoys a game of tennis in his spare time.

Brad Sherrell

Brad is the manager of E-Business for the Life Insurance Division of Pacific Life Insurance Company. He is responsible for the development of Internet applications and specializes in application architecture using Microsoft technologies. Brad is also a lecturer at the University of California, Irvine where he teaches Visual Basic and application architecture to some of the brightest undergraduates in the country. He lives in San Clemente, California, with his wife Christy and their son Justin. Brad would like to thank his wife and son for putting up with him on one of his many projects "that won't take very long...I promise!" When he's not in front of a computer, he spends most of his free time attempting to play golf.

Gopalakrishnan Sreeraman

Gopal Sreeraman is a Senior Consultant with Professional Access Ltd, NY. Currently he is involved in architecting and developing Web applications for large organizations. He was earlier a functional and technical consultant in the Financials area of the ERP system, Ramco Marshal. Gopal holds a BS and MBA.

Table of Contents

Chapter 2: Installation 27

Chapter 3: The Site Server Platform   195

Chapter 4: Building Your First E-Commerce Site   231

Chapter 5: Under the Hood of a Site Server E-Commerce Site — 283

Chapter 7: Pipelines   359

Chapter 11: Analysing Your Site 491

Chapter 12: Personalization and Membership 527

Chapter 13: Advanced E-Commerce Site Concepts 573

Appendix A: The Commerce Interchange Pipeline 599

Appendix B: ASP Reference   607

Appendix C: Third-Party Components   **619**

Introduction

It's not hard to see that in today's world, increased Internet access, user confidence, better payment systems, and rapidly improving web security are fueling the massive growth in what has become known as e-commerce. There are increasing opportunities in this fast changing world, and most businesses know that they need to get onto the Internet to stay in the game. Setting up an e-commerce site can be a daunting prospect, but there is help at hand – this book will show you the way.

Site Server 3.0 from Microsoft can be viewed as an architectural platform for your Internet, intranet, extranet and e-commerce sites. But Site Server Version 3.0 can also be viewed as a set of applications, a suite of tools, utilities and services, that provide you with everything you need for content management, knowledge management, access control, web site traffic analysis and more.

In addition, Site Server 3.0 Commerce Edition enables you to build a transactional e-commerce web site, and provides you with all the tools you need for managing it.

Microsoft Site Server 3.0 is a large product, but in this book, we're going to show you how to tame it, and how to unleash the power of Site Server Version 3.0 Commerce Edition.

What Does this Book Cover?

The aim of this book is to provide an introduction to and an overview of Microsoft's Site Server 3.0 and Site Server 3.0 Commerce Edition. But that also includes getting your hands dirty, as a fully functional commerce site is built, dissected, deconstructed, and reconstructed so that you can better understand what's going on under the covers.

So here's what we'll cover in the book:

- ❑ Installing Site Server is notoriously difficult, but we'll provide you with detailed and comprehensive guidelines for installation of Site Server (along with the other tools and products that must be installed with it), which will allow you to breeze through this process. We'll cover installation on both Windows NT 4.0 and 2000 platforms, with or without SQL Server 6.5 or 7.0.

- ❑ We'll show you how to use the wizards that Site Server provides to build a fully functioning e-commerce site.

- ❑ Additionally, you'll learn how to programmatically add functionality to the commerce site that you create with the Site Builder Wizard, so that you can customize your site to suit your own needs.

- ❑ We'll help you with the design considerations that are so important, both from architectural and from functional perspectives.

- ❑ We'll finish with a wider look at some of the Site Server components, learning more about the technology itself, and what you can do with it.

Who is this Book For?

If you want to know more about e-commerce, and how Site Server and Site Server Commerce Edition can help you get your foot in the door, then this is the book for you. We don't assume any previous knowledge of Site Server: if you're a beginner with the Site Server 3.0 product, Beginning Site Server 3.0 will help you get up and running as quickly as possible, but even more advanced Site Server 3.0 pros will benefit from the technical information here. You will find it useful to have experience with SQL Server (6.5 or 7.0) and Active Server Pages.

As well as a comprehensive step-by-step guide to the installation of Site Server and its Commerce counterpart, we'll show you the tips and tricks you'll need to get around. We'll lead you through practical demonstrations of what to do with Siter Server once you've actually installed it. By the end of the book, you'll have built your own e-commerce site, and will know what you can do to expand and improve on it.

If you think that this book is completely technical, however, you'll be mistaken. There's more to e-commerce than merely the technical ability to use products intelligently to exploit a market niche: e-commerce is business online, bringing with it a whole new understanding of how business should take place.

There's something for everybody here – from those who are tugging at the reins for a product to help unleash their site on the Internet, to those who still need persuasion as to why e-commerce is so important in today's modern world. Managers at all levels will find a good discussion of the 'whys' as well as the 'hows', giving a more complete picture of business in the online community.

What Do I Need To Use This Book?

Many of the chapters in this book cover features available in Site Server 3.0, but to get the most out of the book, you'll need Site Server 3.0 Commerce Edition.

You will also need the following:

- ❑ Microsoft Windows NT Server 4.0, or Windows 2000 Server, Advanced Server or Data Center Server

- ❑ SQL Server 6.5 or 7.0

- ❑ Internet Information Server

- ❑ Internet Explorer 4 (or, if you have NT 4.0 and SQL Server 7.0 installed on the same machine, IE5)

- ❑ Development tool: Visual Studio 6.0 with Visual Studio SP3

Conventions

We have used a number of different styles of text and layout in the book to help differentiate between the different kinds of information. Here are examples of the styles we use and an explanation of what they mean:

Advice, hints and background information comes in an indented, italicized font like this.

> **Important bits of information that you really shouldn't ignore come in boxes like this!**

Bulleted lists appear indented, with each new bullet marked as follows:

- ❑ **Important Words** are in a bold type font.
- ❑ Words that appear on the screen in menus like the File or Window menu are in a similar font to what you see on screen.
- ❑ Keys that you press on the keyboard, like *Ctrl* and *Enter*, are in italics.

Code in this book comes in a number of different styles. If it's a word that we're talking about in the text, for example, when discussing the For...Next loop, it's in a fixed-width font. If it's a block of code that you can type in as a program and run, then it's also in a gray box:

```
Private Sub cmdQuit_Click()
    End
End Sub
```

Sometimes you'll see code in a mixture of styles, like this:

```
Private Sub cmdQuit_Click()
    End
End Sub
```

In this case, we want you to consider the code with the gray background. The code with a white background is code we've already looked at, and that we don't wish to examine further.

These formats are designed to make sure that you know what it is you're looking at – we hope they make life easier.

Downloading the Source Code

As you work through the examples in this book, you might decide that you prefer to type all the code in by hand. Many readers prefer this because it's a good way to get familiar with the coding techniques that are being used.

Whether you want to type the code in or not, we have made all the source code for this book available at our web site, at the following address:

```
http://www.wrox.com
```

If you're one of those readers who likes to type in the code, you can use our files to check the results you should be getting – they should be your first stop if you think you might have typed in an error. If you just don't like typing, then downloading the source code from our web site is a must!

Either way, it'll help you with updates and debugging.

Customer Support

We've tried to make this book as accurate and enjoyable as possible, but what really matters is what the book actually does for you. Please let us know your views, either by returning the reply card in the back of the book, or by contacting us via e-mail at feedback@wrox.com.

Deductions

This book is really much more than a beginner's guide to Microsoft Site Server 3.0 Commerce Edition. That's because Site Server is not only dependent, but is deeply integrated on and with the Windows NT 4.0 and Windows 2000 suite of server products (IIS, MTS, COM+, SQL, etc.).

This book goes above and beyond Site Server 3.0 – it could be looked at as a "Beginner's Guide to Windows NT/2000, Internet Information Server, SQL Server and Site Server in a Web Environment" – or better yet, how about "E-Commerce on the Microsoft Platform". Whatever you call it, however you view it, there's a wealth of information about the design, development, and implementation of Site Server 3.0 e-commerce sites in this book.

Jump in! Have fun! And good luck in your implementations of Site Server 3.0 Commerce. Beginning Site Server 3.0 will get you well on your way!

Site Server and E-Commerce

With the boom of the Internet and its effect on today's worldwide economy, businesses are constantly changing the way that they operate to take advantage of the power of the World Wide Web. By using the different technologies that the Internet can provide, more and more companies are beginning to change the way they do business. These new technologies can improve efficiency, lessen traditional operating costs and help companies adapt more quickly to changes in the new marketplace. Armed with the tools to make their growing businesses more efficient and profitable, companies are turning to electronic commerce as a new way of doing business.

To help you on your way, Microsoft offers **Site Server** and more particularly the **Commerce Edition** to help you build your electronic commerce, more commonly referred to as **e-commerce**, system. Microsoft's Site Server Commerce platform blends the necessary components to manage your site, analyze your usage, provide transaction capabilities, and integrate a comprehensive commerce solution for your business. With the different tools that Site Server provides, you can reduce the development time and even begin immediately to start readying your business for e-commerce. Site Server Commerce Edition can help mold and build your business for business-to-consumer or business-to-business transactions on the Internet.

This book is designed to get your foot in the door of e-commerce using Site Server. Over the next 500 pages or so, we are going to install Site Server, build an e-commerce site and extend that site to incorporate additional functionality that we desire. Providing you take things one step at a time, you'll discover that Site Server isn't as complex to use as you might think.

We are going to start the book not so much with an introduction to Site Server but an introduction to how Site Server functions in the new e-commerce environment. So in this chapter we will see:

- ❑ E-commerce business models
- ❑ The different flavors of Site Server
- ❑ The benefits that Site Server offers in creating an e-commerce solution

E-Commerce Today

As businesses continue to adopt new technology in the workplace, e-commerce is finding itself on the minds and radar screens of many people on both the business and technology side of today's economy. The power of the web is based upon the premise of reaching a national or even global audience through a universal standard such as your web browser. Anywhere and anyone that has an Internet browser can communicate with another person or business anywhere in the world. Companies that were once restricted by geography can move to the web and reach millions upon millions of new customers. As long as you have a presence on the Internet, it doesn't make any difference if you're running your business out of your basement or in an office complex. Companies that fail to take notice of hungry Internet startups might not survive the next round of e-commerce.

E-commerce is changing the way many of us are doing our purchasing and changing the way a lot of companies are doing business. Consumers are becoming more aware of their purchases and companies are becoming more efficient by tying in their partners, vendors and suppliers via the Internet as well. While customers are still going to be doing a percentage of their purchasing in traditional stores, they are being continually drawn to the ease of e-commerce that offer cheap prices, a pleasant experience, no queues and are open twenty-four hours a day. What was once a dream of communicating between their customers and business partners is now becoming a reality by using what the Internet can offer.

The bottom-line behind e-commerce is saving money and making businesses more profitable through technologies such as the Internet. The Internet at its fullest potential can offer a lot to the everyday consumer as well as the corporate powerhouses who manually purchase millions of different products each day. As more and more businesses move into the electronic marketplace, the idea of streamlining their business processes has been integrated with every part of their business. By streamlining their business practices and processes, companies can pass their savings on to you.

A majority of the companies that are taking advantage of the situation in today's marketplace and establishing a presence on the Internet will stand to do better than their counterparts that wait. For those companies that delay, they will not only have to overcome the gap in technology, but also the gap between themselves and the ever-evolving marketplace as it continues to change. The chances are, the longer these businesses delay in their move to on-line businesses, the more likely they are to fail. By using e-commerce to maximize their business practices, companies that are taking advantage of the Internet are going to be at a significant advantage. Furthermore, companies that move into e-commerce at a later stage will not only have missed the short-term opportunities of supernormal profits that are associated with innovation, but will have the difficulties of enticing customers away from competitors who have built brand loyalty.

This chapter is designed to give you a brief overview of e-commerce and how you can begin to think of Microsoft Site Server as you develop your e-commerce solution. The power behind Microsoft Site Server lies in the ability to manage so many parts of an e-commerce solution. With Microsoft Site Server you can monitor and administer your advertising, commerce (tax and shipping components), content, and development and analysis sections of your intranet or Internet site. By keeping a close eye on the traffic numbers and transaction data with Site Server Analysis, you can analyze the transaction data and detect buying patterns to help make your site more successful. By taking advantage of these different tools, you can not only develop a comprehensive solution, but also manage it successfully from beginning to end.

E-Commerce Business Models

In the world of e-commerce, the business world is divided into different solutions, or business models. There are those types of businesses that focus on **business-to-business** e-commerce such as Cisco Systems. A business-to-business solution might have a tightly integrated extranet that brings together a variety of partners, vendors and distributors to streamline their business and minimize their costs. These extranets are becoming more popular because they allow companies to communicate with one another over a secure channel, by using the Internet and a variety of safety measures such as Virtual Private Networks and firewalls to protect their communications. Normally, these functions that are normally attributed to doing business such as purchasing agents, inventory control and communication with the supply chain, can be both expensive and inefficient.

On the other side of the table is **business-to-consumer** e-commerce. Companies such as Amazon.com and CDNow.com are developing their businesses around reducing the middleman and selling directly to you from the distributors. This gives these types of companies a lot of flexibility in price and functionality.

Although each type of business model shares a lot of similar characteristics, such as the technology that they use, the way each does business is completely different. We'll explore these different types of roles as we learn more about business-to-business and business-to-consumer e-commerce.

Business-to-Consumer E-Commerce

The business-to-consumer form of electronic commerce has had the biggest influence on how we go about making purchases of goods and services today. While electronic commerce is not going to replace a traditional shopping experience where shoppers can touch and feel the products they're purchasing, almost every retail market is making a play to gobble up a section of cyberspace in the hope that they can build a strong consumer base of customers.

Everything from electronics to home groceries is now being offered over the Internet as a potential marketplace. Almost anything that you could possibly think of is now being sold over the web in some shape or form. You can think of the Internet as a global flea market with a variety of potential buyers. This can be easily demonstrated with the multitude of auction sites that continue to pop up such as eBay.com, Yahoo!Auctions and OnSale.com.

So why do so many people take advantage of products being sold over the web? There are actually several different answers to that question, and I'll try to make sure they're dealt with accordingly. Basically, consumers want the buying experience to be:

- ❑ Compelling
- ❑ Convenient
- ❑ Cost-effective

Compelling is easy to explain: right now, the Internet is still brand-new and many people are taking advantage of the novelty of buying their purchases on-line. They are having a positive buying experience on-line and are returning to buy more. Essentially, it's "cool" to purchase over the Internet.

The second part of the boom in business-to-consumer e-commerce is how *easy* the process has become. All you need is a few clicks of the mouse in the convenience of your own home, and you can buy almost anything imaginable. You can find anything from the latest car to the oldest comic book. There is no waiting in queues, hassles of traffic, parking, awkward salespeople, or running around from store to store only to find out of stock signs. For those who use the web to stay well informed as to what they want to buy, the web can offer a wonderland of good buys. By not having to wait in lines and working with companies like Fed-Ex or UPS, the purchasing process has never been easier. A good example of this is how shipping companies are even allowing you to track your packages on the Internet with a tracking number. All that you need to do is insert the tracking number into their tracking site and you can find the exact status of your package.

Finally, *price*: people love finding bargains on the web as much as they like to find them in their local department store and the web is full of places where you can save a buck or two depending on how hard you look. With all of the businesses springing up on-line, there is an enormous amount to choose from, and every company wants to compete on price. For example, Buy.com sells many of their products under cost to attract new business! The bottom line remains is that if the Internet wasn't cost-effective and people weren't saving money, it wouldn't matter how great the buying experience was. But since people are saving money and enjoying the convenience and power to buy their goods from their home, e-commerce is taking off.

Business-to-Business E-Commerce

While most of the buzz with what you read in the papers typically deals with large retail e-commerce sites such as Amazon.com, the real power of e-commerce is taking place from business to business. With all of the media excitement, business-to-business e-commerce still makes up roughly seventy-five percent of e-commerce today and is expected to grow as businesses begin to adopt their practices for the Internet.

Businesses sell or buy from other business every day in order to support their own business. Some companies specialize in catering to the needs of other companies while many companies select vendors to supply them with the necessary equipment or tools they need to run their day-to-day operations. Many of these relationships have moved to the web for ease of access and to streamline their business processes.

If you speak to any Chief Financial Officer, they'll be sure to tell you a million ways that they can save their company money. With the Internet however, they now have an effective way that they can make this a reality. By using the Internet as a tool to solve business problems, companies can reduce expenses that would normally account for wasted income and bureaucratic red tape.

In an industry seminar discussing the growth of e-commerce, John Chambers of Cisco Systems was quoted as saying that, "The Internet economy will have the same impact on society that the industrial revolution had 300 years ago." This bold statement begins to show how much effect the Internet economy has begun to have on the way companies are doing business, as we now know it.

Cisco Systems is a perfect model for how companies are turning their everyday efforts to the web to save money. Once faced with overwhelming growth, Cisco began to exploit the best that the web had to offer in hopes of making their business more efficient. By integrating with their suppliers and manufacturers, Cisco is able to account for roughly $28 million dollars a day or 73 per cent of their $8.3 billion revenue on-line.

By using the Internet as a sales and communication tool, Cisco's customers can configure their orders, access technical information and find their order-status on-line...all without talking to a single sales person. This flow of information equates to approximately $550 million dollars per years in saving, which can be reinvested into their company and, most importantly, research and development.

By saving on such traditional costs such as sales, support and purchasing agents, Cisco also speed the "time to market" process by reducing the amount of human interaction from the initial purchase order to delivery of the product to the consumer's door. This creates a tremendous advantage over their competitors who are stuck in traditional loopholes and processes that end up costing valuable time and money.

Enter Microsoft Site Server

Microsoft's offering for intranet/internet solutions and their e-commerce strategy is bundled as a number of components and services called **Site Server (SS)** and **Site Server Commerce Edition (SSCE)**. Site Server 3.0 is built as a solution that requires Internet Information Server 4.0 and Windows NT 4.0.

> *In addition, SS 3.0 and SS 3.0 Commerce Edition is functional on Windows 2000 Server and Windows 2000 Advanced Server with the application of service packs and hot fixes.*

The base Site Server package contains tools and components to provide new functionality to existing sites you may have or provide you with a better set of solutions when envisioning new sites. The Site Server components are accessible via ASP pages that you can customize and build into your existing systems. Site Server 3.0 and Site Server 3.0 Commerce Edition can be seen as toolkits that let you create powerful web based applications that fit your company's internal and external needs. Microsoft's components can be used within templates and exampled sites that can then be modified to fit your needs. The components can also be used for building custom solutions once the technology is understood.

There are also a few NT Services that are installed in Windows NT Server 4.0 that adds greater functionality to web sites. An example of such a service is the Message Builder Service, which is part of the Direct Mail component of Site Server. This component allows you to send personalized bulk e-mail to registered members of your site based on information they have provided. You could easily create custom components to handle these types of business needs but Site Server provides many components that can be used for a lower cost than custom code. Even if you only use a small part of what Site Server offers it is more cost effective than re-building things that have already been built.

What can Site Server Add to my Existing Tool Set?

Site Server's is very flexible. A few of the things Site Server can bring to a developer's tool set are:

- ❏ Greater search functionality
- ❏ Powerful content personalization features
- ❏ Ability to deploy an entire web site across a server farm
- ❏ Managing content for publication
- ❏ Selling products online
- ❏ Streamlining internal corporate purchase processes

Any web developer using Active Server Pages can fairly easily become familiar with the Site Server components and implement them with the correct guidance.

What Is the Difference Between Site Server and Site Server Commerce Edition?

Let's take a minute to go over the differences between Microsoft Site Server and Microsoft Site Server Commerce Edition (SSCE). Microsoft Site Server fills the role of web site management with a set of different tools to help you:

❑ Manage your website

❑ Analyze the traffic statistics (Analysis)

❑ Control your content (Publishing and Content Managment)

❑ Help personalize your content (Personalization & Membership)

❑ Update your content on single or multiple web servers (Content Deployment)

Site Server (the standard edition) does not provide any commerce features to help you sell and begin accepting financial transactions over the Internet. With Site Server 3.0 you can install seven different server services such as Publishing, Analysis, Commerce, Search, Personalization and Membership and Push. These services can help you manage your site, from creating customized Membership databases, and managing the content of your site with Publishing, to monitoring and analyzing your site with the variety of analysis tools.

When you install Site Server for the first time, you have the ability to install only the components that you'll need for your site. This means that you can take advantage of only the parts of Site Server that you'll need and ignore the rest. If you need the other services that you didn't install, you always have the option of installing them at a later date.

Site Server Commerce Edition includes all the web site management tools provided with Site Server, and also provides extre commerce features. These services include the Order Processing Pipeline (OPP) that allows you to start accepting orders, enabling transactions, creating sales promotions and generating business logic for your site. The OPP allows you to plug in components to handle specific tasks that need to occur when taking an order over the Internet. These tasks can include tax calculation, shipping cost calculation and real time credit card processing.

> *SSCE also provides an Ad Server for banner rotation, managing advertising campaigns and generating data that you can use to analyze your traffic in order to increase your marketing advantage and target your users more effectively with Site Server's Analysis services.*

To get you moving in the right direction, SSCE also includes a set of sample commerce sites and a set of Wizards to help you generate your own commerce site. Having these examples and wizards can help you get up and running quickly with Site Server and SSCE. We'll look at these Wizards in more detail in Chapter 4.

What You'll Need to Compete

OK, you know that you want to exploit the web to its fullest potential and invest in an e-commerce site where you can either sell your goods more efficiently or tie-in to your partners network. Electronic commerce is a business that when it is done right can be very profitable, but failures are right around the corner if you don't have a realistic view of what you want to accomplish.

It is common sense that e-commerce should make life easier for your customers and partners, not harder. An electronic business site that alienates and gives a poor experience for the end user can fail miserably in almost any field. By using the web, you want to empower your customers with information and lower prices and at the same time reduce overhead and increase profits.

By integrating such parts of the business as Marketing and IT, you can take advantage of e-commerce to the fullest extent. By using the Site Server Analysis tools, you can generate customized reports that the Marketing department can use to help sell more widgets at your targeted audience. E-commerce is not just about technology: e-commerce is about focusing your entire company on building a smarter business that uses the Internet to its advantage.

Making The Sell

We have previously discussed how e-commerce can be broken up into basically two types, business-to-consumer and business-to-business. These sites all support some way of making some type of transaction between the business and the customer, be it taking credit card purchases from a consumer or exchanging business documents between trading partners. Site Server excels in both of these areas by utilizing a number of pre-built components and ASP, and offering customization to fit your needs. Let's take a look at how Site Server can be implemented to support these two types of business models.

Business-to-Consumer

An online store that sells products to the general public is classified as a business-to-consumer site. For an explanation of how Site Server can be useful in developing one of these sites we'll discuss what Commerce Server brings to the table.

In a situation in which your company would like to develop an online store there are many things you should take into consideration. These are things such as taxes, inventory, retaining receipt information and the product catalog. You are tasked with developing an online store for your company to sell its products on the web. The product catalog is already in place for other systems to access on a SQL Server 7.0 database and you would not like to move the data or duplicate it in anyway. The site requires real time tax calculation as well as real-time credit card processing to take place when an order is placed. Also, inventory must be reduced when an order is placed so that there is never a problem filling an order due to inaccurate data.

Site Server's Commerce Server was developed to be flexible and work with systems that were already in place. The product catalog already in its own table structure on the SQL 7.0 database presents no problem, as Site Server is *schema independent*. This means that any structure can be used and built on. Most of the things required to run an online store have already been developed within Site Server, such as the way the shopping basket is handled, components to format currency and components to provide easier ways to format URL query strings, to name but a few. The **pipeline technology** within a Site Server store allows business rules to be plugged into the site with little change to the surrounding site or ASP pages. Also, there are 3rd party vendors who offer components for tax calculation, credit card processing, shipping cost calculation and many other purposes.

Site Server 3.0 Commerce Edition also is shipped with a number of pipeline components that can be used within your store. This provides functionality without having to write custom components but if a custom component is needed, those can be written in any language that supports COM.

What does Site Server offer when building an online store?

❏ Any database schema can be integrated

❏ Pre-built components to handle data display, formatting, etc.

❏ Pre-built components to handle business logic, inventory checking/reduction, etc.

❏ A wide range of 3rd party components to handle payment processing, shipping and taxes to name a few

❏ The ability to cross sell products based

❏ The ability to create sales or promotions such as buy 2 products get one free

Business-to-consumer e-commerce can be implemented using Site Server Commerce Edition to build an extensible, scalable solution based on the Site Server components and Active Server Pages.

Business-to-Business

Site Server Commerce Edition 3.0 offers many tools for creating sites for the purpose of selling and buying in the business-to-business arena. Let's discuss what Site Server can do for a development effort in which a business-to-business e-commerce site must be built.

Your company sells office supplies to regional trading partners in a traditional relationship. The development team has been tasked with implementing an online solution that will receive and process orders from the current trading partners. To move into using more standards-based technology you would like to implement data transfer using XML, a language that allows document transfer between systems that might otherwise be incompatible. Site Server would be a wonderful choice for implementing this solution because it contains pre-built components that are specialized in many of the tasks needed, can audit the transfer to ensure delivery and is extensible so that changes can be made to the system without a complete re-write. The pipeline architecture for business-to-business communication is designed so that trading partners can exchange their data securely using encrypted data transfers. Site Server also offers components that map to and from XML allowing the data to be exchanged in a format that is platform independent.

How did Site Server aid in this solution?

❏ Extensible architecture

❏ Secure data transfer with signed and encrypted data

❏ Transport-independent data transfer

❏ XML-based standards in use

The technologies implemented in Site Server Commerce Edition can be used to build data transfer systems between companies across EDI or just about any transport necessary. They can also be used to receive orders from an intranet site or extranet site and decrease the time for order turn around in some cases.

Marketing / Data Gathering

There is more to creating a successful site than gathering up the necessary bits of information about your customer base and competitors. A whole industry is dedicated to driving business to your site with an assortment of tools like search engines and targeted advertising. The different types of marketing and data gathering for your site opens up an entire new phase that you can get involved in with Microsoft Site Server.

While your first goal is probably to make money by selling your business over the Internet, you can also generate a large revenue stream by effectively selling your site as prime advertising space. This is where the importance of Microsoft Site Server comes into play. Site Server offers different analysis tools that you can use to generate custom reports and details about users' habits and important trends within your site.

By using the Site Server Commerce tools such as Ad Server and the various Analysis tools, you can target your customers, and evaluate different ways to improve your business. Site Server also offers Personalization and Membership features that you can use to create customer profiles, membership tiers and personalized web pages. By examining the data from Ad Server and Personalization & Membership, you can develop customized marketing generated towards a specific user audience.

Data gathering is the "Holy Grail" of electronic commerce. The idea behind data gathering is to know enough information about your potential customers through attributes such as age, income, likes and dislikes, etc. Most of this you can get from taking a long hard look at each user session that comes across your site, and looking at the referring URL or the last page that your potential customer was viewing before they decided to browse your site. This can give you a better idea as to what parts of your site you would want to market to drive more business to your site.

A successful marketing campaign can have many different features, from the traditional marketing standpoint of paper/radio/commercials, or the more technical gambit of pointed advertising to a specific amount of people.

Not every company or business has the money to spend on public relations to promote his or her e-business, but in the world of cyberspace, market share counts. And it counts a lot. You can think of the Internet as the "wild-wild west" and the new companies that are springing up as the new settlers. Companies such as Amazon.com are becoming larger than ever by grabbing as much market share as they could early on, with their traditional competitors such as Barnes & Noble trying to play catch-up. Although Barnes & Noble were able to still launch their online bookstore, they are still years behind companies like Amazon.com in terms of market share and business.

A good example of Amazon.com's targeted marketing is the different types of recommendations that the site offers depending on your previous purchases. Amazon.com examines your recent buying habits and tries to cross-sell similar products that you might be interested in. With Site Server's Personalization and Membership features, these tools are all available.

Site Server Analysis

The Site Server Analysis tools provide a lot of functionality for examining the log files within your site. What do you do when a link is down or broken? With the Analysis tools, you can monitor and verify the pages of your site as well as view different analysis reports for your site that are generated through Site Server's Content Analyzer. A wonderful feature of Site Server Analysis is the ability to schedule reports so that the reports are ready for the people requesting them when they need them, viewed via the Internet in HTML format or as a Microsoft Word document.

Whenever someone visits your site, your web server logs their visit to a log file. These log files are viewable with a text editor, and they log the visitor's TCP/IP address, any file(s) that was requested and other information that is collected from the client.

The Usage Analyst tool is used to examine the log files and provide usage information and detailed reports for your site. The format of a log file is difficult to read and comprehend: unless you look closely, or know exactly what you're looking for, this log file doesn't make any sense. The Usage Analyst tool can take the important information contained within these files and organize the data so it can be analyzed later, by importing your log files into either an Access or a SQL Server database.

The Content Analyzer tool for Site Server is used to crawl your site and report back usage, such as broken links and a site map. This tool is wonderful, and gives you a detailed graphical view as to how your site is laid out. You can follow your site link by link to help you better plan for the future or make any architecture decisions.

Finally, the Report Writer tool allows you to choose from over 40 report definitions or create customized and detailed reports about a variety of useful topics, such as Executive Summary (Complete), Referral, Advertising, Bandwidth, and many others. This is a great utility to help analyze the data that you're collecting that IIS provides.

Personalization

One of the more popular ways to make your customers feel more at home on your site is to add some **personalization** to your site. Personalization can take many forms for your site such as recognizing the user, saving personal data and credit card information, offering cross-selling capabilities, and offering them special offers that are specific to their user account.

We'll explore the different ways that you can offer personalization and membership for your site with Microsoft Site Server and Personalization and Membership (commonly referred to as P&M). Although we will only cover the basics of the P&M aspects of Site Server, you'll know enough about the details of P&M to add some basic functionality to your site.

The easiest way to offer the benefits of P&M functionality for your site is with cookies. Cookies are a way of placing a little bit of information on the client computer so that your site can recognize the user the next time they return. While cookies can offer a lot of benefits for your site, using cookies and the P&M features within Site Server require a lot of custom Active Server Pages programming, and a staff who can work out the technical issues to offer this functionality.

P&M can take your site to the next level by having a sense of community within your business. Returning customers can be welcomed back and can be targeted with electronic "coupons" and other products that might be similar or might add additional value to products that have previously been purchased.

P&M features are an advanced topic, but some of the basic concepts about the Active User Object and how it ties into Personalization and Membership are discussed in Chapter 12.

Site Server Personalization and Membership Directory

Many web sites are offering registration nowadays to create a sense of community for their businesses so they can better sell their products. Membership functionality allows your web site to store specific information about the people who register for your site.

The Membership server within Site Server can provide a storage directory for user information that you'll use for your Personalization and Membership. By leveraging SQL Server and the Site Server Membership Directory, you can offer a highly flexible solution that can scale to hundreds of thousands of users. Your other option here is Microsoft Access, but for large implementations of a membership database your best option is SQL Server.

Once you setup a Membership Directory, you can use the features within P&M to provide different levels of access that help in identifying and authenticating user accounts. Using this directory, you can also offer specific content directed specifically to your users according to the attributes of their accounts.

Personalized Content

One of the trends in web sites recently is to offer content that is personalized. E-commerce sites use personalization to more accurately target consumers with their products. Specialized content sites use personalization to aim the most appropriate content to a user's preferences. With a web site that offers this feature, the user feels more at home and generally tends to revisit the site more often. The web sites that offer personalization features always seem to have something to offer in an easy to navigate format because it is based on what the user has chosen. You can implement personalization into just about any type of site you may develop. Intranet sites, e-commerce sites, general web sites, online magazines, etc. all are wonderful types of sites to integrate this technology into.

Personalization in E-Commerce

Let's say you are developing an e-commerce site to sell products for your company. One of the design goals is to be able to target the products to the shopper. The products consist of a variety of clothing to gift products for friends or family. You would like to be able to handle a very large amount of users and offer a community feeling as well as display products that meet the interest of the shopper more prominently. With Site Server Personalization you can meet all of these requirements using the same technologies that have made development on a Microsoft platform so easy – Active Server Pages and COM. Personalization & Membership can collect information about the site's visitors, should they choose to enter the information. Site Server stores the users' interests in a membership directory. The next time the shopper logs into the site, you are able to present that person with products that are categorized with their interests. This is a benefit to the shoppers because they do not have to look far for what they are most likely visiting the site to find. P&M also offers the ability to handle a very large user base. This is done using a Lightweight Directory Access Protocol (LDAP) service that connects to the membership directory to retrieve the information stored about the shopper. You can even control access rights to content through P&M on a much greater scale than with a Windows NT domain, in terms of the number of users it can support.

How did you benefit from using Site Server?

❑　Personalization & Membership is designed to store user information and display content based on interests

❑　Millions of users are supported

❑　Access rights can be controlled using P&M to secure content

An e-commerce site that can target the consumer with products effectively has a greater chance of success in the wide variety of vendors that are peddling their wares online.

Personalization in the Intranet

An intranet can have as many user variations as an external site on the World Wide Web. In many companies different departments or divisions have their own web presence within the company offering information about the services they provide to the company. These sites must also target their content to their audience, the employees and present usable and valuable information that is needed for employees to do their job.

Let's talk a little bit about how personalization can enhance the web pages published by the human resource department of a company. Suppose you have been given the task of redesigning the pages. The site must be able to control access to the site using the Windows NT ACLs (Access Control Lists). Based on the user's Windows NT logon, the site must then display the appropriate content that the user should see based on their level within the company. Executive level information should not be viewed by lower management but executives have the opportunity to view all of the content within the web site with the most relevant information being the most prominent and easily accessible.

Site Server Personalization and Membership offers integration with NT security allowing you to define groups and then assign access privileges based on those groups much like the standard NT security model, but with support for a greater amount of users and the ability to add attributes to each user group or user profile.

You are able to tag HTML documents so that they fit within the preferences set up within the groups and set permissions using the Microsoft Management Console so that only users who have access to those documents may view them.

How did Site Server add value to this situation?

❑   Personalized content based on user attributes

❑   Ease of management

Personalization in a site can be a powerful tool when you want to take the extra step in your web site. Site Server's tools and components allow developers to create powerful and robust Internet and intranet applications in a relatively short manner of time.

Content

More and more, e-commerce sites are relying on specific content targeted at their customers in the hope of reaching new audiences and adding more value to their web sites. In the beginning, it was enough to offer a good price and an enjoyable site, but nowadays companies are integrating their sites with content related articles that add additional information for their customers, who might then be tempted to purchase their products.

Having content related articles on your site is a good idea because it keeps your customers coming back to read the articles and purchase more items on your site. For news pages and other real-time sites, content is certainly the key. For an e-commerce site however, the content doesn't have to change three times a day to be successful.

To help your web site's content, Site Server offers different Content Management and Replication tools. The Content Management tools allow you to custom tag your web pages to help automate the approval process within the posting of web pages and source control. Site Server Content Replication allows you to setup custom routes and projects that will let you replicate content from and to your Development, Staging and Production environments. Both of these tools help immensely when trying to manage the content for your site in any environment.

The other side of offering content has to be the extra effort needed to update the content on your site. Depending on how often you think your customers will be returning to your site is roughly how often you should change the content on your site. You can integrate weekly or monthly features that can offer your customers a reason to come back and visit your site on a regular basis, which is the reason for offering content in the first place! However, there are other options, luckily, and they include purchasing content from other sites or just changing the forming of your pages to reflect change.

Site Server Content Management

Managing your web site's content manually can be a timely waste of precious resources. Keeping up to date with the latest content on all of your servers, securing your content, and managing the approval process for all of your web pages can be a difficult task if done manually. With Site Server's Content Management features, you can offload most of this work to the server to free you up to take on more important tasks.

Most web sites have several people involved in submitting and managing the content of the site. The Content Management service supports the submission, editing, approving, and posting of documents to your site so you can have all of your content management done automatically. You can keep track of all of your web pages, spreadsheets, and graphics that are deployed to a single server with Content Management.

Just as you have to manage your content and the approval process, you also are stuck deploying your content and uploading web files manually. This practice of uploading individual files is both tiresome and time consuming. Working with the Content Management service for Site Server allows you to replicate the content of your site to several production servers that you specify by creating specific routes from development servers to your production servers. All that you have to do is deploy your content to one server, and create custom routes that you can use to deploy your content to each server along the way.

With Content Deployment, you can setup custom releases across your development, staging and production servers so that each has a copy of the latest copy of your web content. These projects and routes let you setup content deployment automatically so there won't be any manual intervention. Content Deployment allows you to design a release schedule, configure automatic updates, or even rollback the content of your site regardless of the location of your web servers. Content Deployment will ensure that each server will have the latest and greatest version of your content.

Active Channel Server

Site Server can optionally offer "push" technology to deliver content to subscribed users through the Active Channel Server. When a user subscribes to a channel, they are pointing to a URL that Site Server can use to deliver content down to their desktop. Unfortunately, the main problem with this technology is that Internet Explorer is the only Internet browser that supports the Active Channel or a specification used for creating channels known as the Channel Definition Format (CDF). This will not work with any other browser, which limits its usefulness in the Internet world but is feasible in a controlled browser environment such as an intranet.

Another important part of this equation is making sure on the server end that you have the necessary bandwidth to support feeds from an Active Channel Server. The more subscribers you have, and the larger the content that you're pushing out, the more you will require sufficient bandwidth. It would be a good idea to speak with your ISP before rolling out this service to make sure you'll have enough resources. Without the right amount of bandwidth, you can run into some problems with this server component.

We will not be discussing Active Channel Server again in this book.

Active Channel Multicaster

The Active Channel Multicaster uses IP Multicasting, a method of transferring information by only sending the data once across the network, to deliver its content to the subscribers of this service. Multicast delivers the content down to the subscribers who want to receive the feed, which helps save bandwidth. With the Active Channel Multicaster, subscribers receive the content at specified times without having to outright search for it. The content is delivered to them much like a magazine subscription or a morning newspaper.

We will also not be discussing Active Channel Multicaster again in this book.

Audience Development

Driving people to your site relies on knowing your audience. This can all be thought of as common sense and marketing to some of the strengths of your site and business. If your site deals with financial subscribers, offering stock quotes and investment research are two plus points. You can also target your audience by directing advertising to your customers that they may be interested in. As the e-commerce boom continues to take off, a lot of web companies are now relying on traditional advertising campaigns such as TV, newspapers and radio to get their message across and create buzz towards their site. The importance lies in the fact that the more that people know about your site, the more likely they'll be to come and browse.

There are more methods than you may traditionally be accustomed to in the world of e-commerce. As the web is so crowded, people rely on search engines to find what they are interested in. So instead of looking up a prospective business in a phonebook, they'll turn to search engines such as `Lycos` or `Altavista` to find what they're looking for.

And your next question should be, "How do search engines work?"

Search engines are not proactive, and need to be populated with the latest information as to the sites' development. To make it easier for search engines to do their job, you can insert what are known as meta-tags into your web pages that detail a little about your site and web pages and are used by the search engines.

There are also web sites that will automate the process of driving people to your site by populating each and every major search engine on the Internet, but you will still need to work on working with either the search engines or on-line advertising.

The way most search engines work is that they will look within the content of your site. However, to help the search engines do some of the work, <META> tags are used so search engines don't have to search an entire page when they can parse the <META> symbol in most web pages. Under the <META> tags within the page, web designers place important words about their site so the web search engines can help categorize the site. So when you type if a specific word in a search engine, the web page will be retrieved due to the <META> tags.

For example, if you're looking for a specific page about the food industry, you can type in search words such as "food", "restaurants", or "suppliers". By comparing what the search engine already knows about the food industry and the <META> tags that are found in the web pages, they can relay what you're looking for to your browser. Most search engines work by using an automated "spider" or "robot" to search the content or text of a web site submission.

Submission web sites such as Yahoo! work by people manually sending their links and pages to be included within their directory. Since a person has to physically look at the site to categorize the pages, <META> tags are neither used nor read.

One of the problems with Active Server Pages and using a spider to crawl the content of the site is that ASP technology creates dynamic pages whose content changes all of the time. You can't crawl a site that generates dynamic content upon demand, and expect accurate results from search engines.

Site Server Search

As web sites become larger and larger, a search component of any site is needed. Site Server provides a search component that offers the ability to build a catalog of a specific site as well as the query features so people who visit your site can find the specific pages you'll need. Whether you're going to be setting up search for your own site within your extranet, an e-commerce portal, or crawling your Exchange Public folders, Search can work for you. Search works by creating indexes of information so it can quickly be referenced when a query is made. Instead of searching the entire site, sites, or folders each time a search query is made, a catalog is made in advance to help speed up the query with the latest information. Once the Search server receives the query, the catalog is referenced and the query is sent back to the client with the links to their information. This greatly improves speed and performance when a search is made.

There are many different scenarios in which you will use the Search functionality within Site Server and the best way to make sure you implement Search correctly is to plan accordingly. Setting up Search is not all that difficult within Site Server, but it's important to make sure you plan for the future so that you don't run into scalability problems or extremely slow queries.

Site Server Gatherer service is used to build a catalog of a information so that queries can be made using several different forms of data stores such as Exchange Public Folders, SQL Server tables, HTML and Office documents as well as external web sites. The Site Server Gatherer service for Site Server is used to index the content of your site and the Search service is used for any user or content searches.

For performance and scalability reasons, the Site Server Search Service can reside on a separate server to increase the performance. Each time a query is made on the site, a lot of processor resources are used which can affect the site:

❑ **The Catalog Server:**
Your Catalog build server can be one of many servers that you specify to collect the catalog indexes for your search. Your catalog servers will do the actual work by going out and crawling the sites that you point them at. If you have a small amount of data that you want to catalog, you won't need more than one catalog build server, but if you keep a single catalog build server along with your search server, this can affect performance for your site. It is best to use a dedicated server to perform these duties if you can afford the resources.

❑ **The Search Server:**
Your search server collects the catalog data and executes a search each and every time that a search query is processed. To improve performance, you can use multiple search servers, as long as they have Site Server search installed.

Security

Having a secure web site for your e-commerce platform is a fundamental part of your site, not to mention your business. By securing your site, your customers can feel safe, and you can rest easy making credit card transactions over the web.

We'll explore the issue of security more as we progress through the book, but this topic is of such importance that we are going to mention it more than once. Having a security leak is a surefire way to lose your business. If your customers lose confidence in your ability to provide a secure and safe site for them to shop, you can bet that they'll run to your competitors who may be able to do a better job.

When discussing the various parts of your site, you have to take into account the many different parts of where your security can fail. This will help you to better understand how an e-commerce system works. Microsoft Site Server, like other e-commerce products, is more complicated than it seems after a first glance. Site Server relies on other Microsoft products, such as Internet Information Server, Windows NT, and SQL Server as well as the different programming concepts of your Active Server Pages.

Each part of the system is a potential security leak that you need to be aware of. From the time that the software was initially released, security holes and bugs have been fixed through service packs and hot-fixes. It's your job to make sure that all of the security holes are patched, and your system is locked down as much as possible without compromising the user experience.

Below is a listing of some of the security concerns that you'll have to contain to effectively secure your entire commerce solution:

❑   **Physical Security:**
    The first basis of any security practice starts and finishes with maintaining a degree of physical security for your web servers and other components of your site. Having physical security can take the form of keeping your computers in a locked room, off-site storage of your data, and restricting access to only those who need access to your system.

❑   **Digital ID/Certificates:**
    To allow secure and safe credit card transfers across the Internet, you'll have to obtain a Digital ID from a third-party provider such as `VeriSign` or `Entrust.com`. Once you install your Digital Server Certificate for your web site, you can enable the Secure Socket Layer (SSL) protocol that encrypts the data from the client to the server.

❑   **Software security:**
    Locking down your code is an essential part of making sure that your customers or business competitors don't "borrow" or learn enough information about your site to compromise any data. You can secure your code by placing your business logic in COM components, include statements, or in your `.asp` files that only have execute permissions associated with them. You have many different options, but the less information that you can give away the better.

❑   **Server Security:**
    Because your e-commerce solution is made up of so many different server components from the operating system (Windows NT), web server (IIS), database (SQL) and commerce platform (Site Server), you have to make sure that you can secure your site from unwanted visitors or hackers. When initially installed, there are very few, if any, security measures that are taken to keep anyone from accessing your system.

    Therefore, it is up to you to lock down and secure your servers because in reality it is your data that is at risk. You never want to take anything for granted with your Internet security, and we'll be discussing different security topics in greater detail later on in the book.

❑   **Firewalls/VPN:**
    For any commerce site, you're going to need an extra level of security that only a firewall or Virtual Private Network (VPN) can offer. A firewall can monitor any traffic to and from your site to ensure you that nobody is compromising your security. A VPN can enable secure processing between remote locations such as your ISP or business partners.

As you start to recruit more and more customers to your site, you'll need to reinforce the safety of e-commerce. Consumers are worried about the privacy and security of their on-line transactions. "Although only 2% of Visa International Inc.'s credit-card business relates to Internet transactions, 50% of its disputes and discovered frauds are in that area," said Mark Cullimore a director at Visa International.

Summary

E-commerce is a business that is still being defined each day, evolving as companies move to doing more business online. Site Server covers many aspects of e-commerce with its tools being targeted at selling product or services, from managing the content displayed to the shoppers or users of a site to actually targeting products to specific demographic groups.

Site Server employs technologies that are already in use by many Internet developers and does not bring some radically new, hard to understand technology to the table. With a little guidance, patience and understanding of just what makes up Site Server, powerful and robust web sites can be developed in a relatively short amount of time.

Whether you are developing to allow internal purchasing or plan to sell CDs or books online, Site Server has almost every area of the online business covered. The extensibility allows you to expand with third party components or create your own to accommodate changing business patterns.

Installation

I have performed thousands of Site Server Installations...literally. When I worked on the Olympus (Site Server 3.0) product team, writing architectural components that would be used in the sample sites, my team and I needed to install the latest build of Site Server each day. The installation of Site Server is a meticulous and arduous process.

> **If you skip a step or perform one out of the proper order you are almost guaranteed an unsuccessful installation. And worse yet, there's usually no way to fix an unsuccessful installation, short of wiping your server clean and starting over.**

You'll see later in this chapter that there are five different types of Site Server installations:

- ❑ On the Windows NT 4.0 Platform
    - ❑ Without SQL Server on the box
    - ❑ With SQL Server 6.5 on the box
    - ❑ With SQL Server 7.0 on the box
- ❑ On the Windows 2000 Server Platform
    - ❑ Without SQL Server on the box
    - ❑ With SQL Server 7.0 on the box

The first three start with a base platform of Windows NT 4.0 **Service Pack 3**. I failed an installation just the other day. The network group of the fortune 500 company that I was consulting for installed a server for me. I asked them to take it to a Windows NT 4.0 Service Pack 3 level, and I would take it from there. Two days passed and the network group decided that I must have meant the most current Service Pack at the time, which was Windows NT 4.0 Service Pack 5, so they installed it to that level.

Removing the Service Pack is possible if you choose to create an uninstall directory as an option in the Service Pack install – but unfortunately they did not. I knew that the box would have to be wiped clean and rebuilt to get back to the Service Pack 3 level, and that would take a tremendous amount of time. So I gambled and tried to install from the Service Pack 5 point – following the proper steps in order, but skipping the Service Pack 4 and 5 installations. When it came to the Site Server installation, the computer hung right in the middle of the installation and the box was ruined. I had to wipe the server clean and start completely over.

I tell you that story to show why it's so important to follow the installation steps in this chapter exactly. I've been told that over 90% of the PSS (Microsoft Product Support) calls for Site Server 3.0 are installation related – most people can't even install this beast – but I've outlined the steps very carefully here for you in this chapter, so that you'll be sure of a successful installation.

> **Do yourself a favor – start from scratch. Wipe your box clean with an `FDISK` or equivalent, and repartition your drives as described below. Starting from scratch will guarantee a clean installation.**

In this chapter you'll learn the preparation steps that you need to make before your installation. You'll also be informed of all the potential problems caused by the installation of other Microsoft Server Products on your Site Server. You'll learn how to set up, install and configure the NT 4.0 or Windows 2000 platform that your Site Server will be installed on. You'll also be instructed on when to apply the Service Packs, patches, and "hot-fixes".

Throughout this chapter there are references to URLs on the Microsoft site where you can download Service Packs, patches, etc. At the time of writing, Microsoft Product Support Services is in the process of moving all downloadable support files from the Software Library to the Microsoft Download Center. With the Microsoft Download Center, you will have:

A single starting point for all downloadable files.

The ability to search the entire Microsoft.com site for downloadable files.

Reduced time in finding these files.

If you do not find your files from URLs listed in this chapter, please check the Microsoft Download Center (`http://www.microsoft.com/downloads/search.asp`).

Prerequisite Hardware

Microsoft recommends at least a Pentium 166, with 128Mb of RAM installed and a 4Gb hard drive. Although the product will install with this minimum (with a couple tricks you'll learn in this chapter), even with SQL Server installed on the same box, it will barely run.

Because Site Server is such a monster, it's stating the obvious to say that the more CPU and the more RAM you give it, the better it runs.

- ❑ For a development server (with only a handful of developers hitting off it) you'll be just fine with a minimum install of a Pentium 300 and 256Mb of RAM.

- ❑ Production Servers should have at least 500Mb of RAM, and at least Pentium III 500s.

There are actually some fairly thorough Site Server configuration calculations on the Microsoft Web Site that are dependant on the types of Site Server Technologies that you employ (Personalization and Membership, Content Analysis, Usage Import, etc.) and the number of users you are expecting to hit your Site Server. You can find those calculations and other Capacity and Performance Analyses at `http://www.microsoft.com/siteserver/site/DeployAdmin/CapacityPerform.htm`.

What Else is Needed to Install Site Server?

Site Server and SSCE rely on several foundation services to provide operating system functionality, web services and a data repository. The following are the core components that should be installed before the core Site Server services are loaded:

- ❑ Windows NT 4.0 / Windows 2000
- ❑ SQL Server 6.5/7.0
- ❑ Internet Information Server
- ❑ Development tool: FrontPage98/2000 or Visual Studio 6.0 with Visual Studio SP3

These are the basis for the rest of your Site Server installation, and can make or break your installation if they are configured incorrectly. Installation details can be found later in this chapter.

Microsoft Windows NT 4.0 / 2000

Windows NT and 2000 Server are stable, secure, scalable and high-performance operating systems that are the basis for the entire Site Server platform. Each server component and service that you'll install will need to work and interact with Windows NT/2000 Server. These Windows services provide the basic functionality and security for the entire platform.

The Windows NT Server security model is one of the most important services that it provides for the Site Server platform. This security model is based on the Windows NT user account database, which provides security for all computers within the Windows NT domain. Each user account within the domain has a set amount of permissions that it can use to authenticate people to use resources. Site Server uses this security model to provide security for all of the Site Server services. If you want to use, administer, or change any of the parameters for any Site Server service, you'll need to be a member of the Site Server administrators group for that account.

If you are not using domain security, Windows NT can still use a local account database that acts in a similar way by making sure that each Site Server service has the correct amount of permissions.

Service Packs, Patches, and Hot-fixes

Service Packs are the means by which the Windows Product Updates are distributed. Service Packs keep the product current, extend and update your computer's functionality, include bug fixes, updates, system administration tools, drivers, and additional components. For easy downloading and installation, Service Packs are bundled into a compressed executable.

Site Server has evolved since its original inception, and requires the necessary Services Packs or hot-fixes to function correctly. Windows NT 4.0 Server by itself does not provide the necessary hot-fixes or updates, so you have to rely on the Service Packs for bug fixes and security patches. You'll also need to make sure that you have the latest Windows NT 4.0 Service Pack installed as part of your complete Site Server installation.

Service Packs are cumulative; in other words, each Service Pack contains all the fixes in previous Service Packs, as well as any new fixes. Unfortunately, for a Site Server installation you are not afforded the luxury of simply installing Windows NT 4 Service Pack 6. You must painstakingly install Service Pack 3, and then later in the installation process you must install Service Packs 4 and 6.

Note the absence of Windows NT 4.0, Service Pack 5 from the above paragraph. It is not necessary for our installation process and may even be harmful.

> **Once again: it is vital for a successful installation that you follow exactly *and only* the procedures detailed for your installation. Make sure you follow the directions later in this chapter for your latest Service Pack, and check out the Microsoft Knowledge Base if you have any questions.**

Patches and "**hot-fixes**" are usually smaller compressed executables that fix one particular problem that is missed in a Service Pack. Patches and hot-fixes don't usually require a reboot after installation, whereas a Service Pack does.

Microsoft SQL Server 6.5/7.0

One of the strongest features of SQL Server is its ability to integrate with the Windows NT/2000 and Site Server architecture. This gives SQL Server an inherent advantage over other relational databases such as Oracle, Sybase and IBM's DB2, in both performance terms and interaction with Windows NT and Site Server.

Within the core Site Server services, SQL Server provides the data repository for your Commerce data, Ad server, Analysis and Membership Directory. With each new release of SQL Server, the administration and configuration of the database becomes easier and easier. SQL Server fits in nicely with the entire Site Server platform, with the Site Foundation Wizard examples and pieces of code that demonstrate how to integrate your website with SQL Server. SQL Server 7 also provides a Web Assistant Wizard that can help you publish data contained in a SQL table to a web page.

You have a couple of different options for installing SQL Server into your environment, which offers you a lot of flexibility when it comes to designing your web site solution. You can use either a local installation of SQL Server along with Site Server, or use a dedicated server running SQL Server. Installing both Microsoft SQL Server and Site Server on your local machine might be fine for small sites, where performance and redundancy are not an issue, but for larger sites this will hinder your room to grow. If you decide to use a dedicated SQL Server, you also have the option of using Microsoft Cluster Server for your database, to add another layer of redundancy for your Site Server implementation.

Microsoft Internet Information Server 4.0/5.0

Internet Information Server (IIS) provides your web publishing services and combines much of Site Server's functionality by meshing the rest of your services together. With IIS, you have the combination of a web server, FTP server, and SMTP server for mail services.

Most importantly, IIS provides the necessary platform for **Active Server Pages** (**ASP**) technology. Much of the development that you'll be using later on in this book is built in from the functionality of IIS. Active Server Pages allows you to build highly customizable and dynamic applications that can easily connect to back-end databases or be used to gather information on specific clients.

To learn more about the basics and functionality of Internet Information Server, you can check out Chapter 3 where we go over the product in greater detail.

Microsoft Transaction Server

If you're using Windows NT 4.0, you'll also need to install Microsoft Transaction Server (MTS). MTS is a component-based model for developing, deploying and managing applications. IIS and Site Server use it to enable transactions for your site. We'll see more about transactions in Chapter 6.

If you're using Windows 2000, MTS services will already be installed as part of COM+.

MTS can be obtained from NT Option Pack, or downloaded from Microsoft's web site.

Development: FrontPage 2000 or Visual Studio 6.0

Since this book explores basic development concepts with Site Server, you're going to need to install a development tool onto your development machine so you can work locally if you need to. Microsoft offers several choices of tool for your web site development, and which you choose depends on your level of expertise and the features you require.

For those new to web development, Microsoft FrontPage can get your web site up and running very quickly. FrontPage is a relatively easy development tool to grasp, which offers WYSIWIG (What You See Is What You Get) HTML, web site development and management tools for your site. What you gain in ease of use, you trade off in power and functionality. FrontPage does have a few drawbacks, in terms of generating "pure" HTML that is created by a WYSIWIG tool. And, if you use it to edit an HTML page that was not originally created in Frontpage, it can potentially break that page by introducing problems in the automatically generated HTML.

To combat this, many ASP and HTML developers have taken to the basic text editor, Notepad (or Visual Notepad as it is sometimes referred to), which offers quick and easy results – provided you know HTML.

While Front Page is designed with web authors in mind, more experienced web developers can take advantage of Visual InterDev for more advanced programming and HTML editing. Visual InterDev offers developers a very powerful tool to create dynamic web pages with ASP and connect to back-end databases with ease. The learning curve is greater with Visual InterDev, but the power and functionality more than makes up for that. Visual InterDev contains many different tools and wizards that can have you developing web applications in no time at all.

Although FrontPage and Visual InterDev aren't part of the strict requirements when you install Microsoft Site Server, the installation program will attempt to find the FrontPage program and server extensions. If the installation program can't find FrontPage, you'll be reminded of that during the installation process.

FrontPage Server extensions are very important for the development aspect of your install, when you begin to start creating web projects with Visual InterDev and FrontPage. Server extensions are used to manage your web projects and source control, add additional authors, manipulate and deploy files within your site, and provide a programming free environment to make building your site easier.

You can find the Visual InterDev and FrontPage software that is distributed with your Site Server license. FrontPage 2000 is also available with Office 2000 Premium, and Visual InterDev is one member of the Visual Studio 6.0 platform that also includes Visual J++, Visual Basic, Visual C++ and Visual FoxPro.

Drive Partitioning

Obviously, you'll need quite a bit of drive space for a Site Server installation. 4Gbs of space will more than accommodate the product: most likely, you'll have more than that amount of space. Since Windows NT will only install into a maximum of a 4Gb FAT (File Allocation Table) system partition, you'll also most likely have a multi-partitioned drive.

I normally configure my servers into three different partitions. I have the C:\ drive as the System\Boot drive on a 2Gb FAT partition. FAT partitions are faster than NTFS (Windows NT File System) partitions, so that's where I install Windows NT 4.0 or Windows 2000. Having a 2Gb C:\ partition leaves enough space for the operating system and the page file for your server. However, if you are installing with more than 2Gb of memory, you can increase this as necessary.

Next (in physical, not logical order), I create a 2Gb FAT partition that I tell Windows NT 4.0 or Windows 2000 to use as G:. I use this partition to store my "ghost" images. Norton Ghost is an incredibly powerful program produced by Symantec. Among many other things, Ghost allows you to quickly make (or restore) file images of your FAT or NTFS partitions and store them on a FAT partition.

For instance, on Windows NT 4.0 I always make a "ghost image" of both the FAT and NTFS partitions at the Windows NT Service Pack 3 level. The reason is that, just in case of disaster, I can quickly (normally within 15 minutes) revert back to a platform that took me 4 hours to install and configure. Additionally, I usually make a "ghost" at the NT 4 Option Pack level, and then another when I'm done applying the final Site Server Service Pack 3. On Windows 2000, I always make a ghost image right before installation of Site Server 3.0. Again, this is an optional step, but highly recommended.

Back in the "old" days, it was common to hang your web servers outside the firewall exposed to hackers. If a web server ever got hacked (and they did – and still do), it was painless to simply restore the web server quickly from a ghost image. You can find out more about Norton Ghost at http://www.symantec.com/sabu/ghost/index.html.

After the installation of Windows NT 4.0 or Windows 2000, I use the Windows NT 4.0 Disk Administrator or Windows 2000 Disk Management Utility to change the drive letter of my ghost partition from D: to G:. The Disk Administrator can be found on Windows NT 4.0 by clicking Start, then Programs, then Administrative Tools (Common). The Disk Management Utility can be found on Windows 2000 by clicking Start | Programs | Administrative Tools | Computer Management.

This "ghost" partition is an optional partition that I do not use for Windows NT 4.0 or Windows 2000 system and data files. I simply have it to house the ghost program and any images of the partitions that I make.

And finally I format all the remaining drive space as an NTFS partition with the Windows NT 4.0 Disk Administrator or the Windows 2000 Disk Management Utility. NTFS partitions allow you to apply permissions to the files and folders on the disk. I configure Windows NT 4.0 or Windows 2000 to see the NTFS partition as D: with the Disk Administrator or Disk Management Utility also. This is where I put all data, the web server content (`inetpub`), and Site Server.

> **Site Server needs to be installed on NTFS to run correctly, to apply some of the security SS offers.**

I normally set up the E:\ drive as the CD-ROM device, again with Disk Administrator or Disk Management Utility.

If you use my recommended partitioning set up, your drive partitions will look similar, if not identical to this Windows NT 4.0 Disk Administrator:

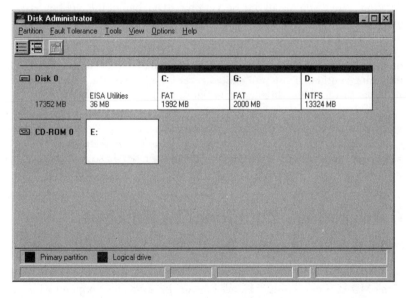

When you're done making all the changes in the Windows NT 4.0 Disk Administrator, make sure to create an emergency repair diskette by running `rdisk.exe`. On Windows 2000, create an emergency repair disk by clicking Start | Programs | Accessories | System Tools | Backup. On the Tools menu, choose Create an Emergency Repair Disk. Along with ghost, an updated emergency repair disk can get you back up quickly and efficiently in case of disaster.

Pre-installation Tips and Tricks

Don't you wish that someone would collect all those little pearls of wisdom and give them to you before you have to say, "I wish someone had told me that before...". Well, here goes.

Windows NT Domain Controllers

Microsoft Site Server 3.0 was designed primarily for installation on NT 4.0 stand alone servers or Windows 2000 member servers. Microsoft recommends that you install Windows NT Server 4.0 or Windows 2000 as a stand-alone or member server, rather than as a domain controller.

One of the by-products of a Site Server installation is group creation. In a stand-alone server, local groups are created. If you install Site Server on a Windows NT 4.0 Primary Domain Controller or Windows 2000 Domain Controller (PDC), then domain groups are created. This is dangerous for many reasons, one of which is that many of your services will have to bind and run as the domain administrator. Having services run by proxy as the domain administrator poses an unnecessary security risk.

Installing Site Server on a Back Up Domain Controller (BDC) is possible, but requires a major manual effort in configuration. When you install Site Server on a BDC, half of the Site Server groups are created, but you have to manually create the shadow groups and accounts that are required for Site Server Personalization and Membership.

Additionally, once you've installed Site Server and join a domain, you cannot remove it from that domain without joining another. If you pull a Site Server out of a domain, many of the services will continue to send broadcast packets while trying to figure out where the domain went...forever.

> *You can read more about the complications of domain installations of Site Server in the Site Server 3.0 Getting Started booklet. Additionally you can read the Knowledge Base Article at* `http://support.microsoft.com/support/kb/articles/q184/7/60.asp` *for more information.*

Microsoft Data Access Components (MDAC)

MDAC (**Microsoft Data Access Components**) and **ADO** (**ActiveX Data Objects**) are almost synonymous.

One of the most common questions for any software developer or network engineer is "How can I tell what version of the MDAC I'm running?" Here's how to check on any computer with a Microsoft operating system (Windows 95 and above). Get a Windows Explorer running and navigate to `\Program Files\Common Files\System\ADO`, which will usually reside on drive `C:`. Locate the most recent version of `msado??.dll` (where ?? is specific to your computer) – most likely it will be `msado15.dll`:

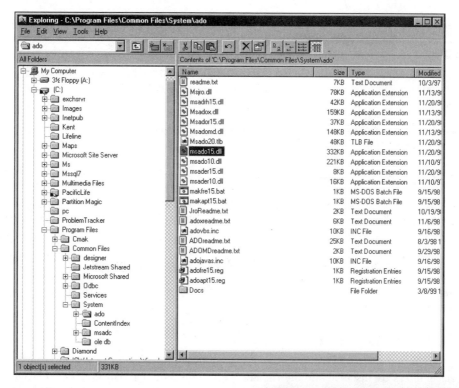

Right click on the `msado??.dll` file and choose **Properties**. Now select the **Version** tab, as shown below. The first two segments of the number highlighted, in this case the 2.10 of 2.10.3513.2.9, is the MDAC version that you are running:

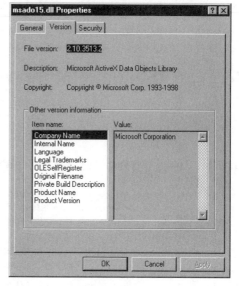

For more granular details of the MDAC versions, refer to:
`http://www.microsoft.com/Data/MDAC21info/MDACinstQ.htm.`

If you carefully follow the installation directions later in this chapter you won't have any problems with the wrong version of the MDAC being installed.

Microsoft Cluster Service / Windows NT Load Balancing Service

Microsoft recommends that you do not install Site Server 3.0 on a computer running Microsoft Cluster Service (MSCS). You can, however, install Site Server onto Windows NT Load Balancing Service (WLBS).

For more details, refer to Knowledge Base Article Q228999 at
`http://support.microsoft.com/support/kb/articles/q228/9/99.asp`.

Microsoft Exchange Server

Microsoft recommends that you do not install Microsoft Exchange Server on a computer with Site Server installed. Because both server products are resource intensive, performance decreases greatly when these products are installed on the same computer

Microsoft BackOffice Small Business Server

Microsoft recommends that you not install Site Server 3.0 on a computer running Microsoft BackOffice Small Business Server.

Microsoft Proxy Server 2.0

When you install Microsoft Proxy Server 2.0, some ISAPI (Internet Server Application Programming Interface) filters are installed and the Default Web Site is modified. For this reason, Microsoft recommends that you do not install Microsoft Proxy Server 2.0 on a computer with Site Server 3.0.

For more details, refer to Knowledge Base article Q216991 at
`http://support.microsoft.com/support/kb/articles/q216/9/91.asp`.

Microsoft Commercial Internet System (MCIS)

Microsoft recommends that you do not install Commerce Server on a computer with Microsoft Commercial Internet System (MCIS) that requires Internet Explorer 5.0.

The Five Types of Site Server Installation

As we mentioned at the start of this chapter, the installation of Microsoft Site Server Version 3.0 has five variations. As the steps of installation for each of these variations can be dramatically different, we've divided this chapter into the following sections:

- ❑ Installing SS3 on Windows NT 4.0 on a computer without SQL Server, go to page 39
- ❑ Installing SS3 on Windows NT 4.0 on a computer with SQL Server 6.5, go to page 73
- ❑ Installing SS3 on Windows NT 4.0 on a computer with SQL Server 7.0, go to page 108
- ❑ Installing SS3 on Windows 2000 on a computer without SQL Server, go to page 141
- ❑ Installing SS3 on Windows 2000 on a computer with SQL Server 7.0, go to page 164
- ❑ Post-Installation Patches, Fixes and Configurations, go to page 186

> **Each section gives you a complete step-by-step guide on how to install Site Server for that scenario. You need only read one of the five installation sections, the one relevant to the installation configuration you will be following, and can skip the others. Whichever installation option you perform, you should then move on to the final section, which has post-installation information.**

The recommended installation is installing Site Server without installing SQL server on the same box.

SQL Server 6.5 was the initial database platform that was designed for both versions of Site Server, but there are many new features of SQL Server that you can take advantage of with version 7.0. With SQL Server 7.0, you have a better performing database, whose features include auto-tuning simple administration practices, and a more "Internet-enabled" database.

The Site Server Installation Matrix below summarizes the major components that need to be installed in their proper installation order for each of the three different NT 4.0 installation scenarios:

	Without SQL	With SQL 6.5	With SQL 7.0
NT4	1	1	1
NT4 SP3	2	2	2
SQL 6.5		3	
SQL 6.5 SP4		4	
IE4 SP2	3	5	3
NT4 OP	4	6	4
FP98 Svr Extns	5	7	5
SS3	6	8	10
SS3 Commerce	7	9	11
NT4 SP4	8	9	6
IE5			7
SQL 7.0			8
SQL 7.0 SP1			9
MDAC2.1SP2	9	12	12
SQL 6.5 SP5a		11	
ADSI 2.5	10	13	13
SS3 SP3	11	14	14
NT4 SP6	12	15	15

Key	
NT4	Windows NT Server 4.0
SP	Service Pack
SQL	Microsoft SQL Server
OP	Option Pack
IE	Microsoft Internet Explorer
FP98	FrontPage 98
SS3	Site Server 3.0
MDAC	Microsoft Data Access Components
ADSI	Active Directory Services Interface

And for the Windows 2000 options:

	Without SQL	With SQL 7.0
Win2K	1	1
SQL 7.0		2
SQL 7.0 SP1		3
SS3W2k	2	4
SS3	3	5
SS3 Commerce	4	6
SS3 SP3	5	7

Key

Win2K	Windows 2000 Server
SS3W2K	SS3W2K.exe patch
SP	Service Pack
SQL	Microsoft SQL Server
SS3	Site Server 3.0

Installing SS3 on Windows NT 4.0 Without SQL Server

> Read this section if your operating system is Windows NT 4.0 and you have a dedicated box for Site Server; that is, if your SQL Server resides on a separate machine.

Windows NT 4.0

Install Microsoft Windows NT Server 4.0. Again, to guarantee a successful Site Server 3.0 Commerce installation I suggest you start with a clean computer, or have the Windows NT 4.0 installation wipe the hard drives clean before starting its installation.

Windows NT 4.0 installation instructions are beyond the scope of this book. There is an abundance of information on how to install the Windows NT 4.0 product on the web, but the product documentation from Microsoft is outstanding. You'll find it on the Windows NT 4.0 CD in the \SUPPORT\BOOKS folder.

Since custom drivers are needed to access the hardware (video, network, etc.) refer to the Microsoft Windows NT 4.0 product documentation and the documentation for the specific hardware that you have in your system. After you complete your Windows NT installation, there is a good chance you will need to install third party (non Microsoft) drivers for the unique hardware (video, network boards, etc.) that you have in your system.

Here are the important points for your Windows NT 4.0 installation:

- ❑ Install Windows NT 4.0 as a **stand-alone** server, if possible.
- ❑ There's no need to install Internet Information Server, although it doesn't hurt. You will be installing Internet Information Server 4.0 in a subsequent step, when you install the Windows NT Option Pack.
- ❑ Although not crucial, it will make your installation quite a bit easier if you have a floppy diskette with updated drivers for your network board. This is especially important if the Windows NT 4.0 installation cannot identify what type of network board you have, or if it does not have a driver for your particular network board.
- ❑ Complete the partitioning, formatting and assigning of drives with the Windows NT 4.0 Disk Administrator when you have completed the Windows NT 4.0 installation. Refer to the Drive Partitioning section above for details.

Windows NT4 Service Pack 3

Install Microsoft Windows NT 4.0 Service Pack 3. You can download the Service Pack from: http://support.microsoft.com/support/ntserver/content/servicepacks/SP3.asp.

> It is very important that you *do not* substitute Windows NT 4.0 Service Pack 4 (or later) at this point.

The installation of Windows NT Service Pack 3 is a simple 4-step wizard. The first step is a splash screen that describes the installation process of the Service Pack. Upon clicking **Next** you will be asked to confirm your intent to install the Service Pack:

Click **Next** and you'll be asked if you want to create an uninstall directory. I always play it safe and create an uninstall directory for any Service Pack that I apply. Murphy's Law will most likely dictate a power failure in the middle of your Service Pack install – if you have an uninstall directory you'll be able to quickly recover:

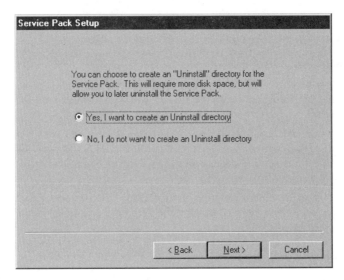

Click **Next** and you will be asked to confirm the installation of Windows NT 4.0 Service Pack 3 by clicking **Finish**. It will take the installation a few minutes to create the uninstall directory, copy the necessary files, do the DLL registrations, and perform the configurations. Upon completion you'll receive a dialog asking you to remove all floppies and CD ROMs because the installation needs to perform a restart of your system:

After the reboot, you'll have a base platform of Windows NT 4.0 Service Pack 3. At this point, although it's certainly not necessary, I recommend making a "ghost". Refer to the Drive Partitioning section of this chapter (above) if you are not familiar with Symantec's Norton Ghost software.

Internet Explorer 4 Service Pack 2

Install Microsoft Internet Explorer 4.01 with Internet Explorer Service Pack 2. You can download Internet Explorer 4.01 and the Service Pack in one executable from:
`http://www.microsoft.com/msdownload/iebuild/ie4sp2_win32/en/ie4sp2_win32.htm`.

> **Do not substitute Internet Explorer 5.0 at this point. If you want to install Internet Explorer 5.0, then install it last, and read the installation notes and caveats that are described at the end of this chapter.**

The installation of the IE4 SP2 uses a wizard. The first screen of the wizard is a splash screen describing the process. Click Next and you'll be presented with the licensing agreement. If you agree with the licensing of IE4, click I accept and then Next. If you downloaded the installation from the Microsoft web site you'll be prompted with Download Options:

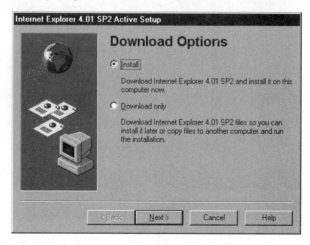

If you have an IE4 SP2 CD, you won't be prompted with Download Options, because you'll have all the installation components on the CD.

If you're doing a "web" installation of IE4, then choose Install and click Next. You'll be prompted with three installation options: Standard Installation, Browser Only installation or a Full Installation. The default choice is the Standard Installation, which installs the IE4 Browser, Outlook Express, Windows Media Player and multimedia enhancements. A standard installation is fine:

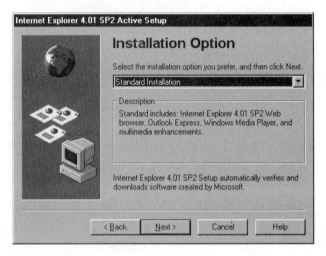

Choose Next, and you'll be presented with a chance to install the Windows Desktop Update, also called the Active Desktop:

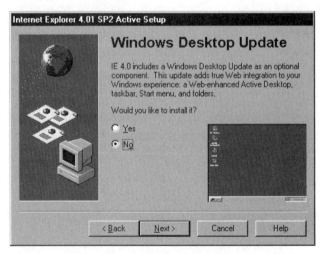

Select No and then click Next, to choose a standard desktop installation.

Now you'll be prompted to choose a region that best represents the country and language of your Active Channel installation. Choose the proper region and click Next.

You'll be prompted for a destination folder for your Internet Explorer 4.0 SP2. If you partitioned your drive and set up your drive mappings as recommended earlier in the chapter, then accept the default on C:.

After copying files and configuring your system, you'll be prompted to restart your system to complete the installation. Choose OK to restart.

Windows NT4 Option Pack

Install the Microsoft Windows NT 4.0 Option Pack. You can download the Option Pack from: http://www.microsoft.com/ntserver/nts/downloads/recommended/NT4OptPk/default.asp.

The Option Pack will install the web services required for Site Server:

❑ The WWW service

❑ The FTP service

❑ The SMTP service

❑ Transaction Server

❑ Index Server

The Option Pack set-up is a web-based installation. If you use an Option Pack CD to do the installation, then the browser will auto start. Choose Install from the left navigation frame in the browser:

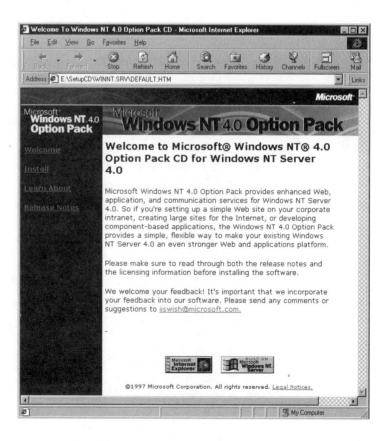

Next in the CD set-up you'll be presented with the choices to install Windows NT 4.0 Service Pack 3 and Internet Explorer 4.01. These are prerequisites for a Windows NT 4.0 Option Pack set up:

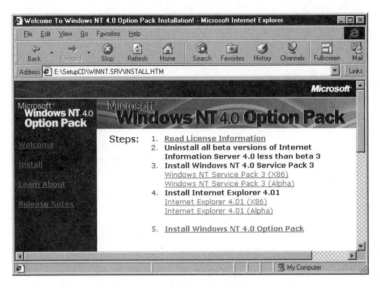

If you've followed the steps outlined above then you have already installed SP3 and IE4, so click Install Window NT 4.0 Option Pack to proceed with the installation. If doing a web installation, and prompted, perform an Upgrade Plus installation. This is critical, since you will need to add specific services. Selecting Upgrade instead of Upgrade Plus will not get you everything you need for a successful Site Server installation.

Next, you'll be presented with a dialog containing a relatively confusing question: "would you like to Run this program from its current location or Save this program to disk?":

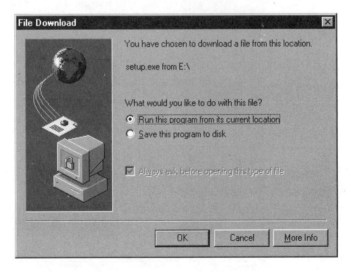

You'll need to understand the implications of this question, because you'll see it quite a bit if you are to download executables from a browser.

If you're running the installation from the Windows NT 4.0 Option Pack CD, Internet Explorer (or any browser for that matter) is not smart enough to know that you have the installation program on a local CD, so it asks you if you want to download it. If you were truly downloading the Windows NT 4.0 Option Pack from the Microsoft web site, then you would Save this program to disk and run it after it's been successfully downloaded. But, if you have a local CD with the Installation software then choose Run this program from its current location.

Next, you get a dialog alerting you of a Security Warning:

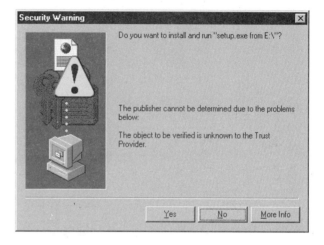

This dialog is alerting you that a certificate authority like VeriSign has not digitally signed the Option Pack setup executable. It's not appropriate to digitally sign controls or executables that modify the operating system (like the Windows NT 4.0 Option Pack) and that's why you have received the security warning. Click Yes to install and run the setup.

After some initialization the Option Pack installation wizard will run. The first screen of the wizard is a splash screen that describes the features that can be installed. Click Next and you'll be presented with the licensing agreement. If you agree with the licensing of the Windows NT 4.0 Option Pack, then click Accept and then Next. Now you'll be offered the three types of installation: Minimum, Typical and Custom:

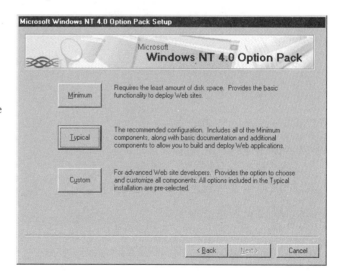

You need to perform a **Custom** installation, so click **Custom** and you will be presented with all the installation options:

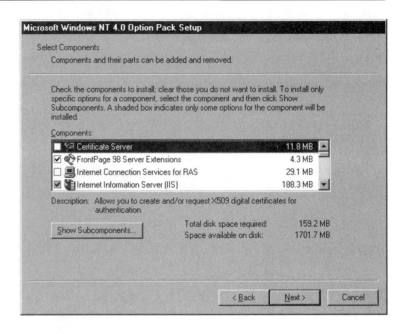

You do not want to install the FrontPage 98 Server Extensions yet (the FrontPage Server Extensions are installed later in the process), so uncheck the FrontPage 98 Server Extensions option.

At this point you should have the following options **checked**:

❑ Internet Information Server (IIS)

❑ Microsoft Data Access Components 1.5

❑ Microsoft Index Server

❑ Microsoft Management Console

❑ Microsoft Script Debugger

❑ NT Option Pack Common Files

❑ Transaction Server

❑ Windows Scripting Host

And you should have the following options **unchecked**:

❑ Certificate Server

❑ FrontPage 98 Server Extensions

❑ Internet Connection Services for RAS

❑ Microsoft Message Queue

❑ Microsoft Site Server Express 2.0

❑ Visual InterDev RAD Remote Deployment Support

Click Next to continue the installation, and you'll be presented with the folder locations for web and FTP publishing, and the folder location for the application files. If you followed the recommended steps for drive partitioning and assigning from earlier in the chapter, then change the C: to D: on the WWW Service and FTP Service, which is the NTFS share on your Windows NT 4.0 server. Leave the Application Installation Point at C:, which is the FAT partition that your operating system (NT 4.0) was installed on:

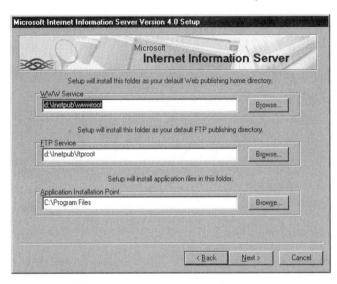

Click Next, and you'll be prompted to choose the folder locations for your Microsoft Transaction Server (MTS) installation. Leave the default of C:\Program Files\Mts, as below:

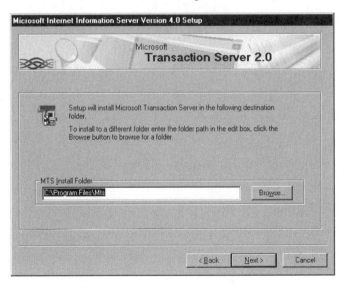

Click Next, and configure MTS for local (not remote) administration by leaving the default as Local. Click Next to continue.

You'll be prompted for the folder for your default index directory. If you followed the recommended steps for drive partitioning and mapping from earlier in the chapter then leave the default of D:\Inetpub:

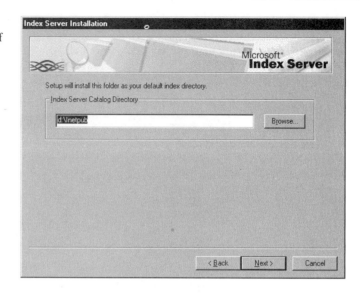

Click Next and you'll be prompted for the folder for your SMTP installation. Again, if you followed the recommended steps for drive partitioning and mapping from earlier in the chapter then leave the default of D:\Inetpub\Mailroot, as below:

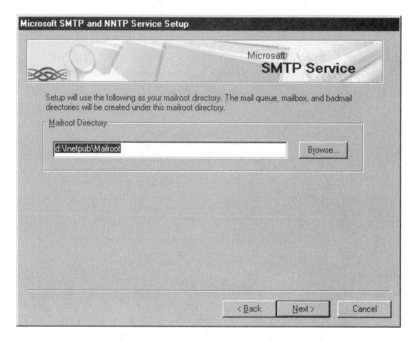

Click Next and the installation will proceed. It may take several minutes depending on the speed of your machine, but you'll be presented with a progress bar so that you can monitor the installation and estimate when it might complete.

Upon completion, click Finish to exit the installation and the Option Pack setup will finalize the settings. You'll be asked if you want to restart to complete the installation, so choose Yes and the computer will restart.

FrontPage 98 Server Extensions

Install the updated FrontPage 98 Server Extensions, version 3.0.2.1706. You can find them at: `http://officeupdate.microsoft.com/frontpage/wpp/license.htm`.

Upon executing the installation program, the software will extract and run the installation. The first screen of the wizard confirms your installation of the software. Click Next and you'll be presented with the licensing agreement. If you agree with the licensing of the FrontPage 98 Server Extensions, click Accept and then Next, and the installation will start.

After a few moments, you'll be presented with a dialog telling you that the installation is complete. Click Finish to complete the installation.

> *You can install the FrontPage 2000 Server Extensions, although this is not recommended with Site Server 3.0 Commerce Edition because of incompatibilities. If you need to install the FrontPage 2000 Server Extensions refer to the Post Installation Configurations section at the end of the chapter.*

(Optional) Install Visual Studio 6.0 or Visual Studio 97

Although you are not required to install any development tools along with your Site Server installation, you can install Visual InterDev or FrontPage, as well as any other third-party development tool such as HomeSite from Alstaire. There are a few points to take into account:

❑ It's always dangerous to install development tools on production servers, so proceed with caution if you are installing a production server.

❑ If you do decide to go ahead with and install Visual Studio 6.0, make sure you don't install the Analyzer component. This component can be resource intensive, and will affect how your server will perform and scale – save this component for your workstations.

❑ Do not install Visual Studio 6.0 Service Pack 3 at this point – it's installed later in the process.

❑ If you install Visual Studio 97, you can also install Visual Studio 97 Service Pack 3. You can download it from `http://msdn.microsoft.com/vstudio/sp/vs97/default.asp`.

Change the SQL Server Client Default Network Library to TCP/IP

As TCP/IP Sockets are faster than Named Pipes when communicating to a SQL server that doesn't reside on the same box, IIS should use TCP/IP sockets when it connects to the SQL Server computer.

To configure the SQL Server client, run
`Windbver.exe`, which lives in
`C:\WINNT\System32`. On the **Net Library**
tab, select **TCP/IP Sockets** as the **Default
Network**, and then click **Done**:

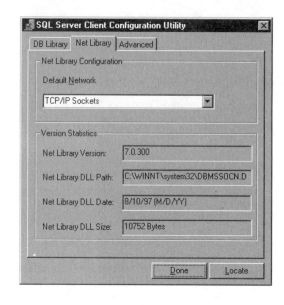

MSDTC Service

The MSDTC service must be started on both the Windows NT Server where Site Server is to be
installed and on the SQL Server computer, and MSDTC should be configured to start automatically.

On the Site Server
machine, go to the
Control Panel (Start |
Settings | Control Panel)
and double-click on
Services. Then navigate
to the **MSDTC** service
and make sure that the
Status is **Started** and that
the **Startup** setting is
Automatic:

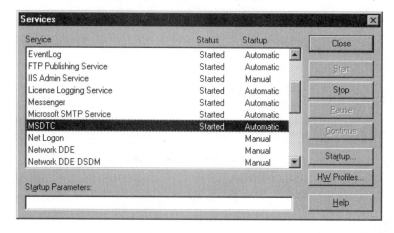

If MSDTC is not configured to start automatically, then click the **Startup** button and change it to
Automatic.

Do the same on the machine that is running SQL Server.

Configure Database Connectivity on the SQL Server

In this install procedure we're not going to install any sample sites, so we don't have to create databases to house the sample site data now. But, we are going to install Ad Server, so we do need to create a database for it to house its data. You'll need to create individual databases for Ad Server and Commerce Server on your SQL server. 20Mb of space is more than adequate to handle the requirements of installation (the actual size will vary depending on your site).

On the SQL Server machine, run the SQL Server Enterprise Manager (Start | Programs | Microsoft SQL Server 7.0 | Enterprise Manager) and create a database called Adserver. If you are using SQL Server 6.5 you'll need to create a database device for the AdServer database to live in, if you don't have space on an existing SQL database device.

To create a database:

❑   Click the + next to Microsoft SQL Servers.

❑   Click the + sign next to SQL Server Group.

❑   Click the + sign next to the name of your server.

❑   Right-click on the Databases folder and choose New Database... This will initiate the New Database Wizard.

If you're using SQL Server 7.0, take all the defaults, including the 1 Mb size, when you create the AdServer database. SQL Server 7.0 will grow the database automatically if you need more space. If you're using SQL Server 6.5 you will have to estimate the size of your AdServer Database. It's completely dependant on the amount of Ads that you will use on the site, but 1 Mb will be fine to get you started. You can increase the size of the database device and database if need be later.

Now you need to create a System DSN to communicate with the AdServer database you just created. On the Site Server machine, go to the Control Panel (Start | Settings | Control Panel), and run the Administrative Tools control panel applet by double-clicking on its icon. Double-click on Data Sources (ODBC), and select the System DSN tab:

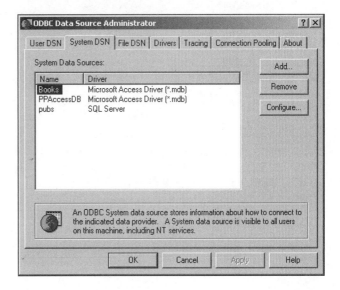

Click **Add**, then choose **SQL Server** from the bottom of the list and click **Finish**. Name the Data source **Adserver**, give a description (**Adserver Database**) and type the name of your server:

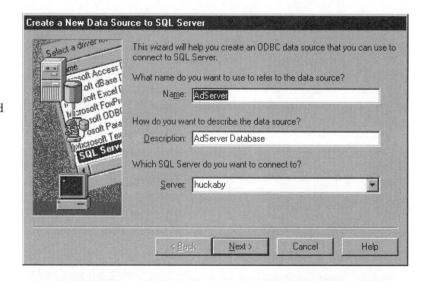

Click **Next**, and you'll be asked to verify the security credentials for the DSN that will be communicating with the SQL Server. Change the verification to **With SQL Server authentication**. Change the **Login Id** to **sa** and type the sa password (this could also be a SQL Server login with at least DBO permissions to the AdServer database, which will prevent the need for using the all powerful sa account for the DSN):

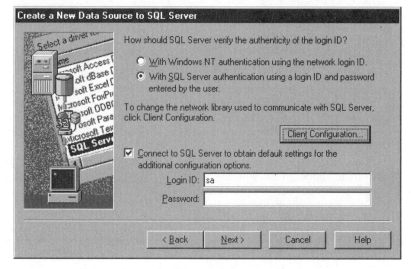

Click **Next**. On the following screen, you'll need to choose the **AdServer** database as the data source that this DSN will communicate to. Click the check box next to **Change the default database to:**, drop down the list of databases and choose **AdServer**:

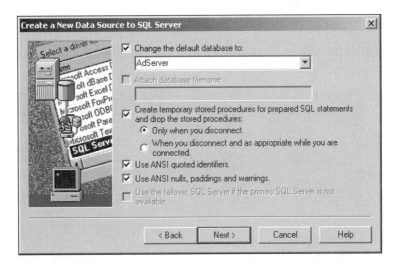

Click **Next**, and then accept all the defaults on the following screen:

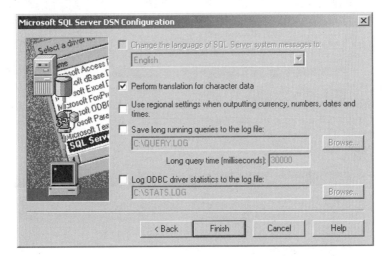

Click **Finish**, and the wizard will summarize all the configuration choices that you have made (and accepted by default). Click the **Test Data Source** button to verify the communication, and then click **OK** on the remaining screens to complete the operation.

Now repeat the procedure to create a database and System DSN for Commerce Server on your Site Server.

Site Server Version 3.0

When you insert the Site Server Version 3.0 CD-ROM, the CD will auto start and you'll be prompted with the main options for installing Site Server 3.0:

Click **Server Installation** to proceed to the Site Server 3.0 installation wizard. Click **Next** to continue, and you'll be presented with the licensing agreement. If you agree with the licensing of Microsoft Site Server Version 3.0, click **Yes**. Now, you'll be prompted to fill in your product and user information. Fill out your **Name, Company, CD Key** and **E-mail address:**

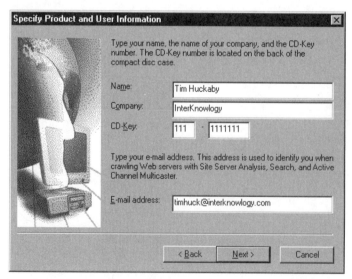

Click **Next** and then click **OK** to confirm your product ID.

Next, you'll be prompted for the Site Server 3.0 folder locations. Site Server needs file permissions (ACLs) painted on its program files directory to run properly, and you'll be warned if you try and install on a FAT partition (which cannot support file permissions). If you have followed the recommended steps for drive partitioning and assigning from earlier in the chapter then change all three defaults of C: to D:, where we have installed the NTFS partition:

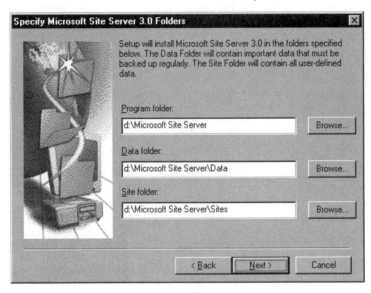

Click Next to continue and you'll be presented with the three types of Site Server 3.0 installations – Typical, Complete, and Custom:

Click the image next to Custom to perform a custom installation.

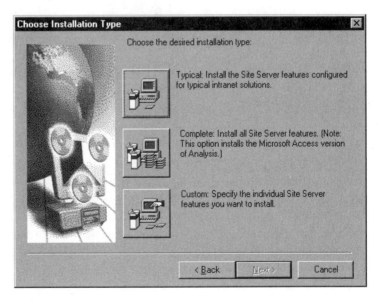

Click the + next to Analysis and change the Analysis database support from its default of Access Database Support by checking SQL Server Database Support. When you select SQL Server Database Support, Access Database Support gets unchecked – it is not possible to install the product with support for both databases:

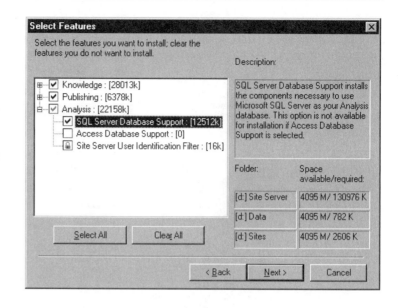

Next, the installation wizard will prompt you to specify a program folder in which to place the Site Server Menu choices. Leave the default of Microsoft Site Server and click Next to continue.

Now you're required to Configure User Accounts for the Publishing and Search services. The Search service requires an Administrative account to run under. The Publishing services simply require enough read and write permissions to publish to folders on the NT shares. For now, set both to run under the local Administrator account. You can always back off the Publishing services permissions later by running under a different account with less than administrative privileges:

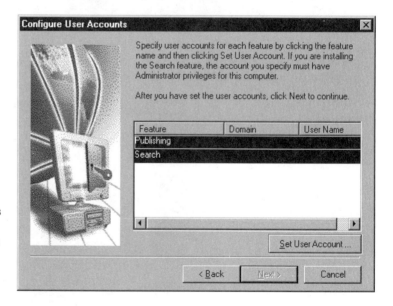

Click the Set User Account button. The dialog will default to Administrator and the name of the computer for the local domain. Type the password twice to set the user account:

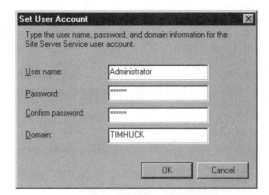

Click **OK**, and then **Next** to continue. The wizard will inform you of all the services it has to stop to proceed with the installation:

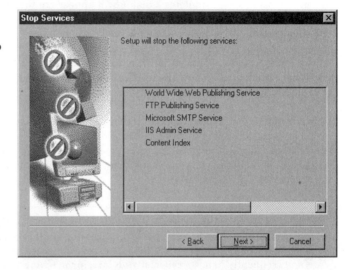

Click **Next** to continue. Click **Next** and the wizard will shut down existing services that need to be modified or are dependant on a service getting modified (like WWW, FTP, IIS Admin, etc.) one by one. The last screen of the wizard will confirm your choices:

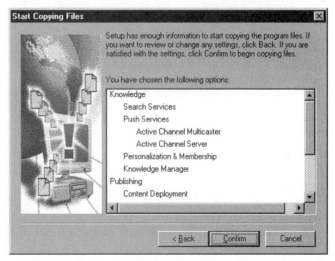

Click Confirm to start copying the files, and the installation of Microsoft Site Server 3.0 will begin. The process could take quite a bit of time depending on the speed of your server hardware.

During the installation, you will be asked to confirm the overwriting of files. This is because Service Packs and the FrontPage 98 Server Extensions that have already been installed were released after the release of Site Server Version 3.0. This is very important: choose **No To All** so as not to overwrite any newer files.

> **If you accidentally overwrite files with older versions you are guaranteed to have an unsuccessful installation.**

When the installation completes a dialog will appear confirming it. You will be given the chance to review the Readme file at that time. It's a good idea to study the Readme file in any NT server component installation. When satisfied, click Finish.

At this point, you may notice a flurry of disk activity. That's because Index Server has been restarted, and it has noticed that 100+ MBs of HTML Help content has appeared as a result of the Site Server installation. Index Server will take over and start indexing all the new content.

This is a requirement, and you'll fail the install if you manually turn the Index Server service off. This isn't that big a deal on a powerful server with lots of RAM, but on a development, staging, or home server, if you start your commerce install (which is the next step) while Index Server is doing its thing on the Site Server content, you'll hang your server – Index Server isn't smart enough to back off while the commerce installation proceeds.

> **Most of the SS3 failed installs are because Index Server runs amok and fails to index all the new content before another installation (in this case Commerce Server) is started. The Commerce installation process competes with Index Server for the CPU and frequently hangs – especially on inferior machines. Make sure that Index Server has completed indexing all the content before rebooting or installing more software.**

So here's the tip for installation on any box: after the reboot immediately following the Site Server 3.0 platform install, get the Task Manager by doing a *CTRL-ALT-Delete*, choose Task Manager, then click on the Processes tab. Sort on processor usage by clicking on the CPU field name. You'll see the cisvc.exe service going wild and the associated cidaemon.exe with it:

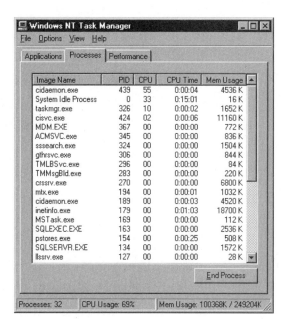

Just wait it out (when the System Idle Process gets to 98% or so), until all the content has been indexed.

> *After the commerce install, the Indexing Service will also need to index all the new content, so you'll need to go through this drill again.*

Site Server 3.0 Commerce Edition

If you have installed the FrontPage 2000 Server Extensions (which was not recommended), you need to edit the Properties of the Default Web Site with the Site Server Service Admin (MMC). On the Home Directory tab, disable the FrontPage Web option. You can enable the FrontPage Web option again once Commerce Server is installed.

Upon inserting the Site Server 3.0 Commerce Edition CD-ROM, the Commerce CD will auto start and you'll be prompted with the main options for installing Commerce Server:

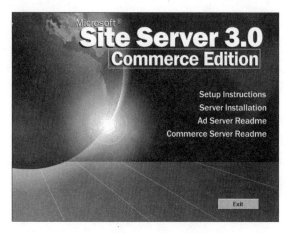

Click Server Installation to proceed to the Site Server 3.0 Commerce Edition installation wizard. Click Next to continue, and you'll be presented with the licensing agreement. If you agree with the licensing of Microsoft Site Server 3.0 Commerce Edition click Yes.

Now, you'll be prompted to fill in your product and user information. Fill out your Name, Company, and CD Key:

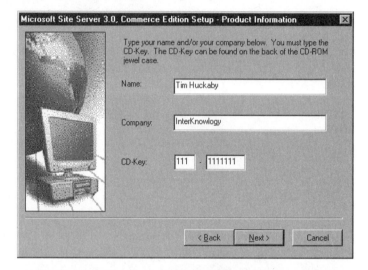

Click Next, and then click OK to confirm your Product ID. Click Next to continue and you'll be presented with the five types of Site Server 3.0 Commerce Edition installations – Typical, Complete, Custom, Ad Server, and Commerce Interchange Pipeline:

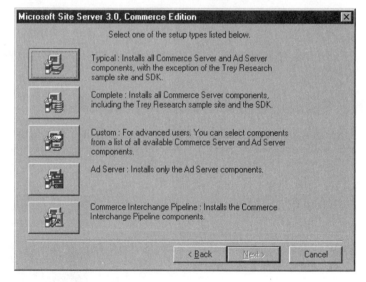

Click the image next to Custom to perform a custom installation.

You'll be prompted to choose which components you wish to install.

There are a number of sample sites that ship with Site Server 3.0 Commerce Edition, but a detailed examination of them is beyond the scope of this book. Professional Site Server 3.0 Commerce Edition (Marco Tabini, ISBN 1-861002-50-5, Wrox Press) has a detailed explanation of the sample sites and how to install and use them.

I don't usually install any sample sites on a production server. And I usually install any sample site (but the Volcano Coffee sample site) on a development server. Let's assume this is a production server and not install any sample sites – the sample sites can always be installed at a later time:

❏ Uncheck the Clocktower, Microsoft Market, Microsoft Press, and Volcano Coffee sample sites

❏ Keep the Trey Research sample site unchecked

❏ Leave Ad Server and Ad Manager checked

❏ If this is a development server check the SDK (System Developers Kit); if not, keep it unchecked

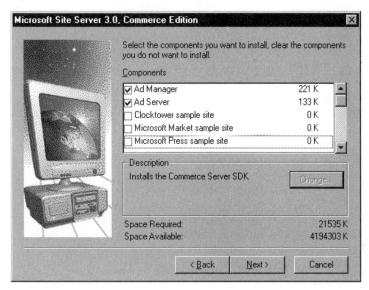

Click Next to continue. A dialog will tell you that you have not chosen to install any of the sample sites, and then ask you if you want to install the Commerce Server core components. Click Yes to continue the installation.

The next screen in the installation wizard will identify the components that you have chosen to install, and notify you that it has enough information to start the installation process:

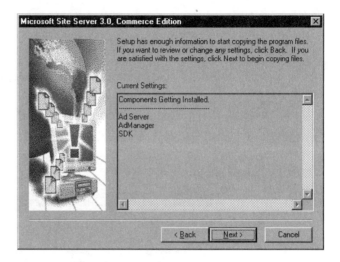

Click Next, and you'll be prompted to select and/or create a DSN for Ad Server. If you've created the database and DSN for Ad Server already – as was recommended earlier – just choose it and click OK.

If you have not created the Ad Server database and DSN yet, run the SQL Server Enterprise Manager on your SQL Server Machine and create a database called AdServer.

Then on the Site Server dialog box, click the ODBC button:

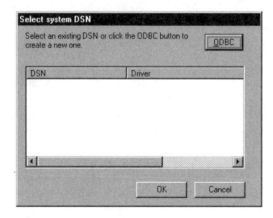

Now create a DSN for the Ad Server database you just created on the SQL Server (refer back to the Configure Database Connectivity section for more details on creating a DSN).

The Commerce Server installation will then start. The length of time it takes to complete the installation is dependent solely on the speed of your machine.

When the installation completes a dialog will appear confirming it. You'll be presented with a choice to review the Readme file at that time. When satisfied, click Finish.

Once again, as in the Site Server installation, you may notice a flurry of disk activity. Index Server has been restarted and the HTML Help files are being indexed. As before, make sure index server has completed indexing all the content before rebooting or installing more software.

Again, to monitor the progress of Index Server, get the Task Manager running by doing a *CTRL-ALT-Delete*, choose **Task Manager**, then click on the **Processes** tab. Sort on processor usage by clicking on the **CPU** field name. Wait until the **System Idle Process** gets to 98% or so, when all the content has been indexed.

Windows NT4 Service Pack 4

Install Microsoft Windows NT 4.0 Service Pack 4. You can download the Service Pack from:
`http://support.microsoft.com/support/ntserver/content/servicepacks/SP4.asp`.

> **Do *not* substitute Windows NT 4.0 Service Pack 5 or later at this point.**

First, you'll be presented with the licensing agreement. If you agree with the licensing of Microsoft NT Version 4.0 Service Pack 4, click **Accept** and then **Install**. When the Service Pack is installed, you'll be required to restart the computer, and you'll then be prompted to install the Y2K updates.

> **Do *not* install the Y2K updates at this time. The Y2K updates are installed by Internet Explorer 4.01 SP2 in a prior step, and by MDAC 2.1 in a subsequent step.**

(Optional) Install Microsoft Internet Explorer 5.0

Internet Explorer 5.0 is not recommended for this configuration. If you do install Internet Explorer 5.0 on a computer with Commerce Server, you should be aware of the following issues:

- ❏ The Site Server Customizable Starter Sites (described in the last section of this chapter) are not compatible with Internet Explorer 5.0.

- ❏ Internet Explorer 5.0 associates the `.prf` extension with PICSRules files, while Site Server associates this extension with Rule Set Files. Therefore, you must perform a custom install of Internet Explorer 5.0, click the **Advanced** button and configure Internet Explorer 5.0 so that it does not associate the `.prf` file extension.

- ❏ Internet Explorer 5.0 prevents the Web Posting Acceptor from allowing Anonymous uploads. At the time of writing Microsoft is developing a fix, but this is not yet available.

(Optional) Install Visual Studio 6 Service Pack 3

If you installed Visual Studio 6.0 in the steps above, then install Visual Studio 6.0 Service Pack 3 at this point. You can download the Service Pack from:
`http://msdn.microsoft.com/vstudio/sp/vs6sp3/vsfixes.asp`.

Upon running the setup (or having the CD auto start), you'll be asked to confirm your intentions to install the Service Pack. Click **Continue** to proceed, and you'll be presented with the licensing agreement. If you agree with the licensing of Visual Studio 6 Service Pack 3, then click **I Agree**.

The installation will begin with copying of files, and then the configuration will proceed. Upon completion you'll receive a dialog pointing you to the Readme file, which contains a summary of many of the problems that are fixed with the installation of the Service Pack.

You'll also be instructed that you need to install Internet Explorer 5.0 to take advantage of the fixes. Remember from above that Internet Explorer 5.0 is not recommended for this configuration:

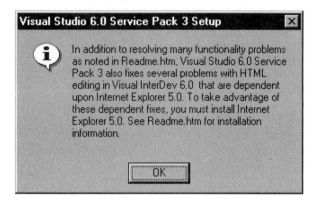

In addition to resolving many functionality problems as noted in Readme.htm, Visual Studio 6.0 Service Pack 3 also fixes several problems with HTML editing in Visual InterDev 6.0 that are dependent upon Internet Explorer 5.0. To take advantage of these dependent fixes, you must install Internet Explorer 5.0. See Readme.htm for installation information.

Click OK and you'll be instructed to restart your computer. After the restart, your Service Pack installation will be complete.

Microsoft Data Access Components 2.1 Service Pack 2

Install MDAC version 2.1.2.4202.3, which is also known as MDAC 2.1 SP2. You can download the MDAC from: `http://www.microsoft.com/data/download.htm`.

Upon running the executable, the first screen is the license agreement. If you agree with the licensing of Microsoft Data Access Components 2.1, click Yes. The file extraction process will begin and then launch the setup wizard.

Screen 1 of the setup wizard confirms your intentions to install Microsoft Data Access Components 2.1. Click Continue. Setup will search for installed components to make sure you have the prerequisites installed. If you've followed the installation procedures as recommended then you do.

To start the installation, click the icon that represents a Complete Installation. The installation will take a few moments depending on how fast your system is. Upon completion, click OK to exit.

Active Directory Services Interfaces Version 2.5

Install Active Directory Services Interfaces Version 2.5. You can download Active Directory Services Interfaces Version 2.5 from:
`http://www.microsoft.com/ntserver/nts/downloads/other/ADSI25/default.asp`.

Upon running the installation executable for Active Directory Services Interfaces (ADSI) Version 2.5, you'll be prompted to confirm your intentions to install. Click Yes to proceed. Now, you'll be presented with the license agreement. If you agree with the licensing of Active Directory Services Interfaces Version 2.5, click Yes and the installation will proceed.

The installation of Active Directory Services Interfaces Version 2.5 will only take a short time. When it's completed, click OK to exit. You will be required to restart your computer when complete – click Yes to do so.

Site Server 3.0 Service Pack 3

Install Site Server 3.0 Service Pack 3. You can download the Service Pack from:
`http://support.microsoft.com/support/siteserver/servicepacks/sp.asp`.

After executing the Service Pack, a number of files will be extracted to your machine. Then, you'll be ready to run the Microsoft Site Server 3.0 Service Pack 3 Setup Wizard. Click Next, and you'll be presented with the licensing agreement. If you agree with the licensing of Microsoft Site Server Version 3.0 Service Pack 3, click I Agree, and then click Next.

You can choose to create an uninstall directory for the Service Pack. It's a good idea to create an uninstall directory, just in case of an installation failure:

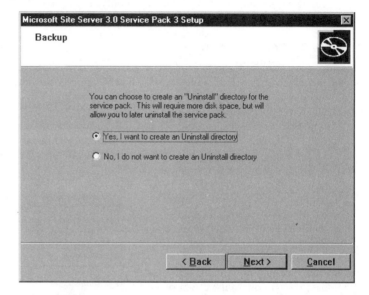

Now, setup has enough information to start copying the files. Click Next to begin. The installation will take a number of minutes depending on the speed of your system. When it has successfully installed click Finish to complete the installation.

> **Important: make sure and read the Site Server Service Pack 3 `Readme.htm` file, which includes the latest release notes and small fixes that need to be made. It is installed in your Site Server Directory in: `\Microsoft SiteServer\sp3\readme.htm`.**

Windows NT4 Service Pack 6

Install Windows NT 4.0 Service Pack 6. You can download the Service Pack from:
`http://www.microsoft.com/ntserver/nts/downloads/recommended/PREM_SP6/allSP6.asp`.

First, you'll be presented with the licensing agreement. If you agree with the licensing of Microsoft Windows NT 4.0 Service Pack 6, click Accept and then Install. The installation will start by inspecting your Windows NT 4.0 configuration, archiving old versions of files and then copying new files.

Upon completion, you will be required to restart your computer to complete the installation. Click Restart and the computer will restart.

Post Installation Notes for your SQL Server Machine

Having successfully installed Site Server, you now need to update your SQL Server, which is running on a separate machine. Refer to the relevant section for whichever version of SQL Server (either 6.5 or 7.0) you are running.

SQL Server Version 6.5

The following is specific to SQL Server 6.5 only. If you have SQL Server 7.0, skip ahead to the following section.

SQL Server 6.5 Service Pack 5a

Before you install SQL Server 6.5 Service Pack 5a on your SQL Server, you need to have a minimum of 3 Mb space (and should have at least 10 Mb) free in your master database. The master database is 25 Mb by default. Let's go through the process of expanding it to 50 Mb.

On your SQL Server 6.5, run the Microsoft SQL Enterprise Manager by clicking Start | Programs | Microsoft SQL Server 6.5 | SQL Enterprise Manager. If this is the first time you've run the SQL Enterprise Manager then you'll need to "register" your server, by typing the name of the server and typing the password for the sa account.

Click the + next to your SQL Server's name to drop down the container of components. First you need to expand the size of the master database device. Click on the + next to Database Devices to drop down the list of database devices on your SQL Server:

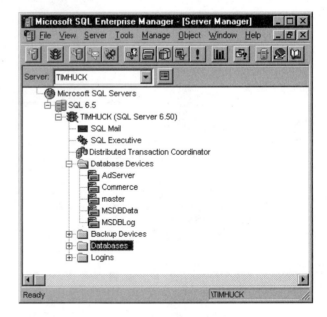

Right-click on **master** and choose
Edit. Change the 25 in the **Size
(MB)** field to 50 and then click
Change Now:

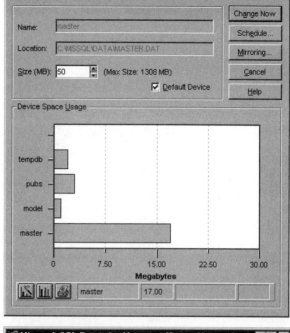

Next, you need to expand the size
of the master database. Click on +
next to **Databases** to drop down
the list of databases on your SQL
Server:

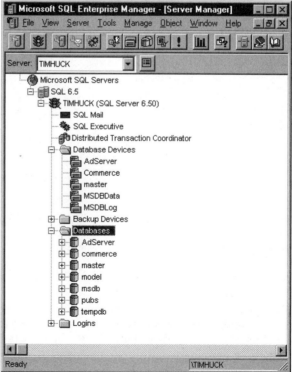

Right-click on master
and choose Edit. You
will default to the
Database tab:

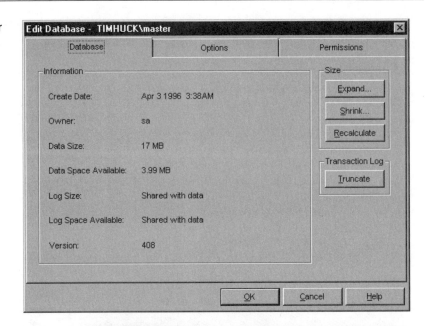

Click the Expand button. Drop
down the Data Device list and
choose master. The Size (MB) will
default to the amount of space that
is available to expand. In this case,
it's 26Mb:

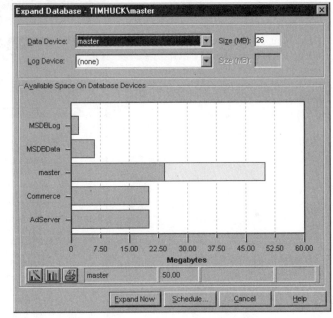

Click Expand Now. After a few short moments the expansion of the master database will be complete.
The Edit Database dialog will reappear; notice that you now have 29.99Mb of available space on your
master database. Click OK to continue, and then exit the SQL Enterprise Manager. You are now ready
to install the SQL Server 6.5 Service Pack 5a.

Install SQL Server 6.5 Service Pack 5a on your SQL Server. You can download the Service Pack, for both the Enterprise and Standard versions of SQL Server, from `http://www.microsoft.com/downloads/release.asp?ReleaseID=12671`.

> **IMPORTANT: if prompted, *do not* install the optional MDAC 2.1 components. It will be installed in a later step.**

After executing the Service Pack, a number of files will be extracted to your machine. Then you'll be ready to run the Microsoft SQL Server 6.5 Service Pack 5a setup wizard.

Click Continue, and you'll be asked for your SA Password (the password for the sa account):

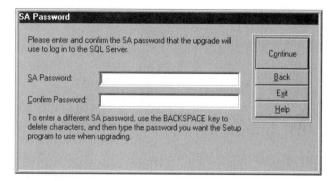

Type the password for your sa account twice and then click Continue. Next, you'll be presented with the licensing agreement. If you agree with the licensing of SQL Server Version 6.5 Service Pack 5a, then click on Page Down 7 times to scroll to the bottom of the License Agreement. Then, click I Agree.

The installation will take a number of minutes depending on the speed of your system. When it has successfully installed click the Finish icon to exit to Windows NT.

MDAC Version 2.1.2.4202.3

Install MDAC version 2.1.2.4202.3, which is also known as MDAC 2.1 SP2. You can download the MDAC from: `http://www.microsoft.com/data/download.htm`.

Upon running the executable, the first screen is the license agreement. If you agree with the licensing of Microsoft Data Access Components 2.1, then click Yes. The file extraction process will begin and will launch the setup wizard.

Screen 1 of the setup wizard confirms your intentions to install Microsoft Data Access Components 2.1. Click Continue, and setup will search for installed components to make sure you have the prerequisites installed. If you have followed the installation procedures as recommended then you do.

To start the installation, click the installation icon that represents a complete installation. The installation will take a few moments depending on how fast your system is. Upon completion, click OK to exit.

Windows NT 4.0 Service Pack 6

Install Windows NT 4.0 Service Pack 6. You can download the Service Pack from: `http://www.microsoft.com/ntserver/nts/downloads/recommended/PREM_SP6/allSP6.asp`.

SQL Server Version 7.0 on Windows NT 4.0

If your SQL Server is a Version 7.0 on Windows NT 4.0 then perform the following three steps on your SQL Server.

SQL Server Version 7.0 Service Pack 1

Install Microsoft SQL Server 7.0 Service Pack 1 on your SQL Server.

If you don't have a CD with the SQL Server 7.0 Service Pack 1, you can download and run the `Sql70sp1i.exe` file. You can download the Service Pack from: `http://www.microsoft.com/sql/support/sp1.htm`. The Service Pack files are extracted to the `C:\SP1` directory. However, you must still run `C:\SP1\Setup.exe` to actually install the Service Pack.

If you have a CD with the SQL Server 7.0 Service Pack 1 on it, get Windows Explorer running, navigate to the `Setup.bat` (in most cases it will be in `\Service Pack 1\x86`) and execute it by double-clicking.

> *Installing SQL 7.0 SP1 can take up to 30 minutes depending on the speed of your machine – that does not include the time it takes to download the Service Pack.*

First, you'll be presented with a screen that confirms your intentions to install the Service Pack. Click Next and you'll be presented with the License Agreement. If you agree with the licensing agreement of Microsoft SQL Server Version 7.0 Service Pack 1, then click Yes to proceed. Next, you'll choose the authentication mode that the setup should use to connect to SQL Server. Keep the default of The Windows NT account...:

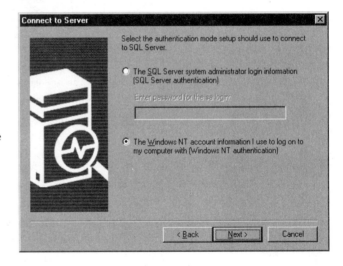

Click Next. After a short period, the setup will determine that it has enough information to proceed. Click Next and the installation will proceed unattended. When it's complete you will be required to restart your computer.

Microsoft Data Access Components 2.1 Service Pack 2

Install MDAC version 2.1.2.4202.3, also known as MDAC 2.1 SP2, on your SQL 7.0 Server. You can download the MDAC from: `http://www.microsoft.com/data/download.htm`.

Upon running the executable, the first screen is the license agreement. If you agree with the licensing of Microsoft Data Access Components 2.1, then click Yes. The file extraction process will begin and will launch the setup wizard.

Screen 1 of the setup wizard confirms your intentions to install Microsoft Data Access Components 2.1. Click Continue, and setup will search for installed components to make sure you have the prerequisites installed. If you have followed the installation procedures as recommended then you do.

To start the installation, click the installation icon that represents a complete installation. The installation will take a few moments depending on how fast your system is. Upon completion, click OK to exit.

Windows NT4 Service Pack 6

Install Windows NT 4.0 Service Pack 6 on your SQL 7.0 Server. You can download the Service Pack from:
`http://www.microsoft.com/ntserver/nts/downloads/recommended/PREM_SP6/allSP6.asp`.

First, you'll be presented with the licensing agreement. If you agree with the licensing of Microsoft Windows NT 4.0 Service Pack 6, click Accept and then Install. The installation will inspect your Windows NT 4.0 configuration, archive old versions of files and then copy new files.

Upon completion, you will be required to restart your computer, so click Restart.

SQL Server Version 7.0 on Windows 2000

If your SQL Server is a Version 7.0 on Windows 2000 then perform the following step on your SQL Server.

SQL Server Version 7.0 Service Pack 1

Install Microsoft SQL Server 7.0 Service Pack 1 on your SQL Server.

If you don't have a CD with the SQL Server 7.0 Service Pack 1, you can download and run the `Sql70sp1.exe` file. You can download the Service Pack from: `http://www.microsoft.com/sql/support/sp1.htm`. The Service Pack files are extracted to the `C:\SP1` directory. However, you must still run `C:\SP1\Setup.exe` to actually install the Service Pack.

If you have a CD with the SQL Server 7.0 Service Pack 1 on it, get Windows Explorer running, navigate to the `Setup.bat` (in most cases it will be in `\Service Pack 1\x86`) and execute it by double-clicking.

> *Installing SQL 7.0 SP1 can take up to 30 minutes depending on the speed of your machine – that does not include the time it takes to download the Service Pack.*

First, you'll be presented with a screen that confirms your intentions to install the Service Pack. Click Next and you'll be presented with the License Agreement. If you agree with the licensing agreement of Microsoft SQL Server Version 7.0 Service Pack 1, then click Yes to proceed. Next, you'll choose the authentication mode that the setup should use to connect to SQL Server. Keep the default of The Windows NT account...:

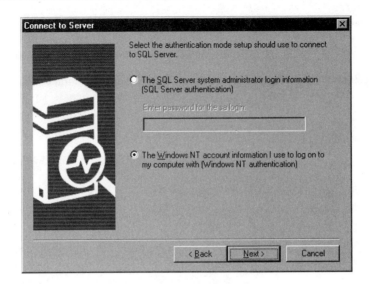

Click Next. After a short period, the setup will determine that it has enough information to proceed. Click Next and the installation will proceed unattended. When it's complete you will be required to restart your computer.

Congratulations! You are installed! Now move on to the final post-installation section.

Installing SS3 on Windows NT 4.0 With SQL Server 6.5

> **Read on if you're installing Site Server on the same box that you are going to install SQL Server 6.5 on, and your operating system is Windows NT 4.0.**

Windows NT 4.0

Install Microsoft Windows NT Server 4.0. Again, to guarantee a successful Site Server 3.0 Commerce installation I suggest you start with a clean computer, or have the Windows NT 4.0 installation wipe the hard drives clean before starting its installation.

Windows NT 4.0 installation instructions are beyond the scope of this book. There is an abundance of information on how to install the Windows NT 4.0 product on the web, but the product documentation from Microsoft is outstanding. You'll find it on the Windows NT 4.0 CD in the \SUPPORT\BOOKS folder.

Since custom drivers are needed to access the hardware (video, network, etc.) refer to the Microsoft Windows NT 4.0 product documentation and the documentation for the specific hardware that you have in your system. After you complete your Windows NT installation, there is a good chance you will need to install third party (non Microsoft) drivers for the unique hardware (video, network boards, etc.) that you have in your system.

Here are the important points for your Windows NT 4.0 installation:

❑ Install Windows NT 4.0 as a stand-alone server, if possible.

❑ There's no need to install Internet Information Server, although it doesn't hurt. You will be installing Internet Information Server 4.0 in a subsequent step, when you install the Windows NT Option Pack.

❑ Although not crucial, it will make your installation quite a bit easier if you have a floppy diskette with updated drivers for your network board. This is especially important if the Windows NT 4.0 installation cannot identify what type of network board you have, or if it does not have a driver for your particular network board.

❑ Complete the partitioning, formatting and assigning of drives with the Windows NT 4.0 Disk Administrator when you have completed the Windows NT 4.0 installation. Refer to the Drive Partitioning section above for details.

Windows NT4 Service Pack 3

Install Microsoft Windows NT 4.0 Service Pack 3. You can download the Service Pack from: `http://support.microsoft.com/support/ntserver/content/servicepacks/SP3.asp`.

> **It is very important that you do not substitute Windows NT 4.0 Service Pack 4 (or later) at this point.**

The installation of Windows NT Service Pack 3 is a simple 4-step wizard. The first step is a splash screen that describes the installation process of the Service Pack. Upon clicking Next you will be asked to confirm your intent to install the Service Pack:

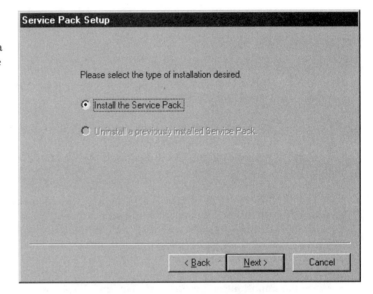

Click Next and you'll be asked if you want to create an uninstall directory. I always play it safe and create an uninstall directory for any Service Pack that I apply. Murphy's Law will most likely dictate a power failure in the middle of your Service Pack install – if you have an uninstall directory you'll be able to quickly recover:

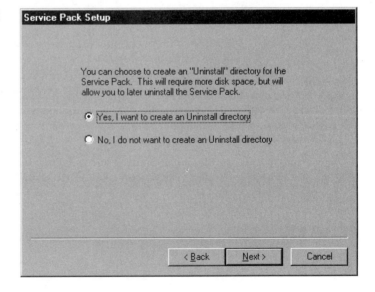

Click Next and you will be asked to confirm the installation of Windows NT 4.0 Service Pack 3 by clicking Finish. It will take the installation a few minutes to create the uninstall directory, copy the necessary files, do the DLL registrations, and perform the configurations. Upon completion you'll receive a dialog asking you to remove all floppies and CD ROMs because the installation needs to perform a restart of your system:

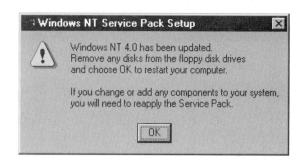

After the reboot, you'll have a base platform of Windows NT 4.0 Service Pack 3. At this point, although it's certainly not necessary, I recommend making a "ghost". Refer to the Drive Partitioning section of this chapter (above) if you are not familiar with Symantec's Norton Ghost software.

SQL Server Version 6.5 (Standard)

When you insert the SQL Server Version 6.5 CD ROM, you will have to navigate to the proper folder on the CD (most likely i386) and run the setup.exe from there. The SQL Server Version 6.5 wizard will start. Click Continue to proceed. You will be prompted for your Name, Company, and Product ID:

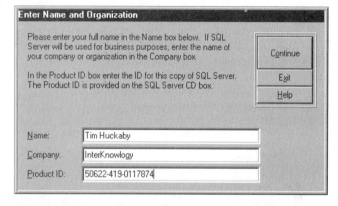

Click Continue to proceed, and you'll be asked to verify your information. Click Continue to move on. Next you'll be presented with the installation options:

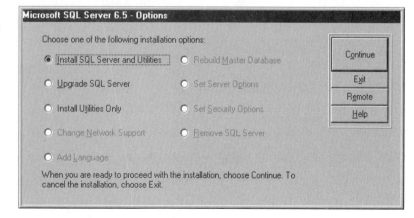

Accept the default of Install SQL Server and Utilities then click Continue. Next, you will be asked to choose the installation folder for SQL Server 6.5:

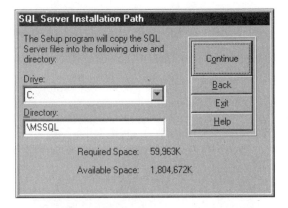

Keep the default of Drive: C: and Directory: \MSSQL so that the SQL Server 6.5 program files will be installed on your FAT partition with the rest of the Windows NT 4.0 operating system files. Click Continue. You will now need to choose where to install your master device. If you have followed the recommended steps for drive partitioning and assigning from earlier in the chapter, change the default from C: to D: so that you can install the Master Device on the NTFS partition:

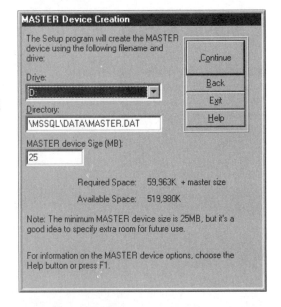

Click Continue. Next, you'll be asked where to install the SQL Server Books Online. The Books Online only take about 15 Mb of space, so I usually choose Install on Hard Disk:

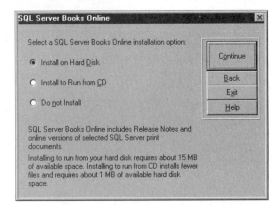

Click Continue. You'll now be prompted with the SQL Server 6.5 Installation Options:

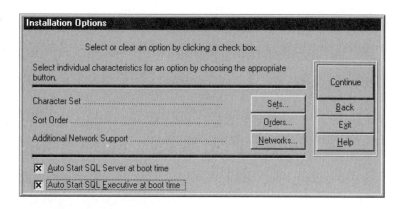

Click the **Networks** button and check **TCP/IP Sockets**. This will add TCP/IP to the protocols that SQL Server 6.5 will talk on. **Named Pipes** will be checked by default.

On the **Installation Options** dialog, check the **Auto Start SQL Server at boot time**, and also check **Auto Start SQL Executive at boot time**. Click Continue.

Next you'll choose how the SQL Executive logs on:

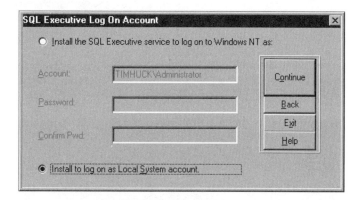

Choose **Install to log on as Local System account**, and click Continue. Next you'll choose the TCP/IP port number that the SQL Server 6.5 will listen on:

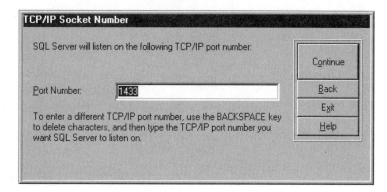

Accept the default of **Port Number: 1433**. Click Continue and the install will start. The speed of the installation is directly related to the speed of your machine. When it's complete, you'll get a dialog that tells you SQL Server 6.5 is installed. You will not have to reboot.

SQL Server 6.5 Service Pack 4

Install Microsoft SQL Server 6.5 Service Pack 4.

> **Do *not* install SQL Server 6.5 Service Pack 5 at this point.**

Service Pack 4 is located on the Site Server CD under:
`\support\QFE\SQL65SP4\i386\Setup.exe`. Run `Setup.exe`, and click Continue on the first screen of the SQL Server 6.5 Service Pack 4 Wizard.

You'll next be prompted for the SA Password. You will need to type it twice to confirm:

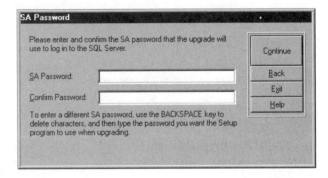

The Service Pack will self extract and install itself. Upon completion, you'll receive a dialog allowing you to exit to Windows NT.

Next you will need to install SQL Server fix 297 (which is also included on the Site Server 3.0 compact disc). First, stop the SQL 6.5 Server service by choosing the SQL Service Manager from Start | Programs | Microsoft SQL Server. Double-click on Stop to stop the MSSQLServer service:

In Windows Explorer navigate to `\support\QFE\SQL297\i386` on the Site Server 3.0 CD. You now need to do a copy and paste on the `sqlserver.exe` file. Copy it from the Site Server CD and paste it over `C:\MSSQL\Binn\sqlservr.exe`:

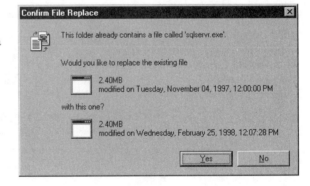

Then navigate back to the SQL Service Manager and restart the MSSQLServer Service by double-clicking Start.

Internet Explorer 4 Service Pack 2

Install Microsoft Internet Explorer 4.01 with Internet Explorer Service Pack 2. You can download Internet Explorer 4.01 and the Service Pack in one executable from:
`http://www.microsoft.com/msdownload/iebuild/ie4sp2_win32/en/ie4sp2_win32.htm`.

> **Do not substitute Internet Explorer 5.0 at this point. If you want to install Internet Explorer 5.0, then install it last, and read the installation notes and caveats that are described at the end of this chapter.**

The installation of the IE4 SP2 uses a wizard. The first screen of the wizard is a splash screen describing the process. Click Next and you'll be presented with the licensing agreement. If you agree with the licensing of IE4, click I accept and then Next. If you downloaded the installation from the Microsoft web site you'll be prompted with Download Options:

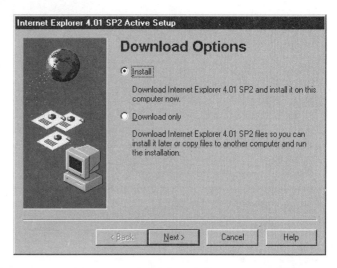

If you have an IE4 SP2 CD, you won't be prompted with Download Options because you'll have all the installation components on the CD.

If you are doing a "web" installation of IE4, then choose Install and click Next. You'll be prompted with three installation options: Standard Installation, Browser Only installation or a Full Installation. The default choice is the Standard Installation, which installs the IE4 Browser, Outlook Express, Windows Media Player and multimedia enhancements. A standard installation is fine:

Choose Next, and you'll be presented with a chance to install the Windows Desktop Update, also called the Active Desktop:

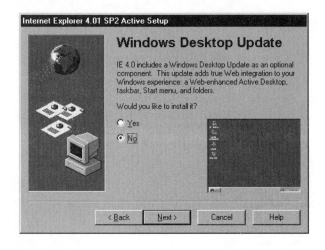

Select No and then click Next, to choose a standard desktop installation.

Now you'll be prompted to choose a region that best represents the country and language of your Active Channel installation. Choose the proper region and click Next.

You'll be prompted for a destination folder for your Internet Explorer 4.0 SP2. If you partitioned your drive and set up your drive mappings as recommended earlier in the chapter, then accept the default on C:.

After copying files and configuring your system, you'll be prompted to restart your system to complete the installation. Choose OK to restart.

Windows NT4 Option Pack

Install the Microsoft Windows NT 4.0 Option Pack. You can download the Option Pack from: http://www.microsoft.com/ntserver/nts/downloads/recommended/NT4OptPk/default.asp.

The Option Pack will install the web services required for Site Server:

❑   The WWW service

❑   The FTP service

❑   The SMTP service

❑   Transaction Server

❑   Index Server

The Option Pack set-up is a web-based installation. If you use an Option Pack CD to do the installation, then the browser will auto start. Choose Install from the left navigation frame in the browser:

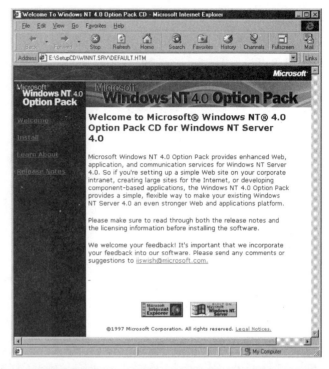

Next in the CD set-up you'll be presented with the choices to install Windows NT 4.0 Service Pack 3 and Internet Explorer 4.01. These are prerequisites for a Windows NT 4.0 Option Pack set up:

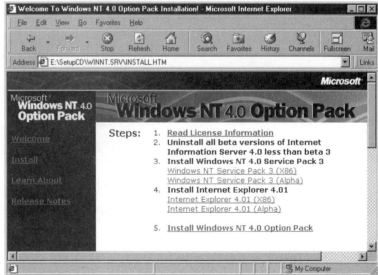

If you've followed the steps outlined above then you have already installed SP3 and IE4, so click Install Window NT 4.0 Option Pack to proceed with the installation. If doing a web installation, and prompted, perform an Upgrade Plus installation. This is critical, since you will need to add specific services. Selecting Upgrade instead of Upgrade Plus will not get you everything you need for a successful Site Server installation.

Next, you'll be presented with a dialog containing a relatively confusing question: "would you like to Run this program from its current location or Save this program to disk?":

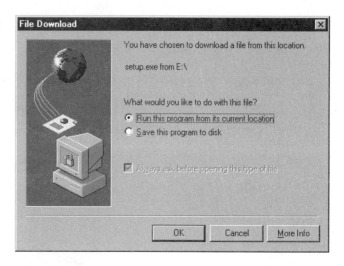

You'll need to understand the implications of this question, because you'll see it quite a bit if you are to download executables from a browser.

If you're running the installation from the Windows NT 4.0 Option Pack CD, Internet Explorer (or any browser for that matter) is not smart enough to know that you have the installation program on a local CD, so it asks you if you want to download it. If you were truly downloading the Windows NT 4.0 Option Pack from the Microsoft web site then you would Save this program to disk and run it after it's been successfully downloaded. But, if you have a local CD with the installation software then choose Run this program from its current location.

Next, you get a dialog alerting you of a Security Warning:

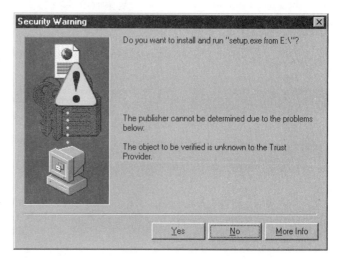

This dialog is alerting you that a certificate authority like VeriSign has not digitally signed the Option Pack setup executable. It's not appropriate to digitally sign controls or executables that modify the operating system (like the Windows NT 4.0 Option Pack) and that's why you have received the security warning. Click Yes to install and run the setup.

After some initialization the Option Pack installation wizard will run. The first screen of the wizard is a splash screen that describes the features that can be installed. Click Next and you'll be presented with the licensing agreement. If you agree with the licensing of the Windows NT 4.0 Option Pack, then click Accept and then Next. Now you'll be offered the three types of installation: Minimum, Typical and Custom:

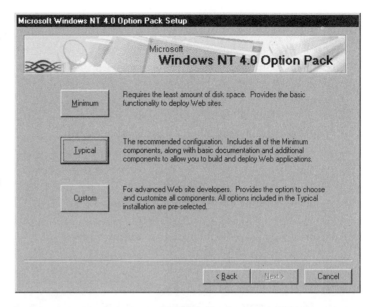

You need to perform a Custom installation, so click Custom and you will be presented with all the installation options:

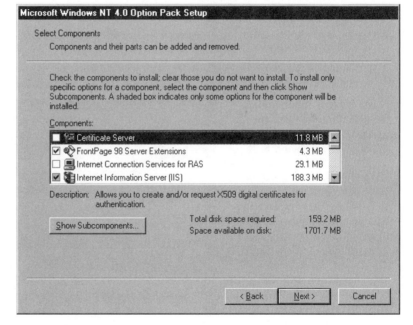

You do not want to install the FrontPage 98 Server Extensions yet (the FrontPage Server Extensions are installed later in the process), so uncheck the FrontPage 98 Server Extensions option.

At this point you should have the following options **checked**:

- ❏ Internet Information Server (IIS)
- ❏ Microsoft Data Access Components 1.5
- ❏ Microsoft Index Server
- ❏ Microsoft Management Console
- ❏ Microsoft Script Debugger
- ❏ NT Option Pack Common Files
- ❏ Transaction Server
- ❏ Windows Scripting Host

And you should have the following options **unchecked**:

- ❏ Certificate Server
- ❏ FrontPage 98 Server Extensions
- ❏ Internet Connection Services for RAS
- ❏ Microsoft Message Queue
- ❏ Microsoft Site Server Express 2.0
- ❏ Visual InterDev RAD Remote Deployment Support

Click Next to continue the installation, and you'll be presented with the folder locations for web and FTP publishing, and the folder location for the application files. If you followed the recommended steps for drive partitioning and assigning from earlier in the chapter, then change the C: to D: on the WWW Service and FTP Service, which is the NTFS share on your Windows NT 4.0 server. Leave the Application Installation Point at C:, which is the FAT partition that your operating system (NT 4.0) was installed on:

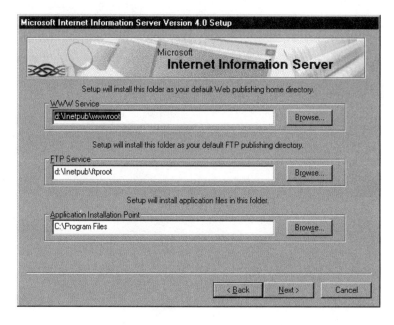

Click Next, and you'll be prompted to choose the folder locations for your Microsoft Transaction Server (MTS) installation. Leave the default of C:\Program Files\Mts:

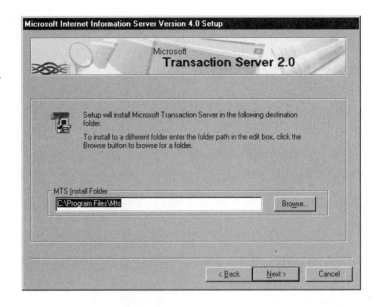

Click Next, and configure MTS for local (not remote) administration by leaving the default as Local. Click Next to continue.

You'll be prompted for the folder for your default index directory. If you followed the recommended steps for drive partitioning and mapping from earlier in the chapter then leave the default of D:\Inetpub:

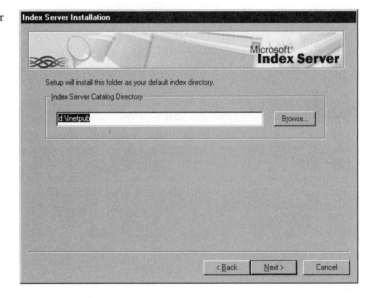

Click Next and you'll be prompted for the folder for your SMTP installation. Again, if you followed the recommended steps for drive partitioning and mapping from earlier in the chapter then leave the default of D:\Inetpub\Mailroot:

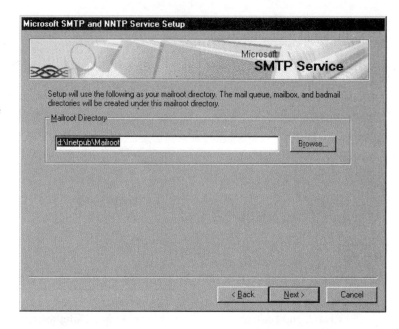

Click Next and the installation will proceed. It may take several minutes depending on the speed of your machine, but you'll be presented with a progress bar so that you can monitor the installation and estimate when it might complete.

Upon completion, click Finish to exit the installation and the Option Pack setup will finalize the settings. You'll be asked if you want to restart to complete the installation, so choose Yes and the computer will restart.

FrontPage 98 Server Extensions

Install the updated FrontPage 98 Server Extensions, version 3.0.2.1706. You can find them at: `http://officeupdate.microsoft.com/frontpage/wpp/license.htm`.

Upon executing the installation program, the software will extract and run the installation. The first screen of the wizard confirms your installation of the software. Click Next and you'll be presented with the licensing agreement. If you agree with the licensing of the FrontPage 98 Server Extensions, click Accept and then Next, and the installation will start.

After a few moments, you'll be presented with a dialog telling you that the installation is complete. Click Finish to complete the installation.

Optionally, you can install the FrontPage 2000 Server Extensions (not recommended with Site Server 3.0 Commerce Edition because of incompatibilities). If you need to install the FrontPage 2000 Server Extensions refer to the Post Installation Configurations section at the end of the chapter.

(Optional) Install Visual Studio 6.0 or Visual Studio 97

Although you are not required to install any development tools along with your Site Server installation, you can install Visual InterDev or FrontPage, as well as any other third-party development tool such as HomeSite from Alstaire. There are a few points to take into account:

❑ It's always dangerous to install development tools on production servers, so proceed with caution if you are installing a production server.

❑ If you do decide to go ahead with and install Visual Studio 6.0, make sure you don't install the Analyzer component. This component can be resource intensive, and will affect how your server will perform and scale – save this component for your workstations.

❑ Do not install Visual Studio 6.0 Service Pack 3 at this point – it's installed later in the process.

❑ If you install Visual Studio 97, you can also install Visual Studio 97 Service Pack 3. You can download it from `http://msdn.microsoft.com/vstudio/sp/vs97/default.asp`.

Change the SQL Server Client Default Network Library to Named Pipes

You want IIS to use Named Pipes (which is faster than TCP/IP when SQL Server and IIS 4.0 are on the same box) when it connects to the SQL Server computer

To configure the SQL Server client, you need to run `Windbver.exe`. It lives in `C:\WINNT\System32`. On the Net Library tab, select Named Pipes as the Default Network, and then click Done:

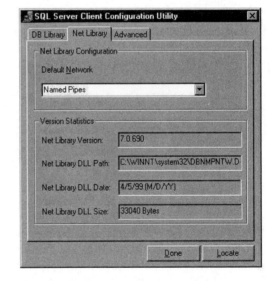

MSDTC Service

The MSDTC service must be started, and MSDTC should be configured to start automatically.

Go to the Control Panel
(Start | Settings | Control
Panel) and double-click on
Services. Then navigate to
the MSDTC service and make
sure that the Status is
Started and that the Startup
setting is Automatic:

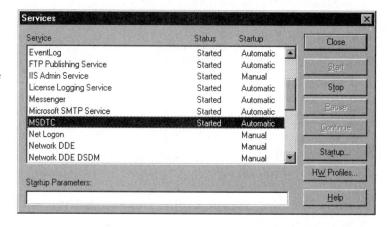

If MSDTC is not configured to start automatically, then click the Startup button and change it to
Automatic.

Configure Database Connectivity on the SQL Server

In this install procedure we're not going to install any sample sites, so we don't have to create databases
to house the sample site data now. But, we are going to install Ad Server, so we do need to create a
database for it to house its data. You'll need to create individual databases for Ad Server and
Commerce Server on your SQL server. 20Mb of space is more than adequate to handle the
requirements of installation (the actual size will vary depending on your site).

Run the SQL Server Enterprise Manager (Start | Programs | Microsoft SQL Server 6.5 | Enterprise
Manager) and create a database called Adserver. With SQL Server 6.5 you'll need to create a database
device for the AdServer database to live in, if you don't have space on an existing SQL database
device.

Now you need to create a System DSN to
communicate with the AdServer database
you just created. Go to the Control Panel
(Start | Settings | Control Panel), and run the
Administrative Tools control panel applet by
double-clicking on its icon. Double-click on
Data Sources (ODBC), and select the
System DSN tab:

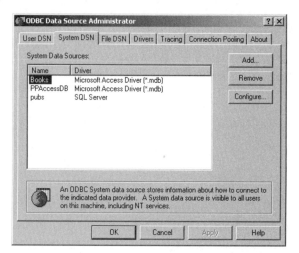

Click Add, then choose SQL Server from the bottom of the list and click Finish. Name the Data source Adserver, give a description (Adserver Database) and type the name of your server:

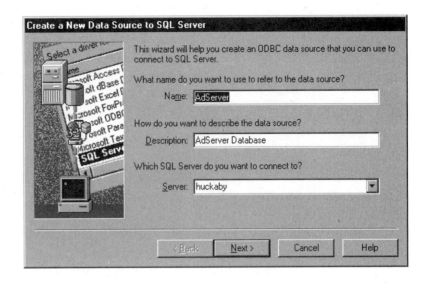

Click Next, and you'll be asked to verify the security credentials for the DSN that will be communicating with the SQL Server. Change the verification to With SQL Server authentication. Change the Login Id to sa and type the sa password (this could also be a SQL Server login with at least DBO permissions to the AdServer database, which will prevent the need for using the all powerful sa account for the DSN):

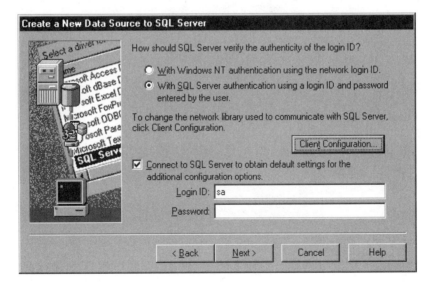

Click Next. On the following screen, you'll need to choose the AdServer database as the data source that this DSN will communicate to. Click the check box next to Change the default database to:, drop down the list of databases and choose AdServer:

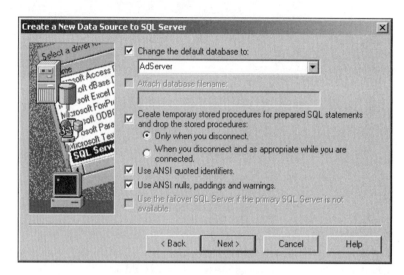

Click Next, and then accept all the defaults on the following screen:

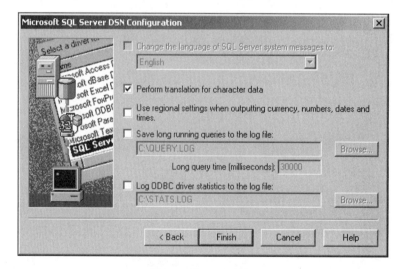

Click Finish, and the wizard will summarize all the configuration choices that you have made (and accepted by default). Click the Test Data Source button to verify the communication, and then click OK on the remaining screens to complete the operation.

Now repeat the procedure to create a database and System DSN for Commerce Server on your Site Server.

Site Server Version 3.0

When you insert the Site Server Version 3.0 CD-ROM, the CD will auto start and you'll be prompted with the main options for installing Site Server 3.0:

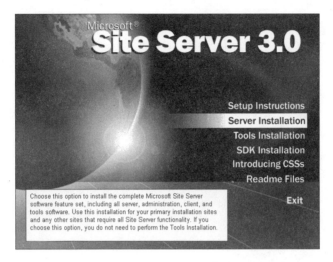

Click Server Installation to proceed to the Site Server 3.0 installation wizard. Click Next to continue, and you'll be presented with the licensing agreement. If you agree with the licensing of Microsoft Site Server Version 3.0, click Yes. Now, you'll be prompted to fill in your product and user information. Fill out your Name, Company, CD Key and E-mail address:

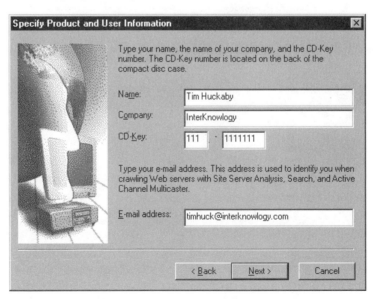

Click Next and then click OK to confirm your product ID.

Next, you'll be prompted for the Site Server 3.0 folder locations. Site Server needs file permissions (ACLs) painted on its program files directory to run properly, and you'll be warned if you try and install on a FAT partition (which cannot support file permissions). If you have followed the recommended steps for drive partitioning and assigning from earlier in the chapter then change all three defaults of C: to D:, where we have installed the NTFS partition:

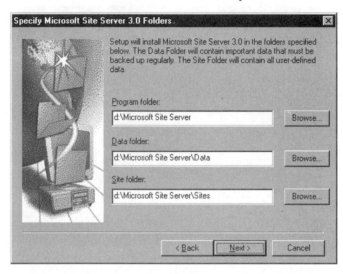

Click Next to continue and you'll be presented with the three types of Site Server 3.0 installations – Typical, Complete, and Custom:

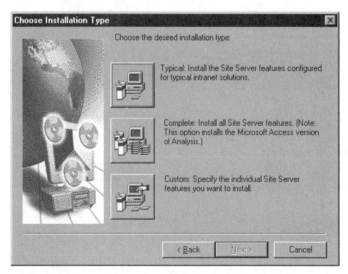

Click the image next to Custom to perform a custom installation. Click the + next to Analysis and change the Analysis database support from its default of Access Database Support by checking SQL Server Database Support. When you select SQL Server Database Support, Access Database Support gets unchecked – it is not possible to install the product with support for both databases:

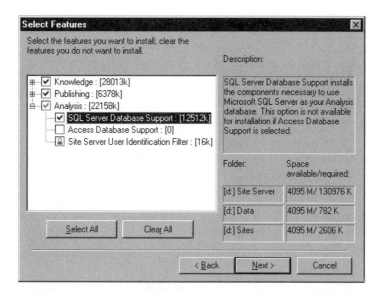

Next, the installation wizard will prompt you to specify a program folder in which to place the Site Server Menu choices. Leave the default of Microsoft Site Server and click Next to continue.

Now you're required to Configure User Accounts for the Publishing and Search services. The Search service requires an Administrative account to run under. The Publishing services simply require enough read and write permissions to publish to folders on the NT shares. For now, set both to run under the local Administrator Account. You can always back off the Publishing services permissions later by running under a different account with less than administrative privileges:

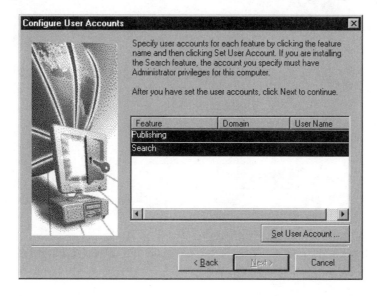

Click the **Set User Account** button. The dialog will default to **Administrator** and the name of the computer for the local domain. Type the password twice to set the user account:

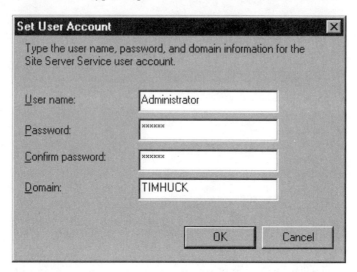

Click **OK**, and then **Next** to continue. The wizard will inform you of all the services it has to stop to proceed with the installation:

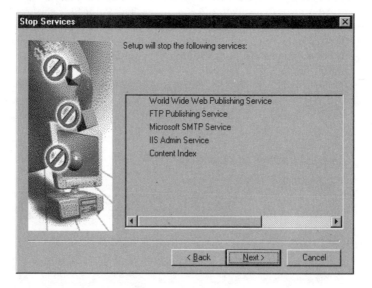

Click **Next** to continue. Click **Next** and the wizard will shut down existing services that need to be modified or are dependant on a service getting modified (like WWW, FTP, IIS Admin, etc.) one by one. The last screen of the wizard will confirm your choices:

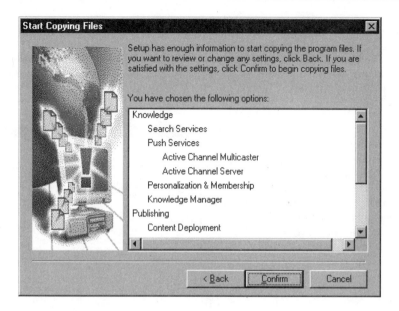

Click **Confirm** to start copying the files, and the installation of Microsoft Site Server 3.0 will begin. The process could take quite a bit of time depending on the speed of your server hardware.

During the installation, you will be asked to confirm the overwriting of files. This is because Service Packs and the FrontPage 98 Server Extensions that have already been installed were released after the release of Site Server Version 3.0. This is very important: choose **No To All** so as not to overwrite any newer files.

> **If you accidentally overwrite files with older versions you are guaranteed to have an unsuccessful installation.**

When the installation completes a dialog will appear confirming it. You will be given the chance to review the Readme file at that time. It's a good idea to study the Readme file in any NT server component installation. When satisfied, click **Finish**.

At this point, you may notice a flurry of disk activity. That's because Index Server has been restarted, and it has noticed that 100+ MBs of HTML Help content has appeared as a result of the Site Server installation. Index Server will take over and start indexing all the new content.

This is a requirement, and you'll fail the install if you manually turn the Index Server service off. This isn't that big a deal on a powerful server with lots of RAM, but on a development, staging, or home server, if you start your commerce install (which is the next step) while Index Server is doing its thing on the Site Server content, you'll hang your server – Index Server isn't smart enough to back off while the commerce installation proceeds.

> Most of the SS3 failed installs are because Index Server runs amok and fails to index all the new content before another installation (in this case Commerce Server) is started. The Commerce installation process competes with Index Server for the CPU and frequently hangs – especially on inferior machines. Make sure that Index Server has completed indexing all the content before rebooting or installing more software.

So here's the tip for installation on any box: after the reboot immediately following the Site Server 3.0 platform install, get the Task Manager by doing a *CTRL-ALT-Delete*, choose Task Manager, then click on the Processes tab. Sort on processor usage by clicking on the CPU field name. You'll see the cisvc.exe service going wild and the associated cidaemon.exe with it:

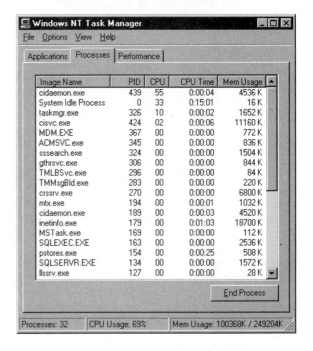

Just wait it out (when the System Idle Process gets to 98% or so), until all the content has been indexed.

After the commerce install, the Indexing Service will also need to index all the new content, so you'll need to go through this drill again.

Site Server 3.0 Commerce Edition

If you have installed the FrontPage 2000 Server Extensions (which was not recommended), you need to edit the Properties of the Default Web Site with the Site Server Service Admin (MMC). On the Home Directory tab, disable the FrontPage Web option. You can enable the FrontPage Web option again once Commerce Server is installed.

Upon inserting the Site Server 3.0 Commerce Edition CD-ROM, the Commerce CD will auto start and you'll be prompted with the main options for installing Commerce Server:

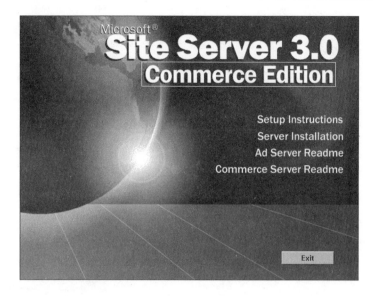

Click **Server Installation** to proceed to the Site Server 3.0 Commerce Edition installation wizard. Click **Next** to continue, and you'll be presented with the licensing agreement. If you agree with the licensing of Microsoft Site Server 3.0 Commerce Edition click **Yes**.

Now, you'll be prompted to fill in your product and user information. Fill out your **Name**, **Company**, and **CD Key**:

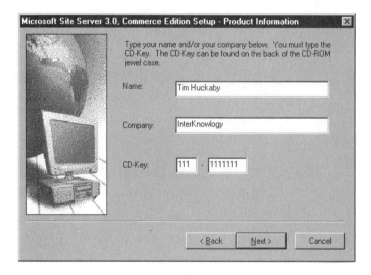

Click **Next**, and then click **OK** to confirm your Product ID. Click **Next** to continue and you'll be presented with the five types of Site Server 3.0 Commerce Edition installations – Typical, Complete, Custom, Ad Server, and Commerce Interchange Pipeline:

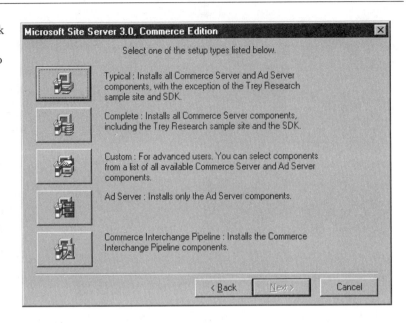

Click the image next to Custom to perform a custom installation.

You'll be prompted to choose which components you wish to install.

There are a number of sample sites that ship with Site Server 3.0 Commerce Edition, but detailed examination of them is beyond the scope of this book. Professional Site Server 3.0 Commerce Edition (Marco Tabini, ISBN 1-861002-50-5, Wrox Press) has a detailed explanation of the sample sites and how to install and use them.

I don't usually install any sample sites on a production server. And I usually install any sample site (but the Volcano Coffee sample site) on a development server. Let's assume this is a production server and not install any sample sites – the sample sites can always be installed at a later time:

❑ Uncheck the Clocktower, Microsoft Market, Microsoft Press, and Volcano Coffee sample sites

❑ Keep the Trey Research sample site unchecked

❑ Leave Ad Server and Ad Manager checked

❑ If this is a development server check the SDK (System Developers Kit); if not, keep it unchecked

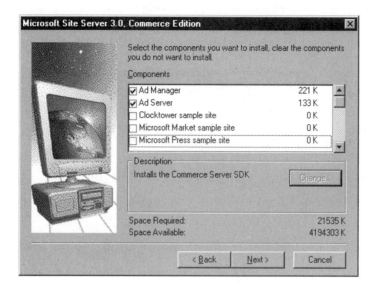

Click **Next** to continue. A dialog will tell you that you have not chosen to install any of the sample sites, and then ask you if you want to install the Commerce Server core components. Click **Yes** to continue the installation.

The next screen in the installation wizard will identify the components that you have chosen to install, and notify you that it has enough information to start the installation process:

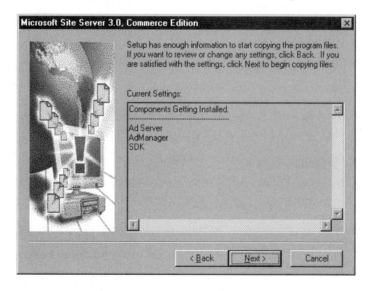

Click **Next**, and you'll be prompted to select and/or create a DSN for Ad Server. If you've created the database and DSN for Ad Server already – as was recommended earlier – just choose it and click OK.

If you have not created the Ad Server database and DSN yet, run the SQL Server Enterprise Manager and create a database called AdServer.

On the Site Server dialog box, click the **ODBC** button:

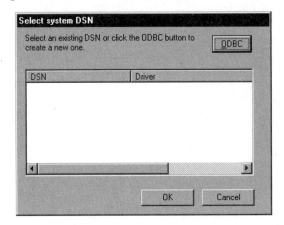

Now create a DSN for the Ad Server database you just created on the SQL Server (refer back to the Configure Database Connectivity section for more details on creating a DSN).

The Commerce Server installation will then start. The length of time it takes to complete the installation is dependent solely on the speed of your machine.

When the installation completes a dialog will appear confirming it. You'll be presented with a choice to review the Readme file at that time. When satisfied, click **Finish**.

Once again, as in the Site Server installation, you may notice a flurry of disk activity. Index Server has been restarted and the HTML Help files are being indexed. As before, make sure index server has completed indexing all the content before rebooting or installing more software.

Again, to monitor the progress of Index Server, get the Task Manager running by doing a *CTRL-ALT-Delete*, choose **Task Manager**, then click on the **Processes** tab. Sort on processor usage by clicking on the **CPU** field name. Wait until the **System Idle Process** gets to 98% or so, when all the content has been indexed.

Windows NT4.0 Service Pack 4

Install Microsoft Windows NT 4.0 Service Pack 4. You can download the Service Pack from:
`http://support.microsoft.com/support/ntserver/content/servicepacks/SP4.asp`.

Do *not* substitute Windows NT 4.0 Service Pack 5 or later at this point.

First, you'll be presented with the licensing agreement. If you agree with the licensing of Microsoft NT Version 4.0 Service Pack 4, click **Accept** and then **Install**. When the Service Pack is installed, you'll be required to restart the computer, and you'll then be prompted to install the Y2K updates.

> **Do *not* install the Y2K updates at this time. The Y2K updates are installed by Internet Explorer 4.01 SP2 in a prior step, and by MDAC 2.1 in a subsequent step.**

(Optional) Install Microsoft Internet Explorer 5.0

Internet Explorer 5.0 is not recommended for this configuration. If you do install Internet Explorer 5.0 on a computer with Commerce Server, you should be aware of the following issues:

- ❏ The Site Server Customizable Starter Sites (described in the final section of this chapter) are not compatible with Internet Explorer 5.0.

- ❏ Internet Explorer 5.0 associates the `.prf` extension with PICSRules files, while Site Server associates this extension with Rule Set Files. Therefore, you must perform a custom install of Internet Explorer 5.0, click the **Advanced** button and configure Internet Explorer 5.0 so that it does not associate the `.prf` file extension.

- ❏ Internet Explorer 5.0 prevents the Web Posting Acceptor from allowing Anonymous uploads. At the time of writing Microsoft is developing a fix, but this is not yet available.

(Optional) Install Visual Studio 6 Service Pack 3

If you installed Visual Studio 6.0 in the steps above, then install Visual Studio 6.0 Service Pack 3 at this point. You can download the Service Pack from:
`http://msdn.microsoft.com/vstudio/sp/vs6sp3/vsfixes.asp`.

Upon running the setup (or having the CD auto start), you'll be asked to confirm your intentions to install the Service Pack. Click **Continue** to proceed, and you'll be presented with the licensing agreement. If you agree with the licensing of Visual Studio 6 Service Pack 3, then click **I Agree**.

The installation will begin with copying of files, and then the configuration will proceed. Upon completion you'll receive a dialog pointing you to the Readme file, which contains a summary of many of the problems that are fixed with the installation of the Service Pack.

You'll also be instructed that you need to install Internet Explorer 5.0 to take advantage of the fixes. Remember from above that Internet Explorer 5.0 is not recommended for this configuration:

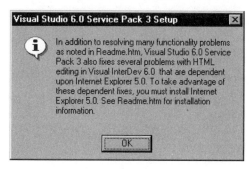

Click **OK** and you'll be instructed to restart your computer. After the restart, your Service Pack installation will be complete.

SQL Server 6.5 Service Pack 5a

Before you install SQL Server 6.5 Service Pack 5a, you need to have a minimum of 3 Mb space (and should have at least 10Mb) free in your master database. The master database is 25 Mb by default. Let's go through the process of expanding it to 50 Mb.

Run the Microsoft SQL Enterprise Manager by clicking Start | Programs | Microsoft SQL Server 6.5 | SQL Enterprise Manager. If this is the first time you've run the SQL Enterprise Manager then you'll need to "register" your server, by typing the name of the Server and typing the password for the sa account.

Click the + next to your SQL server's name to drop down the container of components. First you need to expand the size of the master database device. Click on the + next to Database Devices to drop down the list of database devices on your SQL server:

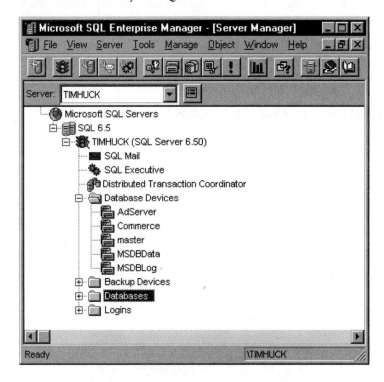

Right-click on master and choose Edit. Change the 25 in the Size (MB) field to 50 and then click Change Now:

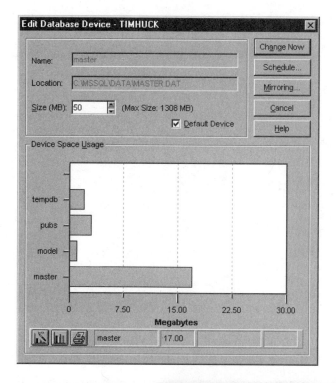

Next, you need to expand the size of the master database. Click on + next to **Databases** to drop down the list of databases on your SQL Server:

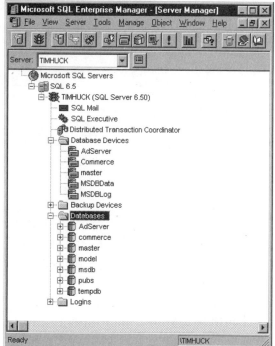

Right-click on master and choose Edit. You will default to the Database tab:

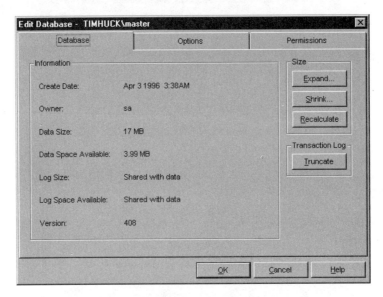

Click the Expand button. Drop down the Data Device list and choose master. The Size (MB) will default to the amount of space that is available to expand. In this case, it's 26Mb:

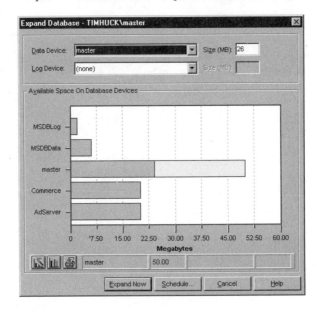

Click Expand Now. After a few short moments the expansion of the master database will be complete. The Edit Database dialog will reappear; notice that you now have 29.99Mb of available space on your master database. Click OK to continue, and then exit the SQL Enterprise Manager.

You are now ready to install the SQL Server 6.5 Service Pack 5a. You can download the Service Pack, for both the Enterprise and Standard versions of SQL Server, from `http://www.microsoft.com/downloads/release.asp?ReleaseID=12671`.

> **IMPORTANT: if prompted, do not install the optional MDAC 2.1 components. It will be installed in a later step.**

After executing the Service Pack, a number of files will be extracted to your machine. Then you'll be ready to run the Microsoft SQL Server 6.5 Service Pack 5a setup wizard.

Click Continue, and you'll be asked for your SA Password (the password for the sa account):

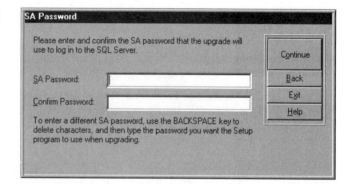

Type the password for your sa account twice and then click Continue. Next, you'll be presented with the licensing agreement. If you agree with the licensing of SQL Server Version 6.5 Service Pack 5a, click on Page Down 7 times to scroll to the bottom of the License Agreement. Then, click I Agree.

The installation will take a number of minutes depending on the speed of your system. When it has successfully installed click the Finish icon to exit to Windows NT.

Microsoft Data Access Components 2.1 Service Pack 2

Install MDAC version 2.1.2.4202.3, which is also known as MDAC 2.1 SP2. You can download the MDAC from: `http://www.microsoft.com/data/download.htm`.

Upon running the executable, the first screen is the license agreement. If you agree with the licensing of Microsoft Data Access Components 2.1, click Yes. The file extraction process will begin and then launch the setup wizard.

Screen 1 of the setup wizard confirms your intentions to install Microsoft Data Access Components 2.1. Click Continue. Setup will search for installed components to make sure you have the prerequisites installed. If you've followed the installation procedures as recommended then you do.

To start the installation, click the icon that represents a Complete Installation. The installation will take a few moments depending on how fast your system is. Upon completion, click OK to exit.

Active Directory Services Interfaces Version 2.5

Install Active Directory Services Interfaces Version 2.5. You can download Active Directory Services Interfaces Version 2.5 from:
`http://www.microsoft.com/ntserver/nts/downloads/other/ADSI25/default.asp.`

Upon running the installation executable for Active Directory Services Interfaces (ADSI) Version 2.5, you'll be prompted to confirm your intentions to install. Click Yes to proceed. Now, you'll be presented with the license agreement. If you agree with the licensing of Active Directory Services Interfaces Version 2.5, click Yes and the installation will proceed.

The installation of Active Directory Services Interfaces Version 2.5 will only take a short time. When it's completed, click OK to exit. You will be required to restart your computer when complete – click Yes to do so.

Site Server 3.0 Service Pack 3

Install Site Server 3.0 Service Pack 3. You can download the Service Pack from:
`http://support.microsoft.com/support/siteserver/servicepacks/sp.asp.`

After executing the Service Pack, a number of files will be extracted to your machine. Then, you'll be ready to run the Microsoft Site Server 3.0 Service Pack 3 Setup Wizard. Click Next, and you'll be presented with the licensing agreement. If you agree with the licensing of Microsoft Site Server Version 3.0 Service Pack 3, click I Agree, and then click Next.

You can choose to create an uninstall directory for the Service Pack. It's a good idea to create an uninstall directory, just in case of an installation failure:

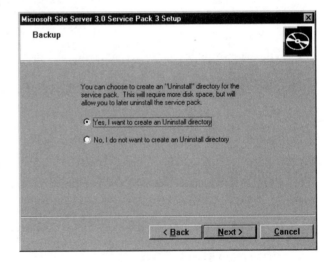

Now, setup has enough information to start copying the files. Click Next to begin. The installation will take a number of minutes depending on the speed of your system. When it has successfully installed click Finish to complete the installation.

> **Important: make sure and read the Site Server Service Pack 3 `Readme.htm` file, which includes the latest release notes and small fixes that need to be made. It is installed in your Site Server Directory in: `\Microsoft SiteServer\sp3\readme.htm`.**

Windows NT4 Service Pack 6

Install Windows NT 4.0 Service Pack 6. You can download the Service Pack from: `http://www.microsoft.com/ntserver/nts/downloads/recommended/PREM_SP6/allSP6.asp`.

First, you'll be presented with the licensing agreement. If you agree with the licensing of Microsoft Windows NT 4.0 Service Pack 6, click Accept and then Install. The installation will start by inspecting your Windows NT 4.0 configuration, archiving old versions of files and then copying new files.

Upon completion, you will be required to restart your computer to complete the installation. Click Restart and the computer will restart.

> **Congratulations! You are installed! Now move on to the final post-installation section.**

Installing SS3 on Windows NT 4.0 With SQL Server 7.0

> **Read on if you're installing Site Server on the same box that you are going to install SQL Server 7.0 on, and your operating system is Windows NT 4.0.**

Windows NT 4.0

Install Microsoft Windows NT Server 4.0. Again, to guarantee a successful Site Server 3.0 Commerce installation I suggest you start with a clean computer, or have the Windows NT 4.0 installation wipe the hard drives clean before starting its installation.

Windows NT 4.0 installation instructions are beyond the scope of this book. There is an abundance of information on how to install the Windows NT 4.0 product on the web, but the product documentation from Microsoft is outstanding. You'll find it on the Windows NT 4.0 CD in the \SUPPORT\BOOKS folder.

Since custom drivers are needed to access the hardware (video, network, etc.) refer to the Microsoft Windows NT 4.0 product documentation and the documentation for the specific hardware that you have in your system. After you complete your Windows NT installation, there is a good chance you will need to install third party (non Microsoft) drivers for the unique hardware (video, network boards, etc.) that you have in your system.

Here are the important points for your Windows NT 4.0 installation:

❑ Install Windows NT 4.0 as a stand-alone server, if possible.

❑ There's no need to install Internet Information Server, although it doesn't hurt. You will be installing Internet Information Server 4.0 in a subsequent step, when you install the Windows NT Option Pack.

❑ Although not crucial, it will make your installation quite a bit easier if you have a floppy diskette with updated drivers for your network board. This is especially important if the Windows NT 4.0 installation cannot identify what type of network board you have, or if it does not have a driver for your particular network board.

❑ Complete the partitioning, formatting and assigning of drives with the Windows NT 4.0 Disk Administrator when you have completed the Windows NT 4.0 installation. Refer to the Drive Partitioning section above for details.

Windows NT4 Service Pack 3

Install Microsoft Windows NT 4.0 Service Pack 3. You can download the Service Pack from: `http://support.microsoft.com/support/ntserver/content/servicepacks/SP3.asp`.

> **It is very important that you do not substitute Windows NT 4.0 Service Pack 4 (or later) at this point.**

The installation of Windows NT Service Pack 3 is a simple 4-step wizard. The first step is a splash screen that describes the installation process of the Service Pack. Upon clicking Next you will be asked to confirm your intent to install the Service Pack:

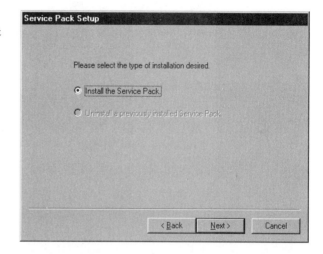

Click Next and you'll be asked if you want to create an uninstall directory. I always play it safe and create an uninstall directory for any Service Pack that I apply. Murphy's Law will most likely dictate a power failure in the middle of your Service Pack install – if you have an uninstall directory you'll be able to quickly recover:

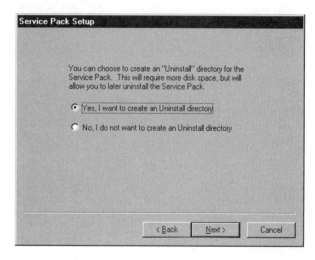

Click Next and you will be asked to confirm the installation of Windows NT 4.0 Service Pack 3 by clicking Finish. It will take the installation a few minutes to create the uninstall directory, copy the necessary files, do the DLL registrations, and perform the configurations. Upon completion you'll receive a dialog asking you to remove all floppies and CD ROMs because the installation needs to perform a restart of your system:

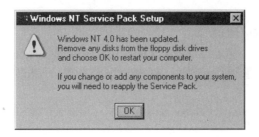

After the reboot, you'll have a base platform of Windows NT 4.0 Service Pack 3. At this point, although it's certainly not necessary, I recommend making a "ghost". Refer to the Drive Partitioning section of this chapter (above) if you are not familiar with Symantec's Norton Ghost software.

Internet Explorer 4 Service Pack 2

Install Microsoft Internet Explorer 4.01 with Internet Explorer Service Pack 2. You can download Internet Explorer 4.01 and the Service Pack in one executable from: `http://www.microsoft.com/msdownload/iebuild/ie4sp2_win32/en/ ie4sp2_win32.htm`.

> **Do not substitute Internet Explorer 5.0 at this point. You will install Internet Explorer 5.0 in a subsequent step.**

The installation of the IE4 SP2 uses a wizard. The first screen of the wizard is a splash screen describing the process. Click Next and you'll be presented with the licensing agreement. If you agree with the licensing of IE4, click I accept and then Next. If you downloaded the installation from the Microsoft web site you'll be prompted with Download Options:

If you have an IE4 SP2 CD, you won't be prompted with Download Options because you'll have all the installation components on the CD.

If you are doing a "web" installation of IE4, then choose Install and click Next. You'll be prompted with three installation options: Standard Installation, Browser Only installation or a Full Installation. The default choice is the Standard Installation, which installs the IE4 Browser, Outlook Express, Windows Media Player and multimedia enhancements. A standard installation is fine:

Choose Next, and you'll be presented with a chance to install the Windows Desktop Update, also called the Active Desktop:

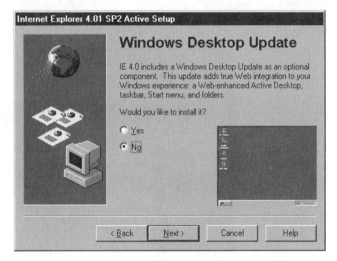

Select No and then click Next, to choose a standard desktop installation.

Now you'll be prompted to choose a region that best represents the country and language of your Active Channel installation. Choose the proper region and click Next.

You'll be prompted for a destination folder for your Internet Explorer 4.0 SP2. If you partitioned your drive and set up your drive mappings as recommended earlier in the chapter, then accept the default on C:.

After copying files and configuring your system, you'll be prompted to restart your system to complete the installation. Choose OK to restart.

Windows NT4 Option Pack

Install the Microsoft Windows NT 4.0 Option Pack. You can download the Option Pack from: `http://www.microsoft.com/ntserver/nts/downloads/recommended/NT4OptPk/default.asp`.

The Option Pack will install the web services required for Site Server:

❑ The WWW service

❑ The FTP service

❑ The SMTP service

❑ Transaction Server

❑ Index Server

The Option Pack set-up is a web-based installation. If you use an Option Pack CD to do the installation, then the browser will auto start. Choose Install from the left navigation frame in the browser:

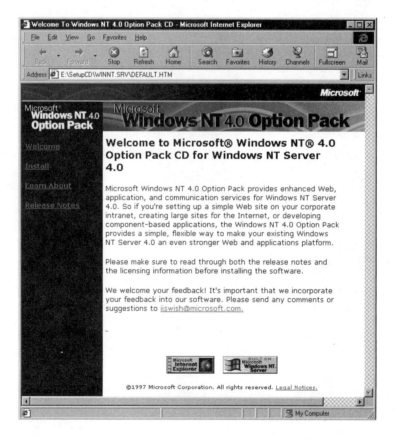

Next in the CD set-up you'll be presented with the choices to install Windows NT 4.0 Service Pack 3 and Internet Explorer 4.01. These are prerequisites for a Windows NT 4.0 Option Pack set up:

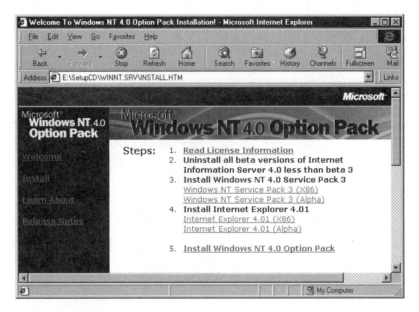

If you've followed the steps outlined above then you have already installed SP3 and IE4, so click Install Window NT 4.0 Option Pack to proceed with the installation. If doing a web installation, and prompted, perform an Upgrade Plus installation. This is critical, since you will need to add specific services. Selecting Upgrade instead of Upgrade Plus will not get you everything you need for a successful Site Server installation.

Next, you'll be presented with a dialog containing a relatively confusing question: "would you like to Run this program from its current location or Save this program to disk?":

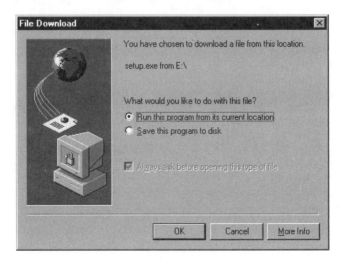

You'll need to understand the implications of this question, because you'll see it quite a bit if you are to download executables from a browser.

If you're running the installation from the Windows NT 4.0 Option Pack CD, Internet Explorer (or any browser for that matter) is not smart enough to know that you have the installation program on a local CD, so it asks you if you want to download it. If you were truly downloading the Windows NT 4.0 Option Pack from the Microsoft web site then you would Save this program to disk and run it after it's been successfully downloaded. But, if you have a local CD with the installation software then choose Run this program from its current location.

Next, you get a dialog alerting you of a Security Warning:

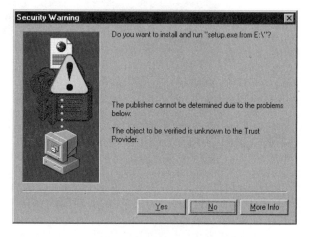

This dialog is alerting you that a certificate authority like VeriSign has not digitally signed the Option Pack setup executable. It's not appropriate to digitally sign controls or executables that modify the operating system (like the Windows NT 4.0 Option Pack) and that's why you have received the security warning. Click Yes to install and run the setup.

After some initialization the Option Pack installation wizard will run. The first screen of the wizard is a splash screen that describes the features that can be installed. Click Next and you'll be presented with the licensing agreement. If you agree with the licensing of the Windows NT 4.0 Option Pack, then click Accept and then Next. Now you'll be offered the three types of installation: Minimum, Typical and Custom:

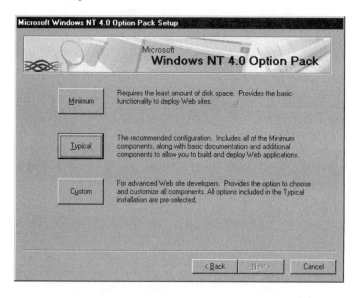

You need to perform a Custom installation, so click Custom and you will be presented with all the installation options:

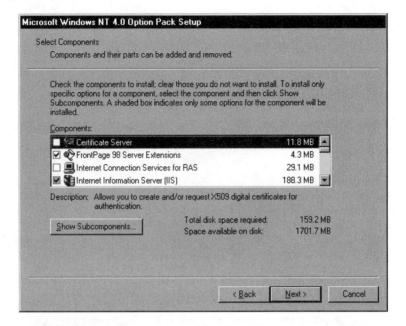

You do not want to install the FrontPage 98 Server Extensions yet (the FrontPage Server Extensions are installed later in the process), so uncheck the FrontPage 98 Server Extensions option.

At this point you should have the following options **checked**:

- ❏ Internet Information Server (IIS)
- ❏ Microsoft Data Access Components 1.5
- ❏ Microsoft Index Server
- ❏ Microsoft Management Console
- ❏ Microsoft Script Debugger
- ❏ NT Option Pack Common Files
- ❏ Transaction Server
- ❏ Windows Scripting Host

And you should have the following options **unchecked**:

- ❏ Certificate Server
- ❏ FrontPage 98 Server Extensions
- ❏ Internet Connection Services for RAS
- ❏ Microsoft Message Queue
- ❏ Microsoft Site Server Express 2.0
- ❏ Visual InterDev RAD Remote Deployment Support

Click Next to continue the installation, and you'll be presented with the folder locations for web and FTP publishing, and the folder location for the application files. If you followed the recommended steps for drive partitioning and assigning from earlier in the chapter, then change the C: to D: on the WWW Service and FTP Service, which is the NTFS share on your Windows NT 4.0 server. Leave the Application Installation Point at C:, which is the FAT partition that your operating system (NT 4.0) was installed on:

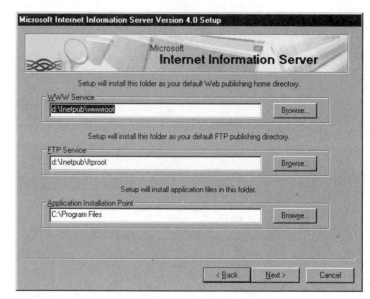

Click Next, and you'll be prompted to choose the folder locations for your Microsoft Transaction Server (MTS) installation. Leave the default of C:\Program Files\Mts, as below:

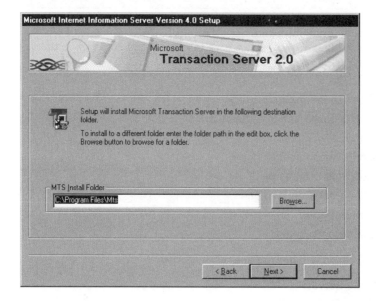

Click Next, and configure MTS for local (not remote) administration by leaving the default as Local. Click Next to continue.

You'll be prompted for the folder for your default index directory. If you followed the recommended steps for drive partitioning and mapping from earlier in the chapter then leave the default of d:\Inetpub, as below:

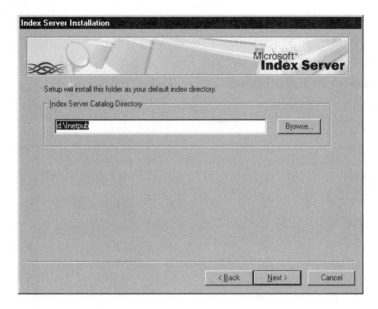

Click **Next** and you'll be prompted for the folder for your SMTP installation. Again, if you followed the recommended steps for drive partitioning and mapping from earlier in the chapter then leave the default of d:\Inetpub\Mailroot, as below:

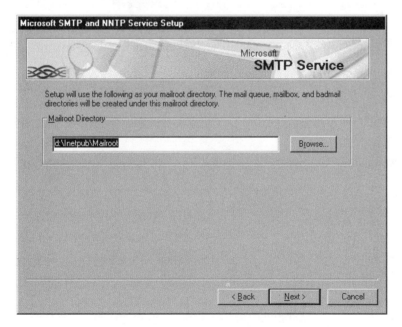

Click Next and the installation will proceed. It may take several minutes depending on the speed of your machine, but you'll be presented with a progress bar so that you can monitor the installation and estimate when it might complete.

Upon completion, click Finish to exit the Installation and the Option Pack setup will finalize the settings. You'll be asked if you want to restart to complete the installation, so choose Yes and the computer will restart.

FrontPage 98 Server Extensions

Install the updated FrontPage 98 Server Extensions, version 3.0.2.1706. You can find them at: `http://officeupdate.microsoft.com/frontpage/wpp/license.htm`.

Upon executing the installation program, the software will extract and run the installation. The first screen of the wizard confirms your installation of the software. Click Next and you'll be presented with the licensing agreement. If you agree with the licensing of the FrontPage 98 Server Extensions, click Accept and then Next, and the installation will start.

After a few moments, you'll be presented with a dialog telling you that the installation is complete. Click Finish to complete the installation.

> *You can install the FrontPage 2000 Server Extensions (not recommended with Site Server 3.0 Commerce Edition because of incompatibilities). If you need to install the FrontPage 2000 Server Extensions refer to the Post Installation Configurations section at the end of the chapter.*

Windows NT4.0 Service Pack 4

Install Microsoft Windows NT 4.0 Service Pack 4. You can download the Service Pack from: `http://support.microsoft.com/support/ntserver/content/servicepacks/SP4.asp`.

> **Do not substitute Windows NT 4.0 Service Pack 5 or later at this point.**

First, you'll be presented with the licensing agreement. If you agree with the licensing of Microsoft NT Version 4.0 Service Pack 4, click Accept and then Install. When the Service Pack is installed, you'll be required to restart the computer, and you'll then be prompted to install the Y2K updates.

> **Do not install the Y2K updates at this time. The Y2K updates are installed by Internet Explorer 4.01 SP2 in a prior step, and by MDAC 2.1 in a subsequent step.**

Internet Explorer 5.0

Install Microsoft Internet Explorer 5.0.

You can download Internet Explorer 5.0 from: `http://www.microsoft.com/ie`.

Note that:

❑ By default, Internet Explorer 5.0 associates the `.prf` extension with PICSRules files. However, Site Server associates this extension with Rule Set Files. To work around this problem, you must perform a custom install of Internet Explorer 5.0, and then click the **Advanced** button and configure Internet Explorer 5.0 so that it does not associate the `.prf` file extension.

❑ Internet Explorer 5.0 can prevent debugging HTML applications with Visual InterDev. Refer to Knowledge base article Q230730 on the Microsoft Web Site at: `http://support.microsoft.com/support/kb/articles/q230/7/30.asp` for details.

❑ Internet Explorer 5.0 may introduce problems with Microsoft Visual Basic, Microsoft Visual InterDev, and Microsoft Visual J++. Refer to Knowledge base article Q230730 on the Microsoft Web Site at: `http://support.microsoft.com/support/kb/articles/q230/7/30.asp` for details.

Upon running the Internet Explorer 5.0 installation wizard, the first screen is the licensing agreement. If you agree with the licensing agreement of Microsoft Internet Explorer Version 5.0 then click **I accept the agreement**, then click **Next** to continue.

Setup will initialize. Next you will be prompted with Screen 2 of the installation wizard. You must select **Install Now – Typical set of components**:

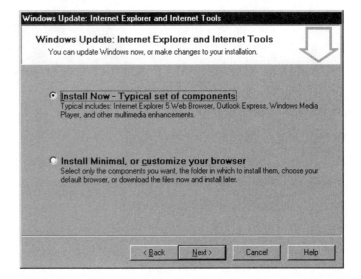

Click Next and the installation will start. The installation can take a while depending on the speed of your system, but there's a good user interface that keeps you updated of the progress.

Upon completion you will be required to click Finish to restart your system.

SQL Server 7.0

When you insert the SQL Server Version 7.0 CD-ROM, the CD will auto start and you'll be prompted with the main options for installing SQL Server Version 7.0:

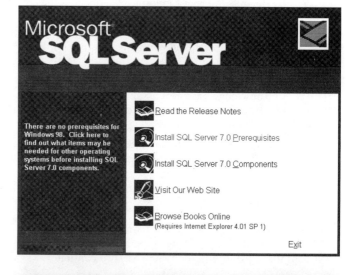

Click Install SQL Server 7.0 Components and you will be prompted with the component options for the SQL Sever Version 7.0 installation:

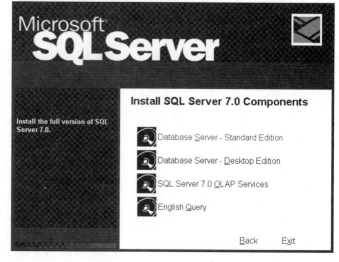

Click **Database Server – Standard Edition** and you start the SQL Server 7.0 installation wizard. Choose the default of **Local Install – Install to the Local Machine**:

Click **Next**. The SQL Server 7.0 installation wizard will search for installed components and then ask you to confirm your intentions to install the product.

Click **Next** and you'll move to the Software License Agreement. If you agree with the licensing agreement of Microsoft SQL Server Version 7.0 then click **Yes**. Now you'll be prompted to enter your **Name** and **Company**:

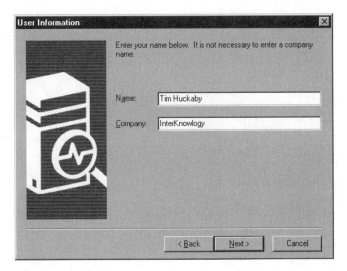

Click Next to continue, and you'll be presented with the Setup Type screen. Choose Typical install. Change the Data Files location to D: by clicking Browse (next to Data Files) and editing the location to d:\MSSQL7:

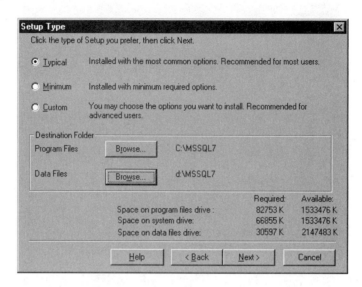

Click Next to continue, and you'll be presented with the Services Accounts screen. It's time to specify which type of security we're going to use for our installation of SQL Server. We can either use Windows NT or Mixed mode, which uses a combination of both SQL Server and Windows NT authentication. For this installation, we're going to use the Local System account for the installation. Check Use the Local System account:

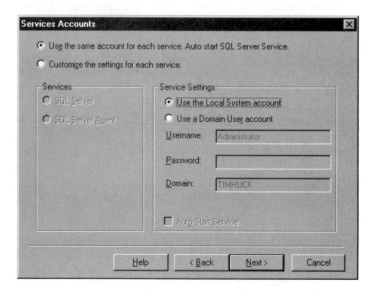

Click **Next** to continue. Now the SQL Server installation is ready to proceed. All that's required now is to enter what type of license you have purchased: Per Seat or Per Client. Choose the appropriate license for your installation and click **Continue**.

The installation will start by copying files. Once the installation is finished, click **Finish** and then exit the SQL Server 7.0 installation wizard by clicking **Exit**. It's a good idea to reboot your server to allow for the SQL Service to start by itself.

Once the reboot has completed, open up SQL Enterprise Manager to test your installation by clicking **Start | Microsoft SQL Server 7.0 | Enterprise Manager**. Click the + next to **Microsoft SQL Servers**. Click the + next to **SQL Server Group**. Your SQL server will appear. If it has a green arrow in the icon, it's running:

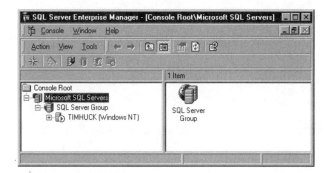

Quit out of the Enterprise Manager and proceed to the SQL Server 7.0 Service Pack 1 installation.

SQL Server Version 7.0 Service Pack 1

Install Microsoft SQL Server 7.0 Service Pack 1.

If you don't have a CD with the SQL Server 7.0 Service Pack 1, you can download and run the `Sql70sp1i.exe` file. You can download the Service Pack from: `http://www.microsoft.com/sql/support/sp1.htm`. The Service Pack files are extracted to the `C:\SP1` directory. However, you must still run `C:\SP1\Setup.exe` to actually install the Service Pack.

If you have a CD with the SQL Server 7.0 Service Pack 1 on it, get Windows Explorer running, navigate to the `Setup.bat` (in most cases it will be in `\Service Pack 1\x86`) and execute it by double-clicking.

> *Installing SQL 7.0 SP1 can take up to 30 minutes depending on the speed of your machine – that does not include the time it takes to download the Service Pack.*

First, you'll be presented with a screen that confirms your intentions to install the Service Pack. Click Next and you'll be presented with the License Agreement. If you agree with the licensing agreement of Microsoft SQL Server Version 7.0 Service Pack 1, then click Yes to proceed. Next, you'll choose the authentication mode that the setup should use to connect to SQL Server. Keep the default of The Windows NT account...:

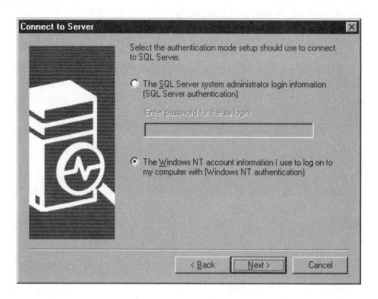

Click Next. After a short period, the setup will determine that it has enough information to proceed. Click Next and the installation will proceed unattended. When it's complete you will be required to restart your computer.

Change the SQL Server Client Default Network Library to Named Pipes

You want IIS to use Named Pipes (which is faster than TCP/IP when SQL Server and IIS 4.0 are on the same box) when it connects to the SQL Server computer

To configure the SQL Server client, you need to run Windbver.exe. It lives in C:\WINNT\System32. On the Net Library tab, select Named Pipes as the Default Network, and then click Done:

MSDTC Service

The MSDTC service must be started, and MSDTC should be configured to start automatically.

Go to the Control Panel (Start | Settings | Control Panel) and double-click on Services. Then navigate to the MSDTC service and make sure that the Status is Started and that the Startup setting is Automatic:

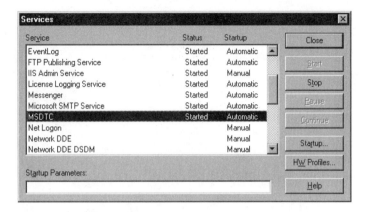

If MSDTC is not configured to start automatically, then click the Startup button and change it to Automatic.

Configure Database Connectivity on the SQL Server

In this install procedure we're not going to install any sample sites, so we don't have to create databases to house the sample site data now. But, we are going to install Ad Server, so we do need to create a database for it to house its data. You'll need to create individual databases for Ad Server and Commerce Server on your SQL server. 20Mb of space is more than adequate to handle the requirements of installation (the actual size will vary depending on your site).

Run the SQL Server Enterprise Manager (Start | Programs | Microsoft SQL Server 7.0 | Enterprise Manager) and create a database called Adserver. To create a database:

❑   Click the + next to Microsoft SQL Servers.

❑   Click the + sign next to SQL Server Group.

❑   Click the + sign next to the name of your server.

❑   Right-click on the Databases folder and choose New Database... This will initiate the New Database Wizard.

Take all the defaults, including the 1 MB size, when you create the AdServer database. SQL Server 7.0 will grow the database automatically if you need more space.

Now you need to create a System DSN to communicate with the AdServer database you just created. Go to the **Control Panel** (Start | Settings | Control Panel), and run the **Administrative Tools** control panel applet by double-clicking on its icon. Double-click on **Data Sources (ODBC)**, and select the **System DSN** tab:

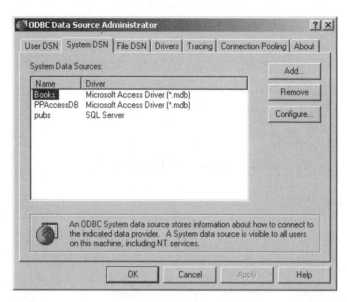

Click **Add**, then choose **SQL Server** from the bottom of the list and click **Finish**. Name the Data source **Adserver**, give a description (**Adserver Database**) and type the name of your server:

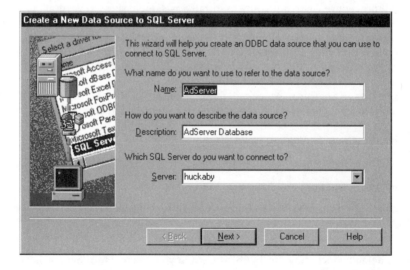

Click Next, and you'll be asked to verify the security credentials for the DSN that will be communicating with the SQL Server. Change the verification to With SQL Server authentication. Change the Login Id to sa and type the sa password (this could also be a SQL Server login with at least DBO permissions to the AdServer database, which will prevent the need for using the all powerful sa account for the DSN):

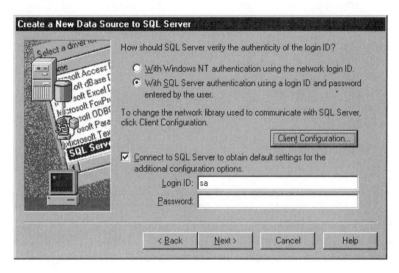

Click Next. On the following screen, you'll need to choose the AdServer database as the data source that this DSN will communicate to. Click the check box next to Change the default database to:, drop down the list of databases and choose AdServer:

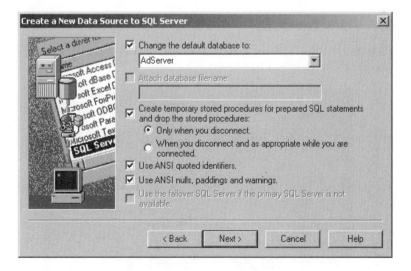

Click **Next**, and then accept all the defaults on the following screen:

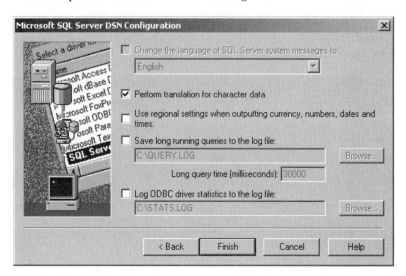

Click **Finish**, and the wizard will summarize all the configuration choices that you have made (and accepted by default). Click the **Test Data Source** button to verify the communication, and then click **OK** on the remaining screens to complete the operation.

Now repeat the procedure to create a database and System DSN for Commerce Server on your Site Server.

Site Server Version 3.0

When you insert the Site Server Version 3.0 CD-ROM, the CD will auto start and you'll be prompted with the main options for installing Site Server 3.0:

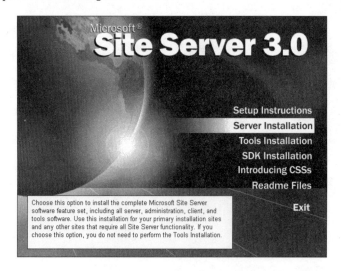

Click **Server Installation** to proceed to the Site Server 3.0 installation wizard. Click **Next** to continue, and you'll be presented with the licensing agreement. If you agree with the licensing of Microsoft Site Server Version 3.0, click **Yes**. Now, you'll be prompted to fill in your product and user information. Fill out your **Name, Company, CD Key** and **E-mail address**:

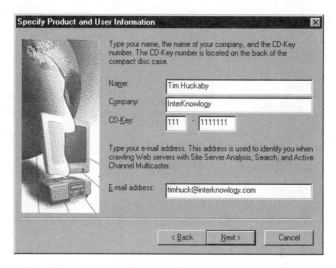

Click **Next** and then click **OK** to confirm your product ID.

Next, you'll be prompted for the Site Server 3.0 folder locations. Site Server needs file permissions (ACLs) painted on its program files directory to run properly, and you'll be warned if you try and install on a FAT partition (which cannot support file permissions). If you have followed the recommended steps for drive partitioning and assigning from earlier in the chapter then change all three defaults of C: to D:, where we have installed the NTFS partition:

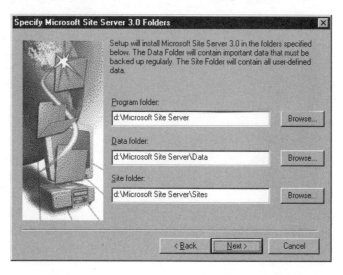

Click **Next** to continue and you'll be presented with the three types of Site Server 3.0 installations –
Typical, **Complete**, and **Custom**:

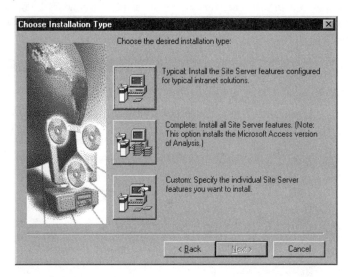

Click the image next to **Custom** to perform a custom installation. Click the + next to **Analysis** and
change the Analysis database support from its default of **Access Database Support** by checking **SQL
Server Database Support**. When you select **SQL Server Database Support**, **Access Database
Support** gets unchecked – it is not possible to install the product with support for both databases:

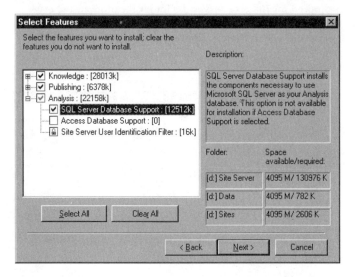

Next, the installation wizard will prompt you to specify a program folder in which to place the Site
Server Menu choices. Leave the default of **Microsoft Site Server** and click **Next** to continue.

Now you're required to **Configure User Accounts** for the **Publishing** and **Search** services. The Search service requires an Administrative account to run under. The Publishing services simply require enough read and write permissions to publish to folders on the NT shares. For now, set both to run under the local Administrator Account. You can always back off the Publishing services permissions later by running under a different account with less than administrative privileges:

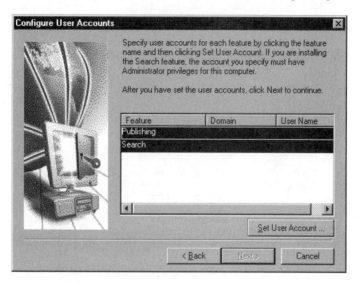

Click the **Set User Account** button. The dialog will default to **Administrator** and the name of the computer for the local domain. Type the password twice to set the user account:

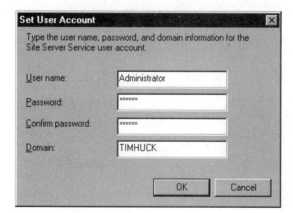

Click **OK**, and then **Next** to continue. The wizard will inform you of all the services it has to stop to proceed with the installation:

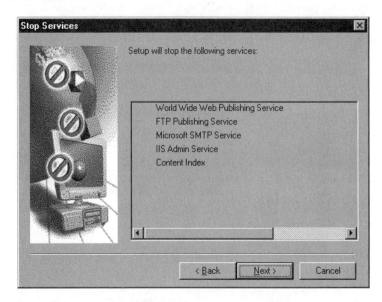

Click **Next** to continue. Click **Next** and the wizard will shut down existing services that need to be modified or are dependant on a service getting modified (like WWW, FTP, IIS Admin, etc.) one by one. The last screen of the wizard will confirm your choices:

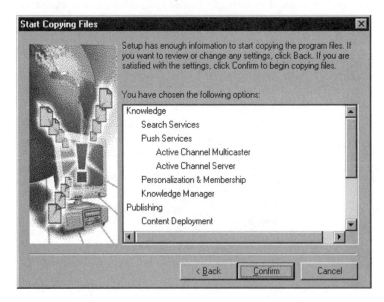

Click Confirm to start copying the files, and the installation of Microsoft Site Server 3.0 will begin. The process could take quite a bit of time depending on the speed of your server hardware.

During the installation, you will be asked to confirm the overwriting of files. This is because Service Packs and the FrontPage 98 Server Extensions that have already been installed were released after the release of Site Server Version 3.0. This is very important: choose **No To All** so as not to overwrite any newer files.

> **If you accidentally overwrite files with older versions you are guaranteed to have an unsuccessful installation.**

When the installation completes a dialog will appear confirming it. You will be given the chance to review the Readme file at that time. It's a good idea to study the Readme file in any NT server component installation. When satisfied, click Finish.

At this point, you may notice a flurry of disk activity. That's because Index Server has been restarted, and it has noticed that 100+ MBs of HTML Help content has appeared as a result of the Site Server installation. Index Server will take over and start indexing all the new content.

This is a requirement, and you'll fail the install if you manually turn the Index Server service off. This isn't that big a deal on a powerful server with lots of RAM, but on a development, staging, or home server, if you start your commerce install (which is the next step) while Index Server is doing its thing on the Site Server content, you'll hang your server – Index Server isn't smart enough to back off while the commerce installation proceeds.

> **Most of the SS3 failed installs are because Index Server runs amok and fails to index all the new content before another installation (in this case Commerce Server) is started. The Commerce installation process competes with Index Server for the CPU and frequently hangs – especially on inferior machines. Make sure that Index Server has completed indexing all the content before rebooting or installing more software.**

So here's the tip for installation on any box: after the reboot immediately following the Site Server 3.0 platform install, get the Task Manager by doing a *CTRL-ALT-Delete*, choose Task Manager, then click on the Processes tab. Sort on processor usage by clicking on the CPU field name. You'll see the cisvc.exe service going wild and the associated cidaemon.exe with it:

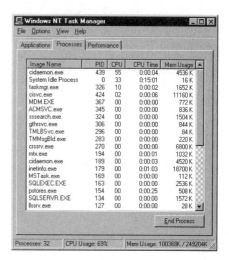

Just wait it out (when the System Idle Process gets to 98% or so), until all the content has been indexed.

After the commerce install, the Indexing Service will also need to index all the new content, so you'll need to go through this drill again.

Site Server 3.0 Commerce Edition

If you have installed the FrontPage 2000 Server Extensions (which was not recommended), you need to edit the Properties of the Default Web Site with the Site Server Service Admin (MMC). On the Home Directory tab, disable the FrontPage Web option. You can enable the FrontPage Web option again once Commerce Server is installed.

.Upon inserting the Site Server 3.0 Commerce Edition CD-ROM, the Commerce CD will auto start and you'll be prompted with the main options for installing Commerce Server:

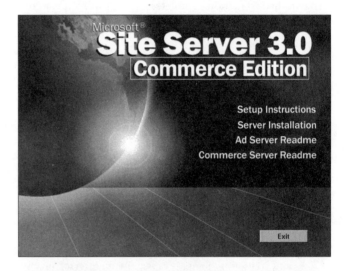

Click Server Installation to proceed to the Site Server 3.0 Commerce Edition installation wizard. Click Next to continue, and you'll be presented with the licensing agreement. If you agree with the licensing of Microsoft Site Server 3.0 Commerce Edition click Yes.

Now, you'll be prompted to fill in your product and user information. Fill out your Name, Company, and CD Key:

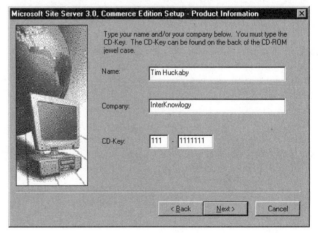

Click Next, and then click OK to confirm your Product ID. Click Next to continue and you'll be presented with the five types of Site Server 3.0 Commerce Edition installations – Typical, Complete, Custom, Ad Server, and Commerce Interchange Pipeline:

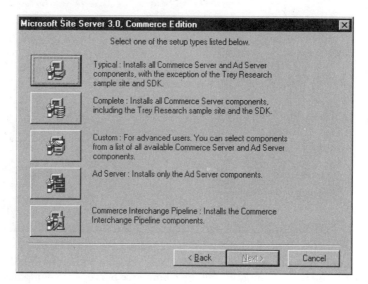

Click the image next to Custom to perform a custom installation.

You'll be prompted to choose which components you wish to install.

> *There are a number of sample sites that ship with Site Server 3.0 Commerce Edition, but detailed examination of them is beyond the scope of this book. Professional Site Server 3.0 Commerce Edition (Marco Tabini, ISBN 1-861002-50-5, Wrox Press) has a detailed explanation of the sample sites and how to install and use them.*

I don't usually install any sample sites on a production server. I usually install any sample site (but the Volcano Coffee sample site) on a development server. Let's assume this is a production server and not install any sample sites – the sample sites can always be installed at a later time:

❑   Uncheck the Clocktower, Microsoft Market, Microsoft Press, and Volcano Coffee sample sites

❑   Keep the Trey Research sample site unchecked

❑   Leave Ad Server and Ad Manager checked

❑   If this is a development server check the SDK (System Developers Kit); if not, keep it unchecked

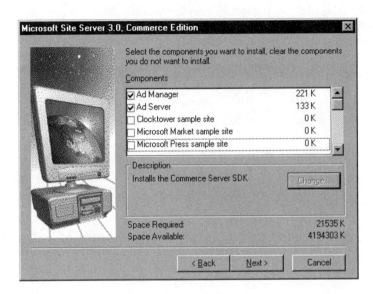

Click Next to continue. A dialog will tell you that you have not chosen to install any of the sample sites, and then ask you if you want to install the Commerce Server core components. Click Yes to continue the installation.

The next screen in the installation wizard will identify the components that you have chosen to install, and notify you that it has enough information to start the installation process:

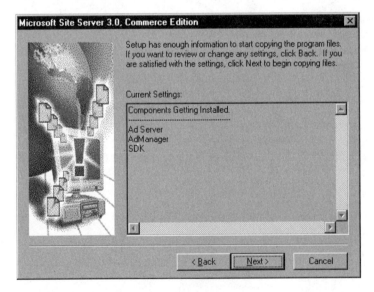

Click **Next**, and you'll be prompted to select and/or create a DSN for Ad Server. If you've created the database and DSN for Ad Server already – as was recommended earlier – just choose it and click **OK**.

If you have not created the Ad Server database and DSN yet, run the SQL Server Enterprise Manager and create a database called AdServer.

On the Site Server dialog box, click the ODBC button:

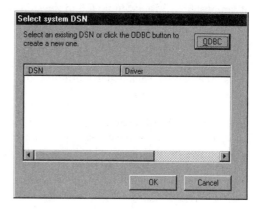

Now create a DSN for the Ad Server database you just created on the SQL Server (refer back to the Configure Database Connectivity section for more details on creating a DSN).

The Commerce Server installation will then start. The length of time it takes to complete the installation is dependent solely on the speed of your machine.

When the installation completes a dialog will appear confirming it. You'll be presented with a choice to review the Readme file at that time. When satisfied, click **Finish**.

Once again, as in the Site Server installation, you may notice a flurry of disk activity. Index Server has been restarted and the HTML Help files are being indexed. As before, make sure index server has completed indexing all the content before rebooting or installing more software.

Again, to monitor the progress of Index Server, get the Task Manager running by doing a *CTRL-ALT-Delete*, choose **Task Manager**, then click on the **Processes** tab. Sort on processor usage by clicking on the **CPU** field name. Wait until the **System Idle Process** gets to 98% or so, when all the content has been indexed.

(Optional) Install Visual Studio 6.0 or Visual Studio 97

Although you are not required to install any development tools along with your Site Server installation, you can install Visual InterDev or FrontPage, as well as any other third-party development tool such as HomeSite from Alstaire. There are a few points to take into account:

❑   It's always dangerous to install development tools on production servers, so proceed with caution if you are installing a production server.

❑   If you do decide to go ahead with and install Visual Studio 6.0, make sure you don't install the Analyzer component. This component can be resource intensive, and will affect how your server will perform and scale – save this component for your workstations.

❑   If you install Visual Studio 97, you can also install Visual Studio 97 Service Pack 3. You can download it from `http://msdn.microsoft.com/vstudio/sp/vs97/default.asp`.

(Optional) Install Visual Studio 6 Service Pack 3

If you installed Visual Studio 6.0 in the steps above, then install Visual Studio 6.0 Service Pack 3 at this point. You can download the Service Pack from: `http://msdn.microsoft.com/vstudio/sp/vs6sp3/vsfixes.asp`.

Upon running the setup (or having the CD auto start), you'll be asked to confirm your intentions to install the Service Pack. Click Continue to proceed, and you'll be presented with the licensing agreement. If you agree with the licensing of Visual Studio 6 Service Pack 3, then click I Agree.

The installation will begin with copying of files, and then the configuration will proceed. Upon completion you'll receive a dialog pointing you to the Readme file, which contains a summary of many of the problems that are fixed with the installation of the Service Pack.

You may be instructed that you need to install Internet Explorer 5.0 to take advantage of the fixes:

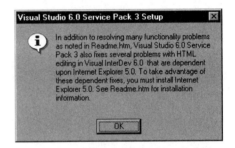

Click OK and you'll be instructed to restart your computer. After the restart, your Service Pack installation will be complete.

Microsoft Data Access Components 2.1 Service Pack 2

Install MDAC version 2.1.2.4202.3, which is also known as MDAC 2.1 SP2. You can download the MDAC from: `http://www.microsoft.com/data/download.htm`.

Upon running the executable, the first screen is the license agreement. If you agree with the licensing of Microsoft Data Access Components 2.1, click Yes. The file extraction process will begin and then launch the setup wizard.

Screen 1 of the setup wizard confirms your intentions to install Microsoft Data Access Components 2.1. Click Continue. Setup will search for installed components to make sure you have the prerequisites installed. If you've followed the installation procedures as recommended then you do.

To start the installation, click the icon that represents a Complete Installation. The installation will take a few moments depending on how fast your system is. Upon completion, click OK to exit.

Active Directory Services Interfaces Version 2.5

Install Active Directory Services Interfaces Version 2.5. You can download Active Directory Services Interfaces Version 2.5 from:

`http://www.microsoft.com/ntserver/nts/downloads/other/ADSI25/default.asp.`

Upon running the installation executable for Active Directory Services Interfaces (ADSI) Version 2.5, you'll be prompted to confirm your intentions to install. Click Yes to proceed. Now, you'll be presented with the license agreement. If you agree with the licensing of Active Directory Services Interfaces Version 2.5, click Yes and the installation will proceed.

The installation of Active Directory Services Interfaces Version 2.5 will only take a short time. When it's completed, click OK to exit. You will be required to restart your computer when complete – click Yes to do so.

Site Server 3.0 Service Pack 3

Install Site Server 3.0 Service Pack 3. You can download the Service Pack from:
`http://support.microsoft.com/support/siteserver/servicepacks/sp.asp.`

After executing the Service Pack, a number of files will be extracted to your machine. Then, you'll be ready to run the Microsoft Site Server 3.0 Service Pack 3 Setup Wizard. Click Next, and you'll be presented with the licensing agreement. If you agree with the licensing of Microsoft Site Server Version 3.0 Service Pack 3, click I Agree, and then click Next.

You can choose to create an uninstall directory for the Service Pack. It's a good idea to create an uninstall directory, just in case of an installation failure:

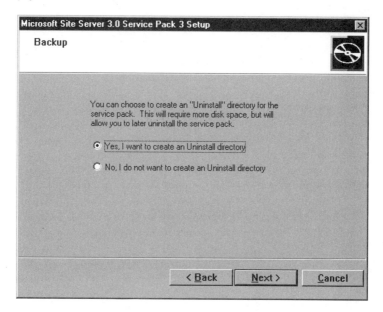

Now, setup has enough information to start copying the files. Click Next to begin. The installation will take a number of minutes depending on the speed of your system. When it has successfully installed click Finish to complete the installation.

> **Important: make sure and read the Site Server Service Pack 3 `Readme.htm` file which includes the latest release notes, and small fixes that need to be made. It is installed in your Site Server Directory in: `\Microsoft SiteServer\sp3\readme.htm`.**

Windows NT4 Service Pack 6

Install Windows NT 4.0 Service Pack 6. You can download the Service Pack from:
`http://www.microsoft.com/ntserver/nts/downloads/recommended/PREM_SP6/allSP6.asp`.

First, you'll be presented with the licensing agreement. If you agree with the licensing of Microsoft Windows NT 4.0 Service Pack 6, click Accept and then Install. The installation will start by inspecting your Windows NT 4.0 configuration, archiving old versions of files and then copying new files.

Upon completion, you will be required to restart your computer to complete the installation. Click Restart and the computer will restart.

> **Congratulations! You are installed! Now move on to the final post-installation section.**

Installing SS3 on Windows 2000 Without SQL Server

> Read this section if your operating system is Windows 2000 and you have a dedicated box for Site Server; that is, if your SQL Server resides on a separate machine.

Windows 2000

Install Microsoft Windows 2000 Server, Advanced Server or Data Center Server. Again, to guarantee a successful Site Server 3.0 Commerce installation, I suggest you start with a clean computer, or have the Windows 2000 installation wipe the hard drives clean before starting its installation.

Windows 2000 installation instructions are beyond the scope of this book. There is adequate information on how to install the Windows 2000 product on the web, but the product documentation from Microsoft is outstanding. You'll find it on the Windows 2000 CD in the \SETUPTXT folder.

One of the truly great things about a Windows 2000 set up is that it can accurately find and identify the devices on your hardware – we didn't have that luxury with Windows NT 4.0. Occasionally though, custom drivers are needed to access the hardware (video, network, etc.). Refer to the Microsoft Windows 2000 product documentation and the documentation for the specific hardware that you have in your system. After you complete your Windows 2000 installation, you may need to install third party (non Microsoft) drivers for the unique hardware (video, network boards, etc.) that you have in your system.

Here are the important points for your Windows 2000 installation:

❑ Install Windows 2000 as a stand-alone or member server, if possible.

❑ Make sure to install Internet Information Server 5.0 with FrontPage 2000 Server Extensions and SMTP. They are part of the default installation.

❑ Make sure to install the Indexing Service. It is part of a default installation.

❑ Complete the partitioning, formatting and assigning of drives with the Windows 2000 Disk Management Utility when you have completed the Windows 2000 Installation. It can be found in the Storage snap-in of the Computer Management MMC from the Administrative Tools menu. Refer to the Drive Partitioning section above for details.

Change the SQL Server Client Default Network Library to TCP/IP

As TCP/IP Sockets are faster than Named Pipes when communicating to a SQL Server that doesn't reside on the same box, IIS should use TCP/IP sockets when it connects to the SQL Server computer.

To configure the SQL Server client, run
Windbver.exe, which lives in
C:\WINNT\System32. On the Net
Library tab, select TCP/IP Sockets as the
Default Network, and then click Done:

MSDTC Service

The MSDTC service must be started on both the Windows 2000 Server where Site Server is to be installed and on the SQL Server computer, and MSDTC should be configured to start automatically.

On the Site Server machine, go to the Control Panel (Start | Settings | Control Panel) and double-click on Services. Then navigate to the MSDTC service and make sure that the Status is Started and that the Startup setting is Automatic:

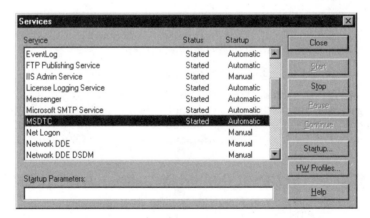

If MSDTC is not configured to start automatically, then click the Startup button and change it to Automatic.

On the Windows 2000 Server, go to Component Services (Start | Programs | Administrative Tools | Component Services). Click on Services (Local), navigate to the MSDTC service, and make sure that it is started and that it's configured to start automatically:

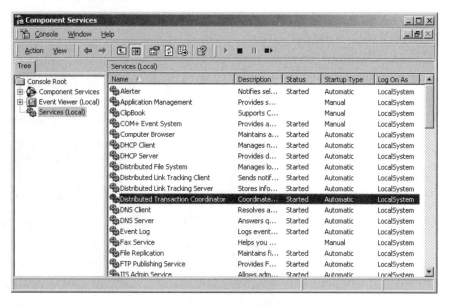

If MSDTC is not configured to start automatically, which is not the default, then double-click on the MSDTC service and change the Startup Type to Automatic.

SS3W2K.exe

Run the SS3W2k.exe patch file. It's part of the Site Server Service Pack 3 package, and you can download the patch file from:
http://www.microsoft.com/siteserver/site/DeployAdmin/SP3.htm.

The SS3W2K.exe file allows Site Server 3.0 to function properly with FrontPage 2000 Server Extensions. Even though the Site Server Service Pack 3 documentation clearly states that this patch file is not necessary for versions of Windows 2000 after Release Candidate 2, I found it necessary even for the RTM (Release To Manufacturing) version of Windows 2000.

The patch file executes quickly and there is no User Interface, so don't be fooled into thinking it didn't run after you've executed it. It doesn't do any harm to run the patch file multiple times, so don't be afraid to run it again if you think it didn't run because it happened so quickly.

Site Server Version 3.0

When you insert the Site Server Version 3.0 CD-ROM, the CD will auto start. Even with the RTM (Release to Manufacturing) Version of Windows 2000, I received the following warning:

Click **Run Program** to proceed with the Site Server 3.0 installation. You'll be prompted with the main options for installing Site Server 3.0:

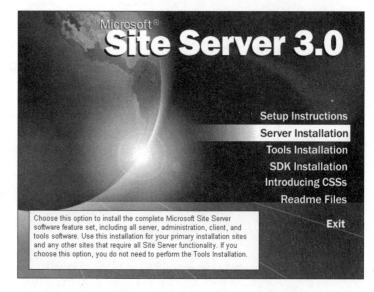

Click **Server Installation** to proceed to the Site Server 3.0 installation wizard. Click **Next** to continue, and you'll be presented with the licensing agreement. If you agree with the licensing of Microsoft Site Server Version 3.0, click **Yes**. Now, you'll be prompted to fill in your product and user information. Fill out your **Name, Company, CD Key** and **E-mail address:**

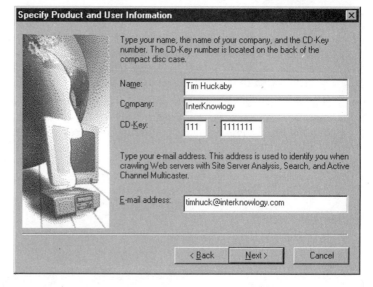

Click Next and then click OK to confirm your product ID.

Next, you'll be prompted for the Site Server 3.0 folder locations. Site Server needs file permissions (ACLs) painted on its program files directory to run properly, and you'll be warned if you try and install on a FAT partition (which cannot support file permissions). If you have followed the recommended steps for drive partitioning and assigning from earlier in the chapter then change all three defaults of C: to D:, where we have installed the NTFS partition:

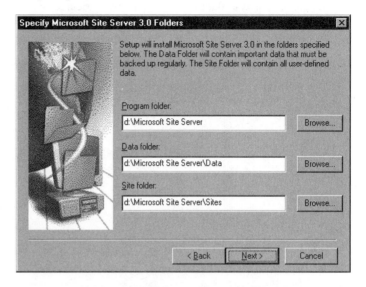

Click Next to continue and you'll be presented with the three types of Site Server 3.0 installations – Typical, Complete, and Custom:

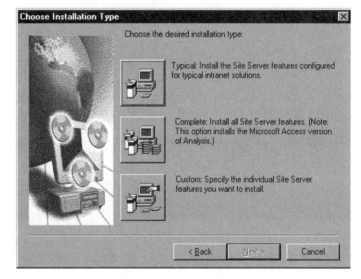

Click the image next to Custom to perform a custom installation. Click the + next to Analysis and change the Analysis database support from its default of Access Database Support by checking SQL Server Database Support. When you select SQL Server Database Support, Access Database Support gets unchecked – it is not possible to install the product with support for both databases:

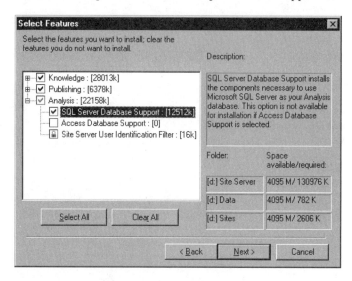

Next, the installation wizard will prompt you to specify a program folder in which to place the Site Server Menu choices. Leave the default of Microsoft Site Server and click Next to continue.

Now you're required to Configure User Accounts for the Publishing and Search services. The Search service requires an Administrative account to run under. The Publishing services simply require enough read and write permissions to publish to folders on the NT shares. For now, set both to run under the local Administrator account. You can always back off the Publishing services permissions later by running under a different account with less than administrative privileges:

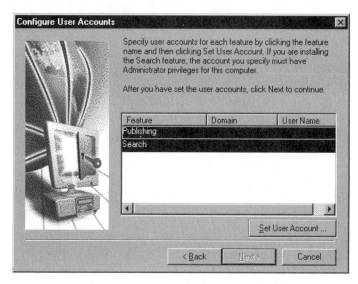

Click the **Set User Account** button. The dialog will default to **Administrator** and the name of the computer for the local domain. Type the password twice to set the user account:

Click **OK**, and then **Next** to continue. The wizard will inform you of all the services it has to stop to proceed with the installation:

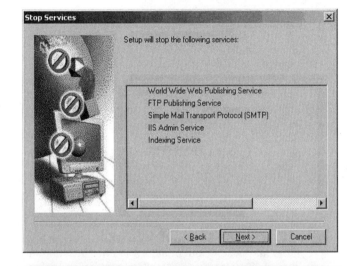

Click **Next** to continue. Click **Next** and the wizard will shut down existing services that need to be modified or are dependant on a service getting modified (like WWW, FTP, IIS Admin, etc.) one by one. The last screen of the wizard will confirm your choices:

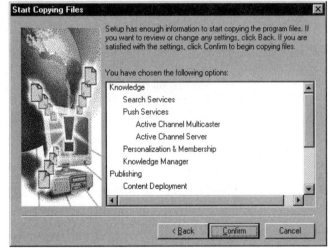

147

Click Confirm to start copying the files, and the installation of Microsoft Site Server 3.0 will begin. The process could take quite a bit of time depending on the speed of your server hardware.

During the installation, you will be asked to confirm the overwriting of files. This is because Windows 2000 installs newer versions of many of the DLLs. This is very important: choose **No To All** so as not to overwrite any newer files.

> **If you accidentally overwrite files with older versions you are guaranteed to have an unsuccessful installation.**

When the installation completes a dialog will appear confirming it. You will be given the chance to review the Readme file at that time. It's a good idea to study the Readme file in any Windows 2000 component installation. When satisfied, click Finish.

At this point, you may notice a flurry of disk activity. That's because the Indexing Service has been restarted, and it has noticed that 100+ MBs of HTML Help content has appeared as a result of the Site Server installation. The Indexing Service will take over and start indexing all the new content.

This is a requirement, and you'll fail the install if you manually turn the Indexing Service off. This isn't that big a deal on a powerful server with lots of RAM, but on a development, staging, or home server, if you start your commerce install (which is the next step) while the Indexing Service is doing its thing on the Site Server content, you'll hang your server – the Indexing Service isn't smart enough to back off while the commerce installation proceeds.

> **Most of the SS3 failed installs are because the Indexing Service runs amok and fails to index all the new content before another installation (in this case Commerce Server) is started. The Commerce installation process competes with the Indexing Service for the CPU and frequently hangs – especially on inferior machines. Make sure that the Indexing Service has completed indexing all the content before rebooting or installing more software.**

So here's the tip for installation on any box: after the reboot immediately following the Site Server 3.0 platform install, get the Task Manager by doing a *CTRL-ALT-Delete*, choose Task Manager, then click on the Processes tab. Sort on processor usage by clicking on the CPU field name. You'll see the cisvc.exe service going wild and the associated cidaemon.exe with it:

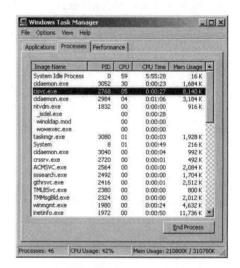

Just wait it out (when the **System Idle Process** gets to 98% or so), until all the content has been indexed.

After the commerce install, the Indexing Service will also need to index all the new content, so you'll need to go through this drill again.

Configure Database Connectivity on the SQL Server

In this install procedure we're not going to install any sample sites, so we don't have to create databases to house the sample site data now. But, we are going to install Ad Server, so we do need to create a database for it to house its data. You'll need to create individual databases for Ad Server and Commerce Server on your SQL Server (which is installed on a separate machine). 20Mb of space is more than adequate to handle the requirements of installation (the actual size will vary depending on your site).

On the SQL Server machine, run the SQL Server Enterprise Manager on your SQL Server (**Start | Programs | Microsoft SQL Server 6.5/7.0 | Enterprise Manager**) and create a database called **Adserver**. If you're using SQL Server 6.5 you'll need to create a database device for the AdServer database to live in, if you don't have space on an existing SQL database device. To create a database:

❑ Click the + next to **Microsoft SQL Servers**.

❑ Click the + sign next to **SQL Server Group**.

❑ Click the + sign next to the name of your server.

❑ Right-click on the **Databases** folder and choose **New Database...** This will initiate the New Database Wizard.

If you're using SQL Server 7.0, take all the defaults, including the 1 Mb size, when you create the AdServer database. SQL Server 7.0 will grow the database automatically if you need more space. If you're using SQL Server 6.5 you will have to estimate the size of your AdServer Database. It's completely dependant on the amount of Ads that you will use on the site, but 1 Mb will be fine to get you started. You can increase the size of the database device and database if need be later.

Now you need to create a System DSN to communicate with the AdServer database you just created. On the Site Server machine, go to the **Control Panel** (**Start | Settings | Control Panel**), and run the **Administrative Tools** control panel applet by double-clicking on its icon. Double-click on **Data Sources (ODBC)**, and select the **System DSN** tab:

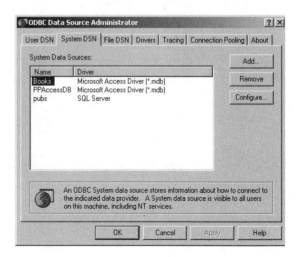

Click Add, then choose SQL
Server from the bottom of the
list and click Finish. Name the
Data source Adserver, give a
description (Adserver Database)
and type the name of your
server:

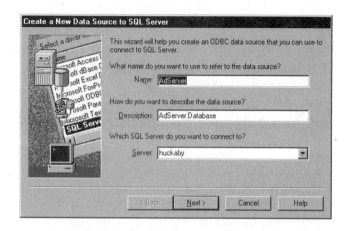

Click Next, and you'll be asked
to verify the security credentials
for the DSN that will be
communicating with the SQL
Server. Change the verification
to With SQL Server
authentication. Change the
Login Id to sa and type the sa
password (this could also be a
SQL Server login with at least
DBO permissions to the
AdServer database, which will
prevent the need for using the all
powerful sa account for the
DSN):

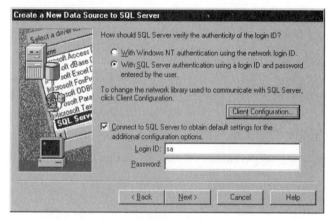

Click Next. On the following
screen, you'll need to choose the
AdServer database as the data
source that this DSN will
communicate to. Click the check
box next to Change the default
database to:, drop down the list
of databases and choose
AdServer:

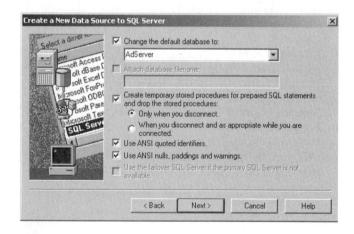

Click **Next**, and then accept all the defaults on the following screen:

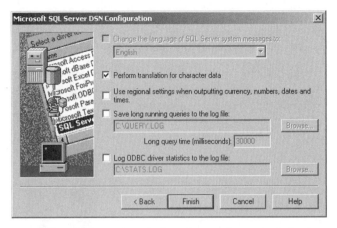

Click **Finish**, and the wizard will summarize all the configuration choices that you have made (and accepted by default). Click the **Test Data Source** button to verify the communication, and then click **OK** on the remaining screens to complete the operation.

Now repeat the procedure to create a database and System DSN for Commerce Server on your Site Server.

Site Server 3.0 Commerce Edition

Upon inserting the Site Server 3.0 Commerce Edition CD-ROM, it will auto start. Even with the RTM (Release to Manufacturing) Version of Windows 2000, I received the following warning:

Click **Run Program** to proceed with the Site Server 3.0 Commerce Edition installation. The Commerce CD will auto start and you'll be prompted with the main options for installing Commerce Server:

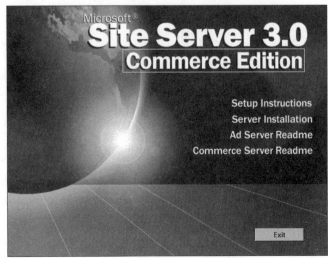

Click **Server Installation** to proceed to the Site Server 3.0 Commerce Edition installation wizard. Click **Next** to continue, and you'll be presented with the licensing agreement. If you agree with the licensing of Microsoft Site Server 3.0 Commerce Edition click **Yes**.

Now, you'll be prompted to fill in your product and user information. Fill out your **Name**, **Company**, and **CD Key**:

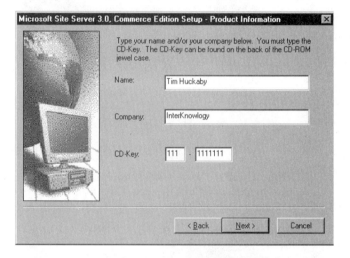

Click **Next**, and then click **OK** to confirm your Product ID. Click **Next** to continue and you'll be presented with the five types of Site Server 3.0 Commerce Edition installations – **Typical**, **Complete**, **Custom**, **Ad Server**, and **Commerce Interchange Pipeline**:

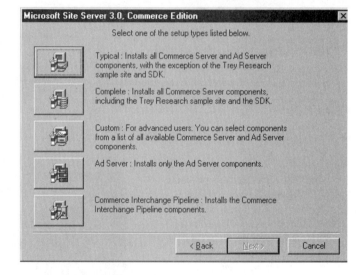

Click the image next to **Custom** to perform a custom installation.

You'll be prompted to choose which components you wish to install.

> *There are a number of sample sites that ship with Site Server 3.0 Commerce Edition, but detailed examination of them is beyond the scope of this book. Professional Site Server 3.0 Commerce Edition (Marco Tabini, ISBN 1-861002-50-5, Wrox Press) has a detailed explanation of the sample sites and how to install and use them.*

I don't usually install any sample sites on a production server. I usually install any sample site (but the Volcano Coffee sample site) on a development server. Let's assume this is a production server and not install any sample sites – the sample sites can always be installed at a later time:

❑ Uncheck the Clocktower, Microsoft Market, Microsoft Press, and Volcano Coffee sample sites

❑ Keep the Trey Research sample site unchecked

❑ Leave Ad Server and Ad Manager checked

❑ If this is a development server check the SDK (System Developers Kit); if not, keep it unchecked

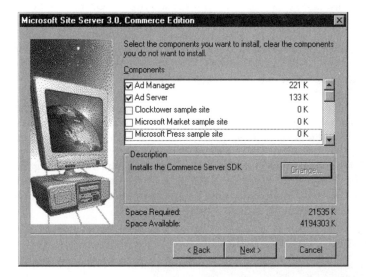

Click Next to continue. A dialog will tell you that you have not chosen to install any of the sample sites, and then ask you if you want to install the Commerce Server core components. Click Yes to continue the installation.

The next screen in the installation wizard will identify the components that you have chosen to install, and notify you that it has enough information to start the installation process:

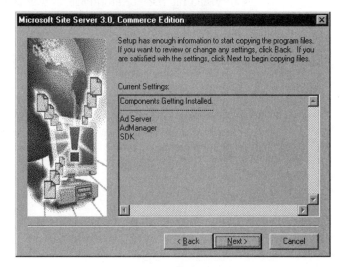

153

Click **Next**, and you'll be prompted to select and/or create a DSN for Ad Server. You've created the database and DSN for Ad Server already, so just choose it and click OK.

The Commerce Server installation will then start. During the installation, it will appear that the installation process has hung, because all activity will stop. Unfortunately, an error message dialog is hiding behind the commerce server installation screen. Press *Alt-Tab* to bring it into focus:

This error message is documented and acknowledged by Microsoft as an insignificant problem, later fixed automatically, and hence it can be ignored: so press the **OK** button. Site Server 3.0 Commerce Edition will install correctly even though you have received this error message.

The length of time it takes to complete the installation is dependent solely on the speed of your machine. When the installation completes a dialog will appear confirming it. You'll be given a chance to review the Readme file at that time. When satisfied, click **Finish**.

Once again, as in the Site Server installation, you may notice a flurry of disk activity. The Indexing Service has been restarted and the HTML Help files are being indexed. As before, make sure index server has completed indexing all the content before rebooting or installing more software.

Again, to monitor the progress of the Indexing Service, get the Task Manager running by doing a *CTRL-ALT-Delete*, choose **Task Manager**, then click on the **Processes** tab. Sort on processor usage by clicking on the **CPU** field name. Wait until the **System Idle Process** gets to 98% or so, when all the content has been indexed.

(Optional) Install Visual Studio 6.0

Although you are not required to install any development tools along with your Site Server installation, you can install Visual InterDev or FrontPage, as well as any other third-party development tool such as HomeSite from Alstaire. It's always dangerous to install development tools on production servers so proceed with caution if you are installing a production server.

If you do decide to go ahead and install Visual Studio 6.0, make sure you don't install the Analyzer component. This component can be resource intensive, and will affect how your server will perform and scale – save this component for your workstations.

> **Do not install Visual Studio 97 on a computer running Windows 2000. Visual Studio 97 is incompatible with Windows 2000.**

(Optional) Install Visual Studio 6 Service Pack 3

If you installed Visual Studio 6.0 in the steps above, then install Visual Studio 6.0 Service Pack 3 at this point. You can download the Service Pack from: `http://msdn.microsoft.com/vstudio/sp/vs6sp3/vsfixes.asp`.

Upon running the setup (or having the CD auto start), you'll be asked to confirm your intentions to install the Service Pack. Click Continue to proceed, and you'll be presented with the licensing agreement. If you agree with the licensing of Visual Studio 6 Service Pack 3, then click I Agree.

The installation will begin with copying of files, and then the configuration will proceed. Upon completion you'll receive a dialog pointing you to the Readme file, which contains a summary of many of the problems that are fixed with the installation of the Service Pack.

You'll also be instructed that you need to install Internet Explorer 5.0 to take advantage of the fixes. Internet Explorer 5.0 is automatically installed with Windows 2000, so this message is not applicable:

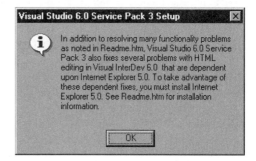

Click OK and you'll be instructed to restart your computer. After the restart, your Service Pack installation will be complete.

Site Server 3.0 Service Pack 3

Install Site Server 3.0 Service Pack 3. You can download the Service Pack from: `http://support.microsoft.com/support/siteserver/servicepacks/sp.asp`.

After executing the Service Pack, a number of files will be extracted to your machine. Then, you'll be ready to run the Microsoft Site Server 3.0 Service Pack 3 Setup Wizard. Click Next, and you'll be presented with the licensing agreement. If you agree with the licensing of Microsoft Site Server Version 3.0 Service Pack 3, click I Agree, and then click Next.

You can choose to create an uninstall directory for the Service Pack. It's a good idea to create an uninstall directory, just in case of an installation failure:

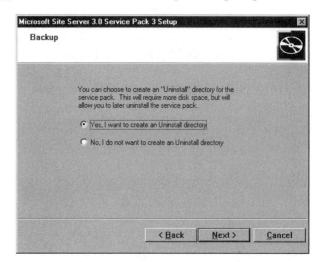

Now, setup has enough information to start copying the files. Click Next to begin. The installation will take a number of minutes depending on the speed of your system. When it has successfully installed click Finish to complete the installation.

> **Important: make sure and read the Site Server Service Pack 3 `Readme.htm` file which includes the latest release notes, and small fixes that need to be made. It is installed in your Site Server Directory in: `\Microsoft SiteServer\sp3\readme.htm`**

Post Installation Configurations

Having successfully installed Site Server, you still need to perform the following updates on your machine running Site Server.

Site Foundation Wizard Updates

When creating a new site using the Site Foundation Wizard, if a Universal Naming Convention (UNC) directory location is specified rather than a local or mapped directory, the site foundation is not created correctly. A new feature in Site Server Service Pack 3, added to the Site Foundation Wizard, will allow you to create configurations that contain multiple web servers and a single file server.

For more information on both the configuration of the hot fix and the known issues associated with it refer to the Knowledge Base article referenced at: `http://support.microsoft.com/support/kb/articles/q243/5/33.asp`.

To install the updated files:

❑ Copy `account.asp`, `directory.asp`, `finish.asp` and `setup.vbs` from the folder: `\Microsoft Site Server\SP3\Commerce` to the folder: `\Microsoft Site Server \SiteServer\Admin\Commerce\Foundation`.

❑ Stop and restart the WWW Service by navigating to the Internet Information Server snap-in within the Site Server Service Admin (MMC) (Start | Programs | Microsoft Site Server | Administration | Site Server Service Admin (MMC)). Right-click on Default Web Site and choose Stop. Right-click on Default Web Site again and choose Start.

Update the CMSample and FPSample Rule Set Files

Update the following files:

❑ Copy all files and folders from: `\Microsoft Site Server\sp3\samples\CmSample` directory to: `\Microsoft Site Server\Data\Publishing\CmSample` directory. Overwrite the existing files and folders.

❑ Copy all files and folders from: `\Microsoft Site Server\sp3\samples\FpSample` directory to: `\Microsoft Site Server\Data\Publishing\FpSample` directory. Overwrite the existing files and folders.

Update the Search ASP Pages

Update the following files:

❑ Copy all files and folders
from: `\Microsoft Site Server\sp3\samples\search` directory
to: `\Microsoft Site Server\Sites\samples\knowledge\search` directory.
Overwrite the existing files and folders.

Post Installation Configurations For Your SQL Server Machine

You now need to update your SQL Server, running on a separate machine

SQL Server Version 6.5 on Windows NT 4.0

If your SQL Server is a Version 6.5 on Windows NT 4.0 then perform the following three steps on your SQL Server.

SQL Server 6.5 Service Pack 5a

Before you install SQL Server 6.5 Service Pack 5a on your SQL Server, you need to have a minimum of 3 Mb space (and should have at least 10 Mb) free in your master database. The master database is 25 Mb by default. Let's go through the process of expanding it to 50 Mb.

On your SQL Server 6.5, run the Microsoft SQL Enterprise Manager by clicking Start | Programs | Microsoft SQL Server 6.5 | SQL Enterprise Manager. If this is the first time you've run the SQL Enterprise Manager then you'll need to "register" your server, by typing the name of the server and typing the password for the sa account.

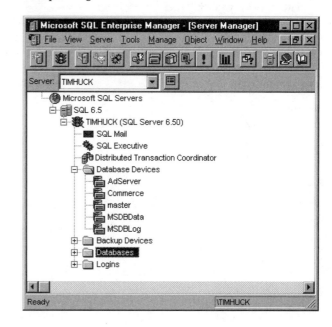

Click the + next to your SQL server's name to drop down the container of components. First you need to expand the size of the master database device. Click on the + next to Database Devices to drop down the list of database devices on your SQL Server:

Right-click on master and choose Edit. Change the 25 in the Size (MB) field to 50 and then click Change Now:

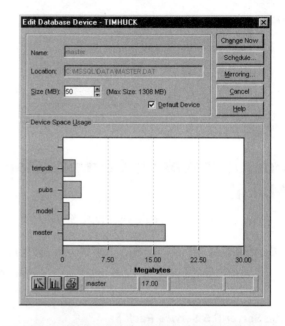

Next, you need to expand the size of the master database. Click on + next to Databases to drop down the list of databases on your SQL Server:

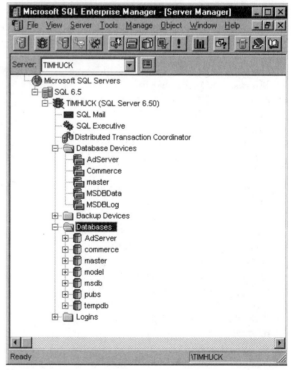

Right-click on master and choose Edit. You will default to the Database tab:

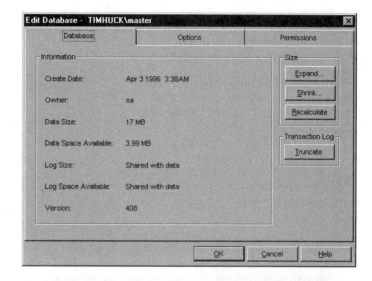

Click the Expand button. Drop down the Data Device list and choose master. The Size (MB) will default to the amount of space that is available to expand. In this case, it's 26Mb:

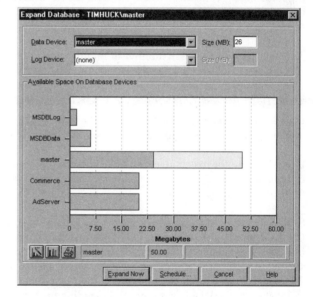

Click Expand Now. After a few short moments the expansion of the master database will be complete. The Edit Database dialog will reappear; notice that you now have 29.99Mb of available space on your master database. Click OK to continue, and then exit the SQL Enterprise Manager. You are now ready to install the SQL Server 6.5 Service Pack 5a.

Install SQL Server 6.5 Service Pack 5a on your SQL Server. You can download the Service Pack, for both the Enterprise and Standard versions of SQL Server, from
`http://www.microsoft.com/downloads/release.asp?ReleaseID=12671`.

> **IMPORTANT: if prompted, do not install the optional MDAC 2.1 components. It will be installed in a later step.**

After executing the Service Pack, a number of files will be extracted to your machine. Then you'll be ready to run the Microsoft SQL Server 6.5 Service Pack 5a setup wizard.

Click Continue, and you'll be asked for your SA Password (the password for the sa account):

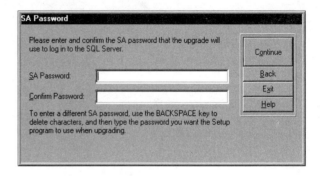

Type the password for your sa account twice and then click Continue. Next, you'll be presented with the licensing agreement. If you agree with the licensing of SQL Server Version 6.5 Service Pack 5a, then click on Page Down 7 times to scroll to the bottom of the License Agreement. Then, click I Agree.

The installation will take a number of minutes depending on the speed of your system. When it has successfully installed click the Finish icon to exit to Windows NT.

Microsoft Data Access Components 2.1 Service Pack 2

Install MDAC version 2.1.2.4202.3, also known as MDAC 2.1 SP2, on your SQL 6.5 Server. You can download the MDAC from: http://www.microsoft.com/data/download.htm.

Upon running the executable, the first screen is the license agreement. If you agree with the licensing of Microsoft Data Access Components 2.1, then click Yes. The file extraction process will begin and then launch the setup wizard.

Screen 1 of the setup wizard confirms your intentions to install Microsoft Data Access Components 2.1. Click Continue, and setup will search for installed components to make sure you have the prerequisites installed. If you have followed the installation procedures as recommended then you do.

To start the installation, click the installation icon that represents a complete installation. The installation will take a few moments depending on how fast your system is. Upon Completion, click OK to exit.

Windows NT4 Service Pack 6

Install Windows NT 4.0 Service Pack 6 on your SQL 6.5 Server. You can download the Service Pack from:
http://www.microsoft.com/ntserver/nts/downloads/recommended/PREM_SP6/allSP6.asp.

First, you'll be presented with the licensing agreement. If you agree with the licensing of Microsoft Windows NT 4.0 Service Pack 6, click Accept and then Install. The installation will inspect your Windows 4.0 configuration, archive old versions of files and then copy new files.

Upon completion, you will be required to restart your computer, so click Restart.

SQL Server Version 7.0 on Windows NT 4.0

If your SQL Server is a Version 7.0 on Windows NT 4.0 then perform the following three steps on your SQL Server.

SQL Server Version 7.0 Service Pack 1

Install Microsoft SQL Server 7.0 Service Pack 1 on your SQL Server.

If you don't have a CD with the SQL Server 7.0 Service Pack 1, you can download and run the `Sql70sp1i.exe` file. You can download the Service Pack from: `http://www.microsoft.com/sql/support/sp1.htm`. The Service Pack files are extracted to the `C:\SP1` directory. However, you must still run `C:\SP1\Setup.exe` to actually install the Service Pack.

If you have a CD with the SQL Server 7.0 Service Pack 1 on it, get Windows Explorer running, navigate to the `Setup.bat` (in most cases it will be in `\Service Pack 1\x86`) and execute it by double-clicking.

> *Installing SQL 7.0 SP1 can take up to 30 minutes depending on the speed of your machine – that does not include the time it takes to download the Service Pack.*

First, you'll be presented with a screen that confirms your intentions to install the Service Pack. Click Next and you'll be presented with the License Agreement. If you agree with the licensing agreement of Microsoft SQL Server Version 7.0 Service Pack 1, then click Yes to proceed. Next, you'll choose the authentication mode that the setup should use to connect to SQL Server. Keep the default of The Windows NT account...:

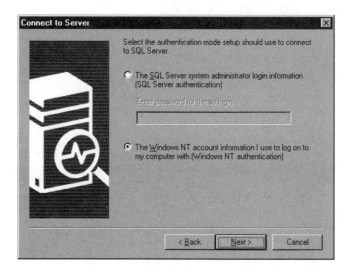

Click Next. After a short period, the setup will determine that it has enough information to proceed. Click Next and the installation will proceed unattended. When it's complete you will be required to restart your computer.

Microsoft Data Access Components 2.1 Service Pack 2

Install MDAC version 2.1.2.4202.3, also known as MDAC 2.1 SP2, on your SQL 7.0 Server. You can download the MDAC from: `http://www.microsoft.com/data/download.htm`.

Upon running the executable, the first screen is the license agreement. If you agree with the licensing of Microsoft Data Access Components 2.1, then click Yes. The file extraction process will begin and will launch the setup wizard.

Screen 1 of the setup wizard confirms your intentions to install Microsoft Data Access Components 2.1. Click Continue, and setup will search for installed components to make sure you have the prerequisites installed. If you have followed the installation procedures as recommended then you do.

To start the installation, click the installation icon that represents a complete installation. The installation will take a few moments depending on how fast your system is. Upon completion, click OK to exit.

Windows NT4, Service, Pack 6

Install Windows NT 4.0 Service Pack 6 on your SQL 7.0 Server. You can download the Service Pack from:
`http://www.microsoft.com/ntserver/nts/downloads/recommended/PREM_SP6/allSP6.asp`.

First, you'll be presented with the licensing agreement. If you agree with the licensing of Microsoft Windows NT 4.0 Service Pack 6, click Accept and then Install. The installation will inspect your Windows 4.0 configuration, archive old versions of files and then copy new files.

Upon completion, you will be required to restart your computer, so click Restart.

SQL Server Version 7.0 on Windows 2000

If your SQL Server is a Version 7.0 on Windows 2000 then perform the following step on your SQL Server.

SQL Server Version 7.0 Service Pack 1

Install Microsoft SQL Server 7.0 Service Pack 1 on your SQL Server.

If you don't have a CD with the SQL Server 7.0 Service Pack 1, you can download and run the `Sql70sp1i.exe` file. You can download the Service Pack from: `http://www.microsoft.com/sql/support/sp1.htm`. The Service Pack files are extracted to the `C:\SP1` directory. However, you must still run `C:\SP1\Setup.exe` to actually install the Service Pack.

If you have a CD with the SQL Server 7.0 Service Pack 1 on it, get Windows Explorer running, navigate to the `Setup.bat` (in most cases it will be in `\Service Pack 1\x86`) and execute it by double-clicking.

> *Installing SQL 7.0 SP1 can take up to 30 minutes depending on the speed of your machine – that does not include the time it takes to download the Service Pack.*

First, you'll be presented with a screen that confirms your intentions to install the Service Pack. Click **Next** and you'll be presented with the License Agreement. If you agree with the licensing agreement of Microsoft SQL Server Version 7.0 Service Pack 1, then click **Yes** to proceed. Next, you'll choose the authentication mode that the setup should use to connect to SQL Server. Keep the default of **The Windows NT account...**:

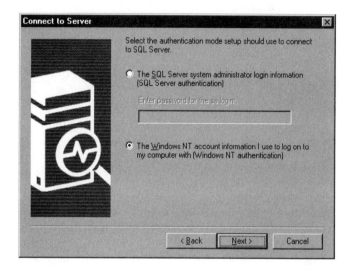

Click **Next**. After a short period, the setup will determine that it has enough information to proceed. Click **Next** and the installation will proceed unattended. When it's complete you will be required to restart your computer.

Congratulations! You are installed! Now move on to the final post-installation section.

Installing SS3 on Windows 2000 With SQL Server 7.0

> Read on if you're installing Site Server on the same box that you are going to install SQL Server 7.0 on, and your operating system is Windows 2000.

Windows 2000

Install Microsoft Windows 2000 Server, Advanced Server or Data Center Server. Again, to guarantee a successful Site Server 3.0 Commerce installation, I suggest you start with a clean computer, or have the Windows 2000 installation wipe the hard drives clean before starting its installation.

Windows 2000 installation instructions are beyond the scope of this book. There is adequate information on how to install the Windows 2000 product on the web, but the product documentation from Microsoft is outstanding. You'll find it on the Windows 2000 CD in the \SETUPTXT folder.

One of the truly great things about a Windows 2000 set up is that it can accurately find and identify the devices on your hardware – we didn't have that luxury with Windows NT 4.0. Occasionally though, custom drivers are needed to access the hardware (video, network, etc.). Refer to the Microsoft Windows 2000 product documentation and the documentation for the specific hardware that you have in your system. After you complete your Windows 2000 installation, you may need to install third party (non Microsoft) drivers for the unique hardware (video, network boards, etc.) that you have in your system.

Here are the important points for your Windows 2000 installation:

❑   Install Windows 2000 as a stand-alone or member server, if possible.

❑   Make sure to install Internet Information Server 5.0 with FrontPage 2000 Server Extensions and SMTP. They are part of the default installation.

❑   Make sure to install the Indexing Service. It is part of a default installation.

❑   Complete the partitioning, formatting and assigning of drives with the Windows 2000 Disk Management Utility when you have completed the Windows 2000 Installation. It can be found in the **Storage** snap-in of the **Computer Management MMC** from the **Administrative Tools** menu. Refer to the Drive Partitioning section above for details.

SQL Server 7.0

When you insert the SQL Server Version 7.0 CD-ROM, the CD will auto start and you'll be prompted with the main options for installing SQL Server Version 7.0:

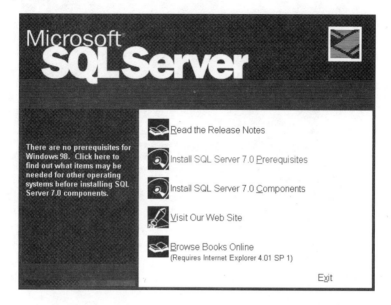

Click Install SQL Server 7.0 Components and you will be prompted with the component options for the SQL Sever Version 7.0 installation:

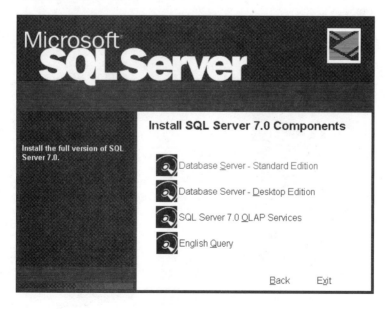

Click Database Server – Standard Edition and you start the SQL Server 7.0 installation wizard. Choose the default of Local Install – Install to the Local Machine:

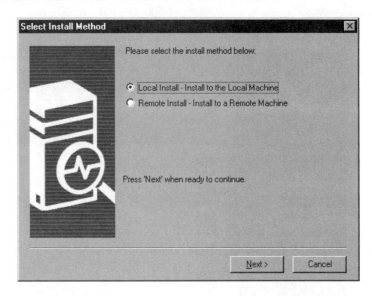

Click Next. The SQL Server 7.0 installation wizard will search for installed components and then confirm your intentions to install the product.

Click Next and you'll move to the Software License Agreement. If you agree with the licensing agreement of Microsoft SQL Server Version 7.0 then click Yes. Now you'll be prompted to enter your Name and Company:

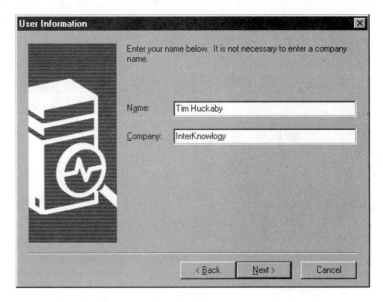

Click **Next** to continue and you will be presented with the **Setup Type** screen. Choose **Typical** install. Change the **Data Files** location to D: by clicking **Browse** (next to **Data Files**) and editing the location to D:\MSSQL7:

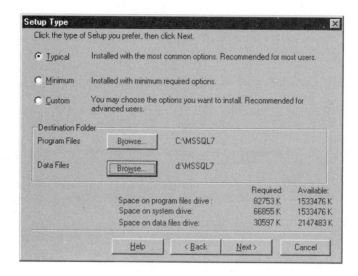

Click **Next** to continue, and you'll be presented with the **Services Accounts** screen. It's time to specify which type of security we're going to use for our installation of SQL Server. We can either use Windows NT or Mixed mode, which uses a combination of both SQL Server and Windows NT authentication. For this installation, we're going to use the Local System account for the installation. Check **Use the Local System account**:

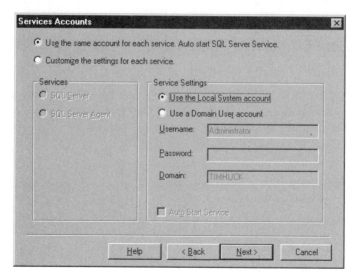

Click **Next** to continue. Now the SQL Server installation is ready to proceed. All that's required now is to enter what type of license you have purchased: Per Seat or Per Client. Choose the appropriate license for your installation and click **Continue**.

The installation will start by copying files. Once the installation is finished, click **Finish** and then exit the SQL Server 7.0 installation wizard by clicking **Exit**. It's a good idea to reboot your server to allow for the SQL Service to start by itself.

Once the reboot has completed, open up SQL Enterprise Manager to test your installation by clicking **Start |Microsoft SQL Server 7.0 | Enterprise Manager**. Click the + next to **Microsoft SQL Servers**. Click the + next to **SQL Server Group**. Your SQL server will appear. If it has a green arrow in the icon, it's running:

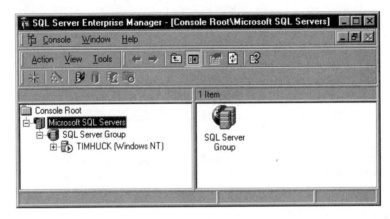

Quit out of the Enterprise Manager and proceed to the SQL Server 7.0 Service Pack 1 installation.

SQL Server Version 7.0 Service Pack 1

Install Microsoft SQL Server 7.0 Service Pack 1.

If you don't have a CD with the SQL Server 7.0 Service Pack 1, you can download and run the `Sql70sp1i.exe` file. You can download the Service Pack from: `http://www.microsoft.com/sql/support/sp1.htm`. The Service Pack files are extracted to the `C:\SP1` directory. However, you must still run `C:\SP1\Setup.exe` to actually install the Service Pack.

If you have a CD with the SQL Server 7.0 Service Pack 1 on it, get Windows Explorer running, navigate to the `Setup.bat` (in most cases it will be in `\Service Pack 1\x86`) and execute it by double-clicking.

Installing SQL 7.0 SP1 can take up to 30 minutes depending on the speed of your machine – that does not include the time it takes to download the Service Pack.

First, you'll be presented with a screen that confirms your intentions to install the Service Pack. Click **Next** and you'll be presented with the License Agreement. If you agree with the licensing agreement of Microsoft SQL Server Version 7.0 Service Pack 1, then click **Yes** to proceed. Next, you'll choose the authentication mode that the setup should use to connect to SQL Server. Keep the default of **The Windows NT account...:**

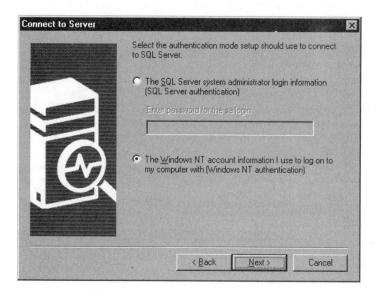

Click **Next**. After a short period, the setup will determine that it has enough information to proceed. Click **Next** and the installation will proceed unattended. When it's complete you will be required to restart your computer.

Change the SQL Server Client Default Network Library to Named Pipes

You want IIS to use Named Pipes (which is faster than TCP/IP when SQL Server and IIS 4.0 are on the same box) when it connects to the SQL Server computer

To configure the SQL Server client, you need to run `Windbver.exe`. It lives in `C:\WINNT\System32`. On the **Net Library** tab, select **Named Pipes** as the **Default Network**, and then click **Done**:

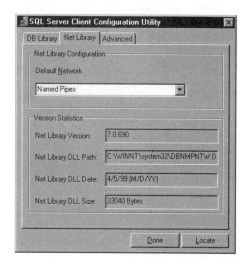

MSDTC Service

The MSDTC service must be started, and MSDTC should be configured to start automatically.

On the Windows 2000 Server, go to Component Services (Start | Programs | Administrative Tools | Component Services). Click on Services (Local), navigate to the MSDTC service, and make sure that it is started and that it's configured to start automatically:

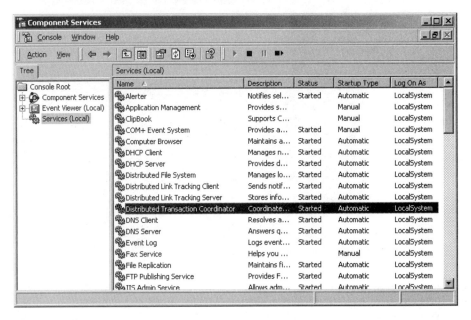

If MSDTC is not configured to start automatically, which is not the default, then double-click on the MSDTC service and change the Startup Type to Automatic.

SS3W2K.exe

Run the SS3W2k.exe patch file. It's part of the Site Server Service Pack 3 package, and you can download the patch file from:
http://www.microsoft.com/siteserver/site/DeployAdmin/SP3.htm.

The SS3W2K.exe file allows Site Server 3.0 to function properly with FrontPage 2000 Server Extensions. Even though the Site Server Service Pack 3 documentation clearly states that this patch file is not necessary for versions of Windows 2000 after Release Candidate 2, I found it necessary even for the RTM (Release To Manufacturing) version of Windows 2000.

The patch file executes quickly and there is no User Interface, so don't be fooled into thinking it didn't run after you've executed it. It doesn't do any harm to run the patch file multiple times, so don't be afraid to run it again if you think it didn't run because it happened so quickly.

Site Server Version 3.0

When you insert the Site Server Version 3.0 CD-ROM, the CD will auto start. Even with the RTM (Release to Manufacturing) Version of Windows 2000, I received the following warning:

Click **Run Program** to proceed with the Site Server 3.0 Installation. You'll be prompted with the main options for installing Site Server 3.0:

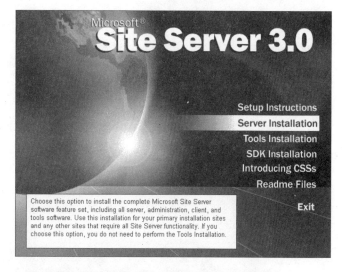

Click **Server Installation** to proceed to the Site Server 3.0 installation wizard. Click **Next** to continue, and you'll be presented with the licensing agreement. If you agree with the licensing of Microsoft Site Server Version 3.0, click **Yes**. Now, you'll be prompted to fill in your product and user information. Fill out your **Name, Company, CD Key** and **E-mail address**:

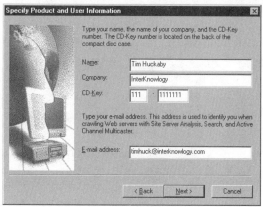

Click **Next** and then click **OK** to confirm your product ID.

171

Next, you'll be prompted for the Site Server 3.0 folder locations. Site Server needs file permissions (ACLs) painted on its program files directory to run properly, and you'll be warned if you try and install on a FAT partition (which cannot support file permissions). If you have followed the recommended steps for drive partitioning and assigning from earlier in the chapter then change all three defaults of C: to D:, where we have installed the NTFS partition:

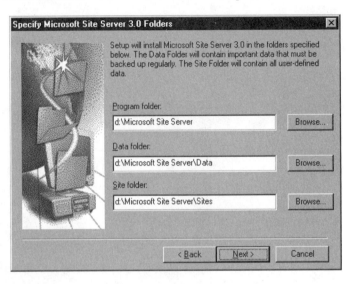

Click Next to continue and you'll be presented with the three types of Site Server 3.0 installations – Typical, Complete, and Custom:

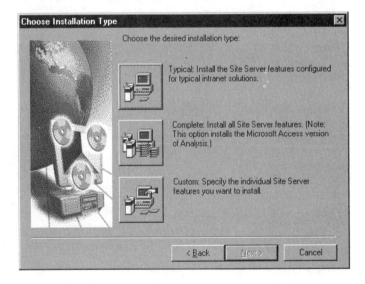

Click the image next to Custom to perform a custom installation. Click the + next to Analysis and change the Analysis database support from its default of Access Database Support by checking SQL Server Database Support. When you select SQL Server Database Support, Access Database Support gets unchecked – it is not possible to install the product with support for both databases:

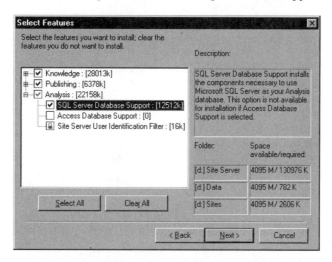

Next, the installation wizard will prompt you to specify a program folder in which to place the Site Server Menu choices. Leave the default of Microsoft Site Server and click Next to continue.

Now you're required to Configure User Accounts for the Publishing and Search services. The Search service requires an Administrative account to run under. The Publishing services simply require enough read and write permissions to publish to folders on the NT shares. For now, set both to run under the local Administrator Account. You can always back off the Publishing services permissions later by running under a different account with less than administrative privileges:

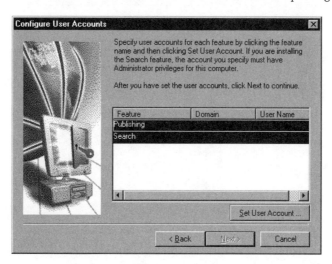

Click the **Set User Account** button. The dialog will default to **Administrator** and the name of the computer for the local domain. Type the password twice to set the user account:

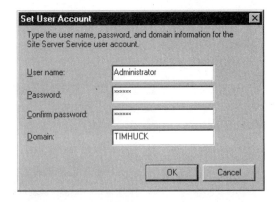

Click **OK**, and then **Next** to continue. The wizard will inform you of all the services it has to stop to proceed with the installation:

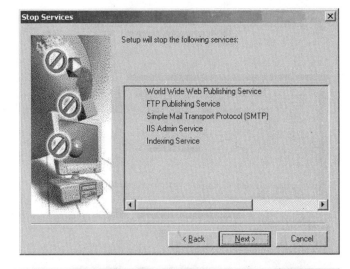

Click **Next** to continue. Click **Next** and the wizard will shut down existing services that need to be modified or are dependant on a service getting modified (like WWW, FTP, IIS Admin, etc.) one by one. The last screen of the wizard will confirm your choices:

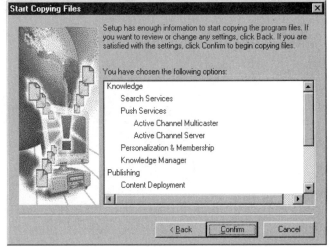

Click **Confirm** to start copying the files, and the installation of Microsoft Site Server 3.0 will begin. The process could take quite a bit of time depending on the speed of your server hardware.

During the installation, you will be asked to confirm the overwriting of files. This is because Windows 2000 installs newer versions of many of the DLLs. This is very important: choose **No To All** so as not to overwrite any newer files.

> **If you accidentally overwrite files with older versions you are guaranteed to have an unsuccessful installation.**

When the installation completes a dialog will appear confirming it. You will be given the chance to review the Readme file at that time. It's a good idea to study the Readme file in any Windows 2000 component installation. When satisfied, click **Finish**.

At this point, you may notice a flurry of disk activity. That's because the Indexing Service has been restarted, and it has noticed that 100+ Mbs of HTML Help content has appeared as a result of the Site Server installation. The Indexing Service will take over and start indexing all the new content.

This is a requirement, and you'll fail the install if you manually turn the Indexing Service off. This isn't that big a deal on a powerful server with lots of RAM, but on a development, staging, or home server, if you start your commerce install (which is the next step) while the Indexing Service is doing its thing on the Site Server content, you'll hang your server – the Indexing Service isn't smart enough to back off while the commerce installation proceeds.

> **Most of the SS3 failed installs are because the Indexing Service runs amok and fails to index all the new content before another installation (in this case Commerce Server) is started. The Commerce installation process competes with the Indexing Service for the CPU and frequently hangs – especially on inferior machines. Make sure that the Indexing Service has completed indexing all the content before rebooting or installing more software.**

So here's the tip for installation on any box: after the reboot immediately following the Site Server 3.0 platform install, get the Task Manager by doing a *CTRL-ALT-Delete*, choose **Task Manager**, then click on the **Processes** tab. Sort on processor usage by clicking on the **CPU** field name. You'll see the **cisvc.exe** service going wild and the associated **cidaemon.exe** with it:

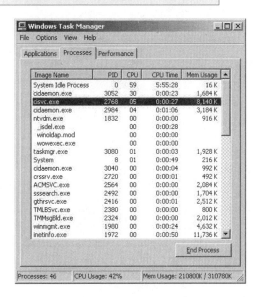

Just wait it out (when the **System Idle Process** gets to 98% or so), until all the content has been indexed.

After the commerce install, the Indexing Service will also need to index all the new content, so you'll need to go through this drill again.

Configuring Database Connectivity for SQL Server

In this install procedure we're not going to install any sample sites, so we don't have to create databases to house the sample site data now. But, we are going to install Ad Server, so we do need to create a database for it to house its data. You'll need to create individual databases for Ad Server and Commerce Server on your SQL Server. 20Mb of space is more than adequate to handle the requirements of installation (the actual size will vary depending on your site).

Run the SQL Server Enterprise Manager (**Start | Programs | Microsoft SQL Server 7.0 | Enterprise Manager**) and create a database called **AdServer**.

❑   Click the + next to **Microsoft SQL Servers**.

❑   Click the + sign next to **SQL Server Group**.

❑   Click the + sign next to the name of your server.

❑   Right-click on the **Databases** folder and choose **New Database…** This will initiate the New Database Wizard.

Take all the defaults, including the 1 MB size, when you create the AdServer database. SQL Server 7.0 will grow the database automatically if you need more space.

Now you need to create a System DSN to communicate with the AdServer database you just created. Go to the **Control Panel** (**Start | Settings | Control Panel**), and run the **Administrative Tools** control panel applet by double-clicking on its icon. Double-click on **Data Sources (ODBC)**, and select the **System DSN** tab:

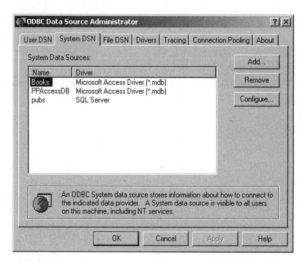

Click **Add**, then choose **SQL Server** from the bottom of the list and click **Finish**. Name the Data source **Adserver**, give a description (**Adserver Database**) and type the name of your server:

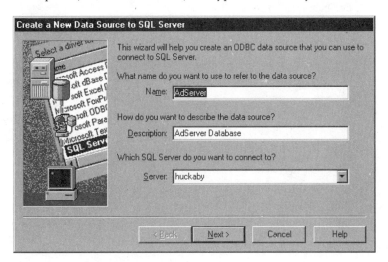

Click **Next**, and you'll be asked to verify the security credentials for the DSN that will be communicating with the SQL Server. Change the verification to **With SQL Server authentication**. Change the **Login Id** to sa and type the sa password (this could also be a SQL Server login with at least DBO permissions to the AdServer database, which will prevent the need for using the all powerful sa account for the DSN):

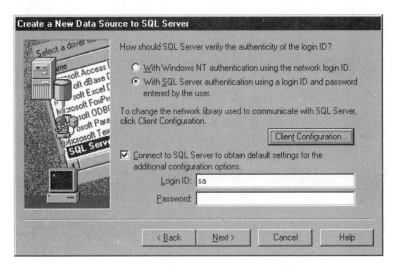

Click Next. On the following screen, you'll need to choose the **AdServer** database as the data source that this DSN will communicate to. Click the check box next to **Change the default database to:**, drop down the list of databases and choose **AdServer**:

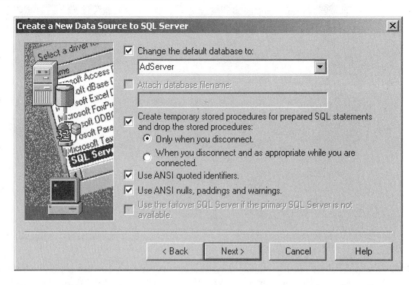

Click Next, and then accept all the defaults on the following screen:

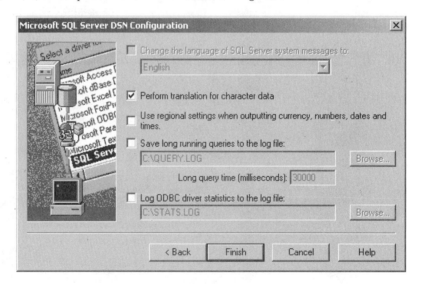

Click **Finish**, and the wizard will summarize all the configuration choices that you have made (and accepted by default). Click the **Test Data Source** button to verify the communication, and then click **OK** on the remaining screens to complete the operation.

Now repeat the procedure to create a database and System DSN for Commerce Server on your Site Server.

Site Server 3.0 Commerce Edition

Upon inserting the Site Server 3.0 Commerce Edition CD-ROM, it will auto start. Even with the RTM (Release to Manufacturing) Version of Windows 2000, I received the following warning:

Click **Run Program** to proceed with the Site Server 3.0 Commerce Edition installation. The Commerce CD will auto start and you'll be prompted with the main options for installing Commerce Server:

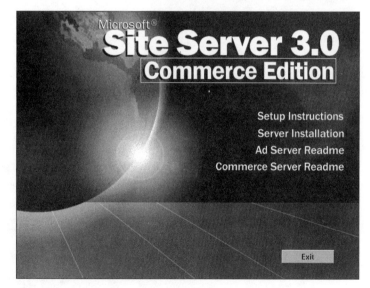

Click Server Installation to proceed to the Site Server 3.0 Commerce Edition installation wizard. Click Next to continue, and you'll be presented with the licensing agreement. If you agree with the licensing of Microsoft Site Server 3.0 Commerce Edition click Yes.

Now, you'll be prompted to fill in your product and user information. Fill out your Name, Company, and CD Key:

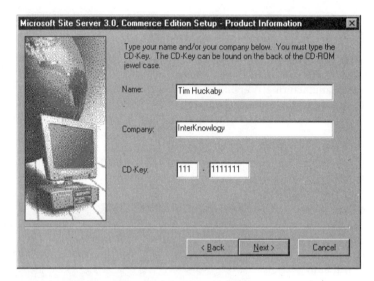

Click Next, and then click OK to confirm your Product ID. Click Next to continue and you'll be presented with the five types of Site Server 3.0 Commerce Edition installations – Typical, Complete, Custom, Ad Server, and Commerce Interchange Pipeline:

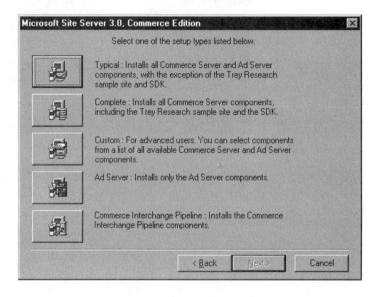

Click the image next to Custom to perform a custom installation.

You'll be prompted to choose which components you wish to install.

There are a number of sample sites that ship with Site Server 3.0 Commerce Edition, but a detailed examination of them is beyond the scope of this book. Professional Site Server 3.0 Commerce Edition (Marco Tabini, ISBN 1-861002-50-5, Wrox Press) has a detailed explanation of the sample sites and how to install and use them.

I don't usually install any sample sites on a production server. And I usually install any sample site (but the Volcano Coffee sample site) on a development server. Let's assume this is a production server and not install any sample sites – the sample sites can always be installed at a later time:

❑ Uncheck the Clocktower, Microsoft Market, Microsoft Press, and Volcano Coffee sample sites

❑ Keep the Trey Research sample site unchecked

❑ Leave Ad Server and Ad Manager checked

❑ If this is a development server check the SDK (System Developers Kit); if not, keep it unchecked

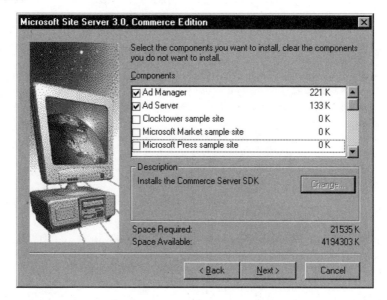

Click Next to continue. A dialog will tell you that you have not chosen to install any of the sample sites, and then ask you if you want to install the Commerce Server core components. Click Yes to continue the installation.

The next screen in the installation wizard will identify the components that you have chosen to install, and notify you that it has enough information to start the installation process:

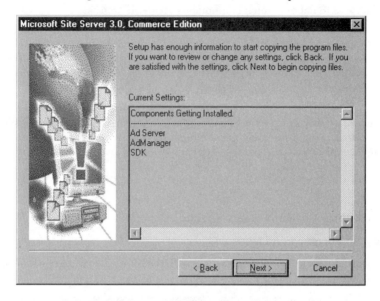

Click Next, and you'll be prompted to select and/or create a DSN for Ad Server. You've created the database and DSN for Ad Server already, so just choose it and click OK.

The Commerce Server installation will then start. During the installation, it will appear that the installation process has hung, because all activity will stop. Unfortunately, an error message dialog is hiding behind the commerce server installation screen. Press *Alt-Tab* to bring it into focus:

This error message is documented and acknowledged by Microsoft as an insignificant problem, later fixed automatically, and hence it can be ignored: so press the OK button.. Site Server 3.0 Commerce Edition will install correctly even though you have received this error message.

The length of time it takes to complete the installation is dependent solely on the speed of your machine. When the installation completes a dialog will appear confirming it. You'll be given a chance to review the Readme file at that time. When satisfied, click Finish.

Once again, as in the Site Server installation, you may notice a flurry of disk activity. The Indexing Service has been restarted and the HTML Help files are being indexed. As before, make sure the Indexing Service has completed indexing all the content before rebooting or installing more software.

Again, to monitor the progress of Index Server, get the Task Manager running by doing a *CTRL-ALT-Delete*, choose **Task Manager**, then click on the **Processes** tab. Sort on processor usage by clicking on the CPU field name. Wait until the **System Idle Process** gets to 98% or so, when all the content has been indexed.

(Optional) Install Visual Studio 6.0

Although you are not required to install any development tools along with your Site Server installation, you can install Visual InterDev or FrontPage, as well as any other third-party development tool such as HomeSite from Alstaire. It's always dangerous to install development tools on production servers so proceed with caution if you are installing a production server.

If you do decide to go ahead and install Visual Studio 6.0, make sure you don't install the Analyzer component. This component can be resource intensive, and will affect how your server will perform and scale – save this component for your workstations.

> **Do not install Visual Studio 97 on a computer running Windows 2000. Visual Studio 97 is incompatible with Windows 2000.**

(Optional) Install Visual Studio 6 Service Pack 3

If you installed Visual Studio 6.0 in the steps above, then install Visual Studio 6.0 Service Pack 3 at this point. You can download the Service Pack from:
`http://msdn.microsoft.com/vstudio/sp/vs6sp3/vsfixes.asp`.

Upon running the setup (or having the CD auto start), you'll be asked to confirm your intentions to install the Service Pack. Click **Continue** to proceed, and you'll be presented with the licensing agreement. If you agree with the licensing of Visual Studio 6 Service Pack 3, then click **I Agree**.

The installation will begin with copying of files, and then the configuration will proceed. Upon completion you'll receive a dialog pointing you to the Readme file, which contains a summary of many of the problems that are fixed with the installation of the Service Pack.

You'll also be instructed that you need to install Internet Explorer 5.0 to take advantage of the fixes. Internet Explorer 5.0 is automatically installed with Windows 2000, so this message is not applicable:

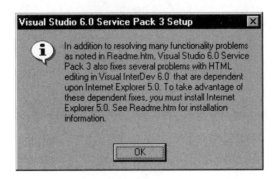

Click OK and you'll be instructed to restart your computer. After the restart, your Service Pack installation will be complete.

Site Server 3.0 Service Pack 3

Install Site Server 3.0 Service Pack 3. You can download the Service Pack from: http://support.microsoft.com/support/siteserver/servicepacks/sp.asp.

After executing the Service Pack, a number of files will be extracted to your machine. Then, you'll be ready to run the Microsoft Site Server 3.0 Service Pack 3 Setup Wizard. Click Next, and you'll be presented with the licensing agreement. If you agree with the licensing of Microsoft Site Server Version 3.0 Service Pack 3, click I Agree, and then click Next.

You can choose to create an uninstall directory for the Service Pack. It's a good idea to create an uninstall directory, just in case of an installation failure:

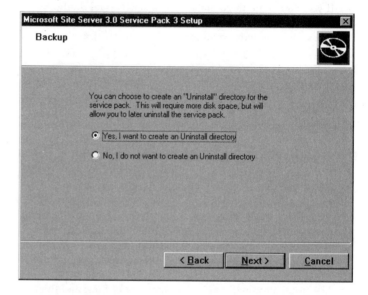

Now, setup has enough information to start copying the files. Click Next to begin. The installation will take a number of minutes depending on the speed of your system. When it has successfully installed click Finish to complete the installation.

> **Important: make sure and read the Site Server Service Pack 3 Readme.htm file which includes the latest release notes, and small fixes that need to be made. It is installed in your Site Server Directory in: \Microsoft SiteServer\sp3\readme.htm.**

Post installation Configurations

Having successfully installed Site Server, you still need to perform the following updates on your machine running Site Server.

Site Foundation Wizard Updates

When creating a new site using the Site Foundation Wizard, if a Universal Naming Convention (UNC) directory location is specified rather than a local or mapped directory, the site foundation is not created correctly. A new feature in Site Server Service Pack 3 added to the Site Foundation Wizard will allow you to create configurations that contain multiple web servers and a single file server.

For more information on both the configuration of the hot fix and the known issues associated with it refer to the Knowledge Base article referenced at:
`http://support.microsoft.com/support/kb/articles/q243/5/33.asp`.

To install the updated files:

- ❑ Copy `account.asp`, `directory.asp`, `finish.asp` and `setup.vbs`
  from the folder: `\Microsoft Site Server\SP3\Commerce`
  to the folder: `\Microsoft Site Server`
  `\SiteServer\Admin\Commerce\Foundation`.

- ❑ Stop and restart the WWW Service by navigating to the Internet Information Server snap-in within the Site Server Service Admin (MMC) (Start | Programs | Microsoft Site Server | Administration | Site Server Service Admin (MMC)). Right-click on Default Web Site and choose Stop. Right-click on Default Web Site again and choose Start.

Update the CMSample and FPSample Rule Set Files

Update the following files:

- ❑ Copy all files and folders
  from: `\Microsoft Site Server\sp3\samples\CmSample` directory
  to: `\Microsoft Site Server\Data\Publishing\CmSample` directory.
  Overwrite the existing files and folders.

- ❑ Copy all files and folders
  from: `\Microsoft Site Server\sp3\samples\FpSample` directory
  to: `\Microsoft Site Server\Data\Publishing\FpSample` directory.
  Overwrite the existing files and folders.

Update the Search ASP Pages

Update the following files:

- ❑ Copy all files and folders
  from: `\Microsoft Site Server\sp3\samples\search` directory
  to: `\Microsoft Site Server\Sites\samples\knowledge\search` directory.
  Overwrite the existing files and folders.

Congratulations! You are installed! Now move on to the final post-installation section.

Post-Installation Patches, Fixes and Configurations

All suggested patches, fixes and configurations in this section are optional, but suggested (especially in production server environments).

Fixes

Most of the many problems that were identified and acknowledged in the Knowledge Base on the Microsoft Site were fixed with Site Server 3.0 Service Pack 3, which shipped in October of 1999. One of the few that slipped through the cracks (or, more likely, was just impossible to fix in a Service Pack) is caused by a lack of communication between the Distributed Transaction Coordinator (DTC) on the Commerce Server computer and the DTC on the SQL Server computer. It may be caused by permissions, or an inability of the services to communicate with each other. This problem has surfaced on almost every commerce site that I have been involved in.

What happens is, when you attempt to execute the transaction pipeline (make a purchase, for instance), the following error occurs:

Error loading the pipeline configuration data from the file:
...config\purchase.pcf SQLItemADO –
...Server execution failed

To prevent this from happening, what you need to do is to change the identity of the System Package in Microsoft Transaction Server by forcing it to run as the Administrator.

Here are the steps to fix the problem:

1. Open the Transaction Server MMC by Clicking Start | Programs | Windows NT 4.0 Option Pack | Microsoft Transaction Server | Transaction Server Explorer.

2. Click the + next to Microsoft Transaction Server.

3. Click the + next to Computers.

4. Click the + next to My Computer.

5. Click the + next to Packages Installed:

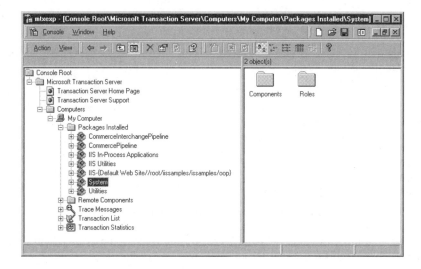

6. Right-click on the System package and choose Properties. Click the Identity tab, click This User and change the user to the local administrative user.

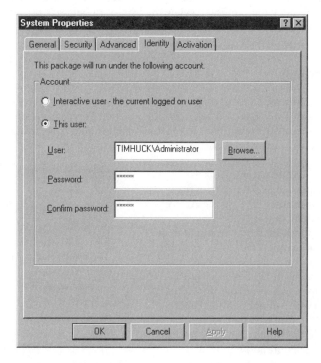

7. Click OK to persist the change.

8. Verify that the DTC service is Started on both computers by checking it in Services from the Control Panel.

Configurations

❑ If you installed the FrontPage 2000 Server Extensions on Windows NT 4.0 and Commerce Server, you must disable the FrontPage 2000 Server Extensions each time you run the Site Foundation Wizard. After you run the Site Foundation Wizard, you must re-enable the FrontPage 2000 Server Extensions.

❑ If you installed any of the Commerce Server sample sites, use the Site Server Microsoft Management Console (MMC) to access Commerce Host Administration. Remove ":80" from the non-secure host name field and ":443" from the secure host name field for all sample stores. Repeat this procedure for all stores that you create.

❑ There is a vulnerability in MDAC that could allow a web site visitor to take unauthorized actions on a web site hosted using Internet Information Server. Web site visitors can gain unauthorized access to the Internet Information server through ODBC data access with Remote Data Services (RDS). Reconfiguring or removing the affected components of MDAC can eliminate the vulnerability. Review the Microsoft Security Bulletin (MS99-025) at:
`http://www.microsoft.com/security/bulletins/ms99-025faq.asp`.

IIS Parent Paths

By default, parent paths are enabled on both Internet Information Server 4.0 and 5.0 when installed as a part of a Windows NT 4.0 Option Pack or Windows 2000 Server installation. Microsoft has confirmed this to be a security problem. Refer to the Knowledge Base article at `http://support.microsoft.com/support/kb/articles/Q184/7/17.asp` for details.

If you are going to disable parent paths as described in the Knowledge Base article, then you will need to make some fixes to the Active Server Pages contained in the Web Administration application. And you might need to make fixes in the samples. Here's an example.

To disable parent paths in IIS 5.0, navigate to the Internet Information Server snap-in within the Site Server Service Admin (MMC). Right-click on Default Web Site and then chose Properties. Choose the Home Directory tab and then click on the Configuration button. Choose the App Options tab and then click Enable Parent Paths to remove the check mark:

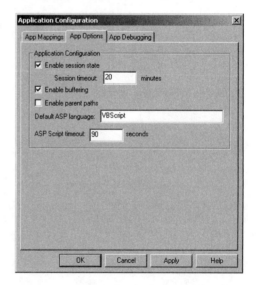

Now, navigate to Site Server Web Administration by choosing Start | Programs | Microsoft Site Server | Administration | Site Server Service Admin (HTML). Choose Membership Directory Manager, which is the third of the seven menu choices on the page. You will get an error similar to this:

Error Type:
Active Server Pages, ASP 0131 (0x80004005)
The Include file '../LibGlobals.asp' cannot contain '..' to indicate the parent directory.
/SiteServer/Admin/Knowledge/DsMgr/Lib\Membership.asp, line 1

To fix this error (and the many errors that you may encounter) you will need to change the relative parent paths in the Active Server Pages to virtual paths.

Open up `Membership.asp` (which is located in `\Microsoft Site Server\SiteServer\Admin\knowledge\dsmgr\lib`) with Visual Interdev or your favorite ASP editor, and look at line 1 where the error occurred. You'll see the following line:

```
<!--#Include File="../LibGlobals.asp"-->
```

If you change line 1 to reference the virtual path, `LibGlobals.asp` as below, the problem will be fixed:

```
<!--#Include Virtual="SiteServer/Admin/Knowledge/dsmgr/LibGlobals.asp"-->
```

You'll need to make fixes like this everywhere on the site where relative parent paths are referenced.

Hint: search your drive for `*.asps` *which contain* `#include file="`.

Buy Now! Templates

Buy Now! Ads are a very quick, 4-step purchase of a single product that is spawned in a separate instance of the browser. The idea is that you can place an advertisement on somebody else's website and sell your stuff from there, without driving traffic off the site. When I was the developer lead at Cooking.com (`http://www.cooking.com/`)it took me over 10 hours to figure out how to write them a Buy Now! Ad.

The URL listed below shows you how to add templates to your Site Server so that Buy Now! Ads are automatically created for you when you run the Site Builder Wizard. You can download the templates with complete instructions on how to install them from:
`http://msdn.microsoft.com/workshop/server/commerce/promotions101.asp`.

Sample and Starter Sites

There are a couple of Site Server sample sites that you might find useful.

Customizable Starter Sites

The Customizable Starter Sites are one of the best-kept secrets in Microsoft Site Server Version 3.0. They are not Commerce sites, but intranet sites that encapsulate all of the features of Site Server 3.0.

If you insert your Site Server Version 3.0 CD, it will auto-start. The last choice off of the main menu is Introducing CSSs. This is an HTML application that describes the Site Server 3.0 Customizable Starter Sites. It's done very well and I recommend that you go through it.

Upon installation, the sites are not pretty, but the engineering behind the scenes (since most of it is Active Server Pages) is completely available for you to use in your sites. They are FrontPage 98 compatible, the management pages are awesome and the installation code is unparalleled. In fact, ServersideConfig.asp is a lesson in Site Server 3.0 COM. That particular Active Server Page (which is used in site setup) is so huge that we actually bombed the IIS heap and the IIS team had to make it bigger, rebuild, and redistribute a new version of Internet Information Server 4.0 in Service Pack 4! The Customizable Starter Sites have a ton of Site Server 3.0 ASP code that you can steal and hack into your web applications.

Unfortunately, the Site Server 3.0 Customizable Starter Sites are not compatible with Internet Explorer 5.0. There is a browser detection component in the Active Server Pages management pages of the Sites that incorrectly rejects every browser except for Internet Explorer 4.0. That's easily fixed, but the real problem is that the browser objects used in the installation wizard are not IE5 compatible. Unfortunately, the Customizable Starter Sites are not scheduled to be updated to be compatible with Internet Explorer 5.0.

Because of the Internet Explorer 5.0 incompatibilities, you can no longer download the Customizable Starter Sites from the Microsoft web site. However, you can download them from: http://www.InterKnowlogy.com/support/SS3/CSS.

Here's a tip for Customizable Starter Sites Installation that is not documented:

1. Stop the wizard after the downloaded CSS executable has extracted by choosing Cancel.

2. Edit \Microsoft Site Server\bin\css\csseis\csseis.inf for the EIS site.

3. Change fdebugServersideConfig=1.

4. Run CSSWizard.exe to install the site. You'll be in "debug mode" and will get dramatically more information as the site installs.

Windows Media Pay-Per-View Sample Site

The starter sites and sample sites that are shipping from Microsoft these days are just awesome. There is a sample site that integrates streaming media, commerce and membership – it's called the Windows Media Pay-Per-View Sample Site.

> *At the time of writing, due to the reorganization of Microsoft's site, the download was not available. Try the following URL for more information:*
> `http://msdn.microsoft.com/workshop/imedia/windowsmedia/Solutions`
> `/payperview.asp.`

After installation pay special attention to the Membership Manager. This is a web based tool for managing your Site Server 3.0 Directory Service that is superior to the Membership Directory Manager (MDM) MMC snap-in in the Site Server Administration MMC.

Site Server 3.0 Client Tools Installation

You can install Site Server Version 3.0 Tools on your clients and servers not running Site Server 3.0: this includes Windows 95, Windows 98, Windows NT Workstation 4.0 and Windows NT Server 4.0 computers not running Site Server. If you perform a Site Server 3.0 Client Tools Installation, you will get:

- ❏ Content Analysis
- ❏ Usage Analysis Report Writer
- ❏ Rule Manager
- ❏ Tag Tool
- ❏ And most importantly the massive amounts of Site Server documentation

To perform a Site Server 3.0 Tools installation, place the Site Server 3.0 CD in your CD ROM drive. The setup program will auto start. Select Tools Installation and the Tools Setup Wizard will start.

Screen 1 of the Tools Setup Wizard confirms your intention to install the Site Server 3.0 Client Tools. Click Next to proceed.

Screen 2 of the Tools Setup Wizard is the license agreement. If you agree with the licensing agreement of Microsoft Site Server 3.0 Client Tools, then click Yes to proceed. You will be prompted for your Name, Company, CD-Key and E-mail address (as in the server install):

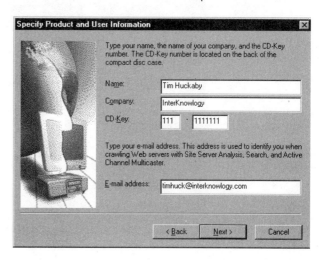

Fill out the required fields and click Next to continue. You'll be asked to confirm your Product ID. Click OK to continue.

Next, you are prompted for an installation location – the default is C:\Microsoft Site Server. Click Next to continue. Next, you'll be prompted to choose the features you want to install. Change the Analysis tools from Access Database Support to SQL Server Support. Leave all the other defaults, which will install all the tools:

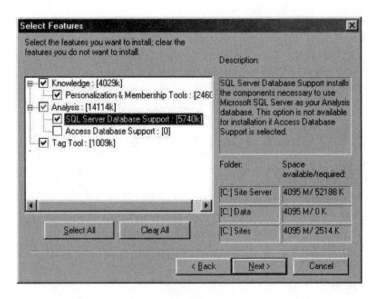

Click Next and you will be prompted for a Program Folder to install the tools under. Leave the default of Microsoft Site Server and click Next to continue. At this point setup has enough information to install Site Server 3.0 Client Tools. You'll receive a dialog confirming your choices:

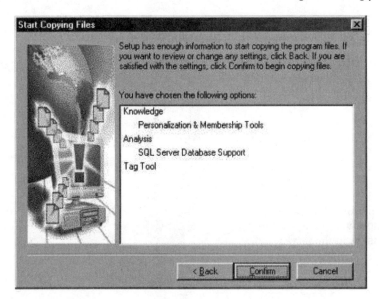

Click Confirm and the installation will start. The Site Server 3.0 Tools installation program may ask if you'd like to overwrite newer files with older ones. Unfortunately there's not a "No to all" choice, so choose No to each older file that the install identifies. You will be required to restart your computer when the installation completes. Click Finish to complete the installation.

Summary

As you've seen, installing the Site Server 3.0 product is no small chore. But, if you have followed the installation steps closely, then you should now have a successful installation. Successful installations of this particular product are rare, unfortunately, and you now know why.

It's a long and arduous process to install Microsoft Site Server 3.0 Commerce Edition, but a successful installation is crucial to maintaining a successful site. There are very few things more difficult than debugging problems in the platform – hopefully, you won't have to!

The Site Server Platform

So you've read Chapter 2, and you've installed Site Server. You may have also had to install SQL Server and maybe even perhaps Internet Information Server. You've gone through one of the most intense installation processes of any product known to man. Over 300 megabytes of DLL's and ASP pages and executables have been successfully placed on your server, so now what? Well, to say that you are going to "start using Site Server" is a little bit misleading. Site Server is an enormous product. Contained in that 300 megabytes of stuff you just installed are several technologies ranging from e-commerce functionality to content management capabilities. Actually what you've just installed is an e-commerce *platform* capable of being used to build just about any kind of business related web site you can dream up.

The purpose of this chapter is to introduce you to the platform you have just installed. So here is our plan of attack for the rest of this chapter:

- ❑ A discussion of web basics and Internet Information Server
- ❑ An introduction to the Site Server administrative tools
- ❑ A quick look at the MTS/COM+ Explorers
- ❑ A very brief introduction to SQL Server

After that you should have an introduction to the platform and you should have a better understanding of how all of the pieces of this gigantic puzzle fit together. One of our goals here is to place Site Server in the proper context in relation to the other technologies on this platform and prepare you for "diving" into Site Server. In order to prepare you for the rest of this book, we'll concentrate mostly on the non-Site Server technologies. Don't worry; we'll keep all of these discussions brief so you can dive right into the details and start building your first e-commerce site in the next chapter.

The Components of a Site Server Platform

Take a look at the following picture:

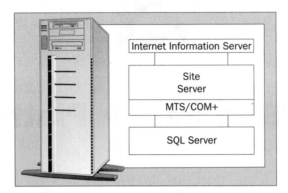

This is a logical view of the platform you have just spent hours installing. So what is going on here? Let's briefly discuss this picture.

At the top of the diagram we have **Internet Information Server (IIS)** which is the web server offering from Microsoft. Your web site is actually housed in IIS. IIS is going to handle the chore of serving web pages to users of your web site, out over the Internet. All of the HTML pages and ASP pages that you are going to develop are going to be "hosted" in IIS.

Underneath IIS, is **Site Server** and all of the functionality it brings to the table. As we mentioned earlier, there is an enormous amount of functionality contained in Site Server. What is important to realize here is that most of this functionality depends on IIS serving web pages. So there is a very tight correlation between IIS and Site Server. Let's look at an example. If you have developed an e-commerce site, and a user starts looking at lists of products and then proceeds to place an order, IIS is taking care of the communication between your web site and the user. Site Server is handling the actual e-commerce specific functionality, like the shopping cart. This is just one example, of the interaction between the numerous Site Server technologies and IIS.

> *Of course, there are Site Server technologies that have nothing to do with web pages at all, like the Site Server Directory Service.*

Next, we have the **MTS/COM+** layer. Site Server is going to hand a lot of work over to MTS. MTS stands for **Microsoft Transaction Server** and it is a component-based transaction processing system. (COM+ is an improved version of MTS for Windows 2000.) What does that mean? Well, what MTS does for us is make it easy to create components, or reusable chunks of functionality, and make them available to Site Server and IIS. One of the keys to a highly scalable web site is to have these components available to many users at the same time. MTS lets us do just that. At the same time, MTS provides a framework for ensuring the integrity of **transactions**. A transaction is a set of operations (typically database updates) that are treated as a single unit. MTS gives developers a way to guarantee the success or failure of transactions and when a transaction fails, MTS can undo all of the unsuccessful work. So what does this have to do with Site Server? Well, if you are developing an e-commerce site and are giving users the ability to purchase products, Site Server will use MTS to guarantee the success or failure of those purchases.

Finally, we have the **SQL Server** layer where all of the data will be stored on this platform. SQL Server is the current enterprise database offering from Microsoft. SQL Server and Site Server are also very tightly coupled. Going back to our e-commerce example, all of the data for products, users and orders will be stored in SQL Server.

So there you have it, a brief explanation of the platform and how the different layers interact with each other. Now we are going to spend the rest of the chapter digging a little deeper into the concepts behind these technologies,

Internet 101

Now that we have spent some time covering the technologies you might encounter in Site Server, let's look at what is really happening when you put a web site in production, out on the Internet.

Web Server Basics

A web server is simply a program or set of programs that provide web pages to requestors or clients. Every web site must have a web server behind it. You have never visited a web site, out on the Internet, and not been accessing a web server.

> *Yes, for those purists out there, you can just put a set of HTML pages on your hard disk and view them using a web browser. You could even call that a web site if you wish. However, you could not put that solution out on the Internet or accommodate very many users with it, so let's just forget about doing that.*

Think of a web server as a waiter at a restaurant. The waiter is the **interface point** between you and the restaurant. The waiter comes to your table, takes your order, gives the order to the chef and when the food is ready brings it to you. While you were waiting for your food, the waiter went to another table, took their order, submitted it to the chef and they received their food. After you are finished eating, your table is cleaned and the next customer arrives to start the process all over again. So the waiter is actually servicing multiple customers at the same time with the support of the restaurant and its staff.

Now let's apply this model to how a web server works. Back to our restaurant example, you could think of the restaurant and its staff as the *infrastructure* behind the waiter. In this same way, you could think of the actual server machine and the operating system and the network containing the server machine as the *infrastructure* behind the web server. A web server is going to use all of the resources at its disposal to handle requests made by users. Since the web server is presumably going to have a lot of resources at its disposal, (and we are dealing in computer speeds now, like nanoseconds) it can service multiple requests from multiple customers at the same time, much like a restaurant.

Back to the web – you type in the address of a web site, in your browser, and land on a web server. The web server then presents you with the requested web page. When you navigate to another portion of the site, the web server is monitoring your every move, probably logging that move to a log file, and when a new page is needed it hands one to your browser. While you were doing this, maybe another 50 to 100, or maybe even 3000 users, were doing the same thing! How a web server actually accomplishes all of its tasks is well beyond the scope of this book.

One thing that is worth mentioning here, in the context of how web servers are designed to handle multiple requests at the same time, is the notion of **state**. When you visit a restaurant, your stay there is what we call **stateful**; at least you better hope it is. Once the waiter has visited your table, you quickly develop a relationship with them, be it good or bad. When you make a request, the waiter knows who you are and if you have developed a good relationship with them, your request is usually fulfilled exactly as you wish. You would not like to go to a restaurant where the waiter forgets who you are between visits to your table. Thinking along these lines, we can say that the waiter is **holding state** between visits to your table, so they can bring you the right items and bill you.

Contrast the above example with how a web server works. Since the web server has to deal with potentially thousands of clients making multiple requests at the same time, the web server *forgets* who you are between requests for resources. Each request sent from a client is independent of all other requests. In other words, the web server is **stateless**. It would require an enormous amount of overhead if the web server had to remember who you were between each request.

In some ways, this statelessness makes writing web applications harder than writing normal software applications. A lot more design is required to make a web application stateless, but useful. This switch to stateless programming is usually one of the stumbling blocks for novice web developers. It requires you to go through a design process where all of the functionality of your application cannot know anything about what has been done or is going to be done. After you write a web application, you are going to appreciate some of the little things you may have taken for granted if you have written any other type of software. State will definitely be one of those things.

> **Each request made to a web server is independent of all other requests.**

Now there are ways for web servers to maintain state between requests, but we are not going to discuss them in any detail here. Your web browser may support **cookies**, which are pieces of information a web site stores on the client machine so it can remember something about you at a later time. Using cookies is referred to as maintaining state on the client. Some web servers do have mechanisms in place to allow for maintaining state on the web server itself during a user's visit. However, you must be careful when using these types of mechanisms because they can be extremely burdensome on the resources of your web server. Suffice to say, if your application requires state to be maintained between requests it can be done. Just know that you are going to have a direct effect on the number of concurrent users you can service if you design a stateful web application. Another way to say this is that you will have a direct effect on the scalability of your app.

Serving Pages Using HTTP over TCP/IP

Don't worry about the above title; by the end of this section, you'll know what we're talking about. When we put our web site into production, our web server is going to need a way to communicate with all of the users out on the Internet. In computing, when we need to make machines, or applications, communicate, at any level, we typically have to use a mechanism called a **protocol**. When communication between two entities occurs, we call these entities **end-points**. All of the communication is occurring between the end-points.

> **A protocol is a set of communication rules that the end-points must adhere to in order for the communication to be successful. In other words, the end-points must understand, or "speak" the protocol.**

In computing, there are many different protocols, some at the hardware level, like network protocols; some protocols allow communication between applications that reside on the same machine; some protocols allow applications residing on different machines to communicate, etc. One good thing about protocols is that they can be made into **standards**. Once a protocol is deemed a standard, more and more people start using it and communication can be expanded to a larger group of people, or in this case computers. In the case of the Internet, there are several protocols that have been deemed a standard. Some standard protocols used in the Internet are:

❑ **TCP** – Transmission Control Protocol

❑ **IP** – Internet Protocol

❑ **HTTP** – Hypertext Transfer Protocol

❑ **FTP** – File Transfer Protocol

❑ **SMTP** – Simple Mail Transfer Protocol

❑ **NNTP** – Network News Transfer Protocol

For the purposes of this chapter, we are only concerned with the first three items in the list. First, TCP and IP are typically combined into a single entity called **TCP/IP**.

> **IP is the protocol that takes care of making sure that data is received by both end-points in communication over the Internet.**

When you type the address of a web site into your browser, IP is what ensures your requests and the fulfillment of those requests make it to the proper destinations. For efficiency, the data being sent back-and-forth between a client and a web server is broken into several pieces, or **packets**. All of these packets do not have to take the same route when they are sent between the client and the web server.

> **TCP is the protocol that keeps track of all these packets and makes sure they get assembled correctly and in the correct order.**

So TCP and IP work together to move data around on the Internet. For this reason, you will almost always see these two protocols combined into TCP/IP.

You'll often hear the phrase **IP address** used in web speak. Every web site on the Internet must have a unique address. This concept is identical to phone numbers and mailing addresses. If the addresses weren't unique how could you ever be sure of finding anything? An IP address is simply a 4-byte number that looks like this: 204.148.170.3. And again, every web site has one. You might be asking yourself, "But I don't type in 204.148.170.3 to get to a web site, I type www.wrox.com. How does this work?" Well, there is yet another standard in use here and it is called the **Domain Name System (DNS)**. What DNS does is allow you to type www.wrox.com into your browser and it figures out that what you really meant was 204.148.170.3.

*When you create your web site and are ready to put it out on the Internet, you will have to register your web site name, or **domain name**. A domain name is the technical term for a web site name. You will have to register this domain name so that it also is unique. If you browse to* http://www.internic.net, *you can find out if your desired domain name is available. Once you find a domain name you can use, you can also link to organizations where, for a fee, you can reserve the name for your use only.*

Typically, your Internet hosting service, or your Internet Service Provider (ISP) will provide you with DNS services, by hosting one or more DNS servers. You will have to give your DNS provider the URL for your site and the corresponding IP address. Then your ISP will make the appropriate entries in their DNS server. Once these entries have been made, there is a system in place for replicating your new DNS entry to all of the other DNS servers, worldwide. Now when you browse the Internet, your ISP is also usually running one of these DNS servers, or buying and accessing DNS from another provider, so that when you type www.wrox.com into your browser, DNS figures out the corresponding IP address and using the IP protocol, you are sent to the correct web site.

HTTP is what we call an application level protocol. When the TCP/IP protocol is used to move data around on the Internet, it does not care what that data looks like. The **Hypertext Transfer Protocol** (HTTP) describes what the data will look like when web pages are sent over the Internet. HTTP data is sent using TCP/IP as the transport mechanism. So that is where we get the title for this section, "Serving Pages Using HTTP over TCP/IP". You have probably noticed that when you browse a web site, the URL in your browser is always prefixed by http://. By specifying http in front of the URL, your browser knows to speak HTTP to the web server on the other end.

If we had put ftp:// *we would be telling the web server to speak FTP.*

Each time you either open a web site in your browser, or click on a link within a web site, your browser sends an **HTTP request** to the appropriate web site using the IP protocol. When the web server receives this request, it formulates one or more **HTTP responses** and sends them back to you, using the IP protocol. Now for each request you make there are going to be several packets of information that are returned to you. Remember, TCP is taking care of making sure all of the packets make it back to you. The content of the packets is governed by the HTTP protocol. Your web browser starts to receive these HTTP responses and takes appropriate action based on what is in the response, like displaying images or formatting text. Eventually your browser renders a complete web page for you to look at.

Internet Information Server (IIS)

Well now it's time to take some of the information we have discussed thus far and apply it to Microsoft's Internet Information Server, or IIS. IIS is a big product. It is an "industrial-strength" web server. My goal here is to expose you to the most important parts of IIS. I want to give you a brief explanation of the parts of IIS that I think you'll need to know in order to successful deploy a web site built using Site Server. The discussion in this chapter will be kept at a high level since there is such an abundance of documentation available, both in the product itself and on the Internet.

Administering IIS

There are actually two user interfaces available for administering IIS: one is a **Microsoft Management Console** snap-in application, or **MMC snap-in**, and the other is a web-based user interface, which is a collection of ASP pages. Their functionality is similar, but not identical.

Most people tend to use the MMC interface if they are afforded the luxury of local administration. For remote administration, there is nothing easier and more powerful than a browser-based interface and that's why Microsoft has included a web-based tool for administrating IIS.

> *Just so you know, by remote we mean you do not have access to your web server over a local area network.*

With the MMC-based IIS admin tool we can actually administer multiple web servers from the same console. So the web-based version of the IIS admin tool comes in very handy when you can only access your web server over the Internet. This will probably be the case if a third-party hosts your web site.

The MMC Administration Interface

After you complete the installation of Site Server, you will actually have two MMC snap-ins at your disposal for administering IIS! Site Server installs its own, slightly enhanced version of the IIS MMC snap-in for administering IIS because of the Site Server P&M directory service. However, we are going to concentrate on the "original" IIS MMC snap-in.

Open the snap-in by going to Start | Programs | Windows NT 4.0 Option Pack | Microsoft Internet Information Server | Internet Service Manager on Windows NT or Start | Programs | Administrative Tools | Internet Service Manager on Windows 2000.

You will be presented with something similar to the following:

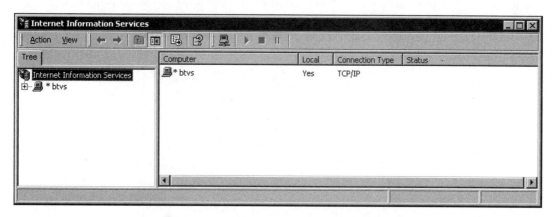

> **All the screenshots in this section are taken of the Windows 2000 version, which is IIS 5.0. If you are using IIS 4.0 (Windows NT 4.0) then you may notice some differences, but for our purposes they are not significant.**

This is the MMC snap-in interface for administering IIS. The user interface is like that used in Windows Explorer. There is a tree control on the left-hand side of the window and the right-hand side contains the details for whatever is highlighted on the tree.

The root of the tree is Internet Information Services or Console Root followed by Internet Information Server depending on your version. Under this we have the local server name. This is the **local host** for this machine (note the Connection Type is TCP/IP).

If you expand your local host node, you will see all the major nodes for this web server. The exact nodes you see will depend on your installation options and the IIS version. However, common to all will be the Default Web Site and Administration Web Site nodes:

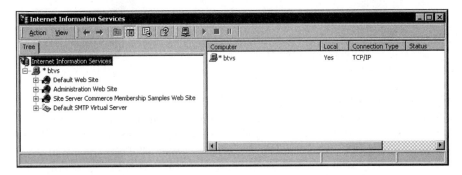

The Administration Web Site is the web-based administration application for IIS that we mentioned earlier, and the Default Web Site is where our sites will be hosted.

First, we are going to look at the properties for the Default Web Site. Again we are not trying to duplicate the IIS documentation, so we will just point out the important elements on each screen. If you right-click on Default Web Site and select Properties, you will bring up the following dialog:

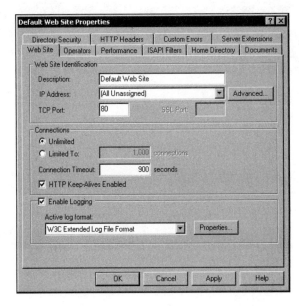

Each of the tabs in the above picture is called a property sheet.

The Web Site Property Sheet (Default Web Site)

IP Address – If you remember from earlier in this chapter, each machine on the Internet must have a unique IP address. If you accept the default for this property, default web will respond to all IP addresses that have been assigned to the machine.

TCP Port – Remember that the protocol used to serve web pages is HTTP. When a client browser asks to establish an HTTP connection with a web server, that connection happens over a **port**. This value specifies the port that HTTP will use for a connection. You will sometimes hear the phrase "bind to a port". By default, HTTP binds to port 80. You can change this value, but web clients will need to know ahead of time.

Enable Logging – You are probably going to want turn on IIS logging and have IIS track details about user visits to your site. Checking the box turns on IIS logging. Log files are simply text files containing web site data (user visits, hits, etc.) stored in a specific format. The Site Server 3.0 Usage Analysis tools can parse these logs and then import them to SQL Server databases in order to allow you to report usage on your web site.

The Operators Property Sheet (Default Web Site)

Take a look under the Operators tab:

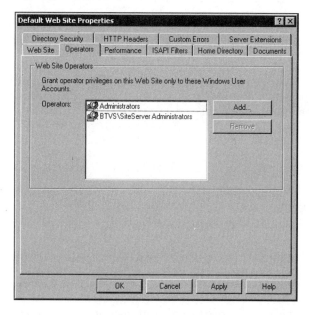

On this property sheet we designate which NT User Accounts can actually administer your web site. Your network administrator will typically control these settings. In the above picture only NT User Accounts in the local Administrators group and the local Site Server Administrators group can administer the web site.

The Home Directory Property Sheet (Default Web Site)

Now take a look under the Home Directory tab:

Every web site hosted with IIS has a **Home Directory**. The Home Directory is the default location where the source web pages can be found for a particular site. This property sheet allows you to change the settings for the Home Directory. You first get to choose where the Home Directory will be located. You can have the Home Directory reside in a file directory on the web server, on a file share on another computer or at a completely different web address. Depending on the setting you choose for When connecting to this resource, the content should come from, the properties you can modify are changed dynamically. Since the most common choice is to have the Home Directory reside on the file system of the web server, we will examine this choice. On sites that are protected with authentication, you will need to place your web pages on an NFTS share.

Local Path

The fully qualified path to the location of the Home Directory. You can click on the Browse... button to use the standard Windows file dialogs to find a location of your choice.

Access Permissions

Read – Allows clients to see and/or download content in the Home Directory or virtual directories. (We'll cover virtual directories later in the chapter.) If you have content in a directory you do not want downloaded from your site, like executable files, you should turn off Read access.

Write – Allows users to upload files to the Home Directory or a virtual directory. With this setting turned on for a particular directory, users can modify existing content in that directory.

You should be aware that these security setting are IIS specific and work in conjunction with the NT file security settings (if the files for your web site are on an NTFS partition). Basically, these IIS permissions need to match the NT file security permissions, or the most restrictive set of permissions takes effect. For example, if in IIS you turn on Write access, but in NT the file permissions are set to Read-Only, users of your web site will not be able to upload files. In this case, the NT permissions are more restrictive and will be enforced.

Directory Browsing – Turn on this option to enable clients to get an HTML directory listing of the contents of this directory. Users can navigate the physical file system when this option is turned on. This option is left off most of the time.

Application Settings

An **application** in IIS is defined as a file, or set of files, that are executed within a defined set of directories. How's that for a technical explanation? Basically, an application is a piece of your web site you want to segregate and treat separately from the rest of the web site. Why would you want to do this? One very important property of applications is that they can be run outside the process space of IIS. Or said another way, if the application fails, it won't cause IIS itself to fail. If the application was running in the same process space as IIS and it failed, IIS could possibly fail.

Name – Simply, the name you want to use to reference the application.

Execute Permissions – This drop-down allows you to specify what type of code can run from the site:

- ❑ None – Nothing is allowed to execute in the directory containing this application.

- ❑ Script – Only applications that contain script can be executed. For script to be processed it must be mapped to a script engine. For example, ASP pages are mapped to the script engine `asp.dll`.

- ❑ Execute – Any type of executable or DLL is allowed to run in this directory. Scripts can also be run.

A word of caution should be given here about the security loopholes created by some combinations of access permissions and execute permissions. If Write and Execute access have been granted on a directory, a user could upload a file to the server, run it on the server and potentially cripple it. Bottom line; be careful!!

Application Protection or Run script in separate memory process – These options allow you to control what process space any executables run under – IIS or an outside surrogate.

We are now finished looking at the important parts of IIS that pertain the **Default Web Site**. Now let's expand the **Default Web Site** node:

There are three different types of nodes under **Default Web Site**:

Directories, Virtual Directories and Applications

A **directory** is simply a physical directory on the hard disk located under the Home Directory for the web site. If you have sub-directories underneath a directory, they will also be visible.

A **virtual directory** is a directory not usually located within the Home Directory of your web server. Virtual directories have an **alias**, which is simply a name that client browsers use to access a physical directory. An alias does not usually indicate the physical location of a directory. You add a virtual directory to your site by right-clicking on **Default Web Site** then selecting **New | Virtual Directory**.

As we covered earlier an **application** is a set of files that are being treated as a separate portion of your web site. An application can have a name, which also acts as its alias. An application can be mapped to a different physical location other than the Home Directory, exactly like a virtual directory. You can add an application by right-clicking on **Default Web Site** then selecting **New | Application**. Alternatively, you can also create an application promoting a directory or virtual directory through the use of a **Create** button on the directory's **Property** pages.

Creating A New Site

Fortunately, adding a new web site in IIS is pretty easy – there is a very easy to follow wizard that walks you through the entire process. Let's go through the process of adding a new web site to your IIS Server.

1. Open the IIS MMC snap-in, right-click on the local host and select New | Web Site from the pop-up menu:

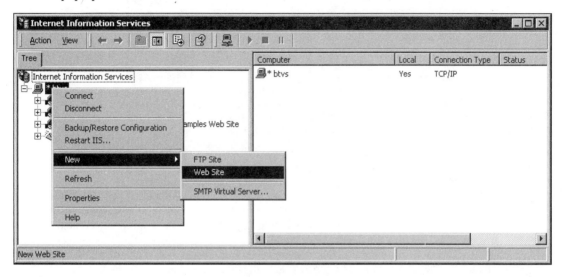

2. The New Web Site Wizard will start and you are on your way. Click Next from the Welcome screen.

3. In the following screen you can pick the name that will appear in the IIS MMC snap-in for your newly created site. For the purposes of this example, just type in Site2 for the Description and then click on Next:

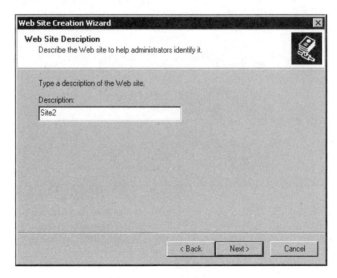

4. Now you get to pick what IP address you want to use for this newly created site, and which port. Keep the defaults and click on Next:

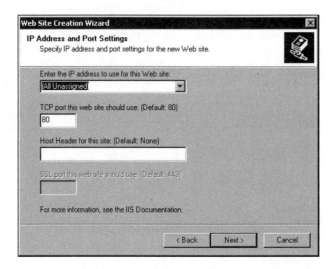

5. Next, you have to select the physical location where the files for your newly created site will reside. You can click on the Browse... button to select a directory. Here you are selecting the Home Directory for your site. Choose any location on your local machine and keep the default for Allow anonymous access. Click on Next when you are finished:

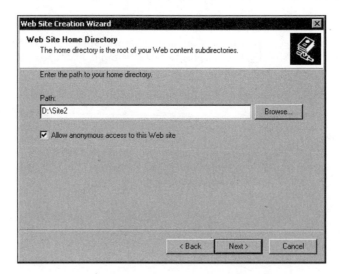

6. Now choose which the directory permissions for the Home Directory. Refer to the earlier discussion on directory permissions if you need help deciding what to choose. For our purposes, the defaults will work just fine. Click Next and then Finish:

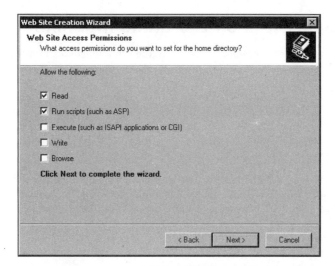

That's all there is to it! After you have completed all of these steps, the IIS MMC snap-in should reflect the fact that you have created a new site. It should look similar to this:

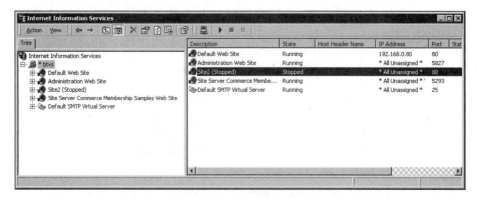

You should notice that your newly created site is not running. The word (Stopped) next to the site name indicates that your site is not accepting requests. If you attempt to start the site by clicking on the "play" button on the toolbar, you will get the following error message:

What happened? Since we have added a new site, there are now two web sites on this machine. When we added Site2, we accepted the defaults for IP address and port number. These settings are in conflict with the Default Web Site. So what are we going to do? Can't we host more than one site on a machine? The answer is yes, and this brings us to our next topic.

Hosting Multiple Sites on the Same Machine

With IIS, you can actually host multiple web sites on the same machine. You will sometimes hear this referred to as **multihosting**. There are three properties that differentiate a web site in IIS:

- ❑ IP Address
- ❑ Port Number
- ❑ Host Header Name

IP addresses and ports were defined earlier. The host header name is simply the name of the site that is being requested. Newer browsers (IE 4.0 or greater and Netscape 4.0 or greater) pass the host header name in the HTTP request. Older browsers do not pass the host header name.

Let's go over the different scenarios for multihosting.

Multihosting Using Different IP Addresses

In this scenario, assume you are going to host www.site1.com and www.site2.com on one machine. For this example, assume that www.site1.com is the Default Web Site and www.site2.com is the newly created web site you added in the prior example (it was called Site2). Assume you have registered DNS entries for both sites as follows:

Site Name	IP Address
www.site1.com	10.4.4.100
www.site2.com	10.4.4.101

You somehow have to come up with two IP addresses on the same machine. There are two ways to do this:

- ❑ First, you could put two network interface cards in the machine and each card would have a different IP address.

- ❑ Secondly, on Windows NT, you can actually have one network interface card have multiple IP addresses! For Windows NT 4.0, the maximum number of IP Addresses per card is five. For Windows 2000, you can have an unlimited number of IP Addresses on one card.

Let's examine the second option in more detail. However, there is some considerable difference in the way to set this up between NT 4.0 and Windows 2000, so read the next section as appropriate to your setup.

Assigning Multiple IP Addresses Using Windows NT 4.0

Click on Start | Settings | Control Panel | Network. Once you are at the Network dialog, click on the Protocols tab, select TCP/IP from the list box and then click the Properties button. You will be presented with the following:

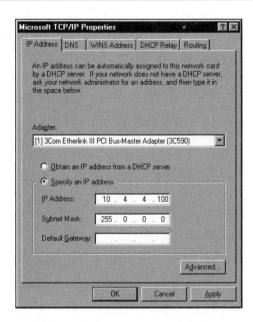

You are now looking at the IP address for this particular network interface card. Now click on the **Advanced...** button. You can then add another IP address for this network interface card. The dialog will look similar to this one:

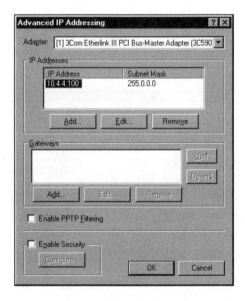

Click on the **Add...** button and simply add another valid IP address. In this case add the `10.4.4.101` IP address. You should see something similar to the following when you are finished:

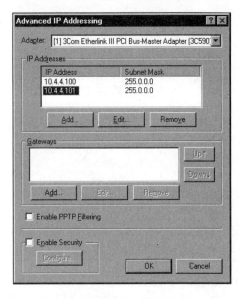

If you click on the OK button, you will have two IP addresses on one network interface card.

Assigning Multiple IP Addresses Using Windows 2000

Open the Network and Dial-up Connections window by going Start | Settings | Network and Dial-up Connections. Each network card installed will be listed as a Local Area Connection. Open the Properties for one of these connections:

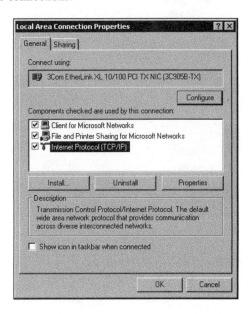

Select the Internet Protocol (TCP/IP) in the list box and press the Properties button:

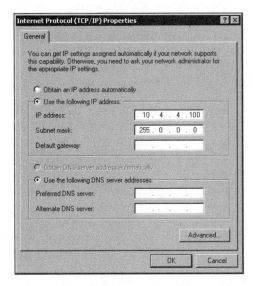

Use the Advanced... button to bring up the Advanced TCP/IP Settings dialog:

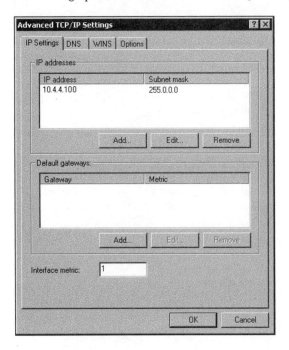

Click on the **Add...** button and simply add another valid IP address. In this case add the `10.4.4.101` IP address. You should see something similar to the following when you are finished:

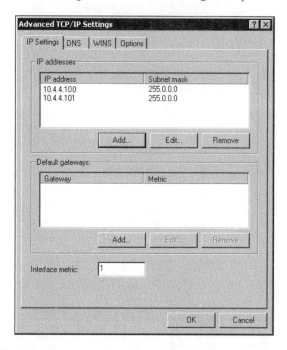

So now, we have two IP addresses on one machine. All that is left is to assign each web site its correct IP address and we are done. Try this out. Right-click on the **Default Web Site** and select **Properties**. Once the dialog appears, on the **Web Site** tab, select 10.4.4.100 from the **IP Address** drop-down list. You should see something similar to the following:

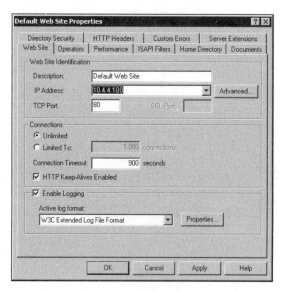

Now repeat this procedure for Site2, but select the 10.4.4.101 IP address from the drop-down list. That's it. You are now hosting two web sites on the same machine. If you try to start Site2, it should start correctly now.

Multihosting Using Different Ports

So how do we host our two web sites on the same machine if, for some reason, we cannot use two IP addresses on the same machine? What if our DNS entries looked like this?

Site Name	IP Address
www.site1.com	10.4.4.100
www.site2.com	10.4.4.100

Well another option is to use a different port. There is actually already an example of this set up on our IIS Server. Open the Properties dialog for our Default Web Site and for the Administration Web Site:

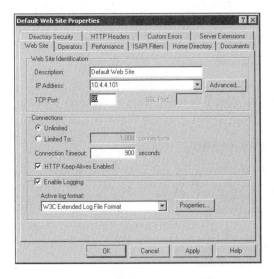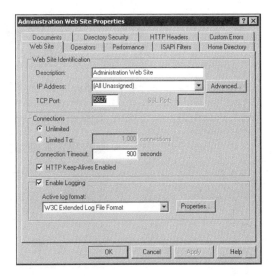

As you can see, the Administration Web Site runs on a port other than the default port 80. This is a security measure, since someone wanting to use the web-based administration tools for IIS would have to know the port number ahead of time. To access this site a user would have to append :5827 behind the name of the web site, (i.e. http://localhost:5827/).

Multihosting Using Different Host Headers

Our last resort if we cannot differentiate our sites using port numbers or IP addresses is to distinguish them by host header name. The host header name is nothing more than the name of the site. It is significant though, because the new browsers (IE 4.0 and greater and Netscape 4.0 or greater) will send this name in the HTTP request, so IIS can use it to route the request to the appropriate site.

Right-click on the Default Web Site and bring up its Properties dialog again. On the Web Site property sheet, click on the Advanced... button:

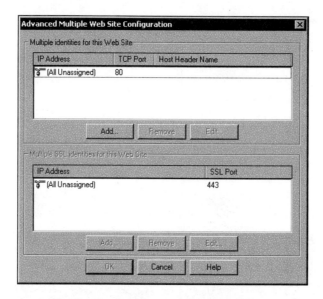

Select the entry in the Multiple identities for this Web Site list that you want to configure the host header for and click the Edit... button. In the Advanced Web Site Identification box enter the host header name of www.site1.com and click on OK when finished:

You would repeat this process for Site2 but enter in www.site2.com for its host header name. Now you can host multiple sites on the same machine that share the same IP address and port, but differ only by host header name.

> *You should consult the IIS documentation on how to enable host header name detection for older browsers.*

This concludes our look at IIS in this context. There are a great many other settings that you specify in IIS, some of which we'll encounter through the rest of the book, but I really do recommend that you familiarize yourself with the ins and outs of IIS to best administer your site.

The Site Server Administrative Tools

What exactly is Site Server? I hear that question a lot. That is why you are reading this book, right? Site Server is really not just one thing; it is a lot of different technologies that are marketed under a single name. This group of technologies enables you to build an e-commerce site, an intranet site or an extranet site. Site Server gives you the tools, or the building blocks, to build all these kinds of web sites.

You can think of Site Server as being divided into five main areas:

- ❑ Publishing
- ❑ Searching
- ❑ Delivering of Content
- ❑ Site Monitoring and Tracking
- ❑ Commerce

For each of these areas there are specific Site Server technologies:

- ❑ Publishing
  - ❑ Content Management
  - ❑ Content Deployment (CRS)
- ❑ Searching
  - ❑ Site Server Search
- ❑ Delivering of Content
  - ❑ Active Channel Server
  - ❑ Active Channel Multicaster
  - ❑ Personalization and Membership (Site Server Directory Service)
- ❑ Site Monitoring and Tracking
  - ❑ Site Server Usage Analysis
- ❑ Commerce
  - ❑ Wizard Generated Commerce Site
  - ❑ Site Server Pipeline

Fortunately for you, there are chapters of this book dedicated to most of these technologies, so we won't go into a discussion on any of these technologies here. However, before we can send you off to the next chapter, we need to talk about the **Site Server administrative tools**.

As you can imagine, there are a lot of tools to administer all of these different technologies. It would take an entire book to cover all of these tools in any depth at all. Again, fortunately for you, you are also going to get the details on what you need to know, from an administrative standpoint, as we go through the book. So what we'll do is introduce you to the two different versions of the Site Server administrative tools and then send you on your way.

Like IIS, there are local and remote versions of the Site Server administration tools:

❑   There is an MMC-based version you can use if you have access to your Site Server machine over a local area network.

❑   There is also a web-based version you can use if you can only access your Site Server machine over the Internet.

To open the MMC-based Site Server admin tool click on Start | Programs | Microsoft Site Server | Administration | Site Server Service Admin (MMC). You will be presented with something that looks like the following:

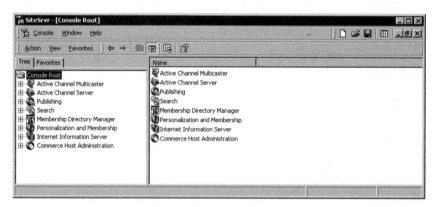

As you can see, this is admin tool is similar in format to the IIS admin tool we covered earlier – after all they are both snap-ins for MMC. There is a tree control on the left hand side of the window and the right-hand side contains the details for what is highlighted on the left-hand side.

On the left-hand side, the top of the tree is the Console Root and beneath it are the Site Server technologies you can administer from this console. Each of the nodes in this tree is a separate snap-in, or program that runs in the MMC. Site Server ships with six MMC snap-ins:

❑   Active Channel Multicaster

❑   Active Channel Server

❑   Publishing

❑   Search

❑   Membership Directory Manager

❑   Personalization and Membership

In addition, it has its own version of the IIS snap-in and when you install Site Server Commerce Edition, it adds the Commerce Host Administration snap-in. There is a considerable amount of material here for you to become familiar with but don't let it bother you. As we move through the rest of this book, you'll get the details on what you really need to know for each of these nodes in the tree.

However, we won't be covering the Active Channel Multicaster or the Active Channel Server in this book.

Did you happen to notice the Internet Information Server node? Guess what? It is the same IIS administration tool we discussed above, but has some Site Server specific elements added to it. Site Server imposes another tab, or property sheet, to the IIS admin tool for **Membership Authentication**. You'll learn about that in Chapter 12.

Before we continue, you need to be aware of the restrictions on accessing the Site Server MMC admin tool. When you install Site Server 3.0, Windows NT security groups are created for the purpose of Site Server administration. These additional groups allow you to limit access to specific Site Server features. Members of the NT group `Administrators` can administer all of the features of Site Server, but they can also administer all of the NT features on the machine as well. So you should be careful about which users you put in the `Administrators` group. There is also a Site Server specific group for most of the Site Server technologies. They are:

- `Site Server Administrators`
- `Site Server Knowledge Administrators`
- `Site Server Membership Administrators`
- `Site Server Directory Administrators`
- `Site Server DirectMail Administrators`
- `Site Server DirectMail Operators`
- `Site Server Search Administrators`
- `Site Server Analysis Administrators`
- `Site Server Publishing Administrators`
- `Site Server Publishing Operators`

In order for someone to access a particular feature of the Site Server MMC admin tool, their NT user id must be a member of a group that has access to that feature. You should consult the Site Server documentation for the privileges associated with each of these groups. For our purposes we are only going to discuss the `Site Server Administrators` group. Members of this group can administer all of the features of Site Server, but not the features of NT (provided they are not in the NT `Administrators` group!).

If you expand each of the nodes, or snap-ins, one level, you will see something similar to the following:

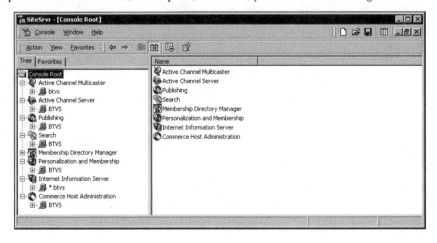

If you haven't used this admin tool yet then some snap-ins might be empty. We'll see how to rectify this in just a second.

With the exception of the Membership Directory Manager node, the next level for each node is the name of the machine being administered for each of these services.

If you right-click on any of these nodes (with the exception of the Membership Directory Manager), you can actually add another machine to administer. The term used to refer to another machine in the Site Server admin tool is **host**. Now each of these services will present slightly different dialogs for adding another host. Basically, they are all asking for the same thing, the name or IP address of another server.

For example, if you right-click on the Commerce Host Administration node then select Add Host... you will be presented with the following dialog:

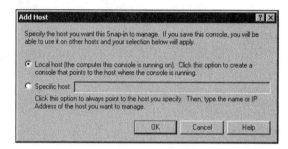

Here you can type in the machine name of another server to administer for Commerce Host Administration, or you can specify an IP address of another server. Alternatively, when you first install Site Server Commerce Edition you will want to register the local host with the Commerce Host Administration snap-in.

If you perform this same procedure on the Search node, you are presented a one-step wizard where you can enter the same information as above:

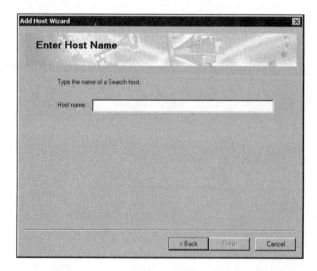

So now you have an idea of what we mean when we say all of these services will ask for the same information, but their presentations will differ.

Now let's take a look at the web based version of the Site Server admin tools. Fire up your browser and type in the following URL: `http://localhost/SiteServer/Admin`. If you are doing this over the Internet, the URL will be `http://<domain name>/SiteServer/Admin`. Either way you will be presented with something similar to this:

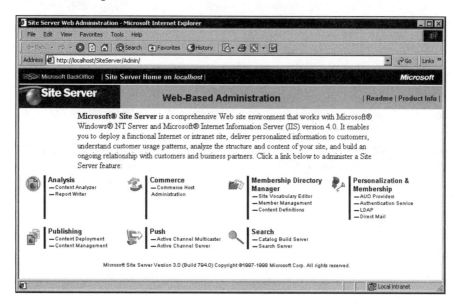

Depending on how you are logged in, you may be presented with a login dialog, in which you must enter a userid and password that belongs to either the NT Administrators group or the Site Server Administrators group. This way, only the people who have been specifically granted administrative access can administer your web site over the Internet. That is a good thing.

Most of these Site Server administrative categories should look familiar, since they are the same as those in MMC-based admin tool.

Again, we won't go into specifics on any particular feature. One thing you should know though, is that to administer the Knowledge Manager and Content Management features of Site Server, you must use the web-based administrative interface.

There's not much else we can do with the administrative interfaces at this point without getting into further detail on the various Site Server tools and services so we'll leave those discussions to their appropriate sections later in the book.

MTS / COM+

We should very briefly touch on the administrative interface for MTS/COM+. We won't go into any detail on these services, as it would require a significant discussion of COM and components, which isn't appropriate here.

For the purposes of this book MTS (Microsoft Transaction Server) and COM+ will be used synonymously. However, COM+ is really the next step on from MTS and contains far greater functionality. COM+ is Windows 2000 specific.

MTS is administered from MTS Explorer and COM+ from the Component Services Explorer, both of which are snap-ins for the MMC.

To open the MTS Explorer go: Start I Programs I Windows NT 4.0 Option Pack I Microsoft Transaction Server I Transaction Server Explorer:

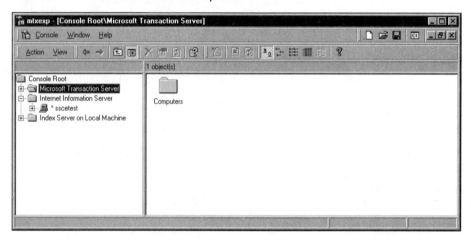

While to open the Component Services Explorer go: Start I Programs I Administrative Tools I Component Services:

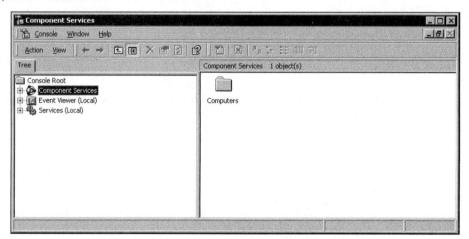

As you can see, both snap-in are quite similar, although the Component Services contains nodes for additional functionality.

The only part of MTS/COM+ that we will concern ourselves with for now is the location of some components installed by Site Server Commerce Edition. In MTS, these components are installed in a **package**, whereas for COM+ the terminology is **COM+ Application**.

We'll look at packages/COM+ applications in more detail in Chapter 6.

Expand the Component Services or Microsoft Transaction Server nodes until you can see the contents of the Packages Installed or COM+ Applications nodes

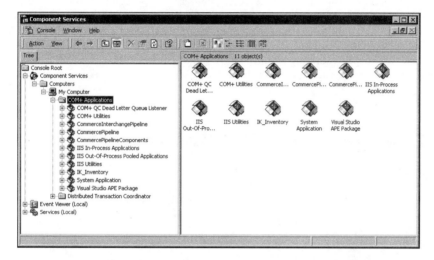

Notice that there are three packages/COM+ applications prefixed by Commerce:

❑ CommerceInterchangePipeline

❑ CommercePipeline

❑ CommercePipelineComponents

We'll discuss pipelines in more detail in Chapters 7 and 8. These components have been installed in MTS/COM+ so as to gain the benefits of being **transactional**. We discussed the advantages of using transactions at the beginning of the chapter.

SQL Server

Before we can wrap up, we should cover some elementary concepts related to SQL Server. SQL Server is the enterprise database platform offering from Microsoft. The main competitors to SQL Server are Oracle and DB2, from IBM. Just so you know, Microsoft Access is considered a desktop database platform and is definitely not in the same class of product as SQL Server. The most current version as of SQL Server, at the time of this writing, is 7.0 Service Pack 1. Site Server can use SQL Server version 6.5 or 7.0. If you can, you should definitely use SQL Server 7.0. I could go on for pages about the differences between versions 6.5 and 7.0 of SQL Server but suffice to say, SQL Server 7.0 is an order of magnitude improvement in both performance and usability.

So what do you need to know about SQL Server? Well, all you really need to know for purposes of this book is how to add databases to the server, how to add tables to a database and how to add fields to a table. You will probably not be the one adding tables and databases to your production SQL Server. Your network administrator or Database Administrator (DBA) will probably handle those duties. They will almost undoubtedly be handling all of the SQL Server security issues as well. The situation changes in your development environment, and this is probably where you will have free reign to do as you wish.

The SQL Server Enterprise Manager

Most of the management activities for SQL Server take place from the **SQL Server Enterprise Manager**.

To start the SQL Server Enterprise Manager, click on Start | Programs | Microsoft SQL Server 7.0 | Enterprise Manager. You will be presented with the following:

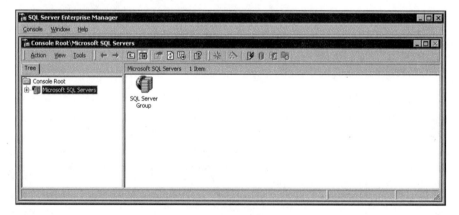

Again, you'll notice that the left-hand side of the window is arranged in a tree structure. Underneath the SQL Server Group is the actual server you will be administrating. Once you are at the server level, you can get to the databases hosted on this server and other services provided by SQL Server. We are only going to concern ourselves with the Databases tree in this chapter.

If you expand the **Databases** tree and select and expand the tree for a database, you will see something like this:

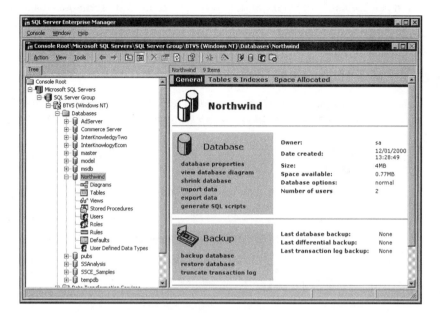

Adding a New Database

Now let's briefly cover how to add a database, add a table to that database and then add some fields to our newly created table. If you right click on the **Databases** and then select **New Database...** from the pop-up menu you will be presented with the following dialog:

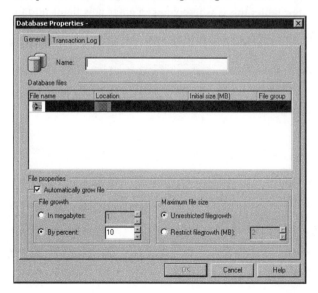

Simply type in a name for your new database in the name field. For our purposes, use Example1 as the database name. You can accept the defaults for all of the other settings and everything will be fine. Click on OK and you are finished! Unlike SQL Server 6.5, version 7.0 handles the details of figuring out how much hard disk space to allocate for your database. If you exceed the allocated amount, SQL Server 7.0 automatically allocates more. It's a very beautiful thing.

Adding a New Table and Fields

Now that you have created a new database, we can add a table to that database. Expand the tree for your newly created database and right-click on Tables then select New Table... and enter a name for your table:

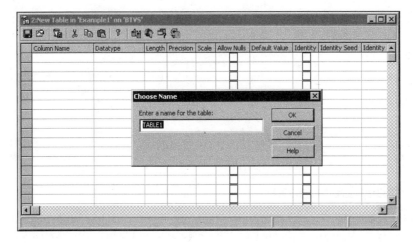

That's it! You have added a new table to your database. After you enter a table name, you are left in design mode for your new table; this is where you can enter new fields into the table:

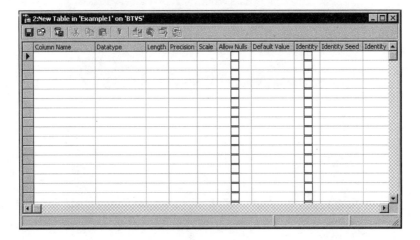

To add fields to a table the only properties you need to define explicitly are the **Column Name** (the name of the field) and the **Datatype** (what format of data will be stored in the field). SQL Server will fill in the other attributes with default settings, although feel free to change them:

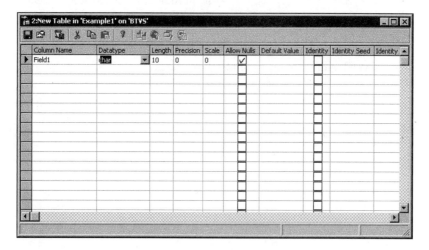

Hopefully, after reading this short introduction to SQL Server you have deduced that SQL Server 7.0 is very easy to use. We will be providing detailed instructions on how to work with SQL Server 7.0 Enterprise Manager whenever necessary in the following chapters.

Summary

You should now have a good conceptual picture of the various components within a Site Server platform. Over the course of the next few chapters you will become more familiar with how they inter-relate as we look at them in action. So you should now:

❑   Have a basic understanding of what is happening out on the Internet and on your web server

❑   How to host multiple sites on a single web server

❑   Be familiar with the basics of the Site Server administration tools

❑   Have a basic functional understanding of working with SQL Server databases

Keep in mind that most of the topics we discussed in this chapter have entire books dedicated to them, so I encourage you to explore further. The following resources might be helpful:

❑   http://www.whatis.com – a web site that defines just about every computing term known to man. Once you locate a term and its definition, they provide links for further information. This site is really helpful for figuring out acronyms, like TCP.

❑   The IIS documentation – I cannot stress enough that the IIS documentation is very good and contains a wealth of information.

❑   http://www.microsoft.com/ntserver/web/default.asp – the portion of the Microsoft web site dedicated to IIS.

❑   http://www.microsoft.com/sql – the portion of the Microsoft web site dedicated to SQL Server.

In the next chapter, we will start putting Site Server to work and use it to generate an e-commerce site that we will then proceed to dig into over the rest of the book.

Building Your First E-Commerce Site

Site Server Commerce Edition contains two very powerful wizards, which when run back-to-back can actually create fully functional e-commerce sites. Upon completion of the **Site Foundation** and **Site Builder** wizards, you will have a functional retail e-commerce site that's complete with registration, shipping, search, billing and tracking of your customer's orders and even shopping baskets.

However, the e-commerce sites generated from the wizards are not pretty – they need significant help with their 'look and feel', and frankly, they're not ready to be immediately put into production. Yet, what they are is a huge leap over the learning curve compared to attempting to build an e-commerce site from scratch.

I would venture to guess that most of the Microsoft Site Server Commerce Sites that are live on the Internet today were created from the wizards.

Through these wizards, you can create your own customizable e-commerce site or work with a copy of the demo sites that you can install, so you can play around and become more familiar with the product.

Over the course of this chapter, I'll show you just how powerful a wizard-generated site can be by exploring the features of such a site. Then, we'll walk through each of the wizards and see how to generate that very commerce site.

Over the course of this chapter we will:

- ❑ Use the Commerce Site Foundation Wizard to build the foundation of our e-commerce site
- ❑ Use the Commerce Site Builder Wizard to generate the functionality for the site
- ❑ Use the Site Manager created by the wizards to add data such as products to our site
- ❑ Use the Site Manager to set up promotions on our site

However, before we can start generating our first site, we'll take a look at the functionality that we will be implementing shortly.

The Wizards

The Commerce Site Foundation Wizard is the first of the wizards that we'll use, when we walk through the steps that it takes to build the foundation for an e-commerce site. This wizard helps you by generating the virtual directory within IIS, the site configuration files, the foundation components and a local account group for the site, to link to a manager's page to begin building the rest of the site. This is the first step to building a finished e-commerce site and is a prerequisite to running the Commerce Site Builder Wizard that will generate the commerce components for the e-commerce site.

Once you've generated the architectural building blocks of the site by running the Site Foundation Wizard, we'll use the Site Builder Wizard to finish creating all of the commerce components and ASP pages for our site. That includes shopping baskets, search functionality, and even different promotions that the e-commerce site can offer.

Generally, before you proceed with running the Site "Foundation" and "Builder" wizards, you would plan out the desired format of your site. You should make some simple decisions about registration, the layout of the site, sales and promotions, tax, shipping, and handling.

Making sure you decide these elements properly is vital to the eventual functionality of your site. However, if you don't like the results of the generated commerce site because of a choice you made in the wizard, it's quite simple to just generate another one. You don't even have to delete the previous commerce site (although you can). Certainly, there are limits to how many commerce sites you can build on your Site Server – depending on system resources, etc. – but realistically you can run these wizards a number of times until you get the combination of features that works best for you.

Once that's done, though, and you've made changes to the HTML and ASP in your wizard-generated site, it's extremely difficult to go back and run the wizard again without destroying the changes that you've made. That's the price we pay for having the flexibility to modify these wizard-generated sites.

> *Once you've finished building your site, you can take a peek at some of the Active Server Pages that make up your sample site to get a better feeling of the nuts and bolts that hold Site Server Commerce Edition together. That's what we'll be doing in the next chapter. Site Server is a very large product to get your hands around, and running through and "re-engineering" some of the code can go a long way into helping you understand how Site Server Commerce Edition works. Having all of the Commerce foundational objects already in place will help you learn and understand how Site Server Commerce Edition works.*

Again, I feel it's necessary to give you fair warning before you get too deep into this chapter. The User Interface (UI) on a wizard-generated commerce site is very basic at best, and lacks marketing appeal in comparison to most e-commerce web sites that you'll run across on the Internet. The wizards that are used to build and install your first e-commerce site are designed for basic functionality only. Most of the sites that you'll see, once you've finished with the wizards, are not production-ready.

Yes, the wizard-generated sites are packed with functionality, but normally you'd add more customization to the wizard-generated site, such as third-party products that will integrate with the billing, tax, shipping and accounting packages that Site Server offers. Site Server covers the framework aspects of e-commerce and lets various third-party software vendors fill in the holes. For every phase of operation on an e-commerce site, with Site Server Commerce Edition, you can find a vendor that can supply you with a third-party product that will enhance your site. This is true for almost any piece of the purchasing process, from tax components, shipping plug-ins, and credit-card verification, as well as billing and accounting systems. See Appendix C for suppliers of third-party products.

The InterKnowlogy Site

We are going to start with a quick run through of our finished site – a fully functional commerce site that we will be generating with the commerce wizards. For now, we won't pay any attention to the look and feel of the site, only the operation. Our fictional site will sell:

❏   Software Components

❏   Media in the form of presentations from Microsoft Conferences on Videotape and CD format (streaming media in Windows Media format)

❏   Books published by Wrox Press

While the site isn't too fancy or graphically appealing, an HTML guru and creative designer would be able to customize the graphics and layout to add some spice and make the site more interesting. However, the wizard-generated code is very functional:

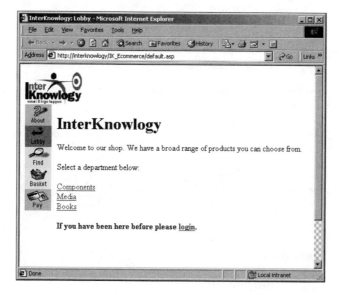

The screen above is the **Lobby** or home page of the site. Notice that the home page of this wizard-generated commerce site contains a number of items:

❏   There is company logo on the top left.

❏   In the main body of the page there is some informational text, and then the departments are listed. Every product that's available for purchase on a wizard-generated site belongs to a department.

❏   Also in the main body of the page, there's a link where previous shoppers to the site can login to identity themselves.

❏   There is a navigation bar on the left of the page, which contains five items (About, Lobby, Find, Basket, and Pay).

The screen below is the "About" section of the commerce site, which is accessed by clicking the About link from the navigation bar:

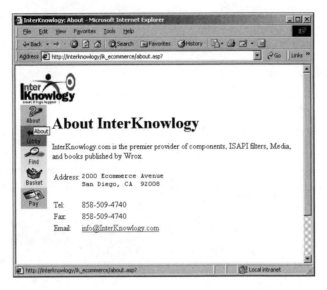

The About section provides company information and an Email link that allows the users of the site to request more information by e-mail.

If you click on the <u>Components</u> link on the home page (Lobby), you receive links to the three types of products that this site sells:

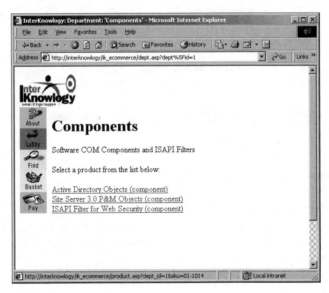

If you were to then click on the link for <u>ISAPI Filter for Web Security (component)</u>, you would move to the Products page. Products pages are generated dynamically depending on the product chosen. Notice from the screen below that there is a product name, a price, a description and an **Add to Basket** button at the bottom of the screen. You could also see a product image (on the far right of the screen), if one was available:

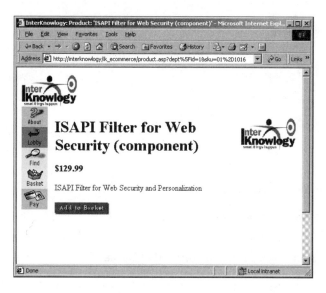

Another great feature of a wizard-generated site is the Product Search. If you were to click on the **Find** button in the navigation bar, you would move to the Product Search page. In the screen below I've typed the word "ISAPI" to search for:

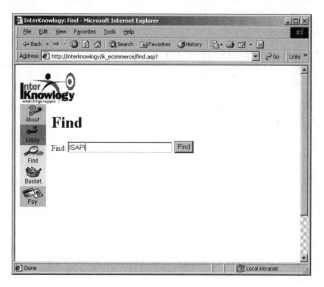

Upon clicking the Find button, 3 items would be retrieved in the Search Results page:

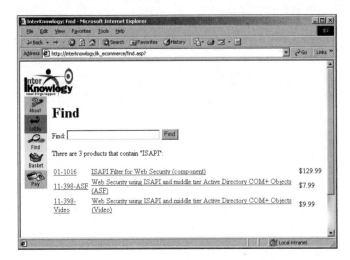

Now, if you were to click on the link for product <u>01-1016</u> you would go to the same Product page we saw a few steps earlier.

From the Product page, if you then click on the Add to Basket button, you will be asked to identify yourself:

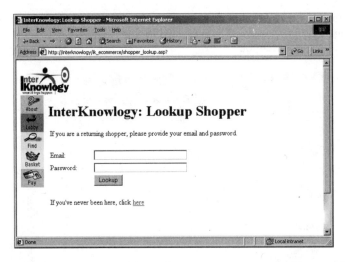

If you were a returning shopper, you could simply type in your e-mail address and password to be authenticated on the site.

> *Note, this is not Windows NT 4.0 or Windows 2000 authentication on the operating system, nor is it an authentication in a directory service on a Site Server 3.0 Membership Server; it's simply a lookup on username and password in the "Shoppers" table of the data store.*

If this were your first purchase at the site you would have to register yourself first, by clicking the here link at the bottom of the page:

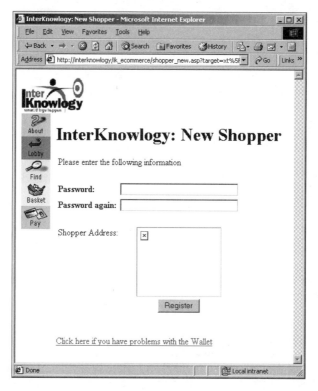

If you look closely at the screen above, you'll notice the broken link next to Shopper Address. This is one of the most disappointing problems you might encounter on a wizard-generated site (although you might not); and it's certainly something that you would want to change or fix before taking your site live. This is an example of a broken or non-installed Microsoft Wallet.

> *Microsoft Wallet is a client side ActiveX control, compatible with Internet Explorer only, which allows you to persist your address and credit card information in a secure manner on your computer.*

I'm using Windows 2000, which installed Internet Explorer Version 5.0. Something is wrong will my Microsoft Wallet installation – most likely, it just wasn't installed as a byproduct of my Internet Explorer 5.0 installation. Unfortunately, the wizard-generated code uses Microsoft Wallet by default when visited by Microsoft Internet Explorer browsers and a broken page results.

It's easy to overcome the problem by clicking the Click here if you have problems with the Wallet link at the bottom of the page. Unfortunately, that's confusing for the users on your site, so you'll most likely want to comment out the Wallet code in the New Shopper page. I've clicked the link, and have moved on to the HTML forms-based new shopper page below:

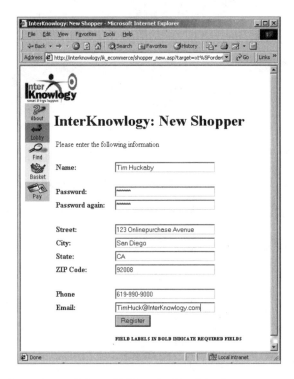

After entering your information and then clicking the Register button, you would move to the Basket page. Remember from above that you clicked the Add to Basket button before being forced to register. The Basket page contains the item you just added and a number of buttons that allow you to purchase the item, empty the basket, update the basket after changing quantities, or remove items from the basket:

Before we check out and make the purchase, I want to show you a promotion that we will set in place in the site. The promotion works like this: if a consumer buys the ISAPI Filter, then they get the Active Directory Objects for free.

So if you go back to the Lobby by clicking the Lobby link in the navigation bar, choose <u>Components</u> and then click on the <u>Active Directory Objects</u> product you will be taken to the Products page below. You could also have clicked the Find button in the navigation bar and searched on the Active Directory Objects product:

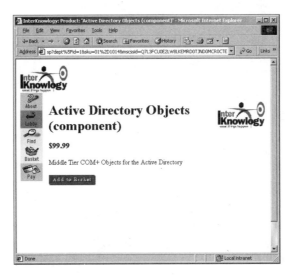

Now if you click on the Add to Basket button to add the Active Directory Objects product to the shopping basket you'll notice that $99.99 has been applied to the Extra Discount column next to the product just added. This has made the item free, which of course is the promotion that's set up on the site:

When you click the Purchase button, you move to the Shipping page:

Notice from the screen above that I've received the Microsoft Wallet problem again – I'll click the link **Click here if you have problems with the Wallet** to move on to an HTML forms-based version of the shipping page:

In the Shipping page, you're allowed to choose the method that you want the products shipped by. The ship-to address fields are automatically populated, because you registered on the site in an earlier step. You can change the data in the ship-to address fields if you so choose.

After clicking the Total button, you'll be taken to the Payment page:

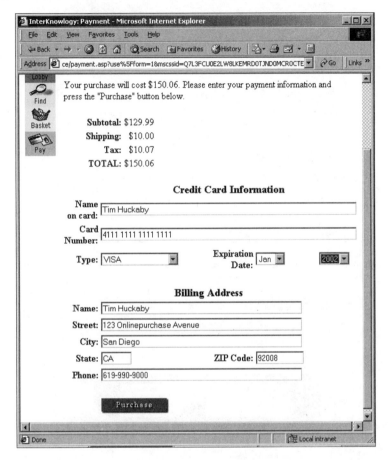

Notice that the purchase is summarized. Type the name as it appears on a fictional credit card and then use the test credit card number for a Visa purchase (4111 1111 1111 1111). The Billing Address fields are again populated automatically, but can be changed if we desire.

Upon clicking the Purchase button, the order is processed and you're taken to the Purchase Confirmation page:

Notice in the Purchase Confirmation screen above that an order number was generated and placed as a link on the page. If you click the link, you get a printable form of the receipt:

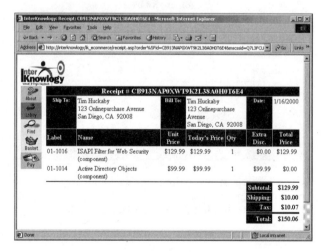

That's a pretty powerful – albeit not highly aesthetical – site, and it's completely wizard-generated. So, now let's generate it for ourselves.

The Commerce Site Foundation Wizard

Now we can finally start examining the basic components of the Site Foundation wizard. This wizard will help you generate the foundation site that you can later use to build your commerce site, and will help you get to know Site Server Commerce Edition a lot better. If you're like most people, once you've finished the Site Server Commerce Edition installation, you're probably still a little vague as to how all of the pieces fit together to form an e-commerce solution. Most likely, you've already digested a lot of information on Site Server, and you're probably still curious as to how these different pieces come together with Active Server Pages.

Part of the difficulty with working with Site Server is that the product is so big and there's so much to learn. This compounds the problem of actually exploring how each of the components work. You probably wouldn't want to change the source code on any development or production Site Server implementation, but with this wizard, you can build multiple sites on a test or development server to see how each of the commerce components work. If you accidentally change any of the code or ASP within the site, you won't have to worry about any production downtime or failure.

So let's begin tackling the **Commerce Site Foundation Wizard** that will help you build your first e-commerce site. As I mentioned, this wizard will help you setup a bland, but functional, e-commerce site that you can use to build on as you move forward to production. Once you get your site up and running, you can then spend some time with experienced HTML and ASP developers and creative design artists, to you help jazz up your site with some creativity and flair and make your online store more appealing.

Prerequisites

Before you begin, you need to make sure that you fulfill the prerequisites for the Wizard. Making sure all of these prerequisites are taken care of before you begin the installation will save you a lot of headaches. Here's a listing of the different software components that you'll need, and things that you'll need to do, before starting:

- ❑ A Windows NT 4.0 or Windows 2000 Server installed with Site Server 3.0 Commerce Edition.

- ❑ A database to store the commerce data for the site (SQL Server or Oracle).

- ❑ A system DSN that communicates with the commerce database.

- ❑ Correct permissions and a user account to use the Site Foundation Wizard. The Administrator account, of course, will work perfectly.

- ❑ A local Windows NT User account on your local machine to manage the Commerce Sites' Manager pages if you are not going to manage with the local Administrator account. You should place this account within the Windows NT Administrator's group so that it will be able to manage the commerce site.

Creating the Database to House the Commerce Data

You will need to create a SQL Server (or Oracle) database that will be used to house all of the data for your commerce site. I suggest using SQL Server 7.0, so we'll go through the process of setting up a SQL database to be used by our commerce site.

1. Open the SQL Server Enterprise Manager (Start | Programs | Microsoft SQL Server 7.0 | Enterprise Manager). Expand the nodes until the Databases folder is visible, and then right-click on the Databases folder to bring up the pop-up menu:

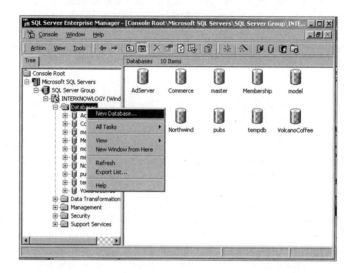

2. Select New Database... from this menu and a Database Properties dialog will appear:

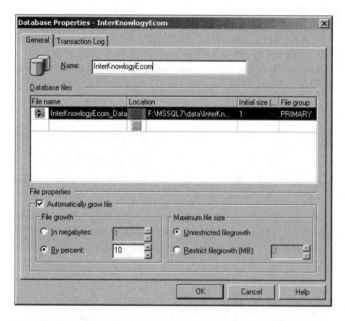

All that you really have to do is give the database a name – in our case, we'll call it InterKnowlogyEcom. SQL Server 7.0 will automatically grow the database as needed by default, so don't worry about the initial size. Click OK to finish.

Creating a DSN to Connect to the Database

SQL Server 7.0 made creating the database very easy – only two steps. Ironically there are more steps (8) involved in creating the DSN (Data Source Name) to connect to the database than creating the database itself! Here's the process:

1. Open the **ODBC Data Source Administrator**. In Windows NT 4.0 this is achieved by running the **ODBC Data Sources** applet in **Control Panel**. Or if you are using Windows 2000 you need to go **Start | Programs | Administrative Tools | Data Sources (ODBC)**.

2. Next, switch to the **System DSN** tab and click the **Add** button:

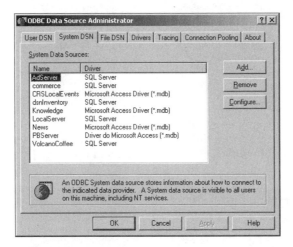

3. From the **Create New Data Source** dialog, scroll down the list of database drivers installed on your machine and choose the driver for you database. In our case we want to choose the **SQL Server** driver to connect to the database we just created:

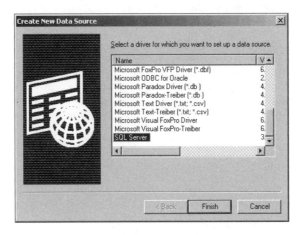

4. Click Finish, and you'll move to the next part of the ODBC Data Source Wizard. Give your DSN a name – I usually give the DSN the exact same name as the database that it connects to, to avoid confusion. You can also give your DSN a description. You'll need to type in the name of a remote SQL server if it's not running on your local server:

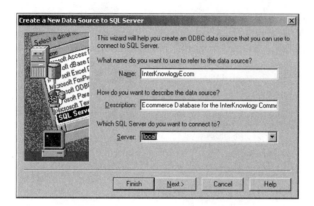

5. Click Next > and you'll be presented with the part of the wizard that lets you choose the authentication method with the SQL Server. Choose SQL Server Authentication, type "sa" for the login ID (or equivalent DBO account) and leave the password blank:

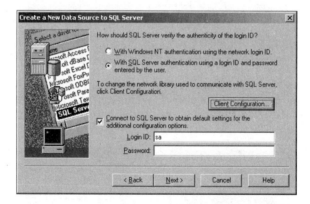

6. Click Next > and you'll be allowed to pick the database on the SQL Server 7.0 that you're going to communicate with. Change the default database to InterKnowlogyEcom from the combo-box:

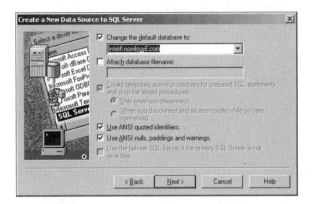

7. Click Next > and you'll be presented with more configuration options:

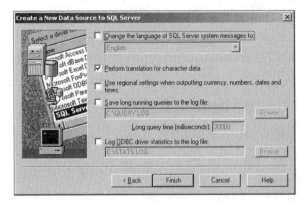

8. There's no need to change any of the configuration options for the commerce site, so simply click Finish. All of the configuration choices will be summarized on another page of the wizard:

9. If you click the Test Data Source button the wizard will test the communication. If you installed and configured your SQL Server as described in Chapter 2, you will receive the screen below:

10. Click OK to acknowledge the successful communication, and then another two OKs to finish the completion of the DSN.

Using the Site Foundation Wizard

Now we are ready to create a commerce site!

1. To begin, make sure you're logged in as the local Administrator (or a user with enough permissions to run the site builder wizard), open up the Site Server Service Admin (MMC) console (Start | Programs | Microsoft Site Server | Administration | Site Server Service Admin (MMC)).

2. Navigate to the Commerce Host Administration snap-in and right-click on the name of the computer that you'll be using to begin the Commerce Site Foundation Wizard. From the pop-up menu, select New | Commerce Site Foundation...:

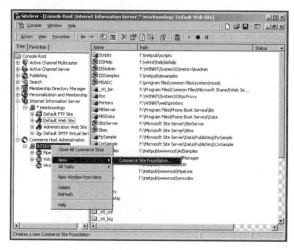

3. The Foundation Wizard is browser-based so you should see Internet Explorer (or whatever your default browser is) launch (if it's not running already). The first page of the Wizard displays a listing of the web sites that are available on your server. Most likely you will only have two web sites listed: the Default Web Site and the Administration Web Site. This selection will be used to create the virtual directory for your new commerce site, which will hold your configuration and ASP files that you will use to help build the site. For our purposes simply choose the Default Web Site option:

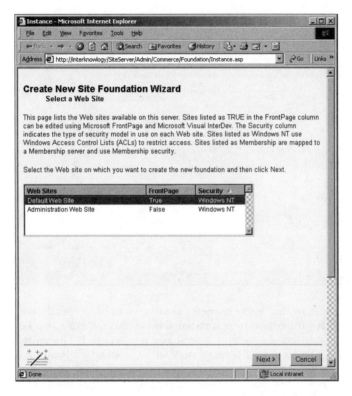

4. Now click the Next > button to move to the next page. This displays a listing of any commerce sites that are already installed on your local machine (in the Reserved list box), and allows you to enter the name for your new site.

We will now choose a Short name and Display name for our commerce site. It makes sense to choose a name that will help us to identify our site and one that we'll remember (although if you forget the name you can always see it in the Site Server Service Admin (MMC)).

It's important to note that if you run this wizard again, you will overwrite all of your existing files. If you use the same short name for your site, you'll overwrite your configuration, and can optionally overwrite the database tables with the default database schema that's created anytime a new site is built. You would lose all of your customization that you've made to the site once the database has been wiped clean with the new configuration. When running the Wizard over an existing database, you'll be warned about existing contents within the database, but obviously, you need to be careful.

We will set the Short name to IK_Ecommerce and the Display name to InterKnowlogy:

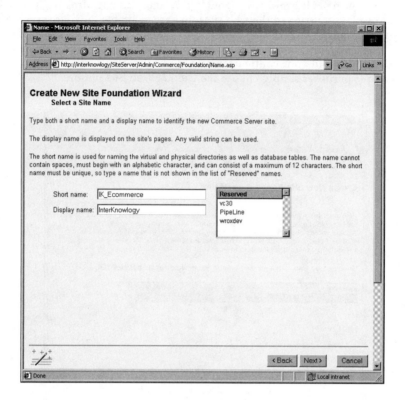

5. Click Next >. Now that we've named our site, we need to specify the location of the source files. It's important to remember this, so that we can come back and examine the source files later to see how they interact on the backend. The most logical, and hence the best way to organize your files is to stick with the standard location of \Inetpub\wwwroot\SITENAME. However, you can place your site directory anywhere that you wish on your local machine, as long as the folder does not already exist – that's a requirement of the Site Foundation.

There are permissions implications with installing your site on FAT partitions, so if you installed SiteServer according to the directions in Chapter 2, you will be installing your wizard-generated sites on the NTFS partition that has "D:" mapped to it.

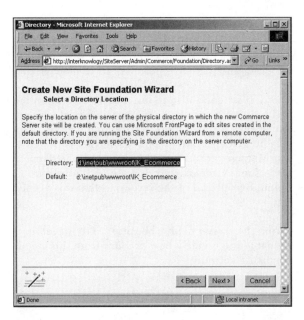

6. Click the Next > button to continue. As one of the prerequisites above, we created a database and DSN prior to starting the Wizard. For the next step, we need to specify where the data store for our site is to be located. We can do this by selecting the DSN for the database we created earlier, and making sure that we connect with a proper database login. Select the InterKnowlogyEcom DSN from the list box, and enter a Database login of sa, leaving the Database password box blank:

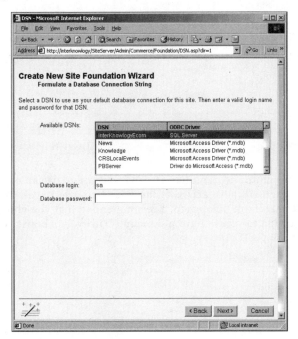

7. Click the Next > button to continue. As security is so important in any e-commerce environment, you need to specify a Windows NT account that will be in charge of managing your site. By default, this account will be placed into a local group, `Commerce_SITENAME`, and will have permissions to manage the site structure.

For security reasons, it's a good idea to use a user account on the local machine of the server as opposed to the domain. Having a specific local user account to manage the web site and commerce pages is much more secure than having a domain account, which could accidentally be given resources across your network and on other computers. If for some reason your Manager account is compromised, the damage would be limited to only one server instead of many across your domain. Administration is also easier to maintain with a local account, because all of the resources that this account will need to access will be on one server.

As you can see from the screen below, because we're logged in with Administrator privileges we're enabled to create a new account from this step of the Wizard. We will chose to use an existing account:

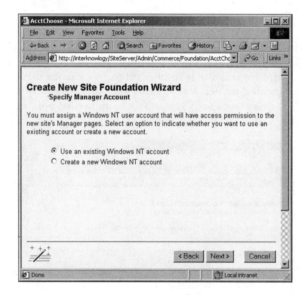

8. Click the Next > button to continue. Having selected to use an existing user, we need to specify which user will have access to the site's Manager pages. First we need to select the domain that the account belongs to. I recommended that you choose a user account on your local machine to separate from domain security, so choose the local server's domain from the list box:

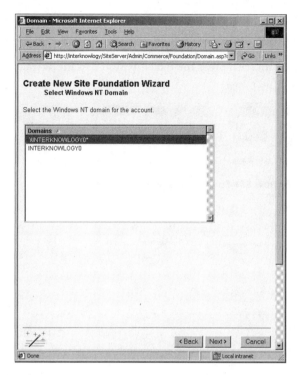

9. Click the Next > button to continue. Now select the local Administrator account from the list box:

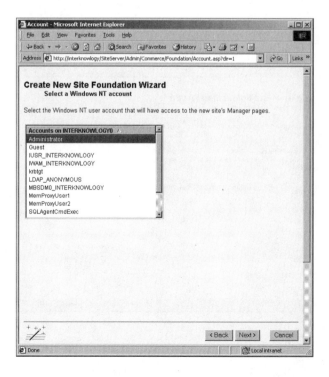

10. Click the Next > button for one last time. Now we have completed gathering all the information necessary to build the commerce foundation site. This is our last chance to go back and change any attributes that we aren't comfortable with. Since we're hopefully satisfied with our choices, press the Finish button and the Wizard will start processing our site:

When processing is complete, we will receive a page with a link that allows us to run the Site Builder Wizard:

The Site Builder Wizard will be used to create your commerce site and generate all the files and database tables that you'll use for your commerce pages. Once your site is built, you can use the Manager's page to change prices of products, close the site, view customer receipts, manage users and perform other important operations.

> *Notice the OK button at the bottom right of the previous screen. If you click this button you'll go to the Commerce Server Administration Page, in this case:*
> `http://localhost/SiteServer/Admin/Commerce/HostAdmin/default.asp`.
> *From the Commerce Server Administration page you can manage any of the commerce sites that are installed on your machine. For now, just leave the browser alone, because in the next step, you will click the URL that's shown as a link*
> `(http://localhost:80/IK_ecommerce/manager/default.asp)` *to run the Site Builder Wizard.*

Summary for the Site Foundation Wizard

The Site Foundation Wizard creates the basic building blocks (or architectural components) that are used in a Site Server 3.0 Commerce site.

By running the Site Foundation Wizard:

❑ Physical directories were created on your server

❑ Virtual directories were created within IIS

❑ Site configuration files were created containing the database connection strings and other site configuration data

❑ Software Components (COM and MTS) were installed and configured

Don't worry about the specifics of these just yet, as we'll be taking an in-depth look at them in the next chapter. For now we simply want to concentrate on getting our site up and running.

The Commerce Site Builder Wizard

Now that we have a site foundation to build upon, we will run the **Commerce Site Builder Wizard**. The Site Builder Wizard will populate the site with the components that make up the Commerce site. The Commerce Site Builder Wizard will help us dramatically by generating the ASP and HTML files, the commerce database tables and the pipeline components for your commerce site. When we are finished with the Wizard, we will have all of the pieces necessary for a fully functional e-commerce site that's ready for customization.

During the Wizard process of building our site, we can select various options that will allow for a significant degree of customization. Over the course of the Wizard, we will have the option of selecting how our site will be laid out, registration options, different departments, product identification, sales specials, as well as a different look and feel for our site.

We'll walk through the creation process for the wizard and I'll explain some of the options that we'll be faced with. Most of the options are simple, but some will need explaining, as they have to deal with commerce functionality that you might not be familiar with.

Using the Site Builder Wizard

1. The first step to using the Site Builder Wizard is to use the Manager site that you generated with the Site Foundation Wizard.

If you've not closed the last page of the Site Foundation Wizard, then simply click the link in the middle of the page (`http://localhost:80/IK_ecommerce/manager/default.asp`) to start the Site Builder Wizard.

Alternatively, you can run the Site Builder Wizard from the Manager page of the commerce site. This can be reached by navigating to the Commerce Host Administration snap-in of the Site Server Service Admin (MMC). You may need to refresh the host, but you should be able to expand the host node to see your newly created site. If you select your new site in the tree structure then in the right-hand pane you will see two links: one to Manage the site, the other to run through the site as a customer. Select the Manage option, right-click and select Browse from the pop-up menu:

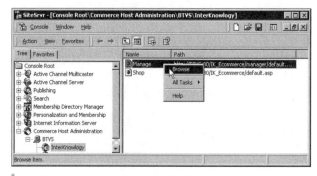

Either way you should now be at the first page of the Site Builder Wizard (again notice that it's browser-based):

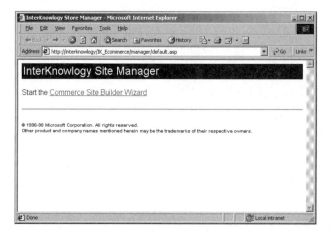

> **Be careful with this Wizard as you can overwrite your files if you're not careful. Once you've used the Site Builder Wizard, you won't want to run the Wizard again unless you're sure you want to overwrite all the files that it originally generated when you ran it the first time.**

2. Click the link Commerce Site Builder Wizard and you will be presented with page 1 of 14 of the Site Builder Wizard. This is the first step to start generating your site:

3. Click the Next > button to continue. The first order of business is to decide whether to customize one of the pre-installed demo sites that can be installed with Site Server Commerce Edition, or to design a fresh customized site. In case you want to customize one of the sample sites, here is a listing of some of sites that are installed:

❑ **Volcano Coffee:** This site was created for coffee lovers everywhere. You can purchase different types of coffees and view the different types of promotions that they offer to help sell their coffee. This is the most popular of the sample sites, and can be used as a great learning tool.

❑ **Microsoft Press:** This site details the process of buying and searching for titles from Microsoft Press. This site is based on the real Microsoft Press Bookstore.

❑ **Clocktower:** The Clocktower site sells specialty household clocks within the site and provides basic components of a commerce site. The Clocktower Sample Commerce site is built on a membership authenticated web site, and has a significant amount of configuration prerequisites before it can be built.

❑ **Microsoft Market:** This somewhat popular site demonstrates some business-to-business e-commerce components. This sample site is based on the Microsoft commerce that can process nearly five thousand orders a week.

As we want to explore all that the Site Builder Wizard can generate, we will chose to use the Create a custom site option:

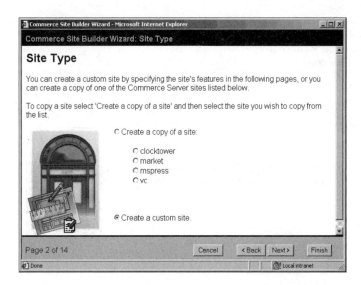

If you followed the installation instructions in Chapter 2 you won't have any of the sample sites installed. In that case, you'll simply be prompted to clicks the Next button at this step.

4. Click the Next > button to continue. You will move to page 3 of 14, which is the Merchant Information page. Here we enter information about our company and/or e-commerce site. The data from this page will be used on the About page, which, if you recall, is a link off the home page of the wizard-generated site:

5. Click the Next > button to continue and we will be prompted to specify the Locale of our site. This will affect the different options that your site will hold for displaying the currency, time, address information and calculating taxes:

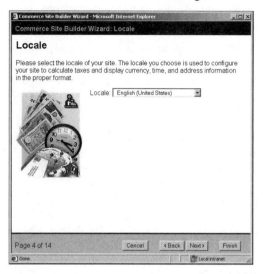

By default, the language will always be English, but choose which option you want to use depending on the country you live in. You'll notice further on in the Wizard the importance of this option when you move onto the Tax section of this Wizard.

6. Click the Next > button to move to page 5 of 14 of the Site Builder Wizard: the Site Style page. This page will help us to start shaping how our site is going to look once we've finished building with the Wizard. These are very basic options that you can change once the Wizard has finished building your site. Leave the top four options as the default settings and check the Use Logo box (we'll see later how to place our logo onto the pages, for now just let the Wizard know to allocate space for it):

7. Click the Next > button to move to the Promotions page. Most likely you're going to be interested in creating different promotions for your site. These different promotions can be used to specify additional discounts (Price promotions) and/or Cross-sell promotions:

❑ **Price Promotions**: Price promotions let you specify different offers and deals to shoppers on your site. You can choose different price promotions for the entire order that you want, depending on what they might buy. For example, you can offer a price promotion for a shopper, for an infinite or limited amount of time, that would give them "X" amount off one product if they bought a specified other product.

Price promotions can help you sell other products that would normally be used in conjunction with one another. If you were selling Palm Pilots on your site, you might offer a 5 % discount if a customer bought a Palm Pilot and Palm Modem, for an infinite or limited amount of time. This is an example of a Price Promotion.

❑ **Cross-Sell Promotions**: Cross-sell Promotions help you sell products that are related to the products you are buying. If you are selling Palm Pilots on your site, you can cross-sell similar products that are attributed with Palm Pilots, such as Palm Modems and Palm accessories. This helps you sell more products, and reminds the shoppers of their different options. This type of sales promotion can be used with Price Promotions for ever-greater profitability.

Choose both Price promotions and Cross-sell promotions:

8. Click the **Next >** button to progress to the Features page. The Features options within the Commerce Site Builder Wizard are very important in the creation of our site:

Firstly, the **Registration** option is used to help us keep track of our customers. There are a lot of opinions within e-commerce sites as to how companies want to get their customers to register with the site. Our options here are:

❑ None

❑ **On Entry**: This option forces the user to logon and register when they first come to visit the site (if they didn't register before). This option can sometimes turn off potential customers who just want to browse around and not buy anything on this visit. One would hope, however, that they would be attracted enough by your site to return at a later date and complete a purchase!

❑ **When Ordering**: Your other option is to have the user register when they are ready to purchase a product or submit their order. This is a good option, because the user isn't forced to do anything out of the ordinary until they are ready to buy something.

> It's important to note here that if you use the Registration options of the Site Builder Wizard, you will not be implementing the Site Server Personalization and Membership feature on your wizard-generated site. Unfortunately, the Commerce Site Foundation and Site Builder Wizards do not generate personalized, membership authenticated commerce sites. That means that if we want to include Personalization and Membership features at a later time, we have to do it ourselves – which would involve a ton of work!

With Departments, we can have multiple department types that will help us to organize the products we're going to be selling. For example, for our site, we will be selling Components, Media, and Books. These are all different Department Type's that can be created easily. The option here is to choose Simple or Variable Depth. A Simple level would mean you have a "flat" organization of the departments, and the Variable Depth option means that you can go many levels deep on the organization of the departments.

Here is an example to further explain both features:

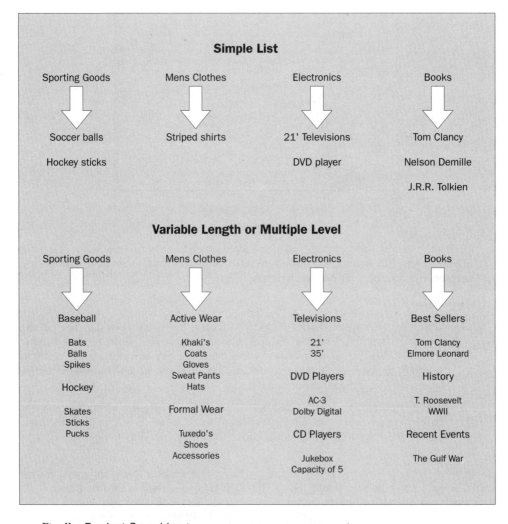

Finally, Product Searching is a must on any e-commerce site.

Choose When Ordering for Registration, Simple (single level) for Department Types, and Product Searching Enabled.

9. Click the Next > button to continue to move to the Product Attribute Type page. With Product Attribute Type you can specify the different attributes that your products will have. If you're only going to be selling a certain type, or products that are uniquely identified by a single SKU (Stock Keeping Unit-Product Number) then you'll want to choose Static Attributes. Static Attributes cannot be changed later, so it's best to be careful when choosing this option. You wouldn't want to pigeonhole yourself later on if you expand into a different type of product structure.

The more flexible, yet more complex option is to select Dynamic Attributes. Dynamic Attributes facilitate a product line where a single SKU might represent multiple products. For instance, a shirt has a SKU, but it contains variable attributes like size and color. You can modify your attributes subsequently in the Manager site. If you were going to be creating a site similar to Amazon.com's different store types, you would need to use the Dynamic Attributes, because you would never know how many attributes you would need in the future.

Since the sample products (Components, Books, and Media) all have a single SKU for each product, we will chose Static Attributes:

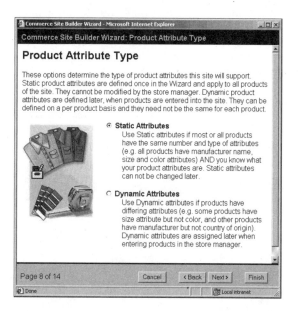

10. Click the Next > button to continue. Screen 9 of 14 of the Site Builder Wizard allows you to choose different product attributes. Since we only need SKU, name, description and price, we don't need to add any optional attributes to our product structure:

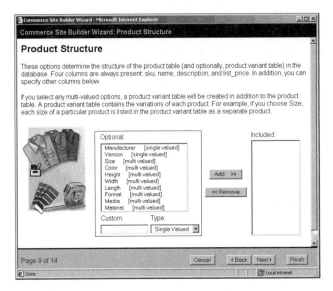

11. Simply click Next > to move to the Shipping and Handling page. This page has some powerful options. As you can control how you want to price your Shipping & Handling methods, you have total control over pricing options. Many e-commerce sites play around with this option, so that their products are very cheap at face value but they make up the difference in price with elevated shipping costs.

This option is frequently circumvented with custom third-party pipeline components from Independent Software Vendors (see Appendix C) that calculate the various shipping costs.

We will simply select the default shipping options for our site:

12. Click the Next > button to continue. Earlier in this wizard, you specified the Locale that you were going to use on the site. This directly affects the Tax option on page 11 – the Site Builder Wizard: SSCE bases your tax listings on your Locale.

With this Wizard, you're permitted to enable which states you want to calculate tax from, and what percentage of the total price tax is going to be. This is a very simplistic calculation of tax. However, American tax law is very complicated, so if you're going to be doing e-commerce on the Internet you'll want to purchase third-party pipeline components that will do all of the calculations for you. It's even more complex when you sell internationally.

Just for the sake of this example, we'll chose to calculate tax on purchases made in California.

Note this in no way covers the consumers tax liability in California for an Internet purchase.

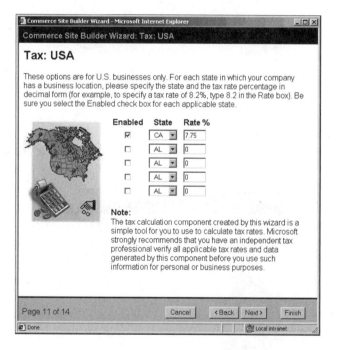

13. Click the Next > button to continue to the Payment Methods page. Site Server Commerce Edition. supports four common credit card Payment Methods that we can use to automate the sales for our site.

Once the Wizard has finished, and you have people shopping on your site, Site Server will only verify that the formation of the numbers on the credit card is valid. You will need additional software – most likely in the form of a Pipeline component that will integrate into your Commerce Interchange Pipeline – that will do real-time processing and transactions for credit cards. Refer to Appendix C for an extensive list of companies that provide these products.

We'll chose to support all four credit cards:

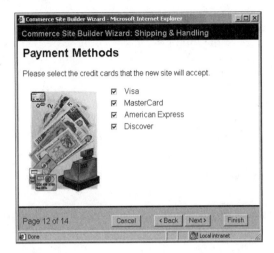

14. Click the Next > button to continue. Part of the power of tracking your users over time is tracking Order History. This is very important when choosing what products to keep within your inventory, seeing what products aren't selling and examining the buying trends of your shoppers.

We want to do this, so check the check box next to Retain Order History and Receipt information:

15. Click the Next > button to continue. We're just about done with the Commerce Site Builder Wizard, so consequently, it's almost time to start auto-generating the different pages that will make up our site. Before we do though, we need to choose the output options of the Wizard.

Really, the only option on the creation of a new site is whether or not to load sample data into the product and department tables. We will choose not to, as this is a completely custom site, so leave the Load Sample Data into Database option unchecked.

The Load Schema into Database option is mandatory for SQL Server so you can create your tables within your commerce database, so make sure to check it. If you were using a different backend database such as Oracle, you wouldn't want to select this option, as the SQL scripts wouldn't update any other database besides Microsoft SQL Server.

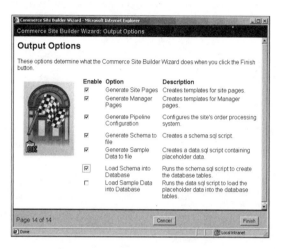

16. Click on Finish and the pages will begin to generate automatically. You will see a listing similar to the screen below:

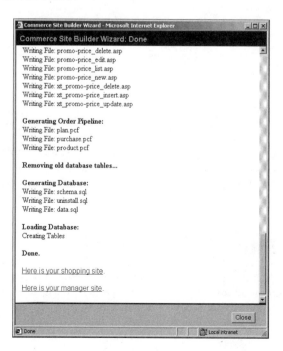

At the bottom of the screen are links to the shopping site and to the manager site, but you can close all the pages on your screen and navigate to either site from the Commerce Host Administration snap-in of the Site Server Service Administrator (MMC).

Summary for the Site Builder Wizard

The Commerce Site Builder Wizard facilitates the construction of a site with the basic commerce components that you would need to start an e-commerce site. You have setup your home page, registration, promotions, and departments, as well as managed your purchasing and shipping components. These basics will let you charge into the next phase of your site, as you populate your site with data and customize its look and feel.

Image File Configuration

Before we start adding products to our e-commerce site from the Manager site, we need to move our images to the appropriate folders on the web site. Notice from the screen shot below that the company logo needs to be named `logo.gif`, and it needs to reside in `...\SITENAME\assets\images` for the wizard-generated commerce site to use it:

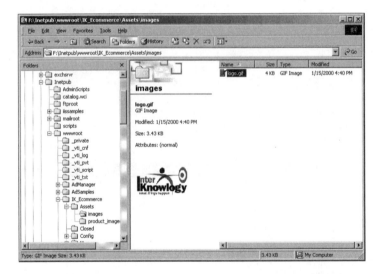

And all the product images need to reside in `...\SITENAME\assets\product_images` for the wizard-generated commerce site to use them. When we add products to the site (later in the chapter), we will be allowed to type the name of the image file for each product, but it must reside in the `product_images` folder.

The Manager Site

Now that we've finished building our first commerce site, it's time to populate the site with our Departments, Products, promotions and customizations to will make it complete. We've used the wizards to build the foundation and commerce components for the site, now it's time to finish the management section.

The **Management Site** helps us manage the different parts of our commerce solution, including the different Departments, Products, Promotions, Orders and managing our Shoppers. Each of these different sections has a separate page: you can add, remove and edit the different sections of your site through the Management web site.

You can navigate to the Manager site from the Commerce Host Administrator snap-in the Site Server Service Admin (MMC). You access it by using the same means as described when starting the Site Builder Wizard (it will no longer run the Wizard):

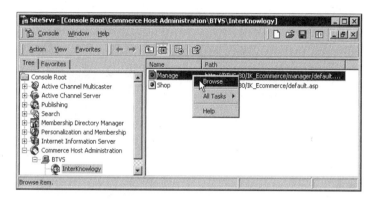

Here is the home page of the Site Manager site:

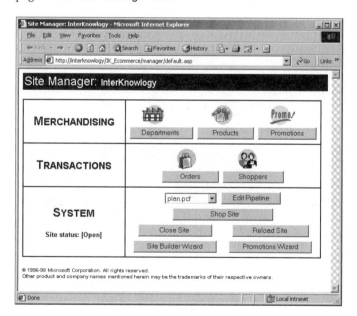

Departments

With the Department page, you can create different departments to organize your site. This is the first level where you can start customizing your site. Depending on what products you're offering on your site, you can create department headings for each of your products. From each department heading, you have the option of specifying and adding different products, inventories, and prices to your new commerce site.

1. Click the Departments button from the main page to be taken to the Departments Management page:

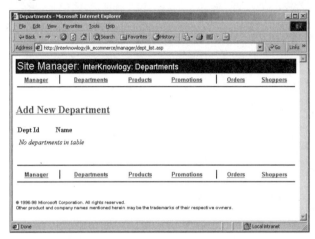

2. We must enter departments before we can enter products, so click the big Add New Department link.

Notice from the screen below that adding a department to the site is simply a matter of coming up with a department ID, a name, and a description:

Enter the details for the first of our departments, Components:

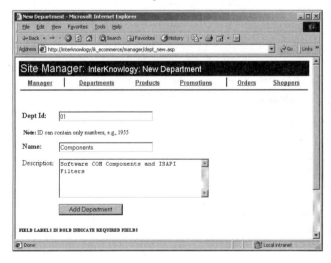

3. After entering the department details click the Add Department button.

4. Add two more departments for `Media` and `Books`, following the steps above. Your Department page will look like this:

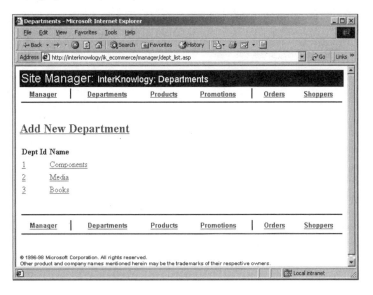

Products

Now, it's time to move on to products.

1. Click the link for <u>Products</u>, and you will receive a screen similar, if not identical to, the one below:

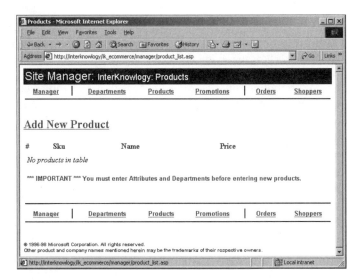

2. Click the <u>Add New Product</u> link to start the process of entering products:

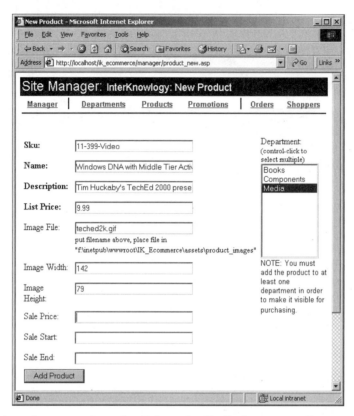

Notice from the screen above that I chose the Media department. I've entered a Sku, Name, Description and List Price.

As mentioned previously, you can type the name of the product image file as long as it resides in the `product_images` folder. The Image Width and Height are in the format of pixels. I used Microsoft Photo Editor to tell me the actual image size in pixels of each of my product images, but almost any drawing or graphics software will be able to tell you. Lastly, you can enter simple price promotions on the Product page with a start and an end, but I've chosen not to with this particular product.

3. Enter all the products to create the screen below:

Now that your products are entered, you can if you want go to the home page of the site and enter a few orders. Remember that you can use the Visa credit card number 4111 1111 1111 1111 for test orders.

Promotions

One of the most powerful features of Site Server sites is the ability to manage different promotions, which help you sell more products to your customers. You can use the Promotions Button to manage, delete, and create different promotions for your products, goods or services. You can create different price and cross-sell promotions, as well as create a 'to-do list' of modifications that you'll need to make to your site in order to allow for the promotions to work.

1. Click the <u>Promotions</u> link on the Site manager, then click the Price Promotions link to receive a screen similar to the one below:

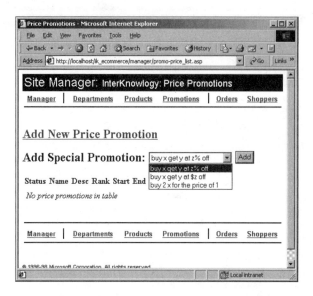

2. We are going to build the promotion that was shown early in the chapter – where if a consumer bought the ISAPI filter they got the Active Directory COM Objects for free. First, select the buy x get y at z% off option from the drop-down, and then click the Add button. You'll be presented with a screen similar to the one below:

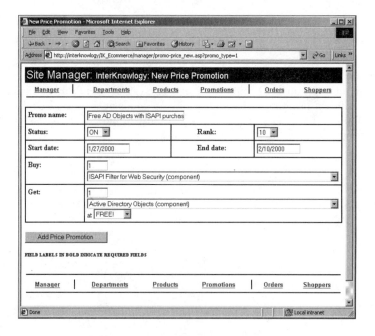

3. Now we need to give our promotion a name and set the other properties:

- ❑ The **Status** of the promotion will be **ON** by default.
- ❑ The **Rank** of the promotion is used to determine what promotions take precedence when multiple promotions apply to a purchase. The lower the number (10 being the lowest choice), the higher the precedence of the promotion.
- ❑ You are allowed to put finite limits on your promotions and have them start in the future with the **Start** and **End** dates.
- ❑ In the **Buy** section, you can trigger the promotion with the product and the amount.
- ❑ In the **Get** section, you define what you receive as a result of qualifying for the promotion. In this case, the consumer gets the Active Directory Objects for free (100% off).

4. After clicking the **Add Price Promotion** button, your promotions page will look similar to the one below:

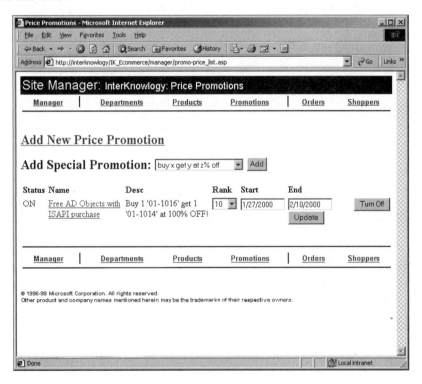

5. If you click on the link of the name of the promotion (Free AD Objects with ISAPI Purchase), and then click the Advanced Attributes link at the bottom of the page, you will get a page that has options to view or change all the attributes of a promotion:

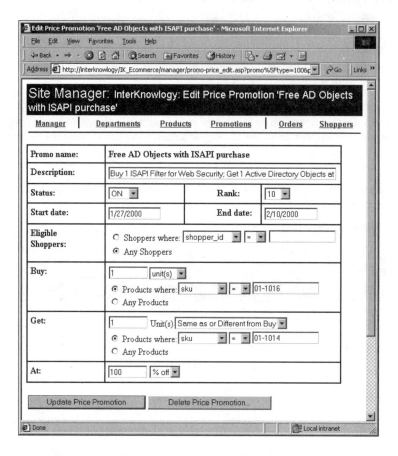

Managing Transactions

Now, why don't you place some orders using the new price promotion that you just added?

Grab a new instance of the browser (so that you can come back to the Site Manager when you're done), navigate to the shoppers site and place a few orders.

Orders

The Orders section of the Site Manager is where orders are aggregated so that you can manage them.

1. Click on the <u>Orders</u> link on the Site Manger site. If you have placed any orders on the site, you will receive a screen, similar to the one below, where all orders are listed:

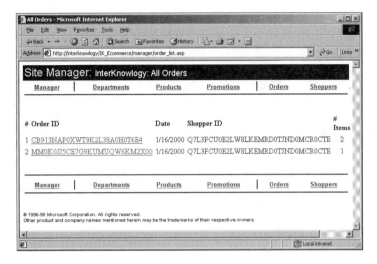

Here is an example from the Manager's site, where we're looking at the orders that have been made. You can use the Order Manger site to view your orders by Month, Year, Product, Shopper or all orders.

2. Click the link on the Order ID to get a complete listing of what was purchased:

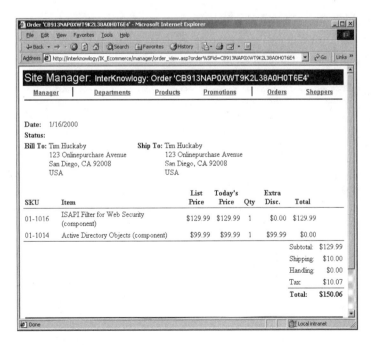

Shoppers

The Shoppers section of the Site Manager is where online shopper data is aggregated so that you can manage them.

3. Now, click the Shoppers link on the Site Manager. You will receive a screen similar to the one below:

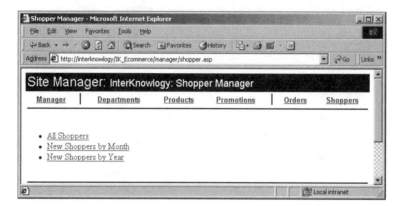

From the Shopper Manager screen you can choose to view your all your shoppers, by month and by year. Since we have probably only entered one shopper on our site, we'll basically get the same view, no matter which we choose.

4. Choose All Shoppers and you'll receive a screen similar to the one below:

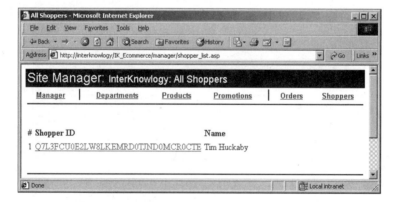

5. In the previous screen shot, you'll see that the Shopper ID is a link. Choose it now to move to a more detailed view of the shopper:

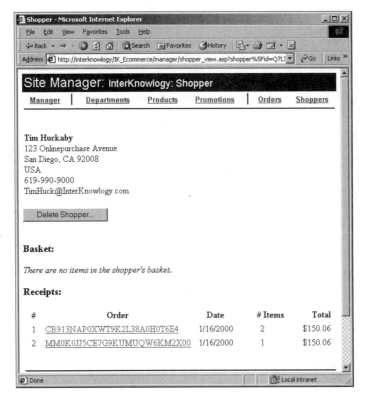

Notice that in addition to the orders that have been placed by this shopper, the actual items of the basket (if there were any) are listed. There is also a button to delete the shopper from this screen, but not an option to change any data, like address or phone numbers. You will probably want to add a page to do that.

Summary

The basis of this chapter was to help get you on your feet and up to speed with the Site Server Commerce Edition Site Generation Wizards. We started by exploring the functionality of a wizard-generated site. Then we actually learned how to build that same site capable of processing user data from within an on-line store.

Through this process we have seen that:

❑ The Commerce Site Foundation Wizard was responsible for building the basic components of the on-line store, connecting to a database, and building the underlying files needed for the architectural foundation of the site.

❑ The Commerce Site Builder Wizard populated the database and directory structure with the necessary commerce objects and web pages.

❏ The Site Manager is used to manage the departments, products, promotions, orders and shoppers.

Now we've finished building our site, in the next chapter, we can start examining the assortment of ASP, HTML and SQL database calls that are automatically generated upon installation. By taking a better look at how each piece fits together, we'll have a better understanding as how the Site Wizards work and we can start enhancing our own wizard-generated e-commerce site.

Under the Hood of a Site Server E-Commerce Site

First, let me set expectations – a Site Server 3.0 Commerce Edition, wizard-generated commerce site contains some seriously advanced-level code. Considering all the functionality that we are given in a wizard-generated site that might go without saying. Unfortunately, all this power comes at a price: Even if you are an experienced ASP and/or COM programmer, you'll find the generated code complex. I've been developing/using the Commerce product for centuries (in Internet years) and there are still a few black boxes that I don't totally understand. Is that a crisis? –Absolutely not. It's not necessary to know every little detail about the Commerce product. It's not necessary to have an advanced level understanding of each component or bit of technology to be effective in customizing your commerce site.

Just the other day I met with a new client. One of the first things he said to me was, "I worked on the NT 3.51 team. I'm a smart guy, I'm an MCSD (Microsoft Certified Solution Developer) and an MCT (Microsoft Certified Trainer) and I have tons of experience developing the HTML, components and ASP of a Windows DNA site, so I ran the wizards and generated a commerce site. After staring at the code, I was overwhelmed. That's why you're here." I smiled and said, "Guess what? I've only heard that a thousand times. Here's what we are going to do. We are going to take to spend some time breaking the site down. You will feel much more comfortable about diving into development on your site after that. I promise."

So that is my intention for this chapter. My mission is to break this monster down into understandable parts. You'll feel much better, after completing this chapter, about the technologies contained in a wizard-generated site. So comfortable, in fact, that you will be ready for Chapter 6, where you jump right in and go through some common custom software development tasks on your commerce site.

Throughout this chapter we will discuss the structure of a wizard-generated site in detail:

❑ The database structure of a wizard-generated store
  First, we will take a look at the table structure of the database that the Site Builder Wizard created for you when you ran it in Chapter 4.

❑   The file structure of a wizard-generated store
     Next, we'll walk through the files that are created by the Site Builder Wizard. We'll go in
     depth into the functionality of the `global.asa`, the ASP pages of the site, the include files
     and the resource files.

❑   The COM object structure of a wizard-generated store
     Lastly, we'll look at some of the most important COM objects that are used in a wizard-
     generated site.

Let's start our discussion with the backend of the site by examining the data structures in the data store.

The Database Structure

Depending on the answers you provided in the Site Builder Wizard, a relational database was created
for you with 6 to 12 tables. The site you built in Chapter 4, contains 9 tables in a SQL Server database.
This database is used to house the basket, department, product, promotion, receipt, and shopper data.

> *Site Server 3.0 Commerce Edition is actually compatible with Oracle databases and the Site
> Builder Wizard can generate sites that use Oracle instead of SQL Server as its backend database,
> but the installation is not as automated and beyond the scope of this book.*

The most common tool to analyze the structure of any SQL Server database is the **SQL Server
Enterprise Manager**. I am using Microsoft SQL Server 7.0 on the same computer that I am running Site
Server (see Chapter 3 for installation details) so I will be examining the SQL Server 7.0 Enterprise
Manager. SQL Server 7.0 tools like the Enterprise Manager can also be installed on a client machine.
The steps will not be dissimilar for SQL Server 6.5.

1.   Run it now (Start | Programs | Microsoft SQL Server 7.0 | Enterprise Manger) from your
         SQL Server or client machine.

> *If this is the first time that you have run the SQL Server 7.0 Enterprise Manager (and it shouldn't
> be since you used it in Chapters 3 and 4) you will need to register your SQL Server. If you need to
> register your SQL server, you can do it by right-clicking on* SQL Server Group *and then clicking
> on* New SQL Server Registration

2.   Expand the Microsoft SQL Servers, SQL Server Group and the name of your database
         server in the left-hand pane so that you can see a list of folders for your server.

3.   Expand the Databases folder so that you can see the list of installed databases on the
         server.

4.   Find the InterKnowlogyEcom database and expand it so you can see the Tables node and
         left-click on it to display the list of tables in the right-hand pane:

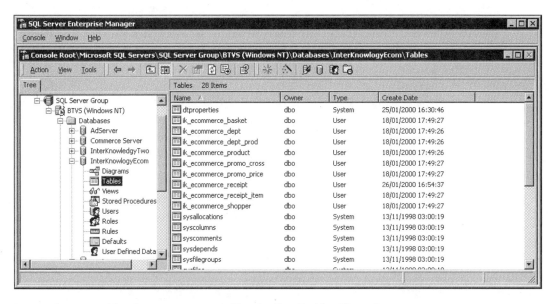

Notice the nine tables that were generated by the Site Builder Wizard.

The other tables (beginning with **sys** *and the* **dtproperties** *table) are system tables that are part of every SQL Server database. Each table subscribes to a naming convention.*

Each table's prefix is the short name of the commerce site and an underscore. In this case it's ik_ecommerce_. This format allows you to store the database tables for multiple commerce sites in the same database.

❑ **The Basket Table**
Contains the shopping basket information for each shopper that has not completed a purchase yet.

❑ **The Dept Table**
Contains the department information for the site.

❑ **The Dept_Prod Table**
Contains the key data that links the products in the Product table to the departments that they belong to in the Dept table.

❑ **The Product Table**
Contains the products available for sale on the wizard-generated commerce site.

❑ **The Promo_Cross Table**
Contains the details of each cross-sell promotion available on the site.

❑ **The Promo_Price Table**
Contains the details of each price promotion available on the site.

❑ **The Receipt Table**
Contains the receipt information for each order header.

❑ **The Receipt_Item Table**
Contains the receipt information for each line item of the orders that are placed on the site.

❑ **The Shopper Table**
Contains the shopper information.

Remember, from the Site Builder Wizard from Chapter 4 that we chose to have the visitors to the site **Register** when ordering. The `Shopper` table is a result of that choice. If we were to choose the **Never** option for the registration option in the Site Builder Wizard then a `Shopper` table would not be created.

5. Right-click on the `Shopper` table (ik_ecommerce_shopper) and notice among all the options on the pop-up menu that you can choose **Design Table**, where you can actually go into a structural edit of the table so that you can add or delete columns (among other things).

6. Now choose **Open Table** | **Return all rows:**

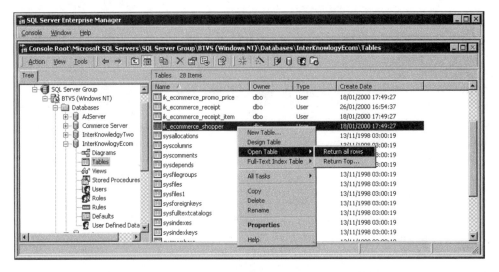

This will perform the Transact SQL statement: `SELECT * FROM Shoppers` thereby returning all the data contained in the table:

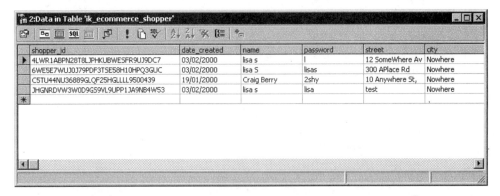

7. Peruse through the shopper data. You will see the data from the shoppers that have registered on your commerce site. If you close this window and right-click on the table again, you can also choose **Properties** on the Shopper table that will display the field properties of the table:

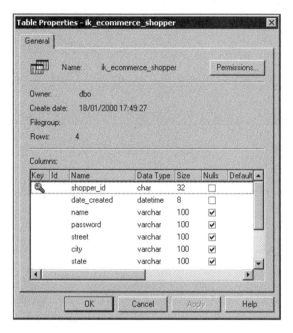

8. Now, Open Table | Return all rows for the Products table (ik_ecommerce_product). The data should look very familiar because it will contain all the products that you entered when you were using the Site Manager in Chapter 4:

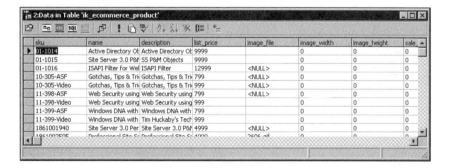

9. Now, Open Table | Return all rows for the Receipts table (ik_ecommerce_receipt). This is where the orders that have been placed on the site are accumulated. Notice that the data is in a different format:

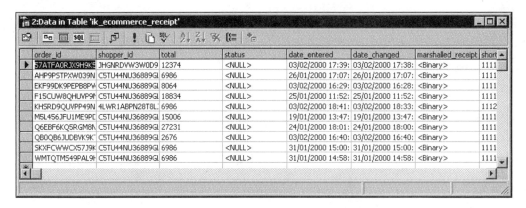

There is a field in the receipts table called marshalled_receipt and it is of **Binary** format. The actual order data is "marshaled" in the database.

10. Explore the rest of the ik_ecommerce_ tables to learn where data such as departments and promotions are stored.

SQL Server Query Analyzer

Now, let's take a look at the **SQL Server Query Analyzer**. You can run it from within the SQL Server Enterprise Manager by clicking Tools from the menu and then selecting SQL Server Query Analyzer. The SQL Query Analyzer can also be executed from the Start menu: Start | Programs | Microsoft SQL Server | Query Analyzer

If you are working with SQL Server, you may want to use this SQL Query Analyzer tool to query the database for information, or test your queries before you insert them into your site to verify that they retrieve the proper information.

The SQL Server Query Analyzer is also available for installation on a client machine by way of a client installation from the SQL Server 7.0 installation CD.

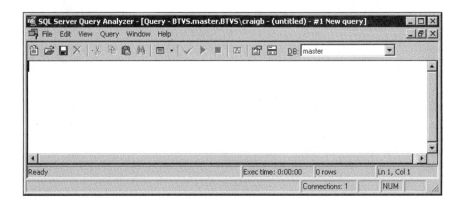

Once you have this tool installed, it is relatively easy to get going. All you have to do is connect to the server you are using via the **Connection** screen that pops up when you start the application and select the database you are going to be querying in the **DB:** drop-down box in the top-right.

However, you still need to type or paste in SQL statements directly, which means you'll need to have at least some knowledge of the language that SQL server speaks in, Transact SQL.

Later in this chapter we will look at the `global.asa` file in the store we created in Chapter 4. In the `global.asa` you will see a number of lines, such as:

```
Set MSCSQueryMap.depts = AddQuery("SELECT dept_id, dept_name, dept_description" & _
                             " FROM ik_ecommerce_dept")
```

The query here is `SELECT dept_id, dept_name, dept_description FROM ik_ecommerce_dept`

You can cut out the query itself, and paste it into your SQL Server Query Analyzer query window and run the query by:

- ❑ Pressing *Control+E* to execute
- ❑ Clicking **Query**, then **Execute** from the menu
- ❑ Pressing the *F5* key
- ❑ Clicking the **Execute Query** button (which is the green triangle)

Remember to select the InterKnowologyEcom database in the DB drop-down.

You will receive the results from the database for that query. In this case, it is the `dept_id`, `dept_name` and `dept_description` columns in the `ik_ecommerce_dept` table:

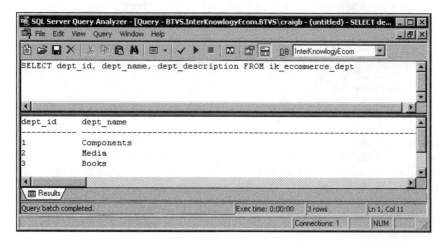

You will need to scroll the Results pane in order to see the dept_description column.

When you modify the queries in your site, it's usually a good idea to use the SQL Server Query Analyzer to try them out before you actually implement them.

Now let me show you some tools that perform the same functionality in a much easier and more powerful manner than the SQL Server Enterprise Manager and the SQL Server Query Analyzer that I just showed you above.

Database Modeling

Database modeling tools are extremely valuable in helping you understand the data structure of any database. These types of tools can help you understand the way the database is built and they give you a very powerful way to change the database tables with a graphical user interface. The built-in database modeling tools that come with Visual Studio are quite impressive. For instance, by creating a Database Project in Visual Interdev you can access both the data, as well as the structure of the database. Let's try it out on the database for the commerce site we generated in Chapter 4.

1. Start Visual Interdev. When the **New Project** dialog appears, navigate to the **Database Projects** folder on the **New** tab and select **New Database Project**. Give the new project the Name IK_DB:

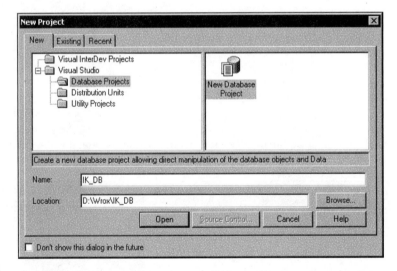

You can use the <u>L</u>ocation setting to place the database project in any folder you have rights to.

2. Click **Open** and you'll be prompted to select the Data Source Name that communicates with your SQL Server database. I am using Visual Studio, which is installed on the server that I installed my commerce site from Chapter 4, so I can use the very same DSN that the site uses. In that chapter we talked about how to set up DSN on your computer.

If you are using Windows NT 4.0 you will get a dialog similar to the following screen, which allows you to choose a DSN from the **Machine Data Source** tab:

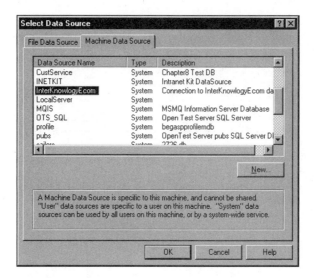

If you are using Windows 2000, you'll get a different looking dialog, but the behavior is still the same. You need to choose the DSN that communicates to your SQL Server by clicking the Connection tab and then choosing the DSN:

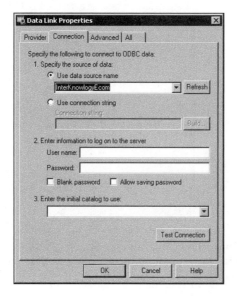

3. Click OK to continue and you will be prompted to authenticate for the sa account (if the sa account is, in fact, the account you used to set up the DSN as per the instructions in the previous chapter):

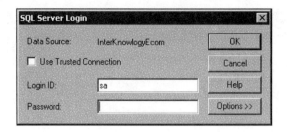

4. Click OK after typing your password (if you have assigned a password to your sa account otherwise leave it blank) to continue. You will end up in the Visual InterDev user interface, with your database opened as a project, which is displayed on the right, in the Project Explorer and Data View windows:

5. In the Data View window, expand the InterKnowlogyEcom database icon. Further explore the database structure by expanding the Tables icon. The tables should look familiar from the Enterprise Manager steps earlier in the chapter, but notice that the system tables have not been included:

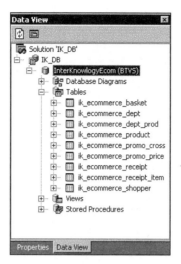

6. Double-click on the ik_ecommerce_dept table and the contents of the table will be displayed for viewing:

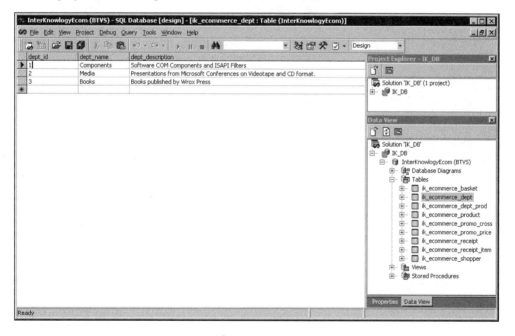

7. Now right-click on Database Diagrams in the Data View window and choose New Diagram. A blank database diagram will appear in the main window of Visual Interdev.

8. Drag the ik_ecommerce_product table onto the blank database diagram.

9. Right-click on the product table in your diagram and choose <u>A</u>dd Related Tables:

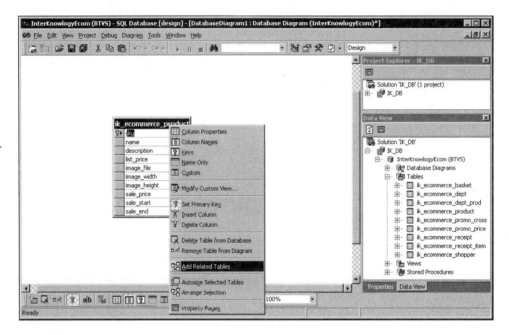

Automatically, the `dept_prod` and `promo_cross` tables are added to the diagram because referential integrity, which in its most simplistic explanation is an enforced relationship between tables, has been enforced on those tables when the wizard created them.

For an in-depth discussion of referential integrity see the Wrox book Professional SQL Server 7.0 (ISBN: 1-861002-31-9).

10. Right-click on the ik_ecommerce_product table again and choose **Arrange Selection**. The tables will be automatically arranged on the database diagram for the best possible viewing of them:

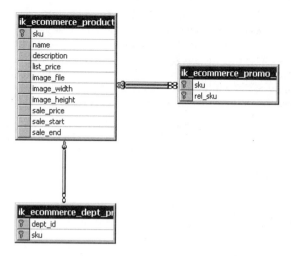

Notice the foreign key/one-to-many relationships that dept_prod *and* promo_cross *share with products – as represented by a small chain with a key.*

11. Now drag the rest of the tables (dept, shopper, basket, promo_price, receipt, and receipt_item) onto the database diagram and print it. This will be a handy reference for you while you dissect your wizard-generated commerce site. Go ahead and save your database diagram. I am sure you will refer to it again and you will want to update it if you add tables or make changes to your commerce site:

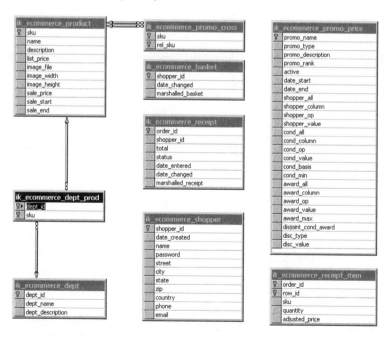

There are more powerful modeling tool such as ERWin from Platinum Software or PowerDesigner DataArchitect from Sybase Inc. whose sole purpose is data modeling. One nice feature of these modeling tools is they generate documentation based on information you have entered – giving you the power of a 20-page addendum to your documentation of the web site with the click of a button. Once you have reverse engineered the generated database schema into your modeling tool, you will be able make changes rapidly and easily within this tool, and then propagate these changes into the database. Your DB tool should be able to generate scripts as well as access the database directly to make changes.

You can download free trial-versions for both these products at their respective sites:

❑   ERWin: `http://www.platinum.com`

❑   PowerDesigner: `http://www.sybase.com`

The Visual Interdev Query Tool

When you create a database project in Visual InterDev you get a query tool that also allows you to run your queries directly on the SQL Server.

1.   Close the diagram window from before.

2.   Double-click on the product table from the **Data View** window and Visual Interdev will open the `Products` table. In fact, what Visual Interdev has done is execute a `SELECT * FROM ik_eccomerce_product` SQL statement.

3.   From the **V**iew menu choose **Toolbars** and then **Query**. This will bring up the **Query** toolbar (if it isn't visible already).

4.   Click the **Show SQL Pane** button on the toolbar and you'll see the Transact SQL that was just executed:

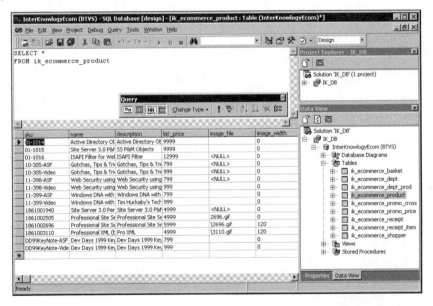

Now that you have the **SQL Pane** available you can type any valid Transact SQL statement in the window and execute it just like you can in the SQL Server Query Analyzer.

5. Add the words ORDER BY sku DESC to the end of the SELECT * FROM ik_ecommerce_product and then click the Exclamation point (Run) button to execute the query. The results will be sorted in sku order descending:

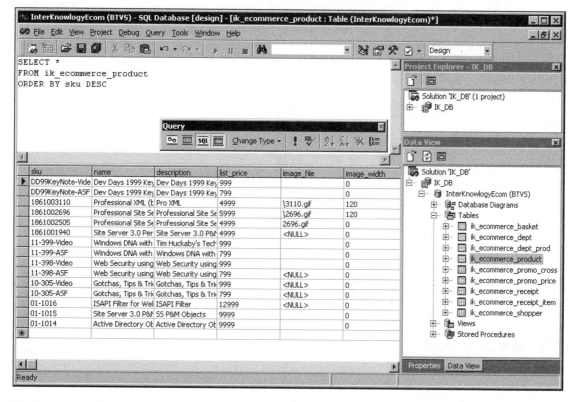

We have just scratched the surface here. The data tools integrated in Visual Studio are very powerful and are well documented in the Visual Studio documentation.

The File Structure

The next step to understanding the functionality of a wizard-generated e-commerce site is to examine the file structure of the store, how the scripts are called, as well as the directory structure that was created for us when we first generated our site in Chapter 4.

The Directory Structure

Let's first look at the **directory structure** of a wizard-generated site. All files are congregated under the virtual directory that was created by the wizard would physically reside under wwwroot by default, but could reside anywhere. In the site that was built in Chapter 4, which, if you followed the recommendations, would be:

    \Inetpub\wwwroot\IK_Ecommerce

Examine the directory structure of the site built in Chapter 4 below:

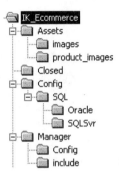

The Site Root

The main root of the site, in this case IK_Ecommerce, contains the majority of the ASP that are executed when a visitor comes to the site. We'll take a look at the files contained in the root of the site in detail later in the chapter.

The Assets Folder

The Assets folder is where all images and multimedia files reside. The Assets folder contains the images that are used in the site (GIFs, JPGs, etc.). The company logo file resides in the images folder and the product image files reside in the product_images folder.

The Closed Folder

The Closed folder contains just one file, closed.asp, which contains the HTML that is rendered to the visitors when the store is closed.

The Config Folder

The Config folder contains the Plan, Product and Purchase pipeline files (*.pcf).

> *Pipelines are explained in detail in Chapter 7, and then we show you how to build pipeline components in Chapter 8.*

The Config folder also houses the site.csc file that contains the hard coded site information, like the DSN used for database access and its password. The Transact SQL (*.sql) scripts that create and populate the database are stored in the SQL\SQLSvr folder off the Config folder.

The Manager Folder

The `Manager` folder contains all of the ASP and include files for the Site Manager Application.

ASP File Types

Now, take a look at the files in the root directory of the site again:

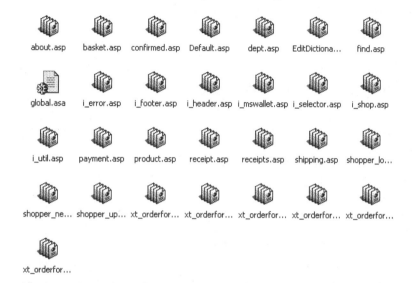

Notice that there are two naming conventions prevalent in the root directory of the site. The first naming convention – files with the prefix `i_` are **include** files.

> **Include files contain common functions and code snippets that are used in many places on your commerce site. They are included in an ASP page with an HTML INCLUDE directive in the format:** `<!-- #INCLUDE FILE="i_shop.asp" -->`
>
> **When a file is included in an ASP page, it becomes part of page and is processed by IIS's Script interpreter as such. By separating out common code into include files, you gain an incredible site maintenance advantage. When it comes time to update or fix code, you only have to fix it one place! Can you imagine having to change a function that is currently contained in** `i_shop.asp` **and it wasn't contained in an include file? You'd have to change it in 100+ places! In addition to being a pain, it would be very risky to make that many changes without accidentally breaking something.**

The next naming convention is files that start with `xt_`. Files with the prefix `xt_` do not contain HTML, only VBScript. Files that start with `xt_` use the `Redirect` method on the `Response` object to redirect users back to the page that called it or another page for processing.

> ASP files in your commerce site that begin with `xt_` have no user interface. They are called and executed from within other ASP files and always `Redirect` back to the original calling ASP or to another ASP files when processing has completed.
>
> Here's the very last line of `xt_orderform_additem.asp`. Notice how it redirects to the Basket page when processing is complete:
>
> ```
> call Response.Redirect("basket.asp?" & _
>                         mscsPage.URLShopperArgs())
> ```

The Pages in the Order Process

The order process on the site that you built in the previous chapter is the process by which consumers place orders on your commerce site. Let's now look at the main Active Server Pages involved in this process.

The Home Page (default.asp)

The start page (Home page or Lobby of the commerce site) welcomes the user with a list of available departments. It is also where you would display special offers and news. Registered shoppers who return to the Home page of the site after placing an order (or return in a separate visit by authenticating with their username and password) are presented with links to monitor their account or view their order history:

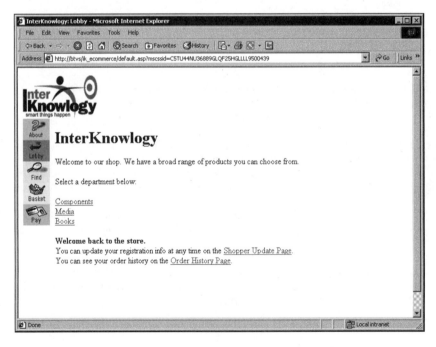

The Departments Page (dept.asp)

When you click on one department from `default.asp`, you get either a sub-department or all the available products for that department displayed on the `dept.asp` page. The `id` of the department selected is passed to this page in the query string:

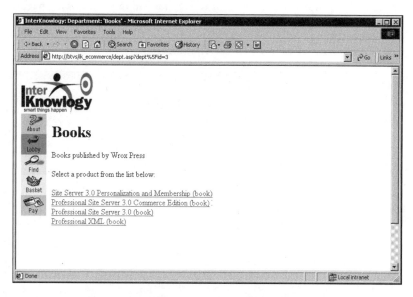

If you proceed by clicking on a product in the list you will end up on the product's Product page.

The Product Pages (product.asp)

The Products pages on your commerce site are where consumers can add products to their shopping baskets. The department `id` and `sku` id are passed to this page in the query string from `dept.asp`:

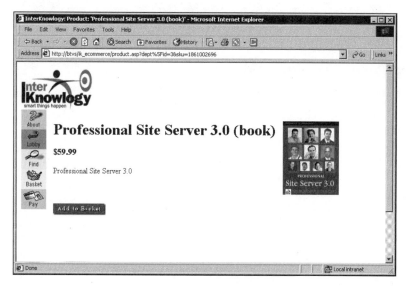

After a product has been added to the basket from a Product page you are redirected to the Basket page.

The Basket Page (basket.asp)

In the Basket page, the contents of the shopper's basket is viewed, and the shopper is given the opportunity to modify the quantity of each item or to continue on to the Shipping page. If the quantity is set to zero, the item is removed automatically. In between the Products page and the Basket page the Lookup Shopper page might be used to determine the ShopperID. This ShopperID is passed to all subsequent pages as the `mscssid` value in the query string:

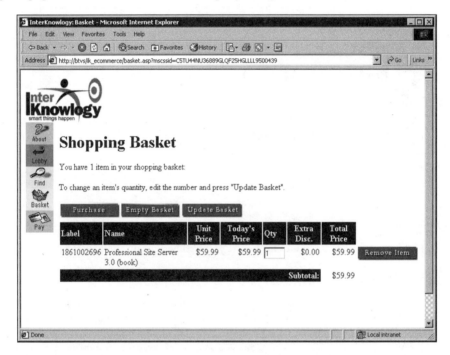

When the Purchase button is hit from this page the Shipping page is loaded.

The Shipping Page (shipping.asp)

The Shipping page is where the shipping method and shipping address information is entered:

The Payment Page (payment.asp)

The Payment page contains the costs of the order subtotaled and totaled. It is also where the credit card information and billing, address are entered:

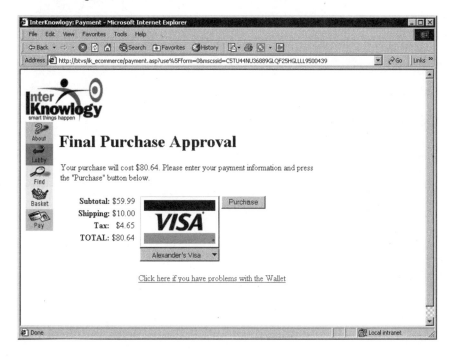

The Order Confirmation Page (confirmed.asp)

When you succeed with your purchase you are redirected to a "Thank you" page that contains a link to a printable receipt for your order. Unfortunately, by default, a wizard-generated commerce site uses a randomly generated, 26-alpha-numerical character order number. Most people find the format of this number unmanageable. Consequently, we will show how to change this to a more manageable number in the next chapter:

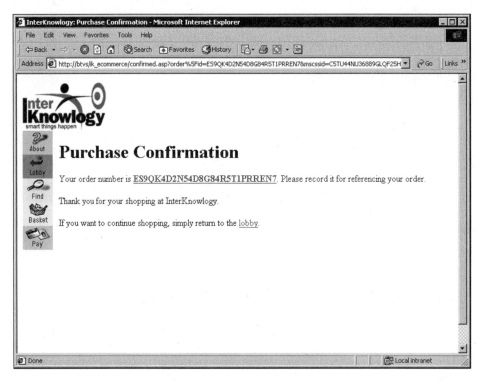

The Receipt Page (receipt.asp)

Finally, if you click the order number on the `confirmed.asp` you are sent to this Receipt page, which can be printed for your records:

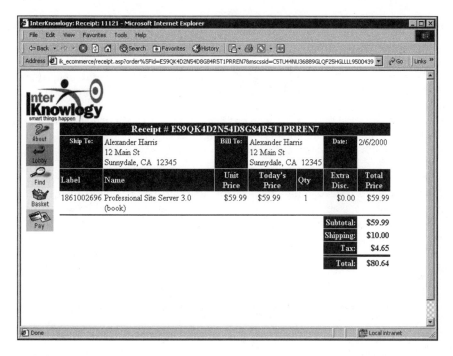

The picture below summarizes the pages in the order process and the relationship between them:

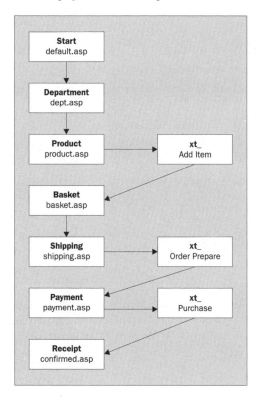

The global.asa File

Each wizard-generated site contains a **global.asa** configuration file that stores event code and objects used by the web application. The `global.asa` or **Global Server file** is probably the most important file within your commerce site because it loads all of your Commerce objects into memory upon startup of the web site. We'll be looking at Commerce objects in the next section of this chapter.

Within the `global.asa` file there is a `Application_OnStart` event, which is responsible for loading all of your Commerce components and Application variables the first time a user touches a page on the site. Application objects are accessible from within any ASP page on the site.

When you start or restart your site or web application, each of these Application level objects in the `global.asa` are loaded/re-loaded into memory the first time a user touches a page on the site. By stopping your site you are essentially stopping the application and all variables are dropped and recreated during startup of the site the first time a user touches a page on the site. Without these Commerce objects defined within your `global.asa`, your site wouldn't be able to function.

Here is `Application_OnStart` event of the `global.asa` file that was created with the Commerce Site Builder Wizard when we built our commerce site in the previous chapter:

```
global.asa - Notepad
File  Edit  Format  Help
<SCRIPT LANGUAGE=VBScript RUNAT=Server>
    Sub Application_OnStart
        vRoot = "IK_Ecommerce"

        Dim MSCSSite
        Dim MSCSQueryMap
        Dim MSCSMessageManager
        Dim MSCSDataFunctions
        Dim MSCSShopperManager

        REM -- Read Store Dictionary
        Set MSCSSite = ReadSiteDict(vroot)

        REM -- Create a Query Map and add all queries:
        set MSCSQueryMap = InitQueryMap()

        REM -- Initialize Message Manager (for use in pipeline) and add all messages:
        set MSCSMessageManager = InitMessageManager()

        REM -- Initialize Shopper Manager for managing shopperId values
        set MSCSShopperManager = InitShopperManager

        REM -- Initialize Data Functions with locale:
        set MSCSDataFunctions = InitDataFunctions

        Set Application("MSCSSite")            = MSCSSite
        Set Application("MSCSQueryMap")        = MSCSQueryMap
        Set Application("MSCSMessageManager")  = MSCSMessageManager
        Set Application("MSCSDataFunctions")   = MSCSDataFunctions
        Set Application("MSCSShopperManager")  = MSCSShopperManager
        Application("MSCSSIDURLKey")           = "mscssid"
    End Sub
```

As mentioned, the sole purpose of the `global.asa` in a wizard-generated commerce site is to instantiate a number of COM objects at the Application level. This means that the objects are generic to the application and not specific to the user as they are in the Session level.

Session level objects are created and available during a users visit to the site, but are destroyed when the user leaves the site (or by timing-out).

Here are a few code snippets from the `global.asa` from the site that we built in the previous chapter to help explain how the Application level objects are used in the commerce site that we built in the prior chapter. Let's examine the `MSCSQueryMap` Application level object that is created to hold the most commonly executed queries on the commerce site.

The MSCSQueryMap Object in global.asa

First, the `MSCSQueryMap` object is created with Application scope in the `global.asa file` by using the `<OBJECT>` tag. This tag is self-contained and is outside of any `<SCRIPT>` tags in the `global.asa`. Again, Application objects declared in the `global.asa` file are not created until the server processes a script that calls that object (a user touches a page). This saves resources by creating only the objects that are needed when they are needed:

```
<OBJECT RUNAT=Server SCOPE=Application ID=MSCSQueryMap
        PROGID="Commerce.Dictionary"></OBJECT>
```

Next, in the `Application_onStart` event, the `MSCSQueryMap` object variable is declared and then set to the value that is returned from the `InitQueryMap` function:

```
Dim MSCSQueryMap

REM -- Create a Query Map and add all queries:
set MSCSQueryMap = InitQueryMap()
```

The `InitQueryMap` function defines a property on the `MSCSQueryMap` object to represent each query. For the sake of explanation, I have edited the function to include only the `depts` query. Notice that the `depts` property is set to the results of the `AddQuery` function:

```
Function InitQueryMap
    REM -- Create Query Map Dictionary
    Set MSCSQueryMap.depts = AddQuery("SELECT dept_id, dept_name,
                                    dept_description FROM ik_ecommerce_dept")

    set InitQueryMap = MSCSQueryMap
End Function
```

Finally, `MSCSQueryMap` is set to Application level scope back in the `Application_onStart` event:

```
Set Application("MSCSQueryMap") = MSCSQueryMap
```

In addition to the `MSCSQueryMap` object, the following Commerce objects are created in the `global.asa`:

❑ **The FileDocument**
Allows you to read the contents of a `Dictionary` object from its binary format in structured storage that is persisted on the disk. In this case, the `ReadDictionaryFromFile` method is used to read the site configuration data from `site.csc` (see the `site.csc` section below).

❑ **The Site Dictionary**
Contain the site configuration data.

❑ **The QueryMap Dictionary**
Contains the SQL queries and eventual result contents used by the wizard-generated commerce site.

❑ **The MessageManager**
Stores the messages used by the pipeline components.

❑ **The StandardSManager**
Initializes the application mode of the commerce site to dictate the manner in which the ShopperID is maintained in state between pages.

❑ **The DataFunctions**
Formats and converts values based on a specific locale (i.e. Japanese). Additionally, performs validation checks on values passed to the pipeline or values saved to the database.

The site.csc File

Another important file is loaded from within the `global.asa` file from the `ReadSiteDict` function. It is the **site.csc** file that contains valuable information about your site. `site.csc` is stored in binary format in structured storage. Unfortunately, and certainly by design because the file contains user and password information to your SQL or Oracle server, neither Notepad nor Visual InterDev can view it, because the file is persisted in binary (structured storage) format. Therefore, in order to edit `site.csc`, you'll need to download the `EditDictionary.asp` file from Microsoft's web site. This is the tool that will allow you to manipulate the data within your site's `site.csc` file.

> **There are security implications of placing an Active Server Page that displays site information on your commerce site. The accompanying documentation that comes with the download will instruct you how to install the file and how to "lock-down" `EditDictionary.asp` from malicious visitors to your site.**

Here is a listing of the different parameters that `site.csc` controls:

❑ **Default Connection String:**
This is your DSN connection that you created to your database.

❑ **ConnectionStringMap:**
The `Dictionary` object used to contain the connection string. This can be used from the Order Processing pipeline.

❑ **DiplayName:**
The name of your site.

❑ **SecureHostName:**
The URL of your web site and port number where a secure connection can be used. SSL Defaults to port 443 if you have a digital certificate installed.

❑ **NonSecureHostName:**
The URL of your site.

❑ **DisableHTTPS:**
If you do not want to use SSL, you can disable this option. The options are 1 for yes, 0 for no.

❑ **ClosedRedirectURL:**
If your site is closed, you can specify a redirection to another URL that will mark the site as closed.

❑ **WebInstance:**
The instance of your commerce site as it is identified by Site Server.

❑ **Status:**
The status of the commerce site store (open or closed).

Here is a screenshot of the `EditDictionary.asp` file in action that is pointing at the `site.csc` file that we created:

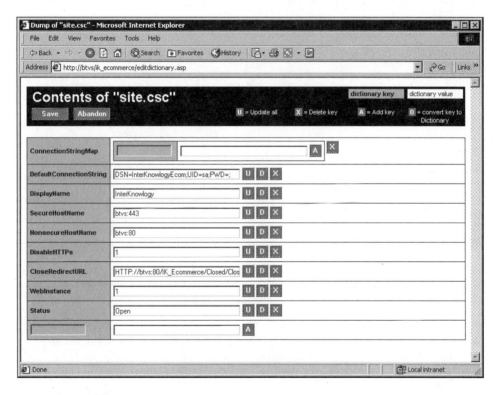

The i_shop.asp File

The `i_shop.asp` file is included in almost every one of the ASP pages that are used within the commerce site. The `i_shop.asp` file is responsible for creating and managing the ShopperID, database connection, and status of the shop, and is used to manage the moving around of the user. You'll notice that this is part of almost every page: this can be seen from the `<!-- #INCLUDE FILE="i_shop.asp" -->` that you'll see within most of your ASP pages.

The i_util.asp File

The i_util.asp file is also included within most of your ASP pages for your site and is responsible for many of the commerce functions that are necessary to manage, access and update the OrderForm object (which you will learn about later in this chapter), shopper information and receipt data. This file is also used to manage the data in the Commerce Interchange Pipeline.

Shopper_new.asp, Shopper_update.asp and Shopper_lookup.asp

Each shopper that registers for your site receives a ShopperID, which is a randomly generated 32-character string that is used to manage their account. By associating a unique ShopperID with each user account, you can make sure that there will never be any possibility that a user will be able to view someone else's shopping cart of sensitive information regarding their account. In order to manage the ShopperID these files are used to either create a new ShopperID, update the information within the ID or lookup the ShopperID that is stored within the Shopper table of your commerce database:

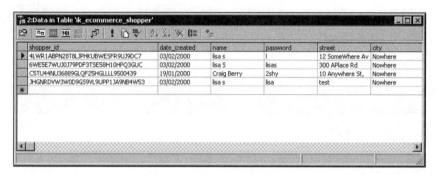

Your ShopperID is passed via the query string or saved in cookies and is used to keep track of registered users as they move around pages on your site.

The Product Search Page (find.asp)

When you chose to include a product search from the Site Builder Wizard, the find.asp page is created. If you look into the code within find.asp you'll see that it is nothing more than a simple ASP file with some ADO (ActiveX Data Objects) that you will learn about in the next chapter.

> It is important to note that this is not Site Server Search, which uses crawl technology to index and catalog disparate data sources like web content, data in Microsoft Exchange Folders, the contents of Microsoft Office Documents, etc. You will learn all about Site Server Search in Chapter 10.

The COM Object Structure

When you installed Microsoft Site Server Commerce in Chapter 3, you installed and registered a number of very powerful COM objects. When you created your online store by using the Site Foundation and Site Builder Wizards in Chapter 4, you put those COM objects to use when they were embedded in the Active Server Pages and pipelines that were created. Many of these COM objects are worth extra attention, as they form an integral part of the functionality of the system.

Throughout this section, we'll walk through some key functionality as well as examine some of the five most commonly used objects.

The StandardSManager Object

The **StandardSManager object** supports methods that facilitate the run time creation, deletion, and retrieval of ShopperIDs.

Functionality in the StandardSManager object includes the creation and return of unique ShopperIDs; retrieving ShopperIDs from cookies, if available; and initializing the object with information that determines how ShopperIDs will be stored and retrieved.

The Page Object

The **Page object** simplifies the layout of HTML pages within of Active Server Pages and the interaction between these pages and the data sources used by your site.

Functionality in the Page object includes the formatting methods of Encode, Option and Check, which are intended to make it possible for you to easily format HTML page items; and where applicable, to determine HTML item values based upon a run time evaluation of other variables used in your page. Additional functionality of the Page object includes the validation methods, which begin by querying the query string; the conversion of those values to given data types based on a locale value; and the validation of these values against a specified range.

The DBStorage Object

The **DBStorage object** supports the mapping of **Dictionary** and **SimpleList** objects to and from the database, primarily for the storage of order information in the form of baskets and receipts.

Functionality in the DBStorage object includes the mapping of a database column to an entry in the OrderForm or Dictionary object that DBStorage object uses to insert and retrieve data. Additional functionally of the DBStorage object includes the finding, inserting, retrieving, deleting, and saving of data to and from the object to the SQL Server tables.

The QueryMap Object

The **QueryMap Dictionary object** saves multiple query descriptions, including the text of each query, enabling queries to be passed conveniently to the Active Server Pages in the site or Order Processing pipeline components. `QueryMap` objects are implemented as `Dictionary` objects, where each name/value pair represents a single query description. Each query description in the query map is also implemented as a `Dictionary` object that specifies properties of each of the queries.

The OrderForm Object

The **OrderForm object** provides for the in-memory storage of customer information (order header information like ship-to and bill-to addresses, etc.) and purchase information (like the items of the order represented in the shopping basket). Wizard-generated sites use the `OrderForm` object to store the items that a customer has chosen to purchase from the shopping basket. Wizard-generated sites also use the `OrderForm` object to store receipt information that reflects a given customer's purchase history.

The `OrderForm` object has a rather complex structure, and is constructed out of `Dictionary` and `SimpleList` objects.

The SimpleList Object

The **SimpleList object** is an array holding simple values, indexed by a number.

This object has just one property, `Count`, which gives the number of items stored in the `SimpleList`. There are also two methods: `Add` for adding items to the `SimpleList` and `Delete` for deleting items from the `SimpleList`:

```
Set objMyList = Server.CreateObject("Commerce.SimpleList")

objMyList.Add("One")
objMyList.Add("Two")
objMyList.Add("Three")

objMyList.Delete(1) ' Deleting the second value, "Two"

For intCount = 0 To objMyList.Count - 1
    Response.Write("<BR>" & intCount & ": " & objMyList(intCount))
Next
```

The Dictionary Object

The **Dictionary object** is a collection object, but is essentially a `SimpleList` object with added functionality. Instead of using indexes to access the contents of the list, it supports a multitude of values that take the form of properties on the object.

To retrieve the value associated with a certain key, you use the `Value` method:

```
Set objMyDict = Server.CreateObject("Commerce.Dictionary")
```

```
objMyDict.First = "One"
objMyDict.Second = "Two"
objMyDict.Third = "Three"

Response.Write("The first value is: " & objMyDict.First)
```

The `Dictionary` object is widely used within SSCE; many of the Application-scope objects declared in `global.asa` are Dictionary objects.

SimpleList and Dictionary Objects in the OrderForm Object

There are three `SimpleLists` within the `OrderForm` object:

❑ The `Items` collection, which holds all the items the shopper intend to purchase.

❑ The `_Basket_errors` collection, which contains errors that were generated when the `OrderForm` object was run though the Order pipeline.

❑ The `_Purchase_Errors` collection, which contain errors that were generated when the `OrderForm` object was run through the Purchase pipeline.

The base of the `OrderForm` object is a `Dictionary` object that contains information that describes the entire order and its header items. This includes customer information, such as the ShopperID, name, and address, as well as order cost information, such as purchase subtotal, tax, shipping, and total.

The real power of the `OrderForm` object is that you can delete or add properties as needed. For instance, if you wanted to add an e-mail address to the `OrderForm` (which would be a common enhancement to your site) you'd simply set the value of `OrderForm.Email` to the e-mail address of the user on the site who typed it into the HTML form most likely contained in `shipping.asp`. The object itself handles the creation of the new property on the object along with setting its value.

The `OrderForm` also has a number of methods. The most commonly used methods on the `OrderForm` object are `AddItem` and `ClearItems` methods, which act on the line items of the order.

The AddItem Method of the OrderForm Object

Within the `OrderForm` object, the `Items` collection holds one `Dictionary` for each `Item` that has been added to the `OrderForm`. When you use the `AddItem` method, it will simply add another entry in the `Items` collection:

```
Set item = OrderForm.AddItem(sku, product_qty, list_price)
```

The sample above calls the `AddItem` method on the `OrderForm` object with the Stock Keeping Unit (or sku), the quantity and the `list_price` of the item. The method returns a reference to the `Dictionary` item that was added, and this is used to assign information such as the name and `dept_id` of the product.

The ClearItems Method of the OrderForm Object

The `ClearItems` method of the `OrderForm` object deletes all the items in the `Items SimpleList`. This is what is done when a visitor to your site clicks the **Empty Basket** button on the `basket.asp` page:

```
If OrderForm.Items.Count > 0 Then
    OrderForm.ClearItems()
End If
```

The script above checks the `Items` collection of the `OrderForm` object to see if there are any items there – if there weren't we don't have to perform the action. We then call the `ClearItems` method.

If you don't want to delete the whole order form, but just remove one product, you must use the `Delete` method of the `Items` collection using an index value:

```
OrderForm.Items.Delete(index)
```

An OrderForm Implementation

Let's walk through a simple purchase on the site from behind the scenes so that we can understand how the `OrderForm` object is instantiated, how it is populated, and how it's used between pages. In the retail commerce site (as opposed to the Site Manager) an `OrderForm` object is first instantiated:

❑ By jumping to a Product page from the Home page and adding an item to the basket from the Product page:

  ❑ (By calling the `xt_orderform_additem.asp` from `product.asp`)

❑ By jumping straight to the Basket page from the Home page where the `OrderForm` object is instantiated first in the Basket page itself and then again by removing, updating, emptying or purchasing:

  ❑ (By running the Plan pipeline in `basket.asp`)

  ❑ (By calling `xt_orderform_delitem.asp` from `basket.asp`)

  ❑ (By calling `xt_orderform_editquantities.asp` from `basket.asp`)

  ❑ (By calling `xt_orderform_clearitems.asp` from `basket.asp`)

  ❑ (By calling `shipping.asp` from `basket.asp`)

❑ By jumping straight to the Shipping page from the Home page where the `OrderForm` object is instantiated first in the Shipping page itself and then again by totaling the order:

  ❑ (By running the Plan pipeline in `shipping.asp`)

  ❑ (By calling `xt_orderform_prepare.asp` from `shipping.asp`)

1. First go to the Home page of your commerce site by running a browser and going to `http://localhost/IK_Ecommerce/default.asp`.

2. Now authenticate on the site by clicking the <u>Login</u> link on the home page.

3. Then, type your username and password and hit the Login button.

4. Notice from the URL that you have been assigned a ShopperID. It was actually retrieved from the `Shoppers` table when you logged in. You will now be sitting on the home page and your URL will look similar to this:

http://localhost/ik_ecommerce/default.asp?mscssid=C5TU44NU36889GLQF25HGLLLL9500439

You will need that ShopperID to instantiate the `OrderForm` object because the code will have to look up the shopper in the `Shopper` table to make sure there's not a shopping basket already populated from a prior visit.

5. Click on one of the three department links to move to the Department page (dept.asp). Notice from the URL that you have carried your ShopperID to the Departments page. You've also carried the DepartmentID in the query string, but we won't look at any code yet because you still don't have an `OrderForm` object:

http://localhost/ik_ecommerce/dept.asp?dept%5Fid=3&mscssid=C5TU44NU36889GLQF25HGLLLL9500439

6. Click on one of the product links to move to the Products page. Now, there are three items carried in the query string of the URL: the ShopperID, the DepartmentID, and the SKU of the product:

http://localhost/ik_ecommerce/product.asp?dept%5Fid=3&sku=1861002696&mscssid=C5TU44NU36889GLQF25HGLLLL9500439

`xt_orderform_additem.asp` is going to need those three values when you click the Add to Basket button next.

7. Click the Add to Basket button on the Products page. You've moved to the Basket page and quite a bit has happened. We are going to take a look at the code in a minute, but first notice from the query string of the URL for the Basket page that the ShopperID has been carried, but you've lost the DeptartmentID and the product SKU:

http://localhost/ik_ecommerce/basket.asp?mscssid=C5TU44NU36889GLQF25HGLLLL9500439

Since the item represented by those two values has already been added to the basket and hence, now lives in the `OrderForm` object, they are no longer needed. Let's look at what happened.

When you clicked the Add to Basket button, `xt_orderform_additem.asp` was called. I am going to describe the entire process of adding an item to a basket with the intention of discovering where the `OrderForm` object gets created and how it is used by the various Active Server Pages.

Open up xt_orderform_additem.asp and i_util.asp in your favorite editor if you want to follow along.

First note that xt_orderform_additem.asp includes i_shop.asp and i_util.asp, which are basically a number of functions. Then it defines it own function, OrderFormAddItem. So in effect xt_orderform_additem.asp has three basic tasks handled in three lines of code.

The first step is to call UtilGetOrderFormStorage. This function lives in i_util.asp. The value that UtilGetOrderFormStorage returns (a DBStorage object) is set to mscsOrderFormStorage:

```
Set mscsOrderFormStorage = UtilGetOrderFormStorage()
```

Second, the local function OrderFormAddItem is called and sent the mscsOrderFormStorage object created in the prior step and the value of the ShopperID:

```
success = OrderFormAddItem(mscsOrderFormStorage, mscsShopperID)
```

The very first thing that OrderFormAddItem does is get an OrderForm object! That's what we've been looking for. Here's how it does it. The first line of OrderFormAddItem calls the function UtilGetOrderForm which lives in i_util.asp:

```
Set mscsOrderForm = UtilGetOrderForm(mscsOrderFormStorage, created)
```

The first task that function UtilGetOrderForm has is to determine is if there's an existing marshaled basket in the Shopper table in SQL Server representing a saved basket from a prior page or visit. It does this by using the GetData method off the DBStorage object that was created a few steps earlier. The GetData method returns an OrderForm object. If it's NULL (which it is in this case) a new one is created with this statement in UtilGetOrderForm:

```
set orderForm = Server.CreateObject("Commerce.OrderForm")
```

Now that we have an OrderForm object, the rest of the mission of xt_orderform_additem.asp is very easy to follow:

❑ First it uses the Department ID and the SKU to look up the product in the SQL Server Products table. It uses a QueryMap object to run the product_info query, which returns the appropriate values of the product that is getting added to the basket.

❑ Armed with the information about the product, it uses the AddItem method off the OrderForm object itself and assigns the product values to the OrderForm object from the recordset returned by the QueryMap object.

❑ Now that the OrderForm object represents the basket (the product just added to the basket) xt_orderform_additem.asp writes the OrderForm object back to disk by calling the function UtilPutOrderForm in i_util.asp.

❑ Now, that the state of the basket is persisted, xt_orderform_additem.asp performs its third and last task, which is simply to redirect to the Basket page

It won't surprise you to find out one of the very first tasks of the Basket page – to create the OrderForm object with the UtilGetOrderForm function in i_util.asp. In fact, in each remaining step involved in making the purchase (shipping.asp, payment.asp) the very first task is to create an OrderForm object with the UtilGetOrderForm function in i_util.asp.

In each remaining step in the purchase, more data is added to the `OrderForm` object and then persisted back to disk (in its marshaled form in the `Basket` table) so it can be retrieved again on the next page:

❑ In the Shipping page, the details of the shipping method and ship-to-address are added to the `OrderForm` object.

❑ In the Payment page, the order totals, the credit card information, and the bill-to-address are added to the `OrderForm` object.

Once the purchase is completed there is no longer a need for an `OrderForm` object, the basket is removed from the `Basket` table and the order is placed in the `Receipts` table by the pipeline components in the Purchase pipeline.

Summary

The basis of this chapter was to help you break down each file and component of a Site Server Commerce Edition wizard-generated site. We started by exploring the database tables that hold the information for our site. Next, we looked at the folder structure of the commerce site that houses the files that live in the site. Then, we looked at many of the files including many of the Active Server Pages files that compromise a wizard-generated site. Next, we learned about many of the COM components that are used from within the Active Server Pages that make up an online store. Lastly, we examined the `OrderForm` object from behind the covers from the start of a purchase all the way through a completed purchase on the site.

Through this process we have seen that:

❑ The database structure of a wizard-generated site is not complex and that the number of tables generated by the wizard is dependant on the features chosen in the Site Builder Wizard.

❑ The folder structure of a wizard-generated site is very simple. Most of the functionality of the site is contained in Active Server Pages that live in the root of the site.

❑ The Active Server Pages that make up the site are very functional and when broken down into pieces their operation and functionality are quite easily understandable.

❑ The COM object implementation of a wizard-generated site is complex and vast. The COM objects used and implemented in the Active Server Pages on a wizard-generated site make the site very powerful.

Although we took a much more detailed than a high-level view into the database structure, the directory structure, the file structure and the COM object structure of a Microsoft Site Server Commerce edition online store, we have only just scratched the surface. An entire book could be written to reference simply the COM object structure of Commerce Server (which is what the Microsoft Site Server, Commerce Edition documentation essentially is).

The foundational knowledge that this chapter provided on the construction of a wizard-generated site will allow us to easily make programmatic enhancements to the site that we created in Chapter 4. So, let's move on to Chapter 6, where you will learn how to programmatically enhance the functionality of your electronic commerce site.

Extending our E-Commerce Site

Well, so far we have created a commerce site in Chapter 4 and we have covered how that site is constructed in Chapter 5. Now it is time to start manipulating that site through its code. When we created the site in Chapter 4, Site Server actually did quite a bit of work for us. A lot of ASP pages and a quite a few database tables were created. As you will see in Chapters 7 and 8, another key piece of the site that was also created was the pipelines. However, you can be certain this "stock" site will not be sufficient for your purposes for long. You will probably be tasked with customizing the site and extending its functionality the second someone else sees it. The inevitable question will be asked, "This is great, but can we add...?"

In this chapter we are going to cover some programming examples that will help you learn your way around Site Server and the sites that Commerce Edition generates. After going through these examples, you should have a better idea of what is required when you are asked to modify, customize or extend your site.

If you haven't figured it out yet, there are a lot of different technologies present in a web site created with Site Server. For a beginner, trying to use all of these technologies to create a solution can be overwhelming. So how do you get started? You start by solving some very simple problems and then working your way up until you can solve the tough ones. In this chapter, we are going to keep the examples pretty simple. The goal here is to expose you to most of these technologies while at the same time providing examples that are useful.

We are going to cover six examples:

- ❑ We will extend the Product table created for us when we ran the Site Builder Wizard in Chapter 4 to add inventory information.

- ❑ We will create an ASP page that uses Microsoft ActiveX Data Objects (ADO) to look in the Product table and report on the inventory of all the products we currently sell on our site. Before actually creating the ASP page we will spend some time covering the basics of ADO.

- ❑ We will create a COM component that performs the same database lookup as the second example. Then we will modify the ASP page we created in the second example, to use the component for doing the database lookup.

❑ We will take the COM component created in the third example and host it under MTS/COM+.

❑ We will modify the appropriate ASP pages so we can display inventory information to users of our web site. We will also show you one way prevent someone from ordering products that are not in stock.

❑ We will create a user-friendly version of the order confirmation number. By default, the order confirmation number created in Site Server is 26 characters long. We'll create a more human-friendly version to work with.

For all of these examples we are going to use the site we created in Chapter 4. Along the way I'll try to provide a high level overview of the technologies we are using.

Extending the Product Table

This happens to be a lot easier than you think. By simply adding fields to a database table, we can extend the data elements that Site Server creates for an e-commerce site. Consider the following problem. Your company has a warehouse full of items that people can purchase using your web site. Wouldn't it be nice to have some way of informing your users when something was out of stock? To keep things simple, we are going to add one data element so we can keep track of how many of each product is in the warehouse. We will be using SQL Server 7.0 for these examples but the steps are similar for SQL Server 6.5.

1. Start the SQL Server Enterprise Manager by going Start | Programs | Microsoft SQL Server 7.0 | Enterprise Manager.

2. Expand the nodes in the tree on the left-hand side of the window until you see the details for the InterKnowlogyEcom database:

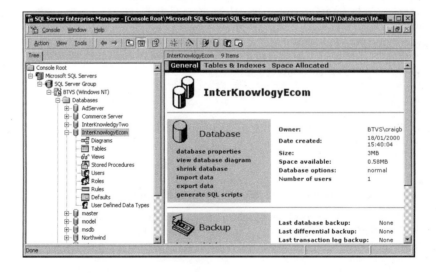

3. Select the Tables node so that all the tables in the database are listed in the right-hand pane.

4. Now right-click on ik_ecommerce_product and select Design Table from the pop-up menu:

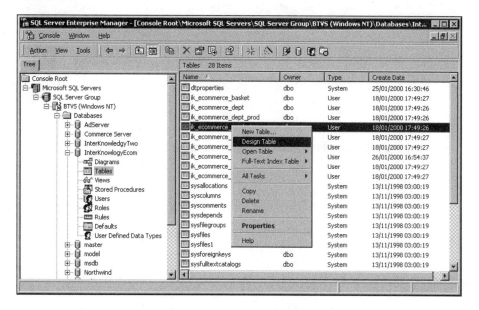

5. You will be presented with the actual fields that make up the Product table for our web site:

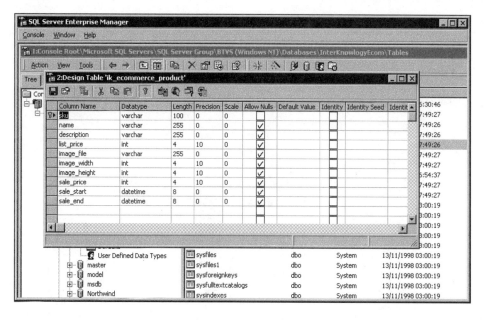

Now click on the row immediately after **sale_end**. We are now ready to add our data field so we can keep track of inventory. Let's call our new field, `quantity_in_stock`. Enter this in the **Column Name**, choose the **int Datatype** and accept the defaults for the rest of the items:

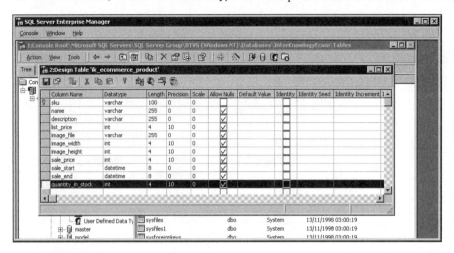

Then close the dialog and your changes will be saved automatically. Now in order for the following examples to work, we need to enter values for this field.

Entering Inventory Information

Ideally, you'd want to write some form of inventory information ASP page or some other more user-friendly means of adding data to the database. However, for our purposes we will simply add the data using the Enterprise Manager.

1. Right-click on the ik_ecommerce_product table again but this time select **Open Table | Return all rows** from the pop-up menu:

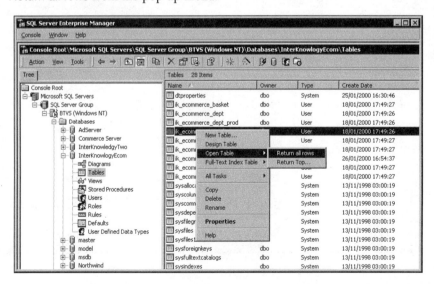

2. You will be presented with the data values for the products stored in the table:

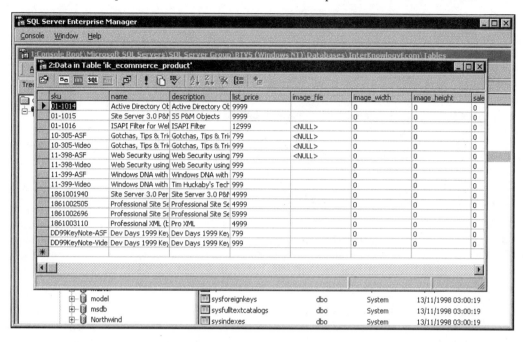

3. Scroll the dialog so that you can see our new `quantity_in_stock` column. Enter some inventory data into the column, giving some products an inventory level of 0:

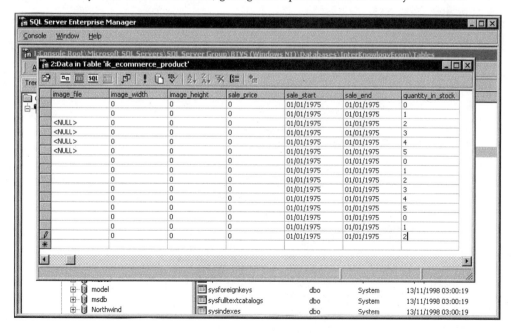

4. Close the dialog and the data will be saved to the database.

Now we are ready to start retrieving this data.

Creating an ASP Page that Displays Inventory Data

Now that we have a newly created data element to help keep track of inventory, we need to use it, right? What are you going to do if someone in your company wants a web page to look at this inventory data? The technology we need here is called **ADO**, or **ActiveX Data Objects**. ADO is one of the technologies from Microsoft that allows developers to query and update databases.

Microsoft's Universal Data Access Strategy

ADO is part of a broader strategy from Microsoft that addresses how developers can access a number of different types of data in the enterprise. This initiative is called the **Universal Data Access** Strategy, or **UDA**. Mainframe databases, applications, directory services, spreadsheets, and even text files are examples of data that might be present at a typical company. The goal of UDA is to provide a common way for the software developer to access all of these different types of data.

Taking the strategy even further, another goal is to have the software developer learn one technology to access all of these different types of data. You are probably asking yourself, "How can Microsoft provide common access to all of the different types of data and only make the programmer learn one technology?" Well, the design of UDA is what allows this to happen. UDA is really two parts: one part to deal with all of the different data sources and one part that the software developer uses. Consider the following picture:

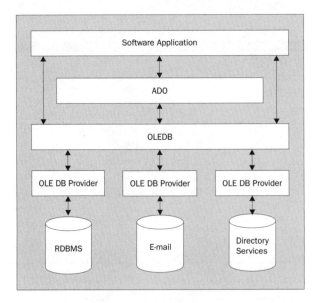

In the UDA strategy, for each different type of data source, there must be an **OLE DB Provider**. An OLE DB Provider knows how to deal with a specific type of data source, how to read from it, write to it, etc., and translate the results of those reads and writes into a common format. Microsoft creates OLE DB Providers for data sources they know how to deal with, such as SQL Server. For other data sources, Microsoft provides a toolkit to create these OLE DB Providers. You, as a software developer writing applications, use ADO, which in turn knows how to talk to OLE DB Providers. So there you have it, you learn one technology, ADO, and you can access all of the different types of data in the enterprise, if there is an OLE DB Provider for each data source.

If you are really brave, you can write code to "talk" directly to OLE DB and bypass ADO. Typically, C/C++ programmers will use this method if they are not getting satisfactory speed from ADO.

ActiveX Data Objects

Since all of the data access in Site Server uses ADO, it might be worthwhile spending some time talking about ADO. Learning ADO is unavoidable if you are going to do much of anything with Site Server. This discussion on ADO is by no means meant to be a tutorial or reference on ADO, but rather to introduce you to the technology.

For a far more detailed discussion of ADO, try one of the ADO titles from Wrox Press: ADO Programmer's Reference or Professional ADO Programming.

Another topic you should become familiar with is SQL, or Structured Query Language. SQL is the language used to write database queries and to perform actions against databases, like deleting records. Of course, Wrox has a good SQL book called Instant SQL Programming by Joe Celko.

The three main objects that we will be covering are:

❏ **The Connection object**

❏ **The Command object**

❏ **The Recordset object**

There are actually more objects in the ADO object model, but these are the objects you will use the most.

The Connection Object

The Connection object is simply a connection to a data source. Other ADO objects can use this connection once it has been established. You can, in a sense, "hand" a Connection object to the other ADO objects. You have a choice as a developer: you can create a Connection object every time you want to access a data source, or you can create a Connection object once and reuse it each time you need to get to the data source. If you choose to reuse the Connection object, you should see an improvement in performance. Establishing a connection to a database is costly because of things like security checking, so reuse connections if you can.

The Connection object has more functionality than just being able to connect to a data source. However, this functionality is really outside of the scope for this discussion on ADO.

The Command Object

The Command object exists to run single commands, or queries, against a data source. The Connection object possesses similar functionality, but the Command object gives the developer more control over how these queries are executed and more control in dealing with the results. For example, a very good use of the Command object is to access **stored procedures** in SQL Server databases. SQL Server stored procedures are compiled versions of SQL statements that are actually stored in the database. When used correctly, they can greatly increase the speed of complex queries.

The Recordset Object

The Recordset is probably the most used object in ADO. Using a recordset is the only way to actually retrieve and modify data using ADO. If you want to display results of a query to a user, you will use the Recordset object. For example, if you wanted to query a database and present the results on an ASP page, you would have to use the Recordset object. So a recordset is simply a collection of rows of data from a database.

The Recordset object allows you to find records, modify records, sort records in any order, and move forwards and backwards through a set of records. Some of the advanced features of the Recordset object include being able to update records directly on the database, or save all of the updates and have them sent to the data source in batch mode. Another advanced feature is the ability for a Recordset object to be disconnected from a connection and passed around between the tiers of a Windows DNA application. For example, a COM component could create a Recordset object, disconnect it and then return that recordset to its caller, say an ASP page. The ASP could then use that Recordset object to display data. These types of Recordset objects are called **disconnected recordsets**.

Another reason you should learn more about ADO is to become familiar with the flexibility of this technology. There are many ways of solving data problems using different combinations of ADO objects. For example, we could use just a Recordset object without any other objects at all; we could use a Connection object, a Command object and a Recordset object; or we could use a Command object and a Recordset object. All of these are valid combinations of how to use the ADO objects to query data in a database.

Using ADO from ASP

Here is the typical scenario you will follow when writing code to access a database using ADO:

- ❑ Create a DSN.
- ❑ Establish a connection to a data source by creating an ADO Connection object using the DSN from Step 1.
- ❑ Create an ADO Recordset using the Connection object from Step 2.
- ❑ Do something with the ADO Recordset object.
- ❑ Close the Recordset object.
- ❑ Close the Connection object.

Now we are going to look at how to implement the above steps from an ASP page to retrieve inventory information from the `Products` table of our site.

1. Before we can start writing any ADO code we need to create a new ASP page. Using the tool of your choice (Notepad, Visual InterDev, FrontPage etc.) create a new ASP page called `GetInventory.asp` and save it in a folder called `TestInventory` which you should create as a sub-folder of our `InterKnowlogy` site. Doing this means that it is already mapped to a virtual directory in IIS and we can view the page in our browser by simply adding `/TestInventory/GetInventory.asp` to the URL.

2. ADO makes use of a lot of constants, which by default are not accessible from our ASP page. However, when you installed ADO a file called `adovbs.inc` was placed on your machine, which allows us to add these constants to our ASP page. You can find this file at `\Program Files\Common Files\System\ado\adovbs.inc`. Copy this file to the same directory as the `GetInventory.asp` file. To make use of this file we need to add a reference to it at the top of our ASP page. Add the following line to `GetInventory.asp`:

```
<!-- #include file=adovbs.inc -->
```

If you're using ASP 3.0 then you can actually reference the ADO 2.5 type library by adding the following META tag:

```
<!-- METADATA TYPE="typelib" FILE="c:\Program Files\Common
Files\System\ado\msado15.dll" -->
```

Now we are ready to start performing the six steps outlined earlier.

3. Create a DSN
We took care of the Step 1 in Chapter 4 when we created the DSN to connect to `InterKnowlogyEcom`.

4. Establish a connection to a data source by creating an ADO Connection object using the DSN from Step 1.
Now add the following lines to establish the connection:

```
<%
'Create ADO connection object
Dim cnInventory
Set cnInventory = Server.CreateObject("ADODB.Connection")

'Open connection to database using System DSN called InterKnowlogyEcom
cnInventory.Open "DSN=InterKnowlogyEcom; UID=sa; PWD=;"
```

Here we use the `Server.CreateObject` method to create an instance of an ADO Connection object. After creating the instance of the Connection object, we call the Connection object's `Open` method. We supply the DSN called `InterKnowlogyEcom` along with an id and password. These parameters to the `Open` method are collectively called a **connection string**.

5. **Create an ADO Recordset using the Connection object from Step 2**.
Add the following code:

```
'Create ADO Recordset object
Dim rsInventory
Set rsInventory = Server.CreateObject("ADODB.Recordset")

'Open a recordset from a query
rsInventory.Open "SELECT * FROM ik_ecommerce_product", cnInventory, _
                 adOpenStatic, adLockReadOnly, adCmdText
```

First, we create in instance of an ADO Recordset object using the `Server.CreateObject` method. Then we execute the `Open` method on the Recordset object and pass in these parameters:

❑ The first parameter is a SQL statement that does nothing but ask for all of the records in the `ik_ecommerce_product` table.

❑ The second parameter is the ADO Connection object we created previously. If we were going to create multiple ADO Recordset objects, we could keep using the `cnInventory` Connection object and realize some performance gains like we mentioned earlier.

❑ Then we pass the ADO constant `adOpenStatic` that tells ADO we want a static cursor where the data we are getting back is fixed and we only want to iterate through it.

❑ The constant `adLockReadOnly` tells ADO we are not going to modify the data in this recordset.

❑ Lastly, we tell ADO to process the first parameter as a SQL statement by passing the constant `adCmdText`.

Again, you really need to consult an ADO reference for the options for all of these parameters.

6. **Do something with the ADO Recordset**.
Now we have established a connection to our data source, the `ik_ecommerce_product` table in the `InterKnowlogy` database, and we have an ADO Recordset object that has all of the rows in the `ik_ecommerce_product` table. Each row of this recordset has several fields. You could look in the SQL Server Enterprise Manager to get a listing of all the fields. First we'll put a simple caption on the page with the following code:

```
Response.Write "<B>Simple ADO Example <BR>"
Response.Write "for Chapter 6 <BR><BR></B>"
```

If you look at the following code we are simply going to loop through all of the rows in the Recordset object and create an HTML table while we are looping through these rows. With the first line below we start an HTML table:

```
'Loop through recordset and create a table while doing so
Response.Write "<TABLE BORDER = '1'>"
```

Next, we setup a loop constraint to loop until we reach an EOF, or End Of File, condition. In ADO, EOF means you have reached the last row of a recordset. When you reach the last row of a recordset, and then try to reach for another row, ADO sets the EOF property to True. The following lines of code produce the body of the HTML table:

```
Do While Not rsInventory.EOF
    Response.Write "<TR><TD>" & rsInventory("sku") & "</TD>"
    Response.Write "<TD>" & Trim(rsInventory("name")) & "</TD>"
    Response.Write "<TD>" & rsInventory("quantity_in_stock") & "</TD></TR>"
    rsInventory.MoveNext
Loop
```

You might notice the statement, rsInventory("sku"). This is shorthand for how we actually get at the value of a field in a row of a recordset. The full syntax would be to call the Value property of the Field, i.e. rsInventory.Fields("sku").Value. So we issue three Response.Write methods to ASP, one for each cell of the table. We then issue the MoveNext method on the Recordset object. This simply moves us to the next row in the recordset. If you wanted to move backwards, you could issue the MovePrevious method. Then we are at the bottom of the loop and we continue the process until we have gone through every row in the recordset. After we are out of the loop, we close the HTML table:

```
Response.Write "</TABLE>"
```

7. Close the Recordset object.
We are almost finished. All we have to do is clean up in the last two steps. First, we close the Recordset object by executing its Close method. Then we set the Recordset object equal to the value Nothing:

```
rsInventory.Close
Set rsInventory = Nothing
```

By setting the Recordset object equal to Nothing, we free the resources being used by Recordset. Simply issuing the Close method does not free resources, but does release the Connection object to be reused.

8. Close the Connection object.
We then repeat this process for the Connection object and we are finished:

```
cnInventory.Close
Set cnInventory = Nothing
%>
```

Congratulations! You have successfully used ADO to access a SQL Server table and display the results on an ASP page.

329

9. Grab a browser and navigate to:

`http://localhost/Ik_ecommerce/TestInventory/GetInventory.asp`

You will receive the following result:

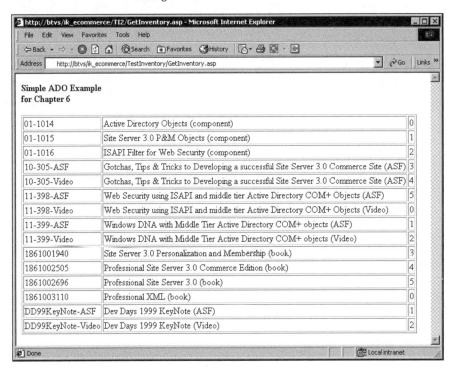

Writing a COM Component that Returns Inventory Data

I have yet to read a simple, beginners-level explanation of COM and I'm not going to try here. Instead, what I am going to do is demonstrate that this technology is approachable at a beginner's level. To fully understand all of the nuances of COM takes a long time. With great tools like Microsoft's Visual Basic, COM components *are not* difficult to develop and implement. What can be difficult is the design of these components. The perception in the industry is that these are very difficult technologies to develop and implement. It is probably because most everything documented is done from the experts' perspective. Well, nothing could be further from the truth and I will show you, step-by-step, in this example how to do it.

Component-Based Development

Component-based development is the tools and techniques that enable the software developer to construct software applications from new and prefabricated components. Component-based development gives you the power and flexibility for reuse among software applications that are surfaced in a number of different ways. The same components that run the business rules in your web-based software applications on your corporate extranet can be (and are) used in your Win32 applications that run on your corporate local area network.

Building applications from components, at first glance, is very attractive from a reuse of code standpoint and was one of the early promises of object-oriented computing. It is particularly attractive for server applications because it provides a natural way to encapsulate business functions in logical places. But, originally, software engineering applications from components were harder than they first appeared. A fundamental weakness of the early object oriented systems was the lack of a common framework that allowed software developers to integrate objects created by different developers into one application, either in the same process or across processes. The **Component Object Model (COM)** addressed this problem.

The Component Object Model (COM)

COM is a software architecture that allows the components made by different software developers to be seamlessly combined into a variety of applications.

> **COM defines a standard for component interoperability, is not dependent on any particular programming language, is available on multiple platforms, and is extensible.**

Why COM? The real question to ask is what would you do without COM? If there were no standard way for programs to communicate with each other, you, as a software developer, would have to create that communication mechanism yourself. In effect, you would be creating a custom communication mechanism for your software programs to talk to each other. What would you do if you needed to make a piece of your software talk to a piece of software written by someone else? What would that other person do? By standardizing on the communication method, you are saving yourself a lot of time and money. Since COM is already available on every Microsoft operating system, why in the world would you not use it?

How do we build these COM components? We can build these components by using tools like Visual Basic and Visual C++. By using these tools, we can create components that "speak" COM. There are actually many different development environments, from several vendors, that can create COM-enabled software. Like application design, there are a lot of books written on the subject of COM and the creation of COM components.

Writing a COM Component

It's time to put some of this theory on components into practice. We are going to go through the process of creating a very simple COM component. This component will perform the exact same functionality as the ASP script we wrote in the previous example. The component will query the `InterKnowlogyEcom` database and return a result to the caller telling the caller the number of items in stock as an ADO Recordset.

The first thing you will need is a development tool capable of creating COM components. Probably the easiest language to use when creating COM components is Visual Basic. Visual Basic masks a lot of the complexities of COM and hides a lot of what is "going on under the hood". If you know how to code in Visual Basic, you are well on your way to being able to write COM components in Visual Basic. If on the other hand, you feel compelled to use Visual C++, you will be forced to learn a lot of low-level details before you will be productive.

1. Start Visual Basic, and when you are presented with the New Project dialog, select ActiveX DLL as the project type:

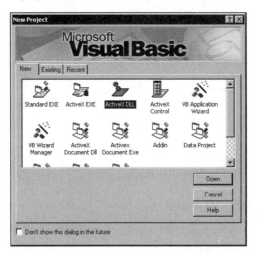

An ActiveX DLL in Visual Basic is synonymous with COM component. The term DLL stands for Dynamic Link Library, which is a compiled piece of code that is only loaded into memory when needed by another program. In other words, it is dynamically loaded at run time when needed by another program.

After you select the project type, you will have a new Visual Basic project that only contains a class module. A class module in Visual Basic is a template from which objects are instantiated. Class modules contain methods and properties. A property is nothing more than a piece of data, or variable, contained in the class. A method is basically a subroutine in the class. As you can see in the picture below, by default, your new project will be called Project1 and the class module will be called Class1:

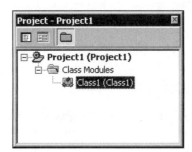

2. Now we're going to change these names to be more descriptive. If you right-click on Project1 in the Project Explorer window then select Project1 Properties, you can change the name of the project to be more descriptive. Let's change the name of the project to IK_Inventory:

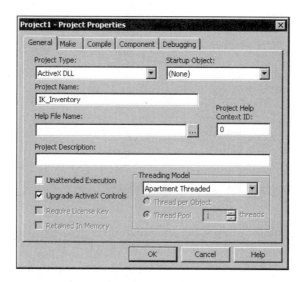

3. The next step is just as easy. Now we need to change the name of the class module. In keeping with our theme, let's change the name to GetInventory. You can do this by right-clicking on Class1 in the Project Explorer window and selecting Properties. You will be presented with the Property sheet for Class1. Change the Name property to GetInventory:

The Project Explorer window should look like this:

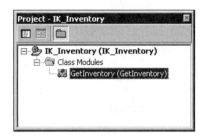

4. Since we know we want to use ADO to access the `InterKnowlogyEcom` database, we need to add a reference to ADO in our Visual Basic project. This way, all of the necessary information about ADO will be added to our project and will also be compiled into our ActiveX DLL. To add a reference to ADO to our project, click on Project | References and scroll down to Microsoft ActiveX Data Access Objects 2.1 Library. Select the check box next to it and click on OK:

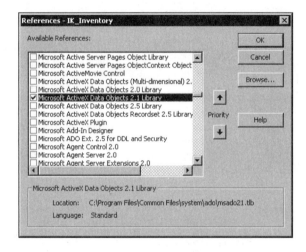

Just a note about the different versions of ADO. ADO has gone through quite a series of revisions in the last year-and-a-half. If you are running on any operating system other than Windows 2000, the most current version of ADO is version 2.1. ADO version 2.5 will be released with Windows 2000. For our purposes, version 2.0 or above will suffice.

Now we are finished with the setup for our project and it is time to start writing code.

5. We really only need one method on our DLL. That method will be called every time a caller wants data from the `ik_commerce_product` table in the `InterKnowlogyEcom` database. So let's add a method to our class. The Visual Basic development environment has a tool to do this.

First, double-click on the `GetInventory` class module in the Project Explorer window and a code window will appear. Make sure to click inside this code window to place the cursor there. Now click on Tools | Add Procedure... and type the name `rsGetProducts` in the Name field and select Function as the type:

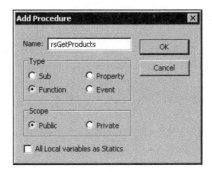

We are going to return an ADO Recordset object to the user so we need a function instead of a sub-routine. Then click on OK. An empty function called `rsGetProducts` will be inserted into the `GetInventory` class module:

```
Public Function rsGetProducts()

End Function
```

6. Once the function has been placed in the class module, we need to modify it. You should notice some similarities between the code we are going to put in this function and the script we wrote earlier.

Firstly, we need to change the return type of the function `rsGetProducts`. This function will actually return an ADO Recordset object to the caller. Make the following change to the function definition:

```
Public Function rsGetProducts() As ADODB.Recordset
```

7. Now we want to declare and create the ADO objects we need:

```
' Declare an ADO Connection object
Dim conIKEcom As ADODB.Connection

' Declare an ADO Recordset object
Dim rsInventory As ADODB.Recordset

' Create instance of ADO Connection object
Set conIKEcom = New ADODB.Connection

' Create instance of ADO Recordset object
Set rsInventory = New ADODB.Recordset
```

8. Now we need to create a connection to our `InterKnowlogyEcom` database, just like we did in the ASP example earlier. The Visual Basic code here is the same as the ASP script we wrote:

```
' Create an ADO Connection object using System DSN InterKnowlogyEcom
conIKEcom.Open "DSN=InterKnowlogyEcom; UID=sa; PWD=;"
```

9. To fill the ADO Recordset we created in Step 7, we will introduce another coding style so you'll recognize it when you see it again. Instead, of passing all of the arguments to the `Open` method of the ADO Recordset object, we are going to set them as properties. We used some of these properties in the ASP example, but we sent them as parameters to the `Open` method of the ADO Recordset, instead of setting each one, like in this example. The only additional property we are using is the `CursorLocation` property:

```
With rsInventory
    .ActiveConnection = conIKEcom
    .CursorLocation = adUseClient
    .Source = "SELECT * FROM ik_ecommerce_product"
    .Open
    Set .ActiveConnection = Nothing
End With
```

By setting `CursorLocation` to `adUseClient`, we are telling ADO we want a recordset that can be disconnected from its ADO Connection object. The actual disconnection occurs with the statement `Set .ActiveConnection = Nothing`. Once, we have disconnected the recordset, we can send it to the client without maintaining a live connection to the database. This technique is a very efficient use of resources. Since we are not going to be editing data in the database, we don't need a connection for very long, just long enough to fill our recordset.

10. After creating and filling the recordset, we want to return our ADO Recordset object to the caller. In Visual Basic, we return values from a function by setting the function name equal to the value we want to return. So the following code will take care of this for us. Notice how we had to use the `Set` keyword. Since we are dealing with objects, you cannot just use an equal sign (=) like with normal variables:

```
' Return disconnected recordset through function name
Set rsGetProducts = rsInventory
```

11. We are almost finished. Notice how we did not use the statement `rsInventory.Close`: when we executed the statement, `Set .ActiveConnection = Nothing`, we took care of closing the recordset. Now we just clean up the resources we used and we are done:

```
' Free resources
Set rsInventory = Nothing
conIKEcom.Close
Set conIKEcom = Nothing
```

12. Now all we have to do is compile our project! Click on File | Make IK_Inventory.dll and you will see the following dialog. There is no need to change the default file name, `IK_Inventory.dll`, but it would be a good idea to place the DLL in the `TestInventory` folder we created earlier:

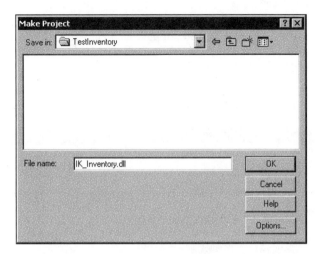

That's it. Congratulations! You have just successfully compiled a pretty cool COM component. It was automatically registered when you compiled it. Now that you have created this component, hopefully you will be inspired to create more COM components. Wrox publishes two good beginner's resources on creating COM components using Visual Basic. The first is *VB COM: Visual Basic Programmer's Introduction to COM* by Thomas Lewis (ISBN: 1-861002-13-0). The second is *Beginning Components for ASP* by Richard Anderson, et al. (ISBN: 1-861002-88-2).

Now, let's use this component in the ASP script we wrote earlier. You really will not have to make that many changes.

13. Open up the GetInventory.asp file and make the following modifications:

```
<%
Dim objIK
Dim rsInventory

'Create instance of object to query Inventory database
Set objIK = Server.CreateObject("IK_Inventory.GetInventory")

'Create ADO Recordset object
Set rsInventory = objIK.rsGetProducts

Response.Write "<B>Simple COM Component Example <BR>"
Response.Write "for Chapter 6 <BR><BR></B>"

'Loop through recordset and create a table while doing so
Response.Write "<TABLE BORDER = '1'>"
Do While Not rsInventory.EOF
    Response.Write "<TR><TD>" & rsInventory("sku") & "</TD>"
    Response.Write "<TD>" & Trim(rsInventory("name")) & "</TD>"
    Response.Write "<TD>" & rsInventory("quantity_in_stock") & "</TD></TR>"
    rsInventory.MoveNext
Loop
Response.Write "</TABLE>"

%>
```

Notice how we just create an instance of the IK_Inventory.GetInventory object and call its method, rsGetProducts. We do not have to do any setup for ADO Connection objects or ADO Recordset objects. Once the call to obj.rsGetProducts is complete, the code is exactly the same as it was in the previous example.

Here is the result from running the script. The results are exactly the same, just as they should be:

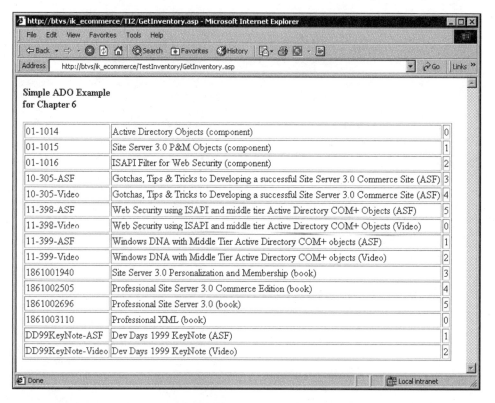

You have now successfully taken some logic that once resided in an ASP page, encapsulated it in a COM component and then used the COM component on another web page. It really wasn't that bad was it? What you have really learned from this example is how to work with components and create components. When you write Site Server applications, you will interact with components a lot. Now you have a base understanding to move forward.

Hosting our COM Component in MTS / COM+

Now we need to start thinking bigger. It would be nice if we could host that component in a single place and have a single point of control for updates. I am now going to introduce you to **Microsoft Transaction Server (MTS)**. MTS is an essential technology for building highly scalable web sites that can handle thousands of users. Site Server makes extensive use of MTS and you should become familiar with MTS if you are going to write Site Server applications.

Throughout this section I will use the terms MTS and COM+ synonymously. This is a gross generalization of comparing the two technologies, but for the purpose of this chapter and this book, it will work OK. In Microsoft Windows NT 4.0 we run our distributed COM components under MTS (Microsoft Transaction Server) and in Microsoft Windows 2000 we run our distributed COM components under COM+.

MTS is a technology that houses COM components written in Visual Basic or Visual C++ or other COM compliant languages. An important concept to keep in mind here is that MTS is a run time environment that is hosting COM components, exactly like the one you just wrote in the previous example. Another way to say this is that "COM components can run under MTS". MTS provides low-level plumbing and extends the functionality of COM components by providing the following:

❑ Component Transactions – MTS monitors the activity of components running under it and can guarantee the success or failure of updates to databases. A transaction is a set of database operations that are treated as a single unit. Either all of the operations succeed, or none of them are allowed to take place. MTS provides an environment that makes creating transactions pretty easy.

❑ Object Brokering – MTS allows components to be shared across multiple machines. Once you have a COM component running under MTS, any machine on your network can access it. These machines become clients of the components running under MTS.

❑ Resource Pooling – MTS monitors what server resources, such as database connections, components are accessing and creates pools of connections to these resources. By providing a pool of connections, components have faster access to these resources.

❑ Security – MTS can control which clients can access the components it is hosting.

❑ Administration – MTS has an MMC-based user interface to control the features listed above.

Building COM components and hosting them under MTS is also the subject of many books and a detailed discussion on the matter is outside the scope of this chapter.

You can find information on how to build COM components and host them under MTS by reading Professional MTS MSMQ with VB and ASP by Alex Homer and David Sussman from Wrox Press (ISBN 1-861001-46-0).

To write a component that takes advantage of all the features of MTS would take us quite a bit of time. So in the spirit of keeping it simple and introductory in nature, let's take the component we just wrote and host it in MTS.

Hosting our Component

It's time to put some of this theory on MTS/COM+ into practice. Although it's possible to modify our component to programmatically access the MTS/COM+ run time it is really outside the scope of this book and given that our component is very simple anyway, not really necessary.

> **However, if you are going to pursue component development for Site Server then this will be something you will need to learn.**

Our component will perform the exact same functionality as before, but this time the run time environment will be under the control of MTS/COM+.

1. Firstly, we need to create a MTS/COM+ **package** to house our newly created component through the relevant MMC snap-in. A package is simply a set of components that perform related functions. In COM+, packages have been renamed to **COM+ Applications**.

The MMC snap-in for MTS is the MTS Explorer which is started at: Start | Programs | Windows NT 4.0 Option Pack | Microsoft Transaction Server | Transaction Server Explorer:

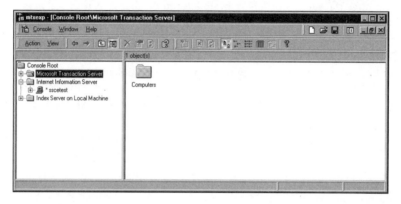

For COM+ this is the Component Services Explorer, which is started at: Start | Programs | Administrative Tools | Component Services:

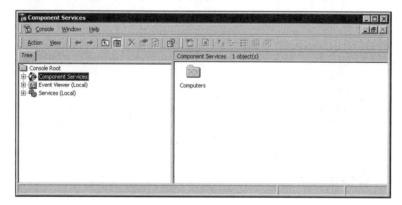

As you can see they are both quite similar.

2. Expand the Console Root folder in the left-hand pane through Component Services, Computers, and MyComputer until you can see a folder called Packages Installed for the MTS Explorer or COM+ Applications for COM+:

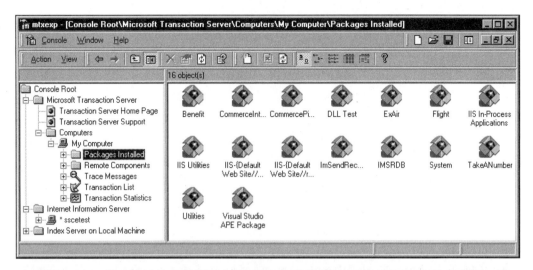

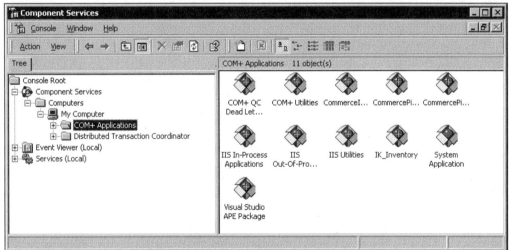

3. Right-click on this folder (Packages Installed or COM+ Applications) and choose New and then either Application or Package as relevant. This will start the Package installation Wizard.

4. Choose to Create an empty package/application and click Next:

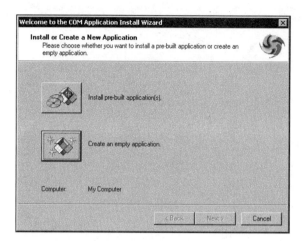

5. Give the package/application the name IK_Inventory:

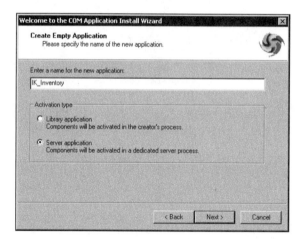

If you are using COM+, leave it as a **Server application** (this is the default setting for MTS) and hit **Next** to continue the Wizard.

6. Next, you'll implement one of the most commonly used features of MTS/COM+ – that is the application identity. Many COM components that you will write will have to run under a security context because of the powerful things they do. For instance, if you wrote a COM component that needed to get some data from the registry, you'd need to run under the context of a user that has rights to do that. The proxy user (in the form IUSR_Machinename) of the web server does not have those types of rights. If you run that component in a Win32 Visual Basic Application you will run under the context of the user that you are logged into the local machine as. But, when you distribute components and run them on web servers, you are running under a "proxied" security context with little or no rights.

Change the radio button from Interactive user to This user and click the Browse button. For this sample application, simply choose the local administrator of the server. The local administrator certainly has enough permissions to run our little COM component. You'll need to type the password for that account twice:

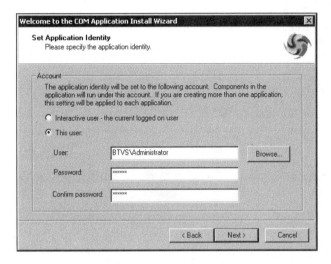

7. Click the Next button and then the Finish button to complete the creation of the package/application.

8. Now, we need to add the component we just compiled to the package. You'll notice that the `IK_Inventory` package/application has appeared under the other MTS packages/COM+ Applications. Expand it by clicking our new IK_Inventory package/application and the Components and Roles folders will appear:

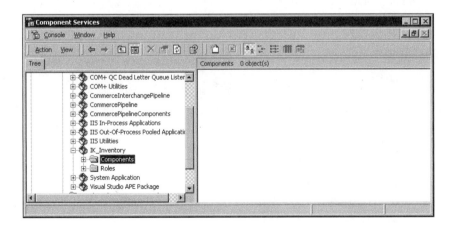

9. Left-click on the Components folder so that the right-hand pane is empty.

10. Now open Windows Explorer and navigate to the `TestInventory` folder where our DLL is located. Arrange Windows Explorer and the MTS/Component Services Explorer on your screen such that you can see both our DLL in Windows Explorer and the right-hand pane of the MTS/Component Services Explorer. Now drag and drop our DLL from Windows Explorer into the right-hand pane of MTS/Component Services Explorer (i.e. into the Components folder for or package/application):

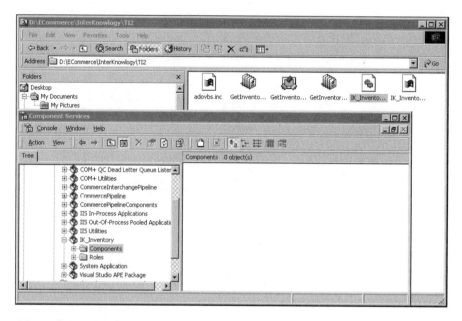

After a flurry of disk activity you will see that the `GetInventory` class has been added as a ball with a cross to the Components folder:

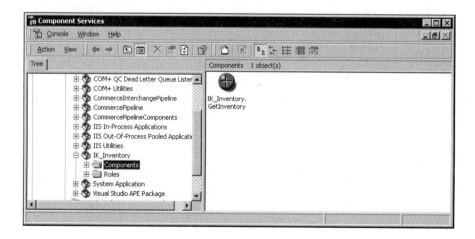

11. Now, let's put it into action to prove that it works. Run the `GetInventory.asp` file again in your browser again. It should take a little longer for the page to load this time but if you refresh the page again you will notice that performance has improved.

This happens because MTS/COM+ has to initially load the package/application the first time but it remains in memory (default is 3 minutes) so that subsequent calls are a lot quicker.

If you are quick, you can move back to MTS/Component Services Explorer and see the "ball spin".

Hopefully through the course of the last three examples, you have gained an understanding of what is required to implement Site Server applications.

Displaying Inventory Status on the Site

It's time to switch gears and work on our e-commerce site we created in Chapter 4. Remember the first example where we extended the data model for the e-commerce site? Let's use that newly created data element and display inventory status (either *in stock* or *out of stock*) when a user browses a list of products.

If a user chooses to see the detail about a particular product, then we'll use the same data element to display the actual quantity of that product we have on hand.

Before we begin, we are going to be using a lot of the objects and pages that were discussed in Chapter 5. If you did not read Chapter 5, you might want to at least go back and have a quick look. In Chapter 5, we deconstruct the site we created in Chapter 4 and briefly describe the important elements of an e-commerce site generated by running the Site Builder Wizard.

The desired effect should look something like this:

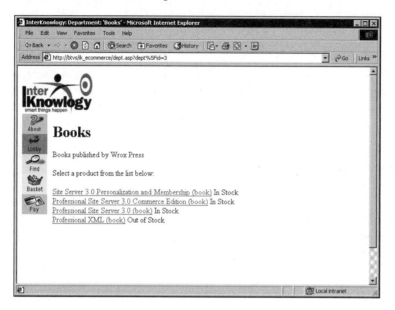

Ok so it's not the prettiest looking of solutions, but the user is informed of the status of the products listed on that page.

1. Browse to the physical location of the site you created in Chapter 4. The location is probably `\inetpub\wwwroot\ik_ecommerce`. Find the `global.asa` file and open it for editing. If you recall the discussions from Chapter 5, there are queries placed in `global.asa` that are available for all of the pages in the site. We need to modify one of these queries to return the newly created data element containing our inventory data. The query used by `dept.asp` to display a list of products for a given department is called `products_by_dept`. Locate the `products_by_dept` query. It should look something like this (note: the text has been modified so we can display it here in print):

```
Function InitQueryMap

REM -- Create Query Map Dictionary
Set MSCSQueryMap.depts = AddQuery("SELECT dept_id, dept_name,
                            dept_description FROM ik_ecommerce_dept")
.

.

Set MSCSQueryMap.products_by_dept = AddQuery("SELECT prod.sku, prod.name
                            FROM ik_ecommerce_product prod,
                            ik_ecommerce_dept_prod dept WHERE _
                            dept.sku = prod.sku and dept.dept_id
                            = :1")
.

.

End Function
```

There are actually quite a few queries in the function InitQueryMap: *we have omitted all of them here except for the one we need to modify.*

2. We need to modify this query to include the field quantity_in_stock. All we do is simply add quantity_in_stock to the SELECT portion of the query. (Again, consult a SQL reference if you are having trouble.) After you are finished, it should look like this:

```
Function InitQueryMap

REM -- Create Query Map Dictionary
Set MSCSQueryMap.depts = AddQuery("SELECT dept_id, dept_name,
                                  dept_description FROM ik_ecommerce_dept")
.
.
Set MSCSQueryMap.products_by_dept = AddQuery("SELECT prod.sku, prod.name
                                  prod.quantity_in_stock FROM
                                  ik_ecommerce_product prod,
                                  ik_ecommerce_dept_prod dept WHERE
                                  dept.sku = prod.sku and dept.dept_id
                                  = :1")
.
End Function
```

3. While we are here, we need to make the same modifications to the products_by_sku query so the second half of this example will function correctly. Simply add the pf.quantity_in_stock field to this query. It should look like this when we are finished.

```
Set MSCSQueryMap.product_by_sku = AddQuery("SELECT pf.sku, pf.name, _
                                  pf.description, pf.list_price,
                                  pf.sale_price, pf.sale_start,
                                  pf.sale_end, pf.image_file,
                                  pf.image_width, pf.image_height,
                                  pf.quantity_in_stock, dept.dept_id,
                                  dept.dept_name FROM
                                  ik_ecommerce_product pf,
                                  ik_ecommerce_dept_prod deptprod,
                                  ik_ecommerce_dept dept
                                  WHERE pf.sku = :1 and pf.sku =
                                  deptprod.sku AND dept.dept_id =
                                  deptprod.dept_id AND
                                  dept.dept_id = :2")
```

4. Save `global.asa`.

You are probably wondering what the `:1` *and* `:2` *are doing. These are placeholders that will be used for a text substitution. In this case, the placeholder is used to denote the* `dept_id`*. So if we want to use this query, we can run another function to substitute a value for* `:1` *or* `:2` *and there will be a value for* `dept_id` *in the query.*

5. Now find `dept.asp` (it should be in the same directory as `global.asa`), and open it for editing. This file is pretty long, so we can't display its entire contents here. First, let's examine where the query `products_by_dept` is used:

```
<%

    if dept_exists then
        cmdTemp.CommandText = _
            Replace(MSCSQueryMap.products_by_dept.SQLCommand,":1",dept_id)
        Set rsProducts = Server.CreateObject("ADODB.Recordset")
        rsProducts.Open cmdTemp, , adOpenStatic, adLockReadOnly

        if rsProducts.EOF then
            products_exist - false
        Else
            products_exist = true
        end if
    end if

%>
```

First, notice how the function `Replace` is called to substitute the value for `dept_id` for `:1`. What is returned is a perfectly formatted SQL statement. That string is assigned to the `CommandText` property of the Command object `cmdTemp`. The recordset `rsProducts` is created using the `cmdTemp` Command object as a parameter.

6. Now we can add the statement we need to hold the value for `quantity_in_stock` by just grabbing the value from the Recordset object `rsProducts` and putting it in the page variable `quantityfield`. Then we can conditionally print the statement in stock or out of stock based on the value of `quantityfield`:

```
<!--#INCLUDE FILE="i_header.asp" -->

<%
    if not dept_exists then %>
        <P>The department you requested is currently not available.
    <% else %>
        <H1><%= mscsPage.HTMLEncode(dept_name) %></H1>

        <P>
```

```
        <%= mscsPage.HTMLEncode(dept_description) %>

        <P>

    <% if products_exist then %>
        Select a product from the list below:

        <UL>
            <%
            set skuField = rsProducts("sku")
            set nameField = rsProducts("name")
            set quantityField = rsProducts("quantity_in_stock")
            do while Not rsProducts.EOF
                %>
            <LI><A HREF="<%= baseURL("product.asp") & _
                mscsPage.URLShopperArgs("dept_id",_
                dept_id, "sku", skuField.value) %>"> _
                    <%= mscsPage.HTMLEncode(nameField.value) %></A>
            <% if quantityField > 0 then %>
                    In Stock
            <% else %>
                    Out of Stock
            <% end if %>
            <% rsProducts.MoveNext
            loop
            rsProducts.Close
            %>
        </UL>
    <% else %>
        <FONT SIZE="2">No products at this time.</FONT>
    <% end if %>

<% end if %>
```

7. Save your changes and browse to dept.asp within your site. You should see the inventory status of each product in each department. That's it!

Now let's take this just a little bit further. Once a user clicks on one of the product links they are taken to a page that displays the detail for that particular product. The page that displays this detail is called product.asp. Once a user lands on product.asp, we could show them the quantity of that item we have in stock. If we don't have any in stock, we could hide the **Add to Basket** button so they cannot order something that is out of stock.

> **Important Note: this example is being used to demonstrate how you might customize a couple of the pages in a Site Server e-commerce site. The issue of inventory control is much more complex than we are making it here.**

8. Find `product.asp` and open it for editing. Add the quantity variable statement around line 47 or so:

```
REM -- get fields from recordset
name = rsProduct("name").value
description = rsProduct("description").value
dept_name = rsProduct("dept_name").value
list_price = rsProduct("list_price").value

sale_price = rsProduct("sale_price").value
sale_start = rsProduct("sale_start").value
sale_end = rsProduct("sale_end").value

image_file = rsProduct("image_file").value
image_width = rsProduct("image_width").value
image_height = rsProduct("image_height").value

quantity = rsProduct("quantity_in_stock").value
```

9. Now add the conditional statement to display the amount on hand or a statement indicating we are out of stock and then conditionally hide the **Add to Basket** button:

```
<% if on_sale then %>
  <P><FONT SIZE="4"><B>ON SALE! <%= MSCSDataFunctions.Money(sale_price)
%></B></FONT>
  <P>Regular Price: <%= MSCSDataFunctions.Money(list_price) %>
<% else %>
  <P><FONT SIZE="4"><B><%= MSCSDataFunctions.Money(list_price) %></B></FONT>
<% end if %>

<P><%= mscsPage.HTMLEncode(description) %>

<% if quantity > 0 then
     InStock = True %>
     <P>We currently have <% =quantity %> of these available
<% else %>
     <P>This item is currently not in stock.
<% end if %>

<% if InStock then %>
   <P>
   <INPUT TYPE="Image"
   SRC="<%= "/" & siteRoot %>/manager/MSCS_Images/buttons/btnaddbskt1.gif"
   WIDTH="112"
   HEIGHT="24"
   BORDER="0"
   ALT="Add to Basket"
   ALIGN="MIDDLE">
<% end if %>
```

The results should look like this if the item is in stock:

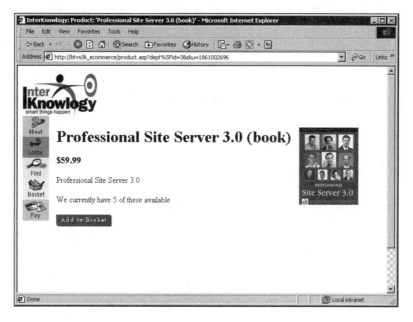

If the item is not in stock the result should look like this:

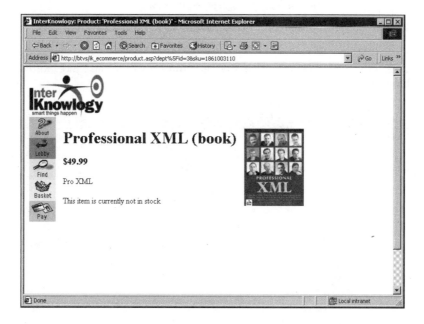

You might have noticed that we did not include any code to decrement the `quantity_in_stock` field when an order is placed. The way to solve this piece of the puzzle is to write a pipeline component that will decrement the field during the order process. What on earth is a pipeline component? Well, you are going to read all about the pipeline and pipeline components in Chapter 7. Then, in Chapter 8 you will get the opportunity to write a `Scriptor` component that actually ties in with this example and decrements the `quantity_in_stock` field when an order is placed.

Creating a Usable Order Confirmation Number

Have you ever seen the order confirmation numbers generated by Site Server? They are 26 characters long! If you can remember one of those, you probably don't need to be reading this book since you possess enormous brainpower. However, for us lesser mortals it is quite likely someone at your company will ask you to change this.

We are going to accomplish this quite simply by the following methodology:

❑ Add a new field to the `ik_ecommerce_receipt` table called `short_order_id`. This field will be an identity field that is automatically incremented every time a new row is added to this table.

❑ Add a new query to `global.asa` called `short_order_id`.

❑ Edit `confirmed.asp` and call the query created in Step 2.

❑ Display the shortened order confirmation number instead of the 26 character version.

❑ Edit `receipt.asp` and call the query created in Step 2.

❑ Display the shortened order confirmation number on the order receipt page.

1. First, open the SQL 7.0 Enterprise Manager and browse to the `InterKnowlogyEcom` database and find the `ik_ecommerce_receipt` table:

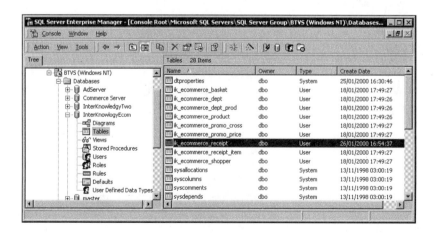

2. Then right-click on ik_ecommerce_receipt and select **Design Table**. We are going to add an **identity** field. This is simply an integer that will be incremented by SQL Server every time a new row is added to ik_ecommerce_receipt, i.e. every time an order is placed. Add a field called short_order_id. You get to pick the initial value for the field, so start out with something other than the default. If you think about this, would you feel confident with a store where your order is order number 1, 2 or even 78? This way, we give the customer the impression that the store has been up and running for a while. Use 11111 as the seed value and increment by 1 each time. You should see something similar to the following after you are finished:

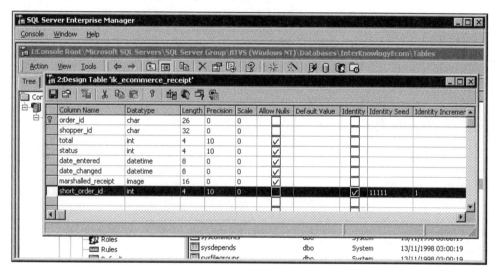

3. Save the changes to the table and close Enterprise Manager.

4. Now we need to edit the global.asa file again. We need to add an entirely new query, instead of editing an existing query. Find the function we modified earlier and add the following query to global.asa at about the same place:

```
Function InitQueryMap
    REM -- Create Query Map Dictionary
    Set MSCSQueryMap.short_order_id = AddQuery("SELECT short_order_id FROM " & _
                                    "ik_ecommerce_receipt WHERE" & _
                                    "order_id = ':1'")
    .
    .
End Function
```

5. Save your changes.

6. The only trick left is to add a placeholder so we can do a text substitution using the Replace function. What we will do is actually look up the row in the database we want by using the 26-character confirmation number. So we will need to use the Replace function to substitute the 26-character confirmation number for :1. Once we have the desired row, we can grab the newly created shortened order confirmation and display it instead.

Find the file confirmed.asp and open it for editing. Add the following code in to confirmed.asp:

```
Your order number is
<%  order_id = mscsPage.HTMLEncode(Request("order_id"))
```

```
<%
Set rsOrder = MSCS.Execute(Replace( _
                    MSCSQueryMap.short_order_id.SQLCommand,":1",order_id))
if not rsOrder.EOF then
  ShortOrderID = rsOrder("short_order_id")
end if
rsOrder.Close
Set rsOrder = Nothing
%>
```

```
<A HREF="<% = baseURL("receipt.asp") & mscsPage.URLShopperArgs("order_id",
Request("order_id")) %>"><STRONG><% = ShortOrderID %></STRONG></A>.
```

Please record it for referencing your order.

We are actually creating an ADO Recordset object here called rsOrder. One way to create a Recordset object is to issue the Execute method of an ADO Command object. MSCS is an ADO Command object that is created in i_shop.asp, which gets included in most pages in an e-commerce site. You should recognize the short_order_id query you added to global.asa and the Replace function where we are substituting the order_id for the :1 placeholder in that query. We then issue the Execute method on MSCS and an ADO Recordset is created. Once we have the Recordset, we can create a page-level variable and grab the contents of the identity field we added in Step 1. Lastly, we display the ShortOrderID variable instead of order_id. The result should look like this:

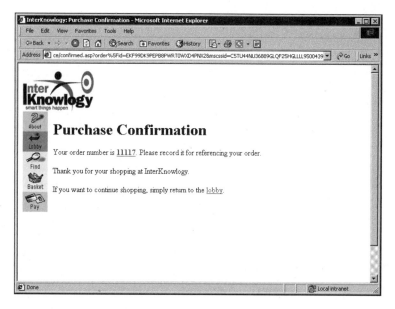

As you can see there is a nice, short, easy to remember order number now displayed on the page instead of the 26-character monster you get by default.

7. One more step and we are finished. You'll notice that the shortened order number on the `confirmed.asp` page is actually a link. That link takes you to `receipt.asp`, which displays all of the detailed information about an order. We need to edit `receipt.asp` to also display the shortened order confirmation number. The process is identical to the one we used in Step 6.

The file `receipt.asp` should be in the same location as `confirmed.asp`. Open `receipt.asp` for editing and insert the following code:

```
<%
order_id = Request("order_id")
Set rsOrder = MSCS.Execute(Replace( _
                MSCSQueryMap.short_order_id.SQLCommand,":1",order_id))
if not rsOrder.EOF then
  ShortOrderID = rsOrder("short_order_id")
end if
rsOrder.Close
Set rsOrder = Nothing
%>

<HTML>
<HEAD>
    <TITLE><%= displayName %>: Receipt: <% =ShortOrderId %></TITLE>
    <META HTTP-EQUIV="Content-Type" CONTENT="text/html; charset=ISO-8859-1">
</HEAD>
<BODY
```

```
        BGCOLOR="#FFFFFF"
        TEXT=    "#000000"
        LINK=    "#FF0000"
        VLINK=   "#FF0000"
        ALINK=   "#FF0000"
>
<!--#INCLUDE FILE="i_header.asp" -->

<% if nitems <> 0 then %>
<TABLE BORDER="0" CELLPADDING="2" CELLSPACING="1">
    <TR>
        <TH BGCOLOR="#000000" VALIGN="TOP" COLSPAN="9">
            <FONT SIZE="4" COLOR="#FFFFFF"><B> Receipt # <% =ShortOrderID %>
            </B></FONT>
        </TH>
    </TR>
```

The code to retrieve the shortened order confirmation number should look familiar. It is nearly the same as the code we used in Step 6. Then we use the variable `ShortOrderId` in the `<TITLE>` tag. When you are finished it should look like this:

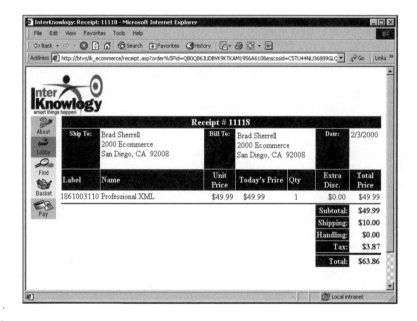

Good job!

Summary

Well we've taken quite a tour through some pretty cool programming examples. Hopefully by now you have gained some confidence and are ready to tackle some more interesting problems than the ones presented here. What have we learned?

- ❑ How to access SQL Server databases using ADO
- ❑ How to write COM components
- ❑ How to host COM components in MTS or COM+
- ❑ How to extend the data model for an e-commerce site created using Site Server's wizards
- ❑ Techniques for customizing some of the pages of an e-commerce site
- ❑ How to create a manageable order confirmation number

I really hope you continue to explore the area of component development using COM and MTS/COM+. In the next chapter, we are going to take a deeper look at the processes running behind the site in the form of pipelines.

Pipelines

You've learned from reading the prior six chapters that the ultimate goal of Site Server is to provide a solid foundation that will help the web developer create a complete and feature-rich e-commerce web presence in an efficient manner. Naturally, what this really means is that Site Server actually lowers the barrier of entry to the online world by giving us a way to get results of professional quality by spending a dramatically less time and money. Similarly, we can use Site Server as the building block of our online solution, which makes it possible to concentrate on our innovation without having to start from scratch and reinvent the wheel every time.

One of the primary mechanisms that Site Server Commerce Edition uses to lower this barrier of entry is pipeline technology. Through the implementation of pipelines, SSCE is able to encapsulate the complex functionality of e-commerce transactions, both business-to-consumer and business-to-business.

In this chapter, we'll look at the pipeline technology in Site Server and at how it can help us build our online stores. Here's a quick breakdown of the topics that we'll be tackling:

- ❑ Pipeline structure and execution
- ❑ The Pipeline Editor
- ❑ The Order Processing Pipeline
- ❑ Manipulating pipelines

First, let's take a closer look at pipelines in Site Server.

Introduction to Pipelines

There's an interesting – and very fitting – comparison that can be made between the innovation brought on by Site Server and another revolution that affected society many years ago. At the beginning of the 20th century, cars were a luxury item that only a few well-off people could afford, since every car was built manually from scratch. The rest of the less fortunate people had to cope with the mileage-per-gallon-of-hay of a carriage, complete – at least in most cases – with horses.

Things have obviously changed since then, considering that you're probably not driving a pony to work today. As it often happens, the transformation began with one man – actually one of my favorite historical figures of this century – Henry Ford, founder of the Ford Motor Company.

Before Ford came along, cars were built using what is now called a **static pipeline**: that is, an assembly line in which cars were built, a piece at a time, in a fixed position within the factory, while workers moved around with their tools and parts and performed their tasks. In addition, most factories used individual employees to take care of more than one task, which often led to a high incidence of mistakes and defects in the vehicles.

Ford is the inventor of the **moving assembly line** (some credit him with the invention of the assembly line in general, but I'm afraid that would be a little too much even for him), in which the workers stay in a fixed place and it's the *cars* that moved around. The result is that a lot less time is wasted on employees moving around, dragging their tools and parts. Every employee can more easily focus on performing an individual task – and therefore, become very good at it – rather than having too many responsibilities and ending up with sloppy results.

Although he did make some mistakes later on in his business career, which ultimately threatened the closure of Ford Motor Company, Mr. Ford's invention has been an undisputable success. The moving assembly line is now used at just about every mass-production facility in the world, and has largely contributed to making many things available to the public-at-large, including the computers we use in our everyday lives.

Pipelines in Site Server

Site Server has its own innovation for the electronic commerce world, called **pipeline technology**, which makes the paragon with Henry Ford so much more fitting.

> A pipeline**, in our case, is a process used to solve a "business problem". By business problem, in this case, I mean a problem that is generally linked to a scenario in which a transaction has to take place, and in which the transaction is usually composed of a number of smaller steps that have to be performed in a particular way.**

For example, let's take into consideration the portion of an online store that takes care of the purchase phase of an order – the moment in which the user has decided that they want to purchase one or more items from the store. As you know, buying something on the Internet involves a number of different steps: covering everything from the collection of personal information (shipping data and credit card numbers etc.) through to the verification of payment availability, to the initiation of the line-of-business procedure that ultimately results in the products being shipped to the recipient.

The issue with these business problems is that the number of steps involved can be significant, and that it might be difficult to handle the relationships between each of them. For example, credit card authorization should not be initiated before all the appropriate information about the user is collected. Similarly, you certainly don't want your store to ship any products until you are reasonably sure that the user will be able to pay for the merchandise they have requested!

The use of pipelines helps us by providing an *atomic* environment in which each "atom" represents a simple business operation. Thus, creating a transaction-handling process becomes simply a matter of putting each individual operation one after the other in the correct order. The result is a powerful technology that lets us solve complex problems with relative ease.

What's more, because pipelines are based on the COM platform, they can be easily extended using a popular programming environment, such as Microsoft Visual Basic or Microsoft Visual C++.

One of the most interesting aspects of pipelines is that they are a completely **open** technology. This means that, based within the working parameters on which they have been designed, they can easily adapt to a number of different situations.

Site Server Pipeline Structure

A pipeline is a software infrastructure that sequentially executes an array of COM components. A pipeline works by executing an arbitrary number of steps in a serial order. Each step is identified by a **component** designed to carry out a specific task. Site Server, as we'll see later on, comes with a number of built-in components that can be used to take care of the most common e-commerce business situations. When these are not enough, it is possible to extend the pipeline's functionality by writing additional components using a language that supports COM, such as Visual Basic or Visual C++.

Pipeline components are grouped into **stages**.

> **A stage is a logical entity used to identify a particular function. You can think of stages as "gearboxes" that contain a group of individual gears (the components) focused on performing a particular operation.**

It's important to understand that stages are simply "logical" containers that help group or categorize pipeline components – they have no effect on the way a pipeline behaves, although they can help you decide what components are going to be inserted in a particular place within the pipeline:

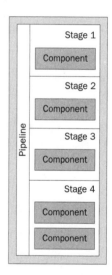

Each pipeline component is designed to operate in one or more stages of a particular pipeline.

> **With the exception of a few components that work in all stages, each component shows affinity with one or more specific stages. This means that the author of the component designed it so that it would work best if it were included in those particular stages.**

As you will see later on when I talk about pipeline creation and editing, this doesn't necessarily mean that the component cannot be included anywhere else, but merely indicates a recommendation as to where it should be added to the pipeline.

Now, let's jump in and take a hands-on look at the technology.

The Pipeline Editor

The **Pipeline Editor** is an application used for editing pipelines. There are two versions of the Pipeline Editor:

❑ The Win32-based Pipeline Editor

❑ The ASP-based (or web-based) Pipeline Editor

The web-based editor can be accessed from the Site Manager pages of your site. (If you built the site from Chapter 4, then the URL will be similar to: `http://localhost/IK_Ecommerce/manager/default.asp` The only difference might be the commerce application name (`IK_Ecommerce`).) Upon navigation to the Manager page for your commerce site, click the Edit Pipeline button and you will load the web-based Pipeline Editor:

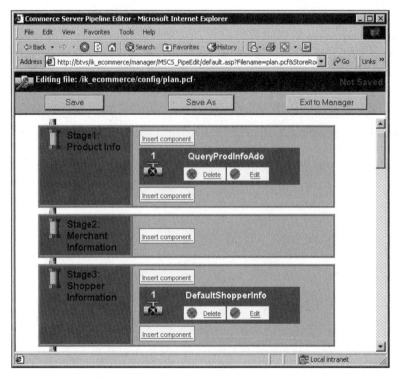

The web-based Pipeline Editor has an advantage over its Win32-based counterpart: **remote administration**. It is a browser-based application, which gives it a broad-reach, but with that power comes feature limitations; like its inability to create new pipeline stages and its inability to create new pipeline configuration files (`.pcf`).

I suggest using the Win32-based Pipeline Editor for these discussions. In fact, I recommend using the Win32-based Pipeline Editor unless you're in a remote administration scenario.

You can open the Win32-based Pipeline Editor from:

Start | Programs | Microsoft Site Server | Commerce | Pipeline Editor

Running the Win32-based Pipeline Editor in Enhanced Mode

There is a relatively unknown and barely documented feature of the Pipeline Editor called **Enhanced Mode**. When you view a pipeline in Enhanced Mode it is easy to see that a pipeline is nothing more than a number of COM objects strewn together. As you will see in the next chapter when you actually build a compiled pipeline component, we will need to run the Pipeline Editor in Enhanced Mode in order to correctly identify a pipeline component.

You can set up the Pipeline Editor to always run in Enhanced Mode when chosen from the Start menu by performing the following steps:

1. Click on the Start button.

2. Select Programs | Microsoft Site Server | Commerce

3. Right-click on Pipeline Editor and choose Properties.

4. Add a /E at the end of the shortcut in the Target box and click OK:

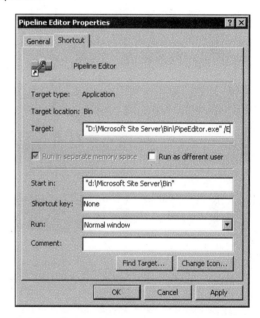

Now the Pipeline Editor will always run in Enhanced Mode when chosen from the Start menu.

Viewing a Pipeline

Let's take a look at one of the pipelines for our InterKnowlogy site. Before opening or modifying any pipeline configurations, it's usually a good idea to make a backup of the .pcf file in the same way we make backups for our source code.

5. Open Windows Explorer and navigate to the Config folder off the main folder of your site. If you built the site from Chapter 4, then the path is: ..\IK_Ecommerce\Config. Make a copy of the purchase.pcf file and create a file called Copy of purchase.pcf in the Config folder. Now if something goes wrong (not that it will of course) you can revert back to this file.

It's important to note that the PCF files are like any other file in your site in that if you make changes to them, they will be overwritten with new files if you run the Site Builder Wizard again.

6. Chose File I Open... or use the Open icon on the toolbar, then navigate to the Config folder off the main folder of your site.

7. Open up the Purchase pipeline (purchase.pcf) and take a look:

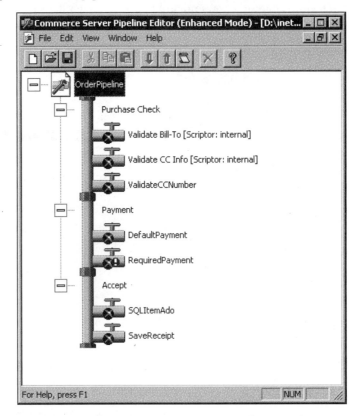

Now that you have opened a pipeline and understand what Pipelines are, before we go on, let me explain some of the concepts. Refer to the screen above.

PCF Files

Commerce Server pipelines are constructed and defined in pipeline configuration (.pcf) files. You create and configure these files using either the Active Server Pages (ASP)-based HTML Pipeline Editor or the Win32-based Pipeline Editor (i.e. we opened purchase.pcf above).

Pipeline Stages

Pipelines are divided into stages, where each stage consists of zero or more pipeline components. In the screen shot of the Purchase pipeline above, notice that there are three stages:

- ❏ Purchase Check
- ❏ Payment
- ❏ Accept

Each stage performs a specific function, and can be custom-tailored to your Commerce Server application.

Pipeline Components

Pipeline components are custom Component Object Model (COM) objects designed to perform operations on some part of the `OrderForm` object or `Dictionary` objects. In the screen shot of the Purchase pipeline above, notice that there are three pipeline components in the **Purchase Check** stage above:

- ❏ Validate Bill-To
- ❏ Validate CC Info
- ❏ ValidateCCNumber

For instance, ValidateCCNumber checks the format of the numbers in the credit card in the **Purchase Check** stage.

The pipeline handles the interaction of pipeline components by passing the `OrderForm` or `Dictionary` objects from one pipeline component to another. Pipeline components are configured to support one of several architectures:

- ❏ The first, the Order Processing Pipeline (OPP), automates order processing in a business-to-consumer (B2C) scenario like in the site that you built in Chapter 4.
- ❏ The second, the Commerce Interchange Pipeline (CIP), is intended to facilitate the packaging and transmission of business documents across a network or the Internet in a business-to-business (B2B) scenario.

Microsoft Site Server 3.0 Commerce Edition comes with a 'canned' set of powerful pipeline components that can be added to a pipeline to support either the B2C or B2B scenarios. In addition, you can create your own components to extend the capabilities of the pipeline architecture. You will learn how to do this in the next chapter.

Configuring a Pipeline Component

Most pipeline components, once added to a pipeline, can be configured by setting their properties. After the Site Builder Wizard has created the pipelines for a store, those components are pre-configured to work with that store. Any new components that are added need to be configured. Each pipeline component usually has its own property page that is distinctive to that component, as well as information such as the CLSID of the pipeline component.

In Chapter 4, when we ran the Site Builder Wizard to create the site, we chose not to charge for handling. Let's assume that after building our site, we've had second thoughts and have decided to charge separately for handing. Obviously we could simply run the Site Builder Wizard again and choose handing this time around, but, if we were to do that, we'd lose all the modifications that we made to the site in the previous chapter. So, let me show you how to do manually what the Site Builder Wizard does automatically:

1. First, because we are going to modify the Plan pipeline, you'll need to make a backup copy of the `plan.pcf` file by making a copy of it like you did in the steps above where you backed up the `purchase.pcf` file.

2. Now that you have made a backup copy of `plan.pcf`, open the Plan pipeline. You don't need to close the Purchase pipeline if you would like to keep it open for reference. If you have the Windows Explorer still open from the steps above where you made the backup copies of the Purchase and Plan pipelines then simply double click on the `plan.pcf` file and it will open in the Win32-based Pipeline Editor automatically (but not in Enhanced Mode). Alternately, you could open the Plan pipeline in the exact same manner that you opened the Purchase pipeline in the steps above.

3. Next, notice that the Plan pipeline has 14 stages – the Purchase pipeline only has three. The 14 stages in the Plan pipeline consist of components that verify the integrity of the OrderForm. Scroll down to the Handling stage. Right-click on the Default Handling component and choose Delete... from the pop-up menu:

Default Handling is used as a placeholder to ensure the integrity of the OrderForm by setting `order._shipping_total` to zero (0). We don't need it anymore because we are going to add a fixed handling charge to the OrderForm every time the Plan pipeline runs, so confirm the deletion when prompted.

4. Right-click on the Handling stage and choose Insert Component... from the pop-up menu:

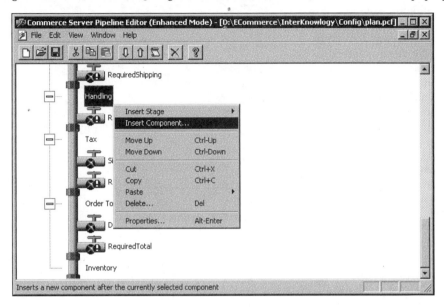

5. Select the FixedHandling pipeline component from the list and then click OK:

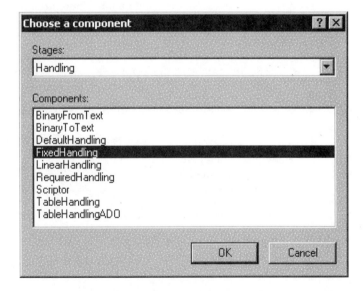

Notice the five types of pipeline components that process handling charges (DefaultHandling, FixedHandling, LinearHandling, TableHandling, and TableHandlingADO). These would not appear if you choose to add a pipeline component into the Shipping or any other stage of the Plan pipeline. All five of these pipeline components were designed specifically to run in the Handling stage of the Plan pipeline. In other words, they have an *affinity* with the Handling stage.

6. The FixedHandling pipeline component will now appear as the first component in the Handling stage of the Plan pipeline. Now that it has been added, either double-click on the FixedHandling pipeline component or right-click on it and chose **Properties** from the pop-up menu. This will bring up the property pages for this component:

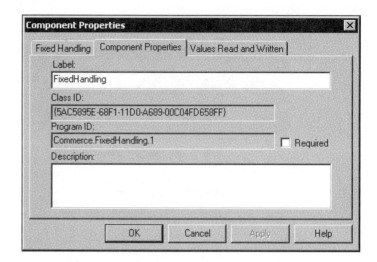

In a compiled pipeline component, the first tab (which is named after the component itself, in this case: **Fixed Handling**) is where the custom properties that are unique to the component are configured. Every compiled pipeline component has a **Component Properties** page (the 2nd tab) and a **Values Read and Written** page (the 3rd tab).

7. Click the **Component Properties** tab. There are four Component properties:

- ❑ The **L**abel property is a user configurable 'friendly name' of the pipeline component.
- ❑ The **Class ID** is the COM CLSID that uniquely identifies the COM component.
- ❑ The **Program ID** is the COM object and class name that is persisted in the registry when a COM component is registered in the operating system.
- ❑ The **D**escription is a user configurable description of the pipeline component.

8. Now, click the **Values Read and Written** tab. It should look similar, if not identical to this screen:

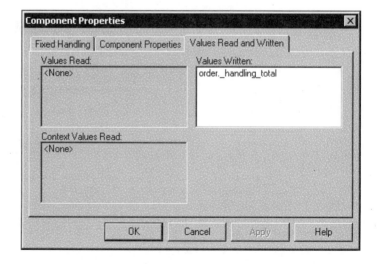

There are three Values Read and Written properties:

❑ The **Values Read** property is the values that this component reads from the `OrderForm` object before it performs its function. In this case, the `FixedHandling` component does not read any values from `OrderForm` object.

❑ The **Values Written** property is the values that the component writes to the `OrderForm` after it has completed its function. In this case, the `FixedHandling` component calculates the fixed handling and then writes the numeric amount to the `_handling_total` property of the **OrderFrom** object (`order._handling_total`).

❑ The **Context Values Read** property is the values that this component reads from the `pipeContext Dictionary` object. The `pipeContext` is passed as a parameter to the Pipeline object's `Execute` method. As you'll learn later in this chapter, the `pipeContext` object is a `Dictionary` object that is passed through the pipeline as a holder of properties needed by pipeline components.

9. Now, click the Fixed Handling tab:

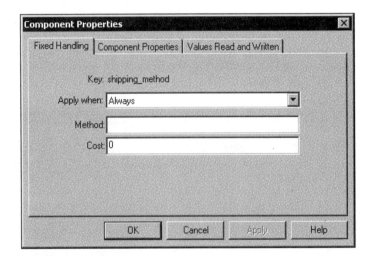

There are four custom properties for Fixed Handling:

❑ The **Key** property is the read-only property used to specify the handling method. The value of this property is compared to the string specified in the **Method** property (see below) to determine whether to apply the handling charge to the order. In this case, we are globally applying a single handling charge to every order, but you could add a number of Fixed Handling pipeline components to the Plan pipeline to conditionally facilitate the application of different fixed handling charges to the order.

❑ The **Apply when** property specifies when to apply the handling charge specified in the Cost property:

❑ **Equal to Method** specifies that the value of the Cost property will be applied only if the value of the property specified for **Key** is the same as the string specified in the **Method** property.

❑ **Has any value** specifies that the value of the Cost property will be applied when the value of the property specified for **Key** has any value on the `OrderForm`. If you select this option, the **Method** property should be left blank since it would be not applicable.

❏ **Always** specifies that the value of the **Cost** property is always applied to the order.

❏ The **Method** property is a placeholder for the value of an item on the `OrderForm` (i.e. `OrderForm.shipping_method = "shipping_method_1"`). If the **Apply when** property has been set to **Equal to Method**, the **Method** property specifies a string (`shipping_method_1`) that the component compares with the value of `shipping_method` on the `OrderForm` to determine whether to apply the handling charge to the order. The value of the **Cost** property will be applied only if there is an exact match. As described above in the **Key** property, the **Method** property helps to conditionally facilitate the application of different fixed handling charges to the order.

❏ The **Cost** property specifies the charge that will be applied if the conditions set by the properties are met. The `MSCSDataFunctions`, as your learned in Chapter 6, are defined in the `global.asa` to define the locale that the site behaves in. In the case of the site we built in Chapter 4, we chose **English-United States (US Dollars)** when running the Site Builder Wizard.

The value of the **Cost** property is 100 times its actual value. For instance, a fixed handling charge of $2.25 is entered in the **Cost** property as `225` (225 / 100 = 2.25). The **Cost** property value is used in calculations appropriately by the pipeline components. It is formatted in the Active Server Pages by methods off the `MSCSDataFunctions` object and rendered to the user in HTML.

10. We want to charge a fixed cost for handling of $6.00 so enter a value of `600` for the value of the **Cost** property:

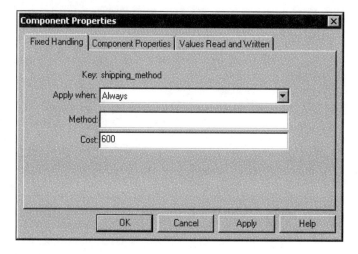

11. Click **OK** to close the property sheet and then save the Plan pipeline (`plan.pcf`) using either the **Save** icon or going **File | Save**.

12. Now browse our site, add something to the basket and proceed to the check out. When you get to the Payment page what happens? Look closely. The handling charge of $6.00 is not displayed individually like shipping is, but it was added to the total price of the order:

49.99 + 10.00 + 3.87 = 63.86, not 69.86. The `FixedHandling` pipeline component that we added to the plan pipeline did its job. It added the $6.00 handling charge to the order, but we have to fix the `Payment.asp` page to display the `orderform.[_handling_total]`. We'll also have to do the same thing on `receipt.asp`.

13. Open `payment.asp` in Microsoft Visual Interdev (or your editor of choice). Scroll down to the HTML table where the subtotal, shipping, tax, and order total values are displayed. Add the code to display the handling total between the shipping and tax values. Let me give you a hint before you start typing. Simply copy the eight lines of code of the HTML Table Row for shipping, paste it directly under and change the two instances of shipping to handling. When you are done it should look like this:

```
<TR>
    <TD ALIGN="RIGHT">
        <B>Shipping:</B>
    </TD>
    <TD ALIGN="RIGHT">
        <%= MSCSDataFunctions.Money(mscsOrderForm.[_shipping_total]) %>
    </TD>
</TR>
```

```
<TR>
    <TD ALIGN="RIGHT">
        <B>Handling:</B>
    </TD>
    <TD ALIGN="RIGHT">
        <%= MSCSDataFunctions.Money(mscsOrderForm.[_handling_total]) %>
    </TD>
</TR>

<TR>
    <TD ALIGN="RIGHT">
        <B>Tax:</B>
    </TD>
    <TD ALIGN="RIGHT">
        <%= MSCSDataFunctions.Money(mscsOrderForm.[_tax_total]) %>
    </TD>
</TR>
```

14. Now, place another order on the site. When you get to the Payment page (`payment.asp`), handling will be uniquely identified like in the screen below:

15. Now, let's fix the Receipt page to uniquely identify handling. Open the Receipt page (`receipt.asp`) in Microsoft Visual Interdev (or your editor of choice). The process will be similar to the fix you just made in the Payment page. Scroll down to the HTML table where the subtotal, shipping, tax, and order total values are displayed. Add the code to display the handling total between the shipping and tax values. Again, like above, let me give you a hint before you start typing. Simply copy the eight lines of code of the HTML Table Row for shipping, paste it directly under and change the three instances of shipping to handling. When you are done it should look like this:

```
<% REM show shipping:  %>
<TR>
    <TD COLSPAN="5"></TD>
    <TH BGCOLOR="#000000" VALIGN="TOP" ALIGN="RIGHT">
        <FONT COLOR="#FFFFFF"><B>Shipping:</B></FONT>
    </TH>
    <TD VALIGN="TOP" ALIGN="RIGHT">
        <B><% = MSCSDataFunctions.Money(receipt.[_shipping_total]) %></B>
    </TD>
</TR>

<% REM show handling:  %>
<TR>
    <TD COLSPAN="5"></TD>
    <TH BGCOLOR="#000000" VALIGN="TOP" ALIGN="RIGHT">
        <FONT COLOR="#FFFFFF"><B>Handling:</B></FONT>
    </TH>
    <TD VALIGN="TOP" ALIGN="RIGHT">
        <B><% = MSCSDataFunctions.Money(receipt.[_handling_total]) %></B>
    </TD>
</TR>

<% REM show tax:  %>
<TR>
    <TD COLSPAN="5"></TD>
    <TH BGCOLOR="#000000" VALIGN="TOP" ALIGN="RIGHT">
        <FONT COLOR="#FFFFFF"><B>Tax:</B></FONT>
    </TH>
    <TD VALIGN="TOP" ALIGN="RIGHT">
        <B><% = MSCSDataFunctions.Money(receipt.[_tax_total]) %></B>
    </TD>
</TR>
```

16. Okay, now go back to the browser and complete the purchase on the site. When you get to the Purchase Confirmation Page (`confirmed.asp`), click on the link for the Order Number. You will proceed to the Receipt Page (`Receipt.asp`) that you just modified to display the handling charge. It will now have the handling charge identified uniquely and look similar to this:

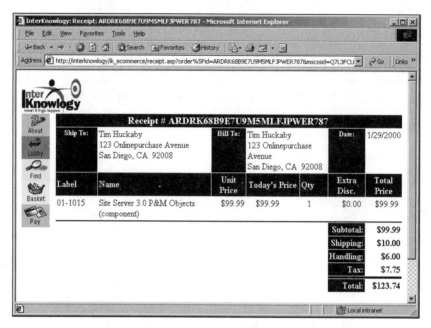

In summary, this example showed the four basic tasks that you would most likely do when adding functionality to your site by adding a pipeline component:

❑ Deleting a pipeline component

❑ Adding a new pipeline component

❑ Modifying the new pipeline component's properties

❑ Modifying the Active Server Pages in the site to make use of the new functionality

The Implementation of Pipelines

In this section, I will cover how the pipelines are implemented and used within a commerce store, and also get you thinking about some of the ways that you might manipulate your pipeline implementations to suit your own store's functionality requirements.

How the Pipelines Are Used

In an online store, like the site we built in Chapter 4, the pipeline components themselves are called via Active Server Pages. The Site Builder Wizard does all of this work for you. The code for creating the objects and executing them can be found in a page called i_util.asp.

Within the i_util.asp page, there are two functions that handle the pipeline execution:

❑ UtilRunPipe()

❑ UtilRunTxPipe()

We will look at each of them and how they operate.

The UtilRunPipe Function

The first function is the UtilRunPipe function, which can be seen here:

```
function UtilRunPipe(file, orderForm, pipeContext)
    Set pipeline = Server.CreateObject("Commerce.MtsPipeline")

    Call pipeline.LoadPipe(Request.ServerVariables("APPL_PHYSICAL_PATH") & _
                        "config\" & file)

    REM Call pipeline.SetLogFile(Request.ServerVariables("APPL_PHYSICAL_PATH") & _
                        "config\pipeline.log")

    errorLevel = pipeline.Execute(1, orderForm, pipeContext, 0)

    UtilRunPipe = errorLevel
end function
```

You will notice that the function requires three arguments:

- ❑ The file, which is the name of the pipeline configuration file to be used (i.e. plan.pcf).
- ❑ The OrderForm object, which has been discussed in detail in Chapter 5.
- ❑ The pipeContext – we will go into the pipeContext later in this section.

After the arguments are passed in, we create the pipeline object using ASP code. Notice the use of Server.CreateObject() instead of just CreateObject(). This will allow IIS to destroy the object once it is no longer used. The next thing that takes place is that the LoadPipe method of the Pipeline object is called and the system path of the file is passed in: this tells the Pipeline object what pipeline configuration file to use and where it is located. You will notice that the next line is REM'd out. The reason for this is that it should only be used during debugging, because the method is not thread-safe and will not support multiple users writing to a log file. The SetLogFile method of the Pipeline object will write a log out to the specified directory. Finally, the function calls the Execute method of the pipeline.

The Execute method's parameters are as follows:

```
Execute(Mode, Order Object, Context, Flag)
```

Where:

- ❑ Mode is the method of execution and is used for backward compatibility with Site Server 2.0.
- ❑ Order Object can be an OrderForm object or a Dictionary object. In a business-to-consumer site using the Order Purchasing Pipeline, this is always an OrderForm object.
- ❑ Context is a Dictionary object containing name/value pairs or pointers to objects used by pipeline components once the pipeline is executed. Again, this will be covered in detail later in the section.
- ❑ Flag is not used at this time and should always be set to zero.

The UtilRunTxPipe Function

The second function found on i_util.asp is called UtilRunTxPipe(). It is identical to
UtilRunPipe() except that the object created is the Commerce.MtsTxPipeline object:

```
function UtilRunTxPipe(file, orderForm, pipeContext)
    Set pipeline = Server.CreateObject("Commerce.MtsTxPipeline")

    Call pipeline.LoadPipe(Request.ServerVariables("APPL_PHYSICAL_PATH") & _
                           "config\" &  file)

    REM Call pipeline.SetLogFile(Request.ServerVariables("APPL_PHYSICAL_PATH") & _
                           "config\txpipeline.log")

    errorLevel = pipeline.Execute(1, orderForm, pipeContext, 0)

    UtilRunTxPipe = errorLevel
end function
```

The Execute method returns one of three values:

❑   **Return value = 1**
    Success – The pipeline encountered no errors.

❑   **Return value = 2**
    Warning – A pipeline component encountered a handled error. For example an invalid credit
    card number.

❑   **Return value = 3**
    Failure – The pipeline component encountered an error, which resulted in failed execution.
    For example, a connection to the database could not be established.

> **Each pipeline component will return an error level of its own. This will "bubble" up
> to the main pipeline. If one pipeline component returns a 2 the pipeline itself will
> return a 2. In the event a pipeline component returns a 2 or above, all components
> following will NOT execute.**

The pipeContext Object

A few times in this chapter we've discussed pipeline components receiving and using the "Context" or
pipeContext object. We discussed how the pipeContext is a required argument for the Execute
method of the two pipeline objects as well.

> **The pipeContext object is a Dictionary object that is passed through the
> pipeline as a keeper of the properties needed by pipeline components.**

The `pipeContext` is passed as a parameter to a pipeline object's `Execute` method. It contains read-only "support" data that the pipeline components use to carry out their functions. This includes database connection strings, configuration values (like you saw in the fixed handling example above), as well as other objects that the components can access during their execution. The Context is created from scratch every time a pipeline is run and destroyed at the end of its execution, and therefore should be considered a read-only storage area. If you must write any values, you should do that in the `Dictionary`.

The `pipeContext` is a way to "hand-off" values that were created within an ASP page to components that are being executed within the pipeline. This is the manner in which state is maintained between the pipeline and the Active Server Pages.

How It Works

We have discussed that the functions necessary to execute a pipeline are found within `i_util.asp` earlier in the chapter. As the `pipeContext` is required to execute a pipeline, the function for setting up the `pipeContext` is also found here. The function is called `UtilGetPipeContext()`.

`UtilGetPipeContext()` sets up the `pipeContext` before it is passed into one of the two pipeline functions – `UtilRunPipe()` or `UtilRunTxPipe()`.

Let's take a look at the `UtilGetPipeContext()` function:

```
function UtilGetPipeContext()
    Set pipeContext = Server.CreateObject("Commerce.Dictionary")
    Set pipeContext("MessageManager")        = MSCSMessageManager
    Set pipeContext("DataFunctions")         = MSCSDataFunctions
    Set pipeContext("QueryMap")              = MSCSQueryMap
    Set pipeContext("ConnectionStringMap")   = MSCSSite.ConnectionStringMap
    pipeContext("SiteName")                  = displayName
    pipeContext("DefaultConnectionString")   = MSCSSite.DefaultConnectionString
    pipeContext("Language")                  = "USA"

    Set UtilGetPipeContext = pipeContext
end function
```

The first line of the function creates the object the `pipeContext` is based upon – the `Dictionary` object:

```
Set pipeContext = Server.CreateObject("Commerce.Dictionary")
```

The `pipeContext`, as complex as it sounds, is nothing more than a `Dictionary` object that is passed into a pipeline object just as the `OrderForm` object is. The `pipeContext` object is passed through the pipeline as a holder of properties needed by pipeline components.

The next lines of the function set the property values of the `pipeContext` object:

```
Set pipeContext("MessageManager")        = MSCSMessageManager
Set pipeContext("DataFunctions")         = MSCSDataFunctions
Set pipeContext("QueryMap")              = MSCSQueryMap
Set pipeContext("ConnectionStringMap")   = MSCSSite.ConnectionStringMap
pipeContext("SiteName")                  = displayName
pipeContext("DefaultConnectionString")   = MSCSSite.DefaultConnectionString
pipeContext("Language")                  = "USA"
```

Notice that most of the property values that are set are set to the Application scope objects defined in the global.asa *file.*

It would be rare problem that demands it, but you could add custom properties to the pipeContext object at the page level and send them to a canned pipeline component that comes with Microsoft Site Server 3.0 Commerce Edition. Most likely, you would do this in configuration properties on the pipeline component itself. An example of doing it though might be if you are using a component that you have written that needs to use an ADODB.Connection object. It would be as simple as writing the following line of code to place a pointer to the object in the pipeContext:

```
Set pipeContext("myConnectionObject") = Server.CreateObject("ADODB.Connection")
```

This is just another area where Site Server's pipeline architecture is very extensible.

The Pipeline Scriptor Component

Before we delve into the meanders of pipeline development in Chapter 8, it's a good idea to introduce a component called the **Pipeline Scriptor** that can be used in any stage of a pipeline. This pipeline component is written in a script language compatible with the Windows Script Host interface (such as Visual Basic Scripting Edition, or VBScript) that has access to configuration properties, the Context object and the Dictionary object just like the compiled pipeline components. With a few limitations (like a 255 line limit, scalability and performance), it can essentially perform the same types of operations that a compiled pipeline component can.

Pipeline Scriptor components work by executing a script that has at least one method called MSCSExecute, whose syntax is below:

```
MSCSExecute (Config, Dictionary, Context, Flags)
```

Where:

❑   Config specifies the parameters that are passed to the script in the form *name=value*

❑   Dictionary is the pipeline's Dictionary (for example, an OrderForm object for an OPP)

❑   Context is the pipeline's Context

❑   Flags is a reserved value.

You will learn how simple pipeline Scriptor components really are by actually building some in the next chapter.

MTS / COM+ in the OPP Pipelines

Microsoft Transaction Server (MTS) on Windows NT 4.0 or **COM+** on Windows 2000 supplies the Site Server pipelines with the ability to handle transactions. What does a pipeline that supports transactions give you? In the event of an error occurring with one of the components during execution, the pipeline will rollback any changes made to your SQL Server database; this will allow your data integrity to be kept intact.. Rolling back all changes made when one of a series of components fails is called *transactional integrity*. This is all handled by MTS/COM+ and the programmer does not have to write extra code to allow a pipeline to roll-back if an error has occurred.

MTS/COM+ communicates with the database via the **Microsoft Distributed Transaction Coordinator** also known as **MSDTC**.

> **The MSDTC service must be running on both the web server and the database server. Site Server Commerce Edition is database independent but for the transactional functionality that can be provided by the transacted pipelines, the database must be a MSDTC compliant database.**

There are two MTS components that create and execute pipelines. They are:

- ❑ Commerce.MTSTxPipeline
- ❑ Commerce.MTSPipeline

The components are identical in their method calls and the only difference is that the Commerce.MTSTxPipeline supports MTS transactions whereas Commerce.MTSPipeline runs under MTS, but does not support transactional integrity.

You will notice by looking through the code generated by the Site Server Site Builder Wizard that the MTSPipeline is used for pages such as the Basket page (basket.asp) and gathering data. This is done because the pipeline does not write any data that cannot be easily reconciled to the database, and if an error occurs no true harm will be done – except for maybe a disgruntled shopper. The actual purchase process (the Purchase pipeline) that is kicked off after a user enters their credit card number is transacted. This is because any reduction of inventory or fulfillment notification takes place at this time. If an error occurs here, the inventory can be reset and no discrepancies with your data will occur.

Pipeline Execution and Branching

When a pipeline is executed, all its components are executed in the *sequential order* in which they appear in the pipeline itself. The execution only stops if one of the components encounters an error that is too critical for the overall operation to complete properly.

This is a very rigid rule, and it has an extremely significant implication: *there is no flow-control in a pipeline*. This means that you cannot decide whether a component will or will not be executed based on external factors (an effect similar to that of an If...Then...Else operation).

The ability to control the flow of execution, sometimes referred to as **branching**, is definitely a very important aspect of programming, and the fact that pipelines do not allow it may look like a significant drawback to the technology. If you consider the elaborate structure of properties on the pipeline components and the way that the properties interact with the fixed shipping and the fixed handling components discussed earlier in the chapter, then it makes much more sense because there is no flow control available in pipelines.

However, there is another simple rule that makes things just a little easier. I call this the **"no-interference" rule**, because it prescribes that a component should only ever write a value to the pipeline's Dictionary if that value is NULL – that is, if a component executed earlier has already written into it, then nothing else should. If components are properly written and arranged, this rule solves many problems that are connected with the lack of support for branching.

For example, let's take a look at the following scenario. Suppose that you have two components, that we will very creatively call Component A and Component B, whose goals are to determine the shipping price of an order. Both work by looking at the number of items in the OrderForm and applying a fixed price for shipping if it is less than a certain quantity:

Component	Less than Quantity	Fixed Shipping
Component A	100	$10
Component B	10	$5

Clearly, we must be careful that the components are executed in the proper order. If Component B is executed before Component A, the end result would always be the value set by Component A. In other words, a fixed shipping amount of $10 would be charged no mater what.

If flow control were available in pipelines, we'd probably want to put an If...Then...Else condition – something similar to the following:

```
If Quantity < 10 Then
    Execute Component B
Else
    Execute Component A
End If
```

However, flow control is not available in the pipeline, and the order that we just outlined – Component A before Component B – is the one that we should use to obtain the desired result *as long as both components respect the no-interference rule.* In fact, what should happen is that Component B writes its value if the number of items is less than 10, and Component A does not interfere with it because it would find a value for shipping in the Orderform object already. Conversely, if the number of items were 11, then Component B would leave the shipping price at its original NULL value and Component A would process it.

This particular way of arranging things is a little difficult to get used to, but it plays a very important role in the pipeline technology. As conditional branching of pipeline components is not available outside the pipeline, the pipeline execution can only take place in one well-defined sequence. This is critical, because in most cases you will be dealing with sensitive procedures (just think of payment processing!) and any use of branching would introduce additional variables in the pipeline's execution that could disrupt the task at hand.

For the Really Tough Situations...

To be perfectly fair, there are a few instances in which the execution of a pipeline *does* require branching. These normally occur when you are dealing with third-party components over whose functionality you have little or no control. Unfortunately, because there is no formal certification process for third-party Site Server components, they often do not strictly follow the no-interference rule that we outlined earlier. As a result, you will end up with two or more components writing over each other – a quite unnerving situation.

There is a solution to this problem, too, but it involves quite a bit of advanced programming. It makes use of a special component called **Micropipe** that ships with Site Server Commerce Edition. A Micropipe makes it possible to execute a single component pipeline on its own, and can be instantiated directly from an ASP script. As a result, you write some dedicated ASP code to handle all your branching needs, and then execute one component at a time using Micropipes. The end result is slightly slower, since each Micropipe has to be instantiated and loaded individually, but serves the purpose of making your life easier in difficult situations.

> *For more information about Micropipes and other advanced Site Server Commerce Edition concepts, check out* Professional Site Server 3.0 Commerce Edition, *by Marco Tabini, published by Wrox Press (ISBN 1-861002-50-5).*

The Pipelines in Site Server 3.0 Commerce Edition

Site Server contains two classes of pipelines that can be used out-of-the box: the **Order Processing Pipeline** and the **Commerce Interchange Pipeline**.

In addition, it is possible to create *custom* pipelines that can better respond to custom needs. Keep in mind that a pipeline is essentially a collection of COM components (since the stages are simply logical groups of components) and therefore you can do just about anything you want with them.

For our discussions here, we will be dealing with the two built-in pipelines:

❑ **The Order Processing Pipeline**
The Order Processing Pipeline (OPP from now on) is used to perform tasks related with the order processing that goes on in a *business-to-consumer* online store. The OPP is really a collection of three different pipelines that are designed to communicate with each other. They have the goal of carrying the purchase process of an online store, from the moment in which the user decides to enter one or more products into the database, to when the Purchase button is pressed.

❑ **The Commerce Interchange Pipeline**
The Commerce Interchange Pipeline, or CIP, is instead used in *business-to-business* transactions, which usually involve the exchange of information between two businesses. B2B transactions are quite different from their B2C counterparts, and they must follow very different rules in order to ensure that the data transmitted from one end reaches the other end – without being corrupted or modified by unauthorized parties en-route.

> *As the Commerce Interchange Pipeline is involved primarily with B2B communications it is not directly relevant to our commerce site, which is B2C. Therefore, we will not be dissecting this class of pipeline in this chapter. We have however, included the information in Appendix A.*

Default Components

As we'll see in the rest of the chapter, several stages in the OPP only contain a **default component**, whose only goal is to simply set the name/value pairs in the pipeline's Dictionary to a default value so that other components will not fail because they are NULL.

I feel compelled to point out that you shouldn't see this apparent lack of functionality as a limitation of the pipeline technology, but rather as an indication of the fact that certain stages required a treatment that is so peculiar that providing catch-all components is essentially impossible. Thus, your best option if you need to add any functionality to one of these stages is to create your own components, either using `Scriptor` – very convenient and easy to debug, in particular, for simple problems – or a COM-compatible compiler for a compiled pipeline component.

Without further ado, let's start looking at the Order Processing Pipeline.

The Order Processing Pipeline

The Order Processing Pipeline is a family of three different pipelines that are used in a business-to-consumer (B2C) store to handle the entire ordering process. The pipelines are:

❑ **The Product Pipeline**
This pipeline can be run when the user requests information about a particular product to generate a set of data that is as accurate and up-to-date as possible, including sale information, discounts and availability.

❑ **The Plan Pipeline**
The Plan pipeline, as seen earlier in the chapter, is used whenever the system must calculate values that relate to an entire shopping basket – including promotions, sales and discounts, as well as shipping, handling and tax-related fees.

❑ **The Purchase Pipeline**
This pipeline, as seen earlier in the chapter, is only run when the system is asked to complete a purchase by the user. It is only run once in the purchase process unlike the Product and Plan pipelines, which can conceivably be run multiple times before the purchase is actually made. Therefore, the goal of the purchase pipeline is essentially that of validating the user's payment information and of initiating the delivery process.

The Product Pipeline

Open the Win32-based Pipeline Editor from:

Start | Programs | Microsoft Site Server | Commerce | Pipeline Editor

Open a `product.pcf` file. If you built the site from Chapter 4, then the path is `..\IK_Ecommerce\Config`:

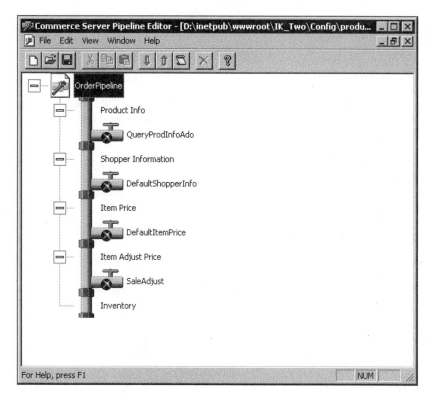

This pipeline contains the following stages.

The Product Info Stage

The **Product Information stage** is generally used in a pipeline to collect all the information about the products in the OrderForm object. This can be done by using QueryProdInfoADO, a pipeline component that runs a query against each item in the OrderForm and adds all the data it retrieves to the items in the OrderForm object.

The QueryProdInfoADO pipeline component uses the QueryMap application object defined in the global.asa in its Context object to run the query product_info.

The Shopper Information Stage

The **Shopper Information stage** is used to retrieve information about the shopper. This can be useful in determining whether the shopper qualifies for certain promotions, or even for the delivery of export-restricted merchandise.

The only built-in component that shows affinity with this stage is DefaultShopperInfo, which essentially takes care of setting the information about the shopper in the OrderForm to a set of default values.

The Item Price Stage

The **Item Price stage** is used to determine the most current price of each item in the OrderForm. The calculation performed at this stage only takes into consideration each individual item, rather than the entire contents of the shopping cart as a whole.

This is particularly important if you consider that certain operations can only take place if the exact quantity and price of all the items in the shopping basket is known, something that, in turn, can only take place once the appropriate calculations have been made to determine such values.

Also in this case, there is only a simple default component, called DefaultItemPrice, that shows affinity with this stage; its task is to simply set the most recent product price – stored in the _iadjust_regularprice name/value pair – to the price that is extracted directly from the Product database.

The Item Adjust Price Stage

In the **Item Adjust Price stage**, the final cost of a particular item is finally calculated by applying the appropriate discounts as determined by a price promotion. At the end of its execution, the pipeline should have set a value in the _iadjust_currentprice name/value pair for each item in the OrderForm.

The Inventory Stage

Finally, the goal of the **Inventory stage** in the Product pipeline is to determine whether any of the items in the OrderForm are actually available for delivery. Naturally, when the Product pipeline is executed the data returned by this stage will, at least in most cases, be for the user's information only, independently from whether your store allows backordering or if an item has to be in stock to be purchased. Many stores consider inventory data highly sensitive information (mostly for security reasons), and therefore only give out vague information (for example, "in stock" or "not in stock" rather than giving out the exact quantity available).

The Plan Pipeline

If not already open, then open the Win32-based Pipeline Editor from:

Start | Programs | Microsoft Site Server | Commerce | Pipeline Editor

Open a plan.pcf file. If you built the site from Chapter 4, then the path is
..\IK_Ecommerce\Config:

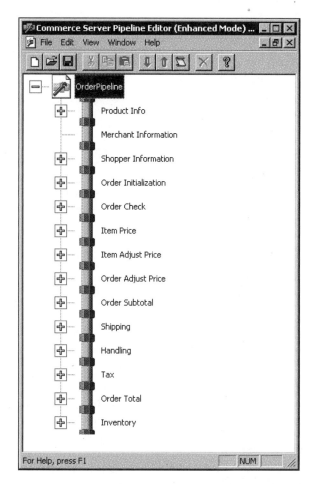

The Plan pipeline is used for repetitive tasks that need to occur during the shopping process. For this reason, the Plan pipeline is executed very frequently. Not only to display the contents of the shopping basket on basket.asp, but the Plan pipeline is executed on many of the other Active Server Pages in the site. One of the by-products of the frequent execution of the Plan pipeline is one of the great features on your site: real-time, up-to-date information is *always* displayed when the shopper views the basket.asp page and other pages on the site. If price changes have occurred or if inventory levels have changed while a shopper is shopping on the site, these will be reflected on those pages automatically warning the shopper of changes. It is conceivable that a product can become obsolete (may no longer be sold) while a shopper is on the site and has it in their basket. In a situation such as this, the product would be removed from the basket and the shopper would be automatically notified that the product is no longer sold and has been removed.

When we discussed the difference between transacted pipelines and non-transacted pipelines, it was mentioned that not all pipelines are usually transacted. A Plan pipeline is generally not transacted because it does not write any data to the database that requires a roll-back. An example is that changes to the product inventory are not written to the database at this point, although, this can change due to customizations that can be made. A Plan pipeline will run more than once during the purchase process.

The Product Info Stage

The **Product Info stage** is the first stage found within the Plan pipeline. The purpose of this stage is to gather all of the information about products in the OrderForm that are required by other components found within the Plan and Purchase pipelines.

One of the pipeline components normally used within the Product Info stage is the QueryProdInfoADO component. This is the very same pipeline component that is used in the Product pipeline and was explained above. Its name is very descriptive: it executes a query to retrieve product data from the database using ADO as its data access component. This component will execute a SQL query for each product found in the OrderForm. The QueryProdInfoADO pipeline component uses the QueryMap application object defined in the global.asa in its Context object to run the query product_info. The information it receives is placed in the OrderForm with a _product prefix to the name/value pair. If the query returns a column named sale_price then the value will be entered into the OrderForm with a name of _product_sale_price.

The Merchant Information Stage

The **Merchant Information stage**, whose goal is to modify the OrderForm so that the identity of the merchant through which a particular transaction went through can be clearly identified, is seldom used. The reason for this is that, usually, only one merchant runs a particular store and, therefore, there is no need to differentiate at the level of the individual order. On the other hand, this stage may come in handy if you need to develop a "virtual mall" of some kind in which more than one retailer sells its merchandise. There are no components that show affinity with this stage.

The Shopper Information Stage

The **Shopper Information stage** is actually optional and could be removed if there is no need to maintain shopper information in the OrderForm. It contains only one component, DefaultShopperInfo, to read the shopper Dictionary object from the pipeContext and write it to the OrderForm into keys starting with _shopper.

The Order Initialization Stage

The **Order Initialization stage** prepares the OrderForm. The Site Builder Wizard adds a Scriptor component called Copy Shopper Info to the Plan pipeline. The Copy Shopper Info pipeline Scriptor component validates the address and telephone information of the shopper and copies it to the appropriate name/value pairs on the OrderForm object.

The Order Check Stage

The **Order Check stage** is a stage dedicated to performing any validation on orders that have been submitted by the shopper. The Site Builder Wizard adds a Scriptor component called Validate Ship-To to the Order Check stage. This Scriptor component, unlike its name implies, validates the shipping method for the order.

The Item Price Stage

There is only one component available at the **Item Price stage**, called DefaultItemPrice, which simply copies the price in the item._product_list_price to the name/value pair of item._iadjust_regularprice. This is done for each item in the Items collection.

The Item Adjust Price Stage

The stage named **Item Adjust Price** is specialized to validate the price for each item the shopper has placed in the `OrderForm`. The components that calculate sale prices and promotions for each individual item are normally used within this stage. These components only affect each individual product's price, not the overall order's price.

There are two components normally used for performing these types of operations:

❑ The `SaleAdjust` component

❑ The `ItemPromo` component

The `SaleAdjust` component uses information entered into the `OrderForm` in the Product Info stage and compares sale start and end dates. If the current date is within the sale dates the component writes the sale price as the current product price:

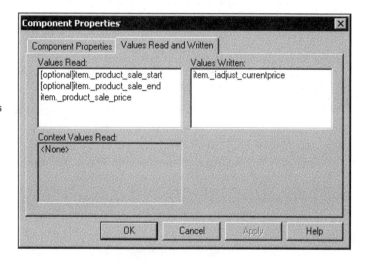

The `ItemPromo` component calculates the cost of the item based on a promotion formula. This can be a "buy two products of the same type and receive a third free" style of promotion.

The Order Adjust Price Stage

The goal of the **Order Adjust Price stage** is to calculate the value of the `_oadjust_adjustedprice` name/value pair for each item in the `OrderForm`. This pair represents the final cost of each item, after applying all the discounts that pertain to it as a single element (for example: on sale at 50% off), as well as to the order as a whole (for example "30% off the purchase of forks if the customer also buys knives).

A very interesting component in this stage is `DBOrderPromoADO`, whose function is to apply promotions to an order based on a set of rules that can be also quite complex. For example, it is possible to specify whether a promotion should be applied when a particular combination of items is in the user's shopping basket, and the promotion itself can come as a percentile discount or as a "buy x get y free" combination. `DBOrderPromoADO` is very flexible and can be directly managed from the store's Store Manager pages if you have chosen to include promotions in your starter site while executing the Site Builder Wizard.

The Order Subtotal Stage

In the **Order Subtotal Stage**, the DefaultOrderSubtotal component just reads the item._oadjust_adjustedprice for all the items, adds them up and writes it to OrderForm._oadjust_subtotal. That is, the subtotal calculated for each item is added up to arrive at the subtotal for the order. Keep in mind that *this* subtotal still doesn't include taxes, shipping or handling – it's just a sum of the cost of all the individual items in the OrderForm, and it's actually what is displayed in the basket page within a Microsoft Site Server 3.0 Commerce Edition store.

The Shipping Stage

The **Shipping stage** contains any code needed to calculate shipping for an order. This calculation is based on the component being used to complete the process.

The shipping pipeline components packaged with Site Server Commerce Edition include:

❑ The DefaultShipping component sets the shipping value to zero. The reason this component is used, like many other default components in the pipeline, is because a shipping total is required for another stage in the pipeline.

❑ The LinearShipping component is per product. The result this component produces is a value that is the sum of a specified field in the OrderForm multiplied by a certain rate. The field is generally a weight field.

❑ FixedShipping is a component that does not produce a variable shipping cost. Shipping is constant based on a shipping method provided.

❑ The TableShippingADO component calculates shipping based on a query specified. The values used come from tables within the database. This component uses ADO as its data access component.

❑ TableShipping operates like TableShippingADO but is supplied for backward compatibility. It does not use ADO as its data access component.

The Handling Stage

As you learned early in the chapter, the **Handling stage** has the function of calculating handling charges for an order. There are five pipeline components supplied with Site Server to calculate handling costs:

❑ The DefaultHandling component

❑ The LinearHandling component

❑ The FixedHandling component

❑ The TableHandlingADO component

❑ The TableHandling component

These components follow the same premise as the Shipping components except they deal with handling costs.

The Tax Stage

The **Tax stage** is used to contain any component that is used to calculate tax. Site Server supplies multiple tax components for calculating tax in the US, Canada (GST, PST), VAT Tax for Europe and Japanese Sales Tax. These components are not recommended for use on a production e-commerce site because of the dynamic nature of international tax law. They are designed for testing purposes and should be replaced by a third-party or custom developed solution.

The components supplied with Site Server are:

❏ The `SimpleUSTax` component

❏ The `SimpleVATTax` component

❏ The `SimpleCanadaTax` component

❏ The `SimpleJapanTax` component

The Order Total Stage

It is in the **Order Total stage** that the total cost of the order is determined, as follows:

```
OrderForm._total_total  =        OrderForm._oadjust_subtotal
                        +        OrderForm._shipping_total
                        +        OrderForm._tax_total
                        +        OrderForm._handling_total
```

The Plan pipeline is run in most of the pages again and again to check and produce the right item, product, price and total on the order.

All of these components described above are configured in a typical default site, depending on the various inputs you gave during the Site Builder Wizard. You could find less or more components in your pipelines.

The Inventory Stage

The **Inventory stage** of the pipeline checks the inventory and reduces inventory. Site Server supplies three components that handle inventory:

❏ The `FlagInventory` component is used to check stock on items that are currently found within the `OrderForm`. The component also allows for the ability to disallow back orders through a select box on the property page of the component. If back orders are not allowed, the component will not allow a product to be ordered if the product's inventory levels are not satisfactory. The component receives its information on inventory levels through a name/value pair called `_product_in_stock` that should be created by the Product Info stage component.

❏ `LocalInventory` is a component very similar to the `FlagInventory` component. This component compares the quantity on hand to the quantity being purchased. The component handles back orders much the same way as the `FlagInventory` component and receives its information from the Product Info stage. `LocalInventory` reads the `_product_local_inventory` name/value pair.

❑ The ReduceLocalInventory component is a component designed to reduce the inventory for an order. The component is available within the inventory stage of a Plan pipeline but it should not be used to reduce inventory because it does not support MTS transactions. It was included for backward compatibility with Commerce Server 2.0. Most likely you would reduce inventory with a custom pipeline component in the Accept stage of the Purchase pipeline. As noted earlier in this chapter, the Plan pipeline may execute multiple times. It actually executes any time the basket page is viewed and then it is executed as the customer enters their shipping and billing information as well. If this pipeline reduces inventory each time the basket page is executed, but a payment has not been taken and the order completed, the inventory data held in the database will not be correct.

This component executes a query that reduces the level of inventory within the database. The query is input directly from the property page but may also be listed within the QueryMap found in the site's global.asa file.

> **Reduction of inventory should be performed within the Purchase pipeline instead of the Plan pipeline because the Plan pipeline is not configured to run as a transacted pipeline by the Site Builder Wizard. If any error should occur on the Plan pipeline and inventory has been reduced, these changes will not roll-back and you will have a discrepancy within your database concerning inventory levels.**

The Purchase Pipeline

If not already open, then open the Win32-based Pipeline Editor from:

Start | Programs | Microsoft Site Server | Commerce | Pipeline Editor

Open a purchase.pcf file. If you built the site from Chapter 4, then the path is
..\IK_Ecommerce\Config:

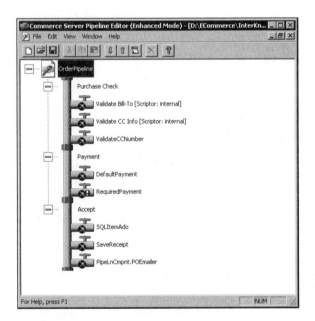

The Purchase pipeline has fewer stages compared to the Plan pipeline. It must always run after the Plan pipeline (not every time, but never before it) so that it has to verify only the payment information of the shopper, authorize the payment and save the receipt.

The Purchase Check Stage

The **Purchase Check stage** is available to allow the programmer to validate any data that has to do with completing the order. The Plan pipeline deals with shipping data because one of its tasks is to calculate shipping cost. Since the Purchase pipeline deals mostly with accepting payment and completing the order, you will most likely be using this stage to validate billing addresses and credit card numbers. It is good practice to try to catch any errors the shopper might have made in this stage due to the processing of credit cards. Many of the real-time credit card processing services charge *per transaction*. If a credit card is rejected due to a shopper's mistake in entry, the shopper must resubmit their credit card number: if this occurs, your site will be billed for two transactions with the credit card processor. In this scenario, data validation can possibly lower or maintain your operating costs of the web site.

The Site Server Site Builder Wizard inserts a `Scriptor` component within the Purchase Check stage that validates entry of the billing address to ensure all of the data was entered. This script does nothing more than check data to make sure it was entered. It is a good idea not to remove this but it can be edited to meet the needs of your store. Site Server also has a component that is supplied to handle credit card checking.

The `ValidateCCNumber` component is supplied to allow the pipeline to verify that the credit card number is a legitimate credit card number. The check is performed on the format of the number being presented: it will run a checksum test based on widely used credit card types and report an error if it does not meet one of these formats.

> The `ValidateCCNumber` component does not perform a check on the shopper's credit card account to ensure that the account is an active account and funds are available. A third-party solution is needed for this type of functionality.

The Payment Stage

The **Payment stage** is used for components that actually handle taking the payment for the order. This can be done in a number of different ways based on the requirements of your store. Some stores may opt to handle payments with purchase orders: a custom component could receive the purchase order and record it to the database in that situation. The standard use of this stage, however, is for the placement of real-time credit card processing components.

There are a number of credit card processing companies that write pipeline components for Microsoft Site Server that interface with their system and require very little changes to a store created with the Site Builder Wizard. The processing company you use depends on which one offers the services best suited for you and your site's needs.

Keep in mind that, if the payment chosen by the user is a credit card, the check performed by the `ValidateCCNumber` component in the Purchase Check stage only determines that the credit card number provided is *mathematically* valid, that is, that it satisfies the algorithm with which those numbers are computed. In order to make sure that the user is actually passing along a *valid* credit card number, your store will also have to connect to a credit card processor and ask for authorization from it. Whether you choose to do this manually off-line or automatically through a pipeline component is a decision yours to make – primarily based on your traffic – just remember that `ValidateCCNumber` alone is not enough!

The Accept Stage

The **Accept stage** of a Purchase pipeline is very general. This is the stage that will handle any processing that must occur to complete the order or which must take place after the order is complete (like sending an e-mail confirmation). The tasks performed here vary from system to system but in general they are things such as writing the order to the database, possibly sending a confirmation e-mail to the shopper, or reducing the inventory levels in the `Product` database.

There are a few components you will see as standard that the Store Builder Wizard places in this stage. Those components are:

❑ The `SQLItemADO` component is used in the Accept stage to write each item found in the `OrderForm` to a table in the database. The way that the function `SQLItemADO` performs, in general, is to execute a SQL query for each item found within the `OrderForm`. Therefore, in the Accept stage this is normally an SQL `INSERT` statement.

❑ The `SaveReceipt` component saves the `OrderForm` as a whole to the `Receipt` table in the database. It works much the same way as the `OrderForm` is saved for use on the basket page but this functionality is wrapped inside a pipeline component. The underlying component for this is the `DBStorage` component, which is received through the `PipeContext`.

There are many other components that can be used within this stage. It would be a good idea to familiarize yourself with these, such as the `MakePO` component, the `POtoFile` component and the `SendSMTP` component. All of these can be used within the Accept stage to make your site more versatile in accepting and processing orders.

> *A tip: should you choose to send receipts to your shoppers via e-mail, it is good practice to use a `Scriptor` or compiled pipeline component with the CDONTS component supplied with Microsoft Internet Information Server instead of the SendSMTP component. The reason for this is that the CDONTS component will queue messages whereas the SendSMTP component does not. If the SendSMTP component cannot connect to a mail server, the entire pipeline will fail and changes will be rolled back (if using a transacted pipeline). If the CDONTS component is used, the mail message is handed off to the IIS SMTP service: if the mail cannot be sent, it does not cause pipeline failure. Chapter 8, shows you how to create a compiled pipeline component that creates a purchase order and then uses CDONTS to send it by e-mail.*

Summary

During the course of this chapter, we've looked at how pipelines work. As you have undoubtedly discovered, pipeline technologies are at the same time incredibly simple and astoundingly complex. In fact, the simplicity of such an open system is dictated by the fact that the goal of these technologies is to provide a framework for executing complex business processes. The complexity, on the other hand, is the consequence of how those processes can vary themselves, to the point where you will most likely have to write your own components to handle at least a few of the situations that you will have to deal with in your applications.

We started off by learning how to edit and manipulate the pipelines to reflect our business and what we wanted to do. Adding and deleting a component to a pipeline is easy, but remember that a pipeline is linear – they do not account for branching, and can only execute components in a strict order, one after the other as they appear in the pipeline. This severity of this rule is, however, alleviated by implementing the *no-interference* rule, where no component should write over a value already written by a previous component. We also saw the implications of adding a business process to the plan pipeline by adding a pipeline component, which added a handling charge to the order. The handling charge was added appropriately in the pipeline, but we needed to go into a couple ASP pages to reflect that handling had actually been added to the order an display that to the consumer.

Moving on, we looked at the Order Processing Pipeline, and then examined the Product, Plan and Purchase pipelines, and how you can implement them in your business. The OPP is useful if we are in a business-to-consumer situation.

In the next chapter, we are going to look at how we can add our own custom functionality to a pipeline by building our very own pipeline components.

Using these technologies in complex applications requires a quite good handling of the entire Commerce Server platform from head to toe. The next logical place for learning more about the technologies are the other Wrox books dedicated to Site Server – Professional Site Server 3.0 (ISBN 1-861002-69-6) and Professional Site Server 3.0 Commerce Edition (ISBN 1-861002-50-5.

Building Pipeline Components

In the last chapter, you learned about pipelines and pipeline components. You learned that pipeline components are nothing more than COM objects or VBScript. You also saw that pipelines are simply a series of pipeline components that are strewn together and run sequentially to serve a business function in whole. Now, I am going to show you how to build pipeline components.

❑ First we'll build a simple pipeline Scriptor component that decrements the quantity_in_stock field, added to the products table in Chapter 5, when an order is placed

❑ Next, I'll show you how to build a compiled pipeline component which creates a purchase order and then emails it

❑ Lastly I'll show you some tools and tricks that will help you in the debugging of pipeline components

Pipeline Scriptor Components

> **The Pipeline Scriptor component is an interpreted, not compiled component, which can be used in any stage of a pipeline. Pipeline Scriptor Components execute scripts written in a Microsoft ActiveX scripting language, such as JScript or VBScript.**

There are three golden rules that you should keep in mind when developing a component as a pipeline Scriptor component:

❑ Scriptor is great for prototyping or short term fixes, but a compiled pipeline component, properly written in Visual Basic, Visual C++, or some other COM compliant language, will provide significantly higher performance, and consequently scale much better than an interpreted pipeline Scriptor component.

❑ The pipeline Scriptor component should always respect the no-interference rule: never overwrite a value in the Dictionary!

❑ Never trap an error unless you're absolutely sure that your script can handle it properly. If the component cannot identify errors that occur in the scripts it runs, the pipeline will not respond properly to error conditions – which may lead to catastrophic results, like an order failing to be processed correctly without properly warning the consumer.

Prerequisites – A Functioning Commerce Site

You will need a functioning commerce site in order to implement the pipeline Scriptor component that we're going to create. In fact, you'll need the commerce site we built in Chapters 4 and 5. Just any old wizard-built site won't do, because our Pipeline Scriptor Component will be dependant on the `quantity_in_stock` field that we added to the `ik_ecommerce_product` table in Chapter 5.

Writing a Simple Pipeline Scriptor Component

Site Server Commerce Edition provides a pre-built Scriptor component framework, which can be inserted anywhere in the pipelines. The script inside can be written in VBScript or JScript. Again, pipeline Scriptor components are powerful as they provide a quick way of prototyping functionality before building them as COM components.

We'll write a small Scriptor component to decrement the `quantity_in_stock` field in the `ik_ecommerce_product` table when an order is placed on the site. Obviously, this isn't double entry accounting, and consequently we won't have a debit or a credit in an inventory transaction database. We will simply decrement the "on hand" bucket to simulate what might happen on a production commerce site.

1. Run the Pipeline Editor: Start | Programs | Microsoft Site Server | Commerce | Pipeline Editor (if you followed the instructions from the earlier chapter, Enhanced Mode will work automatically).

2. Open the Purchase pipeline by navigating to the `Config` folder on our commerce site (...\InterKnowology\Config\purchase.pcf).

3. Navigate to the Accept Stage, right-click on the SaveReceipt component and choose Insert Component | After... from the pop-up menu:

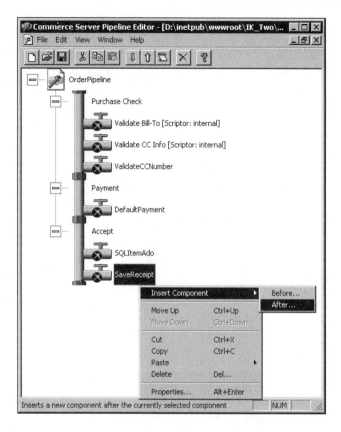

4. You will see various components that are available for the Accept stage:

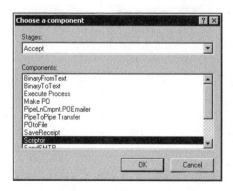

Since we are going to write our own Scriptor code, choose Scriptor and press OK.

5. Double-click on the Scriptor component we just added, and you'll be presented with the property sheet for the scriptor component that we're gong to create:

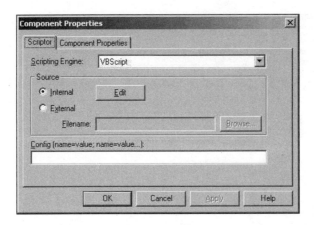

6. Click the Component Properties Tab. Let's give the Scriptor component a name. The "canned" Scriptor components that ship with Microsoft Site Server Commerce Edition follow a naming convention of a simple one or two word description, then the identification of a Scriptor and then whether it's an internal or external Scriptor (we'll cover the internal and external types next). The naming convention of the two Scriptor components in the Purchase Check Stage. They are called Validate Bill-To [Scriptor: internal] and Validate CC Info [Scriptor: internal].

Let's follow the naming convention (although it's not a requirement) and call our Scriptor component Decrement Inventory [Scriptor: external]. Type it into the Label field. Now give the Scriptor a description – something like This external scriptor component decrements the quantity_in_stock field in the ik_ecommerce_product table when an order is placed will do just fine – the Description is not mandatory.

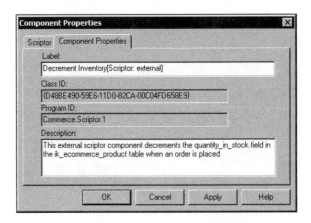

Notice that the other two fields on the dialog are class id and program id – do these sound familiar? They should, because really, all that we're doing in this step is setting properties on a COM object called Commerce.Scriptor.1. Click the Apply button, and then click the Scriptor tab.

7. In the Config property type the following:

DSN=InterKnowlogyEcom; DBUser=sa; DBPwd=; DB=InterKnowlogyEcom

These are 4 configuration parameters that we're going send to the pipeline Scriptor component. They represent the DSN and database parameters that we need to connect to the SQL Server which houses the products table. We need to access the Products table to decrement the quantity_in_stock field.

We could Dim the four variables and set values for them within the script or define constants, but sending the values as configuration parameters makes the scriptor component much more robust. It also makes the scriptor component easier to modify if you change databases or SQL Servers or passwords, because you won't have to edit code.

8. Click the Edit button. You can point the Scriptor component to an External file on your web site, but for the example in this chapter, we'll use an Internal source. You will see entry point functions like those shown below:

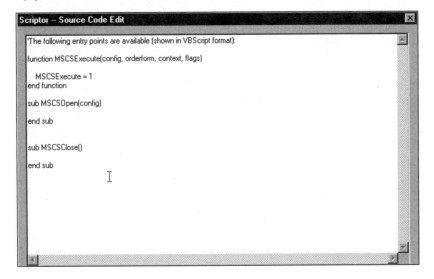

The script that's written for the MSCSOpen subroutine is executed immediately after the Scriptor component is created. The MSCSExit subroutine is executed after the Scriptor component is destroyed. The MSCSOpen and MSCSExit subroutines are not used in any scriptor component that ships with Microsoft Site Server 3.0 Commerce Edition, and we'll not need to use them in our Scriptor component either.

The MSCSExecute function is called after MSCSOpen and before MSCSExit. Of the three exports that make up a default Scriptor component, only the MSCSExecute method is required.

MSCSExecute is the function in which we'll have to write our code to decrement the on-hand inventory amount. MSCSExecute should return 1 if its functional processing is successful.

9. Examine the code below and then type it into the editing window that's used for the internal source, as the body of the function MSCSExecute. (If we were using an external file for source, any HTML editor would suffice to edit the file.)

In the code below we Dim two variables: the cnProducts variable will be the ADO Connection object that we need to talk to the SQL Server, and the strSQL variable will be a string that holds the Transact SQL UPDATE statement that decrements the quantity_in_stock field:

```
Function MSCSExecute(config, orderform, context, flags)
    Dim cnProducts
    Dim strSQL
```

Then we create the ADO Connection object:

```
'Create ADO connection object
Set cnProducts = CreateObject("ADODB.Connection")
```

Next, we open a connection to the database. Notice the use of the configuration parameters sent on the Config object (the first parameter of the MSCSExecute function):

```
'Open connection to database using System DSN
cnProducts.Open "DSN=" & config.DSN & "; UID=" & config.DBUser & "; PWD=" _
                    & config.DBPwd & "; DATABASE=" & config.DB
```

Now, we simply iterate through the Items Simplelist (as we learned in Chapter 5, the items are a Simplelist object that is part of the OrderForm object) on the OrderForm object. At the completion of each iteration of an item on the OrderForm (each line item on the order), we execute the transact UPDATE statement that decrements the quantity_in_stock field of the ik_ecommerce_product table by the value Item.Quantity on the OrderForm object:

```
Set Items = orderform.items

' This code loops through each item in the orderform.
For each item in Items
    'Define Transact SQL Update statement to decrement inventory by the
    'amount purchased
    strSQL = "UPDATE ik_ecommerce_product " & _
            "SET quantity_in_stock = quantity_in_stock - " & Item.Quantity & _
            " WHERE sku ='" & Item.sku & "'"

    'Use the Execute method to issue the query on the database
    cnProducts.Execute(strSQL)
Next
```

Lastly, we destroy the ADO Connection object to free up the resource, and tell the Scriptor component that we've successfully completed by setting `MSCSExecute` to 1.

```
    Set cnProducts = Nothing

    MSCSExecute = 1
End Function
```

10. Click the OK button twice and then save the Plan pipeline.

11. Now order something from the site you built in Chapter 4. Pay special attention to the Product page that tells you how many items are in stock and available for purchase. Upon completion of the order (and consequent successful completion of the pipeline component that you just wrote), go back to the Product page and notice that the quantity on hand is decremented by the amount you just ordered.

Compiled Pipeline Components

As we saw in the previous chapter, a pipeline is merely a series of one or more pipeline components that execute in succession. We've already seen how to add, edit and delete the pipeline components that Site Server Commerce Edition provides for us, so now we're going to build our own compiled component to insert into one of the pipelines of our commerce site. The function of this compiled pipeline component will be to facilitate the automatic creation of a purchase order, and then create and send an e-mail containing the purchase order to a fulfillment partner, accounting entity or whomever you decide to notify of the order.

The **POEmailer pipeline component**, like most compiled pipeline components, has two basic functions:

❑ The first, and most obvious function is to actually create the purchase order and the e-mail, and then send that e-mail by way of the purchase pipeline. It has no user interface.

❑ A truly robust pipeline component must also support a property page, where application level properties can be set and persisted with a user interface. The second function of the compiled pipeline component allows the user to set properties for the compiled component. Allowing the setting of properties through a user interface prevents hard-coding those values into the component itself, forcing it to be recompiled each time a configuration change is required. In this case, we'll set three properties on the pipeline component related to the e-mail:

   ❑ The e-mail addresses of the Sender

   ❑ The e-mail addresses of the Receiver

   ❑ The e-mail addresses of the CC Receiver

   And five properties to set the SQL Server connection data:

   ❑ The DSN for the database

   ❑ The SQL Server user name

    ❑   The password for that user name

    ❑   The name of the database

    ❑   The name of the database table

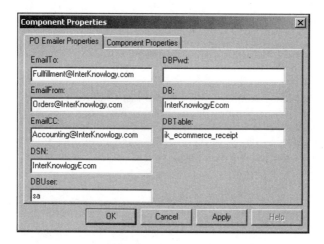

The Development Environment

The most difficult part of building compiled pipeline components is debugging them. In fact, I'll go so far as to say that this is a huge weakness of the compiled pipeline component, and it makes the development of pipeline components difficult.

Although it's possible to debug compiled pipeline components by the cryptic error messages that are returned to the browser when a problem is encountered, you will most likely want to set up your development server to be able to use the debugger to "step into" a compiled pipeline component. Setting up the development environment for debugging is no small chore either and certainly beyond the scope of this case study, but you can find detailed documentation on how to set up your development environment for debugging in the Visual Studio documentation. There is also great information on how to set up the development environment for debugging on the MSDN site at: `http://support.microsoft.com/support/kb/articles/q247/1/88asp` and `http://support.microsoft.com/support/kb/articles/q244/2/72.asp`. However, at the end of this chapter I will provide some tips for debugging.

> *In order to fully understand this project you need a good understanding of COM and especially how it works with VB. However, this is beyond the scope of this book so I will provide you as much information as you need to know but I recommend you read up on*
>
> *COM. A good place to start would be VB COM: A Visual Basic Programmer's Introduction to COM from Wrox Press (ISBN: 1-861002-13-0).*

Creating the Compiled Pipeline Component

1. Open Visual Basic 6.0 and when the New Project dialog comes up, select the New tab and choose ActiveX Control:

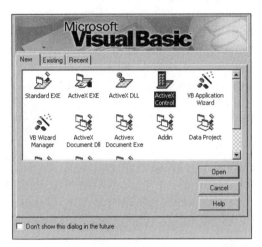

Click the Open button to create the new ActiveX Control project.

2. First let's get rid of the generic names that the project has defaulted. Go to the Project Explorer dialog and select Project1. Then, in the Properties window, change the Name property of the project from Project1 to IK. Now select the default UserControl and change its Name property to POEmailer:

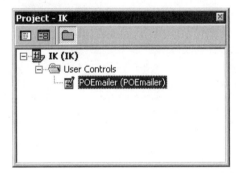

This is will effectively make the ProgID of this COM (compiled pipeline) component `IK.POEmailer`.

3. We need to add three references to the pipeline component project:

❑ Firstly we need the Commerce **pipeline 1.0 Type Library**. The Pipeline library will allow the component to function as a Microsoft Site Server 3.0 Commerce Edition pipeline component.

❑ Secondly, we need the **Microsoft CDO for NTS 1.2 Library**. The CDONTS library supports the automation of sending SMTP emails.

❑ Thirdly, we'll need the **Microsoft ActiveX Data Objects 2.5 library**, because we'll be retrieving the short order id from the SQL server in the receipts table. I've installed Site Server 3.0 Commerce Edition on Windows 2000, so I have ADO 2.5 available. If you've installed Site Server on Windows NT 4.0, then the ADO 2.1 library will work just fine.

Open the **References** dialog by going to the **P**roject menu and then selecting **Refere**n**ces...** Scroll through the list of possible references and check the boxes next to the two type libraries listed above:

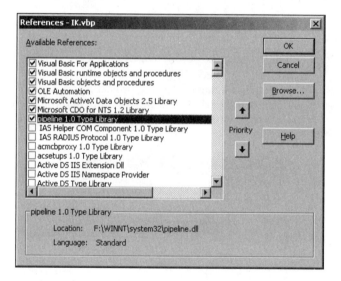

The User Control

1. First, right-click on the **POEmailer** User Control and chose **View Code** to open the code module. Enter the following in the **General Declarations** section.

Use the drop-downs in the top-left and top-right to select this section if you're not sure.

```
Option Explicit
```

```
Private mstrEmailTo As String
Private mstrEmailFrom As String
Private mstrEmailCC As String

Private mstrDSN As String
Private mstrDBUser As String
Private mstrDBPwd As String
Private mstrDB As String
Private mstrDBTable As String

Dim mblnDirty As Boolean
```

Here we've declared three variables to hold the values of the three email addresses, five variables to hold the SQL Server connection data that the component will persist as properties, and one variable (`mblnDirty`) to track whether data from the property page needs to be persisted.

2. Now, we write property procedures that work the member variables we declared above. Enter the following code below our declarations in the code module:

```
Public Property Get EmailTo() As String
    EmailTo = mstrEmailTo
End Property

Public Property Let EmailTo(mailTo As String)
    mstrEmailTo = mailTo
    mblnDirty = True
End Property

Public Property Get EmailFrom() As String
    EmailFrom = mstrEmailFrom
End Property

Public Property Let EmailFrom(mailFrom As String)
    mstrEmailFrom = mailFrom
    mblnDirty = True
End Property

Public Property Get EmailCC() As String
    EmailCC = mstrEmailCC
End Property

Public Property Let EmailCC(mailCC As String)
    mstrEmailCC = mailCC
    mblnDirty = True
End Property

Public Property Get IsDirty() As Boolean
    IsDirty = mblnDirty
End Property
```

```
Public Property Get DSN() As String
    DSN = mstrDSN
End Property

Public Property Let DSN(strDSN As String)
    mstrDSN = strDSN
    mblnDirty = True
End Property

Public Property Get DBUser() As String
    DBUser = mstrDBUser
End Property

Public Property Let DBUser(strDBUser As String)
    mstrDBUser = strDBUser
    mblnDirty = True
End Property

Public Property Get DBPwd() As String
    DBPwd = mstrDBPwd
End Property

Public Property Let DBPwd(strDBPwd As String)
    mstrDBPwd = strDBPwd
    mblnDirty = True
End Property

Public Property Get DB() As String
    DB = mstrDB
End Property

Public Property Let DB(strDB As String)
    mstrDB = strDB
    mblnDirty = True
End Property

Public Property Get DBTable() As String
    DBTable = mstrDBTable
End Property

Public Property Let DBTable(strDBTable As String)
    mstrDBTable = strDBTable
    mblnDirty = True
End Property
```

Note that whereas our member variables were declared as `Private`, the property procedures are `Public`. This means the only external access to the variables will be through the property procedures.

Adding PropertyBag Support

Next, we add property bag support. A **PropertyBag** object holds information that is to be saved and restored across invocations of an object.

A PropertyBag object is passed into an object through the `ReadProperties` event and the `WriteProperties` event, in order to respectively restore and save the state of the object.

1. Add the following code below the property procedures.

The `UserControl_ReadProperties` subroutine reads the property values from the property bag. The property bag is effectively the storage location for the properties that get persisted to disk, even after the `UserControl_WriteProperties` subroutine executes:

```
Private Sub UserControl_ReadProperties(PropBag As PropertyBag)

    mstrEmailTo = PropBag.ReadProperty("EmailTo", "")
    mstrEmailFrom = PropBag.ReadProperty("EmailFrom", "")
    mstrEmailCC = PropBag.ReadProperty("EmailCC", "")

    mstrDSN = PropBag.ReadProperty("DSN", "")
    mstrDBUser = PropBag.ReadProperty("DBUser", "")
    mstrDBPwd = PropBag.ReadProperty("DBPwd", "")
    mstrDB = PropBag.ReadProperty("DB", "")
    mstrDBTable = PropBag.ReadProperty("DBTable", "")

    mblnDirty = False

End Sub
```

The `UserControl_WriteProperties` subroutine writes the values of the properties that we defined to disk so that they may be retrieved and used in the `IPipelineComponent_Execute` method, which actually does the work of the pipeline component:

```
Private Sub UserControl_WriteProperties(PropBag As PropertyBag)

    PropBag.WriteProperty "EmailTo", mstrEmailTo
    PropBag.WriteProperty "EmailFrom", mstrEmailFrom
    PropBag.WriteProperty "EmailCC", mstrEmailCC

    PropBag.WriteProperty "DSN", mstrDSN
    PropBag.WriteProperty "DBUser", mstrDBUser
    PropBag.WriteProperty "DBPwd", mstrDBPwd
    PropBag.WriteProperty "DB", mstrDB
    PropBag.WriteProperty "DBTable", mstrDBTable

    mblnDirty = False

End Sub
```

Adding Pipeline Functionality

So far we've only really added the interface (the property procedures) for our component, so there is nothing specifically making it a pipeline component. Let's do this now.

1. Go back to the General Declarations section and add this line:

```
Option Explicit

Implements IPipeLineComponent

Private mstrEmailTo As String
Private mstrEmailFrom As String
Private mstrEmailCC As String
```

The `Implements` statement specifies an interface or class that will be implemented in the class module (or in this case the user control module of an ActiveX control) in which it appears. In this case, we are implementing the `IPipeLineComponent` interface. This is what makes this component a *pipeline* component.

2. As we're implementing an interface, we must define all the functions of this interface in our user control. This is simpler than it sounds. Once you've added the `Implements` line you can go to the Object drop-down box in the code module (top-left) and you will now find an entry for IPipelineComponent:

Select IPipelineComponent from this drop-down, and then from the Procedure drop-down box you can simply select the required procedures for this interface to automatically generate the stubs in the code module. If you do this for the EnableDesign and Execute procedures you should get the following:

```
Private Sub IPipelineComponent_EnableDesign(ByVal fEnable As Long)

End Sub
```

```
Private Function IPipelineComponent_Execute(ByVal OrderForm As Object, _
                ByVal pdispContext As Object, ByVal lFlags As Long) As Long

End Function
```

The `EnableDesign` procedure is not really needed, but its definition is required by implementation. Only Site Server 3.0 Commerce Edition administrative tools should call this method, which makes it non-applicable for our pipeline component – there is no reason to call it when executing a pipeline.

> Also note that in the `Execute` method, I've changed the `pdispOrder` parameter to the more readable `OrderForm`.

It is in the Execute procedure that the meat of our component resides. This is the function that gets called when the pipeline runs. Take note of the declaration of the CDONTS object.

1. Type the following code into the code view window directly below the Pipeline Component Support declaration (you'll find it similar in function and syntax to the code you used in the Execute method of the Scriptor component earlier in the chapter.

First, we Dim the variables that we're going to use in the function:

```
Private Function IPipelineComponent_Execute(ByVal OrderForm As Object, _
                ByVal pdispContext As Object, ByVal lFlags As Long) As Long
```

```
    Dim Item, Items
    Dim ShortOrderID
    Dim i As Integer
    Dim Body As String
    Dim strSQL As String
    Dim strShortOrderID As String
    Dim objMail As CDONTS.NewMail
    Dim objCon As ADODB.Connection
    Dim objRS As ADODB.Recordset
```

2. Next we create the Collaborative Data Object as an e-mail. Notice how we set the properties of the NewMail object to the properties that we gathered on the property sheet of the pipeline component:

```
    Set objMail = CreateObject("CDONTS.NewMail")

    objMail.To = mstrEmailTo
    objMail.Cc = mstrEmailCC
    objMail.From = mstrEmailFrom
```

3. Now, we need to set the subject of the e-mail to the short order id of the order. We have to do some ADO to grab the short order id from the Receipt table.

First we create the ADO Connection object:

```
    Set objCon = CreateObject("ADODB.Connection")
```

Next, we open a connection to database using a System DSN and database parameters that are defined on the property sheet:

```
    objCon.Open "DSN=" & mstrDSN & "; UID=" & mstrDBUser & "; PWD=" & mstrDBPwd & _
            "; DATABASE=" & mstrDB
```

Then we build the SQL query string, execute the query, and persist the result in a recordset:

```
    strSQL = "SELECT short_order_id FROM " & mstrDBTable & _
            " WHERE order_id = '" & OrderForm.order_id & "'"

    Set objRS = objCon.Execute(strSQL)
```

Lastly, we assign the value of the short order id that was retrieved from the receipts table to a variable. To be safe, in case of disaster, we assign the normal order id to the string if we don't return anything from our query. This should never happen, because the prior pipeline component (SQLADO) must execute successfully or our pipeline component would never start. The Purchase pipeline is a transacted pipeline managed by MTS, so if there were a problem in the SQLADO component the entire thing would roll back:

```
If Not objRS.EOF Then
   strShortOrderID = objRS("short_order_id")
Else
   strShortOrderID = OrderForm.order_id
End If
```

4. Because we no longer need the database, we free up the resources by letting them go. Then we assign the short order id retrieved from the receipts table to the subject line of the e-mail:

```
objRS.Close
objCon.Close
Set objRS = Nothing
Set objCon = Nothing

objMail.Subject = "Purchase Order # " & ShortOrderID & "."
```

5. Now, we go into the painstaking detail of building the body of the e-mail message, which, of course, contains the details of the purchase order:

```
Body = Body & "Order Confirmation #" & vbCrLf
Body = Body & vbTab & OrderForm.order_id & vbCrLf
Body = Body & vbCrLf
Body = Body & "Order Date:" & vbCrLf
Body = Body & vbTab & OrderForm.date_changed & vbCrLf
Body = Body & vbCrLf
Body = Body & "Billing Address:" & vbCrLf
Body = Body & vbTab & OrderForm.bill_to_name & vbCrLf
Body = Body & vbTab & OrderForm.bill_to_street & vbCrLf
Body = Body & vbTab & OrderForm.bill_to_city & " "
Body = Body & vbTab & OrderForm.bill_to_state & ",  " & _
             OrderForm.bill_to_zip & vbCrLf
Body = Body & vbTab & OrderForm.bill_to_country & vbCrLf
Body = Body & vbCrLf
Body = Body & "Shipping Address:" & vbCrLf
Body = Body & vbTab & OrderForm.ship_to_name & vbCrLf
Body = Body & vbTab & OrderForm.ship_to_street & vbCrLf
Body = Body & vbTab & OrderForm.ship_to_city & " "
Body = Body & vbTab & OrderForm.ship_to_state & ",  " & _
             OrderForm.ship_to_zip & vbCrLf
Body = Body & vbTab & OrderForm.ship_to_country & vbCrLf
Body = Body & vbCrLf
```

6. We continue building the body of the e-mail message by simply iterating through the Items Simplelist on the OrderForm object:

```
Set Items = OrderForm.Items

'This code loops through each item.
For Each Item In Items

  'used for numbering each item
  i = i + 1

  Body = Body & "Item #" & (i) & vbCrLf
  Body = Body & vbTab & "Product Name:  " & Item.Name & vbCrLf
  Body = Body & vbTab & "Form Number:  " & Item.Number & vbCrLf
  Body = Body & vbTab & "Quantity:  " & Item.Quantity & vbCrLf
  Body = Body & vbCrLf

Next
```

7. After setting the Body property on the NewMail object with the strBody string that was built, we use the Send method on the NewMail object to send the e-mail:

```
objMail.Body = Body

objMail.Send
```

8. Lastly, we destroy the NewMail object to free up the resource, and tell the component that we've successfully completed by setting IPipelineComponent_Execute to 1:

```
Set objMail = Nothing

' Return 1 for Success
IPipelineComponent_Execute = 1

End Function
```

That's all the code we need for the User Control.

The Property Page

The property page allows you to set configuration parameters (in this case, the e-mail addresses for the TO:, FROM: and CC: on an e-mail message) for the component, so that you don't have to hard-code anything into the component itself.

1. Insert a property page into the project, going to the Project menu and selecting Add Property Page. From the Add PropertyPage dialog, select New | Property Page:

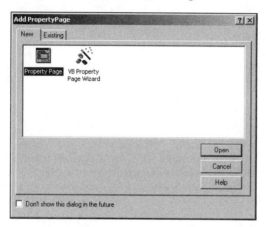

Change the name of the new property page to POEmailerProperties.

2. Follow the previous step again to add another property page, but this time instead of selecting the New Property Page option, select the VB Property Page Wizard.

3. Click Next > to move off the first page of the wizard. We need to choose the property page we want to use with our user control – the wizard will list POEMailerProperties so make sure it's checked:

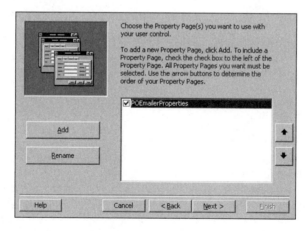

4. Click the Next > button. We now have to choose the properties we want to display on the property page. The wizard will read the available properties that were defined in the code in the User Control. Press the >> button to move all the Available Properties to the POEmailerProperties tab on the right:

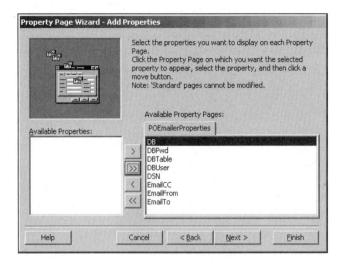

5. Click Next > to move to the final page of the wizard. You'll be prompted to see a summary report on what needs to be done after the property page is built. Click Finish and then click OK.

If you haven't saved your VB Pipeline Component Project already, now would be as good a time as any. I like to save my components in a dedicated components folder, but that's just for organization purposes. COM won't care where the actual component resides when you register it.

6. After reading the Summary Report, take a look at what the Wizard has done. To view the property page simply double click on it in the Project Explorer window:

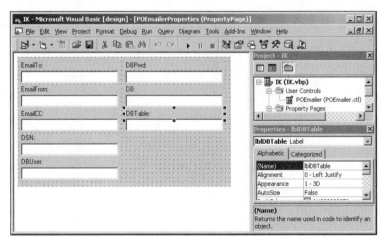

As you can see, the Wizard has placed eight text boxes on the property page to correspond with our eight properties.

7. Now if you right-click on the **POEmailerProperties** property page we just created in the
Project Explorer window and choose **View Code**, you will notice that the Wizard has
already added some code for us (we're going to add to this code in the steps below, so
we'll talk about each section in detail then):

```
Private Sub txtDBTable_Change()
    Changed = True
End Sub


Private Sub txtDB_Change()
    Changed = True
End Sub


Private Sub txtDBPwd_Change()
    Changed = True
End Sub


Private Sub txtDBUser_Change()
    Changed = True
End Sub


Private Sub txtDSN_Change()
    Changed = True
End Sub


Private Sub txtEmailCC_Change()
    Changed = True
End Sub


Private Sub txtEmailFrom_Change()
    Changed = True
End Sub


Private Sub txtEmailTo_Change()
    Changed = True
End Sub


Private Sub PropertyPage_ApplyChanges()
    SelectedControls(0).DBTable = txtDBTable.Text
    SelectedControls(0).DBPwd = txtDBPwd.Text
    SelectedControls(0).DBUser = txtDBUser.Text
    SelectedControls(0).DSN = txtDSN.Text
    SelectedControls(0).EmailCC = txtEmailCC.Text
    SelectedControls(0).EmailFrom = txtEmailFrom.Text
    SelectedControls(0).EmailTo = txtEmailTo.Text
End Sub
```

```
Private Sub PropertyPage_SelectionChanged()
    txtDBTable.Text = SelectedControls(0).DBTable
    txtDBPwd.Text = SelectedControls(0).DBPwd
    txtDBUser.Text = SelectedControls(0).DBUser
    txtDSN.Text = SelectedControls(0).DSN
    txtEmailCC.Text = SelectedControls(0).EmailCC
    txtEmailFrom.Text = SelectedControls(0).EmailFrom
    txtEmailTo.Text = SelectedControls(0).EmailTo
End Sub
```

8. Now we want to add code of our own. Add the following to the General Declarations section:

```
Option Explicit
```

```
Dim mstrEmailTo As String
Dim mstrEmailFrom As String
Dim mstrEmailCC As String

Dim mstrDSN As String
Dim mstrDBUser As String
Dim mstrDBPwd As String
Dim mstrDB As String
Dim mstrDBTable As String
```

Other than the `Option Explicit` statement – which is simply good coding practice because it forces you to explicitly declare your variables – we have simply declared string variables for the eight properties.

9. Next are the `Change` events for all of the properties. The purpose of the `Change` event on each property is to assign the value entered into the text box to the appropriate string variable if the value has changed. There is error processing to handle type mismatches.

If the value is changed, then we store the value locally until the user clicks the Apply button to Apply the changes. Modify the existing code routines as appropriate:

```
Private Sub txtDBTable_Change()
    ' If the value is changed, then store the value locally until
    ' user says ApplyChanges. Also update the text with what we
    ' think is the correct value.

    On Error GoTo ErrHappenned
    mstrDBTable = CStr(txtDBTable.Text)
    Changed = True
    Exit Sub

ErrHappenned:
    ' If type mismatch error, then just assign "" to the field
    If 13 = Err Then
        mstrDBTable = ""
```

```
        Else
            Err.Raise Err.Number
        End If

End Sub

Private Sub txtDB_Change()

        On Error GoTo ErrHappenned
        mstrDB = CStr(txtDB.Text)
        Changed = True
        Exit Sub

ErrHappenned:
        ' If type mismatch error, then just assign "" to the field
        If 13 = Err Then
            mstrDB = ""
        Else
            Err.Raise Err.Number
        End If

End Sub

Private Sub txtDBPwd_Change()

        On Error GoTo ErrHappenned
        mstrDBPwd = CStr(txtDBPwd.Text)
        Changed = True
        Exit Sub

ErrHappenned:
        ' If type mismatch error, then just assign "" to the field
        If 13 = Err Then
            mstrDBPwd = ""
        Else
            Err.Raise Err.Number
        End If

End Sub

Private Sub txtDBUser_Change()

        On Error GoTo ErrHappenned
        mstrDBUser = CStr(txtDBUser.Text)
        Changed = True
        Exit Sub

ErrHappenned:
        ' If type mismatch error, then just assign "" to the field
        If 13 = Err Then
            mstrDBUser = ""
```

```
        Else
            Err.Raise Err.Number
        End If
    End Sub

Private Sub txtDSN_Change()

    On Error GoTo ErrHappenned
    mstrDSN = CStr(txtDSN.Text)
    Changed = True
    Exit Sub

ErrHappenned:
    ' If type mismatch error, then just assign "" to the field
    If 13 = Err Then
        mstrDSN = ""
    Else
        Err.Raise Err.Number
    End If

End Sub

Private Sub txtEmailCC_Change()

    On Error GoTo ErrHappenned
    mstrEmailCC = CStr(txtEmailCC.Text)
    Changed = True
    Exit Sub

ErrHappenned:
    ' If type mismatch error, then just assign "" to the field
    If 13 = Err Then
        mstrEmailCC = ""
    Else
        Err.Raise Err.Number
    End If

End Sub

Private Sub txtEmailFrom_Change()

    On Error GoTo ErrHappenned
    mstrEmailFrom = CStr(txtEmailFrom.Text)
    Changed = True
    Exit Sub

ErrHappenned:
    ' If type mismatch error, then just assign "" to the field
    If 13 = Err Then
        mstrEmailFrom = ""
    Else
```

417

```
            Err.Raise Err.Number
        End If

End Sub

Private Sub txtEmailTo_Change()

    On Error GoTo ErrHappenned
    mstrEmailTo = CStr(txtEmailTo.Text)
    Changed = True
    Exit Sub

ErrHappenned:
    ' If type mismatch error, then just assign "" to the field
    If 13 = Err Then
        mstrEmailTo = ""
    Else
        Err.Raise Err.Number
    End If

End Sub
```

10. Next is the `ApplyChanges` event. The `ApplyChanges` event is fired when the user clicks the **Apply** or **OK** buttons on the property page. In the event, the property page is updated with the values first, and then the values are transferred to the component. Again, modify the code as appropriate:

```
Private Sub PropertyPage_ApplyChanges()

    ' This event is fired when the user clicks the Apply or OK buttons
    ' on the property page.

    ' Update the page with what we think the values are
    txtEmailTo.Text = mstrEmailTo
    txtEmailFrom.Text = mstrEmailFrom
    txtEmailCC.Text = mstrEmailCC
    txtDBTable.Text = mstrDBTable
    txtDBPwd.Text = mstrDBPwd
    txtDB.Text = mstrDB
    txtDBUser.Text = mstrDBUser
    txtDSN.Text = mstrDSN

    'Transfer the values to the component(s) now.
    SelectedControls(0).DBTable = txtDBTable.Text
    SelectedControls(0).DBPwd = txtDBPwd.Text
    SelectedControls(0).DB = txtDB.Text
    SelectedControls(0).DBUser = txtDBUser.Text
    SelectedControls(0).DSN = txtDSN.Text
    SelectedControls(0).EmailCC = txtEmailCC.Text
    SelectedControls(0).EmailFrom = txtEmailFrom.Text
    SelectedControls(0).EmailTo = txtEmailTo.Text
End Sub
```

11. The last bit of code is the `SelectionChanged` event. The firing of this event notifies the property page that the selection of controls has changed, and therefore the display of the current property values may need to be updated. The `SelectionChanged` event is also raised when the property page is first activated in a control. Change the code as detailed here:

```
Private Sub PropertyPage_SelectionChanged()
    txtDBTable.Text = SelectedControls(0).DBTable
    txtDBPwd.Text = SelectedControls(0).DBPwd
    txtDB.Text = SelectedControls(0).DB
    txtDBUser.Text = SelectedControls(0).DBUser
    txtDSN.Text = SelectedControls(0).DSN
    txtEmailCC.Text = SelectedControls(0).EmailCC
    txtEmailFrom.Text = SelectedControls(0).EmailFrom
    txtEmailTo.Text = SelectedControls(0).EmailTo
```

```
    ' the above two calls to update the text fields would have set
    ' Changed to True. Since this is the default state, restore it to False.
    Changed = False
```

```
End Sub
```

That's it – that's all the code we need for the property page.

Compiling the Component

Now it's time to compile the pipeline component:

1. First, if you haven't already saved them, save the project, the user control and the property page.

2. Now choose Make IK.ocx... from the File menu.

3. You will be asked where to place your OCX file. I always dedicate a folder called `objects` off the root of my NTFS share, and place all my components there. Choose a destination and click OK.

The project will be compiled into an OCX file, and will automatically be registered by Visual Basic.

Setting the Version Compatibility

Now our component is compiled we need to change the Version Compatibility on the component – you'll see why in the next section.

1. For now, open the IK Properties option through the Project menu.

2. Click the Component tab, change the Version Compatibility option to Binary Compatibility, and then click OK:

3. Now, compile the component again following the above steps, but this time overwrite the file we created previously.

Implementing the Pipeline Component

In order to use VB components in a pipeline, the components have to be identified in the registry with the Category ID of the Stage of the pipeline that they are to be used in. These entries could be manually added to the registry with `regedit.exe` to associate the IDs with the component.

A better solution however, it to automate the process using Registration Entry Files (REG), which are simple to create. For a pipeline component you need to add two entries to the registry:

❑ The entry enables the component to show up in the all components list in the pipe editor:

```
[HKEY_CLASSES_ROOT\CLSID\{CLSID_COMPONENT}\Implemented Categories\
{CATID_MSCSPIPELINECOMPONENT}]
```

Where:

❑ `CLSID_COMPONENT` is the CLSID of the pipeline component you have created

❑ `CATID_MSCSPIPELINECOMPONENT` is the Category ID generic to a pipeline component

❑ The second entry enables the component to show up in the list of components for the stage you are editing:

```
[HKEY_CLASSES_ROOT\CLSID\{CLSID_COMPONENT}\Implemented Categories\{CATID_STAGE}]
```

Where:

- ❏ CLSID_COMPONENT is the CLSID of the pipeline component
- ❏ CATID_STAGE is the Category ID of the stage that the component is to be used in

If you are unfamiliar with the registry (GUIDs, CLSIDs, CATIDs, etc.) this may seem a little intimidating. Don't worry – I'll show you how to find the two 36 character strings (GUIDs or Globally Unique Identifiers) that we need for the REG file for our pipeline component.

Creating the REG File

First though, let's create the framework for the REG file, which you can then use whenever you need to install a new custom built pipeline component.

1. Open Notepad and add the following:

```
REGEDIT4
[HKEY_CLASSES_ROOT\CLSID\{CLSID_COMPONENT}\Implemented
Categories\{CATID_MSCSPIPELINECOMPONENT}]

[HKEY_CLASSES_ROOT\CLSID\{CLSID_COMPONENT}\Implemented Categories\{CATID_STAGE}]
```

2. Save the file as POEmailer.reg. Note that you need to change the file extension to REG.

All we need to do now is look up the GUIDS that we need.

The Component's CLSID

The first GUID we need is the CLSID of the pipeline component that we have written.

If you are unfamiliar with Microsoft Visual Basic, note that VB normally creates a new, random CLSID every time a project is compiled. To prevent this (and thus avoid having to change the Registration Entries File (*.reg) after every compile), we compiled the component project once, then set the project to use **Binary Compatible** with the just compiled OCX. If you let VB generate a new GUID every time you compiled the project, you'd have to search the registry for the new GUID and then update the Registry Entry file and reregister every time you compiled – not very practical.

3. Run regedit.exe by opening the Run dialog from the Start menu and typing regedit, and then clicking OK.

4. Navigate through the registry to:

HKEY_LOCAL_MACHINE\SOFTWARE\Classes\Ik.POEmailer\Clsid

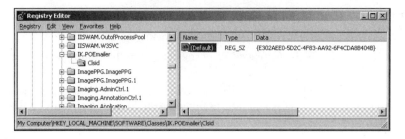

The value of the data in the Clsid key is the CLSID of the component.

5. Double-click on the (Default) label. Then, copy and paste the value from the resulting dialog to the proper places (replace the {CLSID_COMPONENT}) in the REG file hosted in Notepad.

Generic Category ID GUID

One of the GUIDs will always be the same. It's the GUID that enables the component to show up in the all components list in the pipe editor. This GUID will always be:

    {CF7536D0-43C5-11D0-B85D-00C04FD7A0FA}

6. Replace the {CATID_MSCSPIPELINECOMPONENT} in the REG file with the GUID above.

The Stage Category ID

The final GUID that we need is that of the stage in the pipeline where our component is going to be inserted.

7. Run the Commerce Server Pipeline Editor in Enhanced mode so that we can view the properties for each stage.

8. Open up the Purchase pipeline for our InterKnowlogy site
(\..\InterKnowlogy\Config\purchase.pcf).

We are going to insert our component in the Accept stage, which is the very last stage in the Purchase pipeline. Our pipeline component will run last, after every step of the purchase has been completed. Navigate down to the Accept stage and open its Properties by double-clicking on it or using the pop-up menu:

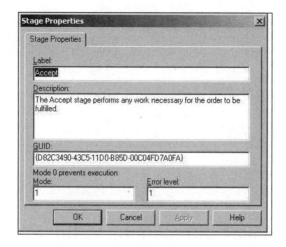

9. Copy and paste the GUID from this property page into your awaiting REG file in place of {CATID_STAGE}.

My completed REG file looked like this:

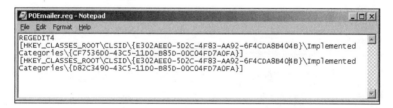

Merging the REG File into the Registry

10. In Windows Explorer, navigate to the REG file we just created (POEmailer.reg).

11. Right-click on the file, and then choose Merge from the pop-up menu. You will be asked if you want to add the contents of the file to the registry. Choose Yes and the contents of the REG file will be added to the registry.

Checking that it Worked

You can view where the information from the registration entries file that you just merged ended up in the registry by navigating in regedit to:

HKEY_CLASSES_ROOT\CLSID\{CLSID_COMPONENT}\Implemented Categories

Where {CLSID_COMPONENT} is the CLSID of the component. There you should find sub-keys for the Category IDs:

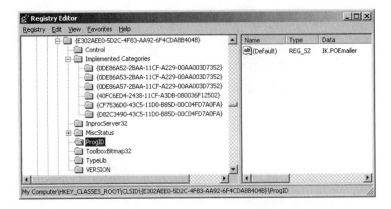

Adding the POEMailer Component to the Pipeline

It's now time to add our custom built component to the Purchase pipeline.

1. If the Pipeline Editor isn't still running then run it now and open the Purchase pipeline.

2. Highlight the SaveReceipt component in the Accept Stage and right-click it to bring up the pop-up menu.

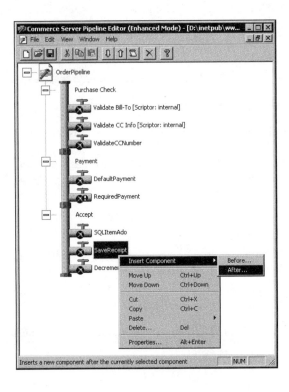

4. Choose Insert Component then After... and you'll be presented with a dialog of all the pipeline components that are available in the Accept stage:

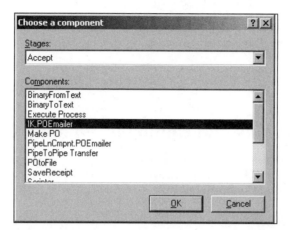

3. Pick the IK.POEmailer component that we just created and click OK. The component will be added as the last component, in the last stage (Accept) of the Purchase pipeline.

4. Now right-click on the pipeline component you just added and chose Properties. What happens? The properties sheet that you created in the VB project for the component appears:

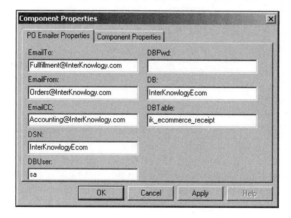

5. Fill in the eight fields as appropriate and then click OK.

If your SMTP server has been configured to send e-mails over the internet then make sure you type e-mail addresses that you'll be able to retrieve e-mail, on because when you start testing the component is going to start firing-off e-mails! Don't worry if you've not configured your SMTP server to send e-mail over the internet, just make sure that the service is installed and running.

If you installed site server according to the directions in Chapter 2, then it is installed and running. We'll look at how to find the e-mails in a moment.

6. Save the pipeline configuration file and quit the Pipeline Editor.

Running and Testing the Compiled Pipeline Component

Now grab a browser and navigate to the commerce site that you've just installed the pipeline component into. Make a purchase. You'll know your purchase is complete and your pipeline component has run if you make it to the Purchase Confirmation page:

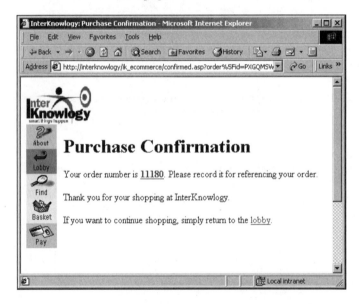

If you have a fully configured and functional SMTP server on your Site Server that sends emails to the Internet you can check the e-mail account now for the purchase order that your component just sent. If not, the e-mail you have created with the compiled pipeline component will most likely be sitting in the queue.

The first time the POEmailer pipeline component ran on my Windows 2000 box, a (BAD) file was sitting in the BadMail directory (\Inetpub\mailroot\BadMail). I opened the (BAD) file in Notepad and quickly deduced that, because I set up Windows 2000 to run DNS (Domain Naming Service), it tried to deliver the e-mails. I turned off the Default SMTP Virtual Server, made another purchase, and the e-mail file (EML) was sitting the Pickup directory (\Inetpub\mailroot\Pickup).

When I ran the `POEmailer` pipeline component on Windows NT 4.0, I received a different behavior from the SMTP Server. If you're running Windows NT 4.0, navigate to the `Mailroot` directory on your server and check the `Queue` folder. The full path will be similar, if not identical to: `\Inetpub\mailroot\Queue`. If you have network access, you may find the e-mail file (EML), and two ST files (STL and SML). If you don't have network access, you'll find two files sitting in the queue: a RTR file and an EML file:

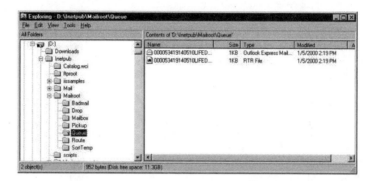

The RTR file is a router file that will include information about the SMTP server's inability to send the mail to the Internet:

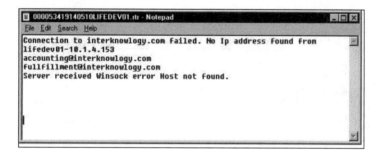

The EML file is the e-mail message. Double-click on it and it will open in Outlook Express:

Debugging the Pipeline

In this section, we'll discuss the different ways to debug the pipeline during the development of your Site Server store.

Most often, error messages from problems in a pipeline component don't "bubble-up" to be rendered in the browser, making it impossible to determine what's gone wrong. As we stated earlier, setting up the Visual Studio and server environments for debugging is difficult, cumbersome and buggy (yes, that's right – the debugging process is buggy!). Debugging alternatives include making use of:

❑   Pipeline log files

❑   The Application Event logs of the operating system, to help understand the error messages when they are displayed

❑   A nifty little script used as a pipeline Scriptor component called DumpOrder.vbs

The Pipeline Log File

The pipeline log file is useful in debugging, in that it shows all values read and written to the `OrderForm` by components in the executing pipeline configuration. You can see where the pipeline is failing: if it was a problem with data being passed into the component, or if it was a previous component that did not perform its job correctly and caused a later component to fail.

The logging is set in the `i_util.asp` file in the `UtilRunPipe()` and the `UtilRunTxPipe()` functions by calling the `SetLogFile` method of the pipeline object. The code is already present in the page, but is REM'd out by the Site Builder Wizard. The code found in the `UtilRunTxPipe()` function is as follows:

```
Call pipeline.SetLogFile(Request.ServerVariables("APPL_PHYSICAL_PATH") _
                         & "config\txpipeline.log")
```

Notice that the physical path of the server is used, and that the file will be placed in the `Config` directory located in the store. The file will be named `txpipeline.log`.

> The user `I_USERmachinename` **must have Write permissions to the** `Config` **directory or the logging will fail. This proxy user that IIS uses does not have those permissions by default – you will have to add them.**

Let me show you a problem that I had when I was writing the pipeline scriptor component that decrements the quantity on hand that we created earlier in this chapter. When I first tested the component, it failed, and the only message I received in the browser was Error 500-Internal Server Error. Frustrated (it being 2:30AM), I turned on pipeline logging as described above.

Let's take a look at a log file that was created. Don't let the length and format of the log file intimidate you – the real answer that I was looking for is at the very bottom of the pipeline log file. But, there is some great info in the pipeline log files if you look at them closely.

Here's the start of my log file:

```
Sink started at 2000/02/01 02:53:19.0311
PIPELINE:++ 2000/02/01 02:53:19.0311  Pipeline Execution starts (lMode==0x1,
lFlags==0x0)
```

Notice below that log tells us that 8 components were called when my site ran the purchase pipeline. If you open the purchase pipeline in enhanced mode you'll see that there are 8 pipeline components executed in 3 pipeline stages. The values from the `OrderForm` object that are used by each pipeline component are displayed after the execution of each in the pipeline log file.

Although, unfortunately, not specifically stated in the pipeline log file (because the ProgID of the actual COM component that ran is `Commerce.Scriptor.1`), this snippet of the pipeline log file represents the execution of the `Validate Bill-To` Scriptor:

```
      8 components in the list (MTS is enabled)
   PIPELINE:++ component[0x0] about to be called ProgID: Commerce.Scriptor.1
   RootObject:  ReadValue  _Purchase_Errors  VT_DISPATCH  PV=[0x25adff8]  VT_EMPTY
   _empty_
   RootObject:  ReadValue  bill_to_name     VT_BSTR       Tim Huckaby        VT_EMPTY
   _empty_
   RootObject:  ReadValue  bill_to_street   VT_BSTR       123 Onlinepurchase Avenue
   VT_EMPTY    _empty_
   RootObject:  ReadValue  bill_to_city     VT_BSTR       San Diego          VT_EMPTY
   _empty_
   RootObject:  ReadValue  bill_to_state    VT_BSTR       CA                 VT_EMPTY
   _empty_
   RootObject:  ReadValue  bill_to_zip      VT_BSTR       92008              VT_EMPTY
   _empty_
   RootObject:  ReadValue  bill_to_country  VT_BSTR       USA                VT_EMPTY
   _empty_
   PIPELINE:-- component [0x0] returned hr: 0x0 in 20 milliseconds
```

And you would find similar snippets representing the execution of the each of the eight pipeline components in the purchase pipeline.

Remember that my purchase failed in the execution of the purchase pipeline at the Accept stage, where I have my decrement inventory scriptor component. That's why the answer to the problem is at the very end, upon execution of the eighth component, which is my decrement inventory Scriptor:

```
PIPELINE:++ component[0x7] about to be called ProgID: Commerce.Scriptor.1
PIPELINE:-- component [0x7] returned hr: 0x80020101 in 461 milliseconds
    Error Description: [InterKnowlogy]Component Execution failed for component[0x7]
hr: 0x80020101

ProgID: Commerce.Scriptor.1

MscsExecute() failed.

Script invocation failed.

[Microsoft][ODBC SQL Server Driver][SQL Server]Login failed for user 'sa'.

Line: 10.

[Microsoft][ODBC SQL Server Driver][SQL Server]Login failed for user 'sa'.
PIPELINE:-- 2000/02/01 02:53:22.0175 Pipeline Execution completed returning hr:
0x80020101

            i:  0x8

      hrLoop:  0x80020101

  *plErrorLevel:  1000

(=====MTS ABORTed=====)
Sink stopped at 2000/02/01 02:53:22.0175
```

Notice that I have a failed SQL Server login for the sa account. I use a number of development servers and most of the time I give the sa account a password. In this server's case I left it in its default state, with no password. When the decrement inventory Scriptor component used a password for the sa account (which it read from the config parameters) it failed the authentication.

In my case, I screwed up by accident. If you want to recreate this debugging scenario, purposely cause your Scriptor to fail by entering an invalid value for the password in the Config parameters of the Decrement Inventory pipeline component. Then make a purchase.

The Application Events

Now, let's look at the results of the same error from the operating system's application event log.

In both Windows NT 4.0 and in Windows 2000 you execute the Event log the same way: Start | Programs | Administrative Tools | Event Viewer.

Choose the Application log (as opposed to the System, Security or some other event log). I found an application event whose source is Microsoft Site Server 3.0 at the very top of the list. When I double-clicked it, I got the following screen:

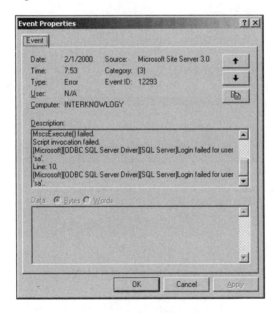

Notice that in this particular error's case, the Application log gives me a little better idea of the problem, because it gives the description and the actual line number of the Scriptor component where it failed.

DumpOrder.vbs

DumpOrder.vbs is a script file installed by the Site Server 3.0 Commerce Edition SDK that can be added to a pipeline via a Scriptor component. This script will generate a text file containing the values of the OrderForm object at the time of pipeline execution.

One technique that is useful is to move the Scriptor around to different places within three different pipelines to see where certain values are written.

Adding DumpOrder.vbs to a Pipeline

1. We'll use the site that we built in Chapter 4. Open the Plan pipeline in the pipeline editor. The Plan pipeline will be found in \Inetpub\wwwroot\IK_Ecommerce\Config\plan.pcf.

2. Add a Scriptor component within the Inventory stage of the pipeline. This should be the only component within the stage:

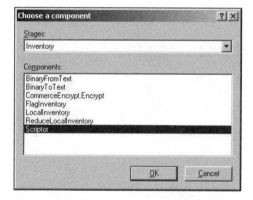

3. To configure the component, open the Properties for that component by either double-clicking on it or using the pop-up menu.

4. This time change the Source option to External. You will receive a prompt asking if you would like to export the internal source code:

5. Choose No. The Filename text box should now be enabled.

6. Press the Browse... button to navigate to the location of DumpOrder.vbs. You'll find this script file at \Microsoft Site Server\SiteServer\Commerce\SDK\Commerce\Samples\DumpOrder.vbs.

7. Now that you have designated which external script to run, DumpOrder.vbs requires a configuration parameter. In the Config text box of the property page, type filename=d:\dumporder.txt (or whatever drive your site is installed on). This tells the script you would like the file written to the D: drive and the name of the file should be dumporder.txt. You property page should now resemble this:

Whichever drive and directory that you choose you will again need to ensure that I_USRMachinename has write access to that directory.

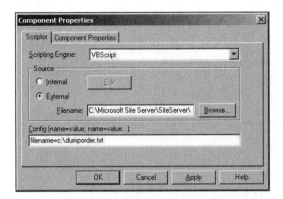

> **Do not give** I_USRMachinename **write access to the root directory of a production server, especially on the drive where the operating system is installed. This would open a huge security hole. I have used this as an example on my development server for debugging purposes only.**

❑ Click **OK** and then save the pipeline. The next time the plan pipeline is executed, it will execute normally, but a new dumporder log will be written to the drive and directory that you specify in the **Config** parameter.

Let's take a look at a sample log file that DumpOrder.vbs creates:

```
** Orderform Contents **
Items List
    Item 1
        Key [SKU] {String} Value [CAT] {String}
        Key [Quantity] {String} Value [1] {Long}
        Key [placed_price] {String} Value [3999] {Long}
        Key [_product_sku] {String} Value [CAT] {String}
        Key [_product_name] {String} Value [The Original Kit Kat Clock] {String}
        Key [_product_list_price] {String} Value [3999] {Long}
        Key [_n_unadjusted] {String} Value [1] {Long}
        Key [_oadjust_adjustedprice] {String} Value [3999] {Long}
        Key [_iadjust_regularprice] {String} Value [3999] {Long}
        Key [_iadjust_currentprice] {String} Value [3999] {Long}
        Key [_oadjust_discount] {String} Value [0] {Long}
End of Items List
Order Key [shopper_id] {String} Value [URHRNJX3FWSH2K0B00836JP14B500439] {String}
Order Key [date_changed] {String} Value [12/4/99 12:15:37 AM] {Date}
Order Key [order_id] {String} Value [UVHRNJX3FWSH2K0B00836JP143] {String}
Order Key is [_Basket_Errors] Start List
```

```
End of List
Order Key is [_Purchase_Errors] Start List
    Value [Unable to complete order. Cannot compute tax.] {String}
End of List
Order Key is [_Verify_With] Start Dictionary
End of Dictionary
Order Key [_oadjust_subtotal] {String} Value [3999] {Long}
Order Key [_shipping_total] {String} Value [1995] {Long}
Order Key [_handling_total] {String} Value [0] {Long}
** End of Orderform Contents **
```

As you can see, each value within the Orderform is "dumped" to the text file. This gives us a reference to go by when checking to make sure all of the correct values are being written to the Orderform by the pipeline.

> **Do not turn on pipeline logging for a production site. The logging method allows only one user to access the pipeline at a time. All other users will receive a permission denied error. Also, the forms of logging available could write sensitive information to a text file. This could be a security issue if these files are not cleared or are not secure.**

Summary

That wasn't that difficult, was it? Many of the pipeline components that we write are prototyped, debugged and tested with a Scriptor component first, and then moved to a compiled pipeline component when completely stable and solid, because they're pretty difficult to debug once compiled. That's probably the method you will choose for implementation of your pipeline components also.

In this chapter, we have seen:

❑   How simple it is to build pipeline Scriptor components

❑   A framework (the VB project you just built) that could be used as a template to build new compiled pipeline components quickly and easily

❑   Three simple methods of debugging pipeline components

To leverage the power of the POEmailer compiled pipeline component, simply make copies of the Visual Basic project, change a few name properties and then replace the code in the Private function IPipelineComponent_Execute event.

Additionally, the logic built in the POEmailer pipeline component can be easily modified to support other transports than email. It would be quite straightforward to modify the code, for instance, to create an XMLdata island (which is simply XML formatted data) from the OrderForm object, and post it to a web page instead of sending it by e-mail.

You're now well on your way (and have made huge leaps over the learning curve) to building your own powerful pipeline components.

Publishing and Content Management

Any organization that has started using the web as its main information-sharing medium will soon realize that content begins to grow almost exponentially, and changes are also frequent. The main challenge is to make all of this up-to-date content available on time, to all users of the information, both internal and external. While there are quite a few individual products available to publish, deploy and manage content, Microsoft has definitely walked that extra mile to provide the **Publishing and Content Management** features as an integrated suite in Site Server 3.0. Other features, like Personalization & Membership and Search, can go hand-in-hand to deliver users the right information at the right time.

The objective of this chapter is to give you a basic grounding in the Content Management process on the Internet/intranet using Site Server. It is broadly divided into the following sections:

- ❑ Content Management
- ❑ The Publishing process
- ❑ Content Deployment
- ❑ Troubleshooting

Content Management

> For the purpose of Content Management we will define content as any resource that will be used to ultimately deliver information over the web.

A typical listing of content we might come across on a web server includes:

- ❑   HTML/ASP files
- ❑   Image files, like GIF, JPEG etc.
- ❑   COM components
- ❑   Other documents like Word, Excel, PDF etc.

With the advent of the information explosion on the web it's no longer possible, even in a small organization, for a single member/team to manage the validity, timeliness and completeness of information published. For example, if there are different divisions in an organization, like Finance, HR, Sales, and Products, it might be convenient to grant each entity ownership of its own information on the corporate intranet/Internet. Then the Webmaster and his team need only be concerned with collecting these and making them available on the web servers. They just need to take care of the web application level details – like development, deployment and maintenance of portals – that lead users to the information.

The emergence of WYSIWYG tools like FrontPage and Visual InterDev have made it easy for even non-technical people to design and develop HTML files. Also, applications like Word, SQL Server etc. allow a user to easily make information available in a format suitable for the Internet.

On one hand, all this has resulted in ease of content development, while on the other, it has led to a proliferation of content. So information will come from different quarters at different times with different updating requests, and your system should be able to deal with it appropriately. Furthermore, with companies starting to employ load balancing or mirror servers, it's imperative that the right content be available everywhere at the right time.

> In short, the challenge of Content Management is to collect content from various sources and automatically make it available to various destinations.

The Publishing Process

More often than not, your work-in-progress server will not be the end production server. All of the content development will be done on a development server, and the tested application will be moved to a production server.

Frequently, there is another server put up between development and production stages, called the staging server. The development server will be used to develop the application, while a staging server will be used to host the application to be tested before sending off to the production server. This intermediate analytical stage is also called the Q/A (Question Analysis) stage, where any bugs could be detected and fixed. This division of stages allows for troubleshooting as well as better performance, since the end users will not be affected while some changes are happening to the content.

A typical setup of this scenario is depicted below:

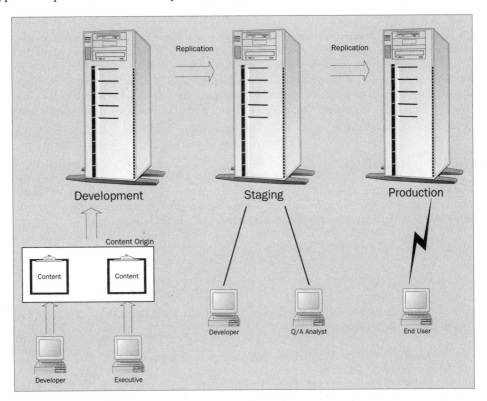

Content Origin

As we already discussed, tools like FrontPage or Visual InterDev can be used to develop web pages easily – not only static HTML pages, but dynamically generated pages too. It's possible to assign a site on the development server to which users connect using FrontPage or InterDev so that they can publish their content directly. To facilitate this a project needs to be created on the client machine that will connect to the site on the server. We'll see how to do this shortly.

For more information on using InterDev refer to Beginning Web Development with Visual Interdev 6 by Andrew Mumford, ISBN 1-861002-94-7, from Wrox Press.

Nowadays, the web is not only about HTML or ASP, but also about sharing any type of document that could either be downloaded or read within a browser – including Word, Excel, PDF documents, and so on. Also, in an intranet, employees can publish their documents on the web so that anyone can access them for specific information. This achieves collaboration and eases work flow in an organization.

The objective of sharing information, whether in the intranet or Internet, would be defeated if users could not find what they want. So a good Content Management system should not only be able to accept content, but also should have the capability to classify content and give users the ability to find what they're interested in.

A simple way to classify documents would be to put content in specific pre-defined directories, but this only works when there's a one-to-one relationship between the classifications and content. In reality, content could belong to various classifications, and there could be attributes on documents (like author, approver and so on) that could be common among documents. The ideal way is to embed any special **content attributes** in the content itself, so that any software that knows what standard is being followed can know more about the document. **Tagging** a document has become a standard way of knowing more about it.

Document Tagging

The **META tag** serves the purpose of conveying hidden information about a document. This information can then be used by applications, like a search engine, to narrow down on specific documents. A META tag is used within the HEAD element in a HTML document.

The common usage of the META tag is:

```
<META NAME=text CONTENT=text>
```

The text for the NAME element will be the document attribute, while the text for CONTENT will describe the value for that attribute. For example:

```
<META NAME="Owner" CONTENT="InterKnowlogyEcom Administrator">
```

Owner is an attribute of the document. There could be several others like DocType, SubmitTime and so on, depending on what meta information you would like to embed into the documents. Site Server provides a simple tool called the **Tag Tool** for administrators to tag content.

The Tag Tool

The Tag Tool can be launched by navigating to:

Start | Programs | Microsoft Site Server | Tools | Tag Tool:

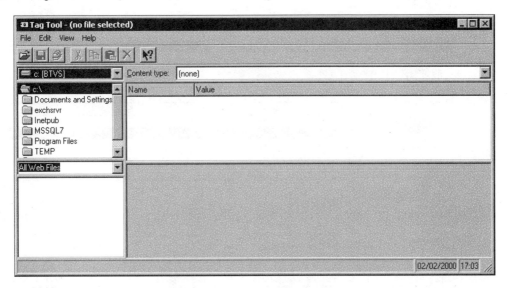

As you can see from the above screenshot, you can select and load a file to insert META tags. To demonstrate this tool, we'll add an Owner META tag to one of the ASP pages for our e-commerce site.

1. Using the drive and file list boxes on the left of the window, navigate to main InterKnowlogy folder for our site and double-click on the about.asp file. You will see the results of the generated ASP file in the lower window:

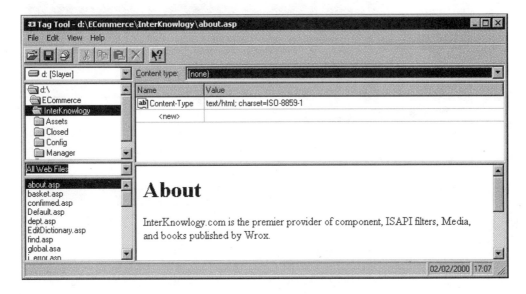

2. As you can see the file already contains a META tag for Content-Type. We want to add our own, which is a simple process. Simply click on the <new> box and it will change to a drop-down combo box. Enter the name of our new META tag, which is Owner, and a new row will be inserted:

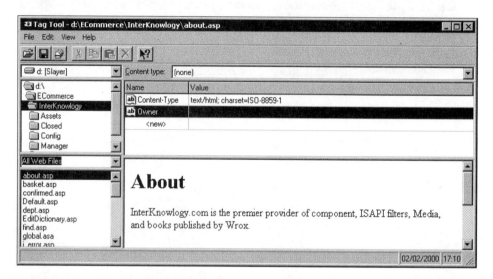

3. Now enter the value for the META tag by double-clicking in the Value column. Once done, save the file:

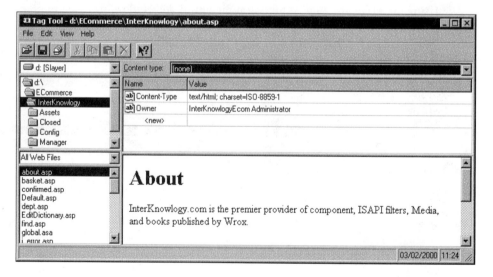

If you were to now open the about.asp file, you would find that it contains the new meta information for Owner:

```
about.asp - Notepad
File  Edit  Format  Help

<!--#INCLUDE FILE="i_shop.asp" -->

<HTML>

<HEAD>
<meta name="Owner" content="InterKnowlogyEcom Administrator">
     <TITLE><%= displayName %>: About</TITLE>
     <META HTTP-EQUIV="Content-Type" CONTENT="text/html; charset=ISO-8859-1">
</HEAD>

<BODY
     BGCOLOR="#FFFFFF"
     TEXT=   "#000000"
     LINK=   "#FF0000"
     VLINK=  "#FF0000"
     ALINK=  "#FF0000"
>
```

This meta information would be used by search engines, as we will see in the next chapter on Search.

The FPSample Application

It can also be convenient to let your users tag their documents themselves. This can be achieved by writing your own application pages in ASP to interact with the user, and help them upload content to the server with appropriate tagging. In fact there are two sample applications, **FPSample** and **CMSample**, that you could customize. These allow users to tag and upload content, along with the functionality of reviewing content. We will take a look at how the FPSample site helps achieve this.

The `FPSample` site can be launched in your browser using the address
`http://localhost/fpsample`:

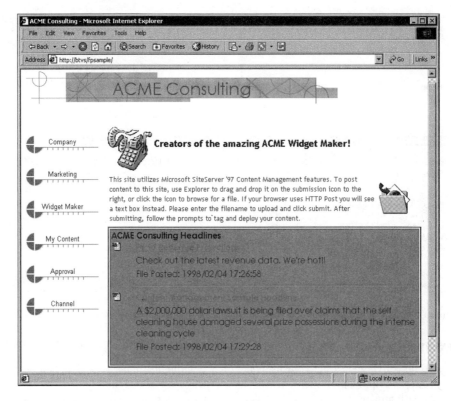

By clicking on the upload icon on the right-hand side of the page you can browse your local machine
and choose the documents you want to publish to the server:

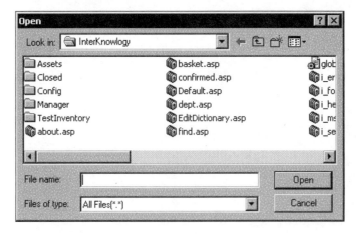

Once you click the **Open** button, the next page that comes up asks you to tag the document with the META tag `ContentType`, which might indicate how the document is classified:

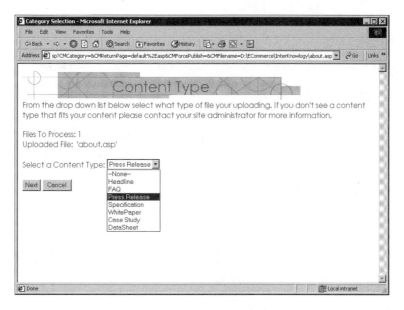

You can see that there are a range of pre-defined values for this META tag. These values are defined in a common repository called the **Site Vocabulary**, usually defined by an administrator. The Site Vocabulary contains the range of values for a META tag that one could apply within the site. This greatly helps in classifying content uniformly rather than each content-author using arbitrary phrases or words. After choosing a `ContentType` and on clicking **Next**, another page is launched that asks for other META tags associated with `ContentType`:

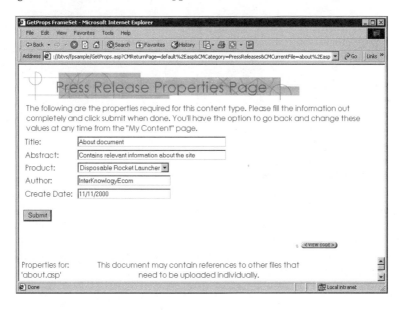

You can observe here again that the META tag Product has a pre-defined range of values that the author can choose from while other tags are author defined. Thus there could be a combination of both.

On pressing the Submit button, the document with associated meta information is sent to the server and the main page returns in the browser. If documents require approval, the documents are not published to the web site immediately. Instead, there will be an approval page that will be used by say an editor who approves the author's document. This sort of workflow could be built in based on custom needs.

The FPSample site is a sample of what Content Management could be on a web site and how it could be achieved. It is just an example that could be customized according to your requirements and not necessarily a complete Content Management solution. For the purpose of this chapter and our discussion, what is important to understand is that content could be created in a decentralized manner by authors, then pushed on to the web site using standard/custom applications like the FPSample site, leading to less intervention by technical personnel.

Content Deployment

By now you will understand that content for the web could be collected in a variety of ways. Users could connect to the server and publish their content using tools like InterDev and FrontPage, or by using a custom application and uploading documents. These documents could be application files from the developers or other documents of various formats from employees. Now how do we push this content to the staging server, and ultimately to the production server? Similarly, how do we propagate any change in content down this line? This deployment process can be achieved in Site Server by replicating your site automatically from one server to another.

Earlier, we talked about a scenario of having separate servers at each of the stages. One extreme of having these sites on separate servers might be that they are in different geographical locations. On the other hand, it's also possible that you'll have the development, staging and the production sites on the same server.

To get to know the basics of content replication, we'll take the simple case of having all the stages on a single server, and see how to replicate content from one site to another. For this example let's assume that we have three web sites on the server, pointing respectively to their content directories:

- ❑ Development: `\Inetpub\wwwroot\Dev`
- ❑ Staging: `\Inetpub\wwwroot\Staging`
- ❑ Production: `\Inetpub\wwwroot\Production`

Replication Example – Local

To replicate content from one place to another, we need to create a **project** using **Site Server Publishing**. A project is where we specify the type of content, source location, destination location and timing of replication.

1. Open the Site Server Administration MMC console. (You could use the web-based admin tool if you wish but for this example we'll use the MMC.)

2. Expand the Publishing node in the MMC, and then expand the local server on which you want to create the project so that you can see three sub-folders.

3. Right-click on Projects and choose New | Project with a Wizard... to launch the New Project Wizard:

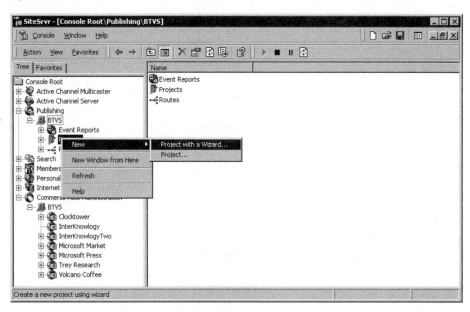

4. After clicking Next on the welcome screen, enter the name of the project. Give it a meaningful name, that lets you know the purpose of this replication, and will be useful for the future. For example, I chose to name the project Dev2Stage, as content will be pushed from the development site to the staging site on the server:

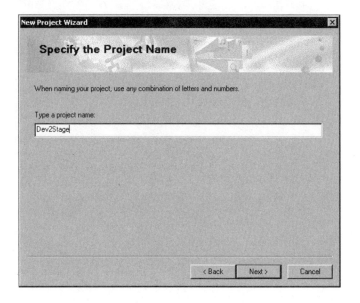

5. Click Next after naming your project. The screen that comes up is where you specify the type of the project. The options make it possible to:

❑ Replicate content from a local directory on the server.

❑ Replicate and remotely install a component. This is needed if you use custom server-side components that you built on the development server. These COM DLLs could be pushed as CAB files to be automatically installed on the target server.

❑ Replicate content by downloading it from an HTTP or FTP server. This option could be used, for example, when you're creating the project at the staging server, and first need to download content from the development server to a local directory. Then you would create a project to replicate this to the production server.

As you can see there are quite a few combinations possible, depending on various configuration factors like whether the source and destination servers are inside/outside the firewall and so on.

Since our case is a single server one, we would like to replicate content from one directory to another. So, choose the first option:

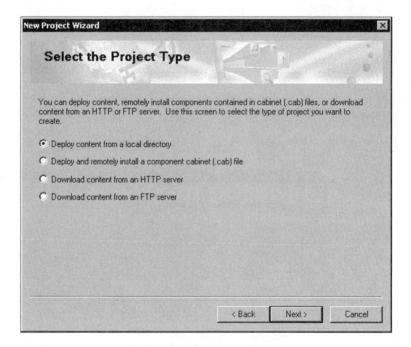

6. Click **Next**. Now type or browse to the development site's directory, as this will be the source of content:

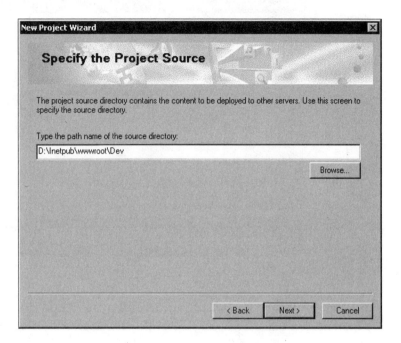

7. On clicking **Next**, you'll be asked to specify the destination of the content. Click **Add...** There are three possible options:

- ❑ Replicate content to a different server from the source server. This is a point-to-point transfer of content.

- ❑ Replicate content using a route. A route is a pre-defined path that the content will take in reaching the final destination. This, as opposed to the **End Point Server** option, means that we could have many mid-point servers on the route. For example, if you have more than one staging server and/or productions servers (which is quite common in a large organization having mirrored sites) this option will be helpful.

- ❑ Replicate content locally. This is what we need for our current example setup.

So choose the Directory option and give the address of the staging site's directory:

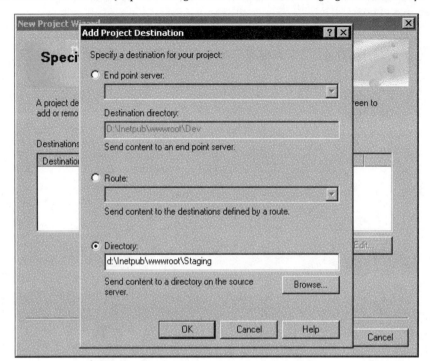

The same project could be used to deploy content to multiple servers at the same time. For example, if we want to replicate content to another standby development server, which might contain a replica of the main development server, we just have to click Add again, and can include as many destinations as we want. That is, a single project could be set up to handle replication to multiple servers or destinations.

8. Let's go with the simplicity of this example. Click OK and then Next. The screen that comes up allows us to create a virtual directory on the source and destination servers. If we didn't have a site for the source or the destination yet, we could use this option. Since we already have a site for development and staging, we'll click Next.

9. This is where scheduling information for the project is entered. Click Add...:

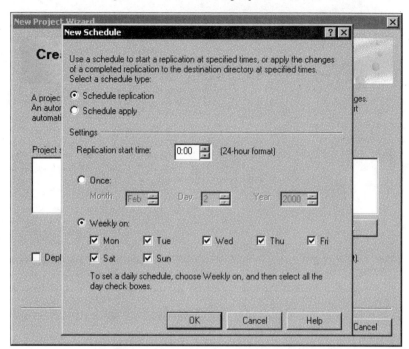

The schedule given here depends on how frequently you want to update content. Content replication on both the source and destination is resource intensive, so it's important to schedule projects accordingly. Usually, content replications to the production server are done during off-peak hours when the load is low. In our case, we've chosen to replicate daily at 0:00 hours. Click OK.

10. There is another option for starting replication – we could schedule Site Server to start replication as soon as the underlying content in the source changes. Probably this depends on the need to have time critical information at as many places as soon as possible. You could in fact choose a combination of these – that's what we've done here by checking the box at the bottom of the dialog:

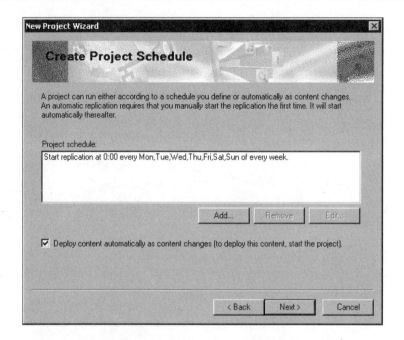

11. On clicking Next, you'll see the summary information for this project:

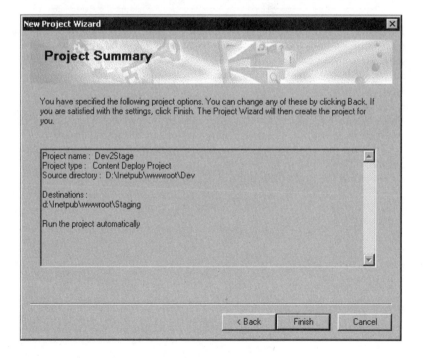

12. Click Finish, and Site Server will create the project with the specifications given on your server:

Before starting the project, let's check out some of the properties of this project, which will be useful in troubleshooting.

In the MMC, right-click on the project we just created and select **Properties**. Most of the tabs in the properties dialog are self-explanatory, but we'll describe a few of them to look at the possibilities for this project:

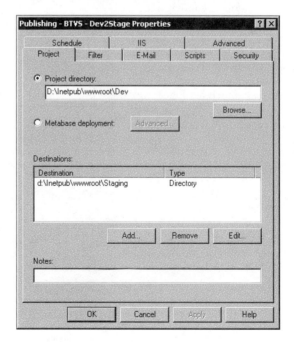

The Filter Tab

While replicating content it's possible that you won't want to send certain type of documents. For example, if your commerce site on the development server has different configurations than your staging/production server, then probably the `global.asa` will have different information on each of the servers. In that case you shouldn't replicate that file, so it should be filtered out.

In short, content can be specifically included or excluded. On the Filter tab you can use the Add button to include/exclude files:

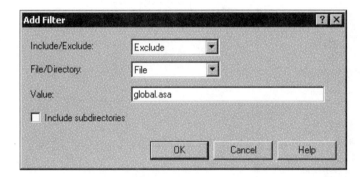

The Security Tab

This tab can be used to set who has access to start, stop or configure the project. Apart from that, there's a facility of replicating not only the content, but also its associated file system security to the destination. These options allow you to preserve security of content while replicating to the destination, avoiding the need to set them again there:

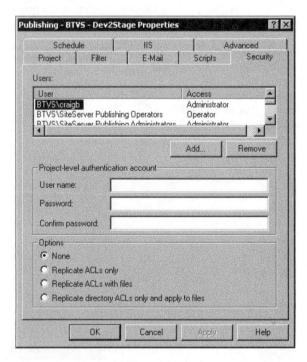

There are other tabs that could be used to specify the e-mail address that would receive success and/or failure of the project, add more schedules or run scripts on the system before/after content replication.

Starting the Project

We have created a Publishing project and looked at some of its configurations. Now what remains is starting the project.

Even though the project is scheduled for automatic execution of content replication, the first time it has to be started manually. We can do this by right-clicking on the project and selecting Start. Similarly clicking Stop will stop a project. What could you do to content that's already sent when you press Stop? Let us digress a bit before starting to replicate.

There is a **rollback** option that will rollback content that was replicated to the destination. This effectively brings back the server to its original state so that whatever content was there before replication is restored. This is convenient in case you found some glitch with the content and would like to correct it before sending again. It is also possible to have up to nine rollback states meaning you could restore to any version of the site up to nine replications back. As you may have guessed Site Server maintains some sort of a transaction log and this process could be resource consuming depending on the number of rollbacks and size of content. These parameters could be configured at the server level by right-clicking on the server under the Publishing node to bring up the Properties pages and selecting the Advanced tab:

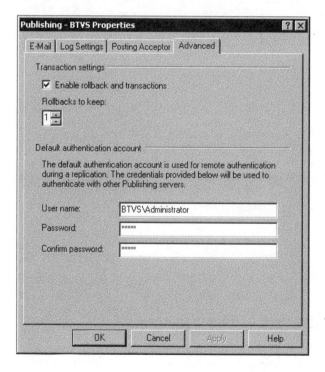

1. Now coming back to starting the project, right-click on the project and then click Start. This is what you'll see:

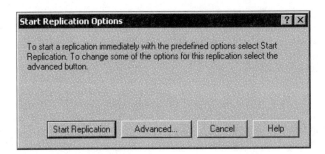

2. Click Start Replication. The Status column in the right-pane of the MMC should indicate the current status of the project: Started, Running, Complete or Idle:

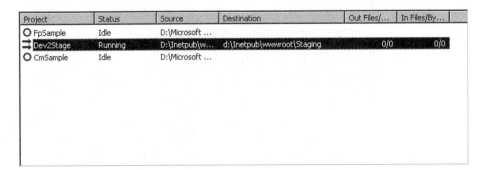

To summarize, our Publishing project involves local content replication, and uses the features:

❑ Triggered replication content change

❑ Scheduled replication

❑ Filtering content to be replicated

❑ Transfer associated security with content

Replication Example – Distributed

In the previous example, we looked at a scenario where replication stages were entirely local. On the other hand, we could have complex scenarios where all the stages are on different servers with several mid point servers on the way.

If we were to replicate content across all of these servers, using the same methodology of specifying one destination server per project as in the last example, we would be creating projects manually on each of the servers. The projects on these servers would receive from the previous machine and replicate to the next machine in the line. To avoid the need to create a project manually on each server and to have the convenience of adding or removing servers in/out of content replication, **routes** are used.

A project could be created on a single server, attaching a route to it. Site Server then automatically creates projects on other servers in the route, and sets them up to receive or send content.

Mid point servers are commonly used in complex content routing scenarios. For example, due to network security restrictions, your development server may not be able to directly connect to the production server. Instead you would replicate first to a mid point server that has access to the production server.

Let's assume that our production server is far away in London, and after we have replicated content to the local staging site in our previous example, we would like to push content to London. The staging site could be used for QA purposes and the site on the London server could be for production.

Creating a Route

The first step in a replication scenario like this is to create a route:

1. Open the Site Server MMC Administration console.

2. Expand the Publishing node and then expand the server node. Right-click on the Routes node and choose New | Route with a Wizard... to launch the New Route Wizard:

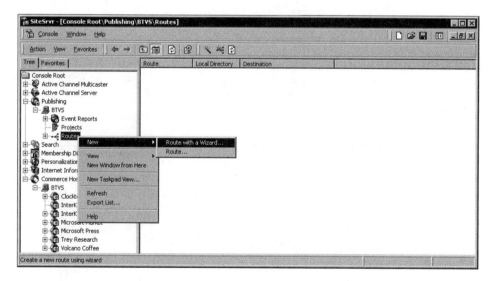

3. Click Next on the welcome screen.

4. You'll first be asked to specify a name for the route. Again, giving a meaningful name will definitely help in easy identification:

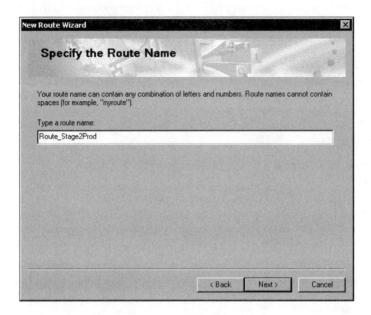

5. Click Next, and you'll be prompted to specify the staging server name. This is the first server in the route, and is the *source* of content for the other servers in the route. Since the staging site is on our local server simply leave this box filled in with the name of the server:

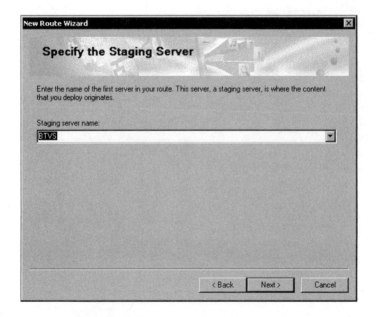

6. On clicking Next you will be asked for the source directory on the machine. In our case, that would be the staging site's directory, i.e. \Inetpub\wwwroot\Staging:

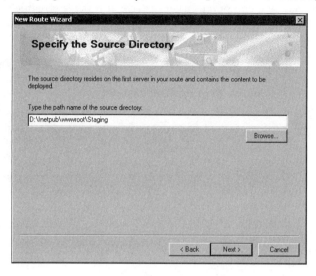

7. Click Next. This is where you can enter mid point servers on the route. Let's say we have a mid point server called MID_LONDON, to which content will be replicated before going to the end point server.

You can click the **Add...** button and add as many mid point servers as you want. The order of replication will be the order of listing of the servers in this screen. You can use the up/down **Move** button to change the order. Also, you could add or remove servers to/from the route at any time. Note that this stage is completely optional and depends on your specific needs:

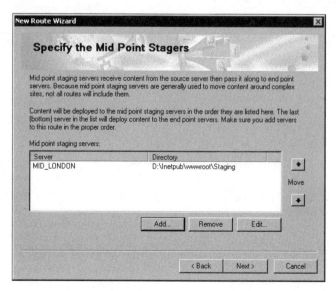

8. Click Next. Now the end point server on the route should be specified. Again there could be more than one end point server – a scenario that's possible where there are lots of mirrored sites for an organization. Just click Add to add each of the end point servers:

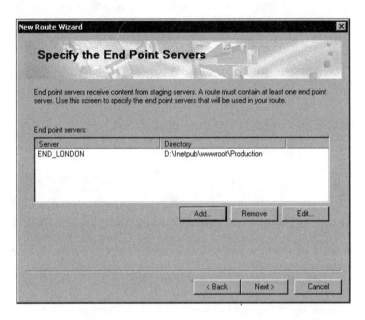

9. On clicking Next and then Finish on the project summary screen, Site Server will try to create a route on each of the servers in the route. You will see one route created on each server, with Destination as the next server in the route. For example on the server where we created the route, this is how it looks:

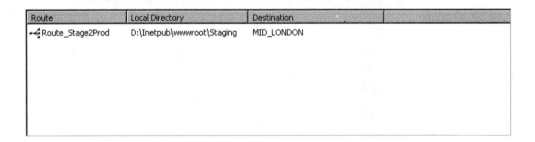

On the MID_LONDON server you would see the Destination as END_LONDON and so on. The name of the route will be the same across the servers.

Using Routes

Once we've created a route, we can create a new project that will be run using this route. The process is the same as we saw in the previous example; only now instead of choosing the **Directory** option, choose the **Route** option and the specific route.

In fact, instead of creating a new project, you could right-click on the `Dev2Stage` project we created earlier, click **Properties** and on the **Project** tab, remove the earlier staging destination we gave using the **Remove** button. Now click **Add...** and change the destination to **Route**:

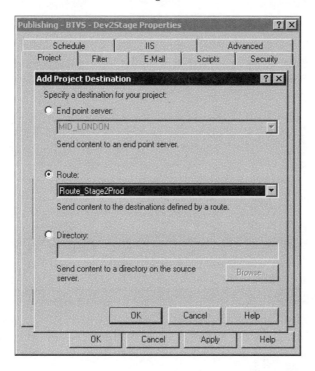

If you modified the existing project, you would see the destination changed to our **Route**:

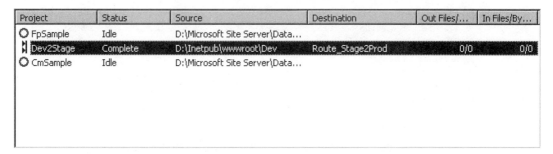

This means that the source will be the development directory while the destination will follow the route, which starts with the staging site, on to the mid point server and ends with the destination server(s). On specifying a route as a destination for a project, Site Server will try to create a similar named project on each of the servers on the route. If it fails, it will give a message asking you to create the project on each server manually.

Troubleshooting

Although there could be a variety of issues that could cause your project to fail, the following checklist includes some useful ways of tracking down errors:

❑ Right-click on the project concerned and click Report. You should see a replication report like that shown below. You could also open the replication report directly from the Local Events node:

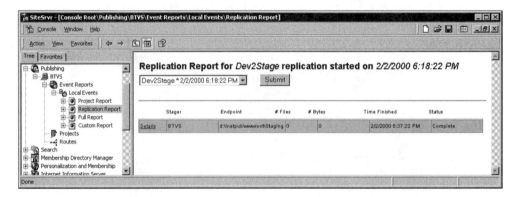

You can click on the Details link to drill down further into the report. As you can see, there are other report options (Project, Full and Custom Reports) that are available under the Local Events node. Going through these reports could identify any cause of errors.

❑ For Publishing to work, check whether the Site Server Content Deployment service is started on the servers:

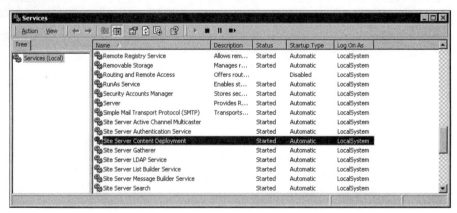

❑ When you are creating projects or routes that involve more than one server, Publishing will use a default account to authenticate with these servers. Check if this account has Publishing privileges on the concerned servers. An account will have these privileges if it's a member of any of the account groups on the destination server, i.e. Administrators, Site Server Publishing Administrators, Site Server Administrators or Site Server Publishing Operators.

You can set the default authentication account by right-clicking on the server under the Publishing node in MMC, select Properties and navigate to the Advanced tab:

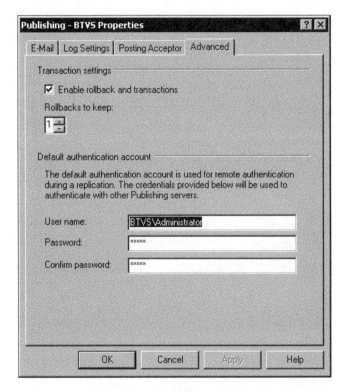

This is default authentication used for Publishing as a whole on a source server and hence will be applicable to all projects on it. It's also possible to set authentication accounts for each project by navigating to the Security tab of the concerned project.

❑ A project could be configured so that whenever it fails an e-mail notification could be sent to both source and target server administrators. They could probably then check various security permissions and settings and/or look into the Event Logs.

❑   To configure e-mail notification, right-click on the project and select **Properties**. Then select the **E-Mail** tab:

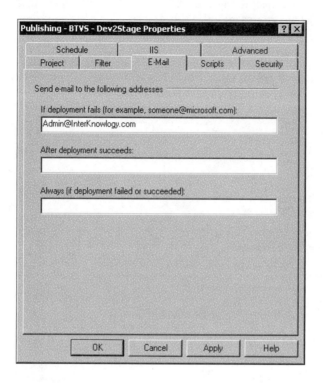

Summary

Content Management could be simple or complex depending on the size of the organization, number of web servers, size of content, users and so on. Nevertheless, as we have seen throughout this chapter, there are ways to manage this proliferation of content.

Site Server provides the necessary infrastructure for collecting, classifying and deploying content. Specifically, content can be collected conveniently using WYSYWIG tools like FrontPage or Visual InterDev, or using an application like FPSample. Then HTML documents could be tagged to classify them. Finally, Publishing features using Projects/Routes can make the job of publishing content to various destinations, in a timely and automatic way, easy and reliable.

Having worked through this chapter, you can take comfort in the knowledge that managing content right from its source to its destination could indeed be achieved with a little help from Site Server Publishing and Content Deployment.

One of the main objectives of Content Management is to make content available to users at the right time. In other words, users should be able to find what they want. That's the topic of the next chapter – Site Server Search.

Site Server Search

There is no greater frustration than struggling to find a piece of information on the web – a place where you are supposed to be able to get information about anything you might want to know in the universe. With thousands of web sites joining the Internet daily, millions and millions of pages are being added to the already existing content maze. You could hardly imagine the time and effort needed to find your way around were it not for search engines like Yahoo, AltaVista and Lycos. In fact, these search engines have added to the popularity and usefulness of the Internet today.

In addition, a lot of sites offer their own search mechanisms to help find information on their own site. This saves the site visitor from the tedious process of going from link-to-link to arrive at the desired document, and can even help verify that the document exists. In fact, providing search facilities as a feature is no longer simply an option – it's more of a necessity if you want to help (and keep) users. With the explosion of information on the web, both on the Internet and intranet, the more help you can give your users to find exactly what they are looking for, the greater appreciated your site will be.

To meet this demand, Site Server provides **Search** functionality. This enables your users to search for information in a variety of content sources, e.g. the file system, ODBC databases, Exchange Folders, News Groups or even other sites on the web.

This chapter will guide you through:

- ❑ The fundamentals of Site Server Search
- ❑ Setting up a search system
- ❑ Practical tips on managing a search system
- ❑ Building custom search pages

First, though, let's look at the basics of the Search functionality that Site Server provides.

The Fundamentals of Site Server Search

Search engines, like Yahoo, provide us with a result set almost immediately when we query using some keywords. From this level of immediacy, we can guess that the result set must have been present already, as it would take a long time to search the entire Internet for a single keyword. From the search engine's perspective, it's also not the most intelligent thing to do, since it would need to perform a new search for *any query* from *any user* – regardless of whether that search had already been done.

In reality, the search is made on pre-defined **catalogs** that are built periodically by crawling out to the Internet. Hence the result set is from the catalog, which in turn will point to the original document.

Site Server Search gives you the ability to build catalogs, propagate catalogs and search catalogs using the **Query object**. However, before we look at that, let's look at some of the basic components in Site Server Search.

Catalogs

A Search catalog is very similar to the catalogs we find in a library. A catalog contains extracts of the original documents that are **indexed** and stored.

> **This makes a catalog a *central repository* containing essential information about the underlying documents, and hence searches can be carried out faster on the catalog.**

For example, a library catalog contains say, the Author, Title, Acquisition Date, Subject, Brief Description and the Bookshelf Number of each of the books. It would be easier to search for your favorite author's books using this catalog than it would by going rack-by-rack and trying to find their works.

A **Site Server Search Catalog** consists of columns that correspond to extracted properties of the documents. For example, a Microsoft Word document contains properties like Author and Title, which correspond to the `DocAuthor` and `DocTitle` columns in a catalog. Which columns are present in the catalog depends on the document type, although some columns are always found in all catalogs by default – e.g. `FileSize`, which indicates the size of the file. Search has the built in ability to catalog documents with the file extensions `asp`, `htm`, `html`, `exch`, `ppt`, `txt`, `xls` and `doc`, although it's also possible to catalog other types as we'll see later.

The Catalog Build Server

The server where a catalog is stored is known as the **Catalog Build Server**. It's the Search service on this server that does the crawling of content and **builds** the catalog, as opposed to the Search Server, which is where these catalogs will be ultimately propagated.

Crawling is basically the processes of gathering the information about documents. Site Server Search has the ability to:

- ❑ Crawl for files in the local file system
- ❑ Crawl for messages in an Exchange Public Folder
- ❑ Crawl across the web by following HTTP links
- ❑ Build a catalog from an ODBC database

The Search Server

Catalogs from the Build Server are propagated to the Search Server. This is the server that actually executes the query for searching against the catalog.

Although it is possible to have both Build and Search on the same server, it's advisable to have them on separate servers when the content size is growing, because both are resource intensive. The **catalog definition** and the **catalog** mark a physical server as Build and Search server, respectively. As a corollary, you could have multiple Build and Search servers.

One case where you might have Build and Search on separate machines is when the production server is separate from a staging server, which is usually the case. Even though it is possible to have catalogs built on the production server itself, it is resource intensive and degrades performance. Thus ideally you would build catalogs on the Build server and push the catalogs on to the Search server. This leads us to the idea that the building itself could be done on multiple servers, depending on the presence of content, and finally pushed to Search server(s).

This figure shows the overall working of a Search system:

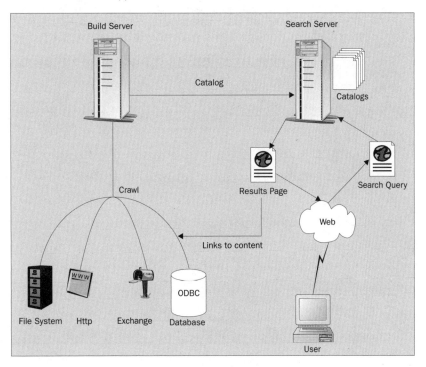

Search vs. Index Server

Search and Index Server (known as the Indexing Service in Windows 2000) are two different products. In case you already have an Index Server based system then knowing the key differences between Search and Index Server will certainly help:

❑ A web site or a virtual directory can be configured to index content by checking the **Index this directory** option on their Home/Virtual directory tab. Then Index Server *automatically* creates indexes on the content, whereas catalogs have to be *explicitly* built using Search. Likewise, Index Server updates changes in content automatically, while it doesn't happen so to catalogs.

❑ The way columns are handled between these two will make a difference while searching for content. For example, Index Server uses the virtual path of a document, displayed as column name `Vpath`, to store the path of the file being indexed. Search stores the absolute address of the file in the `DocAddress` column. Also the default columns vary between Index Server and Search.

❑ Index Server supports hit highlighting whereas Search does not have that ability.

❑ The Index Server indexes and Search catalogs cannot be searched by a single query.

Setting up a Search System

Ok, let's roll up our sleeves and set up a Search system. The Search system is simply the Build and Search servers, the catalog, and associated configurations like security and scheduling.

1. The first step is to define a catalog, which we'll do by launching a wizard. Open the Site Server MMC, expand the **Search** node, right-click the **Catalog Build Server** and select **New Catalog Definition with a Wizard** from the pop-up menu:

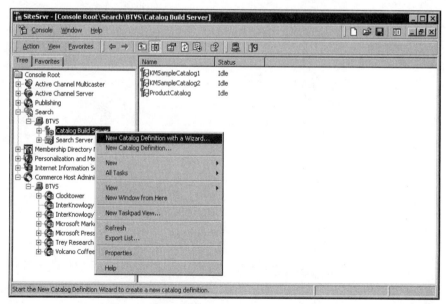

2. Click Next on the welcome screen that appears.

3. Now provide a name for the catalog. For example if you're choosing to build a catalog of content about your products, you might use the name ProductCatalog:

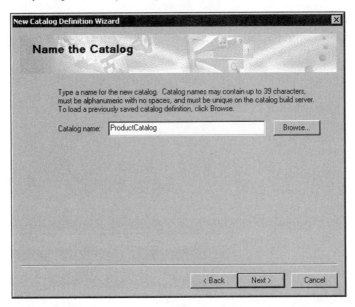

4. Clicking Next will bring you the screen where the crawl type should be defined: you can specify to crawl web links, files in a directory or messages in an Exchange Public Folder. For our system, choose File crawl:

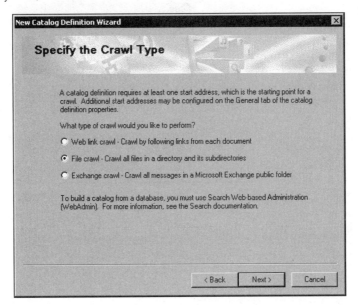

5. When you click Next, the screen that comes up depends on the catalog type you chose. Common to all of them is the starting address to crawl and the depth of crawl. For the file system, the depth is specified in terms of whether to crawl all subdirectories or a restricted number:

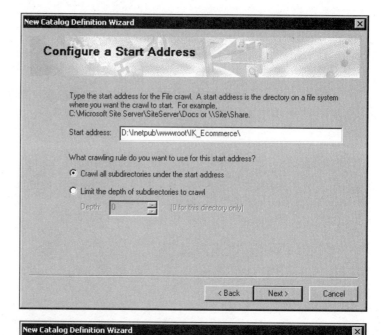

6. Now on clicking Next, we have to say where we want to place the catalog. This could be on the same machine as you're building the catalog, or on a different one. The server that the catalog is propagated to will become the Search Server.
— Choose your host and click Next:

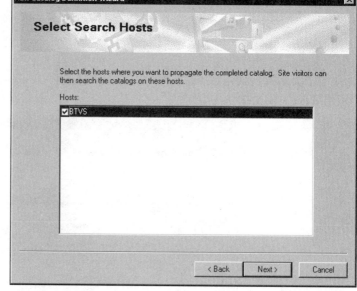

7. You can later add or remove Search Server hosts. Click Next. If you want to start the build immediately, check the Start build now option and click Finish:

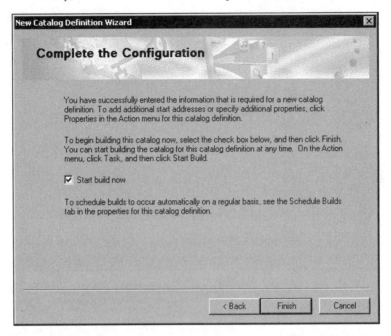

If everything went fine, you should see the catalog definition and the catalog (in this case, ProductCatalog) in the MMC:

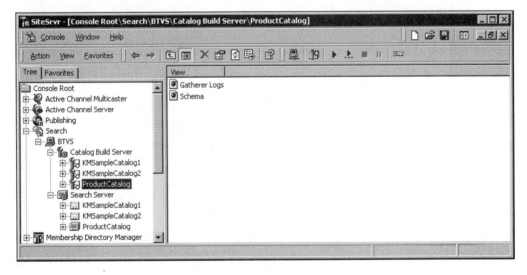

If the directory you specified to be crawled had content, and the build was successful, the Status of the catalog on the Search Server will be Enabled; otherwise it will be Empty:

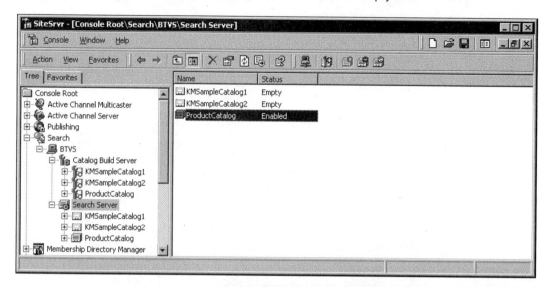

If you right-click on ProductCatalog under Search Server, click Properties and then navigate to the Statistics tab, you can see details like how many documents are in the catalog, and the size of the catalog:

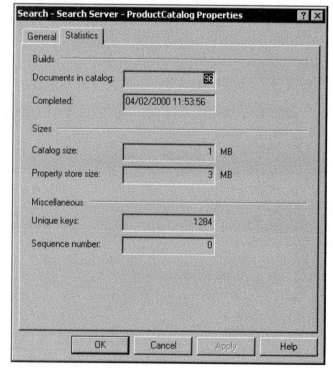

If the build was unsuccessful or there was no content, the documents in the catalog and the catalog size will be 0.

On successful propagation of the catalog, Site Server automatically builds a search and display page for it. To reach the default generated search page, expand the catalog on the Search Server (in our case ProductCatalog). Now when you click the Search node under the catalog, the search page is loaded in the right-hand pane:

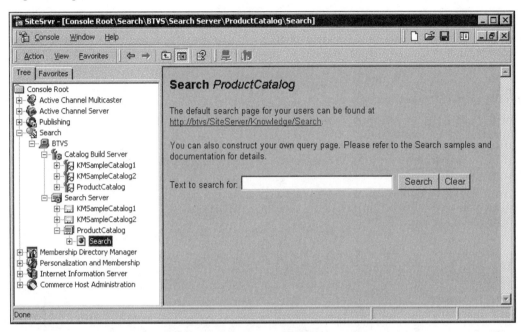

When you enter a Text to search for and press the Search button, the result set (if any) is displayed:

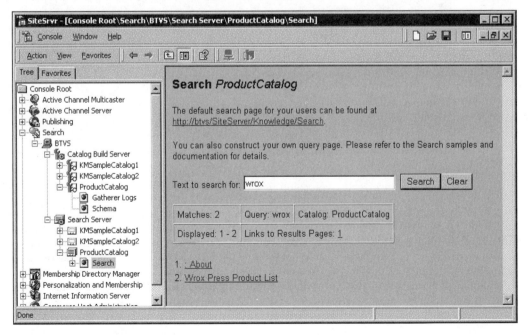

You could customize both the search and result display pages and provide a link from your site, so that visitors can search your products.

Note that the result page gives links to the underlying documents, visible in the status bar.

In a web crawl build, you could give any web address to start with and ask Search to crawl links from it to any depth. It's interesting to note that others could also use their Search systems to crawl content on your site. Let's take a small diversion here to discuss web crawl and its associated features.

Web Crawling

With a web crawl, we can specify the number of page or site hops, i.e. the depth to which Search will go from the Start Address:

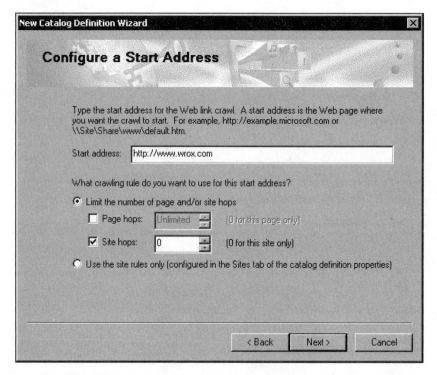

We should be careful in setting these values – since there are innumerable pages and sites on the Internet, if we set them incorrectly, you could find your crawl will go on forever.

Depending on the size of our content, crawl could really drain system resources. On the other hand, the target sites being crawled will also experience degrading performance if too many search engines are crawling them too frequently. Remember, this could happen to your site too, so it's nice to leave a trace of who is crawling. The web master could analyze the log files to know from where most of the HTTP requests are pouring in. You can give an e-mail address that site owners can get back to and also leave information about the user agent (also called a **robot**) that is crawling their site. Right-click on the Catalog Build Server, click Properties and go to the General tab:

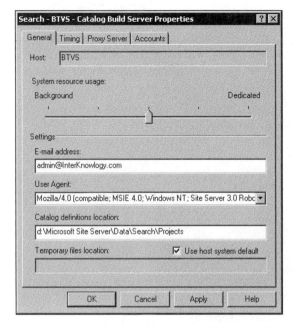

By default, Search requests a site for five documents at a time. Even though you can change this option to request simultaneously an unlimited number of documents, go easy with requests by configuring the site hit frequency using the Timing tab:

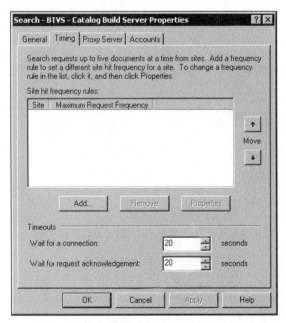

The rule is, if the site you're crawling is not your own, be considerate.

Robots Exclusion

Because of the problem of frequent crawls, sites might restrict access to certain types of robot or to certain areas on their site using **Robot Exclusion files**. Site Server Search obeys robot exclusion, as it checks for the `robot.txt` file on the site being crawled before starting its job. A `robot.txt` file might look like this:

```
# /robots.txt file for http://YOURSITE.com/
# mail webmaster@POSTMASTER.com for comments

User-agent: webbot
Disallow:

User-agent: MyCNNSpider
Disallow: /img

User-agent: WWW Collector
Disallow:

User-agent: *
Disallow: /include
Disallow: /logs
Disallow: /private
```

> *To find out more about the standard, visit*
> *http://info.webcrawler.com/mak/projects/robots/faq.htm.*

Practical Tips

If things didn't go right the first time, don't worry – try a second time! This may not seem much of a recommendation, but patience is truly a virtue for someone who is new to Site Server. All that's required is to systematically check out some of the configurations and try to deduce what's wrong.

First let's bring up the **Properties** page of the **Catalog Build Server**, where there are some configurations to look at:

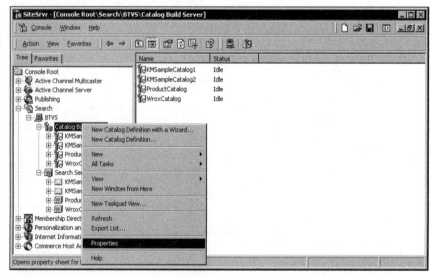

Catalog Security

In the Properties dialog, navigate to the Accounts tab:

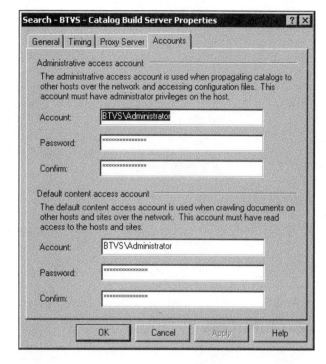

If Content, Build and Search are all on the same physical server then you need not worry about specifying accounts here, but all the three could be on different servers.

The first of the accounts is used to access other servers that may have been configured in your Search system and propagate catalogs to them. This account should be a member of one of the groups (Administrators, Site Server Administrators or Site Server Search Administrators) at each of the Search Servers where the catalog should be propagated.

The second account is used as the Content Access account. If you had configured to crawl on file systems, web sites or Exchange Folders that are on an external machine, this account should have the required privileges on those resources.

A Single Catalog

Suppose you want to put all related content in a single catalog for users to search. The content could come from different sources like files or web sites at the same time. This is possible by adding **sources** to a catalog.

Right-click on the catalog ProductCatalog in the Build server, and click **Properties**. Then just click **Add** in the **General** tab, and add as many sources as you want:

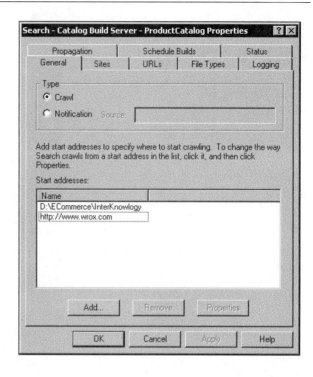

Search Filters

You can specifically include or exclude file types while crawling. We know that catalog building is the process of extracting content and properties from a document, so the crawling software should be able to work with the document in question. Site Server Search supports certain file extensions by default. Switch to the **File Type** tab to see the supported file types:

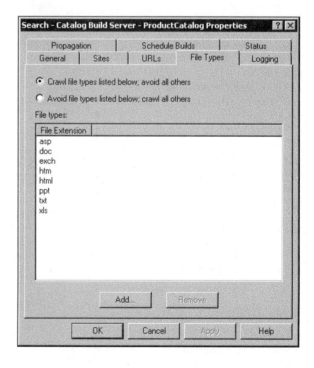

Search provides filters for these file types by default. If you want Search to catalog documents of other file types you need to install those filters by yourself.

> **In short, adding file types just by clicking Add doesn't make Search catalog documents of that file type unless there is a filter associated with the file type.**

You can write your own filters using the Index Server SDK, or obtain them from a third-party.

For example, you can get the Adobe Acrobat PDF filter from Adobe. You can find more information at http://www.adobe.com/support.downloads. *Note that Adobe Acrobat reader should also be installed along with the filter for Search to work.*

Scheduling Builds

Since Search is resource intensive you might want to sequence your schedules in such a way as to optimize machine resources. There are two types of builds:

❑ **An incremental build**
Indexes only those documents that have changed since the last build.

❑ **A full build**
Indexes all documents.

You should schedule for incremental builds frequently – say daily at off-peak hours – while a full build can be done less frequently – say once every weekend.

Scheduling should actually depend on the rate at which the underlying content changes, and the accuracy of search results you desire. For example, if content changes daily and you set up catalog building only on weekends, the accuracy of searches will be found wanting.

To set the scheduling configurations, right-click on the catalog, click **Properties** and go to the **Schedule Builds** tab. Finally select the type of build you want to schedule:

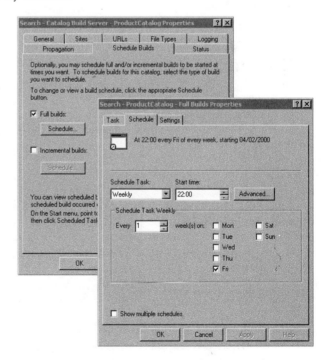

In fact, using the Propagation tab you could even fine tune when catalogs are to be propagated to the Search servers:

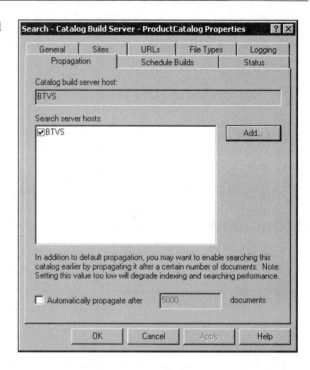

Event Logs

If you want to start finding any errors in the Search process, just click under the catalog in question on the Build server and go to the Gatherer Logs node:

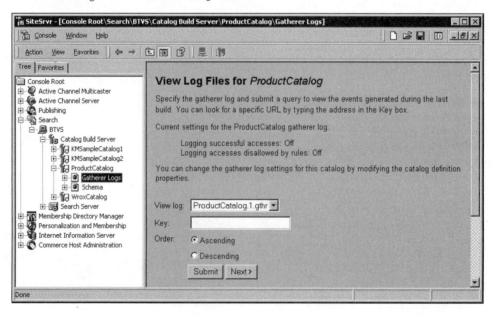

This gives the logs in an easily readable HTML format, with drill downs possible if you need in-depth information. However, as you can see, you can elect what to log and whether to log at all. These setting are controlled in the Logging tab of the Properties dialog for the catalog:

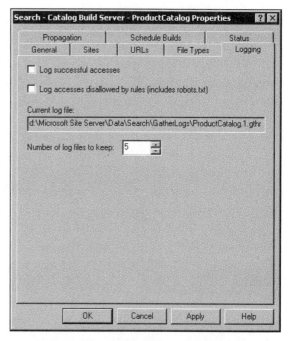

Also, looking at the Windows Event Viewer Application Log will uncover events behind the process. Here's an example on my event log after the ProductCatalog build was started with web crawl added:

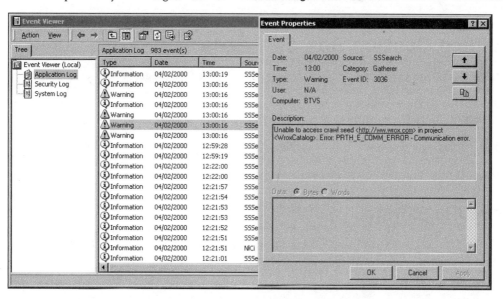

In this example the reason for the error was that the path given as the Start Address for the crawl project, was not found. To correct this problem you would check if a such a path really exists, if it's available now and so on. If the path given was wrong you could go back to the General tab of the catalog concerned and correct it.

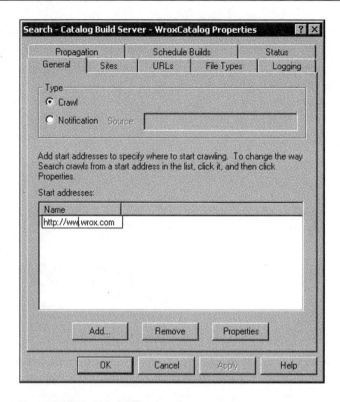

Building Custom Search Pages

As I already said, you could use the default search and result pages generated automatically by Search when you build a catalog. Alternatively you can design your own search pages from the ground up. Ultimately, the **Query object** will be used to execute queries against the catalog. So let's look at a simple example of designing our own search and result pages.

We'll design a simple search form that collects the text to search for, and a results page that will process this query using the Query object, and display the results. The form itself is part of a simple HTML file, SearchPage.htm, and the results page is an ASP, SearchResults.asp.

SearchPage.htm

1. Using the editor of your choice create a new htm file called SearchPage.htm.

2. Add the following code to the new file:

```
<HTML>
<TITLE>Search Page</TITLE>
<BODY>

<H4>Search Form</H4>
```

```
<FORM ACTION="SearchResults.asp" METHOD="POST">

Enter Search Text:  
<INPUT TYPE="text" NAME="txtQuery"><BR><BR>
<FONT COLOR="#0000ff">Search In:</FONT><BR>
<INPUT TYPE="checkbox" NAME="chkProd" VALUE="ProductCatalog" CHECKED>
             Products<BR><BR>
<INPUT TYPE="SUBMIT">

</FORM>

</BODY>
</HTML>
```

The HTML code in the file is pretty straightforward. The search page appears in the browser window as shown:

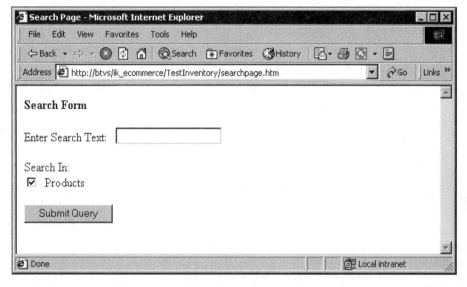

As you can see from the HTML code and the form in the browser, this is a simple form that accepts the search text and the catalog to search in. We have got just a single catalog, Products (you could add more options here as your catalogs).

Basically the search text is the query that is submitted to the Query object. The execution of the query is governed by the **query syntax** of the Query object. For example you could enter master* as the search text and Search will return all documents that have words starting with "master" like masters, mastering and mastered. This is the wildcard querying capability.

> *To know more about various other syntax structures refer to* Using Search Query Syntax *in the Site Server documentation.*

Once the user presses the Submit Query button, control transfers to the SearchResults.asp page.

SearchResults.asp

3. Create a new file in the editor of your choice and call it `SearchResults.asp`.

4. Add the following script:

```
<%
Response.Buffer=True
%>
<HTML>
<TITLE>Search Results</TITLE>
<BODY>
<H4>Search Results</H4>
<%

Dim strQuery, strCatalog
Dim objQuery, objRS

strQuery = Trim(Request.Form("txtQuery"))
strCatalog = Trim(Request.Form("chkProd"))

If(strCatalog="") Then
  Response.Write "Please go back and choose a category to search in"
  Response.End
End If

Set objQuery = Server.CreateObject("MSSearch.Query")

objQuery.Query = strQuery
objQuery.Catalog = strCatalog
objQuery.Columns = "Title,DocAddress,Description"
objQuery.MaxRecords = 20

Set objRS = objQuery.CreateRecordSet("Sequential")

Do While Not objRS.EOF%>
  <A HREF="<% = objRS("DocAddress")%>"> <% = objRS("Title") %></A><BR>
  <% = objRS("Description")%><BR><BR>
  <%
  objRS.MoveNext
Loop
%>

</BODY>
</HTML>
```

The first statement in the page sets up HTTP buffering, since we want to redirect later if there's no catalog selected:

```
<%
Response.Buffer=True
%>
```

Next the standard HTML, BODY, TITLE and heading tags appear.

Then we declare variants to hold the search text, the catalog name, the Query object and the ADO Recordset:

```
Dim strQuery, strCatalog
Dim objQuery, objRS
```

Then fetch the search text and the catalog chosen by the user:

```
strQuery = Trim(Request.Form("txtQuery"))
strCatalog = Trim(Request.Form("chkProd"))
```

If there was no catalog chosen ask the user to choose one:

```
If(strCatalog="") Then
  Response.Write "Please go back and choose a category to search in"
  Response.End
End If
```

The Query object is instantiated like any other COM object in ASP, using the Server.CreateObject method. The ProgId is MSSearch.Query:

```
Set objQuery = Server.CreateObject("MSSearch.Query")
```

Now certain properties of the Query object are set:

```
objQuery.Query = strQuery
objQuery.Catalog = strCatalog
objQuery.Columns = "Title, DocAddress, Description"
objQuery.MaxRecords = 20
```

Using Catalog Columns

There are two ways in which a column in a catalog would be useful.

- ❏ First you could include the column name in the Columns property of the Query object so that values for that column name would be shown in the results. This is what we did above:

  ```
  objQuery.Columns = "Title, DocAddress, Description"
  ```

- ❏ Another way to make use of columns is to include them in the search query itself. For example, the search text can be entered as:

  ```
  @Title = Wrox
  ```

Which will fetch all documents that has in the Catalog property a value of Wrox as the Title.

Ultimately the Query property is set to the actual query to be executed. The Catalog property is set to the catalog chosen by the user, which in our example will be ProductCatalog. To search multiple catalogs, just separate catalogs by commas:

```
objQuery.Catalog = "ProductCatalog, FinanceCatalog, HRCatalog"
```

We assign the `Columns` property all attributes of the documents that we want to be fetched for our results display.

The `MaxRecords` property restricts the number of rows returned in a page. If the number of rows fetched is more than `MaxRecords`, the `MoreRows` extended property of the Recordset object's `Properties` collection is set to `True`. This could be checked to give a link to the results page:

```
<%If (objRS. Properties ("MoreRows")=True) Then%>
   'Link to next page
<%End If%>
```

Meanwhile, the statement:

```
Set objRS = objQuery.CreateRecordSet("Sequential")
```

Creates the result as an ADO Recordset, which will be used to loop through for display in the usual way:

```
<%
...
Do While Not objRS.EOF%>
   <A HREF="<% = objRS("DocAddress")%>"> <% = objRS("Title") %></A><BR>
   <% = objRS("Description")%><BR><BR>
   <%
   objRS.MoveNext
Loop
%>
```

The results page will look something like the following screenshot. Note that a link to the original document address is displayed along with the title and description of the document:

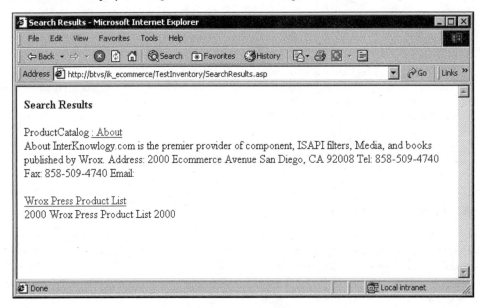

On clicking the link, the relevant document will be fetched to the browser.

There are more parameters and methods to the Query object that could be used to highly fine-tune your search results. Once you have understood the basic concepts of Search outlined throughout this chapter, it's easy to look up further references in the Microsoft Site Server documentation.

Summary

Giving users the power to hit the right information at any time makes your site more powerful and consequently more useful. It makes your visitors feel at home rather than lost in a hyperlink labyrinth. Site Server Search provides a simple yet powerful search system that can be set up with little effort, as we found when we went through the Search basics, setting up a sample Search system and looking behind search query execution by designing our own search pages.

We found that Search is performed on catalogs based on the contents in a file system, web site or Exchange Folders. Once catalogs are built they can then be pushed to a Search server which will typically host the search page and interact with user queries. The search query itself could reference specific columns in the catalog or be free form text.

We've also seen various Search system configuration options and tips, to give you a head start in setting up a search engine for your site.

In the next chapter, we are going to look at another of the services that Site Server provides, that of Analysis.

Analysing Your Site

Say some time back your company put up a web site. It contains content pages, e-commerce and multimedia, and it sure involved a lot of investment in the systems, software, bandwidth and personnel. Now management asks you how the site is doing – meaning whether the web site is useful, directly or indirectly, to the business. They would also like to know the basis for future investments. How do you work out the answers?

As the novelty of a new web site wears off, you are faced with the usual business questions. Questions that are aimed to find out if a web presence can be used to drive a business. The answers are age old: know what customers like and give them the best quality. The "dot com" metaphor is fast becoming your actual business address and a gateway to the world, so it's imperative that you make sure customers see what they want.

In a brick-and-mortar store, the salesperson knows what interests a customer, and quickly attempts to complete the sale. Even if it turns out to be unsuccessful, the reason can most likely be easily deduced – perhaps lack of product quality, unbalanced prices or availability of substitutes. There's a constant feedback mechanism involved in a person-to-person relationship, but how is this time-tested process achieved on a web site?

Site Server comes with tools to help you analyze what you offer on the site, that is content, and the behavior of the users who visit your site. In manufacturing industry parlance, know the quality of the product as well as the customers' response to it.

❏ **User Analysis**
You want to have an idea as to who is coming to your web site, how long they are staying, and what parts of your site are the most popular. The logs that are generated with Internet Information Server make all this possible. Site Server offers the tools to take advantage of this knowledge, so you can analyze your logs and find out more about your customers.

This way, you can adapt your site to meet the ever-changing needs of your users, and hence increase traffic. The reports that are generated with Site Server let you view the traffic patterns, so you'll be able to see the strengths and weaknesses of your site. When integrated with the Personalization and Membership feature, you can even find out what type of users frequent your site.

❑   **Content Analysis**
By analyzing your site content for broken links or load time, it's possible to fine tune content that is displayed on the site. Content could be analyzed from various perspectives, like completeness (no broken links), performance (fast load times), dependency (files that refer to external sites) and so on.

Site Server Analysis is meant to be a comprehensive tool set in your web arsenal – it contains a multitude of options in terms of configurations and reports. So the objective of this chapter is not to analyze everything that we could do with Analysis, but to give you a solid grounding for further exploration.

In this chapter we'll look at:

❑   The basic concepts in Analysis

❑   Using the Content Analyzer tool

❑   Generating reports using the Report Writer

❑   Examples using the Usage Import and Custom Import tools to gather information for analysis

Analysis Concepts

We'll start with a general overview of some of the concepts we'll see in this chapter.

Analyzing Usage

Having said that we can analyze content, web traffic and user-behavior using Analysis tools, how do we feed these tools with the data they need? In the first place, how do we start collecting these data?

Data Sources

There are several data sources that the Analysis tools can use:

❑   IIS log files

❑   User data from the Membership Server

❑   Advertising data from AdServer

❑   Data files generated by the Content Analyzer tool

❑   Custom data files

While the IIS logs are the main source for generating reports about your site, the other key source is the Membership Server. This contains all your member data, including personalization attributes. So in this chapter we will concentrate on the IIS logs and Personalization and Membership data.

Data Import

Broadly speaking, there are two tools used for working on data and generating meaningful information: **Report Writer** and **Content Analyzer**.

You will be using the Report Writer tool of Analysis to generate reports on your data, but it can't work with these various data sources directly; they have to be imported into the **Analysis database** first.

There are two tools that allow you to import data into the Analysis database:

❑ **Usage Import:**
Usage Import is used to import the IIS logs and the AdServer logs

❑ **Custom Import**:
Custom Import is used for importing other data sources, like user data from the Membership Server, Custom files and so on

Analyzing Content

The other important tool in Analysis is the **Content Analyzer**. As the name suggests, it's used to analyze a site's content from various perspectives. Content Analyzer gives a pictorial view of how content flows within your site from the Home Page. It helps you troubleshoot issues like broken links, resources that are oversized, external references and problems with missing files.

Unlike the Report Writer, the data source for this tool is not the Analysis database, but your web site itself, or the file folders on your server.

Content Analyzer crawls content and automatically displays a very useful visual representation of your site and its contents. It also generates some pre-defined reports in HTML format that provide information about the number of resources, file not found problems, external references and so on. A Content Analyzer project file is created, and if you need custom reports on content, you just have to feed the Report Writer with this project file.

How it all Fits Together

The following figure summarizes how all these aspects of Site Server Analysis interact and relate to each other:

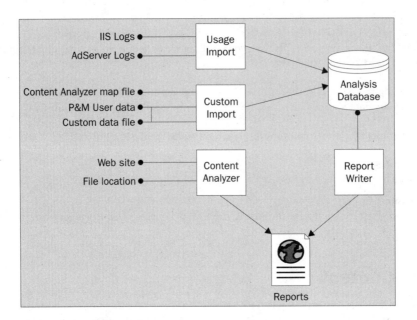

We'll see more about how they actually work throughout this chapter.

Having seen the general concepts of Site Server Analysis, let's get into the practice of using Analysis starting with the Content Analyzer tool.

Content Analyzer

The Content Analyzer is a great tool that enables you to look at your site from different perspectives, and to subject your site to various analyses. It crawls a specified web site or file system, and gives you a detailed blueprint about the site content, detailing information regarding graphics, HTML pages, broken links, graphical layout and an exhaustive listing of each and every file within the site or folder.

Just imagine the work that would be required to perform all of the services that the Content Analyzer tool offers – the saving in terms of man-hours and/or software used is immeasurable. For example, within a few minutes you can know about broken links, missing resources, heavy files and so on.

The best way to get an idea of what Content Analyzer can do is to jump right in and start using it, so that's what we're going to do in this section.

Getting Started with Content Analyzer

When you start Content Analyzer, a project is created and saved as a .wmp file. As soon as you begin a project and start to crawl content, you'll immediately be presented with a cool graphical representation of the site. You can use this as an aid in visual analysis of the site, to look for graphics, links, external references, orphaned resources, etc.

To illustrate how Content Analyzer works, let's create a project to analyze our InterKnowlogy site.

Analyzing Site Content

1. Launch the Content Analyzer by navigating to Start I Programs I Microsoft Site Server I Analysis I Content Analyzer.

2. From the Welcome screen, choose to create a New Project. Alternatively, if you have disabled the Welcome screen, create a project using the File I New I Project from URL... option:

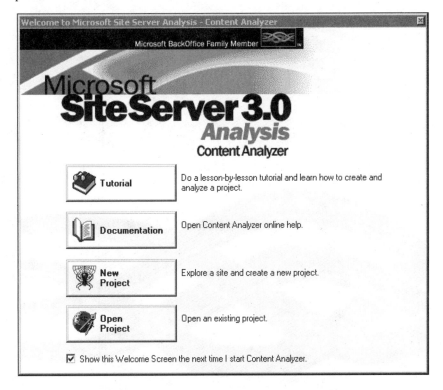

3. In the resulting dialog box, uncheck the Generate site reports option and enter the URL for our e-commerce site. It will be `http://localhost/ik_ecommerce/default.asp`:

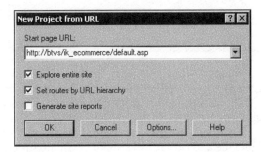

We'll see how to generate site reports later. If you left this option checked then as soon as you created the project, the reports would be generated and the web browser would be launched with the main page of the report.

The Set routes by URL hierarchy option allows you to organise the display map in such a way that the resources are arranged in positions relative to their physical directory structure.

If you check the Explore entire site option the entire site will be crawled, whereas if this option is unchecked we would be able to specify how much of the site in terms of number of pages and levels, can be explored. In case you unchecked the Explore entire site option, on pressing OK you would see this dialog:

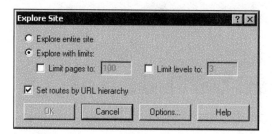

4. Now click the Options... button:

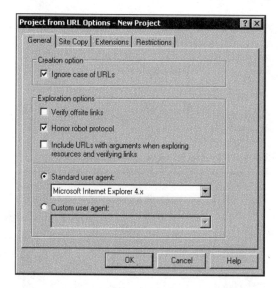

This should remind you of the ideas that were discussed in the chapter on Search, while crawling external sites. Robot exclusion files are standards that are used on web sites to exclude portions of the site from being crawled. It is nice to obey these standards by checking the Honor robot protocol option. Also you can specify which user agent is being used by the Content Analyzer when crawling sites. Another important option to be looked at here is Verify offsite links. It might take a long time to verify the existence of links in your site that point to external sites, so it's better to leave this option unchecked by default.

5. Click OK, both in this dialog and in the **New Project from URL** one. The user agent will now begin crawling. You'll be given a display tracking its progress:

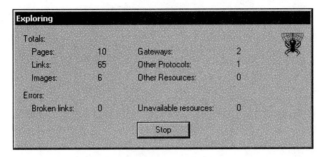

After the crawl is complete you could get a message asking whether to run search queries in case crawl found unavailable resources or broken links (these are shown in the dialog above as Errors). *Say* No *to the message – the various types of search query can be executed on a project at any later time.*

6. Name and save the project by using the menu option **File | Save**, after which the project is saved as a WMP file.

Now Content Analyzer should be showing the site in a colourful graphic representation in the Site window.

The Site Window

The **Site window** consists of two panes: **Outline** and **Hyperbolic**.

Outline is a view of the site in a hierarchical node-to-node fashion. This starts with the Home Page, and shows a tree that has as many nodes as the depth of the site crawled. The icons representing each of the resources on the site – like HTML files, images or links – are different from each other and enable you to distinctly identify the resources as well as the flow of the site from the root:

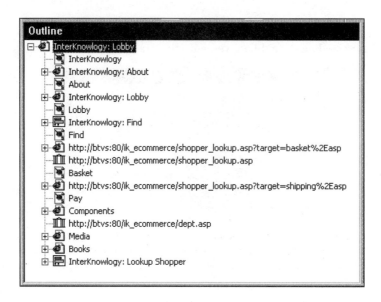

The Hyperbolic view shows your site in terms of a map structure. From this it's easy to see the relationship between various pages on your site. The structure is dynamic, in that when you click on a resource on the Outline pane, that resource becomes the center, and all other resources fan out from it:

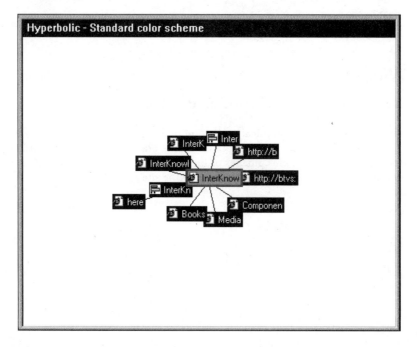

The colors and label texts in the Hyperbolic view have a few special meanings. For example, blue can indicate an external resource, red a broken link and so on. All of these can be customized according to your visual taste and/or any common standards across the sites you maintain.

The color scheme can be changed from the View | Hyperbolic Color Scheme menu, to one of the schemes Standard, Results or Numeric. You can find out what these mean by clicking on View | Color Legends, which will show up the legend of the scheme chosen:

Likewise there are easy menu options that let you change label texts or expand the hierarchy levels displayed.

You can double-click on any resource in either of the views and it will be launched in the browser. Alternatively, you can launch the content, as well as search content using certain standard queries, using the Analysis window.

The Analysis Window

The **Analysis window** allows us to further analyse a specific resource found in the Site window. You can launch the Analysis view from the Site window.

1. Click on the resource that you want to view, then use the menu bar command Window | Analysis Window.

The resulting view shows two panes: one for querying the site, the other for viewing the resource that had focus in the Site window through a browser. For example, when we have focus on the Home Page in the Site window and toggle to the Analysis window we see this view:

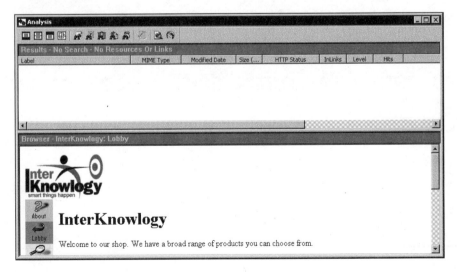

The Results pane currently shows no results, because we've not yet queried on anything. There are several built-in standard query options (called **Quick Searches**) available, which you can view by selecting the Search | Quick Searches menu command.

2. Let's do a Quick Search for Pages with Forms on the site:

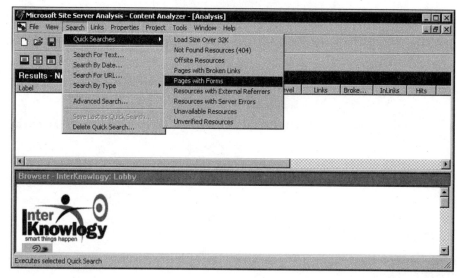

Once the query is executed the results are shown in the Results window. The result includes various properties of the resource, including the URL of the files, number of hits and load size. Now the browser pane will show the resource that has focus in the Results pane:

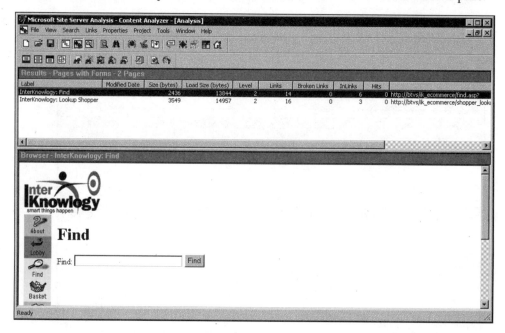

As you see there are many Quick Searches, as well as other search options with text, date etc. There are further powerful search options to save the search results, or search within results. Narrowing down to the exact problem amidst the content jungle seems to be easy now.

The Properties Window

The **Properties window** in Content Analyzer lets you view details about a specific resource within your site on a file-by-file basis. You can launch the window by using the menu option Window | Properties Window. This page lets you explore your site in great detail, by examining the properties of resources – author, expiration date, URL, size, hits or even linked pages. When you find the detail you're looking for, you can examine the different properties of the resources on the site:

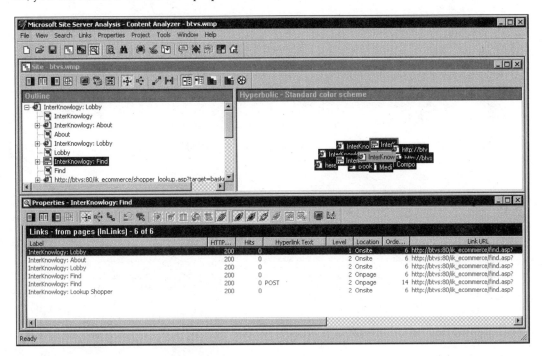

Site Summary Report

Remember that while creating the Content Analyzer project, we unchecked the Generate site reports option. Now we will see how to generate a report for the site project and what it contains.

Created a Site Summary Report

1. Select the Tools | Generate Reports menu option in Content Analyzer. In the resulting dialog, you'll be able to change the directory where reports are to be saved, as well as give an appropriate suffix to the file names for the generated HTML files:

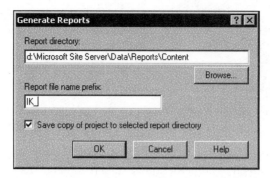

2. Press OK. Analysis generates a number of report files and launches the browser displaying the Site Summary Report page:

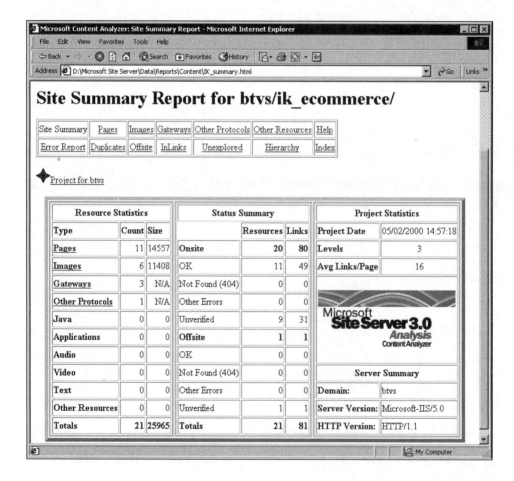

This has links to other detailed report files. Essentially the Site Summary Report is divided into four different sections:

❏ **Resource Statistics**:
The number and size (where relevant) of pages, images, gateways, major MIME types, and other resources in your site. The number of pages reported is the total number of discovered pages. The Explored Onsite Page Report gives a detailed break down of discovered and explored pages.

❏ **Status Summary**:
A listing of the different errors, offsite resources and links.

❏ **Project Statistics**:
Information about the date and time your site was mapped, how many levels deep and the average number of links per page.

❏ **Server Summary**:
Listing of your project's domain name, server type and HTTP version.

By clicking on the various links in the summary page, we can get a detailed drill down. For example, if you click on the link Pages under Resource Statistics in the Summary Report, a separate report page is launched that has both summary and detailed information about pages on your site:

Report Writer

Next we move on to the other powerful information-processing tool in Analysis, the **Report Writer**.

As explained earlier the Report Writer first needs data to be imported to the Analysis database, and that there are two tools to do the job. We'll start with an overview of some of the things we can do with Report Writer. Then we'll set up the Analysis database, followed by a brief discussion on some interesting features in the import tools, before putting them to use.

Reporting Possibilities

The Report Writer is a great tool that you can use to help manage all of the data that you have imported with Usage Import and Custom Import. Report Writer turns out detailed reports in HTML, Word or Excel format. By using your existing log files, or importing custom data from your Site Server services, you can turn out detailed and customized reports about practically anything relating to your web site.

Here is a listing of some of the different options that you could use to generate reports for your site:

❑ **Web server log files**
All activity on your site like visit trends, top resource requests, top organization and countries.

❑ **User data from the Membership Directory**
Which users have been visiting your site, how many are registered, top interests, top cities.

❑ **Search**
Search usage over time, and also what keywords are being submitted for searches on your site.

❑ **Commerce**
Which products are being browsed.

❑ **Content Analyzer**
Analysis data of Types, Topics and Authors.

❑ **Content Management**
Personalization and Membership rules execution statistics.

❑ **Tag Tool**
The number of times a tag was passed to the AdServer GetAd call.

❑ **Proxy Server**
Who and how many visited your site via a proxy server.

❑ **Advertising**
Many different areas, such as placement effectiveness, traffic information and Ad click rate statistics.

Say, for example, your Marketing director wanted to know detailed information about your latest advertising campaign. All you need to do is import the advertising data that you generated with AdServer, and Report Writer would take care of the rest. By making use of this reporting tool, you can get a better understanding as to how you can improve your site, and improve the users' experience.

Thus Site Server Analysis provides a way to analyze your site for various functions and from different angles.

Report Definition

Each report that you can generate using Report Writer has a specified structure. This helps to balance out the reports when it's time to turn the information into Word, Excel or HTML format. Each report that you build has the following characteristics:

- ❑ Sections
- ❑ Calculations
- ❑ Measures
- ❑ Filters
- ❑ Presentations

Sections, calculations, dimensions, measures, and presentations are the basic elements in a **Report Definition**. These elements have a hierarchical relationship: sections contain calculations, and calculations contain dimensions, measures, and presentations.

To help you along the way, there are a variety of preformatted Report Definitions that you can use – all you have to do is import your data and select the report definition that you want to run. This will help you organize your data so that it will be formatted correctly when you're running a report.

Here is an example of a Report Definition that will output an Executive Summary report:

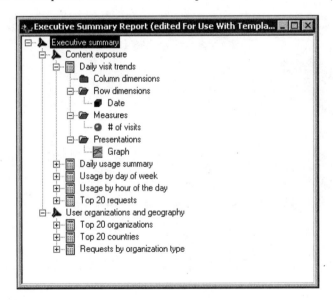

In the example above:

- ❑ Content exposure is a Section
- ❑ Daily visit trends is a Calculation

❑   Date is a Dimension

❑   # of visits is a Measure

❑   Graph is a Presentation

There are quite a few standard pre-defined report definitions from which you can choose initially to generate your reports. Before we start generating reports, however we should have the required data in the Analysis database. The import tools help us gather and import data for Analysis.

Setting up the Analysis Database

Setting up the Analysis database is a fairly straightforward procedure as Site Server provides a wizard to do it for us.

1. Open the Database Setup Wizard by going Start | Programs | Microsoft Site Server | Analysis | Database Setup – SQL Server. If you are using Access you do not need to run the wizard.

2. From the welcome screen click Next.

3. On the Setup Mode screen choose Custom setup as this will allow us to specify such properties as size and location for the database:

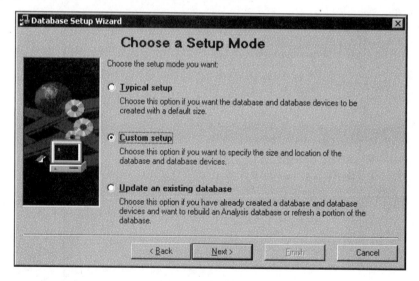

4. Press Next to display the Login dialog. Chose the server where you want to install the Analysis database and enter any relevant login details. Then hit Connect:

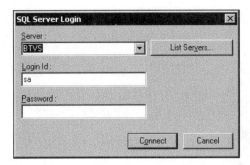

5. Once you have successfully connected the wizard asks for logging information. Accept the defaults and hit Next:

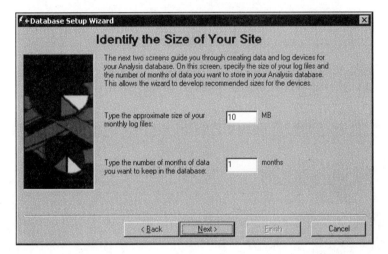

6. The next screen allows you to specify the name, size and location of the data device. Call the device something appropriate like SSAnalysis_Data and set the size and location as appropriate for your server before hitting Next:

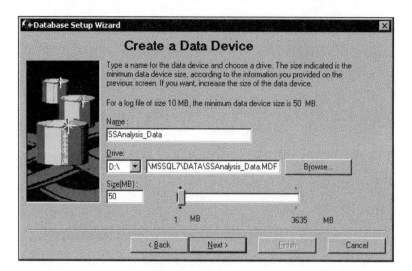

7. The Log Device screen is almost identical to the preceding step. Give the device an appropriate name, such as SSAnalysis_Log, and press Next:

8. The final step before the wizard actually creates the database and devices is to give the database a name. In keeping with our naming scheme call the database SSAnalysis and hit the Create button. The wizard will go away and create the relevant data structures with the settings you have specified:

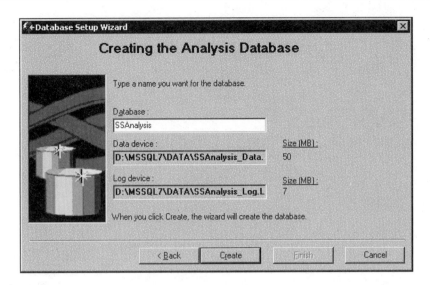

9. Once you have been notified of the successful creation of the database, the wizard moves on to creating a DSN that Site Server's reporting tools will use to communicate with the Analysis database. Enter a name and description for the DSN before hitting Next to create the DSN:

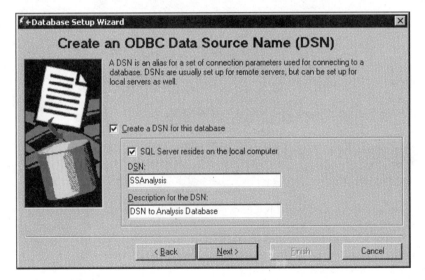

10. After a pause you will get a confirmation screen confirming what you have just done:

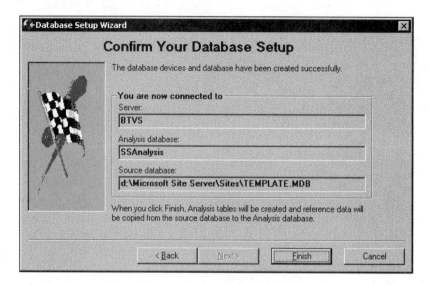

Hit Finish to complete the wizard. The wizard will stop and restart your SQL Server to enable all the changes before loading the device with default data:

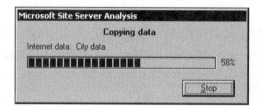

Now we are ready to look at some of the reporting tools

The Usage Import Tool

This tool is used to import data from log files, such as IIS logs and AdServer logs.

The **Server Manager** in Usage Import is a convenient tool that you can use to group the servers that you want to crawl and import into meaningful classifications. For example, if you have a web farm, you might have more than one server with its own IIS logs. In order to centralize the analysis process, you could use Analysis on a single server to group data files on all other servers.

With Server Manager, you essentially let your server know the type of log format you're going to be analyzing, and some characteristics about the home page of the site.

IIS Logging

If you have already enabled logging for your web site then you basically have the client browser-to-web server conversation recorded on file!

To check if your site is enabled for logging, open the Internet Information Server MMC snap-in, either through the Site Server Administration console or on its own (refer to Chapter 3 for details). Expand the nodes until you can see Default Web Site and then right-click and select Properties. Under the Web Site tab you can elect to enable or disable logging:

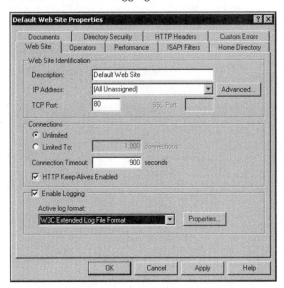

Please note that these screenshots are taken with IIS 5.0 and as such they maybe slightly different from their IIS 4.0 counterparts.

As you can see, there are various possible formats for the logs IIS supports. More often than not you would be logging in the W3C Extended Log File Format. To specify where and how these log files are actually created and stored click the Properties button:

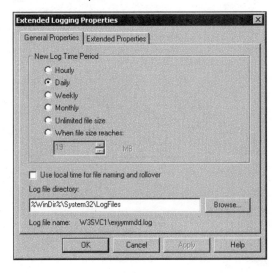

The log files are by default stored in the server's `System32` directory in the `LogFiles` folder, and the file name follows a placeholder format. For example, depending on the **New Log Time Period**, the log file saved for today's hits, assuming today is December 31 1999, could be `ex991231.log`. What this means is that the log file name will have the above said `exyymmdd` format, but a new log file will be created based on the time period chosen from the options.

You can also tweak what is actually logged to these files. If you select the **Extended Properties** tab, you'll be able to specify to IIS what parts of the browser-to-server request-response conversation should be logged:

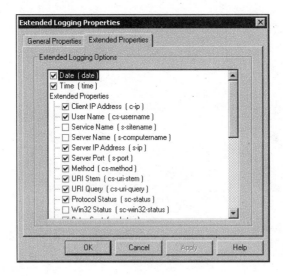

Using Data from Log Files

If we look at a typical IIS log file, we'll find that some of the information (like IP addresses) is not resolved to domain names:

```
ex991209.log - Notepad
File  Edit  Search  Help
20:28:31 206.165.164.118 - GET /admin/Admin/AdminCommon/Images/HomeTitle.gif - 404 623
Mozilla/4.0+(compatible;+MSIE+5.0;+Windows+NT;+DigExt)
SITESERVER=ID=ce39fe889648b4370acab48404fd1e67;+ASPSESSIONIDGGGQGGAA=AOLLABLCFHAIPPGAAMOHOFPL
http://206.41.0.197:86/admin/LogoBar.asp
20:28:31 206.41.0.197 - GET /admin/Admin/Publishing/Default.asp - 404 623
Mozilla/4.0+(compatible;+MSIE+4.01;+Windows+NT)
SITESERVER=ID=7168c58cfcb0136af8b970ce2e8dc7d3;+MemberName=gopal;+MemId=gopk@yahoo.com;+UserID=ad
min;+ASPSESSIONIDGGGQGGAA=KMLLABLCOOJLIEHDMGFIOGBL http://206.41.0.197:86/admin/Home.asp
20:28:32 206.165.164.118 - GET /admin/Admin/Knowledge/PersMbr/Default.asp - 404 623
Mozilla/4.0+(compatible;+MSIE+5.0;+Windows+NT;+DigExt)
SITESERVER=ID=ce39fe889648b4370acab48404fd1e67;+ASPSESSIONIDGGGQGGAA=AOLLABLCFHAIPPGAAMOHOFPL
http://206.41.0.197:86/admin/Home.asp
20:28:33 206.165.164.118 - GET /admin/Admin/AdminCommon/Images/HomeTitle.gif - 404 623
Mozilla/4.0+(compatible;+MSIE+5.0;+Windows+NT;+DigExt)
SITESERVER=ID=ce39fe889648b4370acab48404fd1e67;+ASPSESSIONIDGGGQGGAA=AOLLABLCFHAIPPGAAMOHOFPL
http://206.41.0.197:86/admin/LogoBar.asp
20:28:37 206.165.164.118 - GET /docs/Default.htm - 200 1424
Mozilla/4.0+(compatible;+MSIE+5.0;+Windows+NT;+DigExt)
SITESERVER=ID=ce39fe889648b4370acab48404fd1e67;+ASPSESSIONIDGGGQGGAA=AOLLABLCFHAIPPGAAMOHOFPL
http://206.41.0.197:86/
20:28:37 206.165.164.118 - GET /docs/bar.htm - 200 869
Mozilla/4.0+(compatible;+MSIE+5.0;+Windows+NT;+DigExt)
SITESERVER=ID=ce39fe889648b4370acab48404fd1e67;+ASPSESSIONIDGGGQGGAA=AOLLABLCFHAIPPGAAMOHOFPL
http://206.41.0.197:86/docs/
20:28:37 206.165.164.118 - GET /docs/tocJava.htm - 200 1851
Mozilla/4.0+(compatible;+MSIE+5.0;+Windows+NT;+DigExt)
SITESERVER=ID=ce39fe889648b4370acab48404fd1e67;+ASPSESSIONIDGGGQGGAA=AOLLABLCFHAIPPGAAMOHOFPL
http://206.41.0.197:86/docs/
20:28:37 206.165.164.118 - GET /docs/top_siteserver.htm - 200 5898
Mozilla/4.0+(compatible;+MSIE+5.0;+Windows+NT;+DigExt)
SITESERVER=ID=ce39fe889648b4370acab48404fd1e67;+ASPSESSIONIDGGGQGGAA=AOLLABLCFHAIPPGAAMOHOFPL
http://206.41.0.197:86/docs/
20:28:37 206.165.164.118 - GET /docs/TitleBkGrd.gif - 200 1081
Mozilla/4.0+(compatible;+MSIE+5.0;+Windows+NT;+DigExt)
SITESERVER=ID=ce39fe889648b4370acab48404fd1e67;+ASPSESSIONIDGGGQGGAA=AOLLABLCFHAIPPGAAMOHOFPL
```

It would be nice to know what these domain names are. You might want to have more information about requests coming from certain domains, for example those from which you experience frequent visits.

Usage Import, apart from importing data from the web log files, allows you to enrich the data present in those logs. There are two key features:

❑ **Resolve IP Address:**
The function of IP resolution is to find a domain name for each and every IP address. This requires a DNS server for look up. Ask your network administrator whether you are using proxy servers/firewalls and how to access a DNS server.

❑ **Whois Query:**
The purpose of a `Whois` query is to map an IP address to a specific company or entity that is responsible for the site. For example, if I were to run a `Whois` query against the domain `wrox.com`, my findings would return a listing of who registered the domain, as well as the different technical contacts for the site. However, be warned: if you have a firewall, you must make some tweaks in order to be able to run a `Whois` query.

When you perform a `Whois` query, the domain names in your database that were identified during IP resolution will be interpreted to determine organization name, zip, city, state and region information. You must resolve IP addresses before performing a `Whois` query.

We'll now see an example to give you a feel for using the Report Writer and Usage Import in an integrated manner.

Using Usage Import

In this exercise we're going to import our existing log files with Usage Import and then run a report with Report Writer to gather an Executive Summary of our site:

1. Open up the Usage Import tool from Start Menu I Programs I Microsoft Site Server I Analysis I Usage Import.

2. You will probably get a message box saying that there are no Internet sites configured in the database. Hit OK and the Server Manager will automatically be loaded. You will see a modal Log data source Properties dialog:

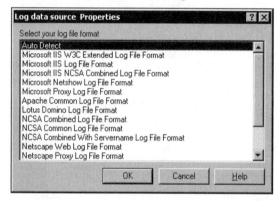

3. Chose the appropriate log source, which is probably Microsoft IIS W3C Extended Log Format, and press OK.

4. The next dialog allows you to specify the web server. You should be able to select the default options and hit OK:

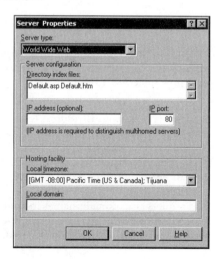

5. You'll then be presented with a **Properties** dialog box:

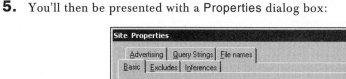
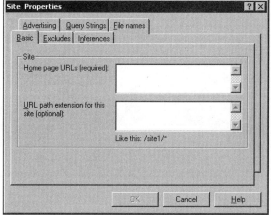

Enter the home page URL, where the address should be pointing to the site that you are trying to analyze. In our case this could be `http://localhost/ik_ecommerce`. Press OK.

You will see the results of your actions in the **Server Manager** window:

6. You can rename the source, the server and the site by just clicking and changing the labels:

7. Now we've setup the server we need to import the data logs. Change the window to **Import Manager** or Click **View | Import Manager**:

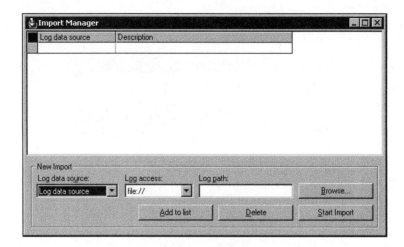

8. Hit the Browse button to select the log files you want to import. Remember IIS stores its log files at \Winnt\System32\LogFiles:

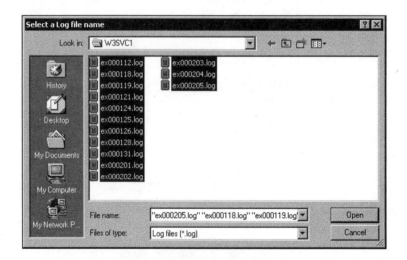

9. Click Open, and add the files to the list by clicking the Add to list button:

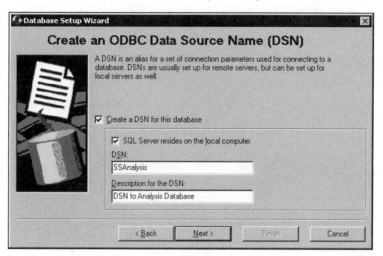

10. Start your import by clicking the Start Import button. You should see the import in progress dialog, and then the import complete dialog. You can check that the import is complete by clicking File | Database Contents:

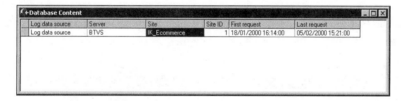

There are a few tools available that let you enhance the Log data you've just imported. All are optional. They can be found under the Tools menu.

❏ Resolve IP addresses
   This step allows you to get a domain name for IP addresses in the log.

❏ Perform a Whois query
   This step allows for geographical data relating to IP addresses to be further defined.

❏ Perform an HTML title lookup
   This simply means that web page titles are associated with site pages.

After finishing this exercise you can explore these yourself.

Report Using Usage Import

Now that you've finished importing, and perhaps enriching, your log files with Usage Import, it's time to use Report Writer to generate a finished report of our findings.

1. Start Report Writer from Start I Programs I Microsoft Site Server I Analysis I Report Writer.

2. You have three options: Report Writer Catalog, New Report Definition and Open an Existing Report Definition. Choose Report Writer Catalog:

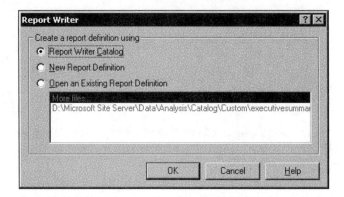

3. From the Report Writer catalog dialog, expand Report Definitions I Summary and select Executive summary report, then click Next:

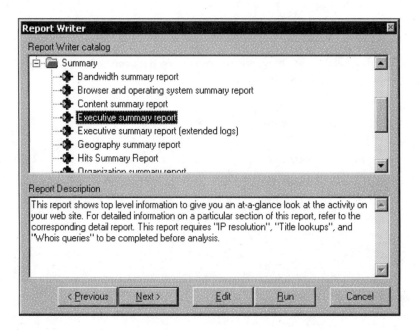

4. If you have more than one site registered in the Server Manager you can choose to generate a report for all the sites or for specific sites. For simplicity, choose the particular site that we added earlier and choose Next:

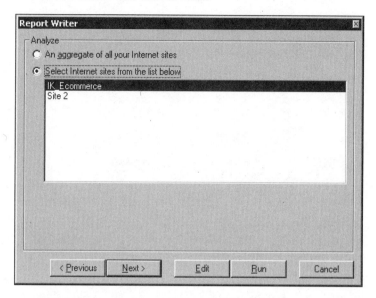

5. You can restrict the report to logs from a certain time range, or choose to include everything imported. Select to use every request imported and press Next:

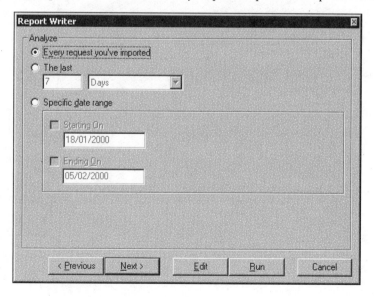

6. Now you could add some more filters. If you want to know how to add these filters, just click on the Examples button:

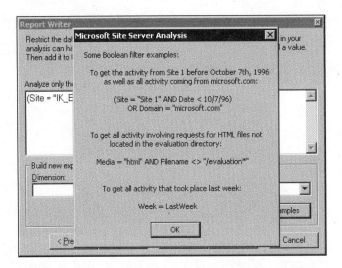

7. Click the Run button to run the report. You will be asked for the Report Document File name: and Format. Leave the format as HTML and add a file name:

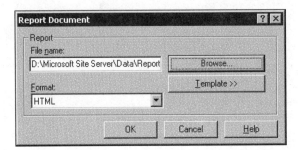

8. When you hit OK Report Writer will start generating the report and open the document in the appropriate application:

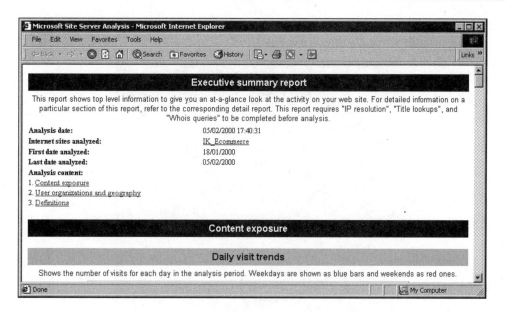

Now that you've generated a report, you can start tweaking the report definition and filters to arrive at the exact report you require.

Custom Import

The Custom Import utility is used to import data from parts of your site that aren't normally logged in a traditional fashion, such as the areas within the Site Server suite. For example, in the Commerce Edition, pipeline logs could be created during the execution of pipelines. These also could be imported using this tool.

> **Since your sources might vary, you have the option of modifying the dimensions in the Analysis database.** Dimensions **are data items around which reports are built from the Analysis database. This feature means that you can extend the Analysis database.**

Once you have imported your custom data into the database, you can then generate detailed custom reports with Report Writer that provides feedback from different areas of the Site Server family like Membership Server and AdServer.

Using Custom Import

By using the Custom Import tool, we could import user data from the Membership Server and generate reports based on that. That's what we're going to do in this exercise.

1. Launch the Custom Import tool using Start | Programs | Microsoft Site Server | Analysis | Custom Import.

2. Click the Get External Data button on the screen. If you don't see this dialog box, click File | Get External Data from the menu:

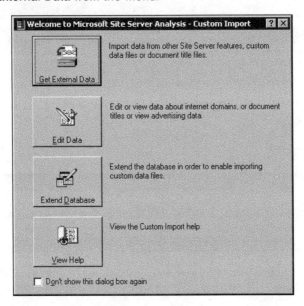

3. In the Get External Data dialog choose User data and then give the application site for which you want the user data import. This site should have been mapped to a Membership Server. Give the user name and password for that Membership Server. Click Import:

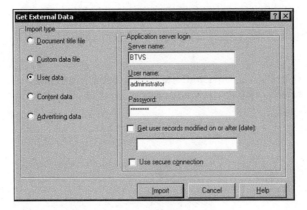

Note that the server name in the above screenshot is the server on which your application, i.e. the web site, runs and not the name of the Membership Server you had mapped to the site.

4. The import may take a long time depending on the amount of data in the Membership Server, the speed of the machine and so on. It's better to have a machine for analysis separate from any production server. You should receive the "Custom import done" message. Click OK.

Reporting Using Custom Import

Now we want to run Report Writer again.

1. Launch Report Writer from Start | Programs | Microsoft Site Server | Analysis | Report Writer.

2. Choose the Report Writer Catalog option in the initial dialog box and click OK.

3. Click the Siteserver node in the resulting dialog box and choose Personalization top user report:

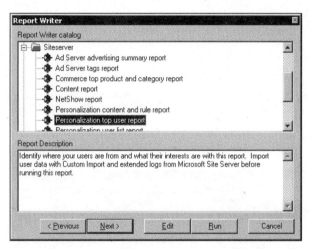

4. Click Next and choose the specific site we registered earlier:

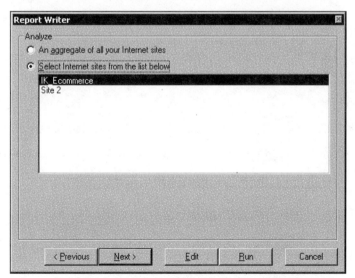

5. Then click Next, and give the date range to limit your analysis:

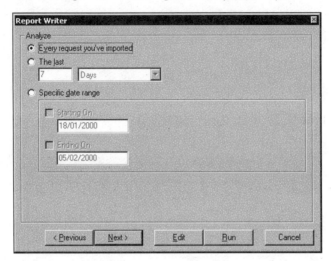

6. After pressing Next, you can enter any filter you want on the analysis, or else just click Run:

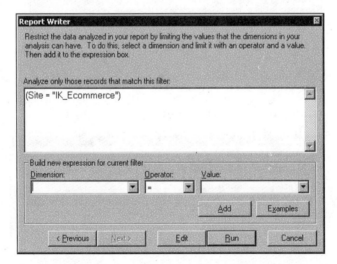

7. As before, you'll need to specify a file location as well as the format of the report file:

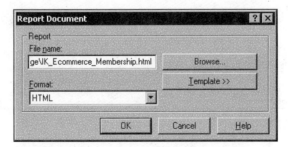

8. Click **OK**. Analysis will start processing to generate the report. After the processing has been completed, Analysis launches the browser with the report file:

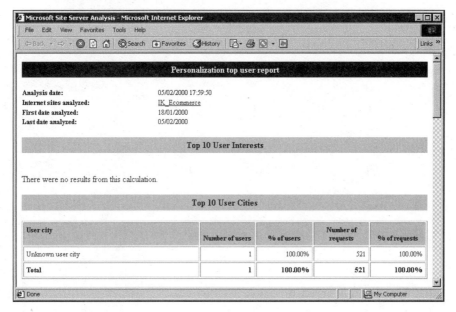

You could open the report definition and tweak the columns, measures, and calculations and so on to make the personalization report more meaningful for you.

Summary

In this chapter, we've taken a look at how Site Server Analysis can help you analyze the services that your site provides:

❑ By using the Content Analyzer's visual structure of your site, as well as the reports it generates, you can make content more complete and user friendly.

❑ By analyzing the habits of your users that you can read from your Analysis reports, you can understand the trends and browsing habits of your users to increase the traffic on your site. Interpreting the reports will give you a good start point in estimating further capacity additions as you would know about site usage, number of users and any bottleneck issues.

This overview of Site Server Analysis tools, has introduced you to methods of importing your log files and user data, and generating reports for your web projects. Site Server Analysis allows you to import log files from your web server, as well as custom information. That includes data from different parts of Site Server, such as Personalization and Membership, Advertising and customized data defined by you.

So having seen some of what's available, now it's time for you to explore all the possibilities Site Server Analysis has to offer for yourself.

In the next chapter, we are going to visit the last of the Site Server services that we are going to be looking at: Personalization and Membership.

Personalization and Membership

As we have seen, Site Server 3.0 is essentially a platform, made up of several components or features: Commerce, Publishing, Personalization and Membership (P&M), Search, Analysis and so on. If we have to name a single feature that pervades throughout this architecture, it has to be P&M. The reason for this is two-fold:

❑ **Personalization** reflects the reality of how business on the web is adapting to its customer. There's a move towards targeting everything that is being offered to the perceived preferences of the customer.

❑ **Membership** reflects another critical aspect of doing business on the web: security. While it might not be common for somebody to enter your shop or factory unauthorized, let alone pilfer goods, it is quite possible that someone from a different continent may be able to break into your web shop, if security is lax.

In this chapter, we'll look at:

❑ The fundamentals of P&M

❑ How to make a web site P&M-enabled for security

❑ How to personalize the user experience

To achieve these objectives, this chapter has a mixed framework mainly of practical head starts backed by corresponding theoretical concepts. However, I should say up front that P&M is a huge topic and entire books can, and have been, written on the subject. All I can hope to do here is give you a brief taste of the subject. To learn more, I recommend you read *Site Server 3.0 Personalization and Membership* from Wrox Press, ISBN: 1-861001-94-0.

The Fundamentals of P&M

Not so long ago, pages on the web consisted of static HTML pages that appeared the same way to all site visitors. Basically the web was a big hyperlink of HTML pages and there was not much interactivity between the user and the system. The pages served were pre-built and had the same content for all users. With the arrival of server-side programming capability (using ASP, Perl etc.), web servers became powerful, introducing an element of interactivity between user and content. This was the first step in the personalization of web services – allowing users to get the content they want.

The next step is to know what the user prefers. This is increasingly essential, since the web is fast becoming an integral part of our life for business, entertainment and information. Browsing has become a daily activity, so users don't want the tediousness of having to enter the same information about themselves and their preferences every time they visit their favorite sites on the web. Knowing user preferences and delivering content based on them brings a personal experience to the users.

Nowadays, a lot of information about an organization's products and services is being shared on the web – both internally and externally. Also, with the advent of online commerce, there has been an increase in companies offering fee-based services on the Internet, and web sites have started accepting a variety of payment mechanisms to sell their products on-line. This all results in the exposure of internal systems (via the web server), as well as privileged content on the site. So establishing who the user is and what they are permitted to access, has become a main concern to web site owners. Thus **authentication** and **authorization** mechanisms need to be well integrated.

> **Authentication is the process of determining if the user is who they say they are, usually by validating a user name and a password against a datastore that holds member information. Authorization is the process of ascertaining that a user has the required permissions to a resource.**

P&M is helping web application designers and developers to implement both security and personalization conveniently, relieving them from old-time homegrown database lookups for users and their preferences and providing them with one central location for user data that is accessible to all applications.

The traditional way to offer personalization features in web sites has been using custom databases to store user information. Building a membership system from the ground up is not an easy job. You have to take care of the database objects, designing how to store members and their privileges, as well as integration with NT security for resource authorization. Furthermore, you have the problem of scaling the application as your site's membership base grows, and making it easy to extend or access the stored user information from other applications.

Although it's not impossible to develop systems like that, it can be very costly. With its Personalization and Membership feature, Site Server offers a ready-made solution. You no longer even have to think about those messy database schemas and changes to maintain a user base.

> **The Membership Server will be the repository for all the user information for your site(s).**

P&M abstracts all that information for you, and gives a neat hierarchical representation of the Membership database to work with. This structure is similar to a telephone directory, so it's easy to look up information and navigate through it. This kind of architecture is called a **directory service**. The directory that holds member information is called the **Membership Directory**.

Directory Services and LDAP

Like the telephone directory, directory services are meant for the fast lookup of information. Instead of connecting to n number of databases individually to access data, we can seek all of the information from a single directory. The directory in turn has the capability to abstract data from primary and secondary data sources. Directory services, unlike databases, don't need to have a Data Source Name, since they are accessible directly on TCP/IP through the **Lightweight Directory Access Protocol (LDAP)**.

Again, while it's possible to design your own directory service, you might get trapped in a non-standard system that makes it difficult for external or new applications to work with your directory. The first open standard for directory services was proposed by the International Telecommunications Union (ITU), and was called the **Directory Access Protocol** or **X.500**. Later, the University of Michigan, USA worked on it and came up with LDAP, which is currently supported by many major software vendors like Microsoft, Netscape, Novell and Sun.

Originally, LDAP was just meant as a protocol that would connect to a directory service. However, when it came down to it, LDAP itself was designed to have a backend database, so that it would act as a directory service by itself. Thus an LDAP service could have its own directory or act as a gateway to other directory services. The service that responds to a client application's request for member information is commonly called the **Membership Server** or **LDAP Server**.

LDAP Data Organization

Even though we may not be concerned with how the LDAP Server stores data physically in the backend database, it is necessary to have some basic knowledge about how data is organized, in order to manipulate the data:

❑ The Membership Directory has a **schema,** much like a typical database schema. This schema will define the objects in the directory.

❑ We will have a list of possible **attributes** in the membership database – similar to database columns. These attributes will have a data type and may be single or multi-valued. Some of the attributes may be defined as *mandatory* meaning that every record will have this attribute.

❑ Every record in the directory will have a **Distinguished Name(DN)**, that is made up of the attributes. A DN could be thought of as a primary key in a traditional relational database.

The Advantages of Personalization and Membership

In short, the Personalization and Membership feature of Site Server uses the LDAP Server to store various types of information, the main type being user data.

Let's see some of the advantages of using the Site Server Personalization and Membership features:

❑ **Membership tiers**
When you register new members for your site with Site Server Personalization and Membership, you can create specific membership tiers and assign each level different user rights and permissions.

For example, you might want to have everyone register on your site to gain free access to some of the content, but have a subscription level as well. Members that have say `Subscribed=True` within the Membership Directory would have access to the subscription-based content of the site. You can examine these properties in your ASP pages to grab the necessary property values.

❑ **Internet Service Provider**
For ISPs who might have tens or hundreds of thousands of customers, having a scalable membership base is a necessity. They'll want to implement a technology that they know can scale, as well as store their membership data. Similarly any large web site with a huge member database will benefit from P&M.

❑ **Custom Content**
With different personalization characteristics, you can deliver custom pages, personalized pages, direct mailings, and specific content to your user community.

❑ **Open Standards**
Since LDAP is based on open standards, it's easier to extend and maintain applications designed to use the directory.

Membership Architecture

A picture is worth a thousand words; especially if the concepts are new, so take a look at the broad picture:

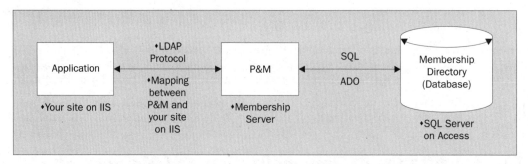

We want to use Membership Server to secure the site and manage users. So, the first step is to create the Membership Server, which is nothing but a service that enables client applications to access the underlying data providers in a uniform way. You might have more than one membership server, each having different data providers. Thus a particular membership server is called an **instance** of the Membership Server.

Membership Server

Membership Servers consist of up to four configurable elements:

- ❑ The Authentication Service
- ❑ The Active User Object (AUO)
- ❑ The LDAP Service
- ❑ The Message Builder Service

A Membership Server is actually an instance of the service called the **Site Server LDAP Service** that needs to be running all the time. You can check this using the Services applet in the Control Panel or Administrative Tools:

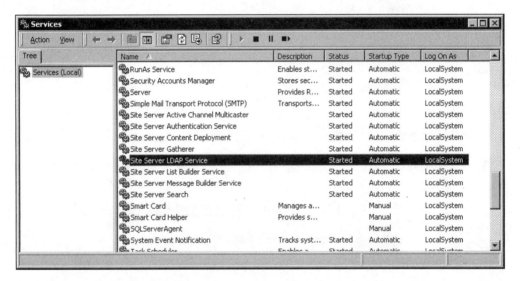

You create a Membership Server instance of this service similar to the way in which a web site is created as an instance of the WWW Publishing Service (the web server). The Membership instance actually talks to the Membership Directory, which is organized to hold data in **containers,** like Members and Groups.

This organization could be seen in the Membership Directory Manager inside the MMC. However, to create the directory structure, we need to first create a Membership Server instance.

Creating a Membership Server Instance

1. Open the Site Server administrator interface using Start I Programs I Microsoft Site Server I Administration I Site Server Service Admin (MMC):

2. Now expand the Personalization and Membership node.

3. Right-click on the host, and select New | Membership Server Instance, which will launch the New Membership Server Wizard:

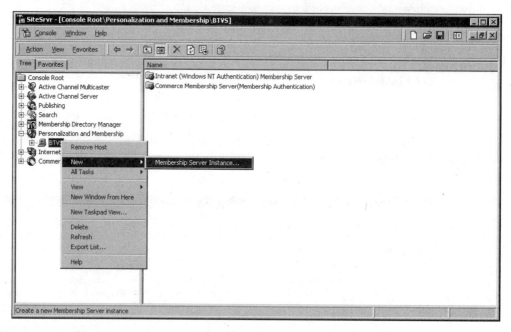

4. Click Next on the welcome page, and then select Custom configuration and click Next:

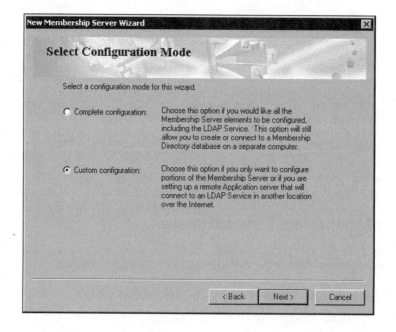

5. Choose all options: that is, AUO, LDAP Service and Message Builder Service. The Message Builder Service is used by Direct Mailer, a tool to send personalized e-mail messages to user lists, which we will see later.

If you do not have the SMTP service installed and running then checking this option will result in a failure to create a Membership Server instance.

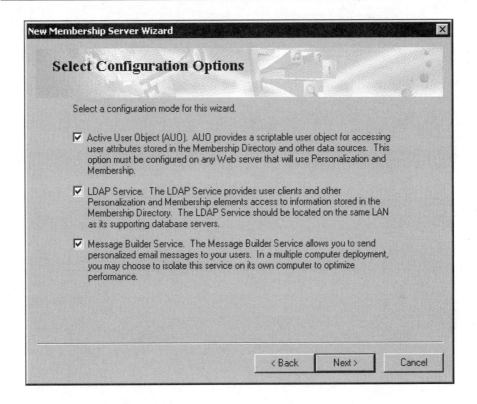

6. Click Next. The following screen concerns the Membership Directory. One option allows you to connect to an existing Membership Directory, which is useful if you've imported the Membership Directory to a new server and would like members to access your web site without needing to register again. Here we'll assume we're creating a fresh membership database, so choose Create a new Membership Directory and click Next:

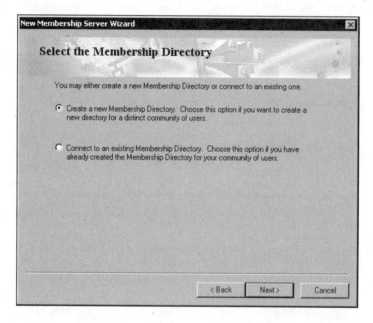

7. The next screen determines how you would like your users to be authenticated:

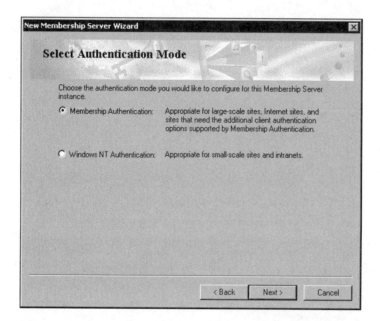

If you choose Windows NT Authentication, the user name and password will be stored in the native NT Security Accounts Manager (SAM) database (which will *not* scale to millions of users) and the user will be authenticated against it; all other attributes like age, address etc. will, however, be stored in the Membership Directory.

Windows NT Authentication can be used for intranet sites where you have less than 50,000 users, a size which Windows NT 4.0 can support. Using NT authentication may also be useful in cases where you would like to use the existing security mechanisms, i.e. when user accounts, groups and permissions are already established on your NT systems. Membership Authentication allows for the support of millions of users. Since all user information is stored at the same place, unlike in NT Authentication mode where user name and password are stored in the NT SAM and the rest in the Membership Directory, it will be faster to retrieve personalization information on users. In addition, the Windows NT Authentication mode does not have other authentication methods that the Membership mode has, like HTML Forms Authentication, Automatic Cookie Authentication and Distributed Password Authentication.

We will choose Membership Authentication and click Next.

8. Give a name to the Membership Directory and enter the password for the administrator for this directory. Click Next:

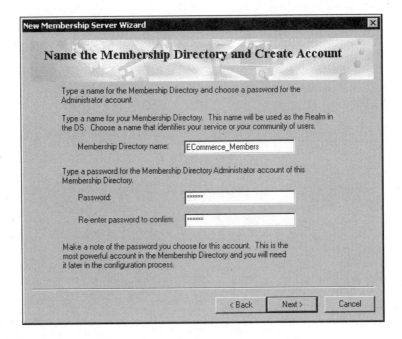

9. Choose to use an
Access database.
We'll use Access
instead of SQL
Server for our
exercise to simplify
matters:

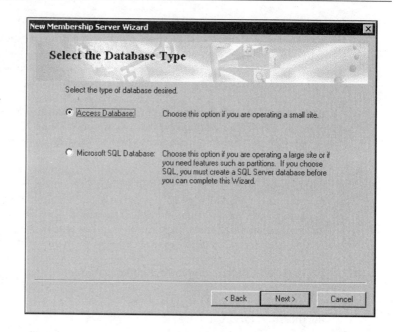

*The database could be on Access or SQL Server: although we choose Access for our demonstration
exercise, obviously for large production databases, SQL Server will be the right choice.*

10. Click Next and
name the database
file:

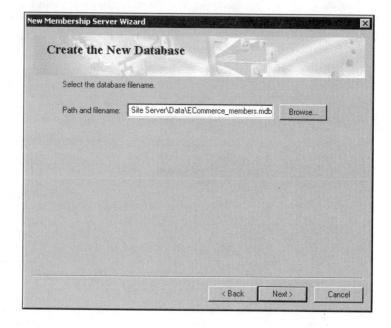

11. Clicking Next will bring up the following screen:

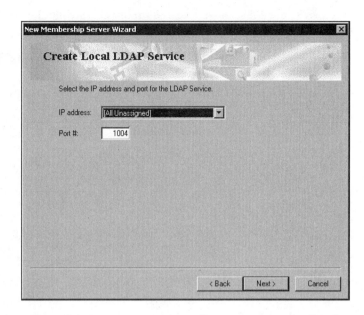

Each Membership Server instance will listen on a unique port. For now, accept the default port and IP address. Click Next.

12. Providing you have a valid SMTP service running you will be asked for the name of the SMTP Mail Server. Accept the local server and press Next:

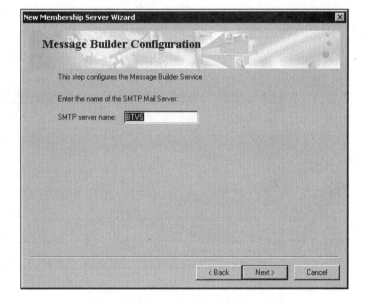

13. You will be shown a screen summarizing your choices. Click **Finish** to accept them and the new Membership Server instance will be created:

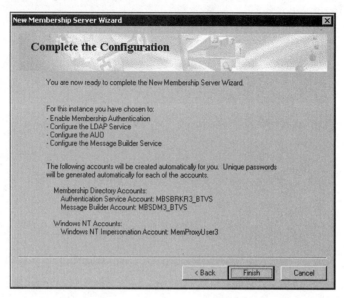

Navigating the Membership Server

Now let's take a quick look at the new Membership Server we created through the wizard.

If you look under the **Personalization and Membership** node in the Site Server MMC, you will see a new Membership Server has been added with a fairly undescriptive name:

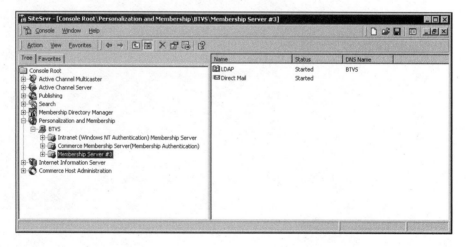

You could right-click on the Membership Server instance and click **Rename** *to give it a meaningful name: it could, perhaps, be* `yoursitename_members` *or for consistency with the examples below:* `ECommerce`*.*

Now it's time to look at how the Membership Server stores information hierarchically, in **containers**.

1. Right-click on the Membership Directory Manager node and select Properties. Give the port number of the Membership Server instance just created and press *Enter*:

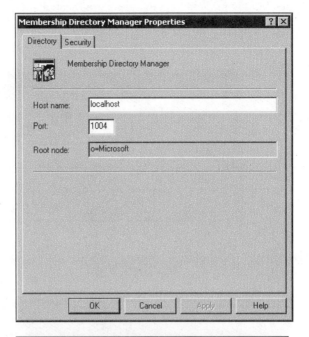

2. If you forget the port number, go to the particular Membership Server instance under the Personalization and Membership node, right-click on the LDAP node under it and click Properties. The TCP port number is the port for this Membership instance:

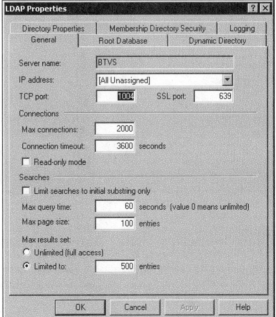

3. On pressing OK in the Membership Directory Manager Properties window you will be asked to log in. Some default users are created automatically in your Membership Database: one is the Anonymous user and the other is the Administrator. Choose Administrator and give the password that was used while creating this Membership instance:

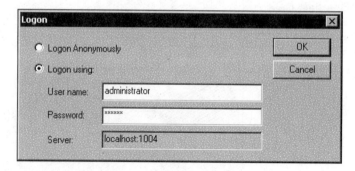

4. Click OK. If you've logged in successfully you should be able to navigate the directory contents:

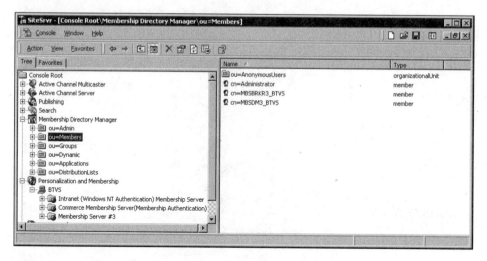

Security Basics

When the New Membership Server Wizard created a new Membership Server instance for us, it also created some specific users and groups to use in the authentication processes.

The wizard created two types of account:

❑ A Windows NT impersonation account

❑ Membership Server groups and accounts

The Windows NT Account

Although we selected Membership Authentication in the wizard, there's one account that is created in the NT SAM (Security Accounts Manager) for this membership server – the **Windows NT impersonation account,** called `MemProxyUser`.

You can check this out by launching the User Manager for Domains from the Start |Programs | Administrative Tools menu for Windows NT 4, or Start | Programs | Administrative Tools | Computer Management and looking in the Users folder of the Local Users and Groups node for Windows 2000:

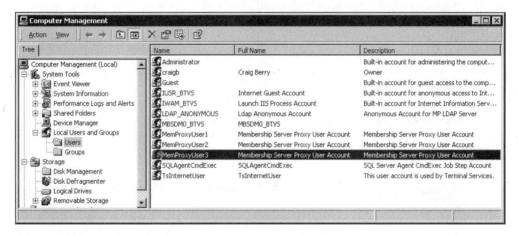

Each time you create a new Membership Server instance you will get a new `MemProxyUser` account. As the server we created was the Membership Server #3 the account was called `MemProxyUser3`.

When you map a site to the Membership Server that's configured for Membership Authentication, users for your site pages are authenticated against the Membership Directory, but still the resources in Window NT need to be authorized. So the `MemProxyUser` account is used to gain authorization to the machine's resources.

Membership Accounts

Now let's see what actual member accounts are created in the Membership Directory. If you navigate to the Membership Directory Manager node in the Site Server Administrator MMC and look in the ou=Members container, you will find user accounts.

For example, in the earlier exercise, these were the accounts created on the Membership Server:

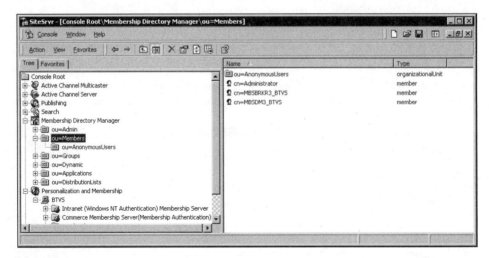

And these were the groups:

> You need to have set up the **Membership Directory Manager** node, as we did in the previous section, otherwise you will see default values.

The accounts (members) you see in the ou=Members container are the Membership accounts, and hence will not be seen in NT SAM.

Creating Users

We will create a user straight away to help demonstrate authentication later.

1. Right-click on the ou=Members container, and select New | User:

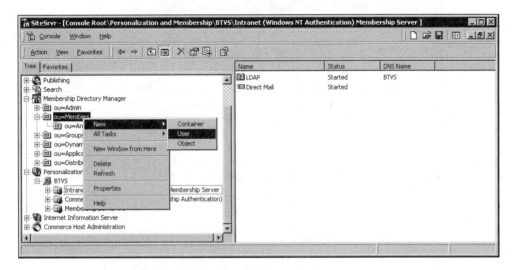

2. Click Next on the welcome page of the wizard.

3. Add the name of the new user and hit Next:

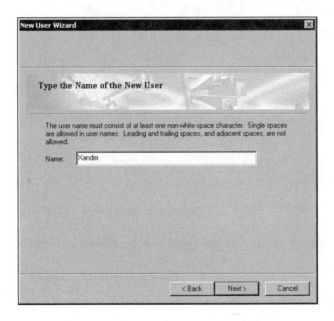

4. In the next stage of the wizard, click the Add Attribute button. There are many standard attributes: choose user-password for now and press OK:

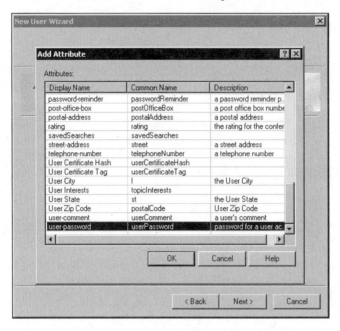

5. Change the user-password attribute's value and click Next:

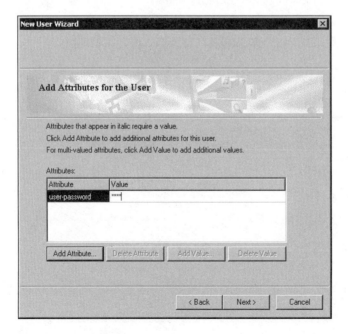

6. Don't bother adding the user to a group: simply click Finish.

Under the ou=members container you can see that cn=Xander is created as a member/user:

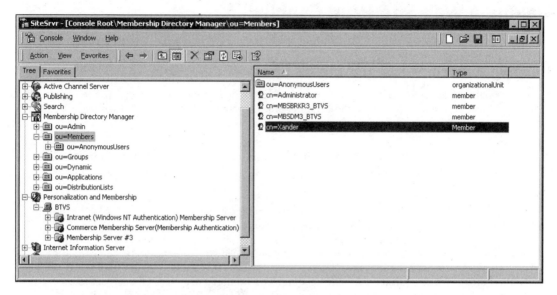

Having successfully created a Membership Server instance and explored it in the Membership Directory Manager, let's take a look at the Membership Directory itself.

The Membership Directory

This is the datastore that stores member information (user name, password, password hint, age, address, etc.) for members in the ou=members container, as well as storing information about other containers in the Membership Directory.

If you open the actual Access (or SQL Server) database where the Membership Directory Service data is persisted, you can see that it contains tables (including classes, attributes and Class_Containers):

It is recommended that no modification be made to this database directly because LDAP has its own method of storing data. Everything should be done using the Membership Directory Manager or programmatically by code contained in scripts.

Making a Web Site P&M Enabled

The first step in this process is, of course, to map the Membership Server instance to a web site.

Mapping Between P&M and the IIS Site

What remains now is to map the IIS site with the Membership Server instance so that all users will be authenticated automatically against the Membership Directory. The mapping process can be easily accomplished with just a few mouse clicks.

1. First, open us the IIS MMC snap-in and browse to the site you want to map to the Membership Directory.

> For the purposes of this example, I will be using the InterKnowlogy site that we created earlier in the book. However, as you recall our site already has membership functionality, which the Site Builder Wizard added for us. Unfortunately, you cannot simply switch to using the Site P&M Services instead. It is possible to use both but it requires a lot of additional complex coding. The standard practice is that if you know you want to use the P&M membership functionality, you do not let the Site Builder Wizard add it but rather you incorporate the functionality at a later date yourself.
>
> Also, this example assumes the site is an instance of the web server and not just a virtual directory under the Default Web Site.

2. Right-click on the site and bring up its Properties dialog.

1. Select the Directory Security tab. Notice that the Edit button under Anonymous access and authentication control is *enabled*, so that you set web permissions the usual way:

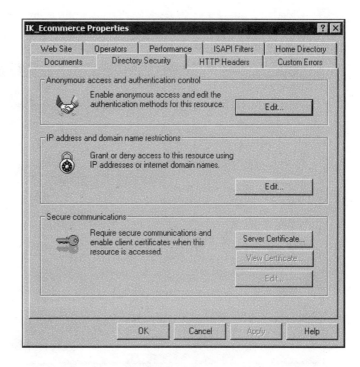

2. Next, visit the ISAPI Filters tab – there will be no filters by default:

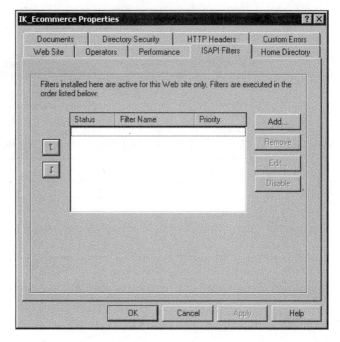

3. Close the dialog and go back to the site node again, right-click and select All Tasks | Membership Server Mapping:

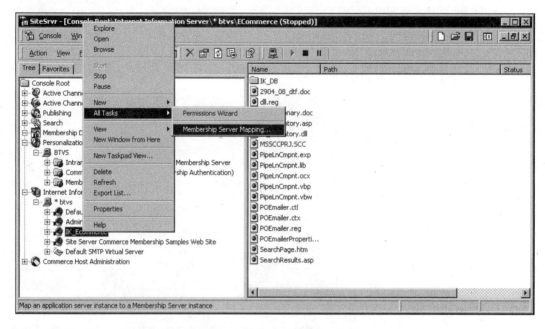

4. Choose the Membership Server instance you created earlier and press OK:

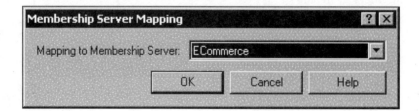

5. If you go back to the Directory Security tab we were discussing just a moment back, you'll find that the Edit button has been disabled, and in fact a new tab called Membership Authentication has been added with some default settings:

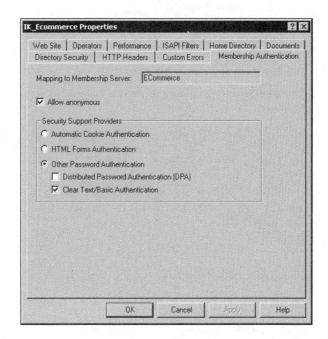

And visiting the ISAPI Filter tab again shows that mapping a Membership Server instance installs an ISAPI filter on the site:

So, whenever a visitor comes to the site, the authentication filter contacts the Membership Server, which in turn consults the Membership Directory database to authenticate the user and allow access to the requested page or resource.

User Validation When Requesting a Resource

The figure below shows the flow when a user requests a resource, product.asp:

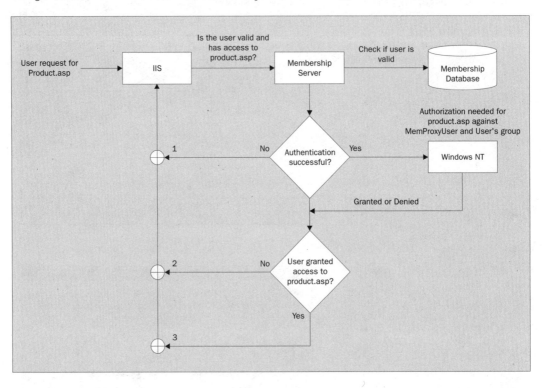

IIS (acting on feedback received from Membership Server) takes one of three courses of action (corresponding to the numbered nodes in the previous figure), depending on the credentials entered by the user:

- ❑ Node 1: Invalid user
- ❑ Node 2: User valid but does not have authorization for product.asp
- ❑ Node 3: User valid and has access to product.asp

Node 1: Invalid user

The user is shown the Logon Troubleshooter page:

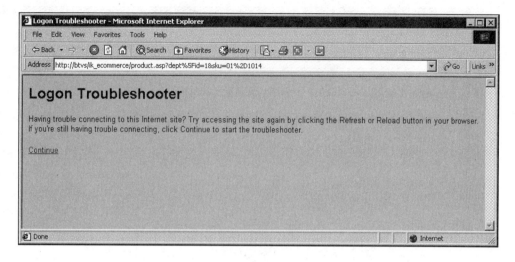

The trouble shooting pages, as well as the forms that handle logins, can be customized to make them appear consistent with the look and feel of your site.

Node 2: User valid but does not have authorization for product.asp

This means that the user's credentials are verified against the Membership Directory, but the resource requested (as secured by NT) is not available. You can simulate this by denying access to Everyone for the product.asp file through Windows Explorer:

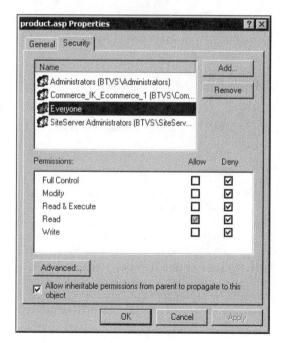

After you remove access, when any user who is not part of any of the groups tries to access the page, the following message will be displayed:

Node 3: User valid and has access to product.asp

In this case `product.asp` is processed by IIS and sent in response to the request:

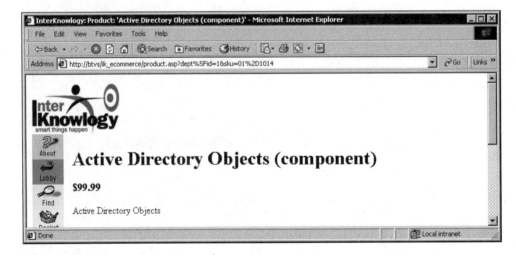

Membership accounts are affiliated to membership groups, which, in turn, are mapped to actual Windows NT groups. For example the cn=Administrator *is a member of the* cn=AdminGroup, *which has a* Site_MemberServer_Members_AdminGroup *local group on the NT SAM. These are groups, along with the* MemProxyUser *account, that will be ultimately used by the Membership Server to get authorization for your Windows NT resources, so take care not to delete any of these accounts or groups through the NT User Manager.*

If you had chosen Windows NT Authentication instead of Membership Authentication, Membership Server would authenticate and authorize against the NT SAM.

> **Use Windows NT Authentication in cases where your site visitors are within the intranet, so that you can use the existing resource authentication and authorization mechanisms. Once your application starts being used on the Internet, however, you could get thousands of users. In this scenario, using Membership Authentication avoids having an individual NT account for each of your site visitors – a security nightmare, as well as a degradation in NT performance.**

Most of us experience security issues while starting with Site Server and P&M. The discussions so far in this section should help you understand what to look for if you run into security issues or want to tighten up security on your site.

If you had any problems when creating the Membership Server instance (from the time you opened the MMC to clicking Finish), please consult Chapter 2 to check that you have installed everything in the proper order, applied the appropriate service packs and fixes, etc.

Disenabling Anonymous Access

Allow anonymous was enabled in the Membership Authentication tab for the site's properties so that any user can anonymously browse through your site without requiring any user name/password credentials verification. Let's uncheck Allow anonymous and see what happens:

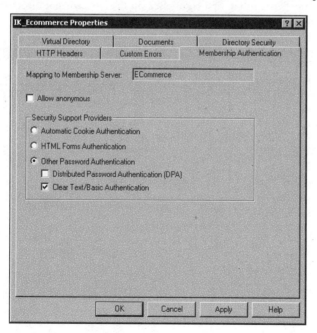

When the user requests the home page again, they are shown a dialog box like the following, where they have to enter their user name and password:

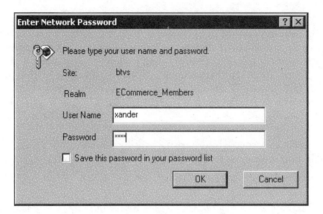

If you were unsuccessful in three attempts to logon, or pressed Cancel, the Logon Troubleshooter page welcomes you. This page is under the `Trouble` directory of the `_mem_bin` virtual directory of your site.

Limiting Anonymous Access

You may not want to ask for credentials as soon as the visitor comes to the homepage. In fact, the homepage should be "window-shoppable" or anonymously browsed, with credentials asked for only at a later business transaction stage. To do that, first right-click on the site's virtual directory and enable Anonymous Authentication as it was before.

Let's assume that the user will be required to give his username/password only on coming to the shopping cart/basket, and that, instead of showing the above authentication box, the user is presented with a login page. So, find `basket.asp` (or any equivalent file) in the right-pane of the MMC, right-click on the file, click Properties and then the Membership Authentication tab. Set HTML Forms Authentication as shown:

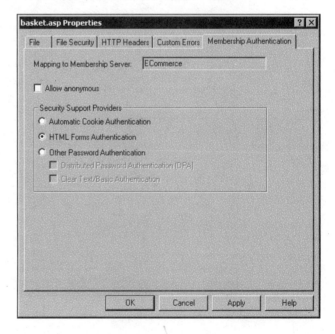

The default authentication filter uses the `FormsLogin.asp` file as the form to accept user credentials. This ASP file shouldn't be renamed, but it can be customized to look consistent with other pages of your site.

> *If you chose **Automatic Cookie Authentication**, then a cookie put by Site Server on the shopper's machine will be automatically used for authentication, without any need for username/password entry.*

Now before the user can see their shopping basket they have to log in:

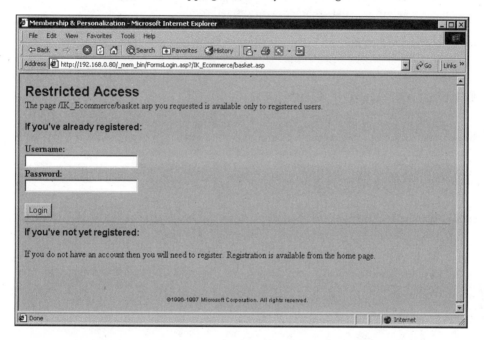

> **Of course this is exactly the functionality that the Site Builder Wizard added to our site so you can see why you need to choose how and when you want to implement authentication through Site Server on your site.**

Personalizing the User Experience

Nowadays, I'm flattered too much whenever I go to my favorite Chinese restaurant. The waitress greets me by name and brings my Buddhist Delight automatically. She knows my name because I told her, but brings me dishes somehow knowing what I like. There seems to be no more debate as to who is the King in the world of business – companies are moving from customer care to customer delight.

> **Showing customers that you know them personally brings them back to you, again and again.**

So far we have talked about the Membership aspect of P&M and getting information about members is the first step to Personalization.

Gathering information about your members can be done using **Explicit Profiling** or **Implicit Profiling**. Explicit profiling is asking the user for information, whereas implicit profiling is based on observing the actions the user takes while at the site. The waitress knew my name because I explicitly told her, while she knew implicitly my favorite food by observing my menu choices.

Once you have information about members, you could use it for various personalization purposes. For example, you could greet members by name, fill in their address automatically once they are placing an order, send mails about topics that are their favorites and so on.

The personalization information can be stored either at the server-side, as a part of member information, or at the client-side, in the form of cookies.

Personalization Using Cookies

A cookie could be put on the client's machine, say, when the user successfully logs in. Storing information in cookies can be a favorable option in certain cases: for example, your home page could always be anonymous and hence you need not wait for users to login to know who they are.

Prior to Site Server, cookies were sent using the ASP Response object:

```
Response.Cookies("MemName") = strMemName
```

In Site Server, you can also use the **Verifusr object** to issue cookies. The Verifusr object contains an `IssueCookie` method which is used for this purpose:

```
Set VerUser = Server.CreateObject("Membership.Verifusr.1")

' Code to validate user - see verifpwd.asp for an example

VerUser.IssueCookie "MemName", strMemName
```

Therefore when the user comes back to your site again, you could greet them on the home page itself by using the `Cookies` collection of the Request object:

```
Response.Write "Welcome " & Request.Cookies("MemName") & " !"
```

Using P&M for Personalization

After the last example you may think, "Why should we store information in P&M at all if we could do it in cookies?" Aside from size limitations of cookies, the answer is evident in the example itself – that is, the client needs to contact the server in order for the server to determine something about the user.

However, there are a lot of business situations where you would like to do some processing based on user information without needing to contact the user, in which case all the processing needs to be done server-side. For example, using **Direct Mailer** in Site Server, you could send personalized mails at specified intervals using mailing lists that contain your users' e-mail addresses.

Adding Personalization Attributes

We know that membership data is actually stored in either Access or SQL Server, but we need not be bothered about its design or how it's stored – that's the beauty of the data abstraction achieved by the Directory Service. But if we want to add a few more attributes to members, how do we do it?

Even though the data design is taken care of by Membership Server, the **schema** is there for you to change. You can look at the schemas under ou=Admin | cn=Schema:

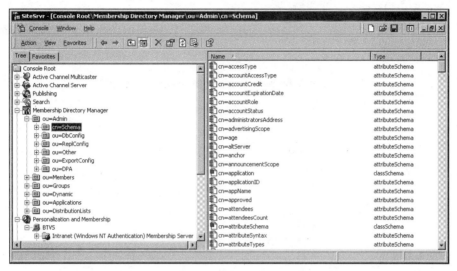

*You'll notice that there are two type of schema: **Class** and **Attribute**. The names are actually quite explanatory, but essentially attributeSchema ares the attributes that define a classSchema. So, for example, cn=member is a classSchema and its attributes, such as cn=userPassword, are attributeSchema.*

If you double-click on the cn=member classSchema, and go to the Class Attributes tab, you should see all the attributes in your current member schema:

The ones that are checked, like the common-name attribute above, are **mandatory attributes**. This means that even though the member schema might contain say 20 attributes, when you create a member, the member need not have all the attributes but it must have those classified as mandatory. So we can always be sure that there is a common-name attribute but not necessarily a birth-date attribute.

Suppose you want to add an attribute that's not in your current schema? Simply click the Add... button and select one of the attributes from the list shown. This is basically a list of all of the attributeSchemas defined in the Membership Directory:

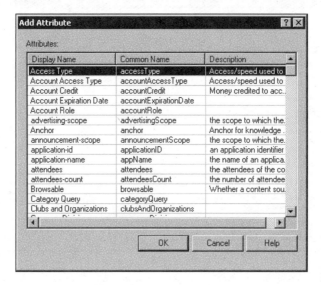

Adding a New Attribute

The information you want to store about your member might need to be modeled differently from any of the available attributes. In that case, you can add an attributeSchema, and then add that attribute to your member class. For example, to add a new member attribute called lastPurchase to your cn=member classSchema you should:

❑   Create a new attributeSchema called lastPurchase

❑   Add the lastPurchase attribute to the cn=member classSchema

Creating a New Attribute Schema

1. Right-click on cn=schema container and select New | Attribute:

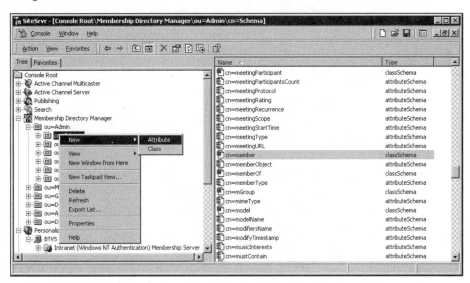

2. Click Next on the welcome screen of the wizard that's launched, then give the name of the attribute to be created. Note there should be no spaces in attributes or class names, but there can be with the Display name. Also check the Multi-valued box at the bottom:

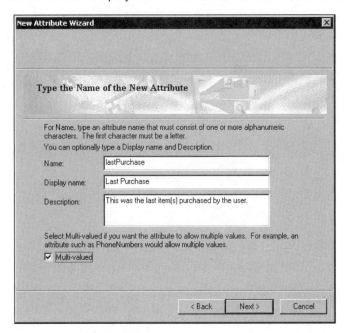

3. Click Next and choose String as the attribute's syntax:

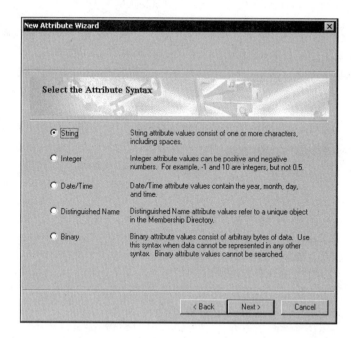

4. Press Next and on the next page choose Syntax Constraints as None:

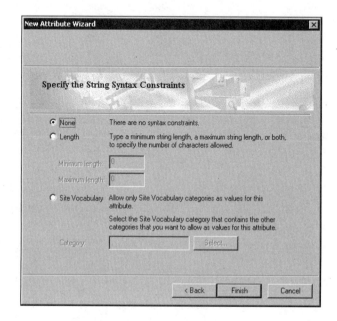

5. Finally click Finish.

6. Now cn=lastPurchase will be part of your attributeSchema, and you can add it to the cn=member schema as explained earlier:

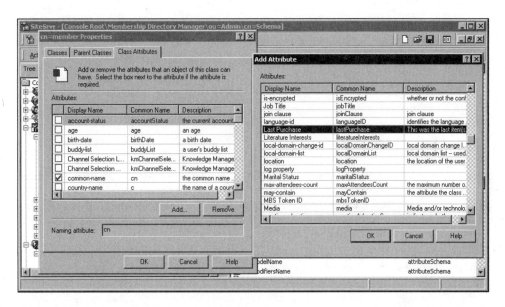

Now that we've seen how to define attributes in a schema for a member, how do we use these attributes in our site?

Working with Attributes

A detailed explanation of how to work with the Membership Directory through code is beyond the scope of this book as there are several methods you can use. What we will do here is provide you with some simple code snippets that work with the **Active User Object (AUO)**.

> *If you want to learn more about coding for P&M then I recommend you read either Professional Site Server 3.0 (ISBN: 1-861002-69-6) or Site Server 3.0 Personalization and Membership (ISBN: 1-861001-94-0) from Wrox.*

When a user is authenticated in the Site Server 3.0 P&M Directory Service, at the page level, if an Active User Object is instantiated it is automatically bound to the currently authenticated or active user. Using this object we can retrieve or set information about the current user.

So to store the lastPurchase attribute for the current user in an e-commerce store we would use the following code, which should go before the OrderForm object is destroyed and released:

```
Dim objAUO
Dim lastPurchases

objAUO = Server.CreateObject("Membership.UserObjects")

For Each key In orderForm
    If (key<>"Items") AND (key <> "_Verify_With") Then
        If(key="pf_id") Then 'add the product code
            lastPurchases = lastPurchases & orderForm.Value(key) & ","
        End if
    End If
Next

objAUO.lastPurchase = lastPurchases
objAUO.SetInfo

Set objAUO = Nothing
```

In the code snippet above, first we iterate through the items of the OrderForm object to build a single string containing the items in the basket that are about to be purchased. Next, we use the AUO object to assign the value of that string to the lastPurchase attribute. Lastly we use the SetInfo method to persist the change. These few lines of code summarize the real power of the AUO object. Attributes are properties on the object itself, making them very simple to add or modify.

> *This is a simple example of setting values to attributes with the AUO object. In reality, since the lastPurchase attribute is multi-valued, we would build an array with the items on the OrderForm object and then use the Put method of the AUO object to persist the array into the multi-valued attribute. Instead of having one long string like in the example above, we'd get each valued segregated in the multi-valued attribute.*

Direct Mailer

Site Server has a utility called **Direct Mailer** that can be used to send automated e-mails to user lists. To facilitate this, P&M has container called ou=DistributionLists where you can create your distribution lists. A distribution list essentially contains an alias for the list and of course the e-mail addresses of the users in the Membership Directory. This assumes that you have the e-mail address of your users in an attribute called say email. The exact attribute used for e-mail could be specified in the schema for the cn=distributionList.

Creating a Distribution List

1. To create a distribution list, right-click on the ou=DistributionLists container and select New | Object:

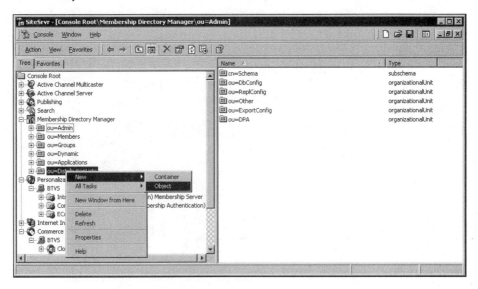

2. Press Next on the welcome splash screen.

3. On the following screen choose distributionList and press Next:

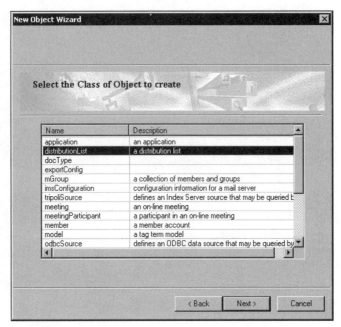

4. Now give the distribution list a name. Since you may create many lists it will be useful to use a meaningful name:

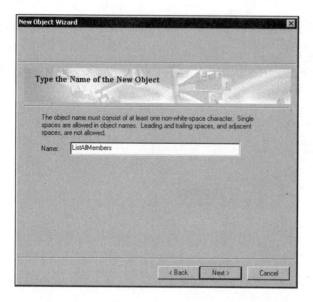

5. Click the Next button and specify the alias for this distribution list. Note that this need not be a valid address:

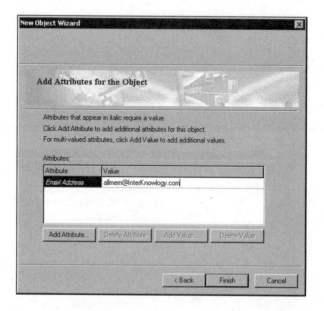

6. Click on the Finish button to create the distribution list.

7. Now open the Properties dialog for the list just created:

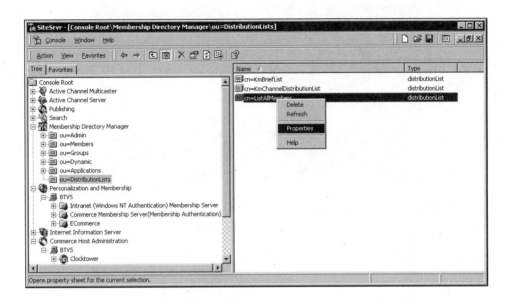

8. In the Properties dialog box that comes up go to the Members tab and click the Add button to include members in this distribution list:

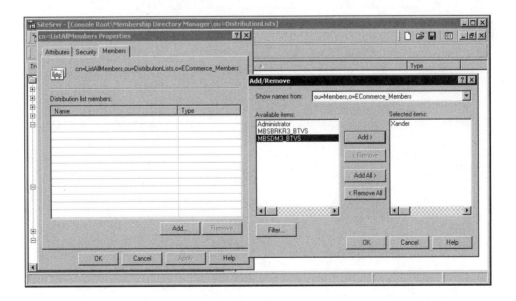

9. Click OK when you have added all the members:

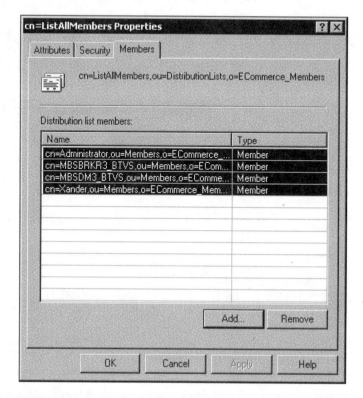

10. Click OK to close the Properties dialog.

Now that the distribution list is ready with members in it, we can use the Direct Mailer to schedule mails.

11. Launch Direct Mailer from Start | Programs | Microsoft Site Server | Tools | Direct Mailer.

12. On launching itself Direct Mailer could show the following dialog box or you can open it by using the menu Tools | Settings:

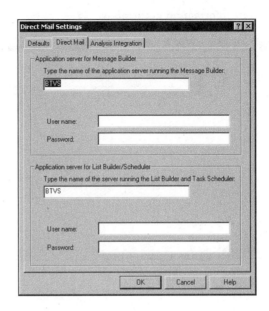

The main concept to note here is that the Application server, i.e. the web site that is mapped to the Membership Server, should be specified and not the Membership Server itself.

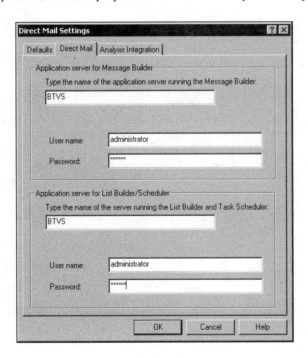

13. If your information in the above screen is right then the main screen appears:

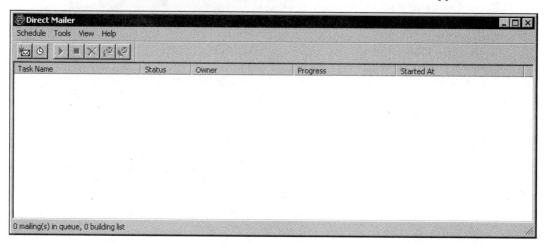

14. To create a new mail schedule click the menu option Schedule | Create Direct Mailing.

15. Give the mail out a name and provide a template URL. Also specify if you want to personalize content. Basically there will be a mailing template ASP file in which the AUO can be used to get each user context and insert content accordingly. Click Next:

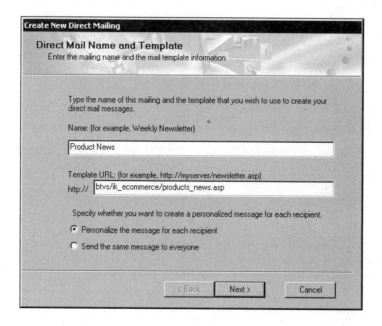

16. In the dialog that comes up, the distribution list alias has to be entered. You can have multiple distribution lists with their aliases separated by commas. Then click Next:

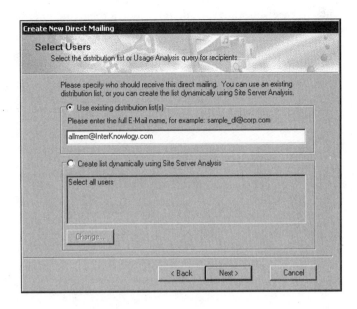

17. In the last screen you can enter the From e-mail address and a subject for this e-mail:

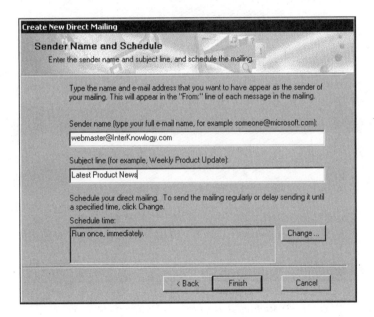

18. In case you want this mailing to be a recurring one, you could schedule it by clicking the Change button:

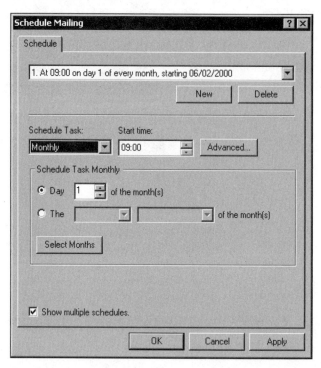

19. Clicking the Finish button will run the mailing list and an e-mail will be sent to the members on the list:

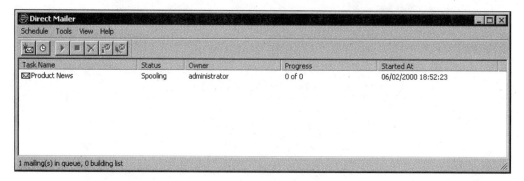

Remember that the Direct Mailer sends mail using the SMTP service on the server. Therefore you should check if the SMTP service is running and has proper routing access to relay servers. Contact your network administrator for more information on the SMTP service and connectivity to external networks.

Summary

Site Server provides us with a powerful way to store and authenticate against member information in the LDAP Server. The Membership Server is used to store personalization information about users and their usage behavior. LDAP provides for fast and unified access to organization wide data, particularly useful on the Internet.

By integrating the different features within P&M, you can create an online community that delivers membership levels, as well as personal features such as custom web pages and direct mail, thus creating a better sense of an online community directed towards your users.

In this chapter we have:

❑   Had a quick look at the P&M architecture

❑   Created a Membership Server instance

❑   Mapped it to a site to be authenticated

❑   Created a member using MMC

❑   Found out how to restrict access to a specific resource

❑   Found how to add new custom attributes to members

❑   Briefly saw how to use Direct Mailer

This should put you on the fast track to working with the Personalization and Membership feature of Site Server. This ends our coverage of main Site Server services and I hope you can begin to see the power behind implementing an e-commerce solution with Site Server. In the final chapter, we will briefly look at some other important aspects that you should consider when deploying an e-commerce site.

Advanced E-Commerce Site Concepts

Through this book we have been exploring the uses and possibilities of Site Server, and learning how to apply it to our own needs. This chapter will focus briefly on other factors that you should consider when implementing a Site Server e-commerce solution.

However, given how large a topic Site Server and its Commerce Edition is, we have only really been able to give you an overview of many of the concepts you need to know in order to produce a successful e-commerce site. However, there are a great many other areas that are not really within the remit of this book, so the purpose of this chapter is to at least make you aware of some of these areas.

The topics discussed in this chapter will give you a broad overview of a few things that should rate highly on an importance scale. They include:

❑ Application architecture
❑ Security
❑ Site design

First, of all let's take a look at the overall design of the way our sites should be constructed.

Application Architecture

So you have been subjected to the glories of Site Server and e-commerce. By now, after all of the topics you have covered so far, you probably feel you can dive straight in and knock up a fantastic e-commerce site in no time at all, right? Well, not so fast. Maybe a little planning is in order – or how about a lot of planning?

There's a lot to think about when authoring an Internet application, especially one that will be deployed on Microsoft Site Server. Why spend a lot of time planning? Well, let's look at the technical requirements for a typical Internet application:

❑ High Availability (24 hours a day, 7 days a week).

❑ Scalable as demand grows. A good Internet application should be able to successfully handle an increasing number of users over time.

❑ Fast.

❑ Secure.

❑ Easily accommodates changing requirements without a lot of coding effort. When changes in company rules and policies change, developers need to be able to modify applications quickly.

❑ Leverages data coming from multiple sources within the organization. Good Internet applications provide users with an easy to use application that can be accessed from anywhere in the world if users have access to the Internet.

❑ Masks the complexity of a heterogeneous computing environment from the user. Even if your application is using data from multiple sources and communicating with multiple types of systems, a user of your application should not be aware of it. For example, a typical environment might include mainframes, Windows-based servers, and UNIX machines. A good Internet application should hide this complexity from the user.

Could you write an application that does all of these things, as well as satisfying all of the business requirements, without some planning? You may possibly be able to do so but it would lengthen the project, increase costs and require more testing. Planning is important to a successful on time, on budget project which saves you the trouble of re-writing code, re-testing, and re-analyzing user requirements.

In this section we are going to explore the issue of application design, and some steps you can take to ensure your Internet application will be a success. By planning ahead and making application design decisions before the development process begins, you will have a much greater chance for success.

Site Server's shopping cart is an example of how to design an Internet application that is highly available, scalable and fast. This application is an example of **n-tier architecture** or **Windows DNA** (Windows Distributed interNet Architecture).

> *Throughout this chapter we'll use the terms n-tier and Windows DNA interchangeably to describe the architecture we are promoting.*

Hopefully, after reading this section you'll be convinced this type of architecture has many advantages, and you'll want to design your applications in much the same way. Most of the concepts we'll be covering are not really specific to any computing platform – these design principles can be applied just about anywhere. However, after introducing the basic concepts, our discussion will be centered on using Microsoft technologies – after all, this is a Site Server book.

A Brief History

Before going into how to design Internet or intranet applications, let's take a look at how we got to this point. Four or five years ago we wrote applications very differently to how we do now. We authored Win32 applications that were written in Visual Basic, Visual C++ or maybe even PowerBuilder. These client applications included business rules and business logic along with data validation. Then, we designed databases – making full use of stored procedures – that contained even more business logic and data validation. Finally, we glued the whole mess together and called it a **client/server** application.

Software developers' lives were actually pretty easy in those days. All we really had to do was keep our client-server applications alive from 8am-5pm, during normal business hours. To help the situation, the only people who used our applications were working for the same company, on our own network or even in the cubicle next to us. When users made changes to the requirements, we made the appropriate coding changes and we re-deployed our application to all of our users. When users complained about our application being slow, we blamed it on the network, or used the excuse that the technology available to us at the time couldn't really support what we were trying to do. Our users didn't know any better and we, as developers, really didn't know of a better way.

Then the Internet burst onto the scene. Suddenly, we were faced with the dilemma of surfacing these client/server applications to users outside of our network and onto the wider world of the Internet. We had to accommodate business-to-business commerce over the Internet. We had to support direct selling of our products to consumers. We had to present data on the Internet from multiple sources within our organization. Our beloved client/server applications now had to run 24 hours a day, 7 days a week, 365 days a year – and they had to be fast.

No longer could we blame the network or inferior technology when things went wrong. OK, we can still blame the Internet for some of our problems, but the real issues are probably still with our application, and for some reason, the new breed of Internet savvy users don't accept excuses. The management in our companies has gotten smarter over time, and demands a return on their investment. They want us to write applications faster and cheaper, and we have to make sure they have a useful life of at least several years. Our lives have become extremely complicated.

The bottom line is that developers are now forced to do a lot more planning and design before they start building Internet applications. The technical requirements for Internet applications are a lot different to those PC developers are used to dealing with. Our mainframe brethren have had to deal with these issues for a long time. Now, the Internet has leveled the playing field and we have to take steps to deal with it.

By taking steps to think ahead and plan your application, and make decisions on architecture before coding begins, you can greatly increase your chances for success.

Application Architecture and Design

By way of an introduction into application architecture, let's examine an online ordering application similar to the one we created in Chapter 4. First we'll go over its basic functionality, and then we'll look at the overall design of an e-commerce application created in Site Server, and discuss the key architectural points.

Basic Functionality

We might expect a typical e-commerce shopping cart application to provide the following functionality:

❑ An e-commerce application should provide the user with the ability to browse through a list of products and see information about them, such as a description, price and maybe a picture. It would also be nice if the user were informed as to whether the products were actually in stock.

❑ Once the user finds a product they would like to purchase, they should be able to easily add it to their shopping cart – just like someone would do if they were shopping in an actual store.

❑ Once the user has selected products to purchase, they should be given the opportunity to "check out", or actually purchase the items they have chosen. Since these purchases are occurring over the Internet, the user will probably have to use a credit card as their form of payment.

❑ Before the checkout process is complete the user is informed of their sales tax and shipping costs, and presented with a final amount that will be billed to their credit card.

❑ If the user decides to make the purchase, the shopping cart application updates the inventory to reflect the purchase, and sends a message to the shipping department that they should expect to be receiving a list of items to ship to our customer.

Your application might not work exactly like this, but I'm sure you get the idea.

Application Architecture

Now let's start to break down this online ordering application and explain the reasoning behind things discussed in the earlier chapters:

❑ First, our application has a **user interface**. The user interface will be the interaction point between the application and the user. In the applications we have worked with in previous chapters, the HTML and ASP pages have been the user interface.

❑ Second, we have a set of **business rules** or **logic** that govern the behavior of the online ordering application. The work done within the pipelines of a Site Server e-commerce site falls within this category.

> **A business rule is a behavior, or a policy, which is being implemented in an application. For example, a life insurance company might have a rule that they do not accept premium payments of less than $50. Business rules can also be calculations or data validations. The term business logic is synonymous with business rules.**

❑ Third, we have a **data source** where all of the product data resides. In Site Server, this is normally SQL Server but as you have learned any ODBC compliant database will suffice.

Take a look at the following diagram:

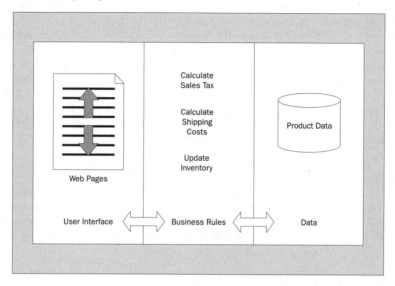

As you can see we have defined three distinct layers or **tiers** within this application, and each of these layers has a very specific function:

❑   The **Presentation Services tier** handles the user interface

❑   The **Business Services tier** handles all of the business logic

❑   The **Data Services tier** is responsible for providing all of the data to the other two layers

If you step back and look at most software applications, they can be broken down into layers like this. What you are doing here is defining the **application architecture** or an **application design**.

Now let's spend some time going over each of the tiers at a conceptual level, and see some guidelines for how to construct each tier.

The Presentation Services Tier

The interaction point between the user and an application, or the user interface, makes up the Presentation Services tier. All of the functionality of an application is exposed to the user through this layer. In a Site Server online ordering application, the shopping cart pages will be the Presentation Services tier.

A key point to remember here is that the functionality contained in the Presentation Services tier should be dedicated to handling user interface issues. Look at how an online ordering application is written in Site Server – the script executed by the ASP pages will update the contents of the pages, and make calls to objects that calculate things like sales tax and shipping cost. The code to calculate these things is not contained in the pages: the actual calculations are part of the Business Services tier.

> **Try not to put business logic in the user interface portion of an application – business logic belongs in the Business Services tier.**

You might be asking yourself, "Where do I put data validation code?" This is an excellent question, and in fact it's sometimes a point of debate. There are so many different ways to classify data validation. For example, should you validate data on the page and not let the user continue until they enter correct data? Or, should you validate that data in the Business Services tier after a form is submitted, and come back to the user if something is wrong? There are ups and downs of both processes for validation. Validating data on the page through client-side scripting is fast and efficient, but you must write code to support all browsers in case the browser does not support the version of script you are writing for. Using the Business Services tier allows you to have more freedom in the code you write, but it can be costly with server resources since you must make another trip to the server each time to validate data. Another problem with using the Business Services tier is that if the user has a slow connection they might have an unpleasant experience while using your application.

You could decide that no data validation belongs in the user interface – after all, the decision on whether something is valid or invalid is business logic. Right? Well, depending on the application, in many cases it may make sense to divide the validation task between tiers. Basic data entry rules such as "you must select a customer" or "data must be numeric" would be best done client-side prior to submitting the form in order to save a trip to the server. More refined business rules such as "purchase amount cannot exceed available credit" would belong in the Business Services tier. It really is up to you, and you should do what makes sense in the context of your application.

The Business Services Tier

The Business Services tier is where all of the "heavy lifting" will be done in a Windows DNA application. This tier is where things like calculating values, and querying and updating inventories will take place. Alternatively, you can think of the Business Services tier as providing a service to the Presentation Services tier for non-user interface functionality.

The overall behavior of an application will be governed by rules located in the Business Services tier. Typically, most of the investment in a large application will be made in the Business Services tier, and as applications grow in size and complexity, so will the size and complexity of this layer.

> **In all situations, the Business Services Tier should be built using components.**

Consider the online ordering application example. We need to calculate tax, query and update inventory, and calculate shipping costs. Wouldn't you agree that it would make sense to have a single place where sales tax is calculated? Or, a single place where shipping costs are calculated?

Components typically exist for a single purpose, so in our online ordering example, we could have a component that handles tax calculations, one that deals with inventory, one that handles the calculation of shipping costs, etc. In fact, this is exactly what is happening in a Site Server e-commerce application – there is a suite of components available to the developer that will handle almost all of the functionality required for the application.

There are plenty of good reasons to use components:

- ❑ Start thinking outside the boundaries of our online ordering application, about all of the other applications that might want to make use of a component that calculates shipping costs. If the business logic is encapsulated in a component, that shipping calculation only needs to be developed once, and then it can be used in every application that needs it.

❑ What happens when the method of calculating these shipping costs changes? If every application were using the same component, there could be a single point of change. All of the applications using that component would automatically receive the new functionality. Also, a component only being used throughout a single application would benefit from this same single point of change.

❑ As you start to build up a collection of components, you will be able to assemble new applications more quickly. A new application could end up being a new user interface that just uses the same components, but in a different way.

❑ You could also purchase components from other companies or experts (see Appendix C for a list). For example, you could purchase tax components for every country with which you do business. That way you don't have to deal with the complexity of different tax laws throughout the world, and you speed up your development time.

❑ What if you have multiple delivery channels? If you really separate your business logic into its own tier, what's stopping you from using that logic in interactive voice applications or Smart TV applications? If you don't have to re-invent the business logic, you can really reduce the amount of work required when new methods of delivering data are developed.

So are you convinced that encapsulating business logic into components and then sharing those components across multiple applications is a good practice?

> **Start thinking about how to encapsulate your business logic into components, and how these components can be shared between multiple applications.**

Data Services Tier

The Data Services tier is actually pretty self-explanatory. All data access for an application should reside in the Data Services tier. In our Site Server online ordering application, there's a SQL Server database that contains all of the data.

But data contained in this tier is not limited to just databases. Directory services, mainframe applications, mail stores and even spreadsheets could all be considered as data stores that would be located in the Data Services tier of an application.

The important point to remember here is that only data should reside at this level, not business logic. In our online ordering application, the SQL Server database contains all of the product data, tax rates, and shipping rates. However, all of the business rules applied to this data reside in components located in the Business Services tier.

This brings us to another point of debate. What about stored procedures in SQL Server?

Under this multi-tier application model, it would go against the "rules" to do something like include business logic in a stored procedure. For example, would it make sense to have a stored procedure to calculate shipping costs, since the data for the shipping rates is already in the database?

The question to ask yourself when deciding whether to put business logic in a stored procedure is, "Is this the best possible place I could put this logic?" In most cases the answer will be no, in which case encapsulate that functionality in a component and move it to the Business Services tier.

But don't get the idea that stored procedures have no place in this model: for executing complex queries, or queries that normally take a long time to execute, stored procedures are definitely the way to go.

> **Try not to mix business logic and data in the Data Services tier. Keep only data in the Data Services tier.**

Now that we've discussed the tiers in more detail we can refine our diagram as follows:

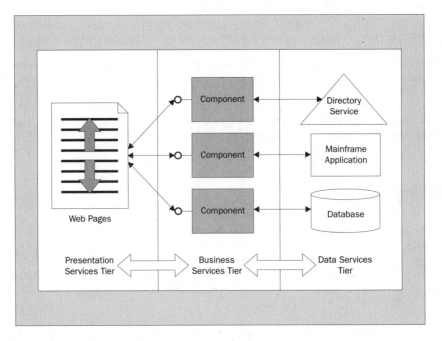

How the Tiers Interact

Now that we've defined the functionality of the tiers, let's discuss how they interact with each other. Here are two simple guidelines to follow:

- ❑ The Business Services tier handles all requests from the Presentation Services tier for anything unrelated to user interface functionality.

- ❑ The Presentation Services tier is not allowed to "talk" directly to the Data Services tier. All requests for data must go through the Business Services tier.

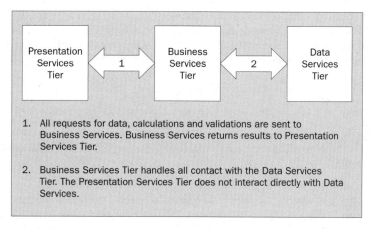

1. All requests for data, calculations and validations are sent to Business Services. Business Services returns results to Presentation Services Tier.

2. Business Services Tier handles all contact with the Data Services Tier. The Presentation Services Tier does not interact directly with Data Services.

The implications of these guidelines are far reaching:

❑ Since all non-user interface requests are going through the Business Services tier, you have a single point of control. Whenever changes are made to the Business Services tier, the Presentation Services tier automatically receives those changes. If you extend this concept and start thinking about sharing components in the Business Services tier across different applications you really start to gain efficiency when changes are made.

❑ By not allowing the Presentation Services tier and the Data Services tier to directly communicate with each other, the details of the data stores in the Data Services tier become hidden from the Presentation Services tier. All the Presentation Services tier knows is that it requests data and it comes from the Business Services tier. This concept is important because we now have the flexibility to change data sources, remove data sources or add new data sources without impacting the Presentation Services tier in any way. Another way to think about this concept is that the Business Services tier *masks* the complexity of the Data Services tier.

There you have it – the basics of Windows DNA, or n-tier architecture. Designing applications where the user interface logic, the business logic, and the data have been segregated gives you an enormous amount of flexibility. As you will see, this flexibility helps you toward successfully meeting all of the technical requirements listed at the beginning of this chapter. You'll also be better able to meet the ongoing demands of your users as their requirements change over time.

Security

Security is one of the single most important aspects of building an e-commerce site. With the fear of credit card theft, a site must be well protected to ensure that customers have confidence in the site. Where to secure your site depends on:

❑ The structure of the site

❑ How/where data is stored

❑ The structure of the network

❑ What type of site it is

On the intranet, dealing with an internal purchasing solution, security isn't as big an issue. Don't get me wrong – it's still an issue – but the data that's usually stored is more likely to be things like PO numbers than credit card numbers. The intranet is usually very secure, and the only people who may have access to the site will be internal employees. This can be looked at from three viewpoints:

❑   The employees are very trustworthy and you never have to worry.

❑   There may be a disgruntled employee that might try to take advantage of access privileges.

❑   Users may accidentally or unknowingly perform an action that can have adverse affects. An example of this would be the accidental deletion of a file or folder that contains important information.

It's very hard to protect against the people who know a systems inside-and-out and have malicious intent, but you can be careful by putting policies and procedures in place to help prevent any problems and to detect them when a security breach occurs. For example, you may want to force password changes through Windows on a scheduled basis. You can also make sure that people have the appropriate level of access privileges, and maintain a tight security policy with permissions on files, servers, etc. There may also be procedures in place for investigating to determine who broke into the system.

Securing an Internet site can require much more technology and planning to accomplish. There are numerous techniques, tactics and technologies that can be employed, and we'll discuss some of the most common in this section. Remember, an Internet site is open to the world, and anyone can potentially access it if the proper security is not in place.

First, let's discuss how the use of a firewall may help prevent unwanted access to certain parts of your infrastructure.

Firewalls/Proxy Servers

> A firewall **is either a software package or a piece of hardware that monitors incoming requests across the Internet. The firewall can prevent connections to certain ports by blocking communication on those ports.**

A firewall can sit in a number of places depending on the functionality and level of security you need. In an instance where you have multiple applications on a web server and need to access ports other than the HTTP port a firewall can sit between a web server and the internal network, keeping all traffic between the Internet and the internal infrastructure regulated:

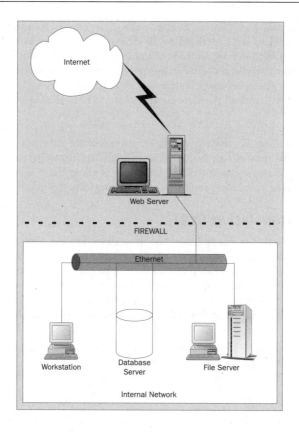

Packet Filtering

Some malicious connections can actually shut a server down or exploit some weakness in your configuration, preventing connections to your server by customers who may be ready to make a purchase. These types of attacks put your business on hold for the duration of the attack.

Firewalls can prevent some of these "denial of service attacks" by filtering out certain types of packets, and stopping them from entering your network and getting to your server. **Packet filtering** is usually selectable on most firewalls or proxy servers.

Communication Port Blocking

In some cases you may wish to only open ports needed for certain applications. A firewall can do this by monitoring the incoming and outgoing traffic, and stopping all packets that are being sent on a specific port or a range of ports.

Web servers communicate via HTTP requests across port 80. This is the default port and can be changed, but most sites don't change it because a port number needs to be specified within the URL to connect to the site. If you change your port number, this can be a problem when you want your site to be accessible to the public; therefore the default is almost always used.

A firewall can sit in front of a web server and only allow communication through port 80, while blocking out all other packets sent/received on all other ports. Another configuration would be to have your web server open to the Internet, in front of the firewall, and your database/file servers behind the firewall. Communication to those servers can be specified for a certain port and opened up in the firewall. For example, SQL Server by default using TCP/IP uses port 1433 to communicate. This port could be opened up on the firewall to allow communication between web server and the SQL Server.

Which configuration you use can depend on the requirements of the project. Some advantages to the server being inside of the firewall are that you can monitor all incoming and outgoing traffic through the firewall. Moving the web server outside of the firewall will allow faster response times because you do not have the firewall layer processing requests and allowing/disallowing connections or packets.

Network Address Translation (NAT)

Network Address Translation is the ability of the firewall to direct connections to computers that may otherwise be unreachable via the Internet. NAT allows us to have computers on a network that may be only accessible from inside the network for some reason or another, respond to requests from outside the firewall. Machines on a corporate LAN might be using invalid IP addresses, because many organizations only have a class C address that just gives them 256 real IP addresses. NAT makes the conversion between the internal, non-routable address and the real IP address.

> *In a Site Server Commerce Edition e-commerce site, any transacted pipelines will NOT function correctly through a NAT firewall.*

Proxy Servers

A **proxy server** is similar to a firewall in that it sits between the internal network and the Internet. The difference is that a true proxy server does not filter packets or block ports. Some serve as a dual proxy/firewall, such as Microsoft's Proxy Server 2.0, but the standard servers are more of a communication tool for use on your network.

The benefit of a proxy server is that it allows only one IP address to be exposed to the Internet, while allowing all of its clients to access resources on the Internet. This protects your internal computers, because there's no way anyone can connect to an internal computer unless the proxy server is configured to allow it. Also, proxy servers provide a cache feature, which makes travel outside to the Internet less needed for highly accessed web sites. When a page is requested that is cached, the proxy server returns the page that is held locally in its cache. The cached page is displayed much faster on the user's computer because the proxy server is on the local network and the request has never had to travel across the Internet.

Encryption

Currently, the only way to protect data entered into web page forms that are being sent across the open Internet or a network is to encrypt it. Cryptography is currently in use worldwide for secure transfer between a client and a server, and encryption applications can be bought or written to secure data stored in a database or on the server.

Public Key Cryptography

Public Key Cryptography is implemented by the exchange of public keys to recipients of encrypted data.

The data is encrypted using the recipient's public key. The data is then sent to the recipient, and their copy of the sender's public key is used to decrypt the information. Usually this exchange of keys happens via certificates.

Microsoft Site Server's Commerce Interchange Pipelines have stages and components aimed at the use of certificates to encrypt information for data or document exchange, allowing companies to safely trade information.

> *The certificates can be generated using Microsoft Certificate Server, which is available as a component of the NT Option Pack and as a service in Windows 2000 Server/Advanced Server. Certificates are also available via trusted third-parties such as Verisign.*

SSL

Secure Sockets Layer (SSL) is the use of certificates to encrypt data that is exchanged between the client's browser and the web server across a default port 443. SSL normally makes use of certificates provided by a Certificate Authority (CA) such as the Verisign certificate, and the public key of that CA is included with most browsers. As an alternative, certificates generated with Microsoft Certificate Server can be used, but users who do not have access to the CA Certificate will receive a message from their browser stating that the certificate cannot be verified. The reason for this is that the certificate has not been added to the list of trusted certificate authorities the browser defaults to.

> *Verisign provides a service to customers by generating these server certificates for use in SSL data transfer. You can view more information on Verisign certificates via their web site at www.verisign.com.*

NTFS

NTFS, which stands for NT File System, was put into use with Microsoft's Windows NT operating systems. This file system format is the most secure of those available on Microsoft platforms, providing more security functionality than the standard FAT (File Allocation Table) or FAT32 file systems. It's recommended that the disk volumes on a web server and database server use NTFS for a more secure system. NTFS also allows for a few other features besides security in which it might be a useful file system to implement. NTFS supports hard disk partitions above 2 GB, which can be important when working with a server that has a large amount of disk space.

Another important feature of NTFS is **fault tolerance**. NTFS allows for software fault tolerance. This means that you have a few methods of protecting your data from corruption, such as hard disk mirroring, where hard disks are identical. Another addition to this functionality is that NTFS itself is fault tolerant. The file system can rollback file system information if a problem is encountered in which data is corrupted. NTFS also has support for file compression. It allows you to compress hard disk data at the file level, letting you choose which files you want to compress and which files to leave uncompressed. This can be very beneficial when trying to save space on the hard drive.

One of the great benefits NTFS provides is the ability to grant or deny access to specific groups of users down to the level of a single file. This can be very important on a web server, where general users may have access to specific directories, but there may be files in that directory intended only for a specified user group.

Database Security

Database security is one of the most important aspects of securing an e-commerce web site. A lot of sensitive information is stored in databases that you don't want to be available to the wrong people. For example, many companies choose to store credit card information in their database, to enable them to bill customers at a later time or to refund cards.

> **This is also one of the most overlooked areas of security with many e-commerce sites on the web today.**

Some common practices for securing databases include:

❑ Grant only the appropriate access to users

❑ Do not use the default system administrator password

❑ Move your database behind a firewall

❑ Encrypt data before it is stored in the database

It's beyond the scope of this book to go into great detail on securing your database, but it would be good design practice to consult your company's database administrator while in the design phase of your web site.

Where To Go From Here

Web site security is not a joking matter and should be taken very seriously. There are numerous resources available from white papers, web sites dedicated to security and also list servers that are dedicated to distributing the latest security techniques and problems.

It would be impossible to list all of the resources but there are a few that you might want to have a look at to get started:

❑ www.microsoft.com/security
❑ The IIS Security Checklist –
    http://microsoft.com/technet/security/iischk.asp

Microsoft has also released a number of bulletins regarding the securing of a Site Server installation. The bulletins may be found at:

❑ http://microsoft.com/technet/security/current.asp
❑ http://Microsoft.com/technet/security/archive.asp

You should always install the latest service packs and hot fixes when performing a Site Server installation.

Site Design

Another thing you should consider before jumping into building an e-commerce site is the actual design of the web site. It's not as simple as throwing together some pages and expecting every shopper to be happy – extensive studies and planning go into the design of successful e-commerce web sites.

In this section we'll cover a few of the main things you need to consider when designing a web site. The areas we'll discuss are:

❑   Designing for performance and scalability

❑   Browser compatibility

❑   Navigation

❑   Graphics

Each of these play an important role in the design of a site, allowing the site to perform well, interact well with users, be consistent and provide an enjoyable experience for the user.

Designing for Performance and Scalability

A slow site will turn away customers very quickly. When surfing the web, people do not want to wait any more than they must. That is why the speed of the site is very important.

ASP Coding Conventions

Many people think of performance as a hardware dependent characteristic of a web site. This is partially true but it is also dependent on the design of the site, the implementation of the code and the level of logic actually found in the Active Server Pages themselves. We'll look at ways you can optimize your ASP code, a few best practices you should follow as well as some things you should not do when coding your site.

ADO – Active X Data Objects

One of the benefits of using Active Server Pages is the ease at which we can access data in a database through the use of server-side components such as ADO. ADO is initially installed as an Apartment-threaded component. For the best performance on a web server, the component should be registered as Free-threaded. Fortunately, Microsoft allows us a means of doing this easily. Within the `\Program Files\Common Files\System\ado\` directory you can run a `.bat` file that will register ADO as a Free-threaded component. The file is named `makfre15.bat` and merges the file `adofre15.reg` into the registry. This should be a common practice for you when setting up and deploying IIS web servers.

> *If at any time you wish to re-register ADO as Apartment-threaded, you may execute the* `makapt15.bat` *file in the same directory.*

Of course, under the DNA model, all data access should really be performed in a Business Services tier component.

Object Scope – Application vs. Session

The scope in which objects are created can be very important to a web application:

❑ Application level objects are created within the global.asa file and are held in memory until the server is stopped, rebooted or the IIS application is reloaded.

❑ Session level objects are created once a user first enters a site and are destroyed via code or when the session times out.

What is placed in each of these objects can affect performance greatly, considering how they are used.

Application objects can be used to enhance the performance of a Site Server e-commerce site by loading information that may remain static into an array and using that throughout the site, instead of making a call to the database to retrieve the information each time it should be displayed. This could be the list of departments shown or possibly the list of products if the list is not too large. We don't want to consume too much of the server's memory here, so the amount of information being stored is very important. Objects that are used a great deal with the same parameters for every user may also be used as Application objects to conserve instantiation time. Some objects of this type, used in the global.asa generated by the Site Server's Store Builder, are the Message Manager object and the Query Map object.

Session variables can be useful but for high capacity sites they are advised against. This is because the server must expend resources to keep track of each user and every single unique user creates objects that are created as Session objects. If your site has 1000 concurrent users, each instantiating objects that must be held in memory for the duration of the session, this can cause a large degradation in performance. It is a good practice on high capacity sites to disable session state either at the page level using <%@ ENABLESESSIONSTATE = FALSE %> at the beginning of every page or by disabling it through the MMC IIS snap-in.

Buffering Output

Another performance consideration is whether or not to buffer the output of the ASP page. There may or may not be reasons when you would want to display the information as it is processed on the server and output but generally you will receive faster performance when buffering. Buffering is not set by default with IIS 4.0 – this must be achieved through code on the page or through enabling it using the MMC IIS snap-in. However, with IIS 5.0 buffering is enabled by default.

Visual Basic DLLs' Threading Model

It is a good practice to move intensive functions and operations to components. The reason for this is that performance is much faster in a compiled component than it is with a scripted language such as VBScript or JScript. This will not only increase the performance of your ASP pages but will also make the code much more manageable if there is a great amount of logic needed to perform an operation. There are however, a few considerations that need to be taken into account when using a component written in Visual Basic. Visual Basic DLLs are Apartment-threaded and should be created and destroyed at the *page level*. This means that for every page the DLL is to be used in, it should be created on that page and then when the component is no longer needed it must be set to nothing. Due to the threading model used for VB DLLs, this may produce problems when they are used at the Application or Session level.

Frames

Although frames can be useful in displaying information there are a few things that must be considered when choosing between frames and a single page to display the information. Browser support for frames hasn't been as widespread over the period of time they have been in use. AOL's browser did not support frames until its version 3.0. Other older browsers did not support frames, so if you are expecting users with very old browsers, frames are not a good choice.

There are also performance issues related to using frames. For the sake of discussion, let's say you have created a web page that uses three frames. This framed page causes three pages to load – potentially tripling the number of calls to the server for each page hit. The client computer may not be a high performance, top of the line machine and having to load three pages simultaneously, with all of the associated graphics files, may put a serious strain on the computer. In this case, even if you are getting response times on the server that are blazing, the user will perceive performance as very slow and may not visit your site again.

Further Reference

ASP Performance is a very broad topic to discuss. It has been around for a few years and has matured since its first inception. Since then, there have been numerous books and articles published on the subject. A few from Wrox Press that should be reviewed are:

❑   Professional Active Server Pages 3.0 – ISBN: 1-861003-38-2

❑   Beginning ASP Components – ISBN: 1-861002-88-2

❑   Alex Homer's Professional ASP Web Techniques – ISBN 1-861003-21-8

Scalability

Much of Site Server's ability to perform on a high level, and scale to industrial-strength levels for performance, is inherited from the Windows platform, which allows you to distribute the Site Server services over a series of different servers or within a **web farm**.

Although you have the option of loading one machine with all of Site Server's components, you can also load each Site Server service onto different computers to increase scalability and performance for your site. This will help off-load the more resource intensive services, such as your database and search functions, onto dedicated servers. If the load on the servers ever begins to increase to the point that performance is suffering, it can be offset by adding more servers.

Site Server by itself is a huge server application, and if you load the entire platform onto one server, by default it will use a large amount of memory, slowing the server. This reduction in performance is due to the amount of resources that are required to run each service that makes up the Site Server platform, therefore it is good practice to stop all services that will not be used.

If you distribute your necessary services to other servers, much of the heavy load can be unloaded from one machine. This lets each service use more resources than would be case if you used just a single server instead of a multiple configuration. The more servers you use for your Site Server network design, the better performance you'll see and the greater your fault tolerance can become.

There's also the issue of **redundancy**. If you distribute your processing, you have a better chance of recovery if one machine should go down – you would still be able to accept transactions while you were getting the rogue machine up and running!

The two most probable resource intensive parts of the Site Server platform are the SQL Server database and the Search components. As these components can take up so much of your processor and memory resources, for scalability and performance reasons it's better to assign them dedicated servers. Otherwise, these resources will be detracting from your web site anytime a hit is made to your database or a search query is run.

Load Balancing

Load balancing is the ability to distribute the load of servers across multiple machines so that the machines do not get "bogged down", decreasing the site's performance – this can also give you redundancy. There are a number of different ways in which you can load balance a server. You may use a hardware-based load balancing solution, such as Cisco's Local Director to direct traffic to each server; a DNS solution, such as a round-robin DNS, in which traffic to each machine is alternated; or you may choose a software-based load balancing solution, such as Microsoft's Windows Load Balancing System.

Commerce Edition and Session State

The Commerce Edition derives its ability to scale from the way it handles the shopper's order form and session tracking. Site Server can use either cookies to help maintain session state or pass information through the query string of the URL. With an e-commerce application it is necessary to maintain state of some type because we must link the shopper's basket with that shopper. The link between the basket and the shopper is needed to display the correct data, calculate the correct pricing for that individual and process the order effectively. There are a number of ways to maintain state on the web and the way you choose to handle this may depend on the requirements of your site.

Session state can sometimes be kept by using the IIS Session object. This allows us to set session variables and let IIS keep track of the session. Session variables can be very resource intensive when used on a large site with a large amount of unique users, instead the data is stored in the database as a Site Server `OrderForm` or `Dictionary` object. Another reason for not using Session variables is that they are unique to the server. Session ID's do not span multiple servers, therefore in a web farm with more than one web server, they become useless.

Another way to keep state might be to use **Dynamic Attributes** that are supplied by Site Server's Personalization and Membership services. For more information regarding this feature, refer to *Site Server 3.0 Personalization and Membership* from Wrox Press, ISBN: 1-861001-94-0.

Browser Compatibility

A design consideration that should be made early on is which browsers should be supported for the web site. This is an important decision and should not be taken lightly, because your choice could prohibit certain users from using your site. The decision should be made with a few things in mind:

❑   The target audience

❑   The functionality required by the site

❑   Environment

We will cover what roles these play in the decision to support different browsers. However, we will not go into detail about the features of each browser because that is beyond the scope of this book.

Target Audience

The target audience plays a role in the determination of which browser you design for. If you would like to reach every conceivable user it is good practice to design for the lowest common denominator. This means your site will need to support at least 3.0 versioned browsers as well as the proprietary online service browsers such as AOL, Prodigy, CompuServe, etc.

What does this mean to you as a developer? This means that you should not use tags that were not available to browsers of these version ranges. The scripting support is either not implemented or barely implemented in these early browsers as well. This means that you must either code for all exceptions or use server-side scripting to offset the difference in scripting support within the browsers.

Functionality Required

The level of functionality required for the site also determines which browsers you may have compatibility problems with. If you are developing a web site that will rely on the newest technology to achieve its design goal, you will be building the site to only support the newest browsers. An example of this would be the use of DHTML within the site to achieve a certain level of functionality, such as drag-and-drop within the browser's window. But this will limit the browser to Internet Explorer 5.0. If you were developing your site to use Layers, then the newest versions of the Netscape browser would be your only compatible choice.

Environment

The environment in which you plan to roll out your web site can be a determining factor of which browser you design for. When would this be relevant? Well, if you are designing a web site or web application for use on a corporate intranet you may be working with a controlled environment. A controlled environment is where the IS departments dictates which browsers are supported on the network. Therefore you will know the browser that will be used and you will have the ability to design *only* for that browser. Many intranets support either Internet Explorer only or Netscape only. This allows the developers to exploit the unique features of the browser they are designing for and some very interesting sites can be built.

Navigation Design

Web sites should be very easy to navigate. With new users arriving every day, it should be obvious how the site works, but the clutter should be kept to a minimum.

Navigation bars provide a good solution. In an e-commerce site, navigation bars might contain links to the available departments, or to the basket pages, utility pages, etc. There are some different types of navigation layouts that can be used easily that have become close to a norm for site design:

❑ Horizontal navigation bar

❑ Vertical navigation bar

❑ Alternatives

These formats present a few advantages and disadvantages that we will discuss.

Horizontal Navigation

Horizontal navigation usually runs along the top portion of the page from left-to-right with options for page navigation:

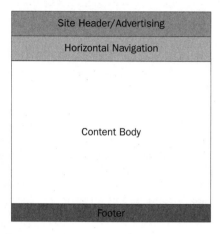

This style of navigation allows for more screen real estate to be used for the main content or the body of the page – more graphics or text can fit onto the screen using this format.

The downside to this style is that the space for your navigation is limited. Adding more navigation options may cause your screen to wrap the options causing it to look different at different screen resolutions.

Vertical Navigation

The style of having the navigation run from top-to-bottom on the side of a page in a table is vertical navigation. This style is very popular in web design, and allows for a greater amount of information to be displayed for the use of navigating the user through the site:

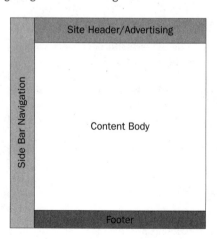

This type of style also gives you more space to add new navigational options without changing the layout of the page for different screen resolutions. The page will just continue to scroll downward as you add new options.

The downside to the style is that you are left with a smaller area on the screen for your actual content. This may or may not be a problem, depending on the size of font you use, and the size of the graphics.

Alternatives

Some alternatives to the standard HTML-based navigation bars are things such as **ActiveX controls** and **Java applets**. These allow for more functional navigation but can sometimes be limiting as well. ActiveX is only supported on Internet Explorer versions 3.0 and above and this would keep users of other browsers from using your site. Java is a good cross-browser solution for later browsers but this also leads to a slower site, because the applet must be downloaded to the user's computer the first and each subsequent time the user visits the site. An example of an effective Java-based navigation scheme is the use of a tree much like that found in Windows Explorer. This allows for information to be categorized and the categories are usually expandable or may be collapsed to allow for more information to be added at later times without affecting the rest of the page.

Content Organization

There are some other things you need to consider when designing a site.

> **You want to keep the number of clicks the user needs to make to get to the information you're providing to a minimum – do not bury your content.**

If you are selling a product online you want all of the product information, price, and availability easily accessible to your users, so that they can make a choice and purchase the product effortlessly. This can lead to increased sales, happier customers and more returning customers. The harder your site is to use, the less time a user will spend on the site and the number of returning customers will be lower.

Graphics

Since the first graphical web browser appeared, the web has become more appealing to the masses. The merge of text with graphics began the use of multimedia on the web, making it more entertaining, more informative and more user-friendly to new computer users just getting online.

There have been some wonderful advances in the use of multimedia and graphics in the past few years, as the Internet has grown. We can see products we are looking to purchase, we can see photographs of homes on the real estate market, and we can even transfer photos of children to family members easily. So what does all of this mean to the web designer?

Graphics can be a wonderful thing when used correctly, but when used badly they can become a nightmare to the 14.4 KBPS modem user who just wants to see the picture of the new lawnmower they ordered. We'll discuss a few of the graphics formats and their uses/limitations in this section, as well as talk about how they can impact your web site.

Graphics Formats

The choice of graphics formats that are used in a web site are important in that they must be able to support fast downloads, display the image efficiently and support the purpose of the image. A wrong choice could end in an image that is either too big for the web, not supported by the browser or just looks plain terrible.

Some of the most common formats you'll encounter are JPG, GIF, TIFF, TGA, and BMP. Since this is a section on web site design, we'll focus on the two most prevalent graphics formats used on the World Wide Web. While the others have their uses they are not as widely in use around the world on web sites.

Joint Photographic Experts Format (JPG)

The JPG image file format is widely used on high-color photography sites. That's what this file format was designed for – displaying photographs.

The JPG image can be compressed into a very small image, and most image editors allow you to change the amount of compression used when saving the image. Each time the file is compressed, data of the image is lost, which means that a highly compressed JPG will lose some of its sharpness and become somewhat blurry. This quality shift depends on how compressed the image is and how many colors were in the image originally.

The benefit to using a JPG is that it can support up to 16-million colors making it very suitable for photographs that are to be displayed on the World Wide Web. The downside is that the format is not suitable for graphics that must be sharp or basic in color, such as a black dividing line or text.

Graphics Interchange Format (GIF)

The GIF file format became prevalent with the online service CompuServe. It was developed to display images to the users of that service, and the specification has filtered onto the Internet because of its usability and special features.

The GIF format is limited in the amount of colors that it can contain. Currently a GIF can only support a 256-color palette, which makes it wonderful for use with basic images but a terrible choice of format for a high-color photograph. The GIF's strong points are in its clarity for simple images – edges remain sharper and base colors appear cleaner.

The GIF also has a secondary spec called the GIF 89a that allows us to use transparent background colors with our images. A color is chosen in the graphics editor to appear transparent, and that color will not show up when the graphic is displayed. This can help add a seamless look to the graphics on a web page.

The GIF 89a spec also has the ability to display simple animations. This is done by adding new image blocks to the file and looping through it. This technique works much the same way as a cartoon, the more image blocks, the faster the images are looped through, the smoother the look of the animation. The downside to this is that the images can become quite large when adding all of these new image blocks to the file.

Both GIF specifications support something called **interlacing**. When a GIF is interlaced, it will appear to fade in gradually as the image is loaded in the web browser. This can be a nice effect and many view this gradual loading of images as causing a perceived faster web site all together. Non-interlaced GIFs do not appear until all of the image data has been downloaded to the web browser.

Graphics Considerations

Let's talk about some of the dos and don'ts of graphics use in web design. There are a few sections we'll touch on briefly that should aid you in designing a great site for your users.

Image Size

When designing a web site, it's important to keep the graphics to a minimum size. The more graphics on a page, the slower it will load. That's why you should make sure your graphics are absolutely necessary, as well as making sure they have been optimized to the lowest possible file size. FrontPage has a nice feature that estimates the download time based on graphic file size for different speed modem users. If you have images that are too large or load too slowly it can adversely affect the performance of the site from the user's perspective – a page that takes 3 minutes to load because of a pretty graphic frustrates the user more than it puts them in awe at your graphic design abilities.

Image Colors

The number of colors your images support might be an issue with certain browsers or graphics cards. Older graphics cards are only capable of up to 256-colors, and graphics that are stored in JPG format with 16-million colors will be displayed with incorrect colors, or might not be discernable at all. It's good practice to stick with basic colors for web site design, and only use high color photographs when absolutely needed. This can help prevent any problems with color shifts in the graphics, and will keep the site looking the same from computer to computer.

Image Usage

One of the biggest problems with graphics on web sites is the overuse of them. Sites that use a large amount of graphics take longer to download, frustrating your user. Browsers have adapted over the years to help with this download time by caching images on the user's computer, therefore many images only have to be downloaded once.

The best practice is to not use graphics that display text, but use standard HTML to display the text. This will load faster, and will also give the user a perception that the site is loading even faster. With the advent of CSS and DHTML, most of the reasons you would use graphics instead of standard text can be accomplished now within the page itself creating a much faster download time.

Animations and Streaming Audio/Video

Ever since the web has become more commercialized, flare has been important in capturing viewers. Graphics became larger and more colorful but the increased download time for truly awe-inspiring graphics made them less feasible on the web. A few technologies have emerged that keep download times low yet provide dramatic, eye-catching flashy sites.

Animations on the web were initially done using the GIF format as we have previously discussed. This was limited by file size and the animations, even today, remain small. To overcome this, the **Flash** format was created. Flash uses a player that can be downloaded as either a Netscape plug-in or an ActiveX control for use with Internet Explorer. Flash offers a number of benefits to those who choose to use it.

Flash files can be created by either using drawing tools that are part of the software or by importing graphics they have created in another graphics editing program. The files are generally very small allowing them to be downloaded quickly making it a great choice for creating animations. The animations can be linked to URLs allowing the animations to actually be used as a user interface on a web site.

The animations created using Flash can be viewed on any size screen resolution and any size monitor, because they are what are called **vector images**. The previously discussed GIF and JPG formats are what are called **raster images**. Raster images cannot be dynamically resized without losing the image's proportions – leading to a distorted image. With vector graphics, you can resize the image without losing any of the image's proportions. This makes the animation seem much smoother, the images appear the same on every screen and they do not lose their "smoothness".

Another choice for "moving" graphics on the web is **streaming video**. Some sites may choose to offer video to the users as a novelty or as an education tool. Training videos on the web are becoming more popular as the technology allows this to evolve. Originally, video on the web was limited to a few small formats, the most prevalent being AVI. These videos were small and usually very large in file size, making for a lengthy download. To give users the ability to view video without the long download process, the technology of "streaming" was introduced. Basically, the server sends information as it is needed and the player interprets the information and starts to translate before the entirety of the file is received. The video begins to play as soon as the stream begins, discarding the information as it is played and requesting the next bit of data that it needs to keep the video going. To keep this smooth, the stream is buffered at different times in the background so that it can stay one step ahead of the video data being played back.

A few of the players for streaming audio/video are the Real Player from Real Networks and the Windows Media Player from Microsoft. When considering streaming audio and video, it is important to remember that the bandwidth requirements are still high from the server-side based on the number of users who are "viewing" the stream.

Summary

Within this chapter we have discussed things that are very important to building e-commerce sites, but beyond the scope of this book. However, the topics in this chapter should be considered due to their importance in building a successful web site.

Think of an e-commerce site not only as a site but also as an *application*. This is one of the greatest considerations you must make, because it must be planned and thought out using the same processes you would use when planning a desktop application:

❑ Use web pages as a presentation layer – Presentation Services tier

❑ Put your business logic in components – Business Services tier

❑ Keep all data in the backend – Data Services tier

We also covered security briefly, and discussed a few of the different ways you could secure your site. The importance of security is something that cannot be stressed enough, and is often the most overlooked aspect of a web site. We discussed a few of the things that can be implemented to help secure your site, and many of these can be implemented at the same time to increase security:

❏ Use a firewall

❏ Use SSL for secure communication between client and server

❏ Use NTFS on the server and database server

❏ Make sure permissions given to users are necessary – tighten up permissions

❏ Use encryption when storing important information such as credit card numbers

Finally, we discussed site design. This is the area where site designers and application programmers seem to separate. Application programmers tend to focus more on the functionality of a site, whereas designers tend to focus on the site's usability and the overall user experience.

We covered the use of navigation and how it may impact your site's success. We discussed how graphics may also be used to enhance a site or, if used the wrong way, can cause problems making the user experience less enjoyable. A few things to remember when designing a site are:

❏ Keep navigation simple

❏ Choose a navigation style that fits your site but keep it functional as well

❏ Choose the correct image format for the type of image you want to display

❏ Keep file sizes down to a minimum

❏ Do not over use graphics

Site Server can be used to build powerful robust sites, but many other things need to be taken into consideration when designing the site.

> *There are too many aspects of web development to list here, but there are many resources available on the web today. One such resource is Microsoft's own MSDN web site, which can be access via* `http://msdn.microsoft.com`. *This site contains many design tips, programming tips, examples, scenarios and ideas to help you get started with building high-powered web server based applications.*

With Site Server you will be able to easily create applications that are almost limitless in scope, allowing you to expand your horizons, sell online, give customers what they are looking for and help build a successful Internet business.

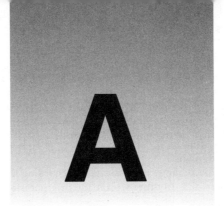

The Commerce Interchange Pipeline

The concept behind business-to-business (B2B) transactions looks deceptively dissimilar to what goes on behind the scenes of a retail online store. In fact, we are used to thinking of a store as a site that *sells* something and that delivers it to us – I *buy* a book at Amazon.com, and Amazon.com *sends* it to me.

Well, that's not really what happens. In fact, all that takes place during a business-to-consumer transaction is an *exchange of information.* Browsing the store corresponds to simply querying a database somewhere using a browser, and receiving information about the merchandise that can be obtained through the store. Similarly, the act of buying means sending to the store personal information so that the merchandise can be delivered to us. As for the process of shipping the goods out, that's not something that the store itself does – usually, it's a completely separated line-of-business system that takes care of that, and all the store does is send a request to it (more information going!) for the shipment to be made.

B2B is *entirely* about exchanging information to facilitate managing the supply chain. In a B2B transaction, two business partners exchange information in a very precise way so that all the data is properly received and understood and that, optionally, the success of the transmission is guaranteed to the highest possible degree of accuracy. For example, the communication that may take place between a store and its line-of-business system when the former receives an order can be considered of B2B type. Similarly, a car factory can order parts from its suppliers using a B2B transmission, and so on. In the `Amazon.com` example above, a B2B transaction might determine which of the warehouses, which are scattered all over the world, would be best to ship the book from.

B2B Transactions

A B2B transaction takes place synchronously using messages called **interchanges**.

> **An interchange is essentially a self-contained set of data that one end of the transaction sends to the other.**

B2B communications always take place based on these fundamental rules:

❑ **Only two partners**
A B2B exchange is like a private phone call – there can only be two partners involved. One originates an interchange, and the other receives it.

❑ **One fundamental language**
The originator of an interchange must format it according to a set of rules that the recipient must be able to understand. In other words, the originator and the recipient must be able to "speak the same language".

❑ **A common carrier**
There has to be a medium through which the two partners of the transaction must be able to communicate. This is an obvious requirement, but a requirement nonetheless, for otherwise the two partners would not be able to communicate!

Additionally, more rules can be established on an individual basis to satisfy particular requirements. The most common rules involve security (since being able to encrypt an interchange so that it cannot be seen from the outside is important when sensitive information travels with it) and guarantee-of-delivery.

Making Sure it Gets There

In a B2B environment, it's often very important to know that a message has reached its intended destination. Since no communication medium is inherently error-free, the only way to ensure the delivery of an interchange is to establish an acknowledgement system, in which the recipient responds to the originator whenever it receives data from it.

This response is also considered an interchange, and is called a **receipt**. Receipts usually contain a certain amount of information to assist the originator with correlating a particular receipt with a transaction, and therefore determining that the latter has indeed reached its destination.

When a receipt procedure is in place, there are certain failsafe systems that must be considered as well. Generally speaking, if the originator does not receive a receipt from the recipient within a certain amount of time, it will attempt to resend the same information, under the assumption that it didn't reach its destination the first time. However, the fact that no receipt ever made its way through could also have been caused by communication problems between the recipient and the originator – the original transmission may actually have been received by the recipient, but the receipt that was sent in response to that interchange got lost somewhere in-between. The result in this scenario is that the recipient gets two copies of the same transaction, and must therefore be able to tell that they are not two separate transactions!

> *Obviously, a receipt should never be acknowledged with another receipt! Doing so would cause an "infinite loop" of receipts to be sent from one end to the other indefinitely.*

Microsoft Site Server 3.0 Commerce Edition and EDI / XML

EDI – acronym for **Electronic Data Interchange** – is the international standard that is used worldwide for the exchange of B2B information on non-internet network platforms. EDI is a very complex standard, mainly because it has to cover an incredible amount of scenarios: clearly, the information exchanged between a factory and its suppliers is very different from whatever information two banks will normally exchange in a financial transaction, even though EDI is used in both cases.

XML – acronym for **eXtensible Markup Language** – is the Internet standard for the exchange of B2B data. XML is structured, obviously, but the creator of the data controls the structure – hence, the "extensibility" feature. As opposed to the rigid standards of EDI, XML is completely user defined. A handful of Internet entities are currently attempting to define XML standards to facilitate the exchange of data over the Internet. For instance, Microsoft's Biztalk Framework for XML defines an XML structure that will seamlessly connect B2B partners.

The Commerce Interchange Pipeline does *not* natively support EDI, but it *does* natively support XML. This means that, if you need EDI for your B2B transactions, you will have to develop the functionality to support it yourself, or integrate a third party pipeline component that does it for you.

Structure of the Commerce Interchange Pipeline

Since there are two partners to a transaction, there are also two types of CIP pipelines. The **Transmit pipeline** is used to create an interchange and send it, while the **Receive pipeline** is used when an interchange is received and has to be interpreted. As you can see, several stages in these pipelines have similar names – in fact, the Receive pipeline is, with a few exceptions, the reverse of the Transmit pipeline.

When a CIP is invoked, two elements have to be passed to it: a Dictionary and a Context. In this case, the latter is still a simple `Dictionary` object that contains essentially the same data as the one passed to the OPP. The Dictionary, on the other hand is not an `OrderForm` – since we're not necessarily dealing with order data in a B2B transaction – but a `Dictionary` object as well, which can contain any amount of information. The Dictionary is then formatted into a pre-defined format (or into a format that you choose) during the transmission process, while the resulting interchange is unpacked into it during the execution of the Receive pipeline.

The Transmit Pipeline

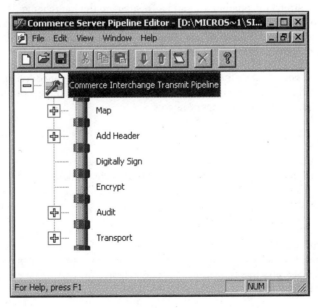

The Transmit pipeline is invoked with three goals:

- ❑ Format and encode the data that will go in the interchange

- ❑ Transmit the data to the recipient

- ❑ Invoke, if necessary, the procedure in the recipient's system that will execute the Receive pipeline (or whatever equivalent exists at the other hand, if a Commerce Server system isn't running there)

The Map Stage

The **Map stage** is used to create the "core" of the interchange, that is the data that actually has to be transmitted with it. As such, its goal is to "map" the contents of the pipeline's Dictionary in a particular format so that they can be sent across the medium chosen for transmission.

The format that you choose is very important, if you consider that – besides the normal requirement of the recipient being able to understand it – the transmission medium sometimes has its own peculiar requirements. For example, if you were to choose Internet e-mail as your transmission medium, you would need to make sure that your encoding didn't include any byte whose value is higher than 127, because e-mail automatically deletes the eighth bit of every byte that is sent across it. Therefore, your data would probably need to undergo further encoding into a well-known mail transport protocol, such as UUEncode.

For the Map stage, Site Server 3.0 Commerce Edition provides a couple of interesting built-in components. The first, called MapToXML, can be used to map the entire contents of the dictionary into XML – a format that is very suitable for interchanges (assuming that the recipient understands it). The second, called MakePO, can be used to encode the whole dictionary into a text file; generally, you could use it to create a comma-delimited database that can contain all the information you need.

The Add Header Stage

In the **Add Header stage**, the pipeline can add a "header" to the interchange. The header is not necessary, although it will prove particularly useful in many cases. A header can contain several pieces of information, such as a unique transaction ID (like the one generated by the AddHeader built-in component), a request for a receipt, the type of the document being sent, and so on.

This stage is also the point in the pipeline in which the interchange is encoded, using the appropriate encoding mechanism for the transmission medium chosen. SSCE provides encoding components for MIME, which is widely used in the most popular Internet protocols.

The Digitally Sign Stage

The next stage, **Digitally Sign**, takes care of adding a digital signature to the interchange. A digital signature is a sort of "digital watermark" that can be used to determine whether the contents of the interchange have been modified en-route. There are a number of good reasons why you may want to use digital signatures, and not all of them have to do with being paranoid about someone intercepting your data – for example, you may want to make sure that no communication errors occurred.

Digital signatures often make use of a digital certificate, and SSCE provides a way to interface to the Microsoft CryptoAPI to take advantage of the most popular Internet encryption systems. If you decide to use these systems, you must make sure that the same encryption algorithms *and* digital certificates are available at both ends of the transaction.

The Encrypt Stage

Keep in mind that, although adding a digital signature to your interchange involves a certain amount of encryption work and deals with the `CryptoAPI`, doing so doesn't in any way protect your data from indiscreet eyes. This is, instead, the role of the **Encrypt stage**, which can be used to encrypt the entire interchange so that it cannot be read en-route.

Once again, while you can provide your own encryption mechanisms, SSCE provides you with the appropriate `CryptoAPI` functionality, which grants you access to a virtually unlimited number of encryption standards.

The Audit Stage

The **Audit stage** – the last stage before the pipeline moves on to actually sending out the interchange – is intended to create a "digital trail" for the transmission, so that it's possible to recognize it later on during handshaking operations with the recipient (that is, to verify that a receipt has been received, and so on).

Having an Audit system – usually stored in a database – is a very important process for a good B2B system. It improves its reliability and robustness, and it also makes it possible to implement certain techniques, such as the use of receipts, that are often required for safety purposes. The CIP contains a complete auditing system that is automatically able to keep track of outgoing interchanges and to link incoming receipts to them.

The Transport Stage

Finally, the **Transport stage** has the double duty of transmitting the completed interchange to the recipient and, where appropriate, also invoking the recipient's system so that it can process the information sent. SSCE provides built-in support for three transport protocols:

❑ **HTTP**
  HTTP is probably the most commonly used, since it works by simply posting the interchange to a specific HTTP address on the recipient's server.

❑ **SMTP**
  Simple Mail Transport Protocol, leverages e-mail. It can be programmed to invoke a script that will, in turn, launch the Receive pipeline.

❑ **DCOM**
  DCOM works by invoking a specific COM object (shipped with SSCE) at the recipient's end; this object will, in turn, invoke the Receive pipeline. Clearly, this system only works if a Windows NT machine running Site Server Commerce Edition is also running at the recipient's end.

Naturally, if required, you can always write your own components to support whatever transmission protocols you choose (for example datapac or EDI); there are also a number of third-party components that provide additional functionality of this kind.

The Receive Pipeline

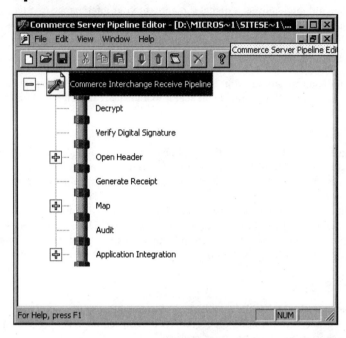

As mentioned earlier, the Receive pipeline works in the opposite way to the Transmit pipeline. This is what we would expect, since its function is to unpack the contents of an interchange, and eventually end up with a Dictionary that contains the original information.

First of all, you'll notice that there is no equivalent of the Transmit stage. This is because the pipeline has already been invoked by some other process that was, in turn, invoked as part of the receiving procedure. For example, if your transmission occurred through HTTP, the Transport stage of the Transmit pipeline will have called up a web page on the receiving server, which in turn will have executed the Receive pipeline.

In general, the other stages of the Receive pipeline perform the opposite task of their counterparts in the Transmit pipeline. The only stages unique to Receive are **Generate Receipt** and **Application Integration**.

The Generate Receipt Stage

This stage takes care of generating a receipt when the sender has required one.

This is usually a two-step process. First, the information to be stored in the receipt (for example, transaction ID, time when the interchange was received, and so on) is computed. Successively, a new Transmit pipeline is invoked that takes care of actually encoding and sending out the receipt as a completely separate interchange.

The Application Integration Stage

The Application Integration stage is used to integrate the pipeline with the rest of your B2B system. In principle, in fact, the pipeline is simply a conduit for your data – you still have to provide your own logic aimed at manipulating it. SSCE provides only basic functionality here, such as writing a text file to disk, or invoking a separate application for processing the interchange.

ASP Reference

This appendix summarizes the objects that make up the ASP object model, listing and describing all the members of each object.

The ASP Object Model

The ASP object model is made up of six objects:

❑ The **Application** object is created when the ASP DLL is loaded in response to the first request for an ASP page from a virtual application. It provides a repository for storing variables and object references that are available to all the pages that all visitors open.

❑ The **ASPError** object is a new object in ASP 3.0, and is available through the `GetLastError` method of the Server object. It provides a range of detailed information about the last error that occurred in ASP.

❑ The **Request** object makes available to the script all the information that the client provides when requesting a page or submitting a form. This includes the HTTP variables that identify the browser and the user, cookies that are stored on the browser for this domain, and any values appended to the URL as a query string or in HTML controls in a `<FORM>` section of the page. It also provides access to a range of server environment variables, the contents of any certificate that the client may be using through **Secure Sockets Layer** (SSL) or other encrypted communication protocol, and properties that help to manage the connection.

❑ The **Response** object is used to access and generate the response that is being created to send back to the client. It makes available information about the content being sent to the browser, and any new cookies that will be stored on the browser for this domain. It also provides a series of methods that are used to create the returned page.

❑ The **Server** object provides a series of methods and properties that are useful in scripting with ASP. The most obvious is the `Server.CreateObject` method, which properly instantiates other COM objects within the context of the current page or session. There are also methods to translate strings into the correct format for use in URLs and in HTML, by converting non-legal characters to the correct legal equivalent.

❑ The **Session** object is created for each visitor when they first request an ASP page from a virtual application, and remains available until the default timeout period (or the timeout period determined by the script) expires, or the session is explicitly ended with the Abandon method. It provides a repository for storing variables and object references that are available just to the pages that this visitor opens during the lifetime of this session.

The following diagram shows conceptually how these objects relate to the client and the server, and the requests made by the client and the responses sent back to them from the server:

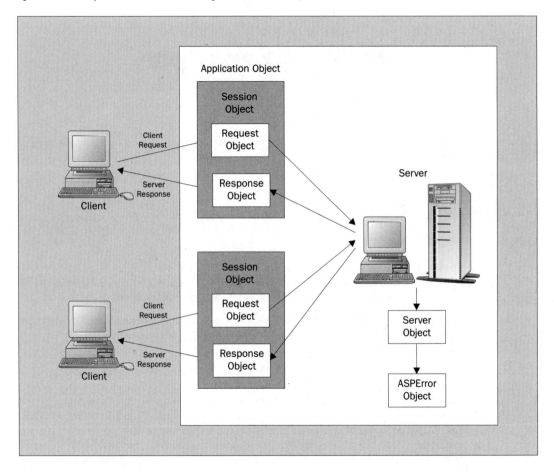

The Application Object

Provides a repository for storing variables and object references that are available to all the pages that all visitors open.

The Application Collections

The Application object provides two collections that are used to access the variables and objects that are stored in the global application space:

Collection Name	Description
Contents	A collection of all of the variables and their values that are stored in the Application object, and are *not* defined using an <OBJECT> element. This includes Variant arrays and Variant-type object instance references.
StaticObjects	A collection of all of the variables that are stored in the Application object by using an <OBJECT> element.

The Application Methods

The Application methods are used to remove values from the global application space, and control concurrent accesses to variables within the space:

Method	Description
Contents.Remove (*variable_name*)	Removes a named variable from the Application.Contents collection.
Contents. RemoveAll()	Removes all variables from the Application.Contents collection.
Lock()	Locks the Application object so that only the current ASP page has access to the contents. Used to ensure that concurrency issues do not corrupt the contents by allowing two users to simultaneously read and update the values.
Unlock()	Releases this ASP page's lock on the Application object.

* You *cannot* remove variables from the Application.StaticObjects collection at runtime.

The Application Events

The Application object exposes two events that occur when an application starts and ends:

Event	Description
onStart	Occurs when the ASP application starts, before the page that the user requests is executed. Used to initialize variables, create objects, or run other code.
onEnd	Occurs when the ASP application ends. This is after the last user session has ended, and after any code in the onEnd event for that session has executed. All variables existing in the application are destroyed when it ends.

The ASPError Object

Provides a range of detailed information about the last error that occurred in ASP.

The ASPError Properties

The ASPError object provides nine properties that describe the error that occurred, the nature and source of the error, and (where possible) return the actual code that caused it:

Property	Description
ASPCode	*Integer*. The error number generated by IIS.
ASPDescription	*String*. A detailed description of the error if it is ASP-related.
Category	*String*. The source of the error: i.e. internal to ASP, the scripting language, or an object.
Column	*Integer*. The character position within the file that generated the error.
Description	*String*. A short description of the error.
File	*String*. The name of the file that was being processed when the error occurred.
Line	*Integer*. The number of the line within the file that generated the error.
Number	*Integer*. A standard COM error code.
Source	*String*. The actual code, where available, of the line that caused the error.

The Request Object

Makes available all the information that the client provides when requesting a page, or submitting a form.

The Request Collections

The Request object provides five collections that we can use to access all kinds of information about the client's request to the web server:

Collection Name	Description
ClientCertificate	A collection of the values of all the fields or entries in the client certificate that the user presented to the server when accessing a page or resource. Each member is read-only.

Collection Name	Description
Cookies	A collection of the values of all the cookies sent from the user's system along with their request. Only cookies valid for the domain containing the resource are sent to the server.
Form	A collection of the values of all the HTML control elements in the <FORM> section that was submitted as the request, where the value of the METHOD attribute is POST. Each member is read-only.
QueryString	A collection of all the name/value pairs appended to the URL in the user's request, or the values of all the HTML control elements in the <FORM> section that was submitted as the request where the value of the METHOD attribute is GET or the attribute is omitted. Each member is read-only.
ServerVariables	A collection of all the HTTP header values sent from the client with their request, plus the values of several environment variables for the web server. Each member is read-only.

The Request Property

The single property of the Request object provides information about the number of bytes in the user's request:

Property	Description
TotalBytes	Read-only. Returns the total number of bytes in the body of the request sent by the client.

The Request Method

The single method of the Request object provides access to the complete content of the part of a user's request that is POSTed to the server from a <FORM> section of a web page:

Method	Description
BinaryRead(count)	Retrieves *count* bytes of data from the client's request when the data is sent to the server as part of a POST request. It returns as a Variant array (or SafeArray). This method *cannot* be used successfully if the ASP code has already referenced the Request.Form collection. Likewise, the Request.Form collection *cannot* be successfully accessed if you have used the BinaryRead method.

The Response Object

Used to access the response that is being creating to send back to the client.

The Response Collection

The Response object provides a single collection that is used to set the values of any cookies that will be placed on the client system:

Collection Name	Description
Cookies	A collection containing the values of all the cookies this will be sent back to the client in the current response. Each member is write-only.

The Response Properties

The Response object provides a range of properties that can be read (in most cases) and modified to tailor the response:

Property	Description
Buffer = true|false	Read/write. *Boolean*. Specifies if the output created by an ASP page will be held in the IIS buffer until all of the server scripts in the current page have been processed, or until the Flush or End method is called. It must be set before any output is sent to IIS, including HTTP header information, so it should be the first line of the .asp file after the <%@LANGUAGE=..%> statement. Buffering is on (true) by default in ASP 3.0, whereas it is off (false) by default in earlier versions.
CacheControl = "*setting*"	Read/write. *String*. Set this property to Public to allow proxy servers to cache the page, or Private to prevent proxy caching taking place.
Charset("*value*")	Read/write. *String*. Appends the name of the character set (for example, ISO-LATIN-7) to the HTTP Content-Type header created by the server for each response.
ContentType "*MIME-type*"	Read/write. *String*. Specifies the HTTP content type for the response, as a standard MIME-type (such as "text/xml" or "image/gif"). If omitted the MIME-type "text/html" is used. The content type tells the browser what type of content to expect.

Property	Description
Expires = *minutes*	Read/write. *Number.* Specifies the length of time in minutes that a page is valid for. If the user returns to the same page before it expires, the cached version is displayed. After that period it expires, and should not be held in a private (user) or public (proxy) cache.
ExpiresAbsolute = #*date*[*time*]#	Read/write. *Date/Time.* Specifies the absolute date and time when a page will expire and no longer be valid. If the user returns to the same page before it expires, the cached version is displayed. After that time it expires, and should not be held in a private (user) or public (proxy) cache.
IsClientConnected()	Read-only. *Boolean.* Returns an indication of whether the client is still connected to and loading the page from the server. Can be used to end processing (with the Response.End method) if a client moves to another page before the current one has finished executing.
PICS("PICS-label-string")	Write-only. *String.* Create a PICS header and adds it to the HTTP headers in the response. PICS headers define the content of the page in terms of violence, sex, bad language, etc.
Status = "code message"	Read/write. *String.* Specifies the status value and message that will be sent to the client in the HTTP headers of the response to indicate an error or successful processing of the page. Examples are "200 OK" and "404 Not Found".

The Response Methods

The Response object provides a set of methods that directly manipulate the content of the page being created on the server for return to the client:

Method	Description
AddHeader("name", "content")	Creates a custom HTTP header using the *name* and *content* values and adds it to the response. Will *not* replace an existing header of the same name. Once a header has been added, it cannot be removed. Must be used before any page content (i.e. text and HTML) is sent to the client.
AppendToLog("string")	Adds a string to the end of the web server log entry for this request when W3C Extended Log File Format is in use. Requires at least the URI Stem value to be selected in the Extended Properties page for the site containing the page.

Method	Description
BinaryWrite(SafeArray)	Writes the content of a Variant-type SafeArray to the current HTTP output stream without any character conversion. Useful for writing non-string information, such as binary data required by a custom application or the bytes to make up an image file.
Clear()	Erases any existing buffered page content from the IIS response buffer when Response.Buffer is true. Does *not* erase HTTP response headers. Can be used to abort a partly completed page.
End()	Stops ASP from processing the page script and returns the currently created content, then aborts any further processing of this page.
Flush()	Sends all currently buffered page content in the IIS buffer to the client when Response.Buffer is true. Can be used to send parts of a long page to the client individually.
Redirect("url")	Instructs the browser to load the page in the string *url* parameter by sending a "302 Object Moved" HTTP header in the response.
Write("string")	Writes the specified *string* to the current HTTP response stream and IIS buffer so that it becomes part of the returned page.

The Server Object

Provides a series of methods and properties that are useful in scripting with ASP and creating instances of other objects.

The Server Property

The single property of the Server object provides access to the script timeout value for an executing ASP page:

Property	Description
ScriptTimeout	*Integer. Default* = 90. Sets or returns the number of seconds that script in the page can execute for before the server aborts page execution and reports an error. This automatically halts and removes from memory pages that contain errors that may lock execution into a loop, or those that stall while waiting for a resource to become available. This prevents the server becoming overloaded with badly behaved pages. You may need to increase this value if your pages take a long time to run.

The Server Methods

The methods of the Server object provide ways to format data, manage page execution, and create instances of other objects:

Method	Description
CreateObject ("*identifier*")	Creates an instance of the object (a component, application or scripting object) that is identified by "*identifier*", and returns a reference to it that can be used in our code. Can be used in the global.asa page of a virtual application to create objects with session-level or application-level scope. The object can be identified by its ClassID (i.e. "{CLSID:FDC8-...-37A9}") value or by a ProgID string such as "ADODB.Connection".
Execute ("*url*")	Stops execution of the current page and transfers control to the page specified in "*url*". The user's current environment (i.e. session state and any current transaction state) is carried over to the new page. After that page has finished execution, control passes back to the original page and execution resumes at the statement after the Execute method call.
GetLastError ()	Returns a reference to an ASPError object that holds details of the last error that occurred within the ASP processing, i.e. within asp.dll. The information exposed by the ASPError object includes the file name, line number, error code, etc.
HTMLEncode ("*string*")	Returns a string that is a copy of the input value "*string*", but with all non-legal HTML characters, such as '<', '>', '&' and double quotes, converted into the equivalent HTML entity – i.e. <, >, &, ", etc.
MapPath ("*url*")	Returns the full physical path and filename of the file or resource specified in "*url*".
Transfer ("*url*")	Stops execution of the current page and transfers control to the page specified in "*url*". The user's current environment (i.e. session state and any current transaction state) is carried over to the new page. Unlike the Execute method, execution *does not* resume in the original page, but ends when the new page has completed executing.
URLEncode ("*string*")	Returns a string that is a copy of the input value "*string*", but with all characters that are not valid in a URL, such as '?', '&' and spaces, converted into the equivalent URL entity – i.e. '%3F', '%26', and '+'.

The Session Object

Provides a repository for storing variables and object references that are available just to the pages that this visitor opens during the lifetime of this session.

The Session Collections

The Session object provides two collections that can be used to access the variables and objects that are stored in the user's local session space:

Collection Name	Description
Contents	A collection of all of the variables and their values that are stored in this particular Session object, and are *not* defined using an `<OBJECT>` element. This includes `Variant` arrays and `Variant`-type object instance references.
StaticObjects	A collection of all of the variables that are stored in this particular Session object by using an `<OBJECT>` element.

The Session Properties

The Session object provides four properties that expose details of the session:

Property	Description
CodePage	Read/write. *Integer*. Defines the code page that will be used to display the page content in the browser. The code page is the numeric value of the character set, and different languages and locales may use different code pages. For example, ANSI code page 1252 is used for American English and most European languages. Code page 932 is used for Japanese Kanji.
LCID	Read/write. *Integer*. Defines the locale identifier (LCID) of the page that is sent to the browser. The LCID is a standard international abbreviation that uniquely identifies the locale; for instance 2057 defines a locale where the currency symbol used is '£'. This LCID can also be used in statements such as `FormatCurrency`, where there is an optional `LCID` argument. The `LCID` for a page can also be set in the opening `<%@..%>` ASP processing directive and overrides the setting in the `LCID` property of the session.
SessionID	Read-only. *Long*. Returns the session identifier for this session, which is generated by the server when the session is created. Unique only for the duration of the parent Application object, and so may be re-used when a new application is started.
Timeout	Read/write. *Integer*. Defines the timeout period in minutes for this Session object. If the user does not refresh or request a page within the timeout period, the session ends. Can be changed in individual pages as required.

The Session Methods

The Session methods are used to remove values from the user-level session space, and terminate sessions on demand:

Method	Description
`Contents.Remove ("variable_name")`	Removes a named variable from the `Session.Contents` collection.
`Contents.RemoveAll()`	Removes all variables from the `Session.Contents` collection.
`Abandon()`	Ends the current user session and destroys the current Session object once execution of this page is complete. You can still access the current session's variables in this page, even after calling the `Abandon` method. However the next ASP page that is requested by this user will start a new session, and create a new Session object with only the default values defined in `global.asa` (if any exist).

* You *cannot* remove variables from the `Session.StaticObjects` collection at runtime.

The Session Events

The Session object exposes two events that occur when a user session starts and ends:

Event	Description
`onStart`	Occurs when an ASP user session starts, before the page that the user requests is executed. Used to initialize variables, create objects, or run other code.
`onEnd`	Occurs when an ASP user session ends. This is when the predetermined session timeout period has elapsed since that user's last page request from the application. All variables existing in the session are destroyed when it ends. It is also possible to end ASP user sessions explicitly in code using the `Session.Abandon` method, and this event occurs when that happens.

Third-Party Components

Site Server 3.0 Commerce Edition is a customizable and extensible software solution that allows you to use custom components at virtually any stage in its processing pipelines. There are a number of custom components available on the market that either replace or extend the pipeline components that ship with Commerce Edition. Third-party components for Site Server 3.0 Commerce Edition broadly fall into the following categories:

- ❑ Catalog Solutions
- ❑ Payment Solutions
- ❑ Tax Calculation
- ❑ Shipping and Handling
- ❑ Configuration
- ❑ Electronic Data Interchange (EDI)

This appendix contains profiles of a number of Independent Software Vendors (ISVs) who provide custom components or solutions that you can integrate into your own commerce solutions. The majority of the ISVs focus on Payment Solutions and Tax Calculations. We have paraphrased the vendors' own advertising material in the first section of this appendix, but for full details of their products, visit their websites.

Microsoft also maintains a list of ISVs on their web site. If you consult the list on Microsoft's web site, you'll find that it is much longer than ours, since it includes those companies that provide their own total commerce solutions (in many cases, built on Site Server 3.0 Commerce Edition).

Profiles of Third-Party Component ISVs

BCE Emergis Inc.

http://www.emergis.com/en/default.htm

BCE Emergis Inc. offers both EDI Commerce and Internet payment-processing products and services. BCE Emergis Inc.'s BuyWay payment service provides a payment-processing gateway that supports the Microsoft Site Server 3.0 Commerce Edition, can accept credit cards from any purchaser at any location in the world, and provide settlement with most North American banks. The solution uses industry-standard security software that supports popular Internet browsers. It will also incorporate future security standards, including the new Secure Electronic Transaction (SET) protocol currently being sponsored by MasterCard and Visa International.

Belarc Inc.

http://www.belarc.com/

Belarc Advisor helps Internet shoppers automatically choose PC hardware and software products that are compatible with their PC systems, without needing to know and understand the products' technical requirements or their PC's configuration. The system consists of a client helper application and an extensive database of product keys, which are updated monthly.

Caledon Card Services

http://www.ccsinc.on.ca/

Caledon Card Services provides credit card processing solutions to North American businesses. They work closely with Canada's major banks, as well as with various credit card processing centers in Canada and the United States. If you need a credit card processing solution for your business, big or small, they probably already have it.

Their software is currently installed in a broad range of companies including call centers, telephone companies, and on many web sites selling everything from software to travel insurance. They are capable of providing solutions ranging from a few transactions a week to thousands of transactions per hour.

Calico Technology

http://www.calicotech.com

Calico eSales Suite offers needs-analysis, configuration, pricing, and quoting of mass-customized complex products and services to field sales reps, telesales reps, distributors, and customers buying directly over the web. Calico eSales Suite integrates seamlessly with Microsoft Site Server Commerce Edition, delivering electronic commerce solutions for complex products and services. Based on Microsoft ActiveX component technology and Active Server Pages, Calico eSales Suite integrates with all popular Windows 95 and Windows NT desktop and sales force automation applications, and can be deployed in laptop, client/server, and Internet applications.

Clarus Corporation

http://www.claruscorp.com

Atlanta-based Clarus Corporation is a pioneer and a leader in providing Web-based Commerce applications that enable organizations to gain control of their operational resources – the non-production goods and services vital to every company's operations. Clarus Commerce leverages web technology to connect large populations of employees, management and suppliers with continuous planning, monitoring and control of resources, which can result in a dramatic impact on the bottom line. The Company's Financial, Human Resources and more recently web-based Commerce solutions are deployed at more than 350 sites for customers including First Data Corporation, MasterCard International, Hyatt Regency Chicago, T. Rowe Price Associates, Inc., Investment Technology Group, Toronto Dominion Bank, The Container Store, Blue Cross and Blue Shield, H.D. Vest Financial Services, Lands' End and Chartwell Re Holdings Corp.

ClearCommerce Corporation

http://www.clearcommerce.com

ClearCommerce Corporation, is a provider in Internet commerce transaction payment, processing, and reporting technology. The company is dedicated to advancing technology and safe commerce practices in the Internet commerce marketplace. Since 1995, ClearCommerce has been helping merchants, banks, and processors implement successful Internet site and transaction processing strategies. ClearCommerce products are entering the third-generation of development. Internet Computing Magazine named ClearCommerce Engine "Net Best Winner" in their March 1998 issue stating, "sites that handle heavy traffic and a multitude of hard and soft goods are best served by ClearCommerce because of its powerful fraud protection module, extensive sales reporting features, ESD and real-time payment processes..."

CyberCash

http://www.cybercash.com/

CyberCash is a technology-driven company that provides software and services to enable secure financial transactions on the Internet. CyberCash provides credit card, check, and cash-based payment services to thousands of merchants worldwide. CyberCash has developed the CyberCash CashRegister Payment Components for Microsoft Site Server 3.0 Commerce Edition to allow merchants and Solution Providers to connect to CyberCash's new CashRegister 3 Service. These Payment Components, available today, allow merchants to accept secure, real-time payments at web storefronts with connectivity to over 95 percent of the merchant acquiring banks in the United States.

CyberSource

http://www.cybersource.com/

Install a single component for Microsoft Site Server Commerce Edition or other Microsoft Commerce Platform, and rapidly implement a suite of mission-critical e-commerce transaction services, including: global payment processing, fraud screening, tax calculation, delivery address verification, fulfillment messaging, digital delivery, and more. Accessing these services over the Internet via the CyberSource Commerce Component ensures you'll maintain total processing control, while our global, mission-critical systems and merchant support services guarantee reliable transaction capability even at peak order volumes.

DataCash LTD

http://www.datacash.com

DataCash 1.0 provides a no-nonsense, easy to install, Payment Gateway component that clips straight into Microsoft Site Server Commerce Edition. It allows merchants to accept credit and debit card transactions securely over the Internet. DataCash provides a full multi-currency system, enabling merchants to trade in up to 155 different currencies and settle in one of the worlds 15 favorite currencies.

Dydacomp Development Corp.

http://www.dydacomp.com/

Dydacomp's Mail Order Manager (M.O.M.) is a completely integrated PC-based program designed to automate the daily activities of any business that takes orders by phone, mail, or the World Wide Web. Customer management, inventory control, order entry, order processing and fulfillment, credit card processing, purchasing, accounting, list maintenance and management, reporting, and contact management are just some of the program's capabilities.

ECWerks

http://www.ecwerks.com/

The GOEWerks family of supply chain management technology solutions provides scalable, real-time solutions, designed to offer comprehensive product management, order management, shipping logistics, and financing. ECWerks has been offering world-class electronic commerce strategies, coupled with customized commerce-enabling applications designed to integrate with traditional corporate procurement and asset management systems since its incorporation in February 1997.

Emercis Corporation

`http://www.emercis.com`

Emercis Corporation helps companies capitalize on the exploding e-commerce trend with software tools that make it easy to create a powerful, flexible and manageable online consumer or business-to-business stores. The Emercis Catalog Server is a rapidly deployable, customizable, Internet-commerce server application that reduces reliance on a company's technical staff by giving non-technical employees the power to control product inventories, promotions, and sales campaigns for online consumer or business stores. The fully-scalable Catalog Server allows business managers to remotely define and organize complex product lines, manage sophisticated promotional campaigns, and implement flexible product comparison and search capabilities.

Edifecs Corporation

`http://www.edifecs.com/content/home/default.asp`

Edifecs is a leading provider of Electronic Data Interchange and business-to-business electronic commerce software tools for pre-production, productivity, and quality assurance. Edifecs will offer EDI and trading partner management software tools that support Microsoft Site Server 3.0 Commerce Edition. The solution will integrate Edifecs' Guideline Management and testing tools, as well as provide comprehensive partner management and legacy EDI support.

GlobeID Software

`http://www.globeid.com/`

GlobeID Software develops and markets world class electronic commerce transaction solutions. Targeted at transaction intensive industries such as Financial and Telecommunication services, billers and utilities, as well as emerging high volume Internet and Commerce service providers, @dvanced Payment is a solution suite that allows high volume Internet payment operators to provide advanced payment services to their online customers. Field based experience has lead GlobeID Software to derive three primary @dvanced Payment solutions:

- ❑ Merchant Acquiring allows authorization and clearing of Internet payment transactions and provides reporting capabilities to both merchants and consumers

- ❑ Ultra-Thin Client addresses the wireless phone market by providing payment services to cellular phone owners

- ❑ E-purse Service allows Smart Card user communities to link to the Internet

These solutions are targeted to readily available markets, addressing the critical requirements of high volume transaction operators for scalability, reliability, openness, integrity and security.

Harbinger Corporation

http://www.harbinger.com

Harbinger Corporation is a world-leading, single-source provider of electronic commerce and EDI solutions serving the industry's largest software and network customer community. Harbinger's TrustedLink EDI translators seamlessly integrate with Microsoft Site Server 3.0 Commerce Edition for delivery of supply chain transaction data. Combining Harbinger's EDI, security, and communications products with Site Server 3.0 Commerce Edition enables customers to rapidly develop electronic commerce solutions that can handle high-volume, formatted EDI transactions for managing their supply chain.

Intelisys Electronic Commerce

http://www.intelisys.com/

Intelisys offers a powerful and complete Internet procurement solution that focuses exclusively on allowing both buyers and suppliers around the world to use the speed and power of the Internet to improve significantly the way they do business.

Intelisys delivers a proven implementation-friendly solution with measurable value that allows buyers to completely control the procurement process from order to payment. And in turn, it provides suppliers with an inexpensive, easily implemented, repeatable and scalable process through the use of open standards and non-proprietary, browser-based thin architecture.

Intell-A-Check

http://www.icheck.com/

Intell-A-Check is a Microsoft Windows-based, Microsoft BackOffice certified, electronic check writing application, which enables companies to accept check payments over the phone, fax, VRU, Internet, and through direct debit programs. By utilizing Microsoft Site Server 3.0 Commerce Edition, Intell-A-Check allows merchants to extend their payment options beyond credit cards, while providing the same level of convenience and security. The Intell-A-Check database can be file-based, or scale to Microsoft SQL Server for printing or immediate electronic deposit via ACH transfer. The Intell-A-Check is a multi-user application that can be accessed from a full-featured 32-bit Windows program, browser or through its Microsoft COM based components for easy integration with legacy systems.

InterShipper.net

http://www.intershipper.net

InterShipper.net provides published shipping rates from multiple carriers including the US Postal Service, Airborne Express, FedEx, RPS, UPS, DHL, and BAX Global. The rates can either be viewed on the InterShipper.net web site, or used to calculate shipping costs during an online transaction. A pipeline component is available for Microsoft Site Server Commerce Edition. Also available are an ActiveX DLL for easy Windows integration, and a Datastream API for integration into just about any platform. By using InterShipper.net to calculate shipping costs, a merchant can now offer several choices to his customers, at fair prices, while always covering his costs. The software and the service are both offered FREE.

Mercado Software, Inc.

http://www.mercadosw.com

Mercado Software is a leader in e-catalog search and integration solutions, and is dedicated to helping companies make their business-to-business and business-to-consumer catalogs more effective. With Mercado products and services, developers can quickly implement or upgrade their existing sites, and their end-users can find the products they're looking for and browse related offerings quickly and easily. This revolutionary capability generates increased revenues and guarantees return on investment for large online sites.

OrderTrust

http://www.ordertrust.com/

OrderTrust LLC is a network-based service provider that allows merchants to easily communicate with their business partners, such as payment processors, fulfillers, suppliers, and customer care centers. The result is a tightly integrated, highly functional business community that will flexibly expand merchants' commerce capacities and reliably drive back-end order processing. A single connection to OrderTrust's fault-tolerant network infrastructure will free merchants from costly network management and interface maintenance.

OrderTrust, the leading order processing network provides services that allow merchants to access and support new sales channels, expand marketing opportunities, and develop relationships with strategic vendors. As a result, merchants attract and retain more customers, increase revenues, and develop brand identity. Customers include Lycos, SkyMall Inc., 1-800-FLOWERS Inc., iParty, and other Internet commerce merchants.

PaylinX

http://www.paylinx.com/

The PaylinX for Site Server payment server is a completely new approach to handling payments from customers. Payment servers provide an enterprise-wide resource for all types of payment, such as payment by credit cards. This approach is unique in its ability to simultaneously support call center agents, automated voice response, mainframe billing systems, Internet payments, and any other part of a company that works with customers. Industrial strength, fast (3 second transactions), high capacity (over 8,000 transactions per hour per server), the PaylinX EnterpriseServer runs on Microsoft Windows NT. PaylinX clients are available for a wide range of platforms.

Preview Systems

http://www.previewsystems.com/

Preview Systems is the market leader in developing ESD systems for the electronic sale, marketing and distribution of software and other soft goods. With ZipLock ESD System – an end-to-end solution for ESD commerce – Preview is changing the way software is bought and sold. ZipLock ESD Gateway for Microsoft Site Server 3.0 Commerce Edition easily integrates with existing wizard-built storefronts to brand, sell, license, and distribute soft goods over the Internet. Preview Systems has worldwide ESD commerce service partners, and partnerships with key distributors around the globe.

SAQQARA Systems, Inc.

http://www.saqqara.com

SAQQARA is a leading provider of catalog management, search, and publishing software. Step Search Professional is a catalog management application for supplier-side business-to-business electronic commerce. It complies with the Microsoft COM and Active Server Page architectures, and includes a sophisticated, generic and extensible data model for businesses to design and maintain structured product information for dynamic web publishing. It features Step Search, an advanced parametric search technology that enables users to quickly search and compare products online to make informed buying decisions

Sterling Commerce

http://www.sterlingcommerce.com/

Sterling Commerce is a leading, global provider of business-to-business electronic commerce software and value-added services. GENTRAN:Server for Microsoft Windows NT, provides messaging support, data transformation, and routes and tracks messages between Microsoft Site Server 3.0 Commerce Edition and order fulfillment applications. It also routes and tracks business-to-business messages between the business and its suppliers, manufacturers, distribution centers, and banks, for complete automation of the supply chain.

T4G

http://www.t4g.com/

T4G's physical point-of-service application, Customers for Life, provides the merchant with the capability of integrating their same back office databases and applications with the Microsoft commerce platform. This allows the electronic store and the physical store to coexist seamlessly. T4G's customer, merchandise, and order fulfillment components allow merchants to deal with one system for relationship marketing, merchandise management, and other selling activities.

TanData Corporation

http://www.tandata.com/

TanData Corporation has been a leading provider of computerized shipping systems for 18 years. In addition to electronic commerce shipping solutions, TanData products are used to manage the "point-of-shipment" business function for medium to large shippers in a variety of industry segments. The Progistics. Merchant Enterprise Edition brings sophisticated transportation management functionality to commerce applications, particularly Microsoft Site Server 3.0 Commerce Edition.

TAXWARE International, Inc.

http://www.taxware.com

The first tax software developer to enter the field of electronic commerce, TAXWARE's leading INTERNET Tax System for on-line transactions has fast become the system of choice for web transactions. TAXWARE's system is the only Internet tax system designed specifically for web transactions, and by taking advantage of TAXWARE's long time partnership with Microsoft, companies can now conduct full-scale commerce on the Internet when using the Microsoft Site Server Commerce Edition.

TAXWARE's software is seamlessly integrated with Microsoft Site Server Order Processing Pipeline, providing customers with a completely automated payment process for their on-line malls. Using TAXWARE, Microsoft Site Server performs real-time sales tax calculations based on product codes, merchant's business nexus, and the ZIP code of the shopper's shipping address. Resulting in the most reliable system available.

Tellan Corporation

http://www.tellan.com/

Tellan's PCAuthorize allows customers using Microsoft Site Server Commerce Edition to authorize and deposit credit card transactions to a wide variety of bank credit authorization networks. Certified on all major U.S. networks, PCAuthorize allows you to choose your bank and your network with proven technology. Both live and periodic batch transactions can be processed, with both private leased line or dial-up connectivity.

Trintech

http://www.trintech.com/

Trintech's PayPurse, PayWare and PayGate suite creates a complete end-to-end payment solution based on the SET standard. PayWare builds a secure bridge between Microsoft Site Server and the financial institution. Chiefly, it manages the payment aspects of an Internet transaction, verifying the identity of all parties using public key cryptography to both the SSL and SET standard. PayWare is operational today in many sites throughout Europe.

TSI International Software, Ltd.

http://www.tsisoft.com/

TSI Software is a leading provider of packaged solutions for integrating enterprise applications. TSI Software's Mercator provides an easy-to-use data transformation solution for organizations that use the Commerce Interchange Pipeline (CIP) facilities of Microsoft Site Server Commerce Edition for creating seamless electronic commerce interfaces to business applications. Using Mercator, customers are able to build electronic commerce applications quickly and cost-effectively, without writing custom interface programs.

VeriFone

http://www.verifone.com/

VeriFone's Internet commerce products provide end-to-end Internet payment solutions for financial institutions, merchants and consumers. VeriFone has spent over a decade solving secure payment problems, and their vPOS and vGATE software provide a customized and secure means for conducting the Internet commerce purchase process.

Vertex Inc.

http://www.vertexinc.com

Vertex is the leading tax compliance software provider in North America. Vertex's Quantum for Sales and Use Tax/CSI 3.0 is integrated with Microsoft Site Server 3.0 Commerce Edition to provide on-line merchants with complete control for taxing transactions over the Internet. Quantum's software and tax databases automate sales and use tax compliance through the research of rules and rates, the accurate calculation of tax amounts, and automated preparation of tax returns.

Choosing Third-Party Components

Site Server Commerce Edition requires you to customize a lot of ASP scripts, and it's no different when you implement a third-party component. You'll have to tailor your scripts to ensure that you collect all of the necessary information that the component requires. As you evaluate third-party components, pay attention to the following:

- ❑ Does the component provide a unique service?
- ❑ Does the component provide a better replacement over an existing component?
- ❑ How well is the component's interface designed?
- ❑ How much ASP scripting work will be required to implement the component?

Good luck implementing your commerce solution!

D

Microsoft Commerce Server Object Model Quick Reference

Configuration Components

AdminFile

Member	Method/Property	Description
ReadFromBinaryFile	Method	Reads an entire file in binary format into memory
ReadFromFile	Method	Reads an entire file in ASCII format into memory

AdminSite

Member	Method/Property	Description
Create	Method	Creates a new store foundation
Delete	Method	Deletes a store
Initialize	Method	Initializes an instance of AdminSite
InitializeFromMDPath	Method	Initializes an instance of AdminSite using an IIS metabase path
IsValidName	Property	Determines whether a store with a particular name exists on a specific instance of IIS

Table Continued on Following Page

Member	Method/Property	Description
ReadDefaultProperties	Method	Reads the Store Dictionary for a particular store
ReadManagerProperties	Method	Reads the Store Dictionary used in the Store Manager of a particular store
WriteDefaultProperties	Method	Writes the Store Dictionary for a particular store
WriteManagerProperties	Method	Writes the Store Dictionary used in the Store Manager of a particular store
Status	Property	Reads/Sets the status of a store (open or closed)

AdminWebServer

Member	Method/Property	Description
GetWebSites	Method	Enumerates all the instances of IIS running on a server
GetWebSiteProperties	Method	Retrieves the IIS metabase for a specific instance of IIS
GetCommerceSites	Method	Enumerates all the MSCS stores installed on a server

Storage Components

SimpleList

Member	Method/Property	Description
Add	Method	Adds an entry to the list
Count	Property	Returns the number of entries in the list
Delete	Method	Deletes an entry from the list
Item	Property	(Default property) Returns a particular entry in the list

Dictionary

Member	Method/Property	Description
Count	Property	Returns the number of name/value pairs in the dictionary
Prefix	Property	Causes the object to filter its name/value pairs during persistency operations
Value	Property	(Default property) Sets or returns a particular name/value pair in the list

FileDocument

Member	Method/Property	Description
ReadDictionaryFromFile	Method	Loads the data of a persisted Dictionary object into another Dictionary object that was previously created
ReadFromFile	Method	Creates a copy of a persisted object
WriteToFile	Method	Persists a particular object to a file

OrderForm

Member	Method/Property	Description
Items	Property	List of products in the object
Items.SKU	Property	SKU of a particular product
Items.Quantity	Property	Quantity of a particular product in the OrderForm
Items.Name	Property	Name of the product
Items.List_price	Property	List price of the product
Items._product_x	Property	Product-specific information retrieved from the database
Items._n_unadjusted	Property	Unadjusted number of items available to the user
Items._oadjust_adjusted price	Property	Total cost of all the items of a specific product available for purchase by the user
Items._iadjust_regular price	Property	The base price of a product

Member	Method/Property	Description
`Items._iadjust_current price`	Property	The current price of the product, considering only product-wide modifiers
`Items.placed_price`	Property	The final price of the product, considering all product- and order-wide modifiers
`Items._tax_total`	Property	Total tax paid on the product
`Items._tax_included`	Property	Tax actually included in the product's price
`Shopper_ID`	Property	ID of the shopper who owns this OrderForm
`Ship_to_*`	Property	Shipping information
`Bill_to_*`	Property	Billing information
`_Basket_errors`	Property	SimpleList containing all errors generated in the Plan pipeline
`_Purchase_errors`	Property	SimpleList containing all errors generated in the Purchase pipeline
`Cc_*`	Property	Credit card fields
`Order_id`	Property	Pipeline-generated, unique ID of the order
`_total_total`	Property	Total cost of the order
`_oadjust_subtotal`	Property	Subtotal of the order, not counting shipping, handling and taxes
`Shipping_method`	Property	Name of the shipping method used to complete the order
`_shipping_total`	Property	Total cost of shipping
`_tax_total`	Property	Total cost of taxes
`_handling_total`	Property	Total cost of handling
`_tax_included`	Property	Amount of tax included in `_oadjust_subtotal`
`_verify_with`	Property	Dictionary object used to determine when the basket's contents have changed without the user being informed
`_payment_auth_code`	Property	The authorization code released by the organization that processed the order

Member	Method/Property	Description
Value	Property	(Default property) Sets or returns a name/value pair in the object
AddItem	Method	Adds one product to the OrderForm
ClearItems	Method	Empties the Items SimpleList
ClearOrderForm	Method	Completely clear all entries in the object

DBStorage

Member	Method/Property	Description
CommitData	Method	Updates data already in the database
DeleteData	Method	Deletes data from the database
DeleteDataKey	Method	Deletes data from the database according to a specified key
GetData	Method	Reads data from a database
InitStorage	Method	Initializes the object to point to a specific database
InsertData	Method	Writes data to the database
LookupData	Method	Retrieves data from the database based on the value of a specific column
LookupMultipleData	Method	Retrieves multiple instances of the same object from the database
Mapping	Property	Establishes how data that is persisted through the object is mapped to the database

User Interface Components

DataFunctions

Member	Method/Property	Description
Locale	Property	Determines the locale used to interpret and format data
CleanString	Method	Removes unwanted characters from a string
ConvertXY	Method	Convert data from type X to type Y, where X or Y can be any of: String Date Time
Convert$Z$	Method	Converts a string from a specific locale into a numeric value of type Z, where Z can be any of: Integer Float Money (in ConvertMoneyStringToNumber)
Date	Method	Converts a date value into a string formatted appropriately for the selected locale
DateTime	Method	Converts a datetime value into a string formatted appropriately for the selected locale
Float	Method	Converts a floating-point value into a string properly formatted for the selected locale
Money	Method	Converts an integer numeric value into a currency representation properly formatted for the selected locale
Number	Method	Converts an integer numeric value into a string properly formatted for the selected locale
Time	Method	Converts a time value into a string formatted appropriately for the selected locale
Validate$K$	Method	Validate a value of type K, where K is one of the following: Number Float DateTime

MessageManager

Member	Method/Property	Description
AddLanguage	Method	Adds an additional language to the object
AddMessage	Method	Adds a new message for a particular language
DefaultLanguage	Method	Sets the default language for the object
GetLocale	Method	Returns the locale for a particular language
GetMessage	Method	Retrieves a message for a particular language

StandardSManager

Member	Method/Property	Description
InitManager	Method	Initializes the object
CreateShopperID	Method	Creates a new shopper ID
GetShipperID	Method	Returns shopper ID from a cookie
PutShopperID	Method	Places shopper ID in a cookie

Page

Member	Method/Property	Description
Check	Method	Creates an HTML checkbox control
GetShopperID	Method	Retrieves the shopper ID for the current user
HTMLEncode	Method	Converts an ASCII string to HTML
Option	Method	Creates an entry of an HTML listbox
ProcessVerifyWith	Method	Determines whether the contents of the user's basket have changed without the user knowing about it
PutShopperID	Method	Saves the shopper ID for the current user so that a session can be maintained

Member	Method/Property	Description
Request*X*	Method	Retrieves a value of type *X* from the HTTP parameter list. *X* can be one of the following: Date Datetime Default (defaults to the optimal type given the data's format) Float MoneyAsNumber Number String Time
SURL	Method	Constructs a secure URL
URL	Method	Constructs an URL
URLArgs	Method	Constructs the query portion of an URL
URLEncode	Method	Converts an ASCII or HTML string in a format suitable for usage in the URL query string
VerifyWith	Method	Creates a digest of the user's basket used by the ProcessVerifyWith method
SiteRoot	Property	Returns the physical directory where the site is located.
SURLPrefix	Property	Sets/Retrieves the prefix to use in building secure URLs
URLPrefix	Property	Sets/Retrieves the prefix to use in building URLs
URLShopperArgs	Property	Returns an URL query parameter that contains the shopper ID for the current user
VirtualDirectory	Property	Returns the name of the virtual directory where the current store resides

Predictor

Member	Method/Property	Description
InitPredictor	Method	Initializes the object
GetPredictions	Method	Returns one or more predictions

Pipeline MS Commerce Server Objects

MtsPipeline and MtsTxPipeline

Member	Method/Property	Description
Execute	Method	Executes a pipeline
LoadPipe	Method	Loads a pipeline configuration file
SetLogFiles	Method	Turns on logging and sets the pathname of the log file

ConfigurationCacheHelper

Member	Method/Property	Description
DeleteFromCache	Method	Deletes a pipeline configuration file from the object's internal cache
LoadFromCache	Method	Loads a pipeline configuration file from the object's internal cache
SaveToCache	Method	Saves a pipeline configuration file in the object's internal cache

Micropipe

Member	Method/Property	Description
Execute	Method	Executes the micropipe
SetComponent	Method	Sets the component that the object will execute
SetLogFile	Method	Turns logging on and sets the pathname of the log file

Support and Errata

One of the most irritating things about any programming book is when you find that bit of code you've just spent an hour typing simply doesn't work. You check it a hundred times to see if you've set it up correctly, and then you notice the spelling mistake in the variable name on the book page. Of course, you can blame the authors for not taking enough care and testing the code, the editors for not doing their job properly, or the proofreaders for not being eagle-eyed enough, but this doesn't get around the fact that mistakes do happen.

We try hard to ensure no mistakes sneak out into the real world, but we can't promise that this book is 100% error free. What we can do is offer the next best thing, by providing you with immediate support and feedback from experts who have worked on the book and try to ensure that future editions eliminate these gremlins. The following section will take you step by step through the process of posting errata to our web site to get that help. The sections that follow, therefore, are:

❑   Wrox Developers Membership

❑   Finding a list of existing errata on the web site

There's also a section covering how to e-mail a question for technical support. This comprises:

❑   What your e-mail should include

❑   What happens to your e-mail once it has been received by us

So that you only need view information relevant to yourself, we ask that you register as a Wrox Developer Member. This is a quick and easy process, that will save you time in the long run. If you are already a member, just update membership to include this book.

Wrox Developer's Membership

To get your FREE Wrox Developer's Membership click on Membership in the navigation bar of our home site – http://www.wrox.com. This is shown in the following screenshot:

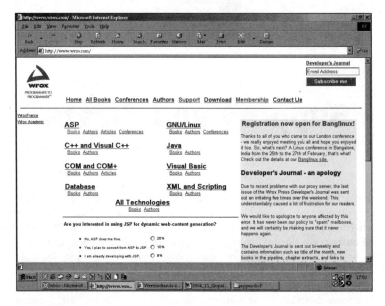

Then, on the next screen (not shown), click on New User. This will display a form. Fill in the details on the form and submit them using the Register button at the bottom. Go back to the main Membership page, enter your details and select Logon. Before you can say 'The best read books come in Wrox Red' you'll get the following screen:

Finding an Errata on the Web Site

Before you send in a query, you might be able to save time by finding the answer to your problem on our web site – http:\\www.wrox.com.

Each book we publish has its own page and its own errata sheet. You can get to any book's page by clicking on Support from the top navigation bar.

From this page you can locate any book's errata page on our site. Select your book from the pop-up menu and click on it.

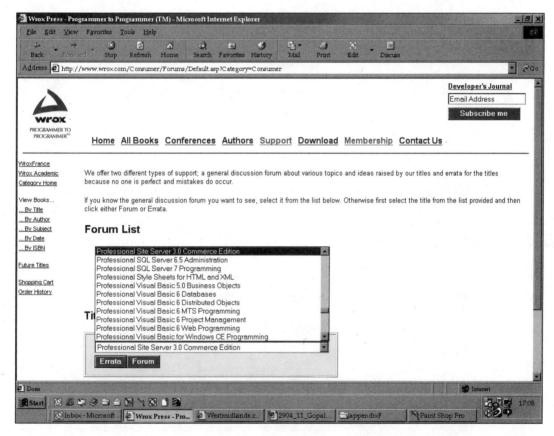

Then click on Errata. This will take you to the errata page for the book. Select the criteria by which you want to view the errata, and click the Apply criteria... button. This will provide you with links to specific errata. For an initial search, you're advised to view the errata by page numbers. If you have looked for an error previously, then you may wish to limit your search using dates. We update these pages daily to ensure that you have the latest information on bugs and errors.

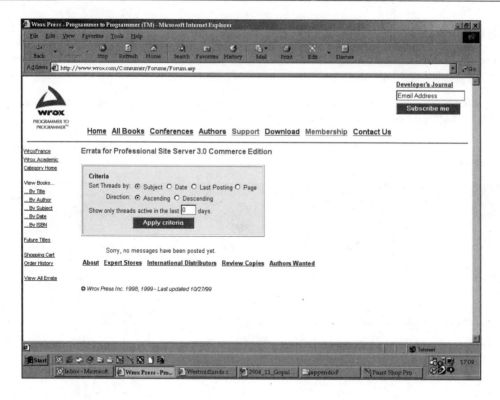

E-mail Support

If you wish to directly query a problem in the book with an expert who knows the book in detail then e-mail support@wrox.com, with the title of the book and the last four numbers of the ISBN in the subject field of the e-mail. A typical e-mail should include the following things:

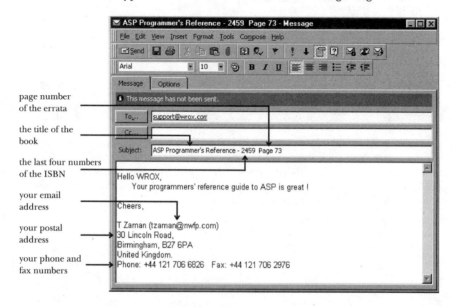

We won't send you junk mail. We need the details to save your time and ours. If we need to replace a disk or CD we'll be able to get it to you straight away. When you send an e-mail it will go through the following chain of support:

Customer Support

Your message is delivered to one of our customer support staff who are the first people to read it. They have files on most frequently asked questions and will answer anything general immediately. They answer general questions about the book and the web site.

Editorial

Deeper queries are forwarded to the technical editor responsible for that book. They have experience with the programming language or particular product and are able to answer detailed technical questions on the subject. Once an issue has been resolved, the editor can post the errata to the web site.

The Authors

Finally, in the unlikely event that the editor can't answer your problem, they will forward the request to the author. We try to protect the author from any distractions from writing. However, we are quite happy to forward specific requests to them. All Wrox authors help with the support on their books. They'll mail the customer and the editor with their response, and again all readers should benefit.

What We Can't Answer

Obviously with an ever-growing range of books and an ever-changing technology base, there is an increasing volume of data requiring support. While we endeavor to answer all questions about the book, we can't answer bugs in your own programs that you've adapted from our code. So, while you might have loved the help desk systems in our Active Server Pages book, don't expect too much sympathy if you cripple your company with a live adaptation you customized from Chapter 12. However, do tell us if you're especially pleased with the routine you developed with our help.

How to Tell Us Exactly What You Think

We understand that errors can destroy the enjoyment of a book and can cause many wasted and frustrated hours, so we seek to minimize the distress that they can cause.

You might just wish to tell us how much you liked or loathed the book in question. Or you might have ideas about how this whole process could be improved, in which case you should e-mail feedback@wrox.com. You'll always find a sympathetic ear, no matter what the problem is. Above all you should remember that we do care about what you have to say and we will do our utmost to act upon it.

Index

Symbols

E

S

wrox

PROGRAMMER TO PROGRAMMER™

Wrox writes books for you. Any suggestions, or ideas about how you want information given in your ideal book will be studied by our team. Your comments are always valued at Wrox.

Free phone in USA 800-USE-WROX
Fax (312) 893 8001

UK Tel. (0121) 687 4100   Fax (0121) 687 4101

Beginning Site Server - Registration Card

Name _____

Address _____

_____

_____

_____

City _____ State/Region _____

Country _____ Postcode/Zip _____

E-mail _____

Occupation _____

How did you hear about this book? _____

☐ Book review (name) _____

☐ Advertisement (name) _____

☐ Recommendation _____

☐ Catalog _____

☐ Other _____

Where did you buy this book? _____

☐ Bookstore (name) _____ City _____

☐ Computer Store (name) _____

☐ Mail Order _____

☐ Other _____

What influenced you in the purchase of this book?

☐ Cover Design

☐ Contents

☐ Other (please specify) _____

How did you rate the overall contents of this book?

☐ Excellent   ☐ Good

☐ Average   ☐ Poor

What did you find most useful about this book? _____

What did you find least useful about this book? _____

Please add any additional comments. _____

What other subjects will you buy a computer book on soon? _____

What is the best computer book you have used this year? _____

Note: This information will only be used to keep you updated about new Wrox Press titles and will not be used for any other purpose or passed to any other third party.

2904   *Check here if you DO NOT want to receive support for this book* ☐   2904

wrox

PROGRAMMER TO PROGRAMMER™

NB. If you post the bounce back card below in the UK, please send it to:

Wrox Press Ltd., Arden House, 1102 Warwick Road,
Acocks Green, Birmingham B27 6BH. UK.

Computer Book Publishers

NO POSTAGE
NECESSARY
IF MAILED
IN THE
UNITED STATES

BUSINESS REPLY MAIL
FIRST CLASS MAIL   PERMIT#64   CHICAGO, IL

POSTAGE WILL BE PAID BY ADDRESSEE

WROX PRESS INC.,
29 S. LA SALLE ST.,
SUITE 520
CHICAGO IL 60603-USA